MCTS: Windows Server 2008 Network Infrastructure Configuration Study Guide

Exam 70-642: TS: Windows Server 2008 Network Infrastructure, Configuring

OBJECTIVE	CHAPTER
CONFIGURING IP ADDRESSING AND SERVICES	
Configure IPv4 and IPv6 addressing. May include but is not limited to: configure IP options, subnetting, supernetting, alternative configuration	2
Configure Dynamic Host Configuration Protocol (DHCP). May include but is not limited to: DHCP options, creating new options, PXE boot, default user profiles, DHCP relay agents, exclusions, authorize server in Active Directory, scopes, server core, Windows Server Hyper-V	4, 7
Configure routing. May include but is not limited to: static routing, persistent routing, Routing Internet Protocol (RIP), Open Shortest Path First (OSPF)	5
Configure IPsec. May include but is not limited to: create IPsec policy, IPsec Authentication Header (AH), IPsec Encapsulating Security Payload (ESP)	2
CONFIGURING NAME RESOLUTION	
Configure a Domain Name System (DNS) server. May include but is not limited to: conditional forwarding, external forwarders, root hints, cache-only, server core, WINS and DNS integration, Windows Server virtualization	3
Configure DNS zones. May include but is not limited to: DNS Refresh no-refresh, intervals, DNS listserv address (NSLOOKUP), primary/secondary zones, Active Directory integration, Dynamic Domain Name System (DDNS), GlobalNames, SOA refresh	3
Configure DNS records. May include but is not limited to: record types, host, pointer, MX, SRV, NS, dynamic updates, Time to Live (TTL)	3
Configure DNS replication. May include but is not limited to: DNS secondary zones, DNS stub zones, DNS scavenging interval, replication scope	3
Configure name resolution for client computers. May include but is not limited to: DNS and WINS integration, configuring HOSTS file, LMHOSTS, node type, Link-Local Multicast Name Resolution (LLMNR), broadcasting, resolver cache, DNS Server list, Suffix Search order, manage client settings by using group policy	3, 4

Sybex®
An Imprint of
WILEY

OBJECTIVE	CHAPTER
CONFIGURING FILE AND PRINT SERVICES	
Configure and monitor print services. May include but is not limited to: printer share, publish printers to Active Directory, printer permissions, deploy printer connections, install printer drivers, export and import print queues and printer settings, add counters to Reliability and Performance Monitor to monitor print servers, print pooling, print priority	8, 9
MONITORING AND MANAGING A NETWORK INFRASTRUCTURE	
Configure Windows Server Update Services (WSUS) server settings. May include but is not limited to: update type selection, client settings, Group Policy object (GPO), client targeting, software updates, test and approval, disconnected networks	9
Capture performance data. May include but is not limited to: Data Collector Sets, Performance Monitor, Reliability Monitor, monitoring System Stability Index	9
Monitor event logs. May include but is not limited to: custom views, application and services logs, subscriptions, DNS log	9
Gather network data. May include but is not limited to: Simple Network Management Protocol (SNMP), Baseline Security Analyzer, Network Monitor	9

Sybex®
An Imprint of
WILEY

OBJECTIVE	CHAPTER
CONFIGURING NETWORK ACCESS	
Configure remote access. May include but is not limited to: dial-up, Remote Access Policy, Network Address Translation (NAT), Internet Connection Sharing (ICS), VPN, Routing and Remote Access Services (RRAS), inbound/outbound filters, configure Remote Authentication Dial-In User Service (RADIUS) server, configure RADIUS proxy, remote access protocols, Connection Manager	5, 6, 7
Configure Network Access Protection (NAP). May include but is not limited to: network layer protection, DHCP enforcement, VPN enforcement, configure NAP health policies, IPsec enforcement, 802.1x enforcement, flexible host isolation	7
Configure network authentication. May include but is not limited to: LAN authentication by using NTLMv2 and Kerberos, WLAN authentication by using 802.1x, RAS authentication by using MS-CHAP, MS-CHAP v2, and EAP	6, 7
Configure wireless access. May include but is not limited to: Set Service Identifier (SSID), Wired Equivalent Privacy (WEP), Wi-Fi Protected Access (WPA), Wi-Fi Protected Access 2 (WPA2), ad hoc versus infrastructure mode, group policy for wireless	6
Configure firewall settings. May include but is not limited to: incoming and outgoing traffic filtering, Active Directory account integration, identify ports and protocols, Microsoft Windows Firewall versus Windows Firewall with Advanced Security, configure firewall by using group policy, isolation policy	7
CONFIGURING FILE AND PRINT SERVICES	
Configure a file server. May include but is not limited to: file share publishing, Offline Files, share permissions, NTFS permissions, encrypting file system (EFS)	8
Configure Distributed File System (DFS). May include but is not limited to: DFS namespace, DFS configuration and application, creating and configuring targets, DFS replication	8
Configure shadow copy services. May include but is not limited to: recover previous versions, set schedule, set storage locations	9
Configure backup and restore. May include but is not limited to: backup types, backup schedules, managing remotely, restoring data	9
Manage disk quotas. May include but is not limited to: quota by volume or quota by user, quota entries, quota templates	8

Sybex®
An Imprint of
WILEY

MCTS
Windows Server® 2008
Network Infrastructure
Configuration
Study Guide

Will Panek

Tylor Wentworth

James Chellis

Wiley Publishing, Inc.

Acquisitions Editor: Jeff Kellum
Development Editor: Stef Jones
Technical Editor: Rodney Fournier
Production Editor: Eric Charbonneau
Copy Editor: Kim Wimpsett
Production Manager: Tim Tate
Vice President and Executive Group Publisher: Richard Swadley
Vice President and Executive Publisher: Joseph B. Wikert
Vice President and Publisher: Neil Edde
Media Project Managers: Laura Moss-Hollister and Jenny Swisher
Media Assistant Producer: Josh Frank
Media Quality Assurance: Kit Malone
Book Designer: Judy Fung
Compositor: Laurie Stewart, Happenstance Type-O-Rama
Proofreaders: Ben Lee; Jen Larsen, Word One
Indexer: Nancy Guenther
Cover Designer: Ryan Sneed

Copyright © 2008 by Wiley Publishing, Inc., Indianapolis, Indiana
Published simultaneously in Canada
ISBN: 978-0-470-26169-9

For general information on our other products and services or to obtain technical support, please contact our Customer Care Department within the U.S. at (800) 762-2974, outside the U.S. at (317) 572-3993 or fax (317) 572-4002.

Wiley also publishes its books in a variety of electronic formats. Some content that appears in print may not be available in electronic books.

Library of Congress Cataloging-in-Publication Data

Chellis, James.
  MCTS : Windows server 2008 network infrastructure configuration study guide (exam 70-642) / James Chellis. -- 1st ed.
     p. cm.
  ISBN 978-0-470-26169-9 (paper/cd-rom)
  1. Electronic data processing personnel--Certification. 2. Microsoft software--Examinations--Study guides. 3. Computer networks--Examinations--Study guides. 4. Microsoft Windows server. I. Title.
  QA76.3.C455 2008
  005.4'476--dc22

                     2008016816

10 9 8 7 6 5 4 3

Dear Reader,

Thank you for choosing *MCTS: Windows Server 2008 Network Infrastructure Configuration Study Guide (70-642)*. This book is part of a family of premium quality Sybex books, all written by outstanding authors who combine practical experience with a gift for teaching.

Sybex was founded in 1976. More than thirty years later, we're still committed to producing consistently exceptional books. With each of our titles we're working hard to set a new standard for the industry. From the paper we print on, to the authors we work with, our goal is to bring you the best books available.

I hope you see all that reflected in these pages. I'd be very interested to hear your comments and get your feedback on how we're doing. Feel free to let me know what you think about this or any other Sybex book by sending me an email at nedde@wiley.com, or if you think you've found a technical error in this book, please visit http://sybex.custhelp.com. Customer feedback is critical to our efforts at Sybex.

Best regards,

Neil Edde
Vice President and Publisher
Sybex, an Imprint of Wiley

Acknowledgments

First I would like to thank my wife, Crystal, and my two daughters, Alexandria and Paige. They put up with me missing many events while working on this project.

Thanks to my co-author Tylor Wentworth for his friendship and laughter. A person could not ask for a better partner and friend.

Thanks to James Chellis for giving me the opportunity to work with him on this project. It is always an honor to have my name next to his on this book.

Thanks to Jeff Kellum for helping me through this process and always being there when I needed guidance. Thanks to Stef Jones for the endless hours of editing. It was a pleasure to work with her on this project. Thanks to Rodney Fournier (another geek like me) who is one of the best Tech Editors a writer could ask for and Eric Charbonneau for guiding me through the finish line. Also, I would like to thank all the other editors and staff at Wiley who helped make this book better. I feel fortunate to have been able to work with all of you.

Finally, I would like to thank Todd Lammle for all his friendship and support. His dedication and guidance to this industry helps motivate us to be better.

—Will Panek

I'd like to start by thanking my wife, Julie, for supporting all my obsessions. I'd also like to thank Travis and Jessie for their support.

I would also like to thank Will for persevering, motivating, and pushing me to go beyond the pondering stage and take action; without him this book would not be in existence.

—Tylor Wentworth

About the Authors

William Panek (MCP®, MCP+I®, MCSA®, MCSA® W/SECURITY & MESSAGING, MCSE – NT (3.51 & 4.0)®, MCSE – 2000 & 2003®, MCSE W/SECURITY & MESSAGING, MCDBA®, MCT®, MCTS® (Windows Server 2008 Active Directory: Configuration, Windows Server 2008 Applications Infrastructure: Configuration, Windows Server 2008 Network Infrastructure: Configuration, Microsoft Windows Vista: Configuration, SQL Server 2005), MCITP®, CCNA®, CHFI®)

After many successful years in the computer industry and a degree in computer programming, William Panek decided that he could better use his talents and his personality as an instructor. He started teaching for The Associates—instructing at such schools as Boston University, Clark University, and Globalnet, just to name a few. In 1998 William started Stellacon Corporation. Stellacon has become one of New England's leading training companies. He brings years of real world expertise to the classroom and strives to ensure that each and every student has an understanding of the course material. Over his 10 years of teaching experience, William has helped thousands of students get certified.

William currently resides in New Hampshire with his wife and their two daughters. In his spare time he is a commercially rated helicopter pilot and volunteer fire fighter.

Tylor Wentworth (MCP®, MCP+I®, MCSA®, MCSA® W/SECURITY & MESSAGING, MCSE – NT (4.0)®, MCSE – 2000 & 2003®, MCSE W/SECURITY & MESSAGING, MCT®, MCTS®, CCNA®, CCNP®, BSEE, FCC RF Licensed)

Tylor Wentworth is a member of the IEEE with membership in the standards committee. Tylor has been involved in computers and networking for over fifteen years. He has worked for large companies such as Computer Associates, Liberty Mutual, Time Warner, Fairpoint Communications, Enterasys, among many others. He has shared his networking knowledge and experience developing and delivering custom curriculum for numerous network infrastructure classes, recently completing VPN, Voice over IP, IPv6, and QoS. He delivers Microsoft Official Curriculum both publicly and privately on a regular basis. Tylor owned Intelligence Quest, a training company which merged with Stellacon Corporation and is now Director of Operations for Stellacon with training locations in Portsmouth and North Conway, New Hampshire as well as Dallas, Texas.

Tylor currently lives in Maine with his wife, Julie. They have a son and a daughter, both of whom are attending college in Maine.

James Chellis, MCSE, has co-authored more than 30 IT certification titles in print. He is currently CEO of Comcourse, Inc., an online education provider.

Contents at a Glance

Table of Contents

Table of Exercises

Introduction

Microsoft has recently changed its certification program to contain three primary series: Technology, Professional, and Architect. The Technology Series is intended to allow candidates to target specific technologies and is the basis for obtaining the Professional Series and Architect Series of certifications. The certifications contained within the Technology Series consist of one to three exams, focus on a specific technology, and do not include job-role skills. By contrast, the Professional Series focuses on a job role and is not necessarily focused on a single technology but rather a comprehensive set of skills for performing the job role being tested. The Architect Series offered by Microsoft contains the premier certifications that consist of passing a review board of previously certified architects. To apply for the Architect Series of certifications, you must have a minimum of 10 years of industry experience.

When obtaining a Technology Series certification, you are recognized as a Microsoft Certified Technology Specialist (MCTS) on the specific technology or technologies on which you have been tested. The Professional Series certifications include Microsoft Certified IT Professional (MCITP) and Microsoft Certified Professional Developer (MCPD). Passing the review board for an Architect Series certification will allow you to become a Microsoft Certified Architect (MCA).

This book has been developed to give you the critical skills and knowledge you need to prepare for the exam requirement for obtaining the MCTS: Windows Server 2008 Network Infrastructure Configuration (exam 70-642).

The Microsoft Certified Professional Program

Since the inception of its certification program, Microsoft has certified more than 2 million people. As the computer network industry continues to increase in both size and complexity, this number is sure to grow—and the need for *proven* ability will also increase. Certifications can help companies verify the skills of prospective employees and contractors.

Microsoft has developed its Microsoft Certified Professional (MCP) program to give you credentials that verify your ability to work with Microsoft products effectively and professionally. Several levels of certification are available based on specific suites of exams. Microsoft has recently created a new generation of certification programs:

Microsoft Certified Technology Specialist (MCTS)   The MCTS is the entry-level certification for the new generation of Microsoft certifications. The MCTS certification program targets specific technologies instead of specific job roles. You must take and pass one to three exams.

Microsoft Certified IT Professional (MCITP)   The MCITP certification is a Professional Series certification that tests network and systems administrators on job roles, rather than only on a specific technology. The MCITP generally consists of passing one to three exams, in addition to obtaining an MCTS-level certification.

Microsoft Certified Professional Developer (MCPD)   The MCPD certification is a Professional Series certification for application developers. Similar to the MCITP, the MCPD is focused on a job role rather than on a single technology. The MCPD generally consists of passing one to three exams, in addition to obtaining an MCTS-level certification.

Microsoft Certified Architect (MCA)   The MCA is Microsoft's premier certification series. Obtaining the MCA requires a minimum of 10 years of experience and requires the candidate to pass a review board consisting of peer architects.

How Do You Become Certified on Windows Server 2008 Network Infrastructure?

Attaining a Microsoft certification has always been a challenge. In the past, students have been able to acquire detailed exam information—even most of the exam questions—from online "brain dumps" and third-party "cram" books or software products. For the current generation of exams, this is simply not the case.

Microsoft has taken strong steps to protect the security and integrity of its new certification tracks. Now prospective candidates must complete a course of study that develops detailed knowledge about a wide range of topics. It supplies them with the true skills needed, derived from working with the technology being tested.

The new generations of Microsoft certification programs are heavily weighted toward hands-on skills and experience. It is recommended that candidates have troubleshooting skills acquired through hands-on experience and working knowledge.

Fortunately, if you are willing to dedicate the time and effort to learn Windows Server 2008 Network Infrastructure, you can prepare yourself well for the exam by using the proper tools. By working through this book, you can successfully meet the exam requirements to pass the Windows Server 2008 Network Infrastructure exam.

This book is part of a complete series of Microsoft certification study guides, published by Sybex, Inc., that together cover the new MCTS, MCITP, MCPD exams, as well as the core MCSA and MCSE operating system requirements. Please visit the Sybex website at www.sybex.com for complete program and product details.

MCTS Exam Requirements

Candidates for MCTS certification on Windows Server 2008 network infrastructure must pass one Windows Server 2008 Network Infrastructure Configuration exam. Other MCTS certifications may require up to three exams. For a more detailed description of the Microsoft certification programs, including a list of all the exams, visit the Microsoft Learning website at www.microsoft.com/learning/mcp.

The Windows Server 2008 Network Infrastructure, Configuring Exam

The Windows Server 2008 Network Infrastructure, Configuring exam covers concepts and skills related to installing, configuring, and managing Windows Server 2008 network infrastructure. It emphasizes network infrastructure support and administration.

This exam is quite specific regarding Windows Server 2008 network infrastructure requirements and operational settings, and it can be particular about how administrative tasks are performed within network infrastructure.

Microsoft provides exam objectives to give you a general overview of possible areas of coverage on the Microsoft exams. Keep in mind, however, that exam objectives are subject to change at any time without prior notice and at Microsoft's sole discretion. Please visit the Microsoft Learning website (www.microsoft.com/learning/mcp) for the most current listing of exam objectives.

Types of Exam Questions

In an effort to both refine the testing process and protect the quality of its certifications, Microsoft has focused its current certification exams on real experience and hands-on proficiency. There is a greater emphasis on your past working environments and responsibilities and less emphasis on how well you can memorize. In fact, Microsoft says that certification candidates should have hands-on experience before attempting to pass any certification exams.

Microsoft will accomplish its goal of protecting the exams' integrity by regularly adding and removing exam questions, limiting the number of questions that any individual sees in a beta exam, limiting the number of questions delivered to an individual by using adaptive testing, and adding new exam elements.

Exam questions may be in a variety of formats: depending on which exam you take, you'll see multiple-choice questions, select-and-place questions, and prioritize-a-list questions. Simulations and case studies are included as well. You may also find yourself taking what's called an *adaptive format exam*. In the following sections, we'll cover the types of exam questions and examine the different testing techniques, so you'll be prepared for all the possibilities.

The Microsoft Windows Server 2008 exams provide a detailed score breakdown, describing which areas you did well in and which areas need improvement.

Multiple-Choice Questions

Multiple-choice questions come in two main forms. One is a straightforward question followed by several possible answers, of which one or more is correct. The other type of multiple-choice question is more complex and based on a specific scenario. The scenario may focus on several areas or objectives.

Select-and-Place Questions

Select-and-place exam questions involve graphical elements that you must manipulate to successfully answer the question. For example, you might see a diagram of a computer network, as shown in the following graphic taken from the select-and-place demo downloaded from Microsoft's website:

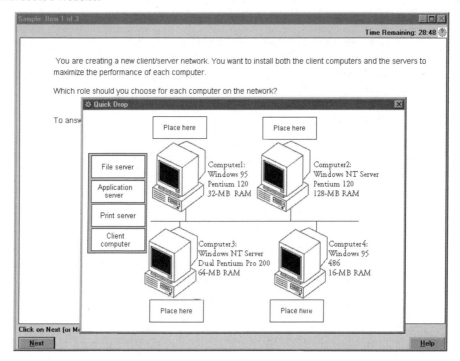

A typical diagram will show computers and other components next to boxes that contain the text *Place here*. The labels for the boxes represent various computer roles on a network, such as a print server and a file server. Based on information given for each computer, you are asked to select each label and place it in the correct box. You need to place *all* of the labels correctly. No credit is given for the question if you correctly label only some of the boxes.

In another select-and-place problem, you might be asked to put a series of steps in order by dragging items from boxes on the left to boxes on the right and placing them in the correct order. One other type requires that you drag an item from the left and place it under an item in a column on the right.

For more information on the various exam question types, go to
www.microsoft.com/learning/mcpexams/policies/innovations.asp.

Simulations

Simulations are the kinds of questions that most closely represent actual situations and test the skills you use while working with Microsoft software interfaces. These exam questions include a mock interface on which you are asked to perform certain actions according to a given scenario. The simulated interfaces look nearly identical to what you see in the actual product, as shown in the following graphic:

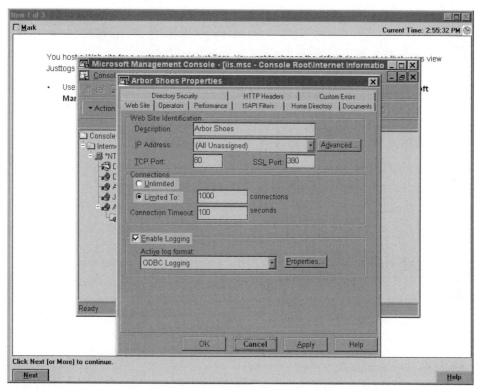

Because of the number of possible errors that can be made on simulations, be sure to consider the following recommendations from Microsoft:

- Do not change any simulation settings that don't pertain to the solution directly.

- When related information has not been provided, assume that the default settings are used.

- Make sure your entries are spelled correctly.

- Close all the simulation application windows after completing the set of tasks in the simulation.

The best way to prepare for simulation questions is to spend time working with the graphical interface of the product on which you will be tested.

Case Studies

Case studies first appeared in the MCSD program. The questions for the case studies present a scenario with a range of requirements. Based on the information provided, you answer a series of multiple-choice and select-and-place questions. The interface for case study questions has a number of tabs, each of which contains information about the scenario. Currently, this type of question appears only in the Design exams.

Microsoft will regularly add and remove questions from the exams. This is called *item seeding*. It is part of the effort to make it more difficult for individuals to merely memorize exam questions that were passed along by previous test-takers.

Tips for Taking the MCTS: Windows Server 2008 Network Infrastructure, Configuring Exam

Here are some general tips for achieving success on your certification exam:

- Arrive early at the exam center so you can relax and review your study materials. During this final review, you can look over tables and lists of exam-related information.

- Read the questions carefully. Don't be tempted to jump to an early conclusion. Make sure you know *exactly* what the question is asking.

- Answer all questions. If you are unsure about a question, then mark the question for review and return to the question at a later time.

- On simulations, do not change settings that are not directly related to the question. Also, assume default settings if the question does not specify or imply which settings are used.

- For questions you're not sure about, use a process of elimination to get rid of the obviously incorrect answers first. This improves your odds of selecting the correct answer when you need to make an educated guess.

Exam Registration

You may take the Microsoft exams at any of more than 1,000 Authorized Prometric Testing Centers (APTCs) around the world. For the location of a testing center near you, call Prometric at 800-755-EXAM (755-3926). Outside the United States and Canada, contact your local Prometric registration center.

Find out the number of the exam you want to take, and then register with the Prometric registration center nearest to you. At this point, you will be asked for advance payment for the exam. The exams are $125 each, and you must take them within one year of payment. You can schedule exams up to six weeks in advance or as late as one working day prior to the date of the exam. You can cancel or reschedule your exam if you contact the center at least two working days prior to the exam. Same-day registration is available in some locations, subject to space availability. Where same-day registration is available, you must register a minimum of two hours before test time.

> You can also register for your exams online at www.prometric.com.

When you schedule the exam, you will be provided with instructions regarding appointment and cancellation procedures, ID requirements, and information about the testing center location. In addition, you will receive a registration and payment confirmation letter from Prometric.

Microsoft requires certification candidates to accept the terms of a nondisclosure agreement before taking certification exams.

Is This Book for You?

If you want to acquire a solid foundation in Windows Server 2008 network infrastructure and your goal is to prepare for the exam by learning how to use and manage the new operating system, this book is for you. You'll find clear explanations of the fundamental concepts you need to grasp and plenty of help to achieve the high level of professional competency you need to succeed in your chosen field.

If you want to become certified as an MCTS, this book is definitely for you. However, if you just want to attempt to pass the exam without really understanding Windows Server 2008 network infrastructure, this study guide is *not* for you. It is written for people who want to acquire hands-on skills and in-depth knowledge of Windows Server 2008 network infrastructure.

What's in the Book?

What makes a Sybex study guide the book of choice for hundreds of thousands of MCTSs? We took into account not only what you need to know to pass the exam but also what you need to know to take what you've learned and apply it in the real world. Each book contains the following:

Objective-by-objective coverage of the topics you need to know   Each chapter lists the objectives covered in that chapter.

> The topics covered in this study guide map directly to Microsoft's official exam objectives. Each exam objective is covered completely.

Assessment test   Directly following this introduction is an assessment test that you should take. It is designed to help you determine how much you already know about Windows Server

2008 network infrastructure. Each question is tied to a topic discussed in the book. Using the results of the assessment test, you can figure out the areas where you need to focus your study. Of course, we do recommend you read the entire book.

Exam essentials   To highlight what you learn, you'll find a list of exam essentials at the end of each chapter. The "Exam Essentials" section briefly highlights the topics that need your particular attention as you prepare for the exam.

Glossary   Throughout each chapter, you will be introduced to important terms and concepts that you will need to know for the exam. These terms appear in italic within the chapters, and at the end of the book, a detailed glossary defines these terms, as well as other general terms you should know.

Review questions, complete with detailed explanations   Each chapter is followed by a set of review questions that test what you learned in the chapter. The questions are written with the exam in mind, meaning that they are designed to have the same look and feel as what you'll see on the exam. Question types are just like the exam, including multiple choice, exhibits, and select-and-place.

Hands-on exercises   In each chapter (with the exception of Chapter 1, which is more an introduction to network infrastructure), you'll find exercises designed to give you the important hands-on experience that is critical for your exam preparation. The exercises support the topics of the chapter, and they walk you through the steps necessary to perform a particular function.

Real-world scenarios   Because reading a book isn't enough for you to learn how to apply these topics in your everyday duties, we have provided real-world scenarios in sidebars. These explain when and why a particular solution would make sense, in a working environment you'd actually encounter.

Interactive CD   Every Sybex study guide comes with a CD complete with additional questions, flashcards for use with an interactive device, and the book in electronic format. Details are in the following section.

What's on the CD?

With this new member of our best-selling Study Guide series, we are including quite an array of training resources. The CD offers bonus exams and flashcards to help you study for the exam. We have also included the complete contents of the study guide in electronic form. The CD's resources are described here:

The Sybex e-book for MCTS: Windows Server 2008 Network Infrastructure Configuration (exam 70-642)   Many people like the convenience of being able to carry their whole study guide on a CD. They also like being able to search the text via computer to find specific information quickly and easily. For these reasons, the entire contents of this study guide are supplied on the CD in PDF. We've also included Adobe Acrobat Reader, which provides the interface for the PDF contents as well as the search capabilities.

The Sybex test engine   This is a collection of multiple-choice questions that will help you prepare for your exam. There are four sets of questions:

- Two bonus exams designed to simulate the actual live exam.
- All the questions from the study guide, presented in a test engine for your review. You can review questions by chapter or by objective, or you can take a random test.
- The assessment test.

Here is a sample screen from the Sybex test engine:

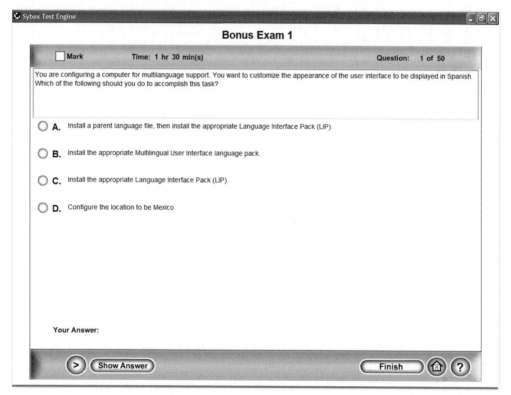

Sybex flashcards for PCs and handheld devices   The "flashcard" style of question offers an effective way to quickly and efficiently test your understanding of the fundamental concepts covered in the exam. The Sybex flashcards set consists of 100 questions presented in a special engine developed specifically for this Study Guide series. Here's what the Sybex flashcards interface looks like:

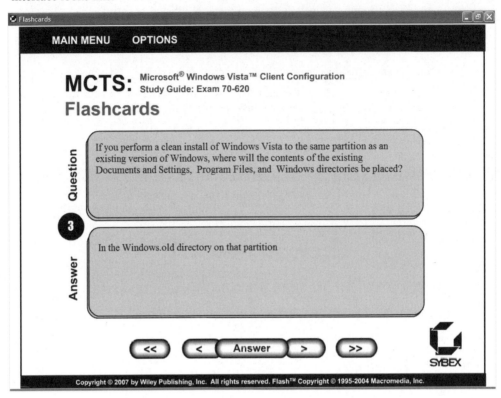

Because of the high demand for a product that will run on handheld devices, we have also developed, in conjunction with Land-J Technologies, a version of the flashcard questions that you can take with you on your Palm OS PDA (including the PalmPilot and Handspring's Visor).

Hardware and Software Requirements

You should verify that your computer meets the minimum requirements for installing Windows Server 2008 (for current Windows 2008 requirements, check out Microsoft's website). We suggest that your computer meets or exceeds the recommended requirements for a more enjoyable experience.

The exercises in this book assume that your computer is configured in a specific manner. Your computer should have at least a 20 GB drive that is configured with the minimum space requirements and partitions. Other exercises in this book assume that your computer is configured as follows:

- 20 GB C: partition with the NTFS filesystem

- Optional D: partition with the NTFS filesystem
- 15 GB or more of free space

Of course, you can allocate more space to your partitions if it is available.

The first exercise in the book assumes you have installed Windows Server 2008 and that your partitions have already been created and formatted as previously specified.

Contacts and Resources

To find out more about Microsoft Education and Certification materials and programs, to register with Prometric, or to obtain other useful certification information and additional study resources, check the following resources:

Microsoft Learning Home Page

www.microsoft.com/learning

This website provides information about the MCP program and exams. You can also order the latest Microsoft Roadmap to Education and Certification.

Microsoft TechNet Technical Information Network

www.microsoft.com/technet

800-344-2121

Use this website or phone number to contact support professionals and system administrators. Outside the United States and Canada, contact your local Microsoft subsidiary for information.

Prometric

www.prometric.com

800-755-3936

Contact Prometric to register to take an exam at any of more than 800 Prometric Testing Centers around the world.

***Microsoft Certified Professional Magazine* Online**

www.mcpmag.com

Microsoft Certified Professional Magazine is a well-respected publication that focuses on Windows certification. This site hosts chats and discussion forums and tracks news related to the MCTS and MCITP programs. Some of the services cost a fee, but they are well worth it.

WindowsITPro magazine

www.windowsITPro.com

You can subscribe to this magazine or read free articles at the website. The study resource provides general information on Windows Vista, Server, and .NET Server.

Assessment Test

1. The time to live (TTL) attached to a DNS record _____.

   A. cannot be used by a resolver; it can be used only by servers making recursive queries

   B. is used only by resolvers

   C. is used to determine how long to cache retrieved results

   D. is refreshed each time the record is modified

2. Which of the following settings cannot be adjusted when using RIP?

   A. The RIP version that can be used for incoming and outgoing traffic on each interface

   B. The set of peer routers from which routes will be accepted

   C. The default announcement interval

   D. The location where received RIP routes are stored

3. You want to set up VPN access for 30 users, and the connections must be encrypted. There is a central Windows Server 2008 domain for your users. Which of the following is the most appropriate VPN solution in this case?

   A. L2TP + IPSec

   B. PPTP

   C. Either A or B

   D. None of the above

4. To enable DHCP-DNS integration, you must do which of the following?

   A. Configure the scope to allow it to use Dynamic DNS only.

   B. Configure the server to allow it to use Dynamic DNS only.

   C. Configure the scope and the server.

   D. Configure the scope or the server.

5. RRAS allows you to create which types of routing-related filters?

   A. Route filters only

   B. Peer filters only

   C. Route and peer filters

   D. Packet filters only

6. What is the IPSec Policy Agent?

   A. It is an optional component that's required when using IPSec with Active Directory.

   B. It is an optional component that's required when using IPSec without Active Directory.

   C. It is an optional component that's required when using IPSec with L2TP.

   D. It is a mandatory component that's required to use IPSec.

7. The seven layers of the OSI model do which of the following?

    A. Map exactly to Windows 2000 networking services and components

    B. Provide a useful conceptual framework for grouping services

    C. A and B

    D. None of the above

8. To test whether a DNS server is answering queries properly, you can use which of the following tools?

    A. The `ping` tool

    B. The `nslookup` tool

    C. The `tracert` tool

    D. The `ipconfig` tool

9. What two modes do RIP routers send updates in?

    A. Link-state database mode

    B. Autostatic update mode

    C. Periodic update mode

    D. Border mode

10. You have installed the DHCP Server service on a member server in your domain and have configured a scope, but clients cannot lease an address. What is the most likely cause of this problem?

    A. The scope is not activated.

    B. There are too many DHCP servers.

    C. The DHCP server is not authorized.

    D. The DHCP server is in another subnet.

11. Which of the following statements about Windows Server 2008 Dynamic DNS is true?

    A. DDNS requires a Microsoft DHCP server to work.

    B. The Windows Server 2008 DDNS server can interoperate with recent versions of BIND.

    C. DDNS clients may not register their own addresses.

    D. DDNS works only with Microsoft clients and servers.

12. VPN connections require which of the following? (Choose two.)

    A. The Windows Server 2008 VPN add-on

    B. The name or IP address of the VPN server

    C. The phone number of the VPN server

    D. An existing TCP/IP connection

13. To reject any incoming call from a client that can't use a specified level of encryption, you would do which of the following?

 A. Turn off the No Encryption check box on the Encryption tab of the remote access policy's profile.

 B. Turn off the No Encryption check box on the Security tab of the server's Properties dialog box.

 C. Create a new remote access profile named Require Encryption.

 D. Check the Require Encryption check box in each user's profile.

14. Which of the following is not an OSI layer?

 A. Session

 B. Application

 C. Presentation

 D. Service

15. DHCP address range exclusions are assigned at which level?

 A. Server level

 B. Scope level

 C. Superscope level

 D. Multicast scope level

16. Which of the following is true about IPSec?

 A. Can be used by itself

 B. Can be used only with L2TP

 C. Cannot be used with L2TP

 D. Requires third-party software for Windows 2000 and newer

17. Which of the following are true of dynamically maintained routing tables? (Choose all that apply.)

 A. They are automatically maintained by the routing protocols.

 B. They are normally not maintained across reboots.

 C. They may be manually edited from the command line.

 D. They consist of multiple entries, each containing a network ID, a forwarding address, and a metric.

18. The DHCP relay agent serves which function on the network?

 A. It listens for DHCP messages on a network and forwards them to a DHCP server on another network.

 B. It accepts DHCP messages from multiple networks and consolidates them for a single DHCP server.

 C. It allows DHCP clients to use WINS services.

 D. It relays DHCP requests to a Dynamic DNS server.

19. Which of the following protocols or services is not required for an Active Directory installation?

    A. TCP/IP

    B. DNS

    C. LDAP

    D. NetBEUI

20. You can control VPN access through which of the following mechanisms? (Choose two.)

    A. Individual user account properties

    B. Remote access policies

    C. Remote access profiles

    D. Group Policy objects

21. What is a mirrored rule?

    A. It is a single rule that specifies the same source and destination for two different protocols.

    B. It is a single rule that specifies the same source and destination for inbound and outbound traffic.

    C. It is a pair of rules specifying the same source and destination for two different protocols.

    D. It is a pair of rules specifying different source and destination addresses for the same protocol.

22. What is the replication of DNS data from one server to another called?

    A. Replication pass

    B. Zone transfer

    C. Replication transfer

    D. Zone replication

23. If settings on a local machine conflict with settings assigned by a DHCP server, which of the following statements are not true? (Choose all that apply.)

    A. None of the conflicting settings will apply.

    B. The DHCP-assigned settings override the locally assigned settings.

    C. Whichever settings are applied first take effect.

    D. The locally assigned settings override the DHCP-assigned settings.

24. To enable dial-up users to get a pooled IP address, you must do which of the following?

    A. Define an address pool on the IP tab of the server's Properties dialog box.

    B. Define an address pool in the remote access policy.

    C. Add a DHCP address range for the dial-up users.

    D. Disable the DHCP address allocator.

25. Which option is used as a tool to compare your desired security settings with your current security settings?

    A. Security template

    B. Security database

    C. Security profile

    D. Security analyst

26. Which policy types are applied to the computer as opposed to users and groups? (Choose all that apply.)

    A. Password policies

    B. Account lockout policies

    C. User rights assignment policies

    D. Security options

27. How do you open the IP Security Monitor in Windows Server 2008?

    A. Select Start ➢ Run, and type **ipsecmon**.

    B. Select Start ➢ Administrative Tools ➢ IP Security Monitor.

    C. Select Start ➢ Accessories ➢ IP Security Monitor.

    D. Add the IP Security Monitor snap-in to the MMC.

28. What is the name of the file that stores information for a DNS zone?

    A. domain_name.dns

    B. LMHOSTS

    C. ZONES

    D. SERVERS

29. Which of the following statements is true regarding caching-only servers?

    A. They are authoritative for a domain.

    B. They perform queries.

    C. They contain zone files.

    D. They participate in zone transfers.

30. Which of the following options determines the permissions and restrictions for users dialing in to a remote access server?

    A. Remote access policies

    B. Remote access profiles

    C. Filter lists

    D. Authentication methods

Answers to Assessment Test

1. C. The TTL indicates how long the record may be safely cached; it may or may not be modified when the record is created. See Chapter 3 for more information on TTL.

2. D. The Routing Information Protocol (RIP) implementation in Windows Server 2008 allows you to mix RIP versions, control which peer routers can send you updates, and control how often your router will broadcast updates to others. However, it does now allow you to change where the routing table data is stored. See Chapter 5 for more information.

3. C. L2TP + IPSec and PPTP can both be encrypted, and with the guidelines set forth in the question, either one would do the job. See Chapter 3 for more information.

4. D. You can enable integration either on one scope only or on all scopes on a server. See Chapter 4 for more information.

5. C. Route filters let you accept or ignore individual routes; peer filters give you control over from which other routers your router accepts routing information. See Chapter 6 for more information.

6. D. The IPSec Policy Agent is the component that downloads IPSec policy settings from the local computer or Active Directory. Accordingly, presence is required for IPSec to function. See Chapter 3 for more information.

7. B. The OSI model is a stylized network model that can be used to compare and contrast implementations from different vendors. See Chapter 1 for more information on the OSI model.

8. B. The `nslookup` tool allows you to look up name and address information. See Chapter 3 for more information.

9. B, C. In periodic update mode, a RIP router sends its list of known routes at periodic intervals (which you define). In autostatic update mode, the RRAS router broadcasts the contents of its routing table only when a remote router asks for it. See Chapter 5 for more information.

10. C. If the DHCP server isn't authorized, it will not answer lease requests; therefore, the client will end up with no address. See Chapter 4 for more information.

11. B. DDNS works with BIND 8.2 and later. See Chapter 3 for more information on DDNS.

12. B, D. VPN connections piggyback on top of regular dial-up or dedicated TCP/IP connections, and you must specify the name or address of the server you're calling. See Chapter 7 for more information.

13. A. The profile associated with each remote access policy controls whether that policy will require, allow, or disallow encryption. To force encryption, create a policy that disallows using no encryption. See Chapter 7 for more information.

14. D. The Session, Application, and Presentation layers are all part of the OSI model, but the Service layer isn't. See Chapter 1 for more information on the OSI layers.

15. B. Scopes or ranges of addresses can be assigned only at the scope level. The scope range includes the exclusion range. See Chapter 4 for more information.

16. A.   IPSec is a stand-alone protocol included in Windows Server 2008 that can be used by itself or in conjunction with Layer 2 Tunneling Protocol (L2TP). See Chapter 2 for more information.

17. A, C, D.   The routing engines maintain the contents of the routing table, although you can add or remove entries manually. Persistent routes, which are the default, are automatically maintained until you delete them manually. See Chapter 5 for more information.

18. A.   The DHCP relay agent allows you to use a DHCP server that resides on one network to communicate with clients that live on a separate network. See Chapter 4 for more information.

19. D.   NetBEUI is deprecated, but the other three protocols are required for Active Directory. See Chapter 2 for more information.

20. A, B.   You can allow users to make VPN connections by modifying individual account properties; if you're using a native mode Windows Server 2008 domain, you can also use remote access policies. See Chapter 6 for more information.

21. B.   A mirrored rule that maps a source address of A and a destination of B actually acts as two rules: source A/destination B for outbound traffic and source B/destination A for inbound traffic. See Chapter 5 for more information.

22. B.   *Zone transfer* is the term used for the transfer of resource records from one zone to another. See Chapter 3 for more information.

23. A, B, C.   Local settings always override settings specified by the DHCP server. See Chapter 4 for more information.

24. A.   To assign static IP addresses to dial-up clients, you have to define a pool of addresses on the server; this pool is used instead of allowing DHCP assignments to clients. See Chapter 4 for more information.

25. A.   Using the Security Configuration and Analysis tool, you can compare the security settings defined in a security template with a specific computer's actual security settings. See Chapter 7 for more information.

26. A, B, D.   Security options apply to computers as opposed to users and groups. See Chapter 7 for more information.

27. D.   In Windows Server 2008, IP Security Monitor is implemented as an MMC snap-in. See Chapter 2 for more information.

28. A.   The `domain_name.dns` file stores name-to-address mappings for DNS. LMHOSTS is used for WINS, and the other two options are not valid. See Chapter 3 for more information.

29. B.   DNS caching-only servers perform queries and cache the results, but they are not authoritative for any domains and do not contain zone files or participate in zone transfers. See Chapter 3 for more information.

30. A.   Remote access policies determine who can log on to the remote access server and provide restrictions such as time of day and callback. Profiles determine the settings that apply after a user has successfully logged on. The other two options apply to IPSec and not to RAS. See Chapter 7 for more information.

Chapter

1

Understanding Windows Server 2008 Networking

Microsoft has put an immense amount of time and effort into building Windows Server 2008. Much is new in the operating system, but it still retains a great deal of core code from Windows 2000, Windows 2003, and even Windows NT, Internet Information Services, and Exchange Server. Windows Server 2008 is a large, complicated, and very powerful operating system. To use it effectively, you have to understand how it works and how to make it do what you want it to do.

This book is a study guide for the Microsoft Windows Server 2008 exam 70-642. So, it only makes sense to start with a discussion of network protocols and which protocols have been included and removed in Windows Server 2008.

Having a good frame of reference helps when discussing network protocols. To establish such a framework, this chapter will start with the OSI network model, a sort of idealized way to stack various protocols together. Then the chapter will cover the different Microsoft Windows network models and which one would work best for your company.

While discussing these topics, we will cover the necessary background information in order for you to be successful on the 70-642 exam as well as work with Windows Server 2008 on the network.

Understanding the OSI Model

The International Organization for Standardization (ISO) began developing the Open Systems Interconnection (OSI) reference model in 1977. OSI has since become the most widely accepted model for understanding network communication; once you understand how the OSI model works, you can use it to compare network implementations on different systems.

When you want to communicate with another person, you need to have two things in common: a communication language and a communication medium. Computer networks are no different; for communication to take place on a network composed of a variety of different network devices, both the language and the medium must be clearly defined. The OSI model (and networking models developed by other organizations) attempts to define rules that cover both the generalities and the specifics of networks:

- How network devices contact each other and, if they have different languages, how they communicate with each other

- Methods by which a device on a network knows when to transmit data and when not to transmit it

- Methods to ensure that network transmissions are received correctly and by the right recipient
- How the physical transmission media is arranged and connected
- How to ensure that network devices maintain a proper rate of data flow
- How bits are represented on the network media

The OSI model isn't a product. It's just a conceptual framework you can use to better understand the complex interactions taking place among the various devices on a network. It doesn't do anything in the communication process; appropriate software and hardware do the actual work. The OSI model simply defines which tasks need to be done and which protocols will handle those tasks at each of the seven layers of the model. The seven layers are as follows:

- Application (layer 7)
- Presentation (layer 6)
- Session (layer 5)
- Transport (layer 4)
- Network (layer 3)
- Data-Link (layer 2)
- Physical (layer 1)

 You can remember the seven layers from top to bottom using a handy mnemonic, such as "All People Seem To Need Data Processing."

Each of the seven layers has a distinct function, which we'll explore a little later in the chapter.

The True IP Protocol Suite

There is another model to represent these same concepts that is truly what the Internet was built upon. The model is known by a few names, including the TCP/IP model, the IP model, or the DoD model (after its designers, the U.S. Department of Defense). The TCP/IP model, as we'll call it, contains only four layers:

- Application
- Transport (sometimes called Host to Host)
- Internet
- Link (also called Network Access)

This model was the one originally used for the design of the Internet. You won't encounter this model on the 70-642 exam, but as a network administrator, you should know that this model exists when you hear your peers talking about it.

Protocol Stacks

The OSI model splits communication tasks into smaller pieces called *subtasks*. Protocol implementations are computer processes that handle these subtasks. Specific protocols fulfill subtasks at specific layers of the OSI model. When these protocols are grouped together to complete a whole task, the assemblage of code is called a *protocol stack*. The stack is just a group of protocols, arranged in layers, that implements an entire communication process. Each layer of the OSI model has a different protocol associated with it. When more than one protocol is needed to complete a communication process, the protocols are grouped together in a stack. An example of a protocol stack is TCP/IP, which is widely used by Unix and the Internet—the TCP and IP protocols are implemented at different OSI layers.

Windows Server 2008 and Windows Vista include the Next Generation TCP/IP protocol stack, which is for both version 4 (IPv4) and version 6 (IPv6) of the Internet Protocol.

Why You Should Care about Protocol Stacks

It may not be incredibly clear right now why you should care about protocol stacks and the OSI model. However, the OSI model and the protocol stacks for Internet communication are the basis upon which the 70-642 exam is built. All things about today's modern network stem from either the OSI or IP model.

Knowing the layers of both models is essential to sound troubleshooting, and though it may not be obvious as you trudge through this background material, knowing the OSI model will help when managing a Windows network. You'll see additional examples of how knowing the OSI model helps when troubleshooting throughout this chapter.

Each layer in the protocol stack receives services from the layer below it and provides services to the layer above it. It can be better explained like this: layer N uses the services of the layer below it (layer N – 1) and provides services to the layer above it (layer N + 1).

For two computers to communicate, the same protocol stacks must be running on each computer. Each layer on both computers' stacks must use compatible protocols in order for the machines to communicate with each other. The computers can have different operating systems and still be able to communicate if they are running the same protocol stacks. For example, a DOS machine running IP can communicate with a Macintosh machine running IP (see Figure 1.1).

FIGURE 1.1   Each layer communicates with its counterparts on other network hosts.

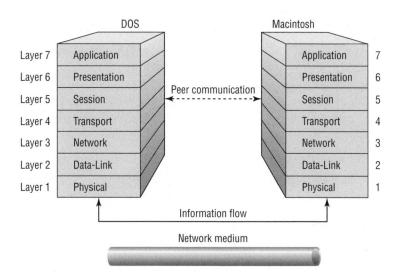

When sending data, each layer in the OSI model places its own information onto the data as it passes down the stack in a process called *encapsulation*. Encapsulation takes place when each layer adds its own header and sometimes trailer information onto the data. When the data is received, it works its way back up the protocol stack, and the corresponding layer of the protocol stack reads this information.

The Physical Layer

The Physical layer is responsible for using electric (or sometimes other types of) signaling to get bits from one computer to another. Physical layer components don't care what the bits *mean*; their job is to get the bits from point A to point B, using whatever kind of optical, electrical, or wireless connection that connects the points. This level defines physical and electrical details, such as what will represent a 1 or a 0, how many pins a network connector will have, and when the network adapter can or cannot transmit the data (see Figure 1.2).

FIGURE 1.2   The Physical layer makes a physical circuit with electrical, optical, or radio signals.

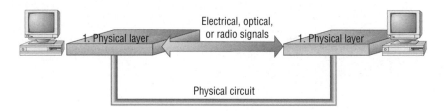

The Physical layer addresses all the small details of the actual physical connection between the computer and the network medium, including the following:

- Network connection types, including multipoint and point-to-point connections.

- Physical topologies, or how the network is physically laid out (for example, bus, star, or ring).

- Which analog and digital signaling methods are used to encode data in the analog and digital signals.

- Bit synchronization, which deals with keeping the sender and receiver in sync as they read and write data.

- Multiplexing, or the process of combining several data channels into one.

- Termination, which prevents signals from reflecting back through the cable and causing signal and packet errors. It also indicates the last node in a network segment.

The Data-Link Layer

The Data-Link layer provides for the flow of data over a single physical link from one device to another. It accepts packets from the Network layer and packages the information into data units called *frames*; these frames are presented to the Physical layer for transmission. The Data-Link layer adds control information, such as the frame type, to the data being sent.

This layer also provides for the error-free transfer of frames from one computer to another. A *cyclic redundancy check* (CRC) added to the data frame can detect damaged frames, and the Data-Link layer in the receiving computer can request that the CRC information be present so that it can check incoming frames for errors. The Data-Link layer can also detect when frames are lost and request that those frames be sent again.

In broadcast networks such as Ethernet, all devices on the LAN receive the data that any device transmits. (Whether a network is broadcast or point-to-point is determined by the network protocols used to transmit data over it.) The Data-Link layer on a particular device is responsible for recognizing frames addressed to that device and throwing the rest away, much as you might sort through your daily mail to separate good stuff from junk. Figure 1.3 shows how the Data-Link layer establishes an error-free connection between two devices.

FIGURE 1.3   The Data-Link layer establishes an error-free link between two devices.

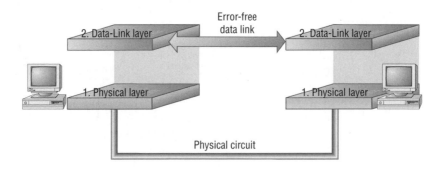

The Institute of Electrical and Electronics Engineers (IEEE) developed a protocol specification known as IEEE 802.X. (802.2 is the standard that divides this layer into two sublayers. The Media Access Control layer, more commonly called the MAC layer, varies depending on the network type and is described further in standards 802.3 through 802.5.) As part of that specification (which today we know as Ethernet), the Data-Link layer is split into two sublayers:

- The Logical Link Control (LLC) layer establishes and maintains the logical communication links between the communicating devices.

- The Media Access Control (MAC) layer acts like an airport control tower—it controls the way multiple devices share the same media channel in the same way that a control tower regulates the flow of air traffic into and out of an airport.

Figure 1.4 illustrates the division of the Data-Link layer into the LLC and MAC layers.

FIGURE 1.4   The IEEE split the ISO Data-Link layer into the LLC sublayer and the MAC sublayer.

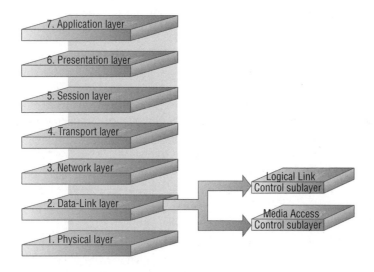

The LLC sublayer provides *service access points* (SAPs) that other computers can refer to and use to transfer information from the LLC sublayer to the upper OSI layers. This is defined in the 802.2 standard.

The MAC sublayer, the lower of the two sublayers, provides for shared access to the network adapter and communicates directly with network interface cards. A unique 48-bit address, commonly represented as a 12-digit hexadecimal MAC address (frequently called the *hardware Ethernet address*), is assigned to network interface cards before they leave the factory where they are made. The LLC sublayer uses MAC addresses to establish logical links between devices on the same LAN. Ethernet is an example of a protocol that exists at the Data-Link layer.

MAC Address Conflicts and Limitations

Historically, one of the more difficult problems to diagnose and fix has been a conflict of MAC addresses between two (or more) devices on a network. Since the MAC address is specific to the hardware, it's sometimes referred to as the *burned-in address*. The MAC consists of 48 bits represented as a 12-digit hexadecimal number. Of those 12 digits, 6 are specific to the vendor that produced the card. For example, the first six numbers on a network card produced by Intel are 00AA00, while on Cisco devices they are 00000C.

On many network cards there is no way to change this address, because it is set at the factory (although some cards do enable the administrator to change the MAC address). When two devices with the same MAC address are connected to the same network segment, a conflict will occur that can be quite difficult to diagnose. Many times the normal troubleshooting techniques won't work since things like pings respond normally. Resolving a MAC conflict sometimes comes down to looking at the MAC address for each device currently reporting problems. On Windows this is accomplished with the `ipconfig /all` command, as you'll see in Chapter 2, "TCP/IP."

MAC addresses don't cross network boundaries. Therefore, when troubleshooting a problem related to a MAC address with a tool called a *sniffer* (a packet sniffer is a utility used to extract packets from a network cable so that the packet information may be examined), you might see one MAC address showing up more often than others. Chances are that this is the address of the router or gateway boundary of the network. Since all traffic coming into the network goes through the router, it assigns its own MAC address to all conversations coming into the network. Many an intrusion analyst or administrator on a network has been confused when seeing large amounts of traffic apparently coming from a single MAC source.

The Network Layer

The Network layer handles moving packets between devices. It makes routing decisions and forwards packets as necessary to help them travel to their intended destination. In larger networks, there may be intermediate devices and subnetworks between any two end systems. The network layer makes it possible for the Transport layer (and layers above it) to send packets without being concerned with whether the end system is on the same piece of network cable or on the other end of a large wide area network.

To do its job, the Network layer translates logical network addresses into physical machine addresses (MAC addresses, which operate at the Data-Link layer). The Network layer also determines the quality of service (such as the priority of the message) and the route a message will take if there are several ways a message can get to its destination.

The Network layer also may split large packets into smaller chunks if the packet is larger than the largest data frame the Data-Link layer will accept. The Network layer reassembles the chunks into packets at the receiving end.

Intermediate systems that perform only routing and relaying functions and do not provide an environment for executing user programs can implement just the first three OSI network layers. Figure 1.5 shows how the Network layer moves packets across multiple links in a network.

FIGURE 1.5 The Network layer moves packets across links to their destination.

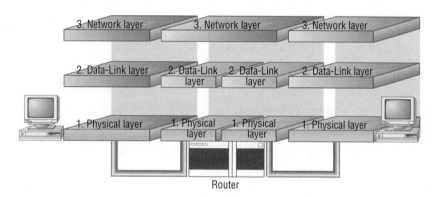

Router

The Network layer performs several important functions that enable data to arrive at its destination. The protocols at this layer may choose a specific route through an internetwork to avoid the excess traffic caused by sending data over networks and segments that don't need access to it. The Network layer serves to support communications between logically separate networks. This layer is concerned with the following:

- Addressing, including logical network addresses and service addresses

- Circuit, message, and packet switching

- Route discovery and route selection

- Connection services, including Network layer flow control, Network layer error control, and packet sequence control

- Gateway services

The Internet Protocol (IP) resides on the Network layer.

The Transport Layer

The Transport layer ensures that data is delivered error-free, in sequence, and with no losses or duplications. This layer also can break large messages from the Session layer into smaller segments to be handed down to the Network layer and sent to the destination computer; it then reassembles segments into messages to be presented to the Session layer. The Transport layer can send an acknowledgment to the originator for messages received (as in Figure 1.6). Most of these services are optional and are not required in the implementation of all Transport layer protocols. The one feature common to all protocols at the Transport layer is upper-layer protocol multiplexing, allowing multiple higher-layer protocol flows to operate simultaneously.

In terms of TCP/IP, this means you could, for example, navigate to a website and download a file at the same time.

Transmission Control Protocol (TCP) and User Datagram Protocol (UDP) are examples of protocols that exist at the Transport layer.

FIGURE 1.6 The Transport layer provides end-to-end communication with integrity and performance guarantees.

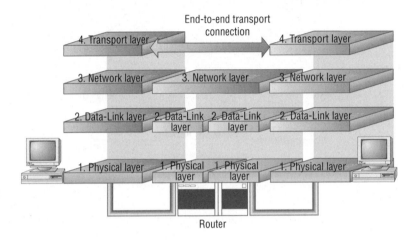

The Session Layer

The Session layer allows applications on separate computers to share a connection called a *session*. This layer provides services that allow two programs to find each other and establish the communication link, such as name lookup and security. The Session layer also provides for data synchronization and check pointing so that in the event of a network failure, only the data sent after the point of failure would need to be re-sent. This layer also controls the dialogue between two processes and determines who can transmit and who can receive at what point during the communication (see Figure 1.7).

NetBIOS, RPC, Named Pipes, PPTP, and SQL are examples of protocols on the Session layer.

The Presentation Layer

The Presentation layer translates data between the formats the network requires and the formats the computer expects. The Presentation layer performs protocol conversion; data translation, compression, and encryption; character set conversion; and the interpretation of graphics commands.

The network redirector, long a part of Windows networking, operates at this level. The redirector is what makes the files on a file server visible to the client computer. The network redirector also makes remote printers act as though they were attached to the local computer. Figure 1.8 shows the Presentation layer's role in the protocol stack.

Graphic formats such as PICT, TIFF, and JPEG are examples of Presentation layer protocols.

FIGURE 1.7   The Session layer allows applications to establish communication sessions with each other.

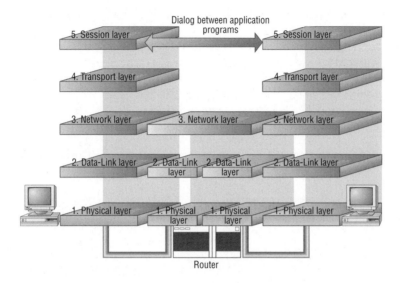

FIGURE 1.8   The Presentation layer allows applications to establish communication sessions with each other.

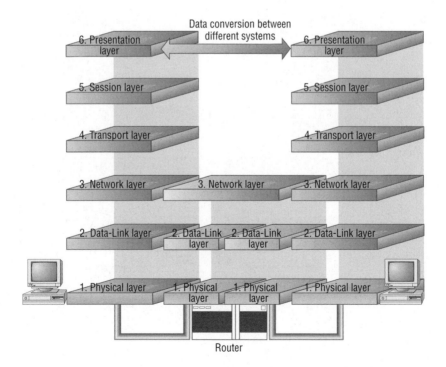

The Application Layer

The Application layer is the topmost layer of the OSI model, and it provides services that directly support user applications, such as database access, email, and file transfers. It also allows applications to communicate with applications on other computers as though they were on the same computer. When a programmer writes an application that uses network services, this is the layer the application will access. For example, Internet Explorer uses the Application layer to make its requests for files and web pages; the Application layer then passes those requests down the stack, with each succeeding layer doing its job (as in Figure 1.9).

File Transfer Protocol (FTP), Hypertext Transfer Protocol (HTTP), Simple Mail Transfer Protocol (SMTP), and others are examples of protocols at the Application layer.

FIGURE 1.9   The Application layer is where the applications function, using lower levels to get their work done.

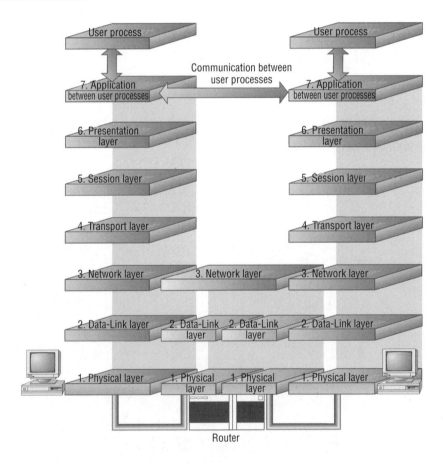

Communication Between Stacks

When a message is sent from one machine to another, it travels down the layers on one machine and then up the layers on the other machine, as shown in Figure 1.10.

As the message travels down the first stack, each layer it passes through (except the Physical layer) adds a header. These headers contain pieces of control information that are read and processed by the corresponding layer on the receiving stack. As the message travels up the stack of the other machine, each layer removes the header added by its peer layer and uses the information it finds to figure out what to do with the message contents (see Figure 1.11).

FIGURE 1.10 Traffic flows down through the stack on one computer and up the stack on the other.

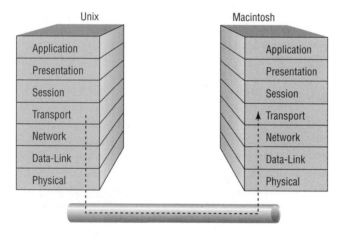

FIGURE 1.11 As packets flow up and down the stacks, each layer adds or removes necessary control information.

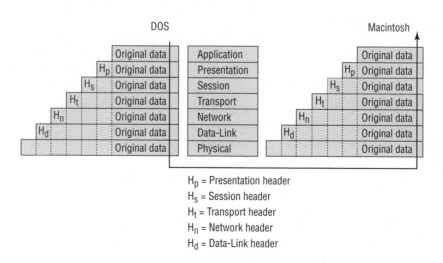

H_p = Presentation header
H_s = Session header
H_t = Transport header
H_n = Network header
H_d = Data-Link header

How Microsoft's Network Components Work with the OSI Model

Because the OSI model is so abstract, it can be hard to tell how its concepts relate to the actual network software and hardware you use in the real world. The following sections will make the link clearer. We will introduce you to some network protocols and show how they apply to the various layers of the OSI model.

In the following sections, we will discuss some protocols that Microsoft Windows Server 2008 no longer supports. We will talk about some of these protocols to help give you a wider range of networking knowledge and to help explain some of the networking concepts in previous Microsoft Windows Server versions.

Device Drivers and the OSI Model

Every hardware device in a computer requires a software-based device driver to make it work. Some drivers—for instance, the driver for an Integrated Device Electronics (IDE) hard disk or for the keyboard—are built into the operating system. Other devices require that drivers be installed separately when the device is attached or installed in the computer. Windows Server 2008 really blurs this distinction because it includes drivers for several hundred different network cards, but if your card isn't on the list, you will need to install the driver provided by the manufacturer.

When Windows 3.11 was introduced, network drivers were vendor-specific for both the operating system and the card. You might, for instance, have had a difficult time if you wanted to put a 3Com Ethernet card and an IBM Token Ring card in the same server. Worse yet, most drivers could be bound only to a single protocol stack and a single card, so you couldn't have two cards using TCP/IP on one server.

A variety of vendors tried to solve this problem by developing driver interfaces that allowed multiple cards to be bound to multiple protocols. Apple and Novell developed the Open Datalink Interface (ODI), and Microsoft countered with the Network Driver Interface Specification (NDIS). Microsoft's operating systems have supported NDIS ever since, making it possible to bind either multiple protocols to one card or the same protocol to multiple cards.

Windows Server 2008 and Windows Vista include Network Driver Interface Specification (NDIS) 6.0.

Network adapter cards and drivers provide the services corresponding to the Data-Link layer in the OSI model. In the IEEE model, the Data-Link layer is split into the LLC sublayer, which corresponds to the software drivers, and the MAC sublayer, which corresponds to the network adapter. You can think of the drivers as intermediaries between the higher layers and the card hardware that handles the business of forming packets and stuffing them into a wire.

Network Protocol Basics

Protocols are nothing more than an agreed-upon way for two objects (people, computers, home appliances, and so on) to exchange information. There are protocols at various levels in the OSI model. In fact, it is the protocols at a particular level in the OSI model that provide that level's functionality. Protocols that work together at one or more layers of the OSI model are known as a *protocol stack* or *protocol suite*. The following sections explain how network protocols move data between machines.

How Protocols Work

A *protocol* is a set of basic steps two or more parties perform according to a predefined or agreed-upon set of standards. A good example of a protocol that follows some unwritten but largely agreed-upon standards is a telephone conversation. When one person places a phone call, they dial the number of another party. The person on the other end answers the phone and says something akin to "Hello," at which point the calling party responds with a similar greeting. The conversation ensues from there. When the conversation is complete, each party (usually) ends the call with some parting words such as "Good-bye." This telephone call followed a routine protocol:

1. Say "Hello."
2. Converse.
3. Say "Goodbye."

In the realm of computers, a protocol follows the same concept. A protocol is a set of predefined standards that both computers must perform in the right order. For instance, for one computer to send a message to another computer, the first computer must perform the steps given in the following general example:

1. Break the data into small sections called *packets* (or *segments*, or another name depending on the layer involved).
2. Add addressing information to the packets, identifying the destination computer.
3. Deliver the data to the network card for transmission over the network.

The receiving computer must perform these steps:

1. Accept the data from the network adapter card.
2. Remove the transmitting information that was added by the transmitting computer.
3. Reassemble the packets of data into the original message.

Each computer needs to perform the same steps, in the same way and in the correct order, so that the data will arrive and be reassembled correctly. If one computer uses a protocol with different steps or even the same steps with different parameters (such as different sequencing, timing, or error correction), the two computers won't be able to communicate with each other.

Network Packets

Ethernet networks running IP and using TCP as the transport protocol primarily send and receive small chunks of data called *packets*. Network protocols construct, modify, and disassemble packets as they move data down the sending stack, across the network, and back up the OSI stack of the receiving computer. An IP packet has the following components:

- A source address specifying the sending computer
- A destination address specifying where the packet is being sent
- Instructions that tell the computer how to pass the data along
- Reassembly information (if the packet is part of a longer message)
- The data to be transmitted to the remote computer (often called the *packet payload*)
- Error-checking information to ensure that the data arrives intact

These components are assembled into slightly larger chunks; each packet contains three distinct parts (listed here and shown in Figure 1.12), and each part contains some of the components listed previously:

Header   A typical header might include an identifier, source and destination addresses, and other options, depending on the protocol.

Data   This is the actual data being sent.

Trailer   The contents of the trailer (or even the existence of a trailer) vary among network types, but it typically includes a CRC. The CRC helps the network determine whether a packet has been damaged in transmission.

FIGURE 1.12   A packet consists of a header, the data, and a trailer.

Protocols and Binding

Many different protocol stacks can perform network functions, and many different types of network interface cards can be installed in a computer. A computer may have more than one card, and a computer may use more than one protocol stack at the same time.

The *binding* process is what links the protocol stack to the network device driver for the network interface adapter. Several protocols can be bound to the same card. In addition, one computer with several interface adapters—for instance, a server that must be able to communicate with both a local area network and a network backbone—can have the same protocol bound to two or more network cards.

The binding process can be used throughout the OSI layers to link one protocol stack to another. The device driver (which implements the Data-Link layer) is bound to the network interface card (which implements the Physical layer). TCP/IP can be bound to the device driver, and the NWLink Session layer can be bound to the device driver.

Determining Connections

Communication between computers can be arranged in two ways:

- Using connectionless protocols
- Using connection-oriented protocols

It's important to understand the differences between them because different Windows Server 2008 services use both types.

Connectionless Protocols

It might seem odd to talk about a connectionless protocol for networks, but you use at least two of them just about every day: radio and television. Connectionless systems assume that all data will get through, so the protocol doesn't guarantee delivery or correct packet ordering. Think of shouting a message out of your window to someone walking by outside—there's no guarantee that they'll hear you, but it's quick and easy. These optimistic assumptions mean that there's no protocol overhead spent on these activities, so connectionless protocols tend to be fast. The User Datagram Protocol (UDP), which is part of the IP protocol suite, is an example of a connectionless Internet transport protocol. In fact, IP itself is connectionless, relying on upper-layer protocols such as TCP to provide the connection. The Domain Name System uses the UDP protocol.

Connection-Oriented Protocols

Connection-oriented systems work more like your telephone—you have to dial a number and establish a connection to the other end before you can send a message. Connection-oriented protocols pessimistically assume that some data will be lost or disordered in most transmissions. They guarantee that transmitted data will reach its destination in the proper sequence and that all data will get through. To accomplish this, connection-oriented protocols that also are considered *reliable* retain the transmitted data and negotiate for a retransmission when needed. Once all the needed data has arrived at the remote end, it can be reassembled into its proper sequence and passed to the higher-level protocols. This means that any application can depend on a connection-oriented transport to reliably deliver data exactly as it was transmitted. TCP is an example of a reliable connection-oriented Internet protocol. Frame Relay is an example of an *unreliable* connection-oriented protocol. Unreliable does not imply undependable. It just means that the protocol does not support the retransmission of lost or errored data.

For local area systems where data isn't likely to be dropped, it makes sense to push serialization and guaranteed delivery up to higher-level protocols that are less efficient because they won't be used often anyway. But in wide area networks like the Internet, it would simply take too much time for higher-level protocols to sort out what data had been sent and what was missing, so the transport protocol takes measures to guarantee that all the data gets through in order.

Network Protocols and Windows Server 2008

A number of protocol stacks are used in the world's networks today. Besides NetWare, Apple-Talk, NetBIOS, and TCP/IP, there are a bunch of specialty protocols such as IBM's Systems Network Architecture (SNA), Digital's (now HP/Compaq's) DECnet, and others. Even though these protocols actually work at different levels of the OSI model, they fall neatly into three distinct groups, as shown in the following list and in Figure 1.13:

- Application protocols provide for application-to-application interaction and data exchange.

- Transport protocols establish communication sessions between computers.

- Network protocols handle issues such as routing and addressing information, error checking, and retransmission requests.

FIGURE 1.13   Each OSI protocol works within one of three groups: Application, Transport, or Network.

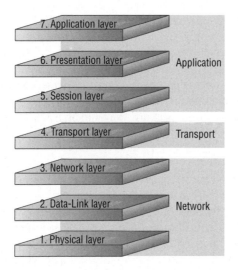

Network Protocols No Longer Supported in Windows Server 2008

In Windows Server 2003, Microsoft supported many different protocol types such as NWLink, AppleTalk, Serial Line Interface Protocol (SLIP), and TCP/IP. In Windows Server 2008, Microsoft supports a different set of protocols.

Support for the following technologies has been removed from Windows Server 2008:

- Bandwidth Allocation Protocol (BAP)

- X.25

- Serial Line Interface Protocol (SLIP)

    SLIP-based connections will automatically be updated to PPP-based connections.

- Asynchronous Transfer Mode (ATM)

- IP over IEEE 1394

- NWLink IPX/SPX/NetBIOS Compatible Transport Protocol

- Services for Macintosh (SFM)

- The Open Shortest Path First (OSPF) routing protocol component in Routing and Remote Access

- Basic Firewall in Routing and Remote Access

    This protocol has been replaced with Windows Firewall.

- Static IP filter APIs for Routing and Remote Access

    This protocol has been replaced with Windows Filtering Platform APIs.

- The SPAP, EAP-MD5-CHAP, and MS-CHAP v1 authentication protocols for PPP-based connections

---

 This list of removed technologies is always subject to change. Microsoft may remove support for additional technologies because of technical or other reasons.

TCP/IP Preferred for Windows Server 2008

Microsoft Windows 2008 supports TCP/IP version 4 and TCP/IP version 6 networking protocols. TCP/IP is a complex transport sufficient for globe-spanning networks such as the Internet, and Microsoft is doing everything possible to position TCP/IP as a one-size-fits-all network protocol. TCP/IP is required to use Active Directory and is the default protocol for Windows Server 2008.

Understanding TCP/IP

TCP/IP is actually two sets of protocols bundled together: the Transmission Control Protocol and the Internet Protocol. The U.S. Department of Defense's Advanced Research Projects Agency (ARPA, or later DARPA) developed TCP/IP and its suite of protocols beginning in 1969. The original goal was to develop network protocols that were robust enough to route communications around damage caused by nuclear war. That design goal was never tested, but some aspects of that design have led to the redundant, distributed whole we call the Internet.

IP is by far the most widely used protocol for interconnecting computers, and it is the protocol of the Internet. This is because although ARPA originally created IP to connect military networks, it provided the protocol standards to government agencies and universities free of charge. The academic world leapt at the chance to use a robust protocol to interconnect their networks, and the Internet was born. Many organizations and individuals collaborated to create higher-level protocols for everything from newsgroups, mail transfer, and file transfer to printing, remote booting, and even document browsing.

Although you'll see it commonly referred to as TCP/IP in Windows and throughout this book, TCP/IP really means the TCP/IP or IP protocol suite, and not necessarily TCP, the Transport layer protocol. UDP is also used, thus making it sort of a misnomer to say TCP/IP while ignoring UDP/IP.

IP is currently the protocol of choice for most networks because of its rapid and widespread adoption. IP is used for networks that span more than one metropolitan area or to connect to (or over) the Internet.

 Real World Scenario

Understanding the OSI Model and Troubleshooting

The company you work for has several regional offices spread around the country. Your job is to make sure the resources on the Windows Server 2008 network, which include manufacturing, inventory, and sales information, are available at all times. If the sales information from the regional offices isn't collected and updated to the manufacturing and inventory programs, the company won't be able to supply its customers effectively. The users of the network aren't particularly interested in the technical nuts and bolts of the system, but they do care when the system is down.

At the same time, you're studying for your MCSE certification and wondering how the abstract notions of the OSI model are relevant to your job. A support call comes in from a user who can't connect to a printer on a Windows Server 2008 machine in another region where an executive management meeting is taking place. The user is down the hall from you, so you drop everything and run down to take a look.

With the OSI model fresh in mind, you approach the problem in terms of layers of functionality. You ping the address of your router, and it comes back fine. You now know that the Physical, Data-Link, and Network layers are working fine, which means you have eliminated cable and basic protocol problems. Your browser also seems to work fine because you can reach random sites. When you ping the name of the Windows Server 2008 machine that hosts the printer, you get the "request timed out" message. But when you ping the IP address directly, the reply shows a healthy connection, implying that you have a name resolution problem. You begin the task of looking at your DNS server.

By breaking down your troubleshooting tactics into the general OSI layers, you can better gauge where the problem lies and which services to look at, depending on where in the OSI model the symptoms appear. Although the OSI model is fairly abstract, when it's applied appropriately, it gives you a structure for thinking about your overall network and provides a framework for following methodical troubleshooting tactics.

IP has some significant advantages:

- Broad connectivity among all types of computers and servers, including direct access to the Internet

- Strong support for routing, using a number of flexible routing protocols

- Support for advanced name and address resolution services (which will be covered in more depth in Chapter 3, "Domain Name System (DNS)"): the Domain Name System (DNS), the Dynamic Host Configuration Protocol (DHCP), and the Windows Internet Name Service (WINS)

- Support for a wide variety of Internet-standard protocols, including protocols for mail transport, web browsing, and file and print services

- Centralized network number and name assignment, which facilitates internetworking between organizations

TCP/IP is the core protocol that Windows Server 2008 depends on for all its network services. In fact, most of this book focuses on TCP/IP and its related services.

Chapter 2 covers TCP/IP in detail.

About Windows Network Models

Now that you have learned how computers communicate with each other, we'll discuss how you choose what kind of network to set up. Before you start setting it up, you have to make an important decision. Specifically, you need to decide what type of network model you need to install. The choice you make here is going to determine how you set up the rest of the computers and servers on your network.

The following sections describe two network models used by Microsoft Windows.

Since this is a Microsoft Windows certification book, the network models that are discussed in this book are Microsoft Windows–related models.

Windows Peer-to-Peer Network

In a Microsoft Windows peer-to-peer network (also referred to as a *workgroup*) all computers on the network are equal. All computers (also referred to as *nodes*) simultaneously act as both clients and servers. This is an advantage for small networks that have 12 or fewer users.

New Features of Windows Peer-to-Peer Network

Windows Vista includes some of the following enhancements to the Windows peer-to-peer network:

People Near Me   This new Windows Vista feature provides four important services:

- Discovery of users on the same subnet
- Ability to invite users to an application
- Publication of objects
- Contact management through the use of the Windows Address Book

New application programming interface (API)   Microsoft has improved and simplified its API's abilities to access Windows peer-to-peer networking capabilities such as name resolution, group creation, and security. This makes it easier for developers to create peer-to-peer applications for Windows.

Group Policy configuration support   Windows Vista allows you to set up a Group Policy to configure Windows peer-to-peer networking settings.

New version of Peer Name Resolution Protocol (PNRP)   Microsoft Windows Vista includes version 2 of the Peer Name Resolution Protocol (PNRP). This version uses less network bandwidth and is more scalable.

> The new version of the PNRP protocol is incompatible with the version that came with the Windows XP Advanced Networking Pack. You can download the PNRP v2 upgrade for Windows XP through the Windows Update utility.

Windows Meeting Space   Windows Vista has included a new peer-to-peer application called Windows Meeting Space. Windows Meeting Space addresses the needs of information workers by providing a means to invite, track, and detect the presence of attendees in a meeting. It also allows screen and window sharing among laptops, tablets, and projectors and file sharing with other meeting attendees.

Windows Peer-to-Peer Network Scenario

Imagine you are planning a network for a small real-estate office with five realtors. Should you set up a client/server-based network and spend money on a powerful machine, Windows 2008 Server, client access licenses (CALs), and a consultant who knows how to set up a Microsoft Active Directory domain? Or should you set up a Microsoft Windows peer-to-peer network? With a peer-to-peer network, all Windows Vista or XP Professional machines can be linked with each other through a small hub, and all users can share resources across the network (see Figure 1.14).

FIGURE 1.14   Microsoft Windows peer-to-peer network

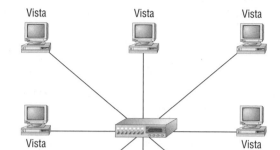

A Microsoft Windows peer-to-peer model has some disadvantages. All data is stored on individual workstations, and the local workstation's owner controls the security. Each user needing to log onto a machine in a peer-to-peer network must have a local username and password. Returning to our example, let's suppose the real-estate office grows to employ 12 realtors. Each realtor needs to be able to log onto any machine in the network:

12 users × 12 computers = 144 user accounts that need to be created

The following are some other disadvantages to a peer-to-peer network:

Scalability   A peer-to-peer network is limited to 12 computers.

Backups   **Backups must be done locally on each computer, instead of backing up one server.**

Decentralized security   Security is controlled by the local workstation's owner. Imagine having 200 files on 12 different workstations. If one user goes on vacation, you might not be able to access a needed file on that user's workstation.

Now, at this point you may be saying to yourself, "We can just install a Windows 2008 file server, and that will solve the backup and decentralized security issues." True. A Windows 2008 file server has a central location to place files for backups and security. But, if you were going to install a Windows 2008 Server anyway, why would you even need to stay on a peer-to-peer network? You could make that server a domain controller and take advantage of all the benefits of a domain (see the next section of this chapter).

A Microsoft Windows peer-to-peer network does have its place in the vast computer universe. It's great for a small company that is trying to save money while still sharing network resources. But if a peer-to-peer network does not fit into your part of the computer universe, you have another Microsoft networking option.

Windows Server 2008 Active Directory Network

IT departments for companies are responsible for maintaining the security of the company's information. This involves planning for, implementing, and managing various network resources. Servers, workstations, and routers are common infrastructure devices that are used to connect users with the information they need to do their jobs. In all but the smallest environments, the effort required to manage each of these technological resources can be great.

That's where Windows Server 2008 and Microsoft Active Directory come in. Active Directory is a data store that allows administrators to manage various types of information within a single distributed database. This is no small task, but many features of this directory services technology allow it to meet the needs of organizations that are small or large in size.

In its most basic definition, a directory is a repository that records information and makes it available to users. The overall design goal for Active Directory is to create a single centralized repository of information that administrators can work with to securely manage a company's user accounts, security, applications, and more.

An Active Directory setup consists of one or more *domains*. A domain is a logical grouping of objects within your organization. Objects within a domain do not have to be physically located near each other.

Active Directory's features include the following:

Hierarchical organization   Active Directory is based on a hierarchical layout. Through the use of various organizational components (or *objects*), a company can create a network management infrastructure and directory structure that mirrors the business organization. For example, if a company called Stellacon.com had several departments (such as sales and human resources), the directory services model could reflect this structure through the use of various objects within the directory (see Figure 1.15). Stellacon.com could then organize its users into the appropriate department containers.

The directory structure can efficiently accommodate the physical and logical aspects of information resources, such as access to other databases, user permissions, and computers. Active Directory also integrates with the network naming service, the DNS. *The* DNS provides for the hierarchical naming and location of resources throughout the company and on the public Internet.

Centralized data storage   All the information within Active Directory resides within a single, distributed, data repository. Users and systems administrators can easily access the information they need wherever they may be within the company. This is one of the most important design goals of the directory service—to provide a secure and centralized location for all your data. The benefits of centralized data storage include reduced administrative requirements, less duplication, higher availability, and increased visibility and organization of data.

FIGURE 1.15   Directory service model

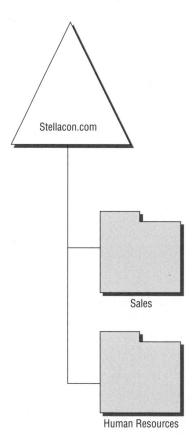

Ease of administration   To accommodate various business models, Active Directory can be configured for centralized or decentralized administration. This gives network and systems administrators the ability to delegate authority and responsibilities throughout the organization while still maintaining security. They allow for making companywide changes with just a few mouse clicks.

Network security   Through the use of a single logon and various authentication and encryption mechanisms, Active Directory can facilitate security throughout an entire enterprise. Through the process of *delegation*, higher-level security authorities can grant permissions to other administrators. For ease of administration, objects in the Active Directory tree inherit permissions from their parent objects. Application developers can take advantage of many of these features to ensure that users are identified uniquely and securely. Network administrators can create and update permissions as needed from within a single repository, thereby reducing the chances of an inaccurate or outdated configuration.

Scalability   Large organizations often have many users and large quantities of information to manage. Active Directory was designed with scalability in mind. Not only does it allow for storing millions of objects within a single domain, it also provides methods for distributing the necessary information between servers and locations. These features relieve much of the burden of designing a directory services infrastructure based on technical instead of business factors.

The biggest disadvantage to an Active Directory model is cost. The following are some of the cost items to consider:

- A powerful enough computer to handle Windows Server 2008
- The cost of personnel (staff IT or consultants) needed to plan, implement, and maintain the Windows Server 2008 Active Directory model

This is why it is important for you to decide which network model is right for your organization. The choice you make here will determine how your network is going to function and grow down the road.

Summary

This chapter covered how the OSI networking model is organized into seven layers (Physical, Data-Link, Network, Transport, Session, Presentation, and Application) and described each level of the OSI stack. You also learned that Windows Server 2008 includes support for TCP/IP v4 and v6. TCP/IP is the primary protocol in use today, and Microsoft encourages you to use TCP/IP exclusively, if possible.

Finally, the chapter discussed the two different Microsoft Windows network models (Windows peer-to-peer and Windows Active Directory networks) and the advantages and disadvantages of these models.

Exam Essentials

Know which protocols Windows Server 2008 supports.   Previous versions of Microsoft Windows Server supported many networking protocols. Windows Server 2008 no longer supports many of these protocols, including BAP, X.25, SLIP, ATM, IP over IEEE 1394, NWLink IPX/SPX/NetBIOS Compatible Transport Protocol, SFM, several components of Routing and Remote Access (OSPF, Basic Firewall, and static IP filter APIs), SPAP, EAP-MD5-CHAP, and MS-CHAP v1 authentication protocols for PPP-based connections.

Review Questions

1. A packet is sent from one computer to another across a network. Various protocols move the packet down the OSI stack from the sending computer and up the OSI stack to the receiving computer. How do the protocols know where to send the packet?

    A. Each packet has a trailer that contains source and destination addresses.

    B. Each packet has a header that contains an alert signal and source and destination addresses.

    C. The data portion of every packet stores all the source and destination information.

    D. Special packets, called *header packets*, that contain only source and destination addresses are sent first. Every packet that follows the header packet is sent to the destination address contained in the header packet.

2. You are the administrator for a software development house that writes small utility programs for a wide range of networks. In addition to supporting its Windows Server 2008 network, you are responsible for verifying that some of the applications that are developed function properly. During these tests, you have to install transport protocols from other development houses that are used by various systems. You have worked out the issues surrounding the different protocols working on Windows Server 2008 by requiring the protocol developers to make sure their protocols are compliant with what standard?

    A. ODI

    B. DLC

    C. NDIS

    D. NetBIOS

3. You administer a very large network that consists of Windows Vista, Windows XP Professional, and Windows Server 2008 computers. You want to implement DNS, DHCP, and WINS, and every computer must have access to the Internet and services on non-Windows machines. You want to be able to configure the network from a central location. Which network protocol provides the ability to do all these things?

    A. NetBEUI

    B. NWLink

    C. TCP

    D. TCP/IP

4. You are the administrator for a Windows NT network that has been internally focused on basic file and print services. You have been charged with upgrading your network to Windows Server 2008 and also allowing the users of the network to find information on the Internet. Currently, the network is running NWLink because of routing needs between two locations and a lack in the IT department of IP experience. You need to change the network protocol to TCP/IP to support Internet connectivity. What layers in the OSI model do you need to consider to allow the workstations to access the Internet for simple browsing? (Choose all that apply.)

   A. Network layer

   B. Application layer

   C. Presentation layer

   D. Transport layer

5. You have just been asked to troubleshoot intermittent communication problems on a fairly old network for a company that builds and repairs elevator motors. You have determined that the network is a straightforward thin-coax Ethernet Windows NT LAN running TCP/IP. The company wants to upgrade to Windows Server 2008, hoping that the now-stable platform will resolve the intermittent problems. You perform the upgrade; all goes smoothly, and initially everything seems to function properly. However, the intermittent problems show up again. What layer in the OSI model is the most likely place for the problems to be occurring?

   A. Physical layer

   B. Data-Link layer

   C. Network layer

   D. Transport layer

   E. Session layer

6. This sublayer, the lower of two sublayers, provides for shared access to the network adapter and communicates directly with network interface cards. A unique 48-bit address, commonly represented as a 12-digit hexadecimal address, is assigned to network interface cards before they leave the factory where they are made. What is the name of this sublayer?

   A. The TCP/IP sublayer

   B. The ISO sublayer

   C. The MAC sublayer

   D. The ARP sublayer

   E. The LLC sublayer

7. This OSI layer handles moving packets between devices. It makes routing decisions and forwards packets as necessary to help them travel to their intended destination. In larger networks, there may be intermediate devices and subnetworks between any two end systems. This OSI layer makes it possible for the Transport layer to send packets without being concerned with whether the end system is on the same piece of network cable or on the other end of a large wide area network. What layer in the OSI model makes this possible?

   A. Physical layer

   B. Data-Link layer

   C. Network layer

   D. Transport layer

   E. Session layer

8. You are the administrator for a small company that makes video games. The company uses Windows XP, Windows Vista, and Windows Server 2008. In the last two days users have been complaining the network has been running much more slowly than usual. You monitor the performance of the server, but the server is showing no signs of problems. You believe that there might be a computer or device on the network that is sending large amounts of broadcast traffic. What type of utility can you use to examine the packets on your network?

   A. Performance Monitor

   B. Ethernet cable tester

   C. `ipconfig /all`

   D. Packet sniffer

9. The OSI layer is responsible for using electric (or sometimes other types of) signaling to get bits from one computer to another. This layer's components don't care what the bits mean; their job is to get the bits from point A to point B, using whatever kind of optical, electrical, or wireless connection that connects the points. What layer in the OSI model are we referring to?

   A. Application layer

   B. Data-Link layer

   C. Network layer

   D. Transport layer

   E. Physical layer

10. You have been hired by a small travel agency to set up a Microsoft Windows network. Currently the travel agency has six travel agents who use Windows XP Professional and Vista. The computers are stand-alone machines with no network connection. The owner of the travel agency wants all the agents to be able to share resources (files and printers), but they are very concerned with minimizing costs. What type of network should you install?

   A. Stand-alone network

   B. Active Directory domain-based network

   C. Peer-to-peer network

   D. Client/server-based network

11. This OSI layer provides for the flow of data over a single physical link from one device to another. It accepts packets from the Network layer and packages the information into data units called *frames*; these frames are presented to the Physical layer for transmission. This OSI layer adds control information, such as the frame type, to the data being sent. This layer also provides for the error-free transfer of frames from one computer to another. Which OSI layer does these tasks?

    A. Application layer

    B. Data-Link layer

    C. Network layer

    D. Transport layer

    E. Physical layer

12. You have been hired by a large food chain to set up a Microsoft Windows network. The food chain currently has 100 computer users, and it plans on increasing that number by 50 percent. Scalability, network security, centralized data storage, and administration are all objectives that must be achieved. What type of network should you install?

    A. Stand-alone network

    B. Active Directory domain-based network

    C. Peer-to-peer network

    D. Client/server-based network

13. This OSI layer ensures that data is delivered error free, in sequence, and with no losses or duplications. This layer also can break large messages from the Session layer into smaller segments to be handed down to the Network layer and sent to the destination computer and then reassemble segments into messages to be presented to the Session layer. This OSI layer can send an acknowledgment to the originator for messages received. Which OSI layer does these tasks?

    A. Application layer

    B. Data-Link layer

    C. Network layer

    D. Transport layer

    E. Physical layer

14. What are the seven OSI Layers in order from top to bottom?

    A. Application, Physical, Session, Transport, Network, Data-Link, Presentation

    B. Application, Physical, Session, Network, Transport, Data-Link, Presentation

    C. Application, Presentation, Session, Network, Transport, Data-Link, Physical

    D. Application, Presentation, Session, Transport, Network, Data-Link, Physical

15. This OSI layer translates data between the formats the network requires and the formats the computer expects. This OSI layer also performs protocol conversion; data translation, compression, and encryption; character set conversion; and the interpretation of graphics commands. What OSI layer are we referring to?

  A. Application layer

  B. Data-Link layer

  C. Network layer

  D. Transport layer

  E. Presentation layer

16. You are the administrator for a Windows peer-to-peer network. All users have Windows Vista on their computers. The owner tells you he needs his employees to have the ability to invite other employees via computer to a meeting where they can share files with other meeting attendees. What application can be used to solve this problem?

  A. Windows Explorer

  B. Windows Meeting Space

  C. Windows Contact Manager

  D. Exchange Server

17. This OSI layer allows applications on separate computers to share a connection. This layer provides services that allow two programs to find each other and establish the communication link, such as name lookup and security. This OSI layer also provides for data synchronization and check pointing so that in the event of a network failure, only the data sent after the point of failure would need to be resent. This layer controls the dialogue between two processes and determines who can transmit and who can receive at what point during the communication. Which OSI layer does this?

  A. Session layer

  B. Data-Link layer

  C. Network layer

  D. Transport layer

  E. Physical layer

18. Which one of the following uses the UDP connectionless protocol?

  A. TCP

  B. FTP

  C. DNS

  D. None of the above

19. What is the name of the process that links the protocol stack to the network device driver for the network interface adapter?

   A. Linking

   B. Binding

   C. Joining

   D. LNIC

20. The TCP/IP model (sometimes called the IP model or the DoD model) is truly what the Internet was built upon. The TCP/IP model has four layers. What are the four layers, in order from top to bottom?

   A. Internet, Application, Transport, and Link

   B. Transport, Internet, Link, and Application

   C. Application, Transport, Internet, and Link

   D. Application, Link, Internet, and Transport

Answers to Review Questions

1. B. Each packet has a header and data and is typically placed in a frame that consists of three parts: a header, data, and a trailer. The packet header includes the source and destination logical addresses.

2. C . Network Driver Interface Specification (NDIS) provides a standard way for protocols to bind to the Data-Link drivers. As long as a developer supports NDIS, the protocol will load in Windows Server 2008. However, this will not make it interoperate with the Windows Server 2008 services. The applications will have to be written to the specific protocols.

3. D. TCP/IP is the most widely used protocol for interconnecting computers and networks. It is the only protocol used on the Internet and the only one compatible with the other protocols mentioned. It works well with very large internetworks.

4. A, B, C, D. TCP sits at the Transport layer, and IP sits at the Network layer; both are necessary to route requests through the Internet. However, you also need a browser such as Netscape or Internet Explorer to provide the HTTP calls to actually connect to the various websites; the browser sits at the Application layer. But any end-to-end communication uses all the levels of the OSI model because each layer communicates with the layer below and the layer above to form the complete chain.

5. A. The Physical layer is concerned with signaling, specifically through electrical, optical, or radio signals. The high voltage associated with large motors can easily cause an interruption in the signaling of coax cable. There have been many cases of people running network cable through elevator shafts in a building because of the ease of access, only to have the network malfunction every time someone summons the car. The other layers are associated with software and are beyond the reach of most electrical interference unless it affects the entire workstation.

6. C. The IEEE split the ISO Data-Link layer into the LLC sublayer and the MAC sublayer. The MAC sublayer, the lower of the two sublayers, provides for shared access to the network adapter and communicates directly with network interface cards. A unique 48-bit address, commonly represented as a 12-digit hexadecimal MAC address (frequently called the *hardware Ethernet address*), is assigned to network interface cards before they leave the factory where they are made.

7. C. To do its job, the Network layer translates logical network addresses into physical machine addresses (MAC addresses, which operate at the Data-Link layer). The Network layer also determines the quality of service (such as the priority of the message) and the route a message will take if there are several ways a message can get to its destination. The Network layer also may split large packets into smaller chunks if the packet is larger than the largest data frame the Data-Link layer will accept. The Network layer reassembles the chunks into packets at the receiving end.

8. D. A packet sniffer is a utility used to extract packets from a network cable so that the packet information may be examined. There are many different packet sniffers on the market, but most will be able to determine what types of packets are being sent. Using a packet sniffer will allow you to determine whether a computer or device is sending high amounts of broadcast traffic.

9. E. The Physical layer is concerned with signaling, specifically through electrical, optical, or radio signals. This layer's components don't care what the bits mean; their job is to get the bits from point A to point B via the optical, electrical, or wireless connection between the points.

10. C. A peer-to-peer network works well with a company that has 12 or fewer users. The advantage of a peer-to-peer network is that users can share resources across a network without spending money on powerful equipment and server software.

11. B. The Data-Link layer provides for the flow of data over a single physical link from one device to another. It accepts packets from the Network layer and packages the information into data units called *frames*; these frames are presented to the Physical layer for transmission. The Data-Link layer adds control information, such as frame type, to the data being sent.

12. B. An Active Directory domain-based network covers all the objectives that the food chain requires. An Active Directory–based network provides security, scalability, centralized data, and administrative ease.

13. D. The Transport layer ensures that data is delivered error free, in sequence, and with no losses or duplications. The Transport layer also can break large messages from the Session layer into smaller segments to be handed down to the Network layer and sent to the destination computer; the Transport layer then reassembles the segments into messages to be presented to the Session layer. The Transport layer can send an acknowledgment to the originator for messages received.

14. D. The OSI layers, in order from top to bottom, are Application, Presentation, Session, Transport, Network, Data-Link, and Physical. The easiest way to remember the seven layers is to use a mnemonic such as "All People Seem To Need Data Processing."

15. E. The Presentation layer translates data between the formats the network requires and the formats the computer expects. The Presentation layer also performs protocol conversion; data translation, compression, and encryption; character set conversion; and the interpretation of graphics commands.

16. B. Windows Vista includes a new peer-to-peer application called Windows Meeting Space. Windows Meeting Space helps information workers address their needs by providing a means to invite, track, and detect the presence of attendees in a meeting. It also allows screen and window sharing between laptops, tablets, and projectors, as well as file sharing with other meeting attendees.

17. A. The Session layer allows applications on separate computers to share a connection called a *session*. This layer provides services that allow two programs to find each other and establish the communication link, such as name lookup and security. The Session layer also provides for data synchronization and check pointing so that in the event of a network failure, only the data sent after the point of failure would need to be resent. This layer also controls the dialogue between two processes and determines who can transmit and who can receive at what point during the communication.

18. C. Domain Name System (DNS) uses the UDP protocol. The *User Datagram Protocol (UDP)*, which is part of the IP protocol suite, is an example of a connectionless Internet transport protocol. In fact, IP itself is connectionless, relying on upper-layer protocols such as TCP to provide the connection.

19. B. The *binding* process links the protocol stack to the network device driver for the network interface adapter.

20. C. The TCP/IP model (also called the IP model or the DoD model) was truly what the Internet was built upon. The TCP/IP model contains four layers: Application, Transport (sometimes called Host to Host), Internet, and Link (also called Network Access).

Chapter
2

TCP/IP

MICROSOFT EXAM OBJECTIVES COVERED IN THIS CHAPTER:

✓ **Configuring IPv4 and IPv6 addressing**

   ▪ May include but is not limited to: configuring IP options, subnetting, supernetting, alternative configuration

✓ **Configuring IPsec**

   ▪ May include but is not limited to: IPsec policy, IPsec Authentication Header (AH), IPsec Encapsulating Security Payload (ESP)

In this chapter, we will discuss the most important protocol used in a Microsoft Windows Server 2008 network: Transmission Control Protocol/Internet Protocol (TCP/IP).

As mentioned in the previous chapter, TCP/IP is actually two sets of protocols bundled together: the Transmission Control Protocol (TCP) and the Internet Protocol (IP). TCP/IP is a suite of protocols developed by the Department of Defense's Advanced Research Projects Agency in 1969.

This chapter is divided into two main topics; we'll talk about TCP/IP version 4 first and then about TCP/IP version 6. TCP/IP version 4 is still used in Windows Server 2008, and it was the primary version of TCP/IP in all previous versions of Windows. However, TCP/IP version 6 is the new release of TCP/IP, and it has been incorporated into Windows Server 2008 as well.

Understanding TCP/IP

We mentioned earlier that TCP/IP is actually two sets of protocols bundled together: TCP and IP. These protocols sit on a four-layer TCP/IP model (see Figure 2.1).

Details of the TCP/IP Model

The four layers of the TCP/IP model are as follows:

Application layer   The Application layer is where the applications that use the protocol stack reside. These applications include File Transfer Protocol (FTP), Trivial File Transfer Protocol (TFTP), Simple Mail Transfer Protocol (SMTP), and Hypertext Transfer Protocol (HTTP).

Transport layer   The Transport Layer is where the two Transport layer protocols reside. These are TCP and the User Datagram Protocol (UDP). TCP is a connection-oriented protocol, and delivery is guaranteed. UDP is a connectionless protocol. This means UDP does its best job to deliver the message, but there is no guarantee.

Internet layer   The Internet layer is where IP resides. IP is a connectionless protocol that relies on the upper layer (Transport layer) for guaranteeing delivery. Address Resolution Protocol (ARP) also resides on this layer. ARP turns an IP address into a Media Access Control (MAC) address. All upper and lower layers travel through the IP protocol.

Link layer   The data link protocols like Ethernet and Token Ring reside in the Link layer. This layer is also referred to as the Network Access Layer.

FIGURE 2.1   TCP/IP model

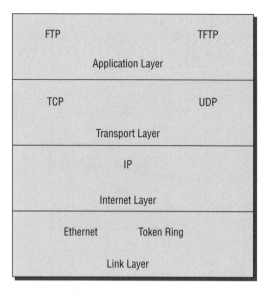

How TCP/IP Layers Communicate

When an application like FTP gets called upon, the application moves down the layers, and TCP is retrieved. TCP then connects itself to the IP protocol and gets released onto the network through the Link layer (see Figure 2.2). This is a connection-oriented protocol (because TCP is the protocol that guarantees delivery).

When an application like TFTP gets called, the application moves down the layers, and UDP is retrieved. UDP then connects itself to the IP protocol and gets released onto the network through the Link layer. This is a connectionless protocol (because the UDP protocol does not have guaranteed delivery).

Understanding Port Numbers

TCP and UDP rely on port numbers assigned by the Internet Assigned Numbers Authority (IANA) to forward packets to the appropriate application process. Port numbers are 16-bit integers that are part of a message header. They identify the application software process that the packet should be associated with.

For example, let's say that a client has a copy of Internet Explorer and a copy of Outlook Express open at the same time. Both applications are sending TCP requests across the Internet to retrieve web pages and email, respectively. How does the computer know which return packets to forward to Internet Explorer and which packets to forward to Outlook Express?

When making a connection, the client chooses a source port for the communication that is usually in the range 1024–65535 (sometimes in the range 1–65535). This source port then communicates with a destination port of 80 or 110 on the server side. Every packet destined for Internet Explorer has a source port number of 80 in the header, and every packet destined for Outlook Express has a source port number of 110 in the header.

FIGURE 2.2 TCP/IP process

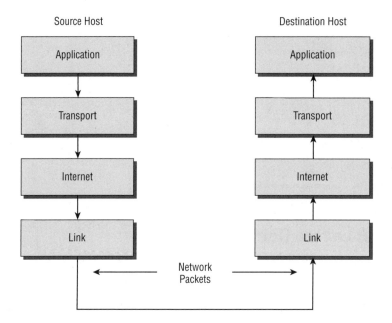

Table 2.1 lists the most common port numbers (you might need to know these for the exam). You can visit www.iana.org to get the most current full list of port numbers. It's good to become familiar with specific port numbers, because it's an asset to be able to determine from memory the ports that, for example, allow or block specific protocols in a firewall. Allowing only port 80, for instance, does not ensure that all web traffic will be allowed. You must also allow port 443 for certain secure web traffic.

Simply because a port is "well known" doesn't mean that a given service must run on it. It's technically valid to run any service on any port, but doing so is usually a bad idea. For example, if you chose to run your web server on TCP port 25, clients would need to type www.example.com:25 in order to reach your website from most browsers.

TABLE 2.1   Common Port Numbers

Port Number	Description
20	FTP data
21	FTP control
23	Telnet
25	Simple Mail Transfer Protocol (SMTP)
53	Domain Name System (DNS)
80	Hypertext Transfer Protocol (HTTP), Web
88	Kerberos
110	Post Office Protocol v3 (POP3)
443	Secure HTTP (HTTPS)

Understanding IP Addressing

Understanding IP addressing is critical to understanding how IP works. An IP address is a numeric identifier assigned to each device on an IP network. This type of address is a logical software address that designates the device's location on the network. It isn't the physical hardware address hard-coded in the device's network interface card.

In the following sections, you will see how IP addresses are used to uniquely identify every machine on a network.

    We'll assume you're comfortable with binary notation and math for the remainder of this discussion.

The Hierarchical IP Addressing Scheme

An IP address consists of 32 bits of information. These bits are divided into four sections (sometimes called *octets* or *quads*) containing 1 byte (8 bits) each. There are three common methods for specifying an IP address:

- Dotted-decimal, as in 130.57.30.56

- Binary, as in 10000010.00111001.00011110.00111000

- Hexadecimal, as in 82 39 1E 38

All of these examples represent the same IP address.

The 32-bit IP address is a structured address, or hierarchical address, as opposed to a flat or nonhierarchical address. Although IP could have used either flat or hierarchical addressing, its designers chose hierarchical addressing—for a very good reason, as you will see.

Why Hierarchical Addressing Is Used

What's the difference between these two types of addressing? A good example of a flat addressing scheme is a U.S. state driver's license number. There's no partitioning to it; the range of legal numbers isn't broken up in any meaningful way (say, by county of residence or date of issue). If this method had been used for IP addressing, every machine on the Internet would have needed a totally unique address, just as each driver's license number in a particular state is unique.

The good news about flat addressing is that it can handle a large number of addresses in 32 bits of data, namely, 4.3 billion. A 32-bit address space with two possible values for each position— either 0 (zero) or 1 (one)—gives you 2^{32} values, which equals approximately 4.3 billion.

The bad news—and the reason why flat addressing isn't used in IP—relates to routing. If every address were totally unique, every router on the Internet would need to store the address of every other machine on the Internet. It would be fair to say that this would make efficient routing impossible, even if only a fraction of the possible addresses were used.

The solution to this dilemma is to use a hierarchical addressing scheme that breaks the address space up into ordered chunks. Telephone numbers are a great example of this type of addressing. The first section of a U.S. telephone number, the area code, designates a very large area; the area code is followed by the prefix, which narrows the scope to a local calling area. The final segment, the customer number, zooms in on the specific connection. By looking at a number such as 603-766-xxxx, you can quickly determine that the number is located in the southern part of New Hampshire (area code 603) in the Portsmouth area (the 766 exchange).

IP Address Structure

IP addressing works the same way. Instead of treating the entire 32 bits as a unique identifier, one part of the IP address is designated as the network address (or network ID) and the other part as a node address (or host ID), giving it a layered, hierarchical structure. Together, the IP address, the network address, and node address uniquely identify a device within an IP network.

The network address—the first two sets of numbers in an IP address—uniquely identifies each network. Every machine on the same network shares that network address as part of its IP address, just as the address of every house on a street shares the same street name. In the IP address 130.57.30.56, for example, 130.57 is the network address.

The node address—the second two sets of numbers—is assigned to, and uniquely identifies, each machine in a network, just as each house on the same street has a different house number.

This part of the address must be unique because it identifies a particular machine—an individual, as opposed to a network. This number can also be referred to as a *host address*. In the sample IP address 130.57.30.56, the node address is .30.56.

Understanding Network Classes

The designers of the Internet decided to create classes of networks based on network size. For the small number of networks possessing a very large number of nodes, they created the Class A network. At the other extreme is the Class C network, reserved for the numerous networks with small numbers of nodes. The class of networks in between the very large and very small ones is predictably called a Class B network.

The default subdivision of an IP address into a network and node address is determined by the class designation of your network. Table 2.2 summarizes the three classes of network, which will be described in more detail in the following sections.

TABLE 2.2   Network Address Classes

Class	Mask Bits	Leading Bit Pattern	Decimal Range of First Octet of IP Address	Assignable Networks	Maximum Nodes per Network
A	8	0	1–126	126	16,777,214
B	16	10	128–191	16,384	65,534
C	24	110	192–223	2,097,152	254

Classless Inter-Domain Routing, explained in detail later in this chapter, has effectively done away with these class designations. You will still hear and should still know the meaning behind the class designations of addresses, because they are important to understanding IP addressing. However, when working with IP addressing in practice, CIDR is more important to know.

To ensure efficient routing, Internet designers defined a mandate for the leading bits section of the address for each different network class. For example, because a router knows that a Class A network address always starts with a 0, the router can quickly apply the default mask, if necessary, after reading only the first bit of the address. Table 2.2 illustrates how the leading bits of a network address are defined. When considering the subnet masking between network and host addresses, the number of bits to mask is important. For example, in a Class A network, 8 bits are masked, making the default subnet mask 255.0.0.0, while in a Class C, 24 bits are masked, making the default subnet mask 255.255.255.0.

Some IP addresses are reserved for special purposes and shouldn't be assigned to nodes. Table 2.3 lists some of the reserved IP addresses. See RFC 3330 for others.

TABLE 2.3   Special Network Addresses

Address	Function
Entire IP address set to all 0s	Depending on the mask, this network (that is, the network or subnet that you are currently a part of) or this host on this network.
A routing table entry of all 0s with a mask of all 0s	Used as the default gateway entry. Any destination address masked by all 0s produces a match for the all-0s reference address. Because the mask has no 1s, this is the least desirable entry but will be used when no other match exists.
Network address 127	Reserved for loopback tests. Designates the local node and allows that node to send a test packet to itself without generating network traffic.
Node address of all 0s	Used when referencing a network without referring to any specific nodes on that network. Usually used in routing tables.
Node address of all 1s	Broadcast address for all nodes on the specified network, also known as a *directed broadcast*. For example, 128.2.255.255 means all nodes on the Class B network 128.2. Routing this broadcast is configurable on certain routers.
169.254.0.0 with a mask of 255.255.0.0	The "link-local" block used for autoconfiguration and communication between devices on a single link. Communication cannot occur across routers. Microsoft uses this block for Automatic Private IP Addressing (APIPA).
Entire IP address set to all 1s (same as 255.255.255.255)	Broadcast to all nodes on the current network; sometimes called a *limited broadcast* or an *all-1s broadcast*. This broadcast is not routable.
10.0.0.0/8 172.16.0.0 to 172.31.255.255 192.168.0.0/16	The private-use blocks for Classes A, B, and C. As noted in RFC 1918, the addresses in these blocks must never be allowed into the Internet, making them acceptable for simultaneous use behind NAT servers and non-Internet-connected IP networks.

In the following sections, we will look at the three network types.

Class A Networks

In a Class A network, the first byte is the network address, and the three remaining bytes are used for the node addresses. The Class A format is `Network.Node.Node.Node`.

For example, in the IP address `49.22.102.70`, the 49 is the network address, and the 22.102.70 is the node address. Every machine on this particular network would have the distinctive network address of 49; within that network, though, you could have a large number of machines.

There are 126 possible Class A network addresses. Why? The length of a Class A network address is 1 byte, and the first bit of that byte is reserved, so 7 bits in the first byte remain for manipulation. This means that the maximum number of Class A networks is 128. (Each of the 7 bit positions that can be manipulated can be either a 0 or a 1, and this gives you a total of 2^7 positions or 128.) But to complicate things further, it was also decided that the network address of all 0s (0000 0000) would be reserved. This means the actual number of usable Class A network addresses is 128 minus 1, or 127. Also, 127 is a reserved number (a network address of 0 followed by all 1s (0111 1111); so, you actually start with 128 addresses minus the two reserved, and you're left with 126 possible Class A network addresses.

Each Class A network has 3 bytes (24 bit positions) for the node address of a machine, which means that there are 2^{24}—or 16,777,216—unique combinations. Because addresses with the two patterns of all 0s and all 1s in the node bits are reserved, the actual maximum usable number of nodes for a Class A network is 2^{24} minus 2, which equals 16,777,214.

Class B Networks

In a Class B network, the first two bytes are assigned to the network address, and the remaining two bytes are used for node addresses. The format is `Network.Network.Node.Node`.

For example, in the IP address `130.57.30.56`, the network address is 130.57, and the node address is 30.56.

The network address is 2 bytes, so there would be 2^{16} unique combinations. But the Internet designers decided that all Class B networks should start with the binary digits 10. This leaves 14 bit positions to manipulate; therefore, there are 16,384 (or 2^{14}) unique Class B networks.

This gives you an easy way to recognize Class B addresses. If the first 2 bits of the first byte can be only 10, that gives you a decimal range from 128 up to 191 in the first octet of the IP address. Remember that you can always easily recognize a Class B network by looking at its first byte—even though there are 16,384 different Class B networks. If the first octet in the address falls between 128 and 191, it is a Class B network, regardless of the value of the second octet.

A Class B network has 2 bytes to use for node addresses. This is 2^{16} minus the two patterns in the reserved-exclusive club (all 0s and all 1s in the node bits), for a total of 65,534 possible node addresses for each Class B network.

Class C Networks

The first 3 bytes of a Class C network are dedicated to the network portion of the address, with only 1 byte remaining for the node address. The format is `Network.Network.Network.Node`.

In the example IP address 198.21.74.102, the network address is 198.21.74, and the node address is 102.

In a Class C network, the first three bit positions are always binary 110. Three bytes, or 24 bits, minus 3 reserved positions leaves 21 positions. There are therefore 2^{21}, or 2,097,152, possible Class C networks.

The lead bit pattern of 110 equates to decimal 192 and runs through 223. Remembering our handy easy-recognition method, this means you can always spot a Class C address if the first byte is in the range 192–223, regardless of the values of the second and third bytes of the IP address.

Each unique Class C network has 1 byte to use for node addresses. This leads to 2^{8}, or 256, minus the two special patterns of all 0s and all 1s, for a total of 254 node addresses for each Class C network.

 Class D networks, used for multicasting only, use the address range 224.0.0.0 to 239.255.255.255 and are used, as in broadcasting, as destination addresses only. Class E networks (reserved for future use at this point) cover 240.0.0.0 to 255.255.255.255. Addresses in the Class E range are considered within the experimental range.

Subnetting a Network

If an organization is large and has lots of computers, or if its computers are geographically dispersed, it makes good sense to divide its colossal network into smaller ones connected by routers. These smaller networks are called *subnets*. The benefits of using subnets include the following:

Reduced network traffic   We all appreciate less traffic of any kind, and so do networks. Without routers, packet traffic could choke the entire network. Most traffic will stay on the local network—only packets destined for other networks will pass through the router and over to another subnet. This traffic reduction also improves overall performance.

Simplified management   It's easier to identify and isolate network problems in a group of smaller networks connected together than within one gigantic one.

An organization with a single network address (comparable to the hotel building mentioned in the sidebar "Understanding the Benefits of Subnetting") can have a subnet address for each individual physical network (comparable to a floor in the hotel building). Each subnet is still part of the shared network address, but it also has an additional identifier denoting its individual subnetwork number. This identifier is called a *subnet address*.

Subnetting solves several addressing problems:

- If an organization has several physical networks but only one IP network address, it can handle the situation by creating subnets.

Understanding the Benefits of Subnetting

To understand one benefit of subnetting, consider a hotel or office building. Say a hotel has 1,000 rooms, with 75 rooms to a floor. You could start at the first room on the first floor and number it 1; then when you get to the first room on the second floor, you could number it 76 and keep going until you reach room 1,000. But someone looking for room 521 would have to guess which floor the room was on. If you were to "subnet" the hotel, you would identify the first room on the first floor with the number 101 (1 = Floor 1 and 01 = Room 1), the first room on the second floor with 201, and so on. The guest looking for room 521 would go to the fifth floor and look for room 21.

- Because subnetting allows many physical networks to be grouped together, fewer entries in a routing table are required, notably reducing network overhead.
- These things combine to collectively yield greatly enhanced network efficiency.

The original designers of the IP protocol envisioned a small Internet with only tens of networks and hundreds of hosts. Their addressing scheme used a network address for each physical network. As you can imagine, this scheme and the unforeseen growth of the Internet created a few problems. The following are two examples:

Not enough addresses   A single network address can be used to refer to multiple physical networks, but an organization can request individual network addresses for each one of its physical networks. If all these requests were granted, there wouldn't be enough addresses to go around.

Gigantic routing tables   If each router on the Internet needed to know about every physical network, routing tables would be impossibly huge. There would be an overwhelming amount of administrative overhead to maintain those tables, and the resulting physical overhead on the routers would be massive (CPU cycles, memory, disk space, and so on). Because routers exchange routing information with each other, an additional, related consequence is that a terrific overabundance of network traffic would result.

Although there's more than one way to approach these problems, the principal solution is the one that we'll cover in this book—subnetting. As you might guess, subnetting is the process of carving a single IP network into smaller logical subnetworks. This trick is achieved by subdividing the host portion of an IP address to create a subnet address. The actual subdivision is accomplished through the use of a subnet mask (covered later in the chapter).

In the following sections, you will see exactly how to calculate and apply subnetting.

Implementing Subnetting

Before you can implement subnetting, you need to determine your current requirements and plan on how best to implement your subnet scheme.

How to Determine Your Subnetting Requirements

Follow these guidelines to calculate the requirements of your subnet:

1. Determine the number of required network IDs: one for each subnet and one for each wide area network (WAN) connection.

2. Determine the number of required host IDs per subnet: one for each TCP/IP device, including, for instance, computers, network printers, and router interfaces.

3. Based on these two data points, create the following:

   - One subnet mask for your entire network

   - A unique subnet ID for each physical segment

   - A range of host IDs for each unique subnet

How to Implement Subnetting

Subnetting is implemented by assigning a subnet address to each machine on a given physical network. For example, in Figure 2.3, each machine on subnet 1 has a subnet address of 1.

FIGURE 2.3   A sample subnet

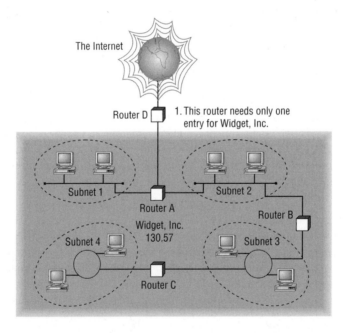

The default network portion of an IP address can't be altered without encroaching on another administrative domain's address space, unless you are assigned multiple consecutive classful addresses. In order to maximize the efficient use of the assigned address space, machines on a particular network share the same of network address. In Figure 2.3, you can see that all the Widget, Inc., machines have a network address 130.57. That principle is constant. In subnetting, it's the host address that's manipulated; the network address doesn't change. The subnet address scheme takes a part of the host address and recycles it as a subnet address. Bit positions are stolen from the host address to be used for the subnet identifier. Figure 2.4 shows how an IP address can be given a subnet address.

Because the Widget, Inc., network is a Class B network, the first two bytes specify the network address and are shared by all machines on the network—regardless of their particular subnet. Here, every machine's address on the subnet must have its third byte read 0000 0001. The fourth byte, the host address, is the unique number that identifies the actual host within that subnet. Figure 2.5 illustrates how a network address and a subnet address can be used together.

FIGURE 2.4   Network vs. host addresses

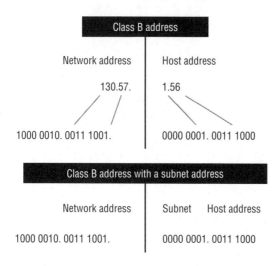

How to Use Subnet Masks

For the subnet address scheme to work, every machine on the network must know which part of the host address will be used as the network address. This is accomplished by assigning each machine a subnet mask.

The network administrator creates a 32-bit subnet mask comprised of 1s and 0s. The 1s in the subnet mask represent the positions in the IP address that refer to the network and subnet addresses. The 0s represent the positions that refer to the host part of the address. Figure 2.6 illustrates this combination.

FIGURE 2.5 The network address and its subnet

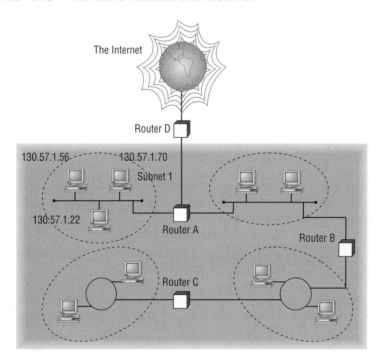

FIGURE 2.6 The subnet mask revealed

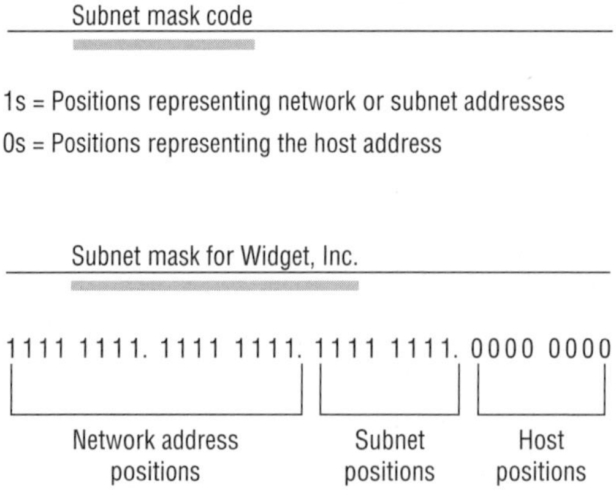

Subnet mask code

1s = Positions representing network or subnet addresses
0s = Positions representing the host address

Subnet mask for Widget, Inc.

1111 1111. 1111 1111. 1111 1111. 0000 0000

Network address   Subnet   Host
positions   positions   positions

In the Widget, Inc., example, the first two bytes of the subnet mask are 1s because Widget's network address is a Class B address, formatted as `Network.Network.Node.Node`. The third byte, normally assigned as part of the host address, is now used to represent the subnet address.

Hence, those bit positions are represented with 1s in the subnet mask. The fourth byte is the only part of the example that represents the host address.

The subnet mask can also be expressed using the decimal equivalents of the binary patterns. The binary pattern of 1111 1111 is the same as decimal 255. Consequently, the subnet mask in the example can be denoted in two ways, as shown in Figure 2.7.

FIGURE 2.7   Different ways to represent the same mask

Subnet mask in binary: 1111 1111. 1111 1111. 1111 1111. 0000 0000

Subnet mask in decimal: 255   .   255   .   255   .   0

(The spaces in the above example are only for illustrative purposes.
The subnet mask in decimal would actually appear as 255.255.255.0.)

Not all networks need to have subnets and therefore don't need to use custom subnet masks. In this case, they are said to have a *default* subnet mask. This is basically the same as saying they don't have a subnet address. Table 2.4 shows the default subnet masks for the different classes of networks.

TABLE 2.4   Default Subnet Masks

Class	Format	Default Subnet Mask
A	Network.Node.Node.Node	255.0.0.0
B	Network.Network.Node.Node	255.255.0.0
C	Network.Network.Network.Node	255.255.255.0

Once the network administrator has created the subnet mask and assigned it to each machine, the IP software applies the subnet mask to the IP address to determine its subnet address. The word *mask* carries the implied meaning of "lens" in this case—the IP software looks at its IP address through the lens of its subnet mask to see its subnet address. Figure 2.8 illustrates an IP address being viewed through a subnet mask.

In this example, the IP software learns through the subnet mask that, instead of being part of the host address, the third byte of its IP address is now going to be used as a subnet address. The IP software then looks in its IP address at the bit positions that correspond to the mask, which are 0000 0001.

The final step is for the subnet bit values to be matched up with the binary numbering convention and converted to decimal. In the Widget, Inc., example, the binary-to-decimal conversion is simple, as illustrated in Figure 2.9.

FIGURE 2.8   Applying the subnet mask

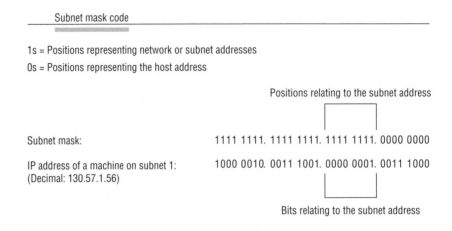

Subnet mask code

1s = Positions representing network or subnet addresses
0s = Positions representing the host address

Positions relating to the subnet address

Subnet mask: 1111 1111. 1111 1111. 1111 1111. 0000 0000

IP address of a machine on subnet 1:   1000 0010. 0011 1001. 0000 0001. 0011 1000
(Decimal: 130.57.1.56)

Bits relating to the subnet address

FIGURE 2.9   Converting the subnet mask to decimal

Binary numbering convention

Position/value: ◄—(continued)	128 64 32 16 8 4 2 1
Widget third byte:	0 0 0 0 0 0 0 1
Decimal equivalent:	0 + 1 = 1
Subnet address:	1

By using the entire third byte of a Class B address as the subnet address, it is easy to set and determine the subnet address. For example, if Widget, Inc., wants to have a subnet 6, the third byte of all machines on that subnet will be 0000 0110 (decimal 6 in binary).

Using the entire third byte of a Class B network address for the subnet allows for a fair number of available subnet addresses. One byte dedicated to the subnet provides eight bit positions. Each position can be either a 1 or a 0, so the calculation is 2^8, or 256. Thus, Widget, Inc., can have up to 256 total subnetworks, each with up to 254 hosts.

Although RFC 950 prohibits the use of binary all 0s and all 1s as subnet addresses, almost all products actually permit this usage today. Microsoft's TCP/IP stack allows it, as does the software in most routers (provided you enable this feature—sometimes it's not enabled by default). This gives you two additional subnets. However, you should not use a subnet of 0 (all 0s) unless all the software on your network recognizes this convention.

How to Calculate the Number of Subnets

The formulas for calculating the maximum number of subnets and the maximum number of hosts per subnet are as follows:

2 × number of masked bits in subnet mask = maximum number of subnets

2 × number of unmasked bits in subnet mask − 2 = maximum number of hosts per subnet

In the formulas, *masked* refers to bit positions of 1, and *unmasked* refers to positions of 0. The downside to using an entire byte of a node address as your subnet address is that you reduce the possible number of node addresses on each subnet. As explained earlier, without a subnet, a Class B address has 65,534 unique combinations of 1s and 0s that can be used for node addresses. The question is, why would you ever want 65,534 hosts on a single physical network? The trade-off is acceptable to most who ask themselves this question.

If you use an entire byte of the node address for a subnet, you then have only 1 byte for the host addresses, leaving only 254 possible host addresses. If any of your subnets will be populated with more than 254 machines, you have a problem. To solve it, you would then need to shorten the subnet mask, thereby lengthening the number of host bits and increasing the number of host addresses; this gives you more available host addresses on each subnet. A side effect of this solution is that it shrinks the number of possible subnets.

Figure 2.10 shows an example of using a smaller subnet address. A company called Acme, Inc., expects to need a maximum of 14 subnets. In this case, Acme does not need to take an entire byte from the host address for the subnet address. To get its 14 different subnet addresses, it needs to snatch only 4 bits from the host address ($2^4 = 16$). The host portion of the address has 12 usable bits remaining ($2^{12} - 2 = 4094$). Each of Acme's 16 subnets could then potentially have a total of 4,094 host addresses; 4,094 machines on each subnet should be plenty.

An Easier Way to Apply Subnetting

Now that you have the basics down of how to subnet, we'll show you an easier way. If you have learned a different way and it works for you, stick with it. It does not matter how you get to the finish line, just as long as you get there. But if you are new to subnetting, Figure 2.11 will make it easier for you.

This chart may look intimidating, but it's really simple to use once you have used it a few times.

> Remember that on this chart that 1s equal subnets and 0s equal hosts. If you get this confused, you will get wrong answers in the following exercises.

Watch the Y column on the lower end of the chart. This represents the number of addresses available to you after the two reserved addresses have been removed. The following sections provide some examples.

FIGURE 2.10   An example of a smaller subnet address

Acme, Inc.

Network address: 132.8 (Class B; net.net.host.host)

Example IP address: 1000 0100. 0000 1000. 0001 0010. 0011 1100

Decimal: 132 .   8   .   18   .   60

Subnet Mask Code

1s = Positions representing network or subnet addresses
0s = Positions representing the host address

Subnet mask:
Binary: 1111 1111. 1111 1111. 1111 0000. 0000 0000
Decimal: 255 .   255 .   240 .   0
(The decimal 240 is equal to the binary 1111 0000.)

Positions relating to the subnet address

Subnet mask: 1111 1111. 1111 1111. 1111 0000. 0000 0000

IP address of a Acme machine: 1000 0100. 0000 1000. 0001 0010. 0011 1100
(Decimal: 132.8.18.60)

Bits relating to the subnet address

Binary-to-Decimal Conversions for Subnet Address

Subnet mask positions:	1	1	1	1	0	0	0	0
	↓	↓	↓	↓				
Position/value: ← (continue)	128	64	32	16	8	4	2	1
Third byte of IP address:	0	0	0	1	0	0	1	0
Decimal equivalent:						0 + 16 = 16		
Subnet address for this IP address:						16		

FIGURE 2.11 TCP/IP v4 subnetting chart

2^(X)-2=Y	128	64	32	16	8	4	2	1
255	1	1	1	1	1	1	1	1
254	1	1	1	1	1	1	1	0
252	1	1	1	1	1	1	0	0
248	1	1	1	1	1	0	0	0
240	1	1	1	1	0	0	0	0
224	1	1	1	0	0	0	0	0
192	1	1	0	0	0	0	0	0
128	1	0	0	0	0	0	0	0
0	0	0	0	0	0	0	0	0

0=Hosts, 1=Subnets

X (POWER)			X		Y
2x	3	=	8	-2	6
2x	4	=	16	-2	14
2x	5	=	32	-2	30
2x	6	=	64	-2	62
2x	7	=	128	-2	126
2x	8	=	256	-2	254
2x	9	=	512	-2	510
2x	10	=	1024	-2	1022
2x	11	=	2048	-2	2046
2x	12	=	4096	-2	4094
2x	13	=	8192	-2	8190
2x	14	=	16384	-2	16382
2x	15	=	32768	-2	32766
2x	16	=	65536	-2	65534
2x	17	=	131072	-2	131070

Subnet Mask Exercise 1: Class C, 10 Hosts per Subnet

You have a Class C address, and you require 10 hosts per subnet.

1. Write down 255.255.255.____. The blank area is the number you need to fill in.

2. Look under the Y column, and choose the first number that is larger than 10 (the number of hosts per subnet you need).

   You should have come up with 14.

3. Move across the page, and look at number in the X (Power) column.

   The power number is 4.

4. Go to the top of the chart, and look for the row with exactly four 0s (hosts). Find the number at the beginning of the row.

   The number at the beginning of the row is 240. That's your answer. The subnet mask should be 255.255.255.240.

Subnet Mask Exercise 2: Class C, 20 Hosts per Subnet

You have a Class C address, and you need 20 hosts per subnet.

1. Write down 255.255.255._____.
2. Look under the Y column, and find the first number that covers 20 (this should be 30).
3. Go across to the power number (5).
4. Go to the top part of the chart, and find the row with exactly five 0s from right to left. The number at the beginning of the row is 224. Your answer should be 255.255.255.224.

Subnet Mask Exercise 3: Class C, 5 Subnets

Now you have a Class C address, and you need five subnets. Remember that subnets are represented by 1s in the chart.

1. First write down 255.255.255._____.
2. Look under the Y column, and find the first number that covers 5 (should be 6).
3. Go across to the power number (should be 3).
4. Go to the top part of the chart, and find which row has exactly three 1s (remember 1s are for subnets) from left to right.

   Your answer should be 255.255.255.224.

Subnet Mask Exercise 4: Class B, 1,500 Hosts per Subnet

This one is a bit harder. You have a Class B address, and you need 1,500 hosts per subnet. Because you have a Class B address, you need to fill in the third octet of numbers. The fourth octet contains eight 0s.

1. Write down 255.255._____.0.
2. Look at the Y column, and find the first number is that covers 1500 (this should be 2046).
3. Go across, and find the power number (this should be 11).
4. Remember, you already have eight 0s in the last octet. So, you need only three more. Find the row with three 0s.

   You should come up with an answer of 255.255.248.0. This actually breaks down to 11111111.11111111.11111000.00000000, and that's how you got the 11 zeros.

Subnet Mask Exercise 5: Class B, 3,500 Hosts per Subnet

You have a Class B address, and you need 3,500 hosts per subnet.

1. Write down 255.255._____.0.
2. Look at the Y column, and find the first number that covers 3500 (this should be 4094).
3. Go across, and find the power number (should be 12).
4. Remember you already have eight 0s in the last octet, so you need only four more. Count for four zeros from right to left.

You should come up with an answer of 255.255.240.0. Again, this actually breaks down to 11111111.11111111.11110000.00000000, and that's how you got the 12 zeros.

 If you get a question that gives you both the hosts and the subnets, always figure out the larger number first. Then, depending on the mask you have decided to use, make sure the lower number also is correct with that mask.

Now try doing the following exercises on your own:

Class B address 1,000 hosts per subnet	Class B address 25 subnets
Class C address 45 hosts per subnet	Class B address 4,000 hosts per subnet
192.168.0.0 10 subnets	Class B address 2,000 hosts per subnet 25 subnets

Here are the answers. If any of your answers are wrong, follow the previous examples, and try to work them out again:

Class B address 1000 hosts per subnet 255.255.252.0	Class B address 25 subnets 255.255.248.0
Class C address 45 hosts per subnet 255.255.255.192	Class B address 4000 hosts per subnet 255.255.240.0
192.168.0.0 10 subnets 255.255.255.240	Class B address 2000 hosts per subnet 25 subnets 255.255.248.0

Applying Subnetting the Traditional Way

Sometimes subnetting can be confusing. After all, it can be quite difficult to remember all those numbers. You can step back a minute and take a look at the primary classes of networks and how to subnet each one. Let's start with Class C because it uses only 8 bits for the node address, so it's the easiest to calculate. In the following sections, we will explain how to subnet the various types of networks.

Subnetting Class C

If you recall, a Class C network uses the first 3 bytes (24 bits) to define the network address. This leaves you 1 byte (8 bits) with which to address hosts. So if you want to create subnets, your options are limited because of the small number of bits available.

If you break down your subnets into chunks smaller than the default Class C, then figuring out the subnet mask, network number, broadcast address, and router address can be confusing. To build a sturdy base for subnetting, study the following techniques for determining these special values for each subnet, but also learn and use the more efficient technique presented in the later section "Quickly Identifying Subnet Characteristics" and the earlier section "An Easier Way to Subnetting." Table 2.5 summarizes how you can break a Class C network down into one, two, four, or eight smaller subnets, and it gives you the subnet masks, network numbers, broadcast addresses, and router addresses. The first three bytes have simply been designated x.y.z. (Note that the table assumes you can use the all-0s and all-1s subnets, too.)

TABLE 2.5 Setting Up Class C Subnets

Number of Desired Subnets	Subnet Mask	Network Number	Router Address	Broadcast Address	Remaining Number of IP Addresses
1	255.255.255.0	x.y.z.0	x.y.z.1	x.y.z.255	253
2	255.255.255.128	x.y.z.0	x.y.z.1	x.y.z.127	125
	255.255.255.128	x.y.z.128	x.y.z.129	x.y.z.255	125
4	255.255.255.192	x.y.z.0	x.y.z.1	x.y.z.63	61
	255.255.255.192	x.y.z.64	x.y.z.65	x.y.z.127	61
	255.255.255.192	x.y.z.128	x.y.z.129	x.y.z.191	61
	255.255.255.192	x.y.z.192	x.y.z.193	x.y.z.255	61
8	255.255.255.224	x.y.z.0	x.y.z.1	x.y.z.31	29
	255.255.255.224	x.y.z.32	x.y.z.33	x.y.z.63	29
	255.255.255.224	x.y.z.64	x.y.z.65	x.y.z.95	29
	255.255.255.224	x.y.z.96	x.y.z.97	x.y.z.127	29
	255.255.255.224	x.y.z.128	x.y.z.129	x.y.z.159	29
	255.255.255.224	x.y.z.160	x.y.z.161	x.y.z.191	29
	255.255.255.224	x.y.z.192	x.y.z.193	x.y.z.223	29
	255.255.255.224	x.y.z.224	x.y.z.225	x.y.z.255	29

For example, suppose you want to chop up a Class C network, 200.211.192.x, into two subnets. As you can see in the table, you'd use a subnet mask of 255.255.255.128 for each subnet. The first subnet would have network number 200.211.192.0, router address 200.211.192.1, and broadcast address 200.211.192.127. You could assign IP addresses 200.211.192.2 through 200.211.192.126—that's 125 additional different IP addresses.

Heavily subnetting a network results in the loss of a progressively greater percentage of addresses to the network number, broadcast address, and router address.

The second subnet would have network number 200.211.192.128, router address 200.211.192.129, and broadcast address 200.211.192.255.

Why It's Best to Use Routers That Support Subnet 0

When subnetting a Class C network using the method in Table 2.5, if you use the 2x – 2 calculation, the subnet 128 in the table doesn't make sense. It turns out that there's a legitimate and popular reason to do it this way, however:

- Remember that using subnet 0 is not allowed according to the RFC standards, but by using it you can subnet your Class C network with a subnet mask of 128. This uses only 1 bit, and according to your calculator, $2^1 - 2 = 0$, giving you zero subnets.

- By using routers that support subnet 0, you can assign 1–126 for hosts and 129–254 for hosts, as stated in the table. This saves a bunch of addresses! If you were to stick to the method defined by the RFC standards, the best you could gain is a subnet mask of 192 (2 bits), which allows you only two subnets ($2^2 - 2 = 2$).

Determining the Subnet Numbers for a Class C Subnet

The first subnet always has a 0 in the interesting octet. In the example, it would be 200.211.192.0, the same as the original nonsubnetted network address. To determine the subnet numbers for the additional subnets, you first have to determine the incremental value:

1. Begin with the octet that has an interesting value (other than 0 or 255) in the subnet mask. Then subtract the interesting value from 256. The result is the incremental value.

   If you again use the network 200.211.192.x and a mask of 255.255.255.192, the example yields the following equation: 256 – 192 = 64. So, 64 is your incremental value in the interesting octet—the fourth octet in this case. Why the fourth octet? That's the octet with the interesting value, 192, in the mask.

2. To determine the second subnet number, add the incremental value to the 0 in the fourth octet of the first subnet.

   In the example, it would be 200.211.192.64.

3. To determine the third subnet number, add the incremental value to the interesting octet of the second subnet number.

   In the example, it would be 200.211.192.128.

4. Keep adding the incremental value in this fashion until you reach the actual subnet mask number.

   For example, 0 + 64 = 64, so your second subnet is 64. And 64 + 64 is 128, so your third subnet is 128. And 128 + 64 is 192, so your fourth subnet is 192. Because 192 is the subnet mask, this is your last subnet. If you tried to add 64 again, you'd come up with 256, an unusable octet value, which is always what you end up with when you've gone too far. This means your valid subnets are 0, 64, 128, and 192.

The numbers between the subnets are your valid host and broadcast addresses. For example, the following are valid hosts for two of the subnets in a Class C network with a subnet mask of 192:

- The valid hosts for subnet 64 are in the range 65–126, which gives you 62 hosts per subnet.

  (You can't use 127 as a host, because that would mean your host bits would be all 1s. The all-1s format is reserved as the broadcast address for that subnet.)

- The valid hosts for subnet 128 are in the range 129–190, with a broadcast address of 191.

As you can see, this solution wastes a few addresses—six more than not subnetting at all, to be exact. In a Class C network, this should not be hard to justify. The 255.255.255.128 subnet mask is an even better solution if you need only two subnets and expect to need close to 126 host addresses per subnet.

Calculating Values for an Eight-Subnet Class C Network

What happens if you need eight subnets in your Class C network?

By using the calculation of 2x, where x is the number of subnet bits, you would need three subnet bits to get eight subnets ($2^3 = 8$). What are the valid subnets, and what are the valid hosts of each subnet? Let's figure it out.

11100000 is 224 in binary and would be the interesting value in the fourth octet of the subnet mask. This must be the same on all workstations.

NOTE   You're likely to see test questions that ask you to identify the problem with a given configuration. If a workstation has the wrong subnet mask, the router could "think" the workstation is on a different subnet than it actually is. When that happens, the misguided router won't forward packets to the workstation in question. Similarly, if the mask is incorrectly specified in the workstation's configuration, that workstation will observe the mask and send packets to the default gateway when it shouldn't.

To figure out the valid subnets, subtract the interesting octet value from 256 (256 − 224 = 32), so 32 is your incremental value for the fourth octet. Of course, the 0 subnet is your first subnet, as always. The other subnets would be 32, 64, 96, 128, 160, 192, and 224. The valid hosts are the numbers between the subnet numbers, except the numbers that equal all 1s in the host bits. These numbers would be 31, 63, 95, 127, 159, 191, 223, and 255. Remember that using all 1s in the host bits is reserved for the broadcast address of each subnet.

The valid subnets, hosts, and broadcasts are as follows:

Subnet	Hosts	Broadcast
0	1–30	31
32	33–62	63
64	65–94	95
96	97–126	127
128	129–158	159
160	161–190	191
192	193–222	223
224	225–254	255

You can add one more bit to the subnet mask just for fun. You were using 3 bits, which gave you 224. By adding the next bit, the mask now becomes 240 (11110000).

By using 4 bits for the subnet mask, you get 14 subnets because $2^4 = 16$. This subnet mask also gives you only 4 bits for the host addresses, or $2^4 - 2 = 14$ hosts per subnet. As you can see, the amount of hosts per subnet gets reduced rather quickly for each host bit that gets reallocated for subnet use.

The first valid subnet for subnet 240 is 0, as always. Because $256 - 240 = 16$, your remaining subnets are then 16, 32, 48, 64, 80, 96, 112, 128, 144, 160, 176, 192, 208, 224, and 240. Remember that the actual interesting octet value also represents the last valid subnet, so 240 is the last valid subnet number. The valid hosts are the numbers between the subnets, except for the numbers that are all 1s—the broadcast address for the subnet.

Table 2.6 shows the numbers in the interesting (fourth) octet for a Class C network with eight subnets.

TABLE 2.6   Fourth-Octet Addresses for a Class C Network with Eight Subnets

Subnet	Hosts	Broadcast
0	1–14	15
16	17–30	31
32	33–46	47

TABLE 2.6   Fourth-Octet Addresses for a Class C Network with Eight Subnets *(continued)*

Subnet	Hosts	Broadcast
48	49–62	63
64	65–78	79
80	81–94	95
96	97–110	111
112	113–126	127
128	129–142	143
144	145–158	159
160	161–174	175
176	177–190	191
192	193–206	207
208	209–222	223
224	225–238	239
240	241–254	255

Subnetting Class B

Because a Class B network has 16 bits for host addresses, you have plenty of available bits to play with when figuring out a subnet mask. Remember that you have to start with the leftmost bit and work toward the right. For example, a Class B network would look like x.y.0.0, with the default mask of 255.255.0.0. Using the default mask would give you one network with 65,534 hosts.

The default mask in binary is 11111111.11111111.00000000.00000000. The 1s represent the corresponding network bits in the IP address, and the 0s represent the host bits. When creating a subnet mask, the leftmost bit(s) will be borrowed from the host bits (0s will be turned into 1s) to become the subnet mask. You then use the remaining bits that are still set to 0 for host addresses.

If you use only 1 bit to create a subnet mask, you have a mask of 255.255.128.0. If you use 2 bits, you have a mask of 255.255.192.0, or 11111111.11111111.11000000.00000000.

As with subnetting a Class C address, you now have three parts of the IP address: the network address, the subnet address, and the host address. You figure out the subnet mask numbers the same way as you do with a Class C network (see the previous section, "Calculating Values for an Eight-Subnet Class C Network"), but you'll end up with a lot more hosts per subnet.

There are four subnets, because $2^2 = 4$. The valid third-octet values for the subnets are 0, 64, 128, and 192 ($256 - 192 = 64$, so the incremental value of the third octet is 64). However, there are 14 bits (0s) left over for host addressing. This gives you 16,382 hosts per subnet ($2^{14} - 2 = 16,382$).

The valid subnets and hosts are as follows:

Subnet	Hosts	Broadcast
x.y.0.0	x.y.0.1 through x.y. 63.254	x.y.63.255
x.y.64.0	x.y.64.1 through x.y.127.254	x.y.127.255
x.y.128.0	x.y.128.1 through x.y.191.254	x.y.191.255
x.y.192.0	x.y.192.1 through x.y.255.254	x.y.255.255

You can add another bit to the subnet mask, making it 11111111.11111111.11100000 .00000000 or 255.255.224.0. This gives you eight subnets ($2^3 = 8$) and 8,190 hosts. The valid subnets are 0, 32, 64, 96, 128, 160, 192, and 224 ($256 - 224 = 32$). The subnets, valid hosts, and broadcasts are listed here:

Subnet	Hosts	Broadcast
x.y.0.0	x.y.0.1 through x.y.31.254	x.y.31.255
x.y.32.0	x.y.32.1 through x.y.63.254	x.y.63.255
x.y.64.0	x.y.64.1 through x.y.95.254	x.y.95.255
x.y.96.0	x.y.96.1 through x.y.127.254	x.y.127.255
x.y.128.0	x.y.128.1 through x.y.159.254	x.y.159.255
x.y.160.0	x.y.160.1 through x.y.191.254	x.y.191.255
x.y.192.0	x.y.192.1 through x.y.223.254	x.y.223.255
x.y.224.0	x.y.224.1 through x.y.255.254	x.y.255.255

The following are the breakdowns for a 9-bit mask and a 14-bit mask:

- If you use 9 bits for the mask, it gives you 512 subnets (2^9). With only 7 bits for hosts, you still have 126 hosts per subnet ($2^7 - 2 = 126$). The mask looks like this:

  11111111.11111111.11111111.10000000 or 255.255.255.128

- If you use 14 bits for the subnet mask, you get 16,384 subnets (2^{14}), but only two hosts per subnet ($2^2 - 2 = 2$). The subnet mask would look like this:

  11111111.11111111.11111111.11111100 or 255.255.255.252

> ### 🌐 Real World Scenario
> #### Subnet Mask Use in an ISP
>
> You may be wondering why you would use a 14-bit subnet mask with a Class B address. This approach is actually very common. Let's say you have a Class B network and use a subnet mask of 255.255.255.0. You'd have 256 subnets and 254 hosts per subnet. Imagine also that you are an Internet service provider (ISP) and have a network with many WAN links, a different one between you and each customer. Typically, you'd have a direct connection between each site. Each of these links must be on its own subnet or network. There will be two hosts on these subnets—one address for each router port. If you used the mask described earlier (255.255.255.0), you would waste 252 host addresses per subnet. But using the 255.255.255.252 subnet mask, you have more subnets available, which means more customers—each subnet with only two hosts, which is the maximum allowed on a point-to-point circuit.
>
> You can use the 255.255.255.252 subnet mask only if you are running a routing algorithm such as Enhanced Interior Gateway Routing Protocol (EIGRP) or Open Shortest Path First (OSPF), discussed in Chapter 5. These routing protocols allow what is called *variable-length subnet masking* (VLSM). VLSM allows you to run the 255.255.255.252 subnet mask on your interfaces to the WANs and run 255.255.255.0 on your router interfaces in your local area network (LAN), using the same classful network address for all subnets. It works because these routing protocols transmit the subnet mask information in the update packets that they send to the other routers. Classful routing protocols, such as RIP version 1, don't transmit the subnet mask and therefore cannot employ VLSM.

Subnetting Class A

Class A networks have even more bits available than Class B and C networks. A default Class A network subnet mask is only 8 bits, or 255.0.0.0, giving you a whopping 24 bits for hosts to play with. Knowing which hosts and subnets are valid is a lot more complicated than it was for either Class B or C networks.

If you use a mask of 11111111.1111111.00000000.00000000, or 255.255.0.0, you'll have 8 bits for subnets, or 256 subnets (2^8). This leaves 16 bits for hosts, or 65,534 hosts per subnet ($2^{16} - 2 = 65534$).

If you split the 24 bits evenly between subnets and hosts, you would give each one 12 bits. The mask would look like this: 11111111.11111111.11110000.00000000, or 255.255.240.0. How many valid subnets and hosts would you have? The answer is 4,096 subnets each with 4,094 hosts ($2^{12} - 2 = 4094$).

The second octet will be somewhere between 0 and 255. However, you will need to figure out the third octet. Because the third octet has a 240 mask, you get 16 (256 − 240 = 16) as your incremental value in the third octet. The third octet must start with 0 for the first subnet, the second subnet will have 16 in the third octet, and so on. This means that some of your valid subnets are as follows (not in order):

Subnet	Hosts	Broadcast
x.0-255.0.0	x.0-255.0.1 through x.0-255.15.254	x.0-255.15.255
x.0-255.16.0	x.0-255.16.1 through x.0-255.31.254	x.0-255.31.255
x.0-255.32.0	x.0-255.32.1 through x.0-255.47.254	x.0-255.47.255
x.0-255.48.0	x.0-255.48.1 through x.0-255.63.254	x.0-255.63.255

They go on in this way for the remaining third-octet values through 224 in the subnet column.

Working with Classless Inter-Domain Routing

Microsoft uses an alternate way to write address ranges, called Classless Inter-Domain Routing (CIDR; pronounced "cider"). CIDR is a shorthand version of the subnet mask. For example, an address of 131.107.2.0 with a subnet mask of 255.255.255.0 is listed in CIDR as 131.107.2.0/24 because the subnet mask contains twenty-four 1s. An address listed as 141.10.32.0/19 would have a subnet mask of 255.255.224.0, or nineteen 1s (the default subnet mask for Class B plus 3 bits). This is the nomenclature used in all Microsoft exams (see Figure 2.12).

FIGURE 2.12   Subnet mask represented by 1s

Subnet mask in binary: 1111 1111. 1111 1111. 1111 1111. 0000 0000

Subnet mask in decimal: 255   .   255   .   255   .   0

(The spaces in the above example are only for illustrative purposes.
The subnet mask in decimal would actually appear as 255.255.255.0.)

Let's say an Internet company has assigned you the following Class C address and CIDR number: 192.168.10.0 /24. This represents the Class C address of 192.168.10.0 and a subnet mask of 255.255.255.0.

Again, CIDR represents the number of 1s turned on in a subnet mask. For example, a CIDR number of /16 stands for 255.255.0.0 (11111111.11111111.00000000.00000000).

The following is a list of all the CIDR numbers (starting with a Class A default subnet mask) and their corresponding subnet masks.

CIDR	Mask	CIDR	Mask	CIDR	Mask
/8	255.0.0.0	/17	255.255.128.0	/25	255.255.255.128

CIDR	Mask	CIDR	Mask	CIDR	Mask
/9	255.128.0.0	/18	255.255.192.0	/26	255.255.255.192
/10	255.192.0.0	/19	255.255.224.0	/27	255.255.255.224
/11	255.224.0.0	/20	255.255.240.0	/28	255.255.255.240
/12	255.240.0.0	/21	255.255.248.0	/29	255.255.255.248
/13	255.248.0.0	/22	255.255.252.0	/30	255.255.255.252
/14	255.252.0.0	/23	255.255.254.0	/31	255.255.255.254
/15	255.254.0.0	/24	255.255.255.0	/32	255.255.255.255
/16	255.255.0.0				

Quickly Identifying Subnet Characteristics Using CIDR

Given the limited time you have to dispatch questions in the structured environment of a Microsoft certification exam, every shortcut to coming up with the correct answer is a plus. The following method, using CIDR notation, can shave minutes off the time it takes you to complete a single question. Since you already understand the underlying binary technology at the heart of subnetting, you can use the following shortcuts, one for each address class, to come up with the correct answer without working in binary.

Identifying Class C Subnet Characteristics

Consider the host address 192.168.10.50/27. The following steps flesh out the details of the subnet of which this address is a member:

1. Obtain the CIDR-notation prefix length for the address by converting the dotted-decimal mask to CIDR notation.

   In this case, /27 corresponds to a mask of 255.255.255.224. Practice converting between these notations until it becomes second nature.

2. Using the closest multiple of 8 that is greater than or equal to the prefix length, compute the interesting octet (the octet that increases from one subnet to the next in increments other than 1 or 0). Divide this multiple by 8. The result is a number corresponding to the octet that is interesting.

   In this case, the next multiple of 8 greater than 27 is 32. Dividing 32 by 8 produces the number 4, pointing to the fourth octet as the interesting one.

3. To compute the incremental value in the interesting octet, subtract the prefix length from the next higher multiple of 8, which in this case is 32. The result (32 − 27) is 5. Raise 2 to the computed value ($2^5 = 32$). The result is the incremental value of the interesting octet.

4. Recall the value of the interesting octet from the original address (50 in this case). Starting with 0, increment by the incremental value until the value is exceeded. The values, then, are 0, 32, 64, and so on.

5. The subnet in question extends from the increment that is immediately less than or equal to the address's interesting octet value to the address immediately before the next increment. In this example, 192.168.10.50/27 belongs to the subnet 192.168.10.32, and this subnet extends to the address immediately preceding 192.168.10.64, which is its broadcast address, 192.168.10.63.

   Note that if the interesting octet is not the fourth octet, all octets after the interesting octet must be set to 0 for the subnet address.

6. The usable range of addresses for the subnet in question extends from one higher than the subnet address to one less than the broadcast address, making the range for the subnet in question 192.168.10.33 through 192.168.10.62. As you can see, 192.168.10.50/27 definitely falls within the subnet 192.168.10.32/27.

Identifying Class B Subnet Characteristics

Using the steps in the previous section, find the subnet in which the address 172.16.76.12 with a mask of 255.255.240.0 belongs:

1. The corresponding CIDR notation prefix length is /20.

2. The next multiple of 8 that is greater than 20 is 24. 24 ÷ 8 = 3. Octet 3 is interesting.

3. 24 − 20 = 4, so the incremental value is 2^4 = 16.

4. The increments in the third octet are 0, 16, 32, 48, 64, 80, and so on.

5. The increments of 64 and 80 bracket the address's third-octet value of 76, making the subnet in question 172.16.64.0, after setting all octets after the interesting octet to 0. This subnet's broadcast address is 172.16.79.255, which comes right before the next subnet address of 172.16.80.0.

6. The usable address range, then, extends from 172.16.64.1 through 172.16.79.254.

Identifying Class A Subnet Characteristics

Try it one more time with 10.6.127.255/14. Combine some of the related steps, if possible:

1. The prefix length is 14. The next multiple of 8 that is greater than or equal to 14 is 16. 16 ÷ 8 = 2, so the second octet is interesting.

2. 16 − 14 = 2, so the incremental value in the second octet is 2^2 = 4.

3. The corresponding second-octet value of 6 in the address falls between the 4 and 8 increments. This means that the subnet in question is 10.4.0.0 (setting octets after the second one to 0) and its broadcast address is 10.7.255.255.

4. The usable address range is from 10.4.0.1 through 10.7.255.254.

Determining Quantities of Subnets and Hosts

The general technique described in the previous section also is useful when trying to determine the total number of subnets and hosts produced by a given mask with respect to the default mask of the class of address in question.

Consider, for example, the Class B address 172.16.0.0 with a subnet mask of 255.255.254.0.

This is a prefix length of 23 bits. When you subtract the default prefix length for a Class B address of 16 from 23, you get the value 7. Raising 2 to the 7th power results in the value 128, which is the number of subnets you get when you subnet a Class B address with the 255.255.254.0 mask.

Determining the number of hosts available in each of these 128 subnets is simple because you always subtract the prefix length that the subnet mask produces—23 in this example—from the value 32, which represents the total number of bits in any IP address. The difference, 9, represents the remaining number of 0s, or host bits, in the subnet mask. Raising 2 to this value produces the total possible number of host IDs per subnet that this subnet mask allows. Remember to subtract 2 from this result to account for the subnet and broadcast addresses for each subnet. This gives you the actual number of usable host IDs per subnet. In this case, this value is $2^9 - 2 = 510$.

Repeated practice with this technique will reduce your time to obtain the desired answer to mere seconds, leaving more time for the more challenging tasks in each question. You have a wealth of examples and scenarios in this chapter, as well as in the review questions, on which to try your technique and build your faith in this faster method.

Understanding IPv6

Internet Protocol version 6 (IPv6) is the first major revamping of IP since RFC 791 was accepted in 1981. Yes, the operation of IP has improved, and there have been a few bells and whistles added (such as NAT, for example), but the basic structure is still being used as it was originally intended. IPv6 has actually been available to use in Microsoft operating systems since NT 4.0, but it always had to be manually enabled. Microsoft Vista is the first Microsoft operating system to have it enabled by default. It is also enabled by default in Windows Server 2008 (and probably will be in all Microsoft operating systems from this point on).

TCP and UDP—as well as the IP applications such as HTTP, FTP, SNMP, and the rest—are still being used in IPv4. So, you might ask, why change to the new version? What does IPv6 bring to your networking infrastructure? What is the structure of an IPv6 address? How is it implemented and used within Windows Server 2008? We'll answer all those questions and more in the following sections.

IPv6 History and Need

In the late 1970s, as the IP specifications were being put together, the vision of the interconnected devices was limited compared to what we actually have today. To get an idea of the growth of the Internet, take a look at Hobbes' Internet Timeline in RFC 2235 (www.faqs.org/rfcs/rfc2235.html). As you can see, in 1984, the number of hosts finally surpassed 1,000—two years after TCP and IP were introduced. With 32 bits of addressing available in IPv4, it handled the 1,000+ hosts just fine. And even with the number of hosts breaking the 10,000 mark in 1987 and then 100,000 in 1989, there were still plenty of IP addresses to go around. But when the number of hosts exceeded 2 million in 1992 and 3 million in 1994, concern in the industry started to build. So, in 1994 a working group was formed to come up with a solution to the quickly dwindling usable address availability in the IPv4 space. Internet Protocol next generation (IPng) was starting.

Have you heard of IP address depletion being a problem today? Probably not as much. When the working group realized it could not have IPv6 standardized before the available addresses might run out, they developed and standardized Network Address Translation (NAT) as an interim solution. NAT—or, more specifically, an implementation of NAT called Port Address Translation (PAT)—is taking care of a big portion of the problem.

NAT works very well, but it does have some limitations, including issues of peer-to-peer applications with their IPv4 addresses embedded in the data, issues of end-to-end traceability, and issues of overlapping addresses when two networks merge. Because all devices in an IPv6 network will have a unique address and no network address translation will take place, the global addressing concept of IPv4 will be brought back (the address put on by the source device will stay all the way to the destination). With the new-and-improved functionality of IPv6, the drawbacks of NAT, and the limitations of IPv4, will be eliminated.

IPv6 New and Improved Concepts

Several elements of the IPv4 protocol could use some enhancements. Fortunately, IPv6 incorporates enhancements as well as new features directly into the protocol specification to provide better and additional functionality.

The new concepts and new implementations of old concepts in IPv6 include the following:

- Larger address space (128-bit vs. 32-bit)
- Autoconfiguration of Internet-accessible addresses with or without DHCP (without DHCP it's called *stateless autoconfiguration*)
- More efficient IP header (fewer fields and no checksum)
- Fixed-length IP header (the IPv4 header is variable length) with extension headers beyond the standard fixed length to provide enhancements
- Built-in IP mobility and security (although available in IPv4, the IPv6 implementation is a much better implementation)
- Built-in transition schemes to allow integration of the IPv4 and IPv6 spaces
- ARP broadcast messages are replaced with multicast request

Here are more details about these features:

128-bit address space   The new 128-bit address space will provide unique addresses for the foreseeable future. Although we would like to say we will never use up all the addresses, history may prove us wrong. The number of unique addresses in the IPv6 space is 2^{128}, or 3.4×10^{38}, addresses. How big is that number? It's enough for toasters and refrigerators (and maybe even cars) to all have their own addresses.

As a point of reference, the nearest black hole to Earth is 1,600 light years away. If you were to stack 4mm BB pellets from here to the nearest black hole and back, you would need 1.51×10^{22} BBs. This means you could uniquely address each BB from Earth to the black hole and back and still have quite a few addresses left over.

Another way to look at it is that the IPv6 address space is big enough to provide more than 1 million addresses per square inch of the surface area of the earth (oceans included).

Autoconfiguration and stateless autoconfiguration   Autoconfiguration is another added/improved feature of IPv6. We've used DHCP for a while to assign IP addresses to client machines. You should even remember that APIPA can be used to automatically assign addresses to Microsoft DHCP client machines in the absence of a DHCP server. The problem with APIPA is that it confines communication between machines to a local LAN (no default gateway). What if a client machine could ask whether there was a router on the LAN and what network it was on? If the client machine knew that, it could not only assign itself an address, but it could also choose the appropriate network and default gateway. The stateless autoconfiguration functionality of IPv6 allows the clients to do this.

Improved IPv6 header   The IPv6 header is more efficient than the IPv4 header because it is fixed length (with extensions possible) and has only a few fields. The IPv6 header consists of a total of 40 bytes, as described in the following list:

- *32 bytes*: Source and destination IPv6 addresses
- *8 bytes*: Version field, traffic class field, flow label field, payload length field, next header field, and hop limit field

You don't have to waste your time with a checksum validation anymore, and you don't have to include the length of the IP header (it's fixed in IPv6; the IP header is variable length in IPv4, so the length must be included as a field).

IPv6 mobility   IPv6 is only a replacement of the OSI layer 3 component, so you'll continue to use the TCP (and UDP) components as they currently exist. IPv6 addresses a TCP issue, though. Specifically, TCP is connection oriented, meaning you establish an end-to-end communication path with sequencing and acknowledgments before you ever send any data, and then you have to acknowledge all the pieces of data sent. You do this through a combination of an IP address, port number, and port type (socket).

If the source IP address changes, the TCP connection may be disrupted. But then, how often does this happen? Well, it happens more and more often, as more people are walking around with a wireless laptop or a wireless Voice over IP (VoIP) telephone. IPv6 mobility establishes a TCP connection with a home address, and when changing networks, it continues to communicate with the original endpoint from a care-of address as it changes LANs, which sends all traffic back through the home address. The handing off of network addresses does not disrupt the TCP connection state (the original TCP port number and address remain intact).

Improved security   Unlike IPv4, IPv6 has security built in. Internet Protocol Security (IPsec) is a component used today to authenticate and encrypt secure tunnels from a source to a destination. This can be from the client to the server or between gateways. IPv4 lets you do this by enhancing IP header functionality (basically adding a second IP header while encrypting everything behind it). In IPv6, you add this as standard functionality by using extension headers. Extension headers are inserted into the packet only if they are needed. Each header has a "next header" field, which identifies the next piece of information. The extension headers currently identified for IPv6 are Hop-By-Hop Options, Routing, Fragment, Destination Options, Authentication, and Encapsulating Security Payload. The Authentication header and the Encapsulating Security Payload header are the IPsec-specific control headers.

IPv4 to IPv6 transmission   Several mechanisms in IPv6 make the IPv4 to IPv6 transition easy:

- A simple dual-stack implementation where both IPv4 and IPv6 are installed and used is certainly an option. In most situations (so far), this doesn't work so well, because most of us aren't connected to an IPv6 network and our Internet connection is not IPv6 even if we're using IPv6 internally. So, Microsoft includes other mechanisms that can be used in several different circumstances.

- Intra-Site Automatic Tunnel Addressing Protocol (ISATAP) is an automatic tunneling mechanism used to connect an IPv6 network to an IPv4 address space (not using NAT). ISATAP treats the IPv4 space as one big logical link connection space.

- 6to4 is a mechanism used to transition to IPv4. This method, like ISATAP, treats the IPv4 address space as a logical link layer with each IPv6 space in transition using a 6to4 router to create endpoints using the IPv4 space as a point-to-point connection (kind of like a WAN, eh?). 6to4 implementations still do not work well through a NAT, although a 6to4 implementation using an application layer gateway (ALG) is certainly doable.

- Teredo is a mechanism that allows users behind a NAT to access the IPv6 space by tunneling IPv6 packets in UDP.

Pseudo-interfaces are used in these mechanisms to create a usable interface for the operating system. Another interesting feature of IPv6 is that addresses are assigned to interfaces (or pseudo-interfaces), not simply to the end node. Your Windows Server 2008 will have several unique IPv6 addresses assigned.

New broadcast methods   IPv6 has moved away from using broadcasting. The three types of packets used in IPv6 are unicast, multicast, and anycast. IPv6 clients then must use one of these types to get the MAC address of the next Ethernet hop (default gateway). IPv6 makes use of multicasting for this along with the new functionality called *neighbor discovery*. Not only does ARP utilize new functionality, but ICMP (also a layer 3 protocol) has been redone and is now known as ICMP6. ICMP6 is used for messaging (packet too large, time exceeded, and so on) as it was in IPv4, but now it's also used for the messaging of IPv6 mobility. ICMP6 echo request and ICMP6 echo reply are still used for `ping`.

IPv6 Addressing Concepts

You need to consider several concepts when IPv6 addressing. For starters, the format of the address has changed. Three types of addresses are used in IPv6 with some predefined values within the address space. You need to get used to seeing these addresses and being able to identify their uses.

IPv6 Address Format

For the design of IPv4 addresses, you present addresses as octets or the decimal (base 10) representation of 8 bits. Four octets add up to the 32 bits required. IPv6 expands the address space to 128 bits, and the representation is for the most part shown in hexadecimal (a notation used to represent 8 bits using the values 0–9 and A–F) Figure 2.13 compares IPv4 to IPv6.

FIGURE 2.13   IPv4/IPv6 comparison

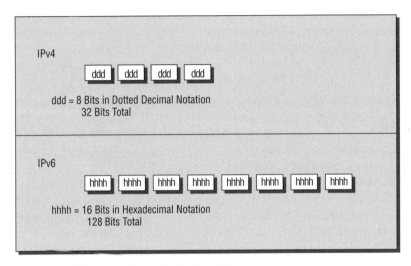

An example of a full IPv6 address looks like this:

```
2001:0DB8:0000:0000:1234:0000:A9FE:133E
```

You can tell the implementation of DNS will make life a lot easier for even those who like to ping the address in lieu of the name. Fortunately, DNS already has the ability to handle IPv6 address with the use of an AAAA record. (*A* is short for *alias*.) An A record in IPv4's addressing space is 32 bits, so an AAAA record—four As—is 128 bits. The Windows Server 2008 DNS server handles the AAAA and the reverse pointer (PTR) records for IPv6.

IPv6 Address Shortcuts

There are several shortcuts for writing an IPv6 address, described in the following list:

- :0: stands for :0000:

- You can omit preceding 0s in any 16-bit word. For example, :DB8: and :0DB8: are equivalent.

- :: is a variable standing for enough zeros to round out the address to 128 bits. :: can be used only once in an address

You can use these shortcuts to represent the example address 2001:0DB8:0000:0000: 1234:0000:A9FE:133E as shown here:

- Compress :0000: into :0:

  ```
  2001:0DB8:0000:0000:1234:0:A9FE:133E
  ```

- Eliminate preceding zeros:

  `2001:DB8:0000:0000:1234:0:A9FE:133E`

- Use the special variable shortcut for multiple 0s:

  `2001:DB8::1234:0:A9FE:133E`

You also now use prefix notation or slash notation when discussing IPv6 networks. For example, the network of the previous address can be represented as `2001:DB8:0000:0000:0000:0000:0000:0000`. This can also be expressed as `2001:DB8::` `/32`. The /32 indicates 32 bits of network, and 2001:DB8: is 32 bits of network.

IPv6 Address Assignment

So, do you subnet IPv6? The answer depends on your definition of subnetting. If you are given 32 bits of network from your ISP, you have 96 bits to work with. If you use some of the 96 bits to route within your network infrastructure, then you are subnetting. In this context, you do subnet IPv6. However, given the huge number of bits you have available, you will no longer need to implement VLSM. For example, Microsoft has a network space of `2001:4898::` `/32`. That gives the administrators a space of 96 bits (2^{96} = 79,228,162,514,264,337,593,543,950,336 unique addresses using all 96 bits) to work with.

You can let Windows Server 2008 dynamically/automatically assign its IPv6 address, or you can still assign it manually (see Figure 2.14). With dynamic/automatic assignment, the IPv6 address is assigned either by a DHCPv6 server or by the Windows Server 2008 machine. If no DHCPv6 server is configured, the Windows Server 2008 can query the local LAN segment to find a router with a configured IPv6 interface. If so, the server will assign itself an address on the same IPv6 network as the router interface and set its default gateway to the router interface's IPv6 address. Figure 2.14 shows that you have the same dynamic and manual choices as you do in IPv4; however, the input values for IPv6 must conform to the new format.

FIGURE 2.14   TCP/IPv6 Properties window

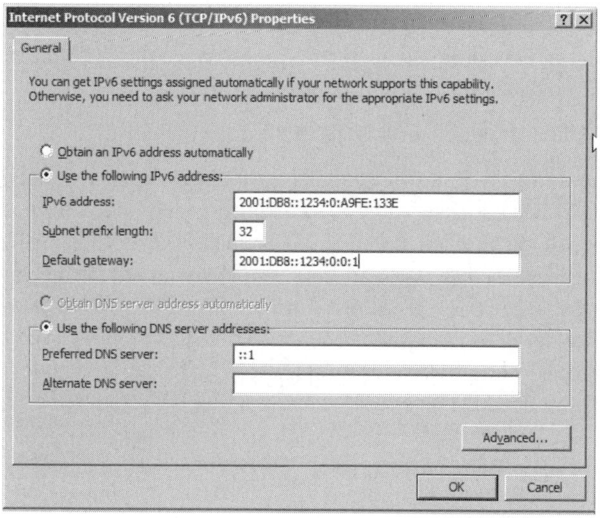

To see your configured IP addresses (IPv4 and IPv6), you can still use the `ipconfig` command. For example, we have configured a static IPv4 address and an IPv6 address on our server. The IPv6 address is the same as used in the earlier IPv6 example address. Figure 2.15 shows the result of this command on Windows Server 2008 for our server.

FIGURE 2.15   IPv6 configuration as seen from the command prompt

IPv6 Address Types

There are three types of addresses in IPv6: unicast, multicast, and anycast.

> Note the absence of the broadcast type, which is included in IPv4. You can't use broadcasts in IPv6; they've been replaced with multicasts.

Anycast addresses   Anycast addresses are not really new. The concept of anycast existed in IPv4 but was not widely used. An anycast address is an IPv6 address assigned to multiple devices (usually different devices). When an anycast packet is sent, it is delivered to one of the devices, usually the closest one.

Unicast addresses   A unicast packet uniquely identifies an interface of an IPv6 device. The interface can be a virtual or pseudo-interface or a real (physical) interface.

Unicast addresses come in several types, as described in the following list:

Global unicast address   As of this writing, the global unicast address space is defined as 2000::/3., The 2001::/32 networks are the IPv6 addresses currently being issued to business entities. As mentioned, Microsoft has been allocated 2001:4898:: /32. A Microsoft DHCPv6 server would be set up with scopes (ranges of addresses to be assigned) within this address space. There are some special addresses and address formats you will see in use as well. You'll find most example addresses listed as 2001:DB8:: /32; this space has been reserved for documentation. Do you remember the loopback address in IPv4, 127.0.0.1? In IPv6 the loopback address is ::1 (or 0:0:0:0:0:0:0:0001). You may also see an address with dotted decimal used.

A dual-stack Windows Server 2008 may also show you FE80::5EFE:192.168.1.200. This address form is used in an integration/migration model of IPv6 (or if you just can't leave the dotted decimal era, we suppose).

Link-local address   Link-local addresses are defined as FE80::/10. If you refer to Figure 2.15 showing the ipconfig command, you will see the link-local IPv6 address as FE80::a425:ab9d:7da4:ccba. The last 8 bytes (64 bits) are random to ensure a high probability of randomness for the link-local address.

The link-local address is to be used on a single link (network segment) and should never be routed.

There is another form of the local-link IPv6 address called the Extended User Interface 64-bit (EUI-64) format. This is derived by using the MAC address of the physical interface and inserting an FFFE between the third and fourth bytes of the MAC. The first byte is also made 02 (this sets the universal/local or U/L bit to 1 as defined in IEEE 802 frame specification). Again looking at Figure 2.15, the EUI-64 address would take the physical (MAC) address 00-03-FF-11-02-CD and make the link-local IPv6 address FE80::0203:FFFF:FE11:02CD. (We've left the preceding zeros in the link-local IPv6 address to make it easier for you to pick out the MAC address with the "FFFE" inserted.)

AnonymousAddress   Microsoft Server 2008 uses the random address by default instead of EUI-64. The random value is called the AnonymousAddress in Microsoft Server 2008. It can be modified to allow the use of EUI-64.

Unique local address   The unique local address can be FC00 or FD00 and is used like the private address space of IPv4. RFC 4193 describes unique local addresses. They are not expected to be routable on the global Internet. They are routable inside a more limited area, such as a site. They may also be routed between a limited set of sites.

Multicast address   Multicast addresses are one-to-many communication packets. Multicast packets are identifiable by their first byte (most significant byte, leftmost byte, leftmost 2 nibbles, leftmost 8 bits, and so on). A multicast address is defined as FF00::/8.

In the second byte shown (the "00" of FF00), the second 0 is what's called the *scope*. Interface-local is 01, and link-local is 02. FF01:: is an interface-local multicast.

There are several well-known (already defined) multicast addresses. For example, if you want to send a packet to all nodes in the link-local scope, you send the packet to FF02::1 (also shown as FF02:0:0:0:0:0:0:1). The all-routers multicast address is FF02::2

You can also use multicasting to get the logical link layer address (MAC address) of a device you are trying to communicate with. Instead of using the ARP mechanism of IPv4, IPv6 uses the ICMPv6 neighbor solicitation (NS) and neighbor advertisement (NA) messages. The NS and NA ICMPv6 messages are all part of the new neighbor discovery protocol (NDP). This new ICMPv6 functionality also includes router solicitation and router advertisements as well as redirect messages (similar to the IPv4 redirect functionality).

Unicast vs. Anycast

Unicast and anycast addresses look the same and may be indistinguishable from each other; it just depends on how many devices have the same address. If only one device has a globally unique IPv6 address, it's a unicast address. If more than one device has the same address, it's an anycast address. Both unicast and anycast are considered one-to-one communication, although you could say anycast is one-to-"one of many."

Table 2.7 outlines the IPv6 address space known prefixes and some well-known addresses.

TABLE 2.7   IPv6 Address Space Known Prefixes and Addresses

Address Prefix	Scope of Use
2000:: /3	Global unicast space prefix
FE80:: /10	Link-local address prefix
FC00:: /7	Unique local unicast prefix
FF00:: /8	Multicast prefix
2001:DB8:: /32	Global unicast prefix use for documentation
::1	Reserved local loopback address
2001:0000: /32	Teredo prefix (discussed later in this chapter)
2002:: /16	6to4 prefix (discussed later in this chapter)

IPv6 Integration/Migration

It's time to get into the mind-set of integrating IPv6 into your existing infrastructure with the longer goal of migrating to IPv6. In other words, this is not going to be a "OK, Friday the Internet is changing over" rollout. You have to bring about the change as a controlled implementation. It could easily take three to five years before a solid migration occurs, and probably longer. We think the migration will take just less than getting the world migrated to the metric system on the overall timeline. The process of integration/migration consists of several mechanisms:

Dual stack   Simply running both IPv4 and IPv6 on the same network, utilizing the IPv4 address space for devices using only IPv4 addresses and utilizing the IPv6 address space for devices using IPv6 addresses

Tunneling   Using an encapsulation scheme for transporting one address space inside another

Address translation   Using a higher-level application to transparently change one address type (IPv4 or IPv6) to the other so end devices are unaware one address space is talking to another

We elaborate on these three mechanisms in the following sections.

IPv6 Dual Stack

The default implementation in Windows Server 2008 is an enabled IPv6 configuration along with IPv4; this is dual stack. The implementation can be dual IP layer or dual TCP/IP stack. Windows Server 2008 uses the dual IP layer implementation (see Figure 2.16). When an application queries a DNS server to resolve a host name to an IP address, the DNS server may respond with an IPv4 address or an IPv6 address. If the DNS server responds with both, Windows Server 2008 will prefer the IPv6 addresses. Windows Server 2008 can use both IPv4 and IPv6 addresses as necessary for network communication. When looking at the output of the `ipconfig` command, you will see both address spaces displayed.

FIGURE 2.16   IPv6 dual IP layer diagram

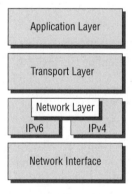

IPv6 Tunneling

Windows Server 2008 includes several tunneling mechanisms for tunneling IPv6 through the IPv4 address space. They include the following:

- Intra-Site Automatic Tunnel Addressing Protocol (ISATAP), which is used for unicast IPv6 communication across an IPv4 infrastructure. ISATAP is enabled by default in Windows Server 2008.

- 6to4, which is used for unicast IPv6 communication across an IPv4 infrastructure.

- Teredo, which is used for unicast IPv6 communication with an IPv4 NAT implementation across an IPv4 infrastructure.

With multiple tunneling protocols available and enabled by default, you might ask what's the difference and why is one used over the others? They all allow you to tunnel IPv6 packets through the IPv4 address space (a really cool thing if you're trying to integrate/migrate). Here are the details:

ISATAP   ISATAP is the automatic tunnel addressing protocol providing IPv6 addresses based upon the IPv4 address of the end interface (node). The IPv6 address is automatically configured on the local device, and the dual stack machine can use either its IPv4 or IPv6 address to communicate on the local network (within the local network infrastructure). ISATAP can use the neighbor discovery mechanism to determine the router ID and network prefix where the device is located, thus making intrasite communication possible even in a routed infrastructure.

The format of an ISATAP address is as follows:

```
[64bits of prefix] [32bits indicating ISATAP] [32bits IPv4 Address]
```

The center 32 bits indicating ISATAP are actually 0000:5EFE (when using private IPv4 addresses). The ISATAP address of the example Windows Server 2008 machine using the link-local IPv6 address is FE80::5EFE:192.168.1.200. Each node participating in the ISATAP infrastructure must support ISATAP. If you're routing through an IPv4 cloud, a border router (a router transitioning from an IPv6 to IPv4 space) must support ISATAP. Windows Server 2008 can be configured as a border router and will forward ISATAP packets. ISATAP is experimental and is defined in RFC 4214.

6to4   6to4 specifies a procedure for IPv6 networks to communicate with each other through an IPv4 space without the IPv6 nodes having to know what's happening. The IPv6 nodes do not need to be dual stacked to make this happen. The border router is the device responsible for knowing about the IPv6 to IPv4 transition. The IPv6 packets are encapsulated at the border router (and decapsulated at the other end or on the way back). There is an assigned prefix for the 6to4 implementation; 2002:: /16. 6to4 is defined in RFC 3056.

Teredo   Teredo (named after a kind of shipworm that drills holes in the wood of ships) is a protocol designed to allow IPv6 addresses to be available to hosts through one or more layers of NAT. Teredo uses a process of tunneling packets through the IPv4 space using UDP. The Teredo service encapsulates the IPv6 data within a UDP segment (packet) and uses IPv4 addressing to get through the IPv4 cloud. Having a layer 4 (Transport layer) available to use as translation functionality is what gives you the ability to be behind a NAT. Teredo provides host-to-host communication and dynamic addressing for IPv6 nodes (dual stack), allowing the nodes to have access to resources in an IPv6 network and the IPv6 devices to have access to the IPv6 devices that have only connectivity to the IPv4 space (like home users who have an IPv6-enabled operating system connecting to IPv6 resources and their home ISP have only IPv4 capabilities). Teredo is defined in RFC 4380.

In Windows Server 2008, an IPv4 Teredo server is identified and configured (using the `netsh` command interface). The Teredo server provides connectivity resources (address) to the Teredo client (the node that has access to the IPv4 Internet and needs access to an IPv6 network/Internet. A Teredo relay is a component used by the IPv6 router to receive traffic destined for Teredo clients and forward the traffic appropriately. The defined prefix for Teredo address is 2001:0000:: /32. Teredo does add overhead like all the implementations discussed. It is generally accepted that you should use the simplest model available. However, in the process of integration/migration for most of us behind a NAT, Teredo will be the process to choose.

From Windows Server 2008, use the `ipconfig /all` command to view the default configurations including IPv4 and IPv6. You may notice a notation we didn't discuss, the percent sign at the end of the IPv6 address (see Figure 2.17). The number after the percent sign is the virtual interface identifier used by Windows Server 2008.

FIGURE 2.17   IPv6 Interface identifier for ipconfig display

```
Link-local IPv6 Address . . . . . : fe80::a425:ab9d:7da4:ccba%10
```

Information Commands Useful with IPv6

You can use numerous commands to view, verify, and configure the network parameters of Windows Server 2008. Specifically, you can use the `netsh` command set and the `route` command set, as well as the standard `ping` and `tracert` functions.

Use the `netsh` command interface to examine and configure IPv6 functionality (as well as the provided dialog boxes if you want). The `netsh` command issued from the command interpreter changes into a network shell (`netsh`) where you can configure and view both IPv4 and IPv6 components.

Don't forget to use the ever-popular `route print` command to see the Windows Server 2008 routing tables (IPv4 and IPv6). The other diagnostic commands are still available for IPv4 as well as IPv6. In previous versions of Microsoft operating systems, `ping` was the IPv4 command, and `ping6` was the IPv6 command. This has changed for Windows Server 2008; `ping` works for both IPv4 and IPv6 to test layer 3 connectivity to remote devices. The IPv4 `tracert` command was `tracert6` for IPv6. The command is now `tracert` for both IPv4 and IPv6 and will show you every layer 3 (IP) hop from source to destination (assuming all the administrators from here to there want you to see the hops and are not blocking ICMP and also assuming there are not IP tunnels your packets are traversing, or you won't see the router hops in the tunnel either).

Overall, the consortium of people developing the Internet and the Internet Protocol have tried to make all the changes to communication infrastructures easy to implement (this is a daunting task with the many vendors and various infrastructures currently in place). The goal is not to daze and confuse administrators; it's to provide the most flexibility with the greatest functionality. IPv6 is going to provide the needed layer 3 (Network layer, global addressing layer, logical addressing layer...call it what you like) functionality for the foreseeable future.

Configuring IPsec

The original specifications for IP made no provisions for any kind of security. That wasn't accidental; it stemmed from two completely different causes. One was the expectation that users and administrators would continue to behave fairly well and not make serious attempts to compromise other people's traffic. The other was that the cryptographic technology needed to provide adequate security wasn't widely available or even widely known about yet.

As the Internet expanded, it became clear that robust authentication and privacy protection were desirable, but they aren't included in version 4 of the IP specification (which is the currently adopted standard). As the installed base of IP-capable devices grew, so too did the complexity of devising a security protocol that wouldn't interfere with the operation of all those devices. Finally, in the late 1990s, vendors began releasing products that incorporated the IP security extensions (better known as just IPsec) into IP version 4.

 Several major vendors, including Microsoft, Cisco, Nortel, and RSA Security, are shipping IPsec products. IPsec is defined by a set of RFCs including RFC 2401, 2402, 2406, 2408, and 2409.

IPsec operates at the Network layer and transparently secures applications. In IPsec terminology, there are *clients* and *servers*, but that's a little misleading. Any Windows 2000 Server, Windows XP, Windows Vista, Windows Server 2003, or Windows Server 2008 machine may be an IPsec client or server—an IPsec client is the computer that attempts to establish a connection to another machine, and an IPsec server is the target of that connection. By choosing appropriate client and server settings, you can fine-tune which computers will use IPsec to talk to each other.

IPsec provides two services: a way for computers to decide whether they trust each other (authentication) and a way to keep network data private (encryption). The IPsec process calls for two computers to authenticate each other before beginning an encrypted connection. At that point, the two machines can use the Internet Key Exchange (IKE) protocol to agree on a secret key to use for encrypting the traffic between them. This process takes place in the context of IPsec security associations (SAs), which you will learn about later in this chapter.

As if that weren't enough, the Windows Server 2003 implementation of IPsec explicitly supports the idea of policy-based security. Instead of running around changing security settings on every machine in a domain, you can set policies that configure individual machines, groups of machines within an organizational unit or domain, or every Windows 2000, Windows XP, Windows Vista, Windows Server 2003, or Windows Server 2008 machine on your network.

When you use IPsec to encrypt or authenticate connections between two machines—called end-to-end mode (or transport mode) because network traffic is protected before it leaves the originating machine—the data remains secured until the receiving machine gets it and decrypts it. There's a second application: using IPsec to secure traffic that's being passed over someone else's wires. This use of IPsec is called tunnel mode because it's used to encrypt traffic to pass over (or through) a tunnel, usually established by the Layer 2 Tunneling Protocol (L2TP).

IPsec Fundamentals

IPsec has two separate features: authentication and encryption. You can use them together or separately, and each feature has a number of options and parameters you can adjust to fine-tune security on your network.

Authentication protects your network, and the data it carries, from tampering. This tampering might take the form of a malicious attacker sitting between a client and a server, altering the contents of packets (referred to as a *man-in-the-middle attack*), or it might take the form of an attacker joining your network and impersonating either a client or a server. IPsec uses an *authentication header* (AH) to digitally sign the entire contents of each packet. This signature provides three separate benefits:

Protection against replay attacks   If an attacker can capture packets, save them until a later time, and send them again, then they can impersonate a machine after that machine is no longer on the network. This is called a *replay attack*. IPsec's authentication mechanism prevents replay attacks by including the sender's signature on all packets.

Protection against tampering   IPsec's signatures provide data integrity, meaning that an interloper can't selectively change parts of packets to alter their meaning.

Protection against spoofing   Usually when you hear about authentication, it refers to the process of a client or server verifying another machine's identity. IPsec authentication headers provide authentication because each end of a connection can verify the other's identity.

Authentication protects your data against tampering, but it doesn't do anything to keep people from seeing it. For that, you need encryption, which actually obscures the payload contents so that it can't be read as it goes by. To accomplish this, IPsec provides the Encapsulating Security Payload (ESP). ESP is used to encrypt the entire payload of an IPsec packet, rendering it undecipherable by anyone other than the intended recipient. ESP provides only confidentiality, but it can be combined with AH to gain maximum security.

In the following sections, you will see how IPsec is integrated into Windows Server 2008 and the specific details of the IPsec negotiation process.

IPsec and Windows Server 2008

Microsoft's IPsec implementation is actually licensed from, and was written by, Cisco, which guarantees good compatibility with other standards-based IPsec clients. Some other Windows Server 2008 features make IPsec more useful, especially Group Policy. Imagine a large network of computers, some running IPsec. When two computers want to communicate, it would be ideal if they could automatically take advantage of IPsec if both ends supported it. You'd also want to ensure that the security settings you wanted were applied to all IPsec-capable machines. With Windows NT, and with most other operating systems, that would mean hand-configuring each IPsec machine to use the settings you wanted.

The solution lies in the Windows Server 2008 Group Policy mechanism. First, you specify the IPsec settings you want to use on your network. Then each Windows 2000, Windows XP, Windows Vista, Windows Server 2003, or Windows Server 2008 machine runs a service called the IPsec Policy Agent. When the system starts, the Policy Agent connects to an Active Directory server, downloads the IPsec policy, and then passes it to the IPsec service. (You will learn more about the Policy Agent in the section "Security Policies" later in this chapter.)

Windows Server 2008 adds several new IPsec features that were either not present in or significantly enhanced since Windows 2000. Some of the features simply add extra layers of security to IPsec, but others actually enhance or replace the management and monitoring tools that you would use in the workplace:

IP Security Monitor   The IP Security Monitor is new for Windows Server 2008. This tool is now implemented as an MMC snap-in and adds several enhancements to the old version. You can now monitor IPsec information on the local computer as well as on remote machines, view details of all IPsec policies, view generic and specific filters, view statistics, view security associations, customize the display, and search for specific filters by IP address.

Stronger cryptographic master key (Diffie-Hellman)   IPsec now includes support for the much stronger Group 3 2048-bit Diffie-Hellman key exchange. The complexity of this key exchange significantly increases the difficulty of computing the secret key. However, if you require backward compatibility with Windows 2000 and Windows XP, you must use Group 2 (medium), which provides a 1024-bit key exchange. You should never use Group 1 (low).

Command-line management with `netsh`   You can now configure IPsec using the updated `netsh` command, which replaced the `IPsecpol.exe` tool a few years ago. With `netsh`, you can script and automate IPsec configuration.

Persistent policies   You can now create a persistent policy for a computer if a local or Active Directory–based policy cannot be applied. The persistent policy is always active and cannot be overridden by any other policy. Persistent policies can be applied only by using the `netsh` command.

Removal of default traffic exemptions   Previously, all broadcast, multicast, Internet Key Exchange (IKE), Kerberos, and Resource Reservation Protocol (RSVP) traffic was exempt from IPsec by default. Now, only IKE traffic is exempt because IKE is required for establishing IPsec-secured communication.

IPsec functionality over NAT   IPsec ESP packets can now pass through Network Address Translation (NAT)–enabled devices that allow UDP traffic to pass with a feature called User Datagram Protocol–Encapsulating Security Payload (UDP-ESP) encapsulation.

IPsec support for Resultant Set of Policy (RSoP)   Resultant Set of Policy (RSoP) is a new feature of Windows Server 2008 that provides the ability to see exactly how the various policies within the domain will apply to a specific user or computer. IPsec provides an extension to the RSoP console that you can use to view detailed settings for the IPsec policy that is being applied.

Security Policies

A security policy is a set of rules and filters that provide some level of security. Microsoft includes a number of prebuilt policies, and you can create your own. (In fact, you'll have to create your own policies for things like Dynamic Host Configuration Protocol [DHCP] and remote access servers.)

You assign policies to computers in a number of ways. The easiest way is to store the policy in Active Directory and let the IPsec Policy Agent apply it to the applicable machines. Once an IPsec policy is assigned to a machine through Active Directory, it remains assigned until another policy is provided, even after the machine leaves the site, domain, or organizational unit (OU) in which it was given the original policy. You can also assign policies directly to individual machines. In either case, you can manually unassign policies when you no longer want a policy in place on a specific machine.

You need to be familiar with three policies within the IP Security Policy Management snap-in:

- The Client (Respond Only) policy specifies that a Windows 2000, Windows XP, Windows Vista, Windows Server 2003, or Windows Server 2008 IPsec client will negotiate IPsec security with any peer that supports it but that it won't attempt to initiate security. Let's say you apply this policy to a Server 2008 computer. When it initiates outbound network connections, it won't attempt to use IPsec. When someone opens a connection to it, though, it will accept IPsec if the remote end asks for it.

- The Secure Server (Require Security) policy specifies that all IP communication to or from the policy target must use IPsec. In this case, all DNS, WINS, and web requests and everything else that uses an IP connection either has to be secured with IPsec or will be blocked. This may not be what you want unless you plan to implement IPsec on your entire network.

- The Server (Request Security) policy is a mix of the two other policies. In this case, the machine will always attempt to use IPsec by requesting it when it connects to a remote machine and by allowing it when an incoming connection requests it. This policy provides the best general balance between security and interoperability.

IPsec Authentication

IPsec supports three separate authentication methods. Which ones you'll use will depend on what kind of network you have (for example, with or without Active Directory) and to whom you're talking. Because the first thing an IPsec client and server want to do is authenticate each other, they need some way to agree on a set of credentials to use. The Windows Server 2008 version of IPsec supports three different authentication methods; they're used only during the initial authentication phase of building the SAs, not to generate encryption keys:

Kerberos   Kerberos is the default authentication protocol for any Windows 2000/2003/2008/ Vista/XP computer. If Kerberos fails, the computer will automatically switch to NT LAN Manager (NTLM) authentication. Kerberos is a widely supported open standard that offers good security and a great deal of flexibility. Because it's natively supported in Windows Server 2008, it's the default authentication method. Many third-party IPsec products include Kerberos support.

Certificates   Certificates are public-key certificates used for authentication. When you use certificate-based authentication, each end of the connection can use the other's public certificate to verify a digitally signed message. This provides great security, with some added overhead and infrastructure requirements. As you add machines to a domain in Windows Server 2008, they're automatically issued machine certificates (which apply to specific computers rather than users) that can be used for authentication; if you want to allow users and computers from other domains or organizations to connect to your IPsec machines, you'll need to explore certificate solutions that allow cross-organization certification.

Preshared keys   Preshared keys are reusable passwords. The preshared key itself is a word, code, or phrase that both computers know. The two machines use this password to establish a trust, but they don't send the plain-text phrase over the network. However, the unencrypted key is stored in Active Directory, so Microsoft recommends against using it in production (because anyone who can see the key can impersonate you or the remote computer). Most of the time you use this mode only when you need to talk to a third-party IPsec product that doesn't yet support certificate or Kerberos authentication.

Summary

Some of the important topics covered in this chapter included how TCP/IP is the primary protocol in use today, and Microsoft encourages you to use TCP/IP exclusively, if possible.

You also learned that the 32-bit IPv4 address is a structured and hierarchical address that is used to uniquely identify every machine on a network. You learned how to determine available IP addresses and implement subnetting. In addition, you learned how the new layer 3 IPv6 protocol is implemented including the structure of the IPv6 address. Finally, we discussed the new functionality included in IPv6 addressing as well as several Windows Server 2008 integration/migration implementations.

This chapter also examined how IPsec provides increased network security by providing or requiring authentication and/or encryption over the normal IP protocol.

Exam Essentials

Understand what subnetting is and when to use it.   If an organization is large and has many computers or if its computers are geographically dispersed, it's sensible to divide its large network into smaller ones connected by routers. These smaller networks are called *subnets*. Subnetting is the process of carving a single IP network into smaller, logical subnetworks.

Understand subnet masks.   For the subnet address scheme to work, every machine on the network must know which part of the host address will be used as the subnet address. The network administrator creates a 32-bit subnet mask consisting of 1s and 0s. The 1s in the subnet mask represent the positions that refer to the network or subnet addresses. The 0s represent the positions that refer to the host portion of the address.

Understand IPv6   Understand the structure of an IPv6 address and how it's displayed. Know the shortcuts and rules (like for displaying 0s) for writing IPv6 addresses. Know the integration/migration components for IPv6 included in Windows Server 2008, including tunneling and dual stack.

Understand how IPsec works.   IPsec operates at the Network layer, and users and applications never need to be aware of whether their traffic is being carried over a secure connection. IPsec primarily provides two services: a way for computers to decide whether they trust each other (authentication) and a way to keep network data private (encryption). The Windows Server 2008 implementation of IPsec explicitly supports the idea of policy-based security.

Review Questions

1. You have a large IP-routed network using the address 137.25.0.0; it is composed of 20 sub-nets, with a maximum of 300 hosts on each subnet. Your company continues on a merger and acquisitions spree, and your manager has told you to prepare for an increase to 50 subnets, with some of them containing more than 600 hosts. Using the existing network address, which of the following subnet masks would work for that requirement from your manager?

    A. 255.255.252.0

    B. 255.255.254.0

    C. 255.255.248.0

    D. 255.255.240.0

2. The company you work for is growing dramatically via acquisitions of other companies. As the network administrator, you need to keep up with the changes because they affect the work-stations, and you need to support them. When you started, there were 15 locations connected via routers, and now there are 25. As new companies are acquired, they are migrated to Win-dows Server 2008 and brought into the same domain as another site. Management says that they are going to acquire at least 10 more companies in the next 2 years. The engineers have also told you that they are redesigning the company's Class B address into an IP addressing scheme that will support these requirements and that there will never be more than 1,000 net-work devices on any subnet. What will be the appropriate subnet mask to support this network when the changes are completed?

    A. 255.255.252.0

    B. 255.255.248.0

    C. 255.255.255.0

    D. 255.255.255.128

3. You work for a small printing company that has 75 workstations. Most of them run standard office applications such as word processing, spreadsheet, and accounting programs. Fifteen of the workstations are constantly processing huge graphics files and then sending print jobs to industrial-size laser printers. The performance of the network has always been an issue, but you have never addressed it. You have now migrated your network to Windows Vista and Windows Server 2008 and have decided to take advantage of the routing capability built into Windows Server 2008. You choose the appropriate server and place two NICs in the machine, but you realize that you have only one network address, 201.102.34.0, which you obtained years ago. How should you subnet this address to segment the bandwidth hogs from the rest of the network while giving everyone access to the entire network?

    A. 255.255.255.192

    B. 255.255.255.224

    C. 255.255.255.252

    D. 255.255.255.240

4. You work for Carpathian Worldwide Enterprises, which has more than 50 administrative and manufacturing locations around the world. The size of these organizations varies greatly, with the number of computers per location ranging from 15 to slightly fewer than 1,000. The sales operations use more than 1,000 facilities, and each of which contains 2 to 5 computers. Carpathian is also in merger talks with another large organization; if the merger materializes as planned, you will have to accommodate another 100 manufacturing and administrative locations, each with a maximum of 600 computers, as well as 2,000 additional sales facilities. You don't have any numbers for the future growth of the company, but you are told to keep growth in mind. You decide to implement a private addressing plan for the entire organization. More than half of your routers don't support variable-length subnet masking. What subnet masks would work for this situation? (Choose all that apply.)

   A. 255.255.224.0

   B. 255.255.240.0

   C. 255.255.248.0

   D. 255.255.252.0

   E. 255.255.254.0

5. Which of the following subnet masks are represented with the CIDR of /27?

   A. 255.255.255.254

   B. 255.255.255.248

   C. 255.255.255.224

   D. 255.255.255.240

6. You administer a network that contains 175 machines. Your manager has assigned the network the IP address 192.168.11.0 with the default subnet mask of 255.255.255.0. A router that has one WAN interface and eight LAN interfaces connects this network to the corporate WAN. You want to subnet the network into three subnets, and you want to reserve a few addresses for a fourth subnet, just in case you need it later. You decide that Subnet A will contain 25 computers, Subnet B will contain 50 computers, and Subnet C will contain 100 computers. In the following exhibit, select the network addresses and subnet masks in the Choices column, and place them in the appropriate boxes in the other three columns. Each item may be used only once.

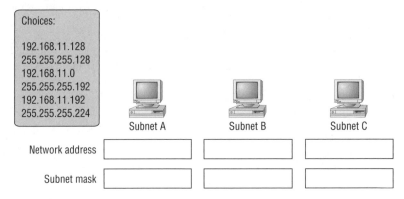

7. You are the administrator of a large internetwork that consists of Windows Server 2008 and Windows Vista computers with statically assigned IP addresses. One of your servers has IP connectivity issues. There are two other computers on the same LAN as the server, each of which reaches the server and the rest of the internetwork with no trouble. The diagram in Exhibit 1 shows the layout of the LAN in question. The server's IP address is 10.89.155.14.

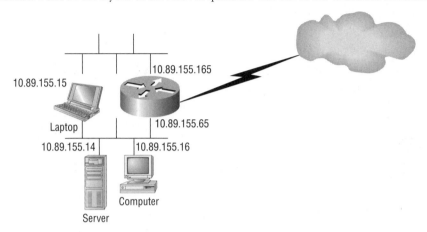

The output in Exhibit 2 was generated by the server and shows the IP routing table that the server uses to make routing decisions.

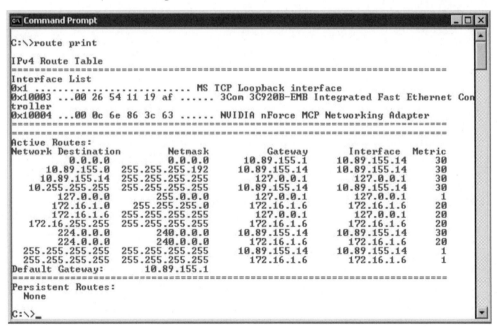

Which of the following two solutions work together to allow the server to have complete connectivity across the internetwork and not affect any other part of the LAN? (Choose two.)

A. Change the IP address of the server to 10.89.155.66.

B. Change the default gateway of the server to 10.89.155.65.

C. Change the local IP address of the router to 10.89.155.1.

D. Change the subnet mask of the server to 255.255.255.128.

E. Change the subnet mask of the server to 255.255.255.0.

F. Change the local subnet mask of the router to 255.255.255.192.

G. Change the IP address of the laptop to 10.89.155.67.

8. You are the administrator of an internetwork that consists of Windows Server 2008 and Windows Vista computers. You are experiencing partial IP connectivity loss. Refer to the following diagram.

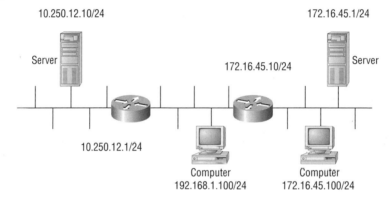

None of the servers or other computers has any static routes configured on them. The server at address 10.250.12.10 has 10.250.12.1 configured as its default gateway. The hosts on the 172.16.45.0 subnet have 172.16.45.10 configured as their default gateway. You execute some ping and traceroute commands and notice the following results: Host 10.250.12.10 and the hosts on the 172.16.45.0 subnet are able to reach host 192.168.1.100. The hosts on the 172.16.45.0 subnet are able to reach one another. The hosts on the 172.16.45.0 subnet are not able to reach host 10.250.12.10. Upon establishing a Telnet session with the router at 10.250.12.1, you discover that this router is configured with a static route to the 172.16.45.0/24 subnet. Which one of the following steps will most likely resolve the connectivity issue you are experiencing?

A. Remove the static route you noticed in the router.

B. Add static routes in the hosts on the 172.16.45.0 subnet to the 10.250.12.0/24 subnet.

C. Add a static route to the 10.250.12.0/24 subnet in the other router.

D. Add two static routes to host 192.168.1.100, each directed toward one of the other two subnets.

E. Configure the hosts on the 172.16.45.0 subnet with the correct default gateway.

9. Which of the following subnet masks are represented with the CIDR of /20?

    A. 255.255.254.0

    B. 255.255.255.254

    C. 255.255.192.0

    D. 255.255.240.0

10. With a /28 mask, which of the following addresses can be assigned to hosts on the same subnet? (Choose all that apply.)

    A. 192.168.1.0

    B. 192.168.1.17

    C. 192.168.1.31

    D. 192.168.1.16

    E. 192.168.1.25

11. Which of the following are subnet boundary addresses that result from the use of the /29 mask? (Choose all that apply.)

    A. 172.20.73.12

    B. 10.8.1.212

    C. 192.168.0.0

    D. 192.168.1.16

    E. 192.168.164.208

12. Which of the following are enhancements/changes to Internet Protocol in version 6? (Choose two.)

    A. Larger IP address space of 128 bits

    B. Expanded TCP and UDP port values 32 bits wide

    C. Broadcast messages are enhanced to provide better ICMP

    D. IP mobility functionality allowing a TCP communicating device to hop between IP networks and maintain TCP connectivity

    E. A variable-length IP header to include a checksum verifying the integrity of the IP/TCP/ Application layer data

    F. New IPv6 packet type of simulcast to allow communication to a single device where multiple devices are configured with the same address

13. Stateless autoconfiguration allows which of the following? (Choose two.)

A. Dynamic configuration of TCP ports for applications using IPv6

B. Dynamic allocation of IPv6 addresses without the use of DHCPv6

C. Device can learn and self assign itself the IPv6 address of the default gateway on its network segment

D. Allocation of its own UDP loopback port for testing

E. Dynamic discovery of Internet routers providing access to IPv6 networks configured via various Internet service providers

14. IPv6 uses an extension header instead or variable-length headers to add functionality to the protocol. As the network administrator, a junior admin wants to know what two headers are added for IPsec. What would you tell the junior admin? (Choose two.)

A. Next-Header

B. Destination Options header

C. Authentication header

D. Encapsulating Security Payload header

E. IPsec ID header

15. Given the IPv6 address 2001:0DB8:0000:0000:0000:BEE0:0000:1234, what would be the appropriate condensed IPv6 address displayed if entered as an interface address on Windows Server 2008?

A. 2001:DB8::BEE0:0:1234

B. 2001:0DB8::BEE:0:1234

C. 2001:DB8::BEE:0:1234

D. 2::1:DB8:0:0:0:BEE0:1234

E. 2001:DB8::BEE0::1234

16. How many bits are there in an IPv6 address, and how many total 16-bit words? (A 16-bit word is four hexadecimal characters separated by a colon.) (Choose two.)

A. 32 bits

B. 64 bits

C. 128 bits

D. 16 words

E. 8 words

F. 32 words

17. Which of the following addresses could be valid representations of a unique IPv6 address seen in the IPv6 space? (Choose all that apply.)

    A. `::`

    B. `::1`

    C. `FF00:2001::12FF:55BC`

    D. `2001:4989::192.168.1.1`

    E. `2001:4989::C0A8`

    F. `2001:4989:G1B5`

18. Which of the following are valid IPv6 address types? (Choose three.)

    A. Unicast

    B. Simulcast

    C. Anycast

    D. Multicast

    E. Broadcast

    F. Staticast

19. You are the network administrator, and your company is migrating to IPv6. You have been testing an IPv6 pilot network within your company and want to access resources in the IPv6 Internet. You are currently using the `10.0.0.0` IPv4 address space internally and have Internet connectivity through a pool of public addresses made available from your ISP. Which of the following mechanisms would be appropriate to test your pilot network implementation? (Choose two.)

    A. IPv6-only stack on your host machines

    B. IPv4-only stack on your host machines

    C. IPv4/IPv6 dual stack on your host machines

    D. Teredo available on your host machines

    E. 6to4 available on your host machines

    F. PAT with Traversal on your host machines

20. You ask one of your technicians to get the IPv6 address of new Windows Server 2008 machine, and she hands you a note with `FE80::0203:FFFF:FE11:2CD` on it. What can you tell from this address? (Choose two.)

    A. This is a globally unique IPv6 address.

    B. This is a link-local IPv6address.

    C. This is a multicast IPv6address.

    D. In EUI-64 format you can see the MAC address of the node.

    E. In EUI-64 format you can see the IPv4 address of the node.

Answers to Review Questions

1. A. A Class B address with a default subnet mask of 255.255.0.0 will support up to 65,534 hosts. To increase the number of networks that this network will support, you need to subnet the network by borrowing bits from the host portion of the address. The subnet mask 255.255.252.0 uses 6 bits from the host's area and will support 64 subnets while leaving enough bits to support 1,022 hosts per subnet. The subnet mask 255.255.248.0 uses 5 bits from the hosts and will support 32 subnetworks while leaving enough bits to support 2,046 hosts per subnet. 255.255.252.0 is the better answer because it leaves quite a bit of room for further growth in the number of networks while still leaving room for more than 1,000 hosts per subnet, which is a fairly large number of devices on one subnet. The subnet mask 255.255.254.0 uses 7 bits from the host's area and will support more than 120 networks, but it will leave only enough bits to support 500 hosts per subnet. The subnet mask 255.255.240.0 uses 4 bits from the hosts and will support only 16 subnetworks, even though it will leave enough bits to support more than 4,000 hosts per subnet.

2. A. The network mask applied to an address determines which portion of that address reflects the number of hosts available to that network. The balance with subnetting is always between the number of hosts and individual subnetworks that can be uniquely represented within one encompassing address. The number of hosts and networks that are made available depends upon the number of bits that can be used to represent them. This scenario requires more than 35 networks and fewer than 1,000 workstations on each network. If you convert the subnet masks as described in the chapter, you will see that the mask in option A allows for more than 60 networks and more than 1,000 hosts. All of the other options are deficient in either the number of networks or the number of hosts that they represent.

3. A. The subnet mask 255.255.255.192 borrows 2 bits from the hosts, which allows you to build four separate networks that you can route through the Windows server. This will allow you to have 62 hosts on each segment. A mask of 255.255.255.128 would have been even better, with two subnets of 126 hosts each, but that wasn't an option, and this solution gives you room for growth in the number of subnets. The subnet mask 255.255.255.224 borrows 3 bits from the hosts; this allows you to create 8 networks, which you don't need, and leaves only enough bits for 30 hosts. The subnet mask 255.255.255.252 borrows 6 bits from the hosts; this allows you to create more than 60 networks, which you don't need, and leaves only enough bits for 2 hosts. The subnet mask 255.255.255.240 borrows 4 bits from the hosts; this allows you to create 16 networks, which you don't need, and leaves only enough bits for 14 hosts per subnet.

4. B, C, D. When you add up the locations that currently need to be given a network address, the total is 3,150, and the maximum number of hosts at any one of these locations is less than 1,000. The subnet masks need to support those requirements. Assuming you choose the Class A private address space 10.0.0.0/8, the subnet masks given in options B, C, and D will provide the address space to support the outlined requirements. The subnet mask 255.255.240.0 supports more than 4,000 subnets and more than 4,000 hosts. The subnet mask 255.255.248.0 supports more than 8,000 subnets and more than 2,000 hosts. The subnet mask 255.255.252.0 supports more than 16,000 subnets and more than 1,000 hosts. Although each of these subnet masks will work, at the rate that this company is growing, 255.255.252.0 is probably the best mask to prepare for the future. It's unlikely that there will ever be more than 1,000 hosts on any given network. In fact,

that number would probably cause performance problems on that subnet. Therefore, it's better to have more subnets available to deploy as the company grows. The subnet mask 255.255.224.0 supports more than 2,000 subnets—an insufficient number to cover the locations. The subnet mask 255.255.254.0 supports more than 32,000 subnets but only 500 hosts per subnet, which are not enough hosts to cover all the locations.

5. C. The CIDR /27 tells you that 27 ones are turned on in the subnet mask. Twenty-seven 1s equals 11111111.11111111.11111111.11100000. This would then equal 255.255.255.224.

6. The network address 192.168.11.192 with a subnet mask of 255.255.255.224 is perfect for Subnet A because it supports up to 30 hosts. The network address 192.168.11.128 with a subnet mask of 255.255.255.192 is perfect for Subnet B because it supports up to 62 hosts. The network address 192.168.11.0 with a subnet mask of 255.255.255.128 is perfect for Subnet C because it supports up to 126 hosts.

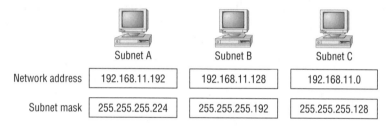

	Subnet A	Subnet B	Subnet C
Network address	192.168.11.192	192.168.11.128	192.168.11.0
Subnet mask	255.255.255.224	255.255.255.192	255.255.255.128

7. B, D. The best way to solve this problem within the parameters of the question is to point the server to the appropriate address to reach the rest of the internetwork, 10.89.155.65. For this to work, however, the server must believe this address is on the same subnet as itself. With the server's current /26 mask, hosts with a fourth-octet value from 1 to 62 are in a different subnet from those with a fourth-octet value from 65 to 126. If the server keeps such a mask, it will always think its default gateway is on a different subnet, which would be poor design if true. In fact, the router is on the same layer-2 segment, so it should be in the same subnet as well. Changing the server's subnet mask to 255.255.255.0 (option E) certainly would convince the server that it was on the same subnet as its router, but it also would affect the server's connectivity to the other Ethernet segment on the other side of the router, causing the server to attempt to communicate directly with those hosts without going through the router. Changing the router's local subnet mask to match that of the server (option F) and placing the server in the fourth-octet range 65 to 126 (option A) would get the server communicating to the rest of the internetwork, but doing so would break the router's connectivity with the other two hosts on the local subnet. Therefore, the best subnet mask for the server in this case is 255.255.255.128, which places all hosts with fourth-octet values from 1 to 126 on the same subnet. Because the other devices on the same LAN as the server already communicate with and through the router, after analyzing the diagram, you'll see that it is likely that they already have /25 masks as well as point to a default gateway of 10.89.155.65. All hosts on the same subnet should have the same subnet mask. Although bringing the router into line with the server's settings (options C and F) would solve the connectivity issues between the server and router, the other two hosts on the local LAN would need reconfiguration to point to the new default gateway address of 10.89.155.1. Although it's possible to place both the server and the laptop within the fourth-octet range from 65 to 126 (options A and G), allowing them to remain in contact with one another as well as allowing the server access to the rest of the internetwork, doing so breaks the server's connectivity with the computer at address 10.89.155.16.

8. C. Because the hosts on the 172.16.45.0 subnet already have default gateways set for their local router, adding static routes to get to a remote network will not change their connectivity. Furthermore, you know that the default gateway configured on the two hosts on that subnet is already correct because each one can reach host 192.168.1.100 without being configured with any static routes. Because the router on the left is already configured to be able to reach the 172.16.45.0 subnet, the problem lies with the router on the right not being able to reach the 10.250.12.0 subnet. Establishing a static route for this purpose in the router on the right will establish full connectivity

9. D. The CIDR /20 tells you that twenty 1s are turned on in the subnet mask. Twenty 1s equal 11111111.11111111.11110000.00000000. This would then equal 255.255.240.0.

10. B, E. Besides not being on the same subnet as the others, when a /28 mask is applied to all five addresses, 192.168.1.0 falls on a subnet boundary and cannot be used for host address assignment. Of the others, only 192.168.1.7 and 192.168.1.25 are valid host addresses on the same subnet when a /28 mask is applied. Although 192.168.1.16 and 192.169.1.31 are both on the same subnet as the two correct answers, they represent the subnet boundary address and the subnet broadcast address, respectively, and are therefore illegal for use in host address assignment.

11. C, D, E. Remember, you can always use the 0 subnet, making option C a valid response. Because $32 - 29 = 3$ and $2^3 = 8$, the subnet boundaries in the fourth octet (32 is the next multiple of 8 higher than 29, and $32 \div 8 = 4$) will be multiples of 8, making options D and E valid as well.

12. A, D. B is incorrect because IPv6 does not change layer 4 (TCP/UDP) functionality. C is incorrect because IPv6 does away with the broadcast functionality altogether. E is incorrect because IPv6 does away with the checksum header in the packet (layer 3) header. F is also incorrect; the functionality described is the anycast type.

13. B, C. iA is incorrect because IPv6 does not assign layer 4 (Transport layer) ports for applications. D is incorrect, because UDP loopback does not exist. E is incorrect because stateless autoconfiguration is for local network parameters, not global like an ISP would be concerned with.

14. C, D. The Next-Header option is the field that defines what extension header (if any) is added to the packet header. The destination options header is used to pass information to a special destination, and an example would be for IP mobility. There is no such thing as an IPsec ID header (at least at this time).

15. A. Remember the rules: use :: only once to replace a word or complete words (four 0s between colons); answers D and E violate this one. Use :0: as a compressed format for one complete word of 0s. You can leave out preceding 0s, but not trailing 0s; B and C violate this rule.

16. C, E. An IPv6 address consists of 128 bits, which are represented using 16-bit words. Dividing 128 bits by 16 bits per word yields 8 words.

17. D, E. The choice :: is all zeros (128 of them) and will not be assigned to a host. ::1 is the reserved loopback address and will not be assigned to a host. Any IPv6 address starting with FF00 is a multicast address and will not be uniquely assigned to a host. The choice 2001:4989:G1B5 is not valid because the character G does not stand for a value in hexadecimal. Choices D and E are actually the same address, one using the ever-popular dotted decimal integrated address, and the other is the hexadecimal representation of the same address.

18. A, C, D. There is no such IP address type as simulcast or staticast. Broadcast is an IPv4 address type. Unicast is the one-to-one address type. Anycast is the one-to-"one of many" address type. Multicast is the one-to-many address type.

19. C, D. Teredo is designed to give IPv4/IPv6 users access to the IPv6 Internet and network resources when the client machines are behind a NAT. There are some caveats and extra implementation steps, but the Teredo implementation in conjunction with a dual-stack node (which supports Teredo, like Windows Server 2008) are the required components.

20. B, D. If the first word of an IPv6 address is FE80 (actually the first 10 bits of the first word yields 1111 1110 10 or FE80:: /10), then the address is a link-local IPv6 address. If it's in EUI-64 format, then the MAC address is also available (unless is randomly generated). The middle FF:FE is the filler and indicator of the EUI-64 space with the MAC address being 00:03:FF:11:02:CD. Remember also the 00 of the MAC becomes 02 in the link-local IPv6 address, flipping a bit to call it *local*.

Chapter

3

Domain Name System (DNS)

MICROSOFT EXAM OBJECTIVES COVERED IN THIS CHAPTER:

✓ **Configure a Domain Name Server (DNS) server**

- May include but is not limited to: conditional forwarding, external forwarders, root hints, cache-only, server core, WINS and DNS integration, Windows Server virtualization

✓ **Configure DNS zones**

- May include but is not limited to: DNS Refresh no-refresh, intervals, DNS listserv address (NSLOOKUP), primary/secondary zones, Active Directory integration, Dynamic Domain Name System (DDNS), GlobalNames, SOA refresh

✓ **Configure DNS records**

- May include but is not limited to: record types, host, pointer, MX, SRV, NS, dynamic updates, Time to Live (TTL)

✓ **Configure DNS replication**

- May include but is not limited to: DNS secondary zones, DNS stub zones, DNS scavenging interval, replication scope

✓ **Configure name resolution for clients computers**

- May include but is not limited to: DNS and WINS integration, configuring HOSTS file, LMHOSTS, Link-Local Multicast Name Resolution (LLMNR), broadcasting, resolver cache, DNS Server list, Suffix Search order, manage client settings by using group policy

DNS is one of the most important topics that you will need to know if you are planning on taking any of the Microsoft administration exams (70-640, 70-642, and so on). Therefore, make sure you have a thorough understanding of DNS before taking any of the Microsoft 2008 exams.

DNS is a requirement of Active Directory, and many important system functions (including Kerberos authentication and finding domain controllers) are handled through DNS lookups. Windows 2000, Windows XP, and Windows Vista clients use DNS for name resolution and also to find Kerberos key distribution centers (KDCs), global catalog servers, and other services that may be registered in DNS.

By the time you finish this chapter, you will have a deeper understanding of how DNS works, plus an understanding of how to set up, configure, manage, and troubleshoot DNS in Microsoft Windows Server 2008.

Introducing DNS

The Domain Name System (DNS) is a service designed to resolve Internet Protocol (IP) addresses to host names. One of the inherent complexities of working in networked environments involves working with various protocols and network addresses. Thanks largely to the tremendous rise in popularity of the Internet, however, most environments have transitioned to using TCP/IP as their primary networking protocol. Microsoft is no exception when it comes to supporting TCP/IP in its workstation and server products. All current versions of Microsoft's operating systems support it, as do most other modern operating systems. Since the introduction of Windows NT 4, TCP/IP has been the default protocol installed.

TCP/IP is actually a collection of different technologies (protocols and services) that allow computers to function together on a single, large, heterogeneous network. Some of the major advantages of this protocol include widespread support for hardware, software, and network devices; reliance on a system of standards; and scalability.

Nowadays, most computer users are quite familiar with navigating to DNS-based resources, such as www.microsoft.com. To resolve these "friendly" names to TCP/IP addresses that the network stack can use, you must have some method for mapping them. Originally, ASCII flat files (often called HOSTS files, as shown in Figure 3.1) were used for this purpose.

In some cases, HOSTS files are still used today in very small networks, because they can help troubleshoot name resolution problems.

FIGURE 3.1   Sample HOSTS file

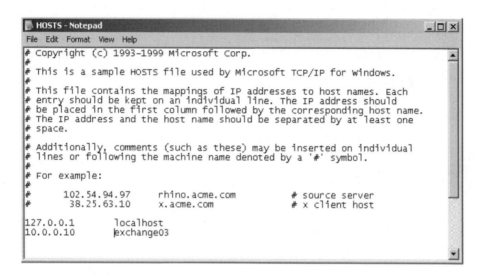

As the number of machines and network devices grew, it became unwieldy for administrators to manage all the manual updates required to enter new mappings to a master HOSTS file and distribute it. Also, years ago many Microsoft networks used WINS servers, which helped turn a NetBIOS (computer) name into a TCP/IP address. Just like with a HOSTS file, someone had to manually configure the ASCII flat-file version of WINS, called the LMHOSTS file. These files did help networks reduce broadcast traffic, but clearly, a better system was needed.

As you can see from the sample HOSTS file in Figure 3.1, you can conduct a quick test of the email server's name resolution:

1. Open the HOSTS file.

2. Add the IP-address-to-host-name mapping.

3. Try to ping the server using the host name to verify that you can reach it using an easy-to-remember name.

Following these steps should drive home the concept of DNS for you because you can see it working to make your life easier. Now you don't have to remember 10.0.0.10, for example; you need to remember exchange03 only.

You can probably also see how this method can become unwieldy if you have many hosts that want to use easy-to-remember names instead of IP addresses to locate resources on your network.

When dealing with large networks, both users and network administrators must be able to locate the resources they require with minimal searching. Users don't care about the actual physical or logical network address of the machine; they just want to be able to connect to it using a simple name that they can remember. From a network administrator's standpoint, however, each machine must have its own logical address that makes it part of the network on which it resides. Therefore, some scalable and easy-to-manage method for resolving a machine's logical name to an IP address was required. DNS was created for this purpose.

DNS is a hierarchically distributed database. In other words, its layers are arranged in a definite order, and its data is distributed across a wide range of machines, each of which can exert control over a portion of the database. DNS is a standard set of protocols defining the following:

- A mechanism for querying and updating address information in the database
- A mechanism for replicating the information in the database among servers
- A schema of the database

DNS is defined by a number of RFCs, though primarily by RFC 1034 and RFC 1035.

DNS was originally developed in the early days of the Internet when the Internet (called ARPAnet at the time) was a small network created by the Department of Defense for research purposes. Before DNS, computer names (or *host names*) were manually entered into a HOSTS file located on a centrally administered server. Each site that needed to resolve host names outside of its organization had to download this file. As the number of computers on the Internet grew, so did the size of this HOSTS file, as well as the problems managing the file. The need for a new system that would offer features such as scalability, decentralized administration, and support for various data types became more and more obvious. DNS, introduced in 1984, became this new system.

With DNS, the host names reside in a database that can be distributed among multiple servers, decreasing the load on any one server and providing the ability to administer this naming system on a per-partition basis. DNS supports hierarchical names and allows the registration of various data types in addition to the host-name-to-IP-address mapping used in HOSTS files. Database performance is ensured through its distributed nature as well as through caching.

The DNS distributed database establishes an inverted logical tree structure called the *domain namespace*. Each node, or domain, in that space has a unique name. At the top of the tree is the root. This may not sound quite right, which is why the DNS hierarchical model is described as being an inverted tree, with the root at the top. The root is represented by the null set " ". When written, the root node is represented by a single dot (.).

Each node in the DNS can branch out to any number of nodes below it. For example, below the root node are several other nodes, commonly referred to as *top-level domains* (TLDs). These are the familiar com, net, org, gov, edu, and other such names. Table 3.1 lists some of these TLDs.

Each of these nodes then branches out into another set of domains, and they combine to form what we refer to as *domain names*, such as microsoft.com. A domain name identifies the domain's position in the logical DNS hierarchy in relation to its parent domain by separating each branch of the tree with a period. Figure 3.2 shows a few of the top-level domains, where the Microsoft domain fits, and a host called Tigger within the `microsoft.com` domain. If someone wanted to contact that host, they would use the fully qualified domain name (FQDN) `tigger.microsoft.com`.

TABLE 3.1   Common Top-Level DNS Domains

Top-Level Domain Name	Type of Organization
com	Commercial (for example, `stellacon.com` for Stellacon Training Corporation).
edu	Educational (for example, `gatech.edu` for the Georgia Institute of Technology).
gov	Government (for example, `whitehouse.gov` for the White House in Washington, D.C.).
int	International organizations (for example, `nato.int` for NATO). This top-level domain is fairly rare.
mil	Military organizations (for example, `usmc.mil` for the Marine Corps). There is a separate set of root name servers for this domain.
net	Networking organizations and Internet providers (for example, `hiwaay.net` for HiWAAY Information Systems). Many commercial organizations have registered names under this domain, too.
org	Noncommercial organizations (for example, `fidonet.org` for FidoNet).
au	Country of Australia.
uk	United Kingdom.
ca	Canada.
us	United States.
jp	Japan.

An FQDN includes the trailing dot (.) to indicate the root node, but it's commonly left off in practice.

FIGURE 3.2   The DNS hierarchy

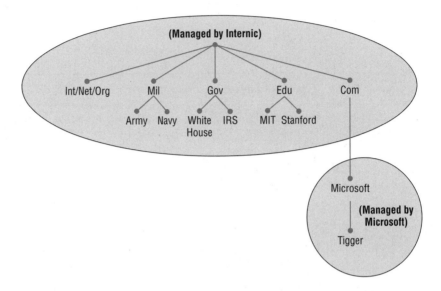

As previously stated, one of the strengths of DNS is the ability to delegate control over portions of the DNS namespace to multiple organizations. For example, the Internet Corporation for Assigned Names and Numbers (ICANN) assigns the control over the TLDs to one or more organizations. Those organizations in turn delegate portions of the DNS namespace to other organizations. For example, when you register a domain name—let's call it example.com—you control the DNS for the portion of the DNS namespace within example.com. The registrar controlling the .com TLD has delegated control over the example.com node in the DNS tree. No other node can be named example directly below the .com within the DNS database.

Within the portion of the domain namespace that you control (example.com), you could create host records and other records (more on these later). You could also further subdivide example.com and delegate control over those to other organizations or departments. These divisions are called *subdomains*. For example, you might create subdomains named for the cities in which your company has branch offices and then delegate control over those subdomains to the branch offices. The subdomains might be named losangeles.example.com, chicago.example.com, stevenspoint.example.com, and so on.

Each domain (or delegated subdomain) is associated with DNS name servers. In other words, for every node in the DNS, one or more servers can give an authoritative answer to queries about that domain. At the root of the domain namespace are the root servers. We'll cover root servers later in this chapter.

Domain names and host names must contain only the characters from *a* to *z* and from *A* to *Z*, the numbers from 0 to 9, and hyphens (-). Other common and useful characters such as the ampersand (&), slash (/), period (.), and underscore (_) are not allowed. This is in conflict with NetBIOS's naming restrictions, but you'll find that Windows Server 2008 is smart enough to take a NetBIOS name, like Server_1, and turn it into a legal DNS name, like `server1.example.com`.

DNS servers work together to resolve hierarchical names. If a server already has information about a name, it simply fulfills the query for the client. Otherwise, it queries other DNS servers for the appropriate information. The system works well because it distributes the authority of separate parts of the DNS structure to specific servers. A *DNS zone* is a portion of the DNS namespace over which a specific DNS server has authority (we discuss DNS zone types in detail later in this chapter).

There is an important distinction to make between DNS zones and Active Directory (AD) domains. Although both use hierarchical names and require name resolution, DNS zones do not map directly to AD domains.

Within a given DNS zone, *resource records* (RRs) contain the hosts and other database information that make up the data for the zone. For example, an RR might contain the host entry for `www.example.com`, pointing it to the IP address `192.168.1.10`.

Understanding Servers, Clients, and Resolvers

You will need to know a few terms and concepts in order to manage a DNS server. Understanding these terms will make it easier to understand how the Windows Server 2008 DNS server works.

DNS server   Any computer providing domain name services is a DNS name server. No matter where in the DNS namespace the server resides, it's still a DNS name server. For example, 13 root servers at the top of the DNS tree are responsible for delegating the TLDs. The root servers provide referrals to name servers for the TLDs, which in turn provide referrals to an authoritative name server for a given domain.

Berkeley Internet Name Domain (BIND) software was originally the only software that used to run the root servers on the Internet. However, a few years ago the organizations responsible for the root servers undertook an effort to diversify the software running on these important servers. Today, the root servers run multiple kinds of name server software. BIND is still primary, however, and it is the most popular for Internet providers as well. None of the root servers run Windows DNS.

Any DNS server implementation supporting service location resource records (see RCF 2782) and dynamic updates (RFC 2136) is sufficient to provide the name service for any operating system running Windows 2000 software and newer.

DNS client   A DNS client is any machine that issues queries to a DNS server. The client host name may or may not be registered in a DNS database. Clients issue DNS requests through processes called *resolvers*. You'll sometimes see the terms *client* and *resolver* used synonymously.

DNS Server list   When setting up a DNS client, you have the ability to set up the DNS Server list. This is the list of DNS servers that the client can contact to resolve names.

DNS suffix search order   Also on a client, you can set up the DNS suffix search order. The suffix name is the name of the DNS zone. For example, if you set up a DNS server for `stellacon.com`, that would be the client's suffix name. If anyone pings Server1, the suffix name `stellacon.com` gets appended, resulting in `Server1.stellacon.com`. You have the ability to set multiple suffix names on the client if you organization has multiple DNS names. Many of the DNS client settings (including suffix search order) can be configured through the use of a Group Policy Object (GPO).

GPOs are discussed in detail in *MCTS: Windows Server 2008 Active Directory Configuration Study Guide* by William Panek and James Chellis (Sybex, 2008).

Resolver   Resolvers are software processes, sometimes implemented in software libraries, that handle the actual process of finding the answers to queries for DNS data. The resolver is also built into many larger pieces of software so that external libraries don't have to be called in order to make and process DNS queries. Resolvers can be what you'd consider client computers or other DNS servers attempting to resolve an answer on behalf of a client.

Query   A query is a request for information sent to a DNS server. Three types of queries can be made to a DNS server: recursive, inverse, and iterative. We'll discuss their differences later in this chapter.

Understanding the DNS Process

To help you understand the DNS process, we will start by covering the differences between dynamic DNS and nondynamic DNS. During this discussion, you will learn how dynamic DNS populates the DNS database. You'll also see how to implement security for dynamic DNS. We will then talk about the workings of different types of DNS queries. Finally, we will discuss caching and time to live. You'll learn how to determine the best setting for your organization.

DDNS and NDDNS

To understand dynamic DNS and nondynamic DNS, you must go back in time (this is where the TV shows always get wavy in a flash back). Many years ago, when we all worked on NT 3.51 and NT 4.0, most networks used Windows Internet Name Service (WINS) to do their

TCP/IP name resolution. Windows versions 95/98 and NT 4.0 Professional all were built on the idea of using WINS. This worked out well for administrators because WINS was *dynamic* (which meant that, once it was installed, it automatically built its own database). Back then, there was no such thing as dynamic DNS. Administrators had to manually enter DNS records into the server. This is important to know even today, because if you have clients still running any of these older operating systems (95/98 or NT 4), these clients cannot use dynamic DNS.

Now let's move forward in time to the release of Windows Server 2000. With that version, Microsoft announced that DNS was going to be the name resolution of choice. Many administrators (including the authors of this book) did not look forward to the switch. Because there was no such thing as dynamic DNS, most administrators had nightmares about manually entering records. But luckily for us, when Microsoft released Windows Server 2000, DNS had the ability to be dynamic.

Now, when you're setting up Windows Server 2008 DNS, you can choose what type of dynamic update you want to use, if any. Let's talk about why you would want to choose one over the other.

The Dynamic DNS (DDNS) standard, described in RFC 2136, allows DNS clients to update information in the DNS database files. For example, a Windows Server 2008 Dynamic Host Configuration Protocol (DHCP) server can automatically tell a DDNS server which IP addresses it has assigned to which machines. Windows 2000, 2003, 2008, XP Professional, and Vista DHCP clients can do this, too—but for security reasons it's better to let the DHCP server do it. The result is that IP addresses and DNS records stay in sync so that you can use DNS and DHCP together seamlessly.

Because DDNS is a proposed Internet standard, you can even use Windows Server 2008's DDNS-aware parts with Unix/Linux-based DNS servers.

Nondynamic DNS (NDDNS) does not automatically populate the DNS database. The client systems do not have the ability to update to DNS.

If you decide to use NDDNS, an administrator will need to populate the DNS database manually. NDDNS is a reasonable choice if your organization is small to midsize and you do not want extra network traffic (clients updating to the DNS server) or if you need to manually enter the computer because of strict security measures.

 DDNS has the ability to be secure, and the chances are slim that a rogue system (a computer that does not belong in your DNS database) could update to a secure DNS server. Nevertheless, some organizations have to follow stricter security measures and are not allowed to have dynamic updates.

The major downside to manually entering records into DNS is if the organization is using DHCP. When using DHCP, there is a possibility that users could end up with different TCP/IP addresses every day. This means that an administrator has to manually update the DNS daily to keep it accurate.

When deciding to allow dynamic DNS, you then need to decide how you want to set up DDNS. When setting up dynamic updates on your DNS server, you have three choices: None, Nonsecure And Secure, and Secure Only (see Figure 3.3).

FIGURE 3.3   Setting the Dynamic Updates option

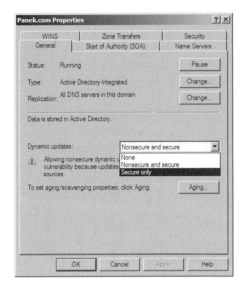

- None means your DNS server is nondynamic.

- Nonsecure And Secure means that any machine (even if it does not have a domain account) can register with DNS. Using this setting could allow rogue systems to enter records into your DNS server.

- Secure Only means that only machines with accounts in Active Directory can register with DNS. Before DNS registers any account in its database, it checks Active Directory to make sure that account is an authorized domain computer.

How Dynamic DNS Populates the DNS Database

On a Microsoft Windows Server 2008 network, TCP/IP is the protocol used for network communications. Users have two ways to receive a TCP/IP number:

- Static (administrators manually enter the TCP/IP information)

- Dynamic (using DHCP)

When an administrator sets up TCP/IP, the administrator can configure DNS.

Once a client gets the address of the DNS server, if that client is allowed to update with DNS, the client sends a registration to DNS or requests DHCP to send the registration. DNS then does one of two things, depending on which Dynamic Updates option is specified:

- Check with Active Directory to see whether that computer has an account (Secure Only updates), and if it does, enter the record into the database.

- Enter the record into its database (Nonsecure And Secure updates).

What if you have clients (95/98 and NT 4.0) that cannot update DNS? Well, there is a solution—DHCP. On the DNS tab in the IPv4 Properties dialog box, check the option labeled "Dynamically update DNS A and PTR records for DHCP clients that do not request updates)," as shown in Figure 3.4.

DHCP, along with dynamic DNS clients, allows an organization to dynamically update its DNS database without the time and effort of having an administrator manually enter DNS records.

FIGURE 3.4   DHCP settings for DNS

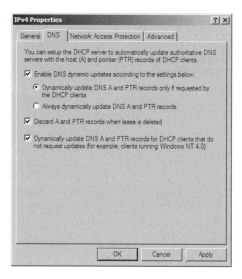

DNS Queries

As stated earlier, a client can make three types of queries to a DNS server: recursive, inverse, and iterative. Remember that the client of a DNS server can be a resolver (what you'd normally call a *client*) or another DNS server.

Iterative Queries

Iterative queries are the easiest to understand. A client asks the DNS server for an answer, and the server returns the best answer. This information likely comes from the server's cache. The server never sends out an additional query in response to an iterative query. If the server doesn't know the answer, it may direct the client to another server through a referral.

Recursive Queries

In a *recursive* query, the client sends a query to a name server, asking it to respond either with the requested answer or with an error message. The error states one of two things:

- The server can't come up with the right answer.
- The domain name doesn't exist.

In a recursive query, the name server isn't allowed to just refer the client to some other name server.

Most resolvers use recursive queries. In addition, if your DNS server uses a forwarder, the requests sent by your server to the forwarder will be recursive queries.

Figure 3.5 shows an example of both recursive and iterative queries. In this example, a client within the Microsoft Corporation is querying its DNS server for the IP address for www.whitehouse.gov.

FIGURE 3.5   A sample DNS query

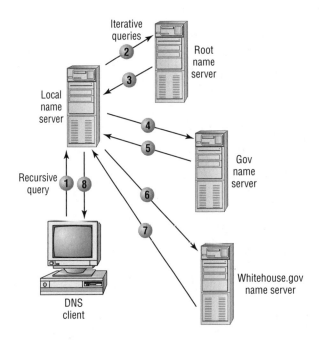

Here's what happens to resolve the request:

1. The resolver sends a recursive DNS query to its local DNS server asking for the IP address of www.whitehouse.gov.

    The local name server is responsible for resolving the name and cannot refer the resolver to another name server.

2. The local name server checks its zones and finds no zones corresponding to the requested domain name.

3. The root name server has authority for the root domain and will reply with the IP address of a name server for the .gov top-level domain.

4. The local name server sends an iterative query for www.whitehouse.gov to the Gov name server.

5. The Gov name server replies with the IP address of the name server servicing the whitehouse.gov domain.

6. The local name server sends an iterative query for www.whitehouse.gov to the whitehouse.gov name server.

7. The whitehouse.gov name server replies with the IP address corresponding to www.whitehouse.gov.

8. The local name server sends the IP address of www.whitehouse.gov back to the original resolver.

Inverse Queries

Inverse queries use PTR records. Instead of supplying a name and then asking for an IP address, the client first provides the IP address and then asks for the name. Because there's no direct correlation in the DNS namespace between a domain name and its associated IP address, this search would be fruitless without the use of the in-addr.arpa domain. Nodes in the in-addr.arpa domain are named after the numbers in the dotted-octet representation of IP addresses. But because IP addresses get more specific from left to right and domain names get less specific from left to right, the order of IP address octets must be reversed when building the in-addr.arpa tree. With this arrangement, administration of the lower limbs of the DNS in-addr.arpa tree can be given to companies as they are assigned their Class A, B, or C subnet addresses or delegated even further down thanks to variable-length subnet masking.

Once the domain tree is built into the DNS database, a special PTR record is added to associate the IP addresses to the corresponding host names. In other words, to find a host name for the IP address 206.131.234.1, the resolver would query the DNS server for a PTR record for 1.234.131.206.in-addr.arpa. If this IP address is outside the local domain, the DNS server would start at the root and sequentially resolve the domain nodes until arriving at 234.131.206.in-addr.arpa, which would contain the PTR record for the desired host.

Caching and Time to Live

When a name server is processing a recursive query, it may be required to send out several queries to find the definitive answer. Name servers, acting as resolvers, are allowed to cache all the received information during this process; each record contains information called *time to live* (TTL). The TTL specifies how long the record will be held in the local cache until it must be resolved again. If a query comes in that can be satisfied by this cached data, the TTL that's returned with it equals the current amount of time left before the data is flushed.

A *negative cache TTL* is used when an authoritative server responds to a query indicating that the record queried doesn't exist and indicates the amount of time that this negative answer may be held. Negative caching is quite helpful in preventing repeated queries for names that don't exist.

The administrator for the DNS zone sets TTL values for the entire zone. The value can be the same across the zone, or the administrator can set a separate TTL for each RR within the zone. Client resolvers also have data caches and honor the TTL value so that they know when to flush.

Real World Scenario

Choosing Appropriate TTL Values

For zones that you administer, you can choose the TTL values for the entire zone, for negative caching, and for individual records. Choosing an appropriate TTL depends on a number of factors, including the following:

- The amount of change you anticipate for the records within the zone

- The amount of time that you can withstand an outage that might require changing an IP address

- The amount of traffic you think the DNS server can handle

Resolvers query the name server every time the TTL expires for a given record. A low TTL, say, 60 seconds, can burden the name server, especially for popular DNS records. (DNS queries aren't particularly intensive for a server to handle, but they can add up quickly if you mistakenly use 60 seconds instead of 600 seconds for the TTL on a popular record.) Set a low TTL only when you need to quickly respond to a changing environment.

A high TTL, say, 604,800 seconds (that's one week), means that if you need to make a change to the DNS record, clients might not see the change for up to a week. This consideration is especially important when making changes to the network, and it's one that's all too frequently overlooked. We can't count the times we've worked with clients who have recently made a DNS change to a new IP for their email or website only to ask why it's not working for some clients. The answer can be found in the TTL value. If the record is being cached, then the only thing that can solve their problem is time.

You should choose a TTL that's appropriate for your environment. Take the following factors into account:

- The amount of time you can afford to be offline if you need to make a change to a DNS record that's being cached

- The amount of load that a low TTL will cause on the DNS server

In addition, you should plan well ahead of any major infrastructure changes and change the TTL to a lower value in order to lessen the effect of the downtime by reducing the amount of time that the record(s) can be cached.

DNS Aging and Scavenging

When using dynamic updates, computers (or DHCP) will register a resource record with DNS. These records get removed when a computer is shut down properly. A major problem in the industry is that laptops are frequently removed from the network without a proper shutdown. Therefore, their resource records continue to live in the DNS database.

Windows Server 2008 DNS supports two features called *DNS aging* and *DNS scavenging*. These features are used to clean up and remove stale resource records. DNS zone or DNS server aging and scavenging flags old resource records that have not been updated in a certain amount of time (determined by the scavenging interval). These stale records will be scavenged at the next cleanup interval. DNS uses time stamps on the resource records to determine how long they have been listed in the DNS database.

DNS Forwarding

In the "Query Types" section earlier in this chapter, we introduced the concept of forwarding. If a DNS server does not have an answer to a DNS request, it may be necessary to send that request to another DNS server. This is *DNS forwarding*. You need to understand the two main types of forwarding:

External forwarding   When a DNS server forwards an external DNS request to a DNS server outside your organization, this is considered external forwarding. For example, a resolver requests the host `www.microsoft.com`. Most likely, your internal DNS server is not going to have Microsoft's web address in its DNS database. So, your DNS server is going to send the request to an external DNS (most likely your ISP).

Conditional forwarding   Conditional forwarding is a lot like external forwarding except that you are going to forward requests to specific DNS servers based on a condition. Usually this is an excellent setup for internal DNS resolution. For example, let's say you have two companies, `stellacon.com` and `stellatest.com`. If a request comes in for Stellacon.com, it gets forwarded to the Stellacon DNS server, and any requests for Stellatest.com will get forwarded to the Stellatest DNS server. Requests are forwarded to a specific DNS server depending on the condition that an administrator sets up.

Introducing DNS Database Zones

As we mentioned earlier in this chapter, a DNS zone is a portion of the DNS namespace over which a specific DNS server has authority. Within a given DNS zone, certain resource records define the hosts and other types of records that make up the database for the zone.

You can choose from several zone types. Understanding the characteristics of each will help you choose which is right for your organization.

   The DNS zones discussed in this book are all Microsoft Windows Server 2008 zones. Non-Windows (such as Unix) systems set up their DNS zones differently.

In the following sections, we will discuss the different zone types and their characteristics.

Understanding Primary Zones

When you're learning about zone types, things can get a bit confusing. But it's really not difficult to understand how they work and why you would want to choose one type of zone over the other.

Basically, zones are databases that store records. By choosing one zone type over another, you are basically just choosing how the database works and how it will be stored on the server.

The *primary* zone is responsible for maintaining all the records for the DNS zone. It contains the primary copy of the DNS database. All record updates occur on the primary zone. You will want to create and add primary zones whenever you create a new DNS domain.

There are two types of primary zone:

- Primary zone
- Primary zone with Active Directory integration (Active Directory DNS)

 NOTE   From this point forward, we refer to a primary zone with Active Directory integration as an Active Directory DNS. When we just use the term *primary zone*, Active Directory is not included.

To install DNS as a primary zone, first you must install DNS using the Server Manager MMC (see Figure 3.6). Once DNS is installed and running, you create a new zone and specify it as a primary zone (see Figure 3.7).

FIGURE 3.6   Using the Server Manager MMC to install a DNS server

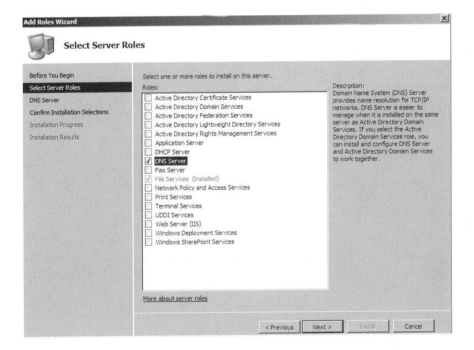

FIGURE 3.7   Choosing a zone type

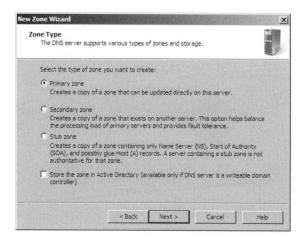

We'll discuss the process of installing DNS and its zones later in this chapter. Step-by-step exercises will also walk you through how to install these components later in this chapter.

Primary zones have advantages and disadvantages. Knowing the characteristics of a primary zone will help you decide when you need the zone and when it fits into your organization.

Local Database

Primary DNS zones get stored locally in a file (with the suffix .dns) on the server. This allows you to store a primary zone on a domain controller or a member server. In addition, by loading DNS onto a member server, you can help a small organization conserve resources. Such an organization may not have the resources to load DNS on an Active Directory domain controller.

Unfortunately, the local database has many disadvantages:

Lack of fault tolerance   Think of a primary zone as a contact list on your cell phone or handheld device. All the contacts in the list are the records in your database. The problem is that if you lose your phone or the phone breaks, you lose your contact list. Until your phone gets fixed or you swap out your phone card, the contacts are unavailable.

It works the same way with a primary zone. If the server goes down or you lose the hard drive, DNS records on that machine are unreachable during the outage. An administrator can install a secondary zone (explained later in this section), which provides temporary fault tolerance. Unfortunately, if the primary zone is down for an extended period of time, the secondary server's information will no longer be valid.

Additional network traffic   Let's imagine that you are looking for a contact number for John Smith. John Smith is not listed in your cell phone directory, but he is listed in your partner's cell phone. You have to contact your partner to get the listing. You cannot directly access your partner's cell contacts.

When a resolver sends a request to DNS to get the TCP/IP address for Jsmith (in this case Jsmith is a computer name) and the DNS server does not have an answer, it does not have the ability to check the other server's database directly to get an answer. So, it forwards the request to another DNS. This causes additional network traffic. When DNS servers are replicating zone databases with other DNS servers, this causes additional network traffic.

No security   Staying with the cell phone example, let's say you call your partner looking for John Smith's phone number. When your partner gives you the phone number over the phone, someone with a scanner picks up your conversation. (Unfortunately, wireless telephone calls are not very secure.)

Now a resolver asks a primary zone for the Jsmith TCP/IP address. If someone on the network has a packet sniffer, they can steal the information in the DNS packets on the network. The packets are not secure unless you implement some form of secondary security. Also, the DNS server has the ability to be dynamic. A primary zone accepts all updates from DNS servers. You cannot set it to accept secure updates only.

Understanding Secondary Zones

In Windows Server 2008 DNS, you have the ability to use secondary DNS zones. Secondary zones are noneditable copies of the DNS database. You use them for *load balancing* (also referred to as *load sharing*), which is a way of managing network overloads on a single server. A secondary zone gets its database from a primary zone.

A secondary zone contains a database with all the same information as the primary zone and can be used to resolve DNS requests. Secondary zones have the following advantages:

- A secondary zone provides fault tolerance, so if the primary zone server becomes unavailable, name resolution can still occur using the secondary zone server.

 It is a good general practice to ensure that each zone has at least one secondary zone server to protect against failures.

- Secondary DNS servers can also increase network performance by offloading some of the traffic that would otherwise go to the primary server.

  Secondary servers are often placed within the parts of an organization that have high-speed network access. This prevents DNS queries from having to run across slow wide area network (WAN) connections. For example, if there are two remote offices within the `stellacon.com` organization, you may want to place a secondary DNS server in each remote office. This way, when clients require name resolution, they will contact the nearest server for this IP address information, thus preventing unnecessary WAN traffic.

Having too many secondary zone servers can actually cause an increase in network traffic because of replication (especially if DNS changes are fairly frequent). Therefore, you should always weigh the benefits and drawbacks and properly plan for secondary zone servers.

Understanding Active Directory–Integrated DNS

In Windows Server 2000, Active Directory–integrated DNS was introduced to the world. This zone type was unique zone, and it was a separate choice during setup. In Windows Server 2003, this zone type became an add-on to a primary DNS zone. In Windows Server 2008 it works the same as in Windows Server 2003. After choosing to set up a primary zone, you check the box labeled "Store the zone in Active Directory" (see Figure 3.8).

FIGURE 3.8   Active Directory–integrated zone type

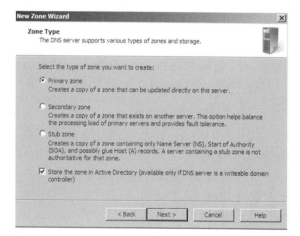

    Microsoft covers Active Directory–integrated DNS on most of the DNS-related exams. Knowing the characteristics of this zone type will help you answer many exam questions. Remember, this is an infrastructure exam (70-642), so you can bet that DNS zones will be covered in depth.

Disadvantages of Active Directory–Integrated DNS

The main disadvantage of Active Directory–integrated DNS is that it has to reside on a domain controller because the DNS database is stored in Active Directory. As a result, you cannot load this zone type on a member server, and small organizations might not have the resources to set up a dedicated domain controller.

Advantages of Active Directory–Integrated DNS

The advantages of using an Active Directory–integrated DNS zone well outweigh the disadvantage just discussed. The following are some of the major advantages to an Active Directory–integrated zone:

Full fault tolerance   Think of an Active Directory–integrated zone as a database on your server that stores contact information for all your clients. If you need to retrieve John Smith's phone number, as long as it was entered, you can look it up on the software.

If John Smith's phone number was stored only on your computer and your computer stopped working, no one could access John Smith's phone number. But since John Smith's phone number is stored in a database that everyone has access to, if your computer stops working, other users can still retrieve John Smith's phone number.

An Active Directory–integrated zone works the same way. Since the DNS database is stored in Active Directory, all Active Directory DNS servers can have access to the same data. If one server goes down or you lose a hard drive, all other Active Directory DNS servers can still retrieve DNS records.

No additional network traffic   As previously discussed, an Active Directory–integrated zone is stored in Active Directory. Since all records are now stored in Active Directory, when a resolver needs a TCP/IP address for Jsmith, any Active Directory DNS server can access Jsmith's address and respond to the resolver.

When you choose an Active Directory–integrated zone, DNS zone data can be replicated automatically to other DNS servers during the normal Active Directory replication process.

DNS security   An Active Directory–integrated zone has a few security advantages over a primary zone:

- An Active Directory–integrated zone can use secure dynamic updates.
- As explained earlier, the dynamic DNS standard allows secure-only updates or dynamic updates, not both.
- If you choose secure updates, then only machines with accounts in Active Directory can register with DNS. Before DNS registers any account in its database, it checks Active Directory to make sure it is an authorized domain computer.
- An Active Directory–integrated zone stores and replicates its database through Active Directory replication. Because of this, the data gets encrypted as it is sent from one DNS server to another.

Background zone loading   Background zone loading (discussed in more detail later in this chapter) allows a DNS Active Directory–integrated zone to load in the background. As a result, a DNS server can service client requests while the zone is still loading into memory.

Understanding Stub Zones

Stub zones work a lot like secondary zones—the database is a noneditable copy of a primary zone. The difference is that that the stub zone's database contains only the information necessary (three record types) to identify the authoritative DNS servers for a zone (see Figure 3.9). You should not use stub zones to replace secondary zones, and you should not use them for redundancy and load balancing.

FIGURE 3.9   DNS stub zone type

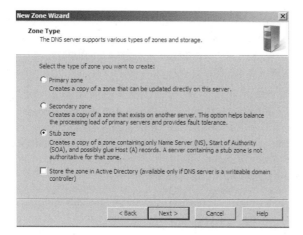

 Stub zones databases contain only three record types: the name server (NS), the start of authority (SOA), and glue host (A) records. Knowing about these records will help on the Microsoft certification exams. Microsoft asks many questions about stub zones on all DNS-related exams.

Understanding Zone Transfers and Replication

DNS is such an important part of the network that you should not use just a single DNS server. With a single DNS server, you also now have a single point of failure, and in fact many domain registrars encourage the use of more than two name servers for a domain. Secondary servers or multiple primary Active Directory–integrated servers play an integral role in providing DNS information for an entire domain.

As previously stated, secondary DNS servers receive their zone databases through zone transfers. When you configure a secondary server for the first time, you must specify the primary server that is authoritative for the zone and that will send the zone transfer. The primary server must also permit the secondary server to request the zone transfer.

Zone transfers occur in one of two ways: full zone transfers (AXFR) and incremental zone transfers (IXFR).

When a new secondary server is configured for the first time, it receives a full zone transfer from the primary DNS server. The full zone transfer contains all the information in the DNS database. Some DNS implementations always receive full zone transfers.

Real World Scenario

When to Use Stub Zones

Stub zones become particularly useful in a couple of scenarios.

Consider what happens when two large companies, example.com and example.net, merge. In most cases, the DNS zone information from both companies must be available to every employee. You could set up a new zone on each side that acts as a secondary for the other side's primary zone, but administrators tend to be very protective of their DNS databases, so they probably wouldn't agree to this plan.

A better solution is to add a stub zone to each side that points to the primary server on the other side. When a client in example.com (which you help administer) makes a request for a name in example.net, the stub zone on the example.com DNS server would send the client to the primary DNS server for example.net without actually resolving the name. At this point, it would be up to example.net's primary server to resolve the name.

An added benefit is that even if the administrators over at example.net change their configuration, you don't have to do anything because the changes will automatically replicate to the stub zone just as they would for a secondary server.

Stub zones can also be useful when you administer two domains across a slow connection.

Let's change this example a bit and assume you have full control over example.com and example.net, but they connect through a 56Kbps line. In this case, you wouldn't necessarily mind using secondary zones because you personally administer the entire network, but it could get messy to replicate an entire zone file across that slow line. Instead, stub zones would refer clients to the appropriate primary server at the other site.

After the secondary server receives its first full zone transfer, subsequent zone transfers are incremental. The primary name server compares its zone version number with that on the secondary server and sends only the changes that have been made in the interim. This significantly reduces network traffic generated by zone transfers.

 Windows NT 4 does not support incremental zone transfers.

Zone transfers are typically initiated by the secondary server when the refresh interval time for the zone expires or when the secondary or stub server boots. Alternatively, you can configure notify lists on the primary server that notify the secondary or stub servers whenever any changes to the zone database occur.

When you consider your DNS strategy, you must carefully consider the layout of your network. If you have a single domain with offices in separate cities, you want to reduce the number of zone transfers across the potentially slow or expensive WAN links, although this is becoming less of a concern as bandwidth seems to multiply daily.

Active Directory–integrated zones do away with traditional zone transfers altogether. Instead, they replicate across Active Directory with all the other AD information. This replication is secure since it uses the Active Directory security.

Understanding How DNS Notify Works

Windows Server 2008 supports DNS Notify, which is a mechanism that allows the process of initiating notifications to secondary servers when zone changes occur (RFC 1996). DNS Notify uses a push mechanism for communicating to a select set of secondary zone servers when their zone information is updated.

After being notified of the changes, secondary servers can then start a pull zone transfer and update their local copies of the database.

> Many different mechanisms use the push/pull relationship. Normally one object pushes information to another object, and that other object pulls the information from the first object.

To configure the DNS Notify process, you create a list of secondary servers to notify. List the IP address of the server in the primary master's Notify dialog box (see Figure 3.10). You can open the Notify dialog box by clicking the Notify button on the Zone Transfers tab in the Zone Properties dialog box (see Figure 3.11).

FIGURE 3.10   DNS Notify dialog box

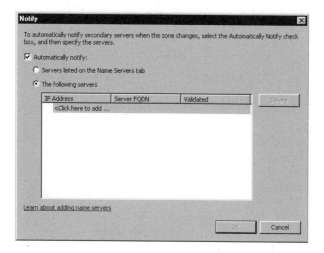

FIGURE 3.11   DNS Zone Transfer tab

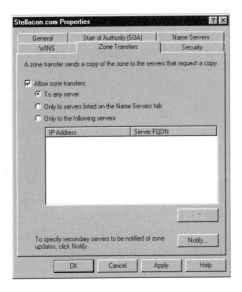

Configuring Stub Zone Transfers with Zone Replication Scope

In the preceding section, we talked about how to configure secondary server zone transfers. What if you wanted to configure settings for stub zone transfers? This is where zone replication scope comes into play.

Only Active Directory–integrated primary and stub zones can configure their replication scope. Secondary servers do not have this ability.

You can configure zone replication scope configurations in two ways. An administrator can set configuration options through the DNS snap-in or through a command-line tool called dnscmd.

To configure zone replication scope through the DNS snap-in, follow these steps:

1. Click Start ➢ Administrative Tools ➢ DNS.

2. Right-click the zone you want to set up.

3. Choose Properties.

4. In the zone's Properties dialog box, click the Change button next to Replication (see Figure 3.12).

5. Choose the replication scope that fits your organization.

FIGURE 3.12   DNS zone replication scope

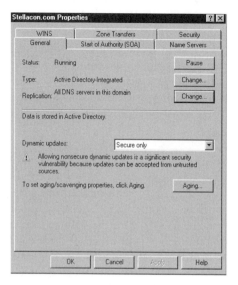

New Functionality in Windows Server 2008 DNS

Microsoft Windows Server 2008 has improved its version of DNS in many ways. The following sections will cover this new functionality. Here are some of the new DNS features we will discuss:

- Background zone loading
- Support for TCP/IP version 6 (IPv6)
- Read-only domain controllers
- GlobalName zone
- Windows Server virtualization
- Server Core installation

Background Zone Loading

In the past, if an organization had to restart a DNS server with an extremely large AD-integrated DNS zone database, a problem commonly occurred. Specifically, after the DNS restart, it could take hours for DNS data to be retrieved from Active Directory. During this time, the DNS server was unable to service any client requests.

Microsoft Windows Server 2008 DNS has addressed this problem by implementing *background zone loading*. As the DNS restarts, the Active Directory zone data now populates the database in the background. This allows the DNS server to service client requests for data from other zones almost immediately after a restart.

Background zone loading accomplishes this task by loading the DNS zone using separate threads. This allows a DNS server to service requests while still loading the rest of the zone. If a client sends a request to the DNS server for a computer that has not loaded into memory yet, the DNS server retrieves the data from Active Directory and updates the record.

Support for IPv6 Addresses

Over the past few years, the Internet has starting running into a problem that was not foreseen when it was first created—it started running out of TCP/IP addresses. As you probably already know, when the Internet was created, it was used for government and academic purposes only. Then, seemingly overnight, the Internet grew to be the information superhighway. Now, asking someone for their email address is as common as asking for their phone number.

In the past, the common version of TCP/IP was version 4 (IPv4). The release of TCP/IP version 6 (IPv6) has solved the lack of IP addresses problem. IPv4 addresses were 32 bits long, but IPv6 addresses are now 128 bits long. The longer lengths allow for a much greater number of globally unique TCP/IP addresses.

Microsoft Windows Server 2008 DNS has built-in support to accommodate both IPv4 and IPv6 address records (DNS records are explained later in this chapter). DHCP can also issue IPv6 addresses, which lets administrators allow DHCP to register the client with DNS, or the IPv6 client can register their address with the DNS server.

Support for Read-Only Domain Controllers

Windows Server 2008 has introduced a new type of domain controller called the *read-only domain controller* (RODC). This is a full copy of the Active Directory database without the ability to configure Active Directory. The RODC gives an organization the ability to install a domain controller in an area or location (onsite or offsite) where security is a concern.

Microsoft Windows Server 2008 DNS has implemented a new type of zone to help support an RODC. A primary read-only zone allows a DNS server to receive a copy of the application partition (including ForestDNSZone and DomainDNSZones) that DNS uses. This allows DNS to support an RODC because DNS now has a full copy of all DNS zones stored in Active Directory.

A primary read-only zone is just what it says—a read-only zone. So, to make any changes to it, you have to change the primary zones located on the Active Directory–integrated DNS server.

GlobalName Zones

Earlier in this chapter we talked about organizations using WINS to resolve NetBIOS names (also referred to as *computer names*) to TCP/IP addresses. Many organizations even today still use WINS along with DNS for name resolution. Unfortunately, WINS is slowly becoming obsolete.

To help organizations move forward with an all-DNS network, Microsoft Windows Server 2008 DNS supports *GlobalName zones*. These use single-label names (DNS names that do not contain a suffix such as `.com`, `.net`, and so on) the same way WINS does. Unlike WINS, GlobalName zones are not intended to support peer-to-peer networks and workstation name resolution, and they don't support dynamic DNS updates.

GlobalName zones were designed to be used with servers. Since GlobalNames zones are not dynamic, an administrator has to manually enter the records into the zone database. In most organizations, the servers have static TCP/IP addresses, and this works well with the GlobalName zone design. GlobalName zones are usually used to map single-label CNAME (alias) resource records to an FQDN.

Windows Server 2008 Hyper-V

Windows Server 2008 has a role-based utility called *Hyper-V*, which is a hypervisor-based virtualization feature. (A *hypervisor* is a virtual machine monitor.) It includes all the necessary features to support machine virtualization. Using machine virtualization allows a company to reduce costs, improve server utilization, and create a more dynamic IT infrastructure.

Server Core Installation

With 2008, you can now install Windows Server on a server in a special minimum server installation called *Server Core*. Server Core allows an IT department to install Windows Server 2008 with a low-maintenance server environment that has limited functionality. One of the functions that Server Core can provide is DNS.

Because Server Core has limited functionality, it actually provides some strong benefits including reduced servicing and management requirements, reduced attack surface, and reduced disk space usage.

Besides DNS, Server Core functionality includes the following:

- Active Directory (AD)
- Active Directory Lightweight Directory Services (AD LDS)
- DHCP server
- File server
- Media services
- Print server

Introducing DNS Record Types

No matter where your zone information is stored, you can rest assured that it contains a variety of DNS information. Although the DNS snap-in makes it unlikely that you'll ever need to edit these files by hand, it's good to know exactly what data is contained there.

As stated previously, zone files consist of a number of resource records. You need to know about several types of resource records to effectively manage your DNS servers, which is why we'll discuss them in the following sections.

Part of a resource record is its *class*. Classes define the type of network for the resource record. There are three classes: Internet, Chaosnet, and Hesoid. By far, the Internet class is the most popular. In fact, it's doubtful that you'll see either Chaosnet or Hesoid classes in the wild.

Prior to jumping into resource records, several bits of information are contained in a given zone file that define the zone and set some default properties for the zone.

 The following are some of the more important records in a DNS database. For a complete listing of records in a Microsoft DNS database, visit Microsoft's website.

Start of Authority Records

The first record in a database file is the *start of authority* record. The SOA defines the general parameters for the DNS zone, including the identity of the authoritative server for the zone.

The SOA is the following format:

```
@ IN SOA primary_master contact_e-mail serial_number
refresh_time retry_time expiration_time time_to_live
```

Here is a sample SOA from the domain example.com:

```
@  IN SOA win2k3r2.example.com. hostmaster.example.com. (
                        5           ; serial number
                        900         ; refresh
                        600         ; retry
                        86400       ; expire
                        3600      ) ; default TTL
```

Table 3.2 lists the attributes stored in this SOA record.

TABLE 3.2   The SOA Record Structure

Field	Meaning
Current zone	This is the current zone for the SOA. This can be represented by an @ symbol to indicate the current zone or by naming the zone itself. In the example, the current zone is example.com. The trailing dot (.com.) indicates the zone's place relative to the root of the DNS.

TABLE 3.2   The SOA Record Structure *(continued)*

Field	Meaning
Class	This will always likely be the letters IN for the Internet class.
Type of record	This is the type of record follows; in this case it's SOA.
Primary master	This is the primary master for the zone on which this file is maintained.
Contact email	This is the Internet email address for the person responsible for this domain's database file. There is no @ symbol in this contact email address since @ is a special character in zone files. The contact email address is separated by a single dot (.). So, the email address of root@example.com would be represented by root.example.com in a zone file.
Serial number	This is the "version number" of this database file. This increases each time the database file is changed.
Refresh time	This is the amount of time (in seconds) that a secondary server will wait between checks to its master server to see whether the database file has changed and a zone transfer should be requested.
Retry time	This is the amount of time (in seconds) that a secondary server will wait before retrying a failed zone transfer.
Expiration time	This is the amount of time (in seconds) that a secondary server will spend trying to download a zone. After this time limit expires, the old zone information will be discarded.
Time to live	This is the amount of time (in seconds) that another DNS server is allowed to cache any resource records from this database file. This is the value that is sent out with all query responses from this zone file when the individual resource record doesn't contain an overriding value.

Name Server Records

Name server (NS) records list the name servers for a domain. This record allows other name servers to look up names in your domain. A zone file may contain more than one name server record. The format of these records is simple:

```
example.com.    IN    NS    hostname.example.com
```

Table 3.3 explains the attributes stored in this NS record.

TABLE 3.3   The NS Record Structure

Field	Meaning
Name	The domain that will be serviced by this name server. In this case, we used example.com.
AddressClass	Internet (IN).
RecordType	Name server (NS).
NameServerName	The FQDN name of the server responsible for the domain.

Any domain name in the database file that is not terminated with a period will have the root domain appended to the end. For example, an entry that has just the name sales will be expanded by adding the root domain to the end, whereas sales.example.com. won't be expanded.

Host Records

A *host record* (also called an *A record* for TCP/IP v4 and *AAAA record* for TCP/IP v6) is used to statically associate a host's name to its IP addresses. The format is pretty simple:

```
host_name optional_TTL IN  A  IP_Address
```

Here's an example from our DNS database:

```
www  IN  A  192.168.0.204
SMTP IN  A  192.168.3.144
```

The A or AAAA record ties a host name (which is part of an FQDN) to a specific IP address. This makes these records suitable for use when you have devices with statically assigned IP addresses; in this case, you create these records manually using the DNS snap-in. As it turns out, if you enable DDNS, your DHCP server can create these for you; that automatic creation is what enables DDNS to work.

Notice that an optional TTL is available for each resource record in the DNS. This value is used to set a TTL that is different from the default TTL for the domain. For example, if you wanted a 60-second TTL for the www A or AAAA record, it would look like this:

```
www 60 IN  A  192.168.0.204
```

Alias Records

Closely related to the host record is the *alias* or *canonical name* (CNAME) record. The syntax of an alias record looks like the following:

```
alias optional_TTL  IN  CNAME  hostname
```

Aliases are used to point more than one DNS record toward the host for which an A record already exists. For example, if the host name of your web server was actually chaos, you would likely have an A record like this:

```
chaos IN A 192.168.1.10
```

Then you could make an alias or CNAME for the record so that www.example.com would point to chaos:

```
www IN CNAME chaos.example.com.
```

Note the trailing dot (.) on the end of the CNAME record. This means the root domain is not appended to the entry.

Pointer Records

A or AAAA records are probably the most visible component of the DNS database because Internet users depend on them to turn FQDNs such as www.microsoft.com into IP addresses that browsers and other components require to find Internet resources. However, the host record has a lesser-known but still important twin: the *pointer* (PTR) record. The format of a pointer record looks like the following:

```
reversed_address.in-addr.arpa. optional_TTL IN PTR targeted_domain_name
```

The A or AAAA record maps a host name to an IP address, and the PTR record does just the opposite—mapping an IP address to a host name—through the use of the in-addr.arpa zone.

The PTR record is necessary because IP addresses begin with the least-specific portion first (the network) and end with the most-specific portion (the host), whereas host names begin with the most specific portion at the beginning and the least specific at the end.

Consider the example 192.168.1.10 with a subnet mask 255.255.255.0. The portion 192.168.1 defines the network, and the final .10 defines the host, or the most specific portion of the address. DNS is just the opposite. The host name www.example.com. defines the most-specific portion, www, at the beginning and then traverses the DNS tree to the least-specific part, the dot (.) at the root of the tree.

Reverse DNS records, therefore, need to be represented in this most specific to least specific manner. The PTR record for mapping 192.168.1.10 to www.example.com would look like this:

```
10.1.168.192.in-addr.arpa. IN PTR www.example.com.
```

Now a DNS query for that record can follow the logical DNS hierarchy from the root of the DNS tree all the way to the most-specific portion.

Mail Exchanger Records

The *mail exchanger* (MX) record is used to specify which servers accept mail for this domain. Each MX record contains two parameters—a preference and a mail server—as shown in the following example:

```
domain IN MX preference mailserver_host
```

The MX record uses the preference value to specify which server should be used if more than one MX record is present. The preference value is a number. The lower the number, the more preferred the server. Here's an example:

```
example.com    IN   MX   0   mail.example.com.
example.com    IN   MX   10  backupmail.example.com.
```

In the example, `mail.example.com` is the default mail server for the domain. If that server goes down for any reason, the `backupmail.example.com` mail server is used by mailers.

Service Records

Windows Server 2008 depends on some other services, such as the Lightweight Directory Access Protocol (LDAP) and Kerberos. Using a *service record*, which is another type of DNS record, a Windows 2000, XP, or Vista client can query DNS servers for the location of a domain controller. This makes it much easier (for both the client and the administrator) to manage and distribute logon traffic in large-scale networks. For this approach to work, Microsoft has to have some way to register the presence of a service in DNS. Enter the service (SRV) record.

SRV records tie together the location of a service (like a domain controller) with information about how to contact the service. SRV records provide seven items of information. Let's look at an example to help clarify this powerful concept (Table 3.4 explains the fields in the following example):

```
ldap.tcp.example.com   SRV   10   100   389   hsv.example.com
ldap.tcp.example.com   SRV   20   100   389   msy.example.com
```

TABLE 3.4   The SRV Record Structure

Field	Meaning
Domain name	Domain for which this record is valid: `ldap.tcp.example.com`.
TTL	Time to live (86,400 seconds).

TABLE 3.4   The SRV Record Structure *(continued)*

Field	Meaning
Class	This field is always IN, which stands for Internet.
Record type	Type of record (SRV).
Priority	Specifies a preference, similar to the preference field in an MX record. The SRV record with the lowest priority is used first (10).
Weight	Service records with equal priority are chosen according to their weight (100).
Port number	The port where the server is listening for this service (389).
Target	The FQDN of the host computer (hsv.example.com and msy.example.com).

You can define other types of service records. If your applications support them, they can query DNS to find the services they need.

Configuring DNS

In the following sections, we'll explain the actual DNS server. We will start with an exercise to install DNS. Then we will talk about different zone configuration options and what they mean. We will follow this with an exercise that covers configuring dynamic DNS, delegating zone, and manually entering records.

Installing DNS

Let's start by installing DNS (see Exercise 3.1).

EXERCISE 3.1

Installing and Configuring the DNS Service

1. Open the Configure Your Server Wizard by selecting Start ➢ Administrative Tools ➢ Server Manager.

2. Under Roles Summary, click the Add Role link.

3. Click the DNS Server item in the Server Role list, and click Next to continue.

4. Click Next on the Summary page to complete the DNS installation. You may need to insert the Windows Server 2008 CD into the CD/DVD drive.

5. If your computer is configured with a dynamic IP address, you are prompted to use a static address. At this point, the Local Area Connection Properties dialog box will appear. Once you have made the necessary changes, click OK.

6. The Configure A DNS Sever Wizard automatically appears. Click Next to dismiss the Welcome screen.

7. Select the Create Forward Lookup Zones radio button, and click Next to continue.

8. Select Yes, Create A Forward Lookup Zone Now, and click Next to continue.

9. Select the Primary Zone option. If your DNS server is also a domain controller, do not check the box to store the zone in Active Directory. Click Next when you are ready.

10. Enter a new zone name in the Zone Name field, and click Next to continue.

11. Leave the default zone filename, and click Next.

12. Select the Do Not Allow Dynamic Updates radio button, and click Next.

13. Select No, Don't Create a Reverse Lookup Zone Now, and click Next to continue.

14. Click Finish to end the wizard. The Configure Your Server Wizard reappears and informs you that the DNS service was successfully installed. Click Finish.

Load Balancing with Round Robin

Like other DNS implementations, the Windows Server 2008 implementation of DNS supports load balancing through the use of *round robin*. Load balancing distributes the network load among multiple network cards if they are available. You set up round-robin load balancing by creating multiple resource records with the same host name but different IP addresses for multiple computers. Depending on the options that you select, the DNS server responds with the addresses of one of the host computers.

If round robin is enabled, when a client requests name resolution, the first address entered in the database is returned to the resolver and is then sent to the end of the list. The next time a client attempts to resolve the name, the DNS server returns the second name in the database (which is now the first name) and then sends it to the end of the list, and so on. Round robin is enabled by default.

Configuring a Caching-Only Server

Although all DNS name servers cache queries that they have resolved, caching-only servers are DNS name servers that only perform queries, cache the answers, and return the results. They are not authoritative for any domains, and the information they contain is limited to what has been cached while resolving queries. Accordingly, they don't have any zone files, and they don't participate in zone transfers. When a caching-only server is first started, it has no information in its cache; the cache is gradually built over time.

Caching-only servers are very easy to configure. After installing the DNS service, simply make sure that the root hints are configured properly.

1. Right-click your DNS server, and choose the Properties command.

2. When the server's Properties dialog box appears, switch to the Root Hints tab (see Figure 3.13).

3. If your server is connected to the Internet, you should see a list of root hints for the root servers maintained by ICANN and the Internet Assigned Numbers Authority (IANA). If not, use the Add button to add root hints as defined in the `cache.dns` file.

    You can obtain current `cache.dns` files on the Internet by using a search engine. Just search for *cache.dns*, and download one (I always try to get `cache.dns` files from a university or a company that manages domain names).

FIGURE 3.13   The Root Hints tab of the DNS server's Properties dialog box

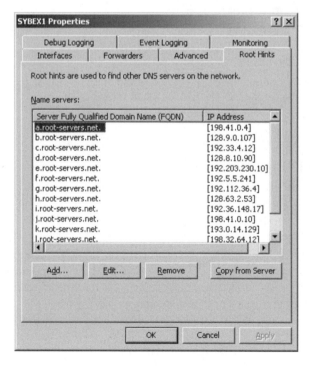

Setting Zone Properties

You'll see six tabs in the zone's Properties dialog box for a forward or reverse lookup zone (see Figure 3.14). You use the Security tab only to control who can change properties and make dynamic updates to records on that zone. We'll discuss the other tabs in the following sections.

FIGURE 3.14   The General tab of the zone's Properties dialog box

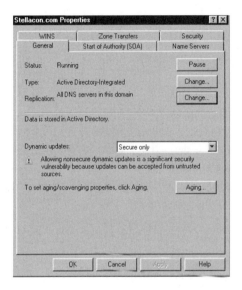

 Secondary zones don't have a Security tab, and their SOA tab shows you the contents of the master SOA record, which you can't change.

General Tab

The General tab (Figure 3.14) includes the following:

- The Status indicator and the associated Pause button let you see and control whether this zone can be used to answer queries. When the zone is running, the server can use it to answer client queries; when it's paused, the server won't answer any queries it gets for that particular zone.

- The Type indicator and its Change button allow you to select the zone type. The options are Standard primary, Standard secondary, and AD-integrated. (See the "Introducing DNS Database Zones" section earlier in this chapter.) As you change the type, the controls you see below the horizontal dividing line will change too. For primary zones, you'll see a field that lets you select the zone filename. For secondary zones, you'll get controls that allow you to specify the IP addresses of the primary servers. However, the most interesting controls are the ones you see for AD-integrated zones. When you change to the AD-integrated zone, you have the ability to make the dynamic zones secure only.

- The Replication indicator and its Change button allow you to change the replication scope if the zone is stored in Active Directory. You can choose to replicate the zone data to any of the following:

  - All DNS servers in the Active Directory forest

  - All DNS servers in a specified domain

  - All domain controllers in the Active Directory domain (required if you use Windows 2000 domain controllers in your domain)

  - All domain controllers specified in the replication scope of the application directory partition

- The Dynamic Updates field gives you a way to specify whether you want to support dynamic DNS updates from compatible DHCP servers. As you learned earlier in the section "DDNS and NDDNS" section, the DHCP server or DHCP client must know about and support DDNS in order to use it, but the DNS server has to participate too. You can turn dynamic updates on or off, or you can require that updates be secured.

Start Of Authority (SOA) Tab

The following options in the Start Of Authority (SOA) tab control the contents of the SOA record for this zone (Figure 3.15):

- The Serial Number field indicates which version of the SOA record the server currently holds; every time you change another field, you should increment the serial number so that other servers will notice the change and get a copy of the updated record.

- The Primary Server and Responsible Person fields indicate the location of the primary NS for this zone and the email address of the administrator responsible for maintaining this zone, respectively. The standard username for this is *hostmaster*.

- The Refresh Interval field controls how often any secondary zones of this zone must contact the primary and get any changes that have been posted since the last update.

- The Retry Interval field controls how long secondary servers will wait after a zone transfer fails before they try again. They'll keep trying at the interval you specify (which should be shorter than the refresh interval) until they eventually succeed in transferring zone data.

- The Expires After field tells the secondary servers when to throw away zone data. The default of 1 day (24 hours) means that a secondary server that hasn't gotten an update in 24 hours will delete its local copy of the zone data.

- The Minimum (Default) TTL field sets the default TTL for all RRs created in the zone; you can assign specific TTLs to individual records if you want.

- The TTL For This Record field controls the TTL for the SOA record itself.

FIGURE 3.15 The Start Of Authority (SOA) tab of the zone's Properties dialog box

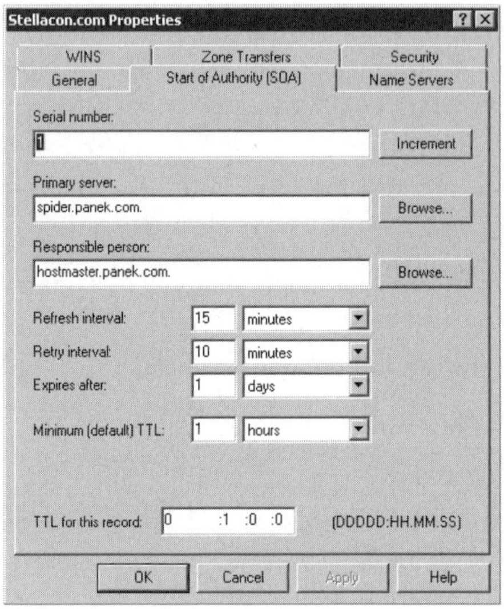

Name Servers Tab

The name server record for a zone indicates which name servers are authoritative for the zone, which usually means the zone primary and any secondary servers you've configured for the zone (remember, secondary servers are authoritative read-only copies of the zone). You edit the NS record for a zone using the Name Servers tab (see Figure 3.16). The tab shows you which servers are currently listed, and you use the Add, Edit, and Remove buttons to specify which name servers you want included in the zone's NS record.

WINS Tab

The WINS tab allows you to control whether this zone uses WINS forward lookups. These lookups pass on queries that DNS can't resolve to WINS for action. This is a useful setup if you're still using WINS on your network. You must explicitly turn this option on with the Use WINS Forward Lookup check box on the WINS tab for a particular zone.

Zone Transfers Tab

Zone transfers are necessary and useful because they're the mechanism used to propagate zone data between primary and secondary servers. For primary servers (whether AD-integrated or not), you can specify whether your servers will allow zone transfers (see Figure 3.17) and, if so, to whom.

FIGURE 3.16   The Name Servers tab of the zone's Properties dialog box

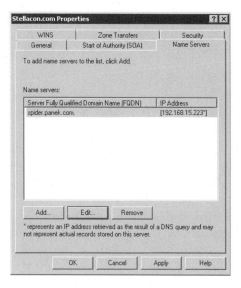

FIGURE 3.17   DNS Zone Transfers tab

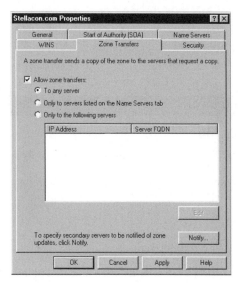

You can use the following controls on the Zone Transfers tab to configure these settings per zone:

- The Allow Zone Transfers check box controls whether the server will answer zone transfer requests for this zone at all. When it's not checked, no zone data will be transferred. The Allow Zone Transfers selections are as follows:

    - To Any Server allows any server anywhere on the Internet to request a copy of your zone data.

    - Only To Servers Listed On The Name Servers Tab (the default) limits transfers to servers you specify. This is a more secure setting than To Any Server because it limits zone transfers to other servers for the same zone.

    - Only To The Following Servers controls allow you to specify exactly which servers are allowed to request zone transfers. This list can be larger or smaller than the list specified on the Name Servers tab.

- The Notify button is for setting up automatic notification triggers that are sent to secondary servers for this zone. Those triggers signal the secondary servers that changes have occurred on the primary server so that the secondary servers can request updates sooner than their normally scheduled interval. The options in the Notify dialog box are similar to those on the Zone Transfers tab. You can enable automatic notification and then choose either Servers Listed On The Name Servers Tab or The Following Servers.

Configuring Zones for Dynamic Updates

In Exercise 3.2, you will modify the properties of a forward lookup zone, configuring the zone to use WINS to resolve names not found by querying the DNS namespace. In addition, you'll configure the zone to allow dynamic updates.

EXERCISE 3.2

Configuring Zones for Dynamic Updates

1. Open the DNS management snap-in by selecting Start ➤ Administrative Tools ➤ DNS.

2. Click the DNS server to expand it, and then expand the Forward Lookup Zones folder.

3. Right-click the zone you want to modify (which may be the one you created in the previous exercise), and choose Properties.

4. Switch to the WINS tab, and click the Use WINS Forward Lookup check box.

5. Enter the IP address of a valid WINS server on your network, click Add, and then click OK.

6. Click the General tab.

7. Change the value of the Allow Dynamic Updates control to Yes. Click OK to close the Properties dialog box. Notice that there's now a new WINS lookup RR in your zone.

Delegating Zones for DNS

DNS provides the ability to divide up the namespace into one or more zones, which can then be stored, distributed, and replicated to other DNS servers. When deciding whether to divide your DNS namespace to make additional zones, consider the following reasons to use additional zones:

- A need to delegate the management of part of your DNS namespace to another location or department within your organization

- A need to divide one large zone into smaller zones for distributing traffic loads among multiple servers for improving DNS name resolution performance or for creating a more fault-tolerant DNS environment

- A need to extend the namespace by adding numerous subdomains at once, such as to accommodate the opening of a new branch or site

Each new delegated zone requires a primary DNS server just like a regular DNS zone. When delegating zones within your namespace, be aware that for each new zone you create, you need to place delegation records in other zones that point to the authoritative DNS servers for the new zone. This is necessary both to transfer authority and to provide correct referral to other DNS servers and clients of the new servers being made authoritative for the new zone.

In Exercise 3.3, you'll create a delegated subdomain of the domain you created in Exercise 3.1. Note that the name of the server to which you want to delegate the subdomain must be stored in an A or CNAME record in the parent domain.

Creating a Delegated DNS Zone

1. Open the DNS management snap-in by selecting Start ➢ Administrative Tools ➢ DNS.

2. Expand the DNS server, and locate the zone you created in Exercise 3.1.

3. Right-click the zone, and choose the New Delegation command.

4. The New Delegation Wizard appears. Click Next to dismiss the initial wizard page.

5. Enter **ns1** (or whatever other name you like) in the Delegated Domain field of the Delegated Domain Name page. This is the name of the domain for which you want to delegate authority to another DNS server. It should be a subdomain of the primary domain (for example, to delegate authority for huntsville.example.net, you'd enter **huntsville** in the Delegated Domain field). Click Next to complete this step.

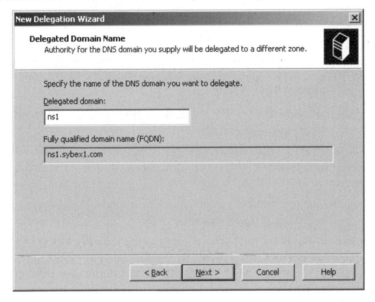

6. When the Name Servers page appears, use the Add button to add the name and IP address(es) of the servers that will be hosting the newly delegated zone. For the purpose of this exercise, enter the zone name you used in Exercise 3.1. Click the Resolve button to automatically resolve this domain name's IP address into the IP address field. Click OK when you are done. Click Next to continue with the wizard.

7. Click the Finish button. The New Delegation Wizard disappears, and you'll notice the new zone you just created appear beneath the zone you selected in step 3. The newly delegated zone's folder icon is drawn in gray to indicate that control of the zone is delegated.

Manually Creating DNS Records

From time to time you may find it necessary to manually add resource records to your Windows Server 2008 DNS servers. Although dynamic DNS frees you from the need to fiddle with A and PTR records for clients and other such entries, you still have to create other resource types (including MX records, required for the proper flow of SMTP email) manually. You can manually create A, PTR, MX, SRV, and many other record types.

There are only two important things to remember:

- You must right-click the zone and use either the New Record command or the Other New Records command.

- You must know how to fill in the fields of whatever record type you're using.

  For example, to create an MX record, you need three pieces of information (the domain, the mail server, and the priority), but to create an SRV record, you need several more.

In Exercise 3.4, you will manually create an MX record for the mailtest server in the domain you created in Exercise 3.1.

EXERCISE 3.4

Manually Creating DNS RRs and Host Records

1. Open the DNS management snap-in by selecting Start ➤ Administrative Tools ➤ DNS.

2. Expand your DNS server, right-click its zone, and select the New Mail Exchanger (MX) command.

3. Enter **mailtest** in the Host Or Child Domain field, enter **mailtest.*yourDomain.com*** (or whatever domain name you used in Exercise 3.1) in the Fully Qualified Domain Name (FQDN) Of Mail Server field, and then click OK. Notice that the new record is already visible.

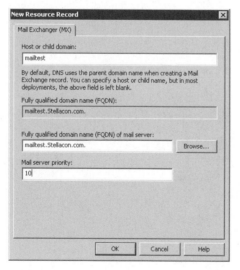

4. Next, create an alias (or CNAME) record to point to the mail server. (It is assumed that you already have an A record for mailtest in your zone.) Right-click the target zone, and choose Other New Records. When the Resource Record Type dialog box appears, find Alias in the list, and select it.

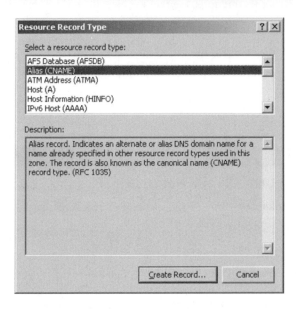

5. Click the Create Record button. The New Resource Record dialog box appears.

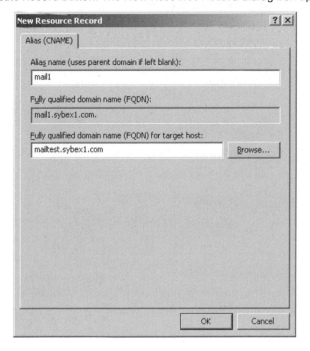

> **EXERCISE 3.4** *(continued)*
>
> 6. Type **mail** in the Alias Name field.
>
> 7. Type **mailtest.***yourDomain.com* in the Fully Qualified Domain Name (FQDN) For Target Host field.
>
> 8. Click the OK button, and then close the Resource Record Type dialog box.
>
> 9. With the DNS server still expanded (see step 1), right-click its zone, and select the New Host (A) record command.
>
> 10. Enter the name of the host computer and its corresponding IP address. Click OK.
>
> 11. Exit the DNS MMC.

Link-Local Multicast Name Resolution

Despite all that DNS can do for you, in some cases you might still decide not to use DNS in all locations of your network. DNS is a requirement of Active Directory, so if you want to install a domain controller, DNS will be present on the network. But what if you do not use a domain? What if you are installing remote offices and don't currently have the ability to use DNS? That's where Link-Local Multicast Name Resolution (LLMNR) can help.

LLMNR is a peer-to-peer name resolution protocol that broadcasts to neighboring hosts to help resolve host names. LLMNR can work with both IPv4 and IPv6. Because LLMNR uses broadcasts, routers will not pass LLMNR protocol traffic. LLMNR is a good solution for small temporary networks. You can disable Multicast Name Resolution by using a GPO.

Monitoring and Troubleshooting DNS

Now that you have set up and configured your DNS name server and created some resource records, you will want to confirm that it is resolving and replying to client DNS requests. A couple of tools allow you to do some basic monitoring and managing. Once you are able to monitor DNS, you'll want to start troubleshooting.

The simplest test is to use the `ping` command to make sure the server is alive. A more exhaustive test would be to use `nslookup` to verify that you can actually resolve addresses for items on your DNS server.

In the following sections, we'll cover some of these monitoring and management tools, as well as how to troubleshoot DNS.

Monitoring DNS with the DNS Snap-In

You can use the DNS snap-in to do some basic server testing and monitoring. More important, you use the snap-in to monitor and set logging options. On the Event Logging tab of the server's Properties dialog box (Figure 3.18), you can pick which events you want logged. The more events you select, the more log information you'll get. This is useful when you're trying to track what's happening with your servers, but it can result in a very, very large log file if you're not careful.

The Monitoring tab (Figure 3.19) gives you some testing tools. When the check box A Simple Query Against This DNS Server is selected, a test is performed that asks for a single record from the local DNS server; this is useful for verifying that the service is running and listening to queries, but not much else. When the check box A Recursive Query To Other DNS Servers is selected, the test is more sophisticated—a recursive query checks whether forwarding is working OK. The Test Now button and the Perform Automatic Testing At The Following Interval check box allow you to run these tests now or later, as you require.

FIGURE 3.18   The Event Logging tab of the server's Properties dialog box

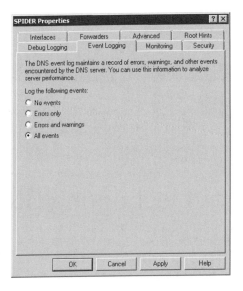

 If the simple query fails, check that the local server contains the zone 1.0.0.127.in-addr.arpa. If the recursive query fails, check that your root hints are correct and that your root servers are running.

In Exercise 3.5, you will enable logging, use the DNS MMC to test the DNS server, and view the contents of the DNS log.

FIGURE 3.19   The Monitoring tab of the server's Properties dialog box

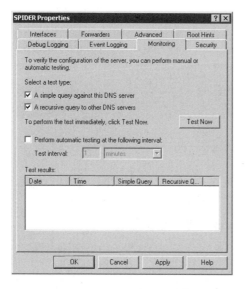

EXERCISE 3.5

Performing Simple DNS Testing

1. Open the DNS management snap-in by selecting Start ➢ Administrative Tools ➢ DNS.

2. Right-click the DNS server you want to test, and select Properties.

3. Switch to the Debug Logging tab, check all the debug logging options except Filter Packets By IP Address, and enter a full path and filename in the File Path And Name field.

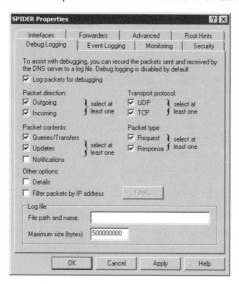

EXERCISE 3.5 *(continued)*

Click the Apply button.

4. Switch to the Monitoring tab, and check both A Simple Query Against This DNS Server and A Recursive Query To Other DNS Servers.

5. Click the Test Now button several times, and then click OK.

6. Using Windows Explorer, navigate to the folder you specified in step 3, and use WordPad to view the contents of the log file.

Troubleshooting DNS

When troubleshooting DNS problems, ask yourself the following basic questions:

- What application is failing? What works? What doesn't work?
- Is the problem basic IP connectivity, or is it name resolution? If the problem is name resolution, does the failing application use NetBIOS names, DNS names, or host names?
- How are the things that do and don't work related?
- Have the things that don't work ever worked on this computer or network? If so, what has changed since they last worked?

Windows Server 2008 provides several useful tools, discussed in the following sections, that can help you answer these questions:

- You can use nslookup to perform DNS queries and to examine the contents of zone files on local and remote servers.
- You can use the command-line utility dnslint for troubleshooting many common DNS issues.
- ipconfig allows you to perform the following tasks:
  - View DNS client settings.
  - Display and flush the resolver cache.
  - Force a dynamic update client to register its DNS records.
- The DNS log file monitors certain DNS server events and logs them for your edification.

Using *nslookup*

nslookup is a standard command-line tool provided in most DNS server implementations, including Windows Server 2008. Windows Server 2008 gives you the ability to launch nslookup from the DNS snap-in.

When launching nslookup from the DNS snap-in, a command prompt window opens automatically. You enter nslookup commands in this window.

nslookup offers the ability to perform query testing of DNS servers and to obtain detailed responses at the command prompt. This information can be useful for diagnosing and solving name resolution problems, for verifying that resource records are added or updated correctly in a zone, and for debugging other server-related problems. You can do a number of useful things with nslookup:

- Use it in noninteractive mode to look up a single piece of data.
- Enter interactive mode, and use the debug feature.
- Perform the following from within interactive mode:
  - Set options for your query.
  - Look up a name.
  - Look up records in a zone.
  - Perform zone transfers.
  - Exit nslookup.

When you are entering queries, it is generally a good idea to enter FQDNs so you can control what name is submitted to the server. However, if you want to know which suffixes are added to unqualified names before they are submitted to the server, you can enter **nslookup** in debug mode and then enter an unqualified name. You can configure suffix search order for clients manually on the client station or by using a GPO.

Using *nslookup* on the Command Line

To use nslookup in plain old command-line mode, enter the following in the command prompt window:

nslookup *DNS_name_or_IP_address server_IP_address*

This command will look up a DNS name or address using a server at the IP address you specify.

Using *nslookup* in Interactive Mode

The nslookup tool is a lot more useful in interactive mode because you can enter several commands in sequence. Entering **nslookup** by itself (without specifying a query or server) puts it in interactive mode, where it will stay until you type **exit** and press Enter. Before that point, you can look up lots of useful stuff. The following are some of the tasks you can perform with nslookup in interactive mode:

Setting options with the set command   While in interactive mode, you can use the set command to configure how the resolver will carry out queries. Table 3.5 shows a few of the options available with set.

TABLE 3.5   Command-Line Options Available with the set Command

Option	Purpose
set all	Shows all the options available with the set option.
set d2	Puts nslookup in debug mode so you can examine the query and response packets between the resolver and the server.
set domain=*domain name*	Tells the resolver what domain name to append for unqualified queries.
set timeout=*timeout*	Tells the resolver which timeout to use. This option is useful for slow links where queries frequently time out and the wait time must be lengthened.
set type=*record type*	Tells the resolver which type of resource records to search for (for example, A, PTR, or SRV). If you want the resolver to query for all types of resource records, type **set type=all**.

Looking up a name   While in interactive mode, you can look up a name just by typing it: **stellacon.com**. In this example, *stellacon* is the owner name for the record you are looking for, and *.com* is the server that you want to query.

You can use the wildcard character (*) in your query. For example, if you want to look for all resource records that have *k* as the first letter, just type **k*** as your query.

Looking up a record type   If you want to query for a particular type of record (for instance, an MX record), use the set type command. The command set type=mx tells nslookup that you're interested only in seeing MX records that meet your search criteria.

Listing the contents of a domain   To get a list of the contents of an entire domain, use the ls command. To find all the hosts in the apple.com domain, you'd type **set type=a** and then type **ls -t apple.com**.

Troubleshooting zone transfers   You can simulate zone transfers by using the ls command with the -d switch. This can help you determine whether the server you are querying allows zone transfers to your computer. To do this, type the following: **ls -d *domain_name*.**

nslookup Responses and Error Messages

A successful nslookup response looks like this:

```
Server: Name_of_DNS_server
Address: IP_address_of_DNS_server
Response_data
```

`nslookup` might also return an error. Table 3.6 lists some of the common messages.

TABLE 3.6   Common `nslookup` Error Messages

Error message	Meaning

`DNS request timed out.`
`Timeout was x seconds.`
`*** Can't find server name for address IP_Address:`
`Timed out`
`*** Default servers are not available`
`Default Server: Unknown`
`Address: IP_address_of_DNS_server`
	The resolver did not locate a PTR resource record (containing the host name) for the server IP address you specified. nslookup can still query the DNS server, and the DNS server can still answer queries.

`*** Request to Server timed-out`	A request was not fulfilled in the allotted time. This might happen, for example, if the DNS service was not running on the DNS server that is authoritative for the name.
`*** Server can't find Name_or_IP_address_queried_` `for: No response from server`	The server is not receiving requests on User Datagram Protocol (UDP) port 53.
`*** Server can't find Name_or_IP_address_queried_` `for: Non-existent domain`	The DNS server was unable to find the name or IP address in the authoritative domain. The authoritative domain might be on the remote DNS server or on another DNS server that this DNS server is unable to reach.
`*** Server can't find Name_or_IP_address_queried_` `for: Server failed`	The DNS server is running but is not working properly. For example, it might include a corrupted packet, or the zone in which you are querying for a record might be paused. However, this message can also be returned if the client queries for a host in a domain for which the DNS server is not authoritative. You will also receive the error if the DNS server cannot contact its root servers, it is not connected to the Internet, or it has no root hints.

In Exercise 3.6, you'll get some hands-on practice with the `nslookup` tool.

EXERCISE 3.6

Using the nslookup **Command**

1. Open a Windows Server 2008 command prompt by selecting Start ➢ Command Prompt.

2. Type **nslookup**, and press the Enter key. (For the rest of the exercise, use the Enter key to terminate each command. We won't continue to mention it.)

3. Try looking up a well-known address by typing **www.microsoft.com**. Notice that the query returns several IP addresses. (Microsoft load-balances web traffic by using multiple servers in the same DNS record.)

4. Try looking up a nonexistent host by typing **www.example.ccccc**. Notice that your server complains that it can't find the address. This is normal behavior.

5. Type **exit** at the prompt. Type **exit** again to leave the command prompt.

Using *dnslint*

Microsoft Windows Server 2008 DNS can use the dnslint command-line utility to help diagnose some common DNS name resolution issues and to help diagnose potential problems of incorrect delegation. You need to download dnslint from the Microsoft Download Center.

dnslint uses three main functions to verify DNS records and generate a report in HTML:

- dnslint /d helps diagnose reasons that cause "lame delegation" and other related DNS problems.

- dnslint /ql helps verify a user-defined set of DNS records on multiple DNS servers.

- dnslint /ad helps verify DNS records pertaining to Active Directory replication.

Here is the syntax for dnslint:

```
dnslint /d domain_name | /ad [LDAP_IP_address] | /ql input_file
[/c [smtp,pop,imap]] [/no_open] [/r report_name]
[/t] [/test_tcp] [/s DNS_IP_address] [/v] [/y]
```

The following are some sample queries:

```
dnslint /d stellacon.com
dnslint /ad /s 192.168.36.201
dnslint /ql dns_server.txt
dnslint /ql autocreate
dnslint /v /d stellacon.com
dnslint /r newfile /d stellacon.com
dnslint /y /d stellacon.com
dnslint /no_open /d stellacon.com
dnslint /s 192.168.36.201 /d labs.stellacon.com
```

Table 3.7 explains the dnslint command options.

TABLE 3.7 dnslint Command Options

Command Option	Meaning
/d	Specifies the domain name that is being tested.
/ad	Resolves DNS records that are used for Active Directory forest replication.
/s	Specifies the TCP/IP address of host.
/ql	Requests DNS query tests from a list. This switch sends DNS queries specified in an input file.
/v	Turns verbose mode on.
/r filename	Allows you to create a report file.
/y	Overwrites an existing report file without being prompted.
/no_open	Prevents a report from opening automatically.

Using *ipconfig*

You can use the command-line tool ipconfig to view your DNS client settings, to view and reset cached information used locally for resolving DNS name queries, and to register the resource records for a dynamic update client. If you use the ipconfig command with no parameters, it displays DNS information for each adapter, including the domain name and DNS servers used for that adapter. Table 3.8 shows some command-line options available with ipconfig.

TABLE 3.8 Command-Line Options Available for the ipconfig Command

Command	What It Does
ipconfig /all	Displays additional information about DNS, including the FQDN and the DNS suffix search list.
ipconfig /flushdns	Flushes and resets the DNS resolver cache.
ipconfig /displaydns	Displays the contents of the DNS resolver cache.
ipconfig /registerdns	Refreshes all DHCP leases and registers any related DNS names. This option is available only on Windows 2000 and newer computers that run the DHCP Client service.

You should know and be comfortable with the ipconfig commands related to DNS for the exam.

Using the DNS Log File

You can configure the DNS server to create a log file that records the following information:

- Queries
- Notification messages from other servers
- Dynamic updates
- The content of the question section for DNS query messages
- The content of the answer section for DNS query messages
- The number of queries this server sends
- The number of queries this server has received
- The number of DNS requests received over a UDP port
- The number of DNS requests received over a TCP port
- The number of full packets sent by the server
- The number of packets written through by the server and back to the zone

The DNS log appears in *systemroot*\System32\dns\Dns.log. Because the log is in RTF format, you must use WordPad or Word to view it.

Once the log file reaches the maximum size, Windows Server 2008 writes over the beginning of the file. You can change the maximum size of the log. If you make the size value higher, data persists for a longer time; however, the log file consumes more disk space. If you make the value smaller, the log file uses less disk space; however, the data persists for a shorter time.

Do not leave DNS logging turned on during normal operation because it sucks up both processing and hard disk resources. Enable it only when diagnosing and solving DNS problems.

Summary

DNS was designed to be a robust, scalable, high-performance system for resolving friendly names to TCP/IP host addresses. We started this chapter by presenting an overview of the basics of DNS and how DNS names are generated. We then covered the many new features available in the Microsoft Windows Server 2008 version of DNS and focused on how to install, configure, and manage the necessary services. Microsoft's DNS is based on a widely accepted set of standards. Because of this, Microsoft's DNS can work with both Windows and non-Windows networks.

Exam Essentials

Understand the purpose of DNS.   DNS is a standard set of protocols that defines a mechanism for querying and updating address information in the database, a mechanism for replicating the information in the database among servers, and a schema of the database.

Understand the different parts of the DNS database.   The SOA record defines the general parameters for the DNS zone, including who the authoritative server is for the zone. NS records list the name servers for a domain; they allow other name servers to look up names in your domain. A host record (also called an *address* or an *A record*) statically associates a host's name with its IP addresses. Pointer records (PTRs) map an IP address to a host name, making it possible to do reverse lookups. Alias records allow you to use more than one name to point to a single host. The MX record tells you which servers can accept mail bound for a domain. SRV records tie together the location of a service (such as a domain controller) with information about how to contact the service.

Know how DNS resolves names.   With iterative queries, a client asks the DNS server for an answer, and the client, or resolver, returns the best kind of answer it has. In a recursive query, the client sends a query to one name server, asking it to respond either with the requested answer or with an error. The error states either that the server can't come up with the right answer or that the domain name doesn't exist. With inverse queries, instead of supplying a name and then asking for an IP address, the client first provides the IP address and then asks for the name.

Understand the difference between DNS servers, clients, and resolvers.   Any computer providing domain name services is a DNS server. A DNS client is any machine issuing queries to a DNS server. A resolver handles the process of mapping a symbolic name to an actual network address.

Know how to install and configure DNS.   DNS can be installed before, during, or after installing the Active Directory service. When you install the DNS server, the DNS snap-in is installed, too. Configuring a DNS server ranges from very easy to very difficult, depending on what you're trying to make it do. In the simplest configuration, for a caching-only server, you don't have to do anything except make sure the server's root hints are set correctly. You can also configure a root server, a normal forward lookup server, and a reverse lookup server.

Know how to create new forward and reverse lookup zones.   You can use the New Zone Wizard to create a new forward or reverse lookup zone. The process is substantially the same for both types, but the specific steps and wizard pages differ somewhat. The wizard will walk you through the steps, such as specifying a name for the zone (in the case of forward lookup zones) or the network ID portion of the network that the zone covers (in the case of reverse lookup zones).

Know how to configure zones for dynamic updates.   The DNS service allows dynamic updates to be enabled or disabled on a per-zone basis at each server. This is easily done in the DNS snap-in.

Know how to delegate zones for DNS.   DNS provides the ability to divide the namespace into one or more zones, which can then be stored, distributed, and replicated to other DNS servers. When delegating zones within your namespace, be aware that for each new zone you create, you'll need delegation records in other zones that point to the authoritative DNS servers for the new zone.

Understand the tools that are available for monitoring and troubleshooting DNS. You can use the DNS snap-in to do some basic server testing and monitoring. More important, you use the snap-in to monitor and set logging options. Windows Server 2008 automatically logs DNS events in the event log under a distinct DNS server heading. `nslookup` offers the ability to perform query testing of DNS servers and to obtain detailed responses at the command prompt. You can use the command-line tool `ipconfig` to view your DNS client settings, to view and reset cached information used locally for resolving DNS name queries, and to register the resource records for a dynamic update client. Also you can configure the DNS server to create a log file that records queries, notification messages, dynamic updates, and various other DNS information. Finally you can use `dnslint`. Microsoft Windows Server 2008 DNS can use the `dnslint` command-line utility to help diagnose some common DNS name resolution issues and to help diagnose potential problems of incorrect delegation.

Review Questions

1. You are the network administrator for a large sales organization with four distinct regional offices situated in different areas of the United States. Your Windows Server 2008 computers are all in place, and you have almost finished migrating all the workstations to XP Professional and Vista. Your next step is to implement a single Active Directory tree, but you want to put your DNS infrastructure in place before you start building your tree. Because DNS is a critical component for the proper functioning of Active Directory, you want to make sure that each region will have service for local resources as well as good performance. What should you do to realize these requirements?

   A. Install a single DNS server at your location, and create a separate domain name for each region for the resolution of local resources.

   B. Install a DNS server at each regional location, and create a single domain name for all the regions for the resolution of local resources.

   C. Install a single DNS server at your location, and create a single domain name for all the regions for the resolution of local resources.

   D. Install a DNS server at each regional location, and create a separate domain name for each region for the resolution of local resources.

2. The following diagram outlines DNS name resolution through recursion. Move each item into the correct position so that the flow of DNS traffic is correct.

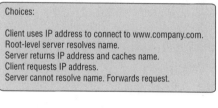

Choices:

Client uses IP address to connect to www.company.com.
Root-level server resolves name.
Server returns IP address and caches name.
Client requests IP address.
Server cannot resolve name. Forwards request.

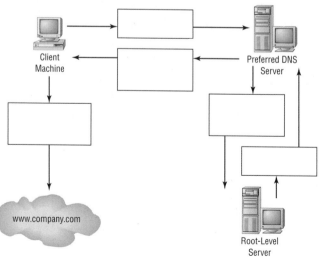

3. After upgrading your Windows NT network to Windows Server 2008, you decide to install Active Directory. Your network consists of 3 Windows Server 2008 computers, 65 XP Professional workstations, and 3 Unix workstations. One of the Unix station is running a large laser printer, and another is running a fax server. You've been using a DNS server on one of the Unix boxes for Internet browsing only, but now you'll need DNS for Active Directory. You deploy the Windows Server 2008 DNS service, replacing the DNS on the Unix box and configuring it for dynamic updates. After you deploy Active Directory, everything appears to work fine—the users can connect to resources on the network through host names. However, it becomes apparent that the fax server and the laser printer are no longer accessible via their host names. What is the most likely cause of this problem?

    A. You need to disable dynamic updates on the DNS server.

    B. You need to install WINS to resolve the host names on the Unix machines.

    C. You need to manually add A resource records for the Unix machines.

    D. You need to integrate the primary DNS zone into Active Directory.

4. You have been brought into an organization that has a variety of computer systems. Management is trying to tie these systems together and to minimize the administrative efforts required to keep the network-provided services running. The systems consist of 4 Windows NT servers, 7 Windows Server 2008 computers, 300 Vista and XP Professional workstations, 100 Windows NT workstations, 30 Unix clients, and 3 Unix servers. Management wants to continue the migration toward the new versions of Windows and also to expand the number of Unix servers as the need arises. Currently, they are using WINS on the Windows NT servers and a DNS service on one of the Unix servers that points to an ISP and provides all the host name resolution. What would be your recommendation for providing name resolution service for this organization?

    A. Install the Windows Server 2008 DNS service on the Windows Server 2008 computer.

    B. Install the WINS service on the Unix server.

    C. Upgrade the DNS on the Unix server to the Windows Server 2008 DNS.

    D. Use the standard DNS service that is already on the Unix server.

5. Jerry wants to configure a Windows Server 2008 DNS server so that it can answer queries for hosts on his intranet but not on the Internet. He can accomplish this by doing which of the following? (Choose two.)

    A. Installing the DNS server inside his company's firewall

    B. Configuring his server as a root server and leaving out root hints for the top-level domains

    C. Leaving forwarding turned off

    D. Disabling recursive lookups

6. Your company has been extraordinarily successful with its e-commerce site. In fact, because your customers have come to expect such a high level of reliability, you want to build several servers that mirror each other. Just in case one of them fails, you will still be able to provide excellent service for your customers. The name of the web server is www.example.com, which you are duplicating on machines on different subnets, and you have made all the necessary host records in the DNS. After a while you notice that only one machine is responding to client requests. You are not the original administrator for the company, so you suspect some of the default settings were changed before you arrived. What must you do so that your customers can utilize all the mirrored web servers?

   A. Enable DNS sharing.

   B. Enable IIS sharing.

   C. Enable round robin.

   D. Enable request redirector.

   E. Configure the proper priorities metric for this host name.

7. You are the network administrator for a Windows Server 2008 network. You have multiple remote locations connected to your main office by slow satellite links. You want to install DNS onto these offices so that clients can locate authoritative DNS servers in the main location. What type of DNS servers should be installed in the remote locations?

   A. Primary DNS zones

   B. Secondary DNS zones

   C. Active Directory–integrated zones

   D. Stub zones

8. The organization you work for has five Windows Server 2008 servers all running as domain controllers. Your DNS servers are all currently running as primary DNS zones. You need to set up a DNS strategy that allows all DNS servers to hold the same database, and the company requires the use of secure DNS dynamic updates. What type of DNS strategy do you need to implement?

   A. Upgrade one server as a primary master and the rest as stub zones.

   B. Upgrade one server as a primary master and the rest as secondary servers.

   C. Upgrade all servers to Active Directory–integrated servers.

   D. Keep all servers primary servers, and set up replication.

9. The company you work for has six locations around the country. You are part of the administrative team based in the central office, and you have finished upgrading the workstations and servers to Vista and Server 2008. Your team is now in the process of deploying DNS in order to support your manager's planned implementation of a single Active Directory tree so you can support the network from your central location. Because you must support name resolution for six offices, you want to provide an efficient and responsive service for the users. Which of the following is the best approach to support your plans for a single Active Directory tree and provide efficiency and responsiveness for the users in this situation?

A. Create a single second-level name, and maintain all the DNS servers at your central office to ease administration.

B. Create a single second-level name, and deploy a DNS server at each location in the network.

C. Create a second-level name for each city, and maintain all the DNS servers at your central office to ease administration.

D. Create a second-level name for each city, and deploy a DNS server at each location in the network.

10. You want to quickly verify that your DNS service is running and listening to queries. What would you click or look at in the dialog box in order to do this?

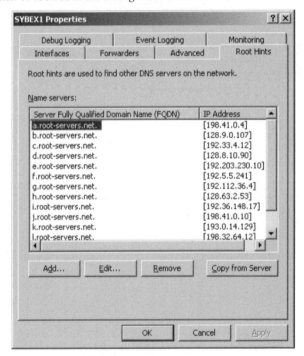

A. The Name Servers area of the Root Hints tab

B. The Add button

C. The Monitoring tab

D. The Interfaces tab

11. Acme Bowling Pin Company, with offices in 4 states, has been acquired by Roadrunner Enterprises, which has offices in 14 states and is a highly diversified organization. Although the various companies are managed independently, the parent company is very interested in minimizing costs by taking advantage of any shared corporate resources; it also wants to have overall central control. This means that you, the network administrator for Acme Bowling Pin Company, will manage your own DNS namespace but will still be under the umbrella of the parent organization. Which of the following will best accomplish these goals?

    A. Have each location, including yours, register its own namespace and manage its DNS system independently.

    B. Register a single domain name for Roadrunner Enterprises, and use delegated subdomains on a single DNS server at corporate headquarters to provide name resolution across the enterprise.

    C. Register a single domain name for Roadrunner Enterprises, and use delegated subdomains on DNS servers installed at each location to provide name resolution across the enterprise.

    D. Have each location, including yours, register its own namespace and add it on a single DNS server at corporate headquarters to provide name resolution across the enterprise.

12. A DNS client sends a recursive query to its local DNS server, asking for the IP address of www.bigbrother.gov. The DNS server finds no local zones corresponding to the requested domain name, so it sends a request to a root name server. What does the root name server reply with?

    A. The IP address of the name server for the bigbrother.gov domain

    B. The DNS name of the .gov top-level domain

    C. The IP address of www.bigbrother.gov

    D. The IP address of the name server for the .gov top-level domain

13. You have a private network that contains several DNS zones and servers, including a couple of root name servers. You never need to change any of your DNS data. You find that the load on one of your name servers is inordinately high. What can you do to reduce this load?

    A. Increase the TTL on the affected name server.

    B. Decrease the TTL on the affected name server.

    C. Add a service record to the affected name server.

    D. Edit the directory command in the DNS boot file.

14. You are charged with upgrading your Windows NT network to Windows Server 2008. You plan on installing Active Directory and upgrading all your client machines to Vista. Your company does not allow Internet access because the company president still views it, as well as email, as a time-wasting toy that distracts the employees. Despite what you think is a short-sighted view by management, you begin to design the upgrade process. You realize that DNS is an important component of Windows Server 2008, even though you won't be using it to locate resources on the Internet. What DNS records must you include in the configuration of the Windows Server 2008 DNS service in this environment? (Choose all that apply.)

   A. Host record

   B. Pointer record

   C. Alias record

   D. Name server records

   E. Start of authority record

   F. Mail exchanger record

   G. Service record

15. A spammer is attempting to send junk mail through an unsuspecting mail server. The spammer uses a fake DNS name from which he thinks the mail server will accept mail, but he is rejected anyway. How does the mail server know to reject the spammer's mail?

   A. The spammer's DNS name is not in the cache file of the primary DNS server that serves the mail server's domain, so it gets rejected.

   B. A fake DNS name is automatically detected if the IP address isn't recognized by the mail server.

   C. The mail server employs a reverse lookup zone to verify that DNS names are not fake.

   D. The spammer does not have an MX record in the database of the DNS server that serves the mail server's domain.

16. Your web server's host name within the LAN is chaos.example.com. However, you need to add a DNS entry so that it can be found with the name www.example.com. What type of record should you add to the DNS zone for example.com in order for this to be configured properly?

   A. An alias/CNAME record

   B. An A record

   C. An SRV record

   D. A PTR record

17. You have two master servers operating in your environment, a primary master and a secondary master. These DNS servers are authoritative for the zone `example.com`. When the secondary master transfers the domain, what part of the DNS zone does it use to determine whether the zone data has changed?

   A. The TTL, or time to live

   B. The NS record

   C. The serial number

   D. The database record tombstone

18. This type of DNS query results in the server returning its best answer from the cache or local data.

   A. Recursive

   B. Iterative

   C. Forward

   D. NS

19. You're troubleshooting an error whereby a client computer seems to have old DNS data. You've used `ipconfig` to see what DNS servers the client is using, and you've used `ping` to verify connectivity to those servers. What command should you use in order to clear the DNS cache on the client so that it will start building a new cache of DNS lookups?

   A. `ipconfig /cleardns`

   B. `nslookup /flushdns`

   C. `dns /register`

   D. `ipconfig /flushdns`

20. Your organization has two DNS servers located at the home office location. However, clients in remote offices are reporting sporadic DNS lookup failures. The network team has informed you that some of the WAN links to the remote offices are nearing saturation. To relieve some of the burden, you decide to implement secondary DNS servers in the remote offices. However, the DNS servers will not be official name servers for the domain, and therefore you don't need to set up NS records for each server. You configure half of the new DNS servers to attempt zone transfer from the primary master and the other half from the secondary master server. After deploying the servers, you notice that none of the servers is able to complete a zone transfer. What is likely the cause of this?

   A. The primary master server's firewall is not configured for zone transfer data.

   B. The primary and secondary master servers are not configured to allow zone transfers from the new DNS servers.

   C. The new DNS servers cannot perform zone transfers from secondary servers.

   D. The primary server is configured to allow recursive queries only.

Answers to Review Questions

1.   B. A DNS server installed at each regional location will provide name and service resolution even if the WAN links go down. The local location will also have better performance because the requests will not have to travel through the WAN links. A single domain name for all the locations is needed because your requirement is to have one Active Directory tree with a contiguous namespace.

2.   The client machine places its request with its preferred DNS server. If the DNS server doesn't have an entry in its DNS database, it forwards the request to a root-level server. The root-level server resolves the name and returns it to the preferred DNS server. The DNS server caches the name so that any future requests don't need to be forwarded, and then it sends the IP address to the client. The client then uses the IP address to reach the intended target.

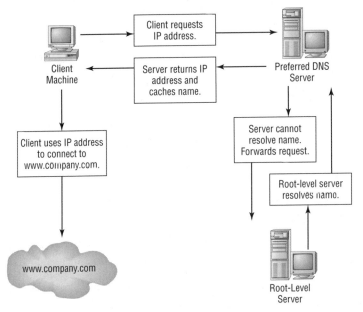

3.   C. Windows 2000 and newer computers will register themselves in the DNS through dynamic updates. However, the Unix machines will not register themselves in the DNS. These machines will have to be added manually into the DNS so that the other clients can locate them. If you disabled the dynamic DNS updates, you would then have to add all the workstations on the network to the DNS manually.

4. A. Installing the Windows DNS service on the Windows Server 2008 computer will provide dynamic updates. This will allow the newer Windows machines to publish themselves and locate the Active Directory services through the SRV records that this version of DNS supports. The Windows Server 2008 DNS will also provide standard DNS services to the Unix and Windows NT machines. In addition, it can point to the DNS server that your ISP is supplying for searches beyond the local network.

No WINS service is available for Unix. It may remain on the Windows NT server until the upgrade is complete and the NetBIOS name resolution is no longer necessary.

5. B, C. Configuring his server as a root server and leaving forwarding off means that the server will either answer a query (for addresses it knows) or return a failure (for addresses it doesn't know).

6. C. The round-robin option allows you to list a host name with multiple IP addresses and then, as each request comes into the DNS server, to rotate that list, presenting each of the IP addresses in turn. This will balance out the load across all the servers you have mirrored and configured in the DNS.

7. D. Stub zones are very useful for slow WAN connections. These zones store only three types of resource record: NS records, glue host (A) records, and SOA records. These three records are used to locate authoritative DNS servers.

8. C. Upgrading all the DNS servers to Active Directory–integrated zones will allow all DNS servers to share the same Active Directory DNS database. Active Directory–integrated zones also allow secure dynamic updates.

9. B. Installing a DNS server at each city as well as the central office allows the workstations in each city to obtain their name resolution from local servers, thereby providing good response time. If all the DNS servers were in the central office, name resolution would have to cross the routers, introducing latency and the potential for no service if the link ever went down. The namespace in a single Active Directory tree must be contiguous. If you create a second-level domain for each city, you would need to create multiple Active Directory trees.

10. C. From the Monitoring tab, you can perform simple and recursive queries to see whether DNS servers are running and listening to queries. You can either run the tests immediately or set a schedule on which the tests will run.

11. C. DNS has the capability to create subdomains of a central corporate domain, and a subdomain can be delegated to a DNS server in each location for independent management. The entire company could use a single DNS server at corporate headquarters with the multiple domains, but then each namespace would not be managed locally at each location.

12. D. The root name server has authority for the root domain and will reply with the IP address of a name server for the `.gov` top-level domain. With the IP address of the top-level domain, the system can now query it for the `bigbrother` address.

13. A. If the TTL is too small, the load on the DNS server will increase.

14. A, D, E, G. Even though it's best practice to have all the records associated with DNS as part of each installation, name resolution will still function properly with just the fundamental records. The host record, or A record, is the basic record that contains the mapping between the logical name and the IP address. This is the heart of DNS. The name server records identify the DNS servers that are available for this network. The start of authority record, or SOA record, contains the basic configuration of the DNS service. The service record, while not essential to a traditional DNS, is critical to Active Directory because it's used to identify the domain controllers for login and other query information. The pointer record is used for reverse lookups; although it's very useful, it's not required for standard functionality. The alias record is needed only if you plan to have different names associated with the same physical address. The mail exchanger record is necessary only if you are using DNS to locate mail servers.

15. C. Most mail servers can be configured to reject incoming mail from servers whose IP addresses cannot be resolved with a reverse lookup.

16. A. Though it's possible to set up another A record pointing www.example.com to the IP address of the server, such a record would not be configured properly. A CNAME record, sometimes called an *alias* record, should be configured to point www at chaos.example.com. Options C and D would not solve the problem.

17. C. Secondary servers use the serial number to determine whether the zone data has changed. By default, this value is automatically updated with Windows Server 2008 DNS server. The zone's TTL is used to determine when to query for an update of the zone file from the master server unless the master server has sent a Notify in the interim.

18. B. An iterative query results in the server sending back its best guess from data residing in its cache or local zones. A recursive query is one in which the server goes out and attempts to find the answer by querying other DNS servers.

19. D. The command ipconfig /flushdns clears the local DNS cache.

20. B. Since you didn't set up the new secondary servers with their own NS records, they aren't listed on the Name Servers tab of the zone's Properties dialog box. Therefore, by default these servers cannot transfer zone data. By going into the Zone Transfers tab, you can configure the servers to receive updates. Option A is incorrect because the main secondary master server can indeed receive zone transfers. Option C is incorrect because DNS servers can perform zone transfers from other secondary servers. Option D has nothing to do with zone transfers and cannot be true since the main secondary master can perform zone transfers.

Chapter

4

Managing Dynamic Host Configuration Protocol (DHCP)

MICROSOFT EXAM OBJECTIVES COVERED IN THIS CHAPTER:

✓ **Configure Dynamic Host Configuration Protocol**

- DHCP Options
- Creating new options
- PXE boot
- Default user profiles
- DHCP relay agents
- Exclusions
- Authorize server in Active Directory
- Scopes
- Node Type
- Server core
- Windows Server Hyper-V

In Chapter 2, "TCP/IP," we briefly discussed the Dynamic Host Configuration Protocol (DHCP) and how to configure DHCP clients. Planning for and using DHCP in Windows Server 2008 is pretty straightforward, but there's a lot you need to know to make sure your installation proceeds without trouble.

In this chapter, you'll learn how to install and manage DHCP, including how to set up plain DHCP scopes, superscopes, and multicast scopes. You'll also learn how to set up integration between Dynamic DNS and DHCP as well as how to authorize a DHCP server to integrate with Active Directory.

Overview of DHCP

As you saw in Chapter 3, "Domain Name System (DNS)," TCP/IP is the priority protocol for Windows Server 2008. There are two ways to have clients and servers get TCP/IP addresses:

- You can manually assign the addresses.

- The addresses can be assigned automatically.

Manually assigning addresses is a fairly simple process. An administrator goes to each of the machines on the network and assigns TCP/IP addresses. The problem with this method arises when the network becomes midsize or larger. Think of an administrator trying to individually assign 4,000 TCP/IP addresses, subnet masks, default gateways, and all other configuration options needed to run the network.

DHCP's job is to centralize the process of IP address and option assignment. You can configure a DHCP server with a range of addresses (called a *pool*) and other configuration information and let it assign all the IP parameters—addresses, default gateways, DNS server addresses, and so on.

 DHCP is defined by a series of Request for Comment (RFC) documents, notably 2131 and 2132.

Introducing the DORA Process

An easy way to remember how DHCP works is to learn the acronym DORA. DORA stands for Discover, Offer, Request, and Acknowledge. In brief, here is DHCP's DORA process:

1. *Discover*: When IP networking starts up on a DHCP-enabled client, a special message called a DHCPDISCOVER is broadcast within the local physical subnet.

2. *Offer*: Any DHCP server that hears the request checks its internal database and replies with a message called a DHCPOFFER, which contains an available IP address.

    The contents of this message depend on how the DHCP server is configured—there are numerous options aside from an IP address that you can specify to pass to the client on a Windows Server 2008 DHCP server.

3. *Request*: The client receives one or more DHCPOFFERs (depending on how many DHCP servers exist on the local subnet), chooses an address from one of the offers, and sends a DHCPREQUEST message to the server in order to signal acceptance of the DHCPOFFER.

    This message might also request additional configuration parameters.

    Other DHCP servers that sent offers take the request message as an acknowledgment that the client didn't accept their offer.

4. *Acknowledge*: When the DHCP server receives the DHCPREQUEST, it marks the IP address as being in use (usually, but it's not required to). Then it sends a DHCPACK to the client.

    The acknowledgment message might contain requested configuration parameters.

    If the server is unable to accept the DHCPREQUEST for any reason, it sends a DHCPNAK message. If a client receives a DHCPNAK, it begins the configuration process over again.

5. When the client accepts the IP offer, the address is assigned to the client for a specified period of time, called a *lease*. After receiving the DHCPACK message, the client performs a final check on the parameters (sometimes it sends an ARP request for the offered IP address) and makes note of the duration of the lease. The client is now configured.

    If the client detects that the address is already in use, it sends a DHCPDECLINE.

   If the DHCP server has given out all the IP addresses in its pool, it won't make an offer. If no other servers make an offer, the client's IP network initialization will fail. In the following sections, we will examine the advantages and disadvantages of DHCP and take a closer look at the DHCP process.

Advantages and Disadvantages of DHCP

DHCP was designed from the start to simplify network management. It has some significant advantages, but it also has some drawbacks.

Advantages of DHCP

The following are advantages of DHCP:

- Configuration of large and even midsize networks is much simpler. If a DNS server address or some other change is necessary to the client, the administrator doesn't have to physically touch each device in the network to reconfigure it with the new settings.

- Once you enter the IP configuration information in one place—the server—it's automatically propagated to clients, eliminating the risk that a user will misconfigure some parameters and require you to fix them.

- IP addresses are conserved because DHCP assigns them only when requested.

- IP configuration becomes almost completely automatic. In most cases, you can plug in a new system (or move one) and then watch as it receives a configuration from the server. For example, when you install new network changes such as a gateway or DNS server, the client configuration is done at only one location—the DHCP server.

- Allows a preboot execution environment (PXE) client to get a TCP/IP address from DHCP. PXE clients—also called Microsoft Remote Installation Services (RIS) clients—can get an IP address without needing to have an operating system installed. This allows RIS clients to connect to a RIS server through the TCP/IP protocol and download an operating system remotely.

Disadvantages of DHCP

Unfortunately, there are a few drawbacks with DHCP:

- DHCP can become a single point of failure for your network. If you have only one DHCP server and it's not available, clients can't request or renew leases.

- If the DHCP server contains incorrect information, the misinformation will automatically be delivered to all your DHCP clients. To fix the problem, you might have to visit each machine and reconfigure it.

- If you want to use DHCP on a multisegment network, you must put either a DHCP server or a relay agent on each segment, or you must ensure that your router can forward Bootstrap Protocol (BOOTP) broadcasts.

 Real World Scenario

DHCP on a Segmented Network

The disadvantage of using DHCP on a multisegment network is important but often overlooked. By design, DHCP network traffic doesn't cross subnets. This means that DHCP messages don't cross router boundaries. If there's a router between two segments of network clients and the clients aren't on the same side as the DHCP server, the clients won't be able to use the server.

DHCP messages don't cross router boundaries because they are sent as broadcasts within a network. It's a bad idea to automatically forward broadcasts through a router. This practice can propagate broadcast storms that can effectively down an entire network.

You can work around this limitation. Many, but not all, routers include a setting allowing you to forward DHCP messages to connected network segments. This option might be called a *relay agent* or *BOOTP helper*. Cisco, a popular router choice, calls this option a *helper-address*. A Cisco device configured with an IP helper-address will forward broadcasts received on one interface to a specified address, presumably a DHCP server connected through another interface.

When configuring DHCP in the real world, be aware of network boundaries and the capabilities of your network gear in handling DHCP messages.

The DHCP Lease Process

As you've already seen, the DHCP lease process is a pretty simple. It involves four stages (DORA):

1. DHCP discovery
2. DHCP lease offer
3. DHCP lease request
4. DHCP lease acknowledgment

At the end of the process (if all goes well), the client has an IP address and whatever other parameters the DHCP server owner wanted to supply. Because an IP address is required to communicate with other devices on an IP network, the DHCP negotiation happens early in the Windows boot cycle.

> Each network adapter in a system has its own IP address; if you have multiple network interface cards (NICs) that are configured to use DHCP, in the following sections you'll see the lease process occurring for each DHCP-aware NIC.

In the following sections, we will further describe each of the stages of the DHCP lease process. In addition, you will see how to renew and release a lease and get a closer look at some `ipconfig` switches that are particularly useful in the context of DHCP.

Step 1: DHCP Discovery

The first step in the DHCP lease process is the discovery stage. It's triggered the first time a client's DHCP-configured IP stack starts or when you switch from using an assigned IP address to using DHCP. It can also occur when a specific IP address is requested but unavailable or immediately after a formerly used IP address is released.

At the time of the lease request, the client doesn't know what its IP address is, and it doesn't know the IP address of the server. To work around this, the client uses 0.0.0.0 as its address and 255.255.255.255 for the server's address. It then sends out a broadcast *DHCP discover message* on UDP port 68 and destination port 67. The discover message contains the client's hardware MAC address.

> DHCP discover message broadcasts aren't heard outside the client's local subnet unless your routers support BOOTP forwarding or the DHCP relay agent. For more detail, see Chapter 7, "Managing Security for Remote Access Services."

On Windows 2000, Windows XP, Windows Vista, Windows Server 2003, and Windows Server 2008, if no DHCP server responds, the client repeats its request five more times at 0-, 4-, 8-, 16-, and 32-second (plus a random amount of time from −1 to 1 second) intervals. If the client still doesn't get a response, it reverts to Automatic Private IP Addressing (APIPA) or its alternate configuration and continues to broadcast discover messages every five minutes until it gets an answer.

RFC 2131 defines the interval for retransmission and requires a random interval between –1 and 1 second. The RFC also specifies the doubling of the retransmission time, up to a maximum interval of 64 seconds. However, the longest retransmission interval used by Windows is 32 seconds.

With APIPA, the client automatically picks what it thinks is an unused address (from the 169.254.*x*.*y* address block) instead of waiting indefinitely for an answer. Even though it now has an address, the DHCP client continues to poll every five minutes for a DHCP server. When the DCHP server becomes available, the client switches back to a DHCP-assigned address.

Step 2: DHCP Lease Offer

In the second phase of the DHCP lease process, any DHCP server that received the discover message broadcast and that has valid address information responds with an offer message. (This feature allows you to configure multiple DHCP servers so that you're protected against a single point of failure.)

You must register a Windows Server 2008 DHCP server in Active Directory. The server won't begin offering leases until it successfully registers in the directory (see "Authorizing DHCP for Active Directory" later in this chapter).

The offer message is a proposal from the server to the client. It contains an IP address, usually along with other options including a subnet mask, a lease period (in days), and a default gateway. Windows DHCP servers (and many others) temporarily reserve any offered IP address so that the server doesn't offer the same address to multiple clients. All offers are sent directly to the requesting client's hardware MAC address.

Step 3: DHCP Lease Selection

Once the client receives at least one offer, the third phase of the DHCP lease process begins. In this phase, the client machine selects an offer from those it received. Windows 2000, XP, Vista, Server 2003, and Server 2008 clients typically accept the first offer that arrives. To signal acceptance, the client broadcasts an acceptance message containing the IP address of the server it selected. This broadcast allows the servers whose offers weren't selected to unreserve (pull back) the addresses they offered.

Step 4: DHCP Lease Acknowledgment

Once the chosen DHCP server receives the acceptance message from the client, it marks the selected IP address as leased and sends an acknowledgment message, called a *DHCPACK*, to the client.

If there's a problem, the server sends a negative acknowledgment, or *DHCPNACK*, to the client. DHCPNACKs are most often generated in the following cases:

- The client is attempting to renew a lease for its old IP address after that address has been reassigned elsewhere.

- The requesting client has an inaccurate IP address because it has physically changed locations to an alternate subnet.

The DHCPACK message includes any DHCP options specified by the server along with the IP address and subnet mask. When the client receives this message, it integrates the parameters into the IP stack, just as though the user had manually given it new configuration parameters.

NOTE   Manually configured entries on the client override any DHCP-supplied entries.

This four-step process may seem overly complicated, but each step is necessary. The process results in exactly one server assigning exactly one address to exactly one client. If parts of the process were left out—for example, if each server offering a lease immediately assigned an IP address to a requesting workstation—there would soon be no addresses left to assign. Likewise, if the DHCP client decided whether to accept or reject the lease (instead of waiting for a DHCPACK or DHCPNACK message), a slow client could cause the server to mark an assigned address as free and assign it somewhere else—leaving two clients with the same offer.

DHCP Lease Renewal

What happens when the lease expires or needs to be renewed? No matter how long the lease period is, the client sends a new lease request message directly to the DHCP server when the lease period is half over (give or take some randomness required by RFC 2131). This period goes by the name *T1* (not to be confused with the T1 type of network connection). If the server hears the request message and there's no reason to reject it, it sends a DHCPACK to the client. This resets the lease period, just as signing a renewal rider on a car lease does.

If the DHCP server isn't available, the client realizes that the lease can't be renewed. The client continues to use the address; once 87.5 percent of the lease period has elapsed (again, give or take some randomness), the client sends out another renewal request. This interval is also known as T2. At that point, any DHCP server that hears the renewal can respond to this *DHCP request message* (which is a request for a lease renewal) with a DHCPACK and renew the lease.

If at any time during this process the client gets a negative DHCPNACK message, it must stop using its IP address immediately and start the leasing process over from the beginning by requesting a new lease.

When a client initializes its IP networking, it always attempts to renew its old address. If the client has time left on the lease, it continues to use the lease until its end. If the client is unable to get a new lease by that time, all IP functions stop until a new, valid address can be obtained.

DHCP Lease Release

Although leases can be renewed repeatedly, at some point they might run out. Furthermore, the lease process is an "at-will" process—the client or server can cancel the lease before it ends. In addition, if the client doesn't succeed in renewing the lease before it expires, the client loses its lease and reverts to APIPA. This release process is important for reclaiming extinct IP addresses used by systems that have moved or switched to a non-DHCP address.

ipconfig Lease Options

The ipconfig command-line tool is useful for working with network settings. Its /renew and /release switches make it particularly handy for DHCP clients. These switches allow you to request renewal of, or give up, your machine's existing address lease. You can do the same thing by toggling the Obtain An IP Address Automatically button in the Internet Protocol (TCP/IP) Properties dialog box, but the command-line option is useful especially when you're setting up a new network.

For example, we spend about a third of our time teaching MCSE classes, usually in temporary classrooms set up at conferences, hotels, and so on. Laptops are used in these classes, with one brawny laptop set up as a DNS/DHCP/DC server. Occasionally, a client will lose its DHCP lease (or not get one, perhaps because a cable has come loose). The quickest way to fix it is to pop open a command-line window and type **ipconfig /renew**.

You can configure DHCP to assign options only to certain classes. Classes, defined by an administrator, are groups of computers that require identical DHCP options. The /setclassid *classID* switch of ipconfig is the only way to assign a machine to a class.

More specifically, the switches do the following:

ipconfig /renew   Instructs the DHCP client to request a lease renewal. If the client already has a lease, it requests a renewal from the server that issued the current lease. This is equivalent to what happens when the client reaches the half-life of its lease. Or, if the client doesn't currently have a lease, it is equivalent to what happens when you boot a DHCP client for the first time. It initiates the DHCP mating dance, listens for lease offers, and chooses one it likes.

ipconfig /release   Forces the client to immediately give up its lease by sending the server a DHCP release notification. The server updates its status information and marks the client's old IP address as "available," leaving the client with no address bound to its network interface. When you use this command, most of the time it will be immediately followed by ipconfig /renew. The combination releases the existing lease and gets a new one, probably with a different address. (It's also a handy way to force your client to get a new set of settings from the server before lease expiration time.)

ipconfig /setclassid *classID*   Sets a new class ID for the client. You will see how to configure class options later in the section "Setting Scope Options for IPv4." For now, you should know that the only way to add a client machine to a class is to use this command. Note that you need to renew the client lease for the class assignment to take effect.

If you have multiple network adapters in a single machine, you can provide the name of the adapter (or adapters) you want the command to work on, including an asterisk (*) as a wildcard. For example, one of our servers has two network cards: an Intel EtherExpress (ELNK1) and a generic 100Mbps card. If you want to renew DHCP settings for both adapters, you can type **ipconfig /renew** *. If you just want to renew the Intel EtherExpress card, you can type **ipconfig /renew ELNK1**.

Understanding Scope Details

By now you should have a good grasp of what a lease is and how it works. To learn how to configure your servers to hand out those leases, though, you need to have a complete understanding of some additional topics: scopes, superscopes, exclusions, reservations, address pool, and relay agents.

Scope

Let's start with the concept of a *scope*, which is a contiguous range of addresses. There's usually one scope per physical subnet, and a scope can cover a Class A, Class B, or Class C network address or a TCP/IP v6 address. DHCP uses scopes as the basis for managing and assigning IP addressing information.

Each scope has a set of parameters, or *scope options*, that you can configure. Scope options control what data is delivered to DHCP clients when they're completing the DHCP negotiation process with a particular server. For example, the DNS server name, default gateway, and default network time server are all separate options that can be assigned. These settings are called *option types*; you can use any of the types provided with Windows Server 2008, or you can specify your own.

Superscope

A *superscope* enables the DHCP server to provide addresses from more than one scope to clients on the same physical subnet. This is helpful when clients within the same subnet have more than one IP network and thus need IPs from more than one address pool. Microsoft's DHCP snap-in allows you to manage IP address assignment in the superscope, though you must still configure other scope options individually for each child scope.

 You should understand what a superscope is for the exam.

Exclusions and Reservations

The scope defines what IP addresses could potentially be assigned, but you can influence the assignment process in two additional ways by specifying exclusions and reservations:

- *Exclusions* are IP addresses within the range that you never want automatically assigned. These excluded addresses are off-limits to DHCP. You'll typically use exclusions to tag any addresses that you never want the DHCP server to assign at all. You might use exclusions to set aside addresses that you want to permanently assign to servers that play a vital role in your organization.

- *Reservations* are IP addresses within the range for which you want a permanent DHCP lease. They essentially reserve a particular IP address for a particular device. The device still goes through the DHCP process (that is, its lease expires, and it asks for a new one), but it always obtains the same addressing information from the DHCP server.

Exclusions are useful for addresses that you don't want to participate in DHCP at all. Reservations are helpful for situations in which you want a client to get the same settings each time they obtain an address.

An address cannot be simultaneously reserved and excluded at the same time. Be aware of this fact for the exam, possibly relating to a troubleshooting question.

Using Reservations and Exclusions

Deciding when to assign a reservation or exclusion can sometimes be confusing. In practice, you'll find that there are certain computers in the network that greatly benefit by having static IP network information. Servers such as DNS servers, the DHCP server itself, SMTP servers, and other low-level infrastructure servers are good candidates for static assignment. There are usually so few of these servers that the administrator is not overburdened if a change in network settings requires going out to reconfigure each individually. Chances are that the administrator would still need to manually reconfigure these servers (by using ipconfig /release and then ipconfig /renew), even if they did not have IP addresses reserved. Even in large installations, we find it much more preferable to manage these vital servers by hand than to rely on DHCP.

Reservations are also appropriate for application servers and other special but nonvital infrastructure servers. With a reservation in DHCP, the client device will still go through the DHCP process but will always obtain the same addressing information from the DHCP server. The premise behind this strategy is that these nonvital servers can withstand a short outage if DHCP settings change or if the DHCP server fails.

Address Pool

The range of IP addresses that the DHCP server can assign is called its *address pool*. For example, let's say you set up a new DHCP scope covering the 192.168.1 subnet. That gives you 255 IP addresses in the pool. After adding an exclusion from 192.168.1.240 to 192.168.1.254, you're left with 241 (255 – 14) IP addresses in the pool. That means (in theory, at least) that you can service 241 unique clients at a time before you run out of IP addresses.

DHCP Relay Agent

By design, the DHCP protocol is intended to work only with clients and servers on a single IP network to communicate. But RFC 1542 sets out how BOOTP (upon which DHCP is based) should work in circumstances in which the client and server are on different IP networks. If no DHCP server is available on the client's network, you can use a DHCP relay agent to forward DHCP broadcasts from the client's network to the DHCP server. The relay agent acts like a radio repeater, listening for DHCP client requests and retransmitting them through the router to the server.

Installing and Authorizing DHCP

Installing DHCP is easy using the Windows Server 2008 installation mechanism. Unlike some other services discussed in this book, the installation process installs just the service and its associated snap-in, starting it when the installation is complete. At that point, it's not delivering any DHCP service, but you don't have to reboot.

Installing DHCP

Exercise 4.1 shows you how to install DHCP Server using Server Manager.

EXERCISE 4.1

Installing the DHCP Service

1. Select Start ➢ Administrative Tools ➢ Server Manager.

2. Click the DHCP Server box, and then click Next.

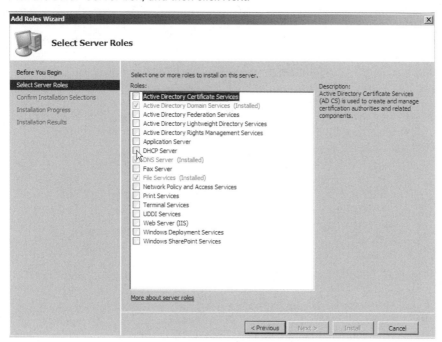

EXERCISE 4.1 *(continued)*

3. If the Introduction to DHCP page appears, click Next.

4. When the Select Network Connection Bindings page appears, make sure your TCP/IP address is checked. Click Next.

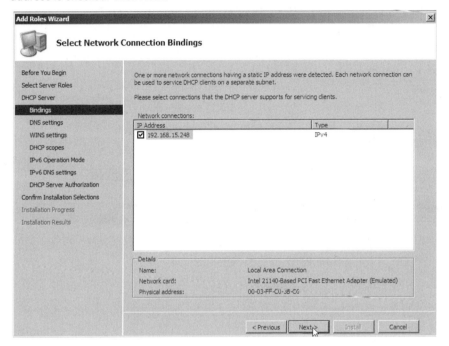

5. On the Specify DNS Server Settings page, make sure your domain name (example: mycompany.com) appears in the Parent Domain field.

6. In the box labeled Preferred DNS Server IP Address, enter the TCP/IP address of your DNS server, and then click Validate. A green Valid check mark will appear. Click Next.

EXERCISE 4.1 *(continued)*

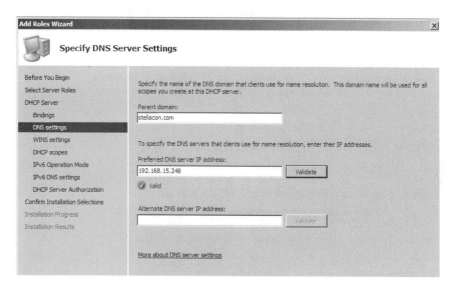

7. On the Specify WINS Server Settings page, click Next.

8. On the Add Or Edit DHCP Scopes page, click the Add button.

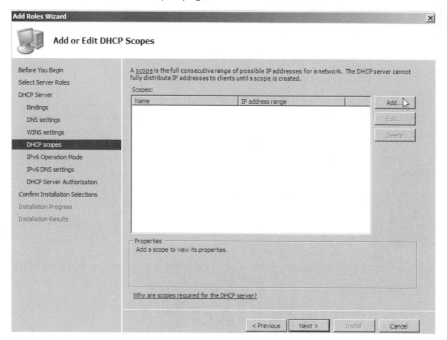

9. In the Add Scope dialog box, enter the following:

    Scope Name: **Test Scope**

    Starting IP Address: **192.168.20.100**

    Ending IP Address: **192.168.20.200**

    Subnet Mask: **255.255.255.0**

    Default Gateway: **192.168.20.1**

    Subnet Type: **Wired (lease duration will be 6 days)**

    Click the Activate This Scope check box, and then click OK.

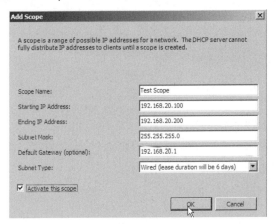

10. On the Select IPv6 DHCP Server Operation Mode page, make sure Yes is checked, and then click Next.

11. On the Specify IPv6 DNS Server Settings page, make sure your domain name (example: mycompany.com) appears in the Parent Domain field. Then click Next.

    Do not put the TCP/IP address of your DNS server in the second box.

12. On the Authorize DHCP Server page, make sure the administrator account is entered in the first box, and click Next.

13. On the Confirm Installation Selections page, confirm all your settings, and click Install.

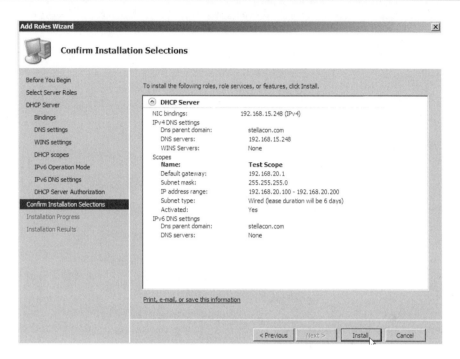

14. On the Installation Results page, click Close once the installation has completed successfully.

15. Close Server Manager.

Introducing the DHCP Snap-In

When you install the DHCP server, the DHCP snap-in is installed, too. You can open it by selecting Start ➢ Administrative Tools ➢ DHCP. Figure 4.1 shows the snap-in.

As you can see, the snap-in follows the standard MMC model. The left pane displays IPv4 and IPv6 sections and which servers are available; you can connect to servers other than the one to which you're already connected. A Server Options folder contains options that are specific to a particular DHCP server. Each server contains subordinate items grouped into folders. Each scope has a folder named after the scope's IP address range. Within each scope, four subordinate views show you interesting things about the scope, such as the following:

- The Address Pool view shows you what the address pool looks like.

FIGURE 4.1   DHCP snap-in

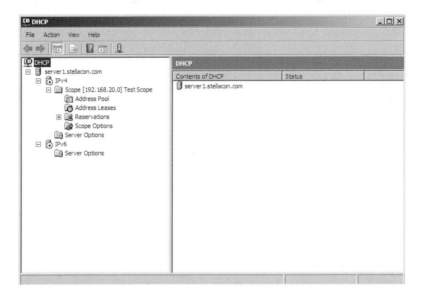

- The Address Leases view shows one entry for each current lease. Each lease shows the computer name to which the lease was issued, the corresponding IP address, and the current lease expiration time.

- The Reservations view shows you which IP addresses are reserved and which devices hold them.

- The Scope Options view lists the set of options you've defined for this scope.

Authorizing DHCP for Active Directory

Authorization creates an Active Directory object representing the new server. It helps keep unauthorized servers off your network. Unauthorized servers can cause two kinds of problems. They may hand out bogus leases, or they may fraudulently deny renewal requests from legitimate clients.

When you install a DHCP server using Windows Server 2008 and Active Directory is present on your network, the server won't be allowed to provide DHCP services to clients until it has been authorized. If you install DHCP on a member server in an Active Directory domain or on a stand-alone server, you'll have to manually authorize the server. When you authorize a server, you're adding its IP address to the Active Directory object that contains the IP addresses of all authorized DHCP servers.

You also have the ability to authorize a DHCP server during the installation of DHCP (this is what you did in Exercise 4.1).

At start time, each DHCP server queries the directory, looking for its IP address on the "authorized" list. If it can't find the list or if it can't find its IP address on the list, the DHCP service fails to start. Instead, it adds a message to the event log, indicating that it couldn't service client requests because the server wasn't authorized.

 DHCP authorization works only with Windows 2000 Server, Server 2003, and Server 2008 DHCP servers. To authorize a DHCP server, you must be logged on as a member of the Administrators or Enterprise Admins groups.

Exercise 4.2 shows you how to unauthorize a DHCP server in an Active Directory domain.

EXERCISE 4.2

Unauthorizing a DHCP Server

1. Select Start ➢ Administrative Tools ➢ DHCP to open the DHCP snap-in.

2. Right-click the server you want to unauthorize, and choose the Unauthorize command.

3. Wait a short time (30–45 seconds) to allow the unauthorization to take place.

4. Right-click the server again. Verify that the Authorize command appears in the pop-up menu; this indicates that the server is now unauthorized.

Exercise 4.3 shows you how to authorize a DHCP server in an Active Directory domain.

EXERCISE 4.3

Authorizing a DHCP Server

1. Select Start ➢ Administrative Tools ➢ DHCP to open the DHCP snap-in.

2. Right-click the server you want to authorize, and choose the Authorize command.

3. Wait a short time (30–45 seconds) to allow the authorization to take place.

4. Right-click the server again. Verify that the Unauthorize command appears in the pop-up menu; this indicates that the server is now authorized.

⊕ **Real World Scenario**

Rogue DHCP Servers

Not allowing a Windows server to provide DHCP services until it is authorized does absolutely nothing to prevent another DHCP server from performing these duties. For example, many routers can perform DHCP services on a network regardless of their authorization state with Active Directory (they don't know or care about Active Directory).

Be aware that the discussion of DHCP authorization covers only Windows and doesn't prevent other DHCP servers in the network from working. Therefore, if you authorize a Windows DHCP server in the network and have conflicting information, be sure to look for rogue devices performing DHCP in the network.

Creating and Managing DHCP Scopes

You can use any number of DHCP servers on a single physical network if you divide the range of addresses you want assigned into multiple scopes. Each scope contains a number of useful pieces of data, but before you can understand them, you need to know some additional terminology.

You can perform the following management tasks on DHCP scopes:

- Create a scope.
- Configure scope properties.
- Configure reservations and exclusions.
- Set scope options.
- Activate and deactivate scopes.
- Create a superscope.
- Create a multicast scope.
- Integrate Dynamic DNS and DHCP.

We will cover each task in the following sections.

Creating a New Scope in IPv4

Like many other things in Windows Server 2008, the process of creating a new scope is driven by a wizard. You will most likely create a scope while installing DHCP, but you may need to create more than one. The overall process is simple, as long as you know beforehand what the wizard is going to ask. If you think about what defines a scope, you'll be well prepared. You need to know the following:

- The IP address range for the scope you want to create
- Which IP addresses, if any, you want to exclude from the address pool
- Which IP addresses, if any, you want to reserve
- Values for the DHCP options you want to set, if any

  This item isn't strictly necessary for creating a scope. However, to create a useful scope, you'll need to have some options to specify for the clients.

To create a scope, under the server name, right-click the IPv4 option in the DHCP snap-in, and use the Action ➤ New Scope command. This starts the New Scope Wizard (see Figure 4.2). We will look at each page of the wizard in the following sections.

FIGURE 4.2 Welcome page of the New Scope Wizard

Setting the Screen Name

The Scope Name page allows you to enter a name and description for your scope. These will be displayed by the DHCP snap-in.

 It's a good idea to pick sensible names for your scopes so that other administrators will be able to figure out what the scope is for. For example, the name DHCP is likely not very helpful, whereas a name like 1st Floor Subnet is more descriptive and can help in troubleshooting.

Defining the IP Address Range

The IP Address Range page (Figure 4.3) is where you enter the start and end IP addresses for your range. The wizard does minimal checking on the addresses you enter and automatically calculates the appropriate subnet mask for the range. You can modify the subnet mask if you know what you're doing.

FIGURE 4.3   IP Address Range page of the New Scope Wizard

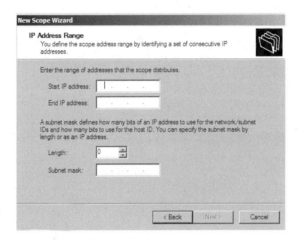

Adding Exclusions

The Add Exclusions page (Figure 4.4) allows you to create exclusion ranges. Exclusions are TCP/IP numbers that are in the pool, but they do not get issued to clients. To exclude one address, put it in the Start IP Address field. To exclude a range, also fill in the End IP Address field.

 Although you can always add exclusions later, it's best to include them when you create the scope so that no excluded addresses are ever passed out to clients.

Setting a Lease Duration

The Lease Duration page (Figure 4.5) allows you to set how long a device gets to use an assigned IP address before it has to renew its lease. The default lease duration is eight days. You may find that a shorter or longer duration makes sense for your network. If your network is highly dynamic, with lots of arrivals, departures, and moving computers, set a shorter lease duration; if it's less active, make it longer.

FIGURE 4.4   Add Exclusions page of the New Scope Wizard

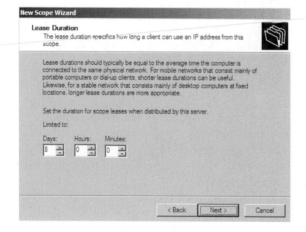

FIGURE 4.5   Lease Duration page of the New Scope Wizard

Remember that renewal attempts begin when approximately half of the lease period is over (give or take a random interval), so don't set them too short.

Configuring Basic DHCP Options

The Configure DHCP Options page (Figure 4.6) allows you to choose whether you want to set up basic DHCP options such as default gateway and DNS settings. The options are described in the following sections. If you choose not to configure options, you can always do so later. However, you should not activate the scope until you've configured the options you want assigned.

FIGURE 4.6 Configure DHCP Options page of the New Scope Wizard

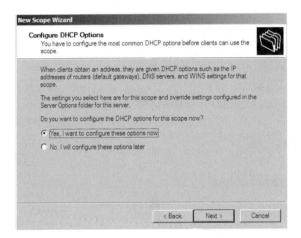

Configuring a Router

The first option configuration page is the Router (Default Gateway) page (Figure 4.7), in which you to enter the IP addresses of one or more routers (more commonly referred to as *default gateways*) that you want to use for outbound traffic. After entering the IP addresses of the routers, use the Up and Down buttons to order the addresses. Clients will use the routers in the order specified when attempting to send outgoing packets.

Providing DNS Settings

On the Domain Name And DNS Servers page (Figure 4.8), you specify the set of DNS servers and the parent domain you want passed down to DHCP clients. Normally, you'll want to specify at least one DNS server by filling in its DNS name or IP address. You can also specify the domain suffix that you want clients to use as the base domain for all connections that aren't fully qualified. For example, if your clients are used to navigating based on server name alone rather than the fully qualified domain name (FQDN) of `server.stellacon.com`, then you'll want to place your domain here.

FIGURE 4.7   Router (Default Gateway) page of the New Scope Wizard

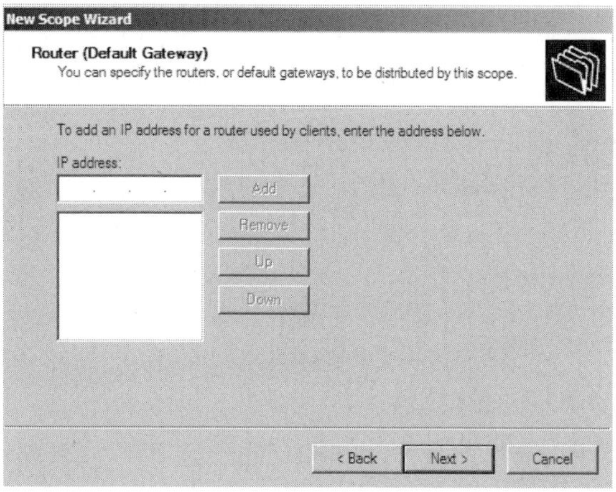

FIGURE 4.8   Domain Name And DNS Servers page of the New Scope Wizard

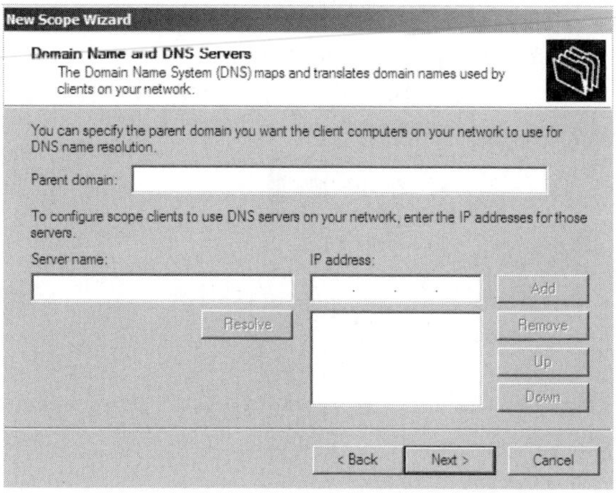

Providing WINS Settings

If you're still using Windows Internet Name Service (WINS) on your network, you can configure DHCP so that it passes WINS server addresses to your Windows clients. (If you want the Windows clients to honor it, you'll also need to define the WINS/NBT Node Type option for the scope.) As on the DNS server page, on the WINS Servers page (Figure 4.9) you can enter the addresses of several servers and move them into the order in which you want clients to try them. You can enter the DNS or NetBIOS name of each server, or you can enter an IP address.

Here are some of the more common options you can set on a DHCP server:

- *003 Router*: Used to provide a list of available routers or default gateways on the same subnet

- *006 DNS Servers*: Used to provide a list of DNS servers

- *015 DNS Domain Name*: Used to provide the DNS suffix

- *028 Broadcast Address*: Used to configure the broadcast address, if different than the default, based on the subnet mask

- *044 WINS/NBNS Servers*: Used to configure the IP addresses of WINS servers

- *046 WINS/NBT Node Type*: Used to configure the preferred NetBIOS name resolution method. There are four settings for node type:

  - *B node (0x1)*: Broadcast for NetBIOS resolution

  - *P node (0x2)*: Peer-to-peer (WINS) server for NetBIOS resolution

  - *M node (0x4)*: Mixed node (does a B node and then a P node)

  - *H node (0x8)*: Hybrid node (does a P node and then a B node)

- *051 Lease*: Used to configure a special lease duration

FIGURE 4.9 WINS Servers page of the New Scope Wizard

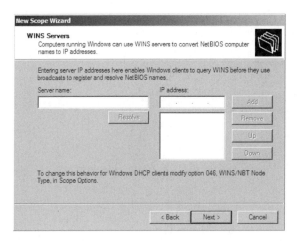

Activating the Scope

The Activate Scope page (Figure 4.10) gives you the option to activate the scope immediately after creating it. By default, the wizard assumes you want the scope activated unless you select the No, I Will Activate This Scope Later radio button, in which case the scope will remain dormant until you manually activate it.

Real World Scenario

Sessions and Routers

Using DHCP through multiple default gateways (or routers) can be both a blessing and a curse. On the one hand, it is useful for clients to be able to reroute their messages if there are problems with the main gateway. In such a scenario, if the main gateway goes down, clients automatically use the next valid gateway as defined in the DHCP settings. For many clients, this transition will be seamless, and they won't even know that "the Internet just went down."

However, programs that rely on session state—such as some web applications—stop working when the client switches to a new gateway. If the local computer gives a false positive—in other words, thinks the default gateway has a problem when it does not—it will switch gateways unnecessarily. This might cause such programs to stop working more frequently than they otherwise would and hurt performance when the network is operating normally. In such cases, it's better not to use multiple gateways.

FIGURE 4.10   Activate Scope page of the New Scope Wizard

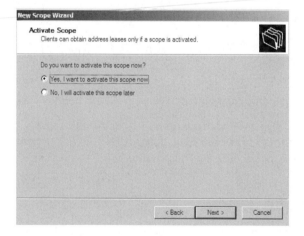

 Be sure to verify that there are no other DHCP servers assigned to the address range you choose!

In Exercise 4.4, you will create a new scope for the 192.168.0 private Class C network. You need to complete Exercise 4.1 before beginning this exercise.

EXERCISE 4.4

Creating a New Scope

1. Open the DHCP snap-in by selecting Start ≻ Administrative Tools ≻ DHCP.

2. Right-click the IPv4 folder, and choose New Scope. The New Scope Wizard appears.

3. Click the Next button on the welcome page.

4. Enter a name and a description for your new scope, and click the Next button.

5. On the IP Address Range page, enter **192.168.0.2** as the start IP address for the scope and **192.168.0.250** as the end IP address. Leave the subnet mask controls alone (though when creating a scope on a production network, you might need to change them). Click the Next button.

6. On the Add Exclusions page, click Next without adding any excluded addresses.

7. On the Lease Duration page, set the lease duration to 3 days, and click the Next button.

8. On the Configure DHCP Options page, click the Next button to indicate that you want to configure default options for this scope.

9. On the Router (Default Gateway) page, enter **192.168.0.1** for the router IP address, and then click the Add button. Once the address is added, click the Next button.

10. On the Domain Name And DNS Servers page, enter the IP address of a DNS server on your network in the IP address field (for example, you might enter **192.168.0.251**), and click the Add button. Click the Next button.

11. On the WINS Servers page, click the Next button to leave the WINS options unset.

12. On the Activate Scope page, if your network is currently using the 192.168.0.x range, select the No, I Will Activate This Scope Later radio button. Click the Next button. When the wizard's summary page appears, click the Finish button to create the scope.

Creating a New Scope in IPv6

Now that you have seen how to create a new scope in IPv4, we'll go through the steps to create a new scope in IPv6.

To create a scope, under the server name, right-click the IPv6 option in the DHCP snap-in, and select the Action ≻ New Scope command. This starts the New Scope Wizard. Just as with creating a scope in IPv4, the welcome page of the wizard tells you that you've launched the New Scope Wizard. We will look at each page of the wizard in the following sections.

Setting the Screen Name

The Scope Name page (Figure 4.11) allows you to enter a name and description for your scope. These will be displayed by the DHCP snap-in.

FIGURE 4.11   IPv6 Scope Name page of the New Scope Wizard

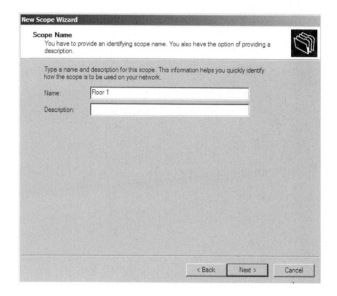

 It's a good idea to pick a sensible name for your scopes so that other admin-istrators will be able to figure out what the scope is for.

Scope Prefix

The Scope Prefix page (Figure 4.12) gets you started creating the IPv6 scope. IPv6 has three types of addresses, which can be categorized by type and scope:

- *Unicast addresses*: One-to-one. A packet from one host is delivered to another host. The following are some examples of IPv6 unicast:

  - The unicast prefix for site-local addresses is FEC0::/48.

  - The unicast prefix for link-local addresses is FE80::/64.

    Figure 4.12 shows the link-local prefix filled in.

- The 6to4 address allows communication between two hosts running both IPv4 and IPv6. The way to calculate the 6to4 address is by combining the global prefix 2002::/16 with the 32 bits of a public IPv4 address of the host. This gives you a 48-bit prefix. 6to4 is described in RFC 3056.

- *Multicast addresses*: One-to-many. A packet from one host is delivered to multiple hosts (but not everyone). The prefix for multicast addresses is FF00::/8

- *Anycast addresses*: A packet from one host is delivered to the nearest of multiple hosts (in terms of routing distance).

FIGURE 4.12   Scope Prefix Page of the New Scope Wizard

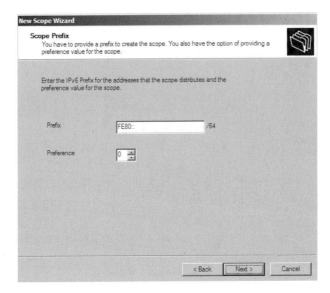

    IPv6 does not use broadcast messages.

Adding Exclusions

As with the IPv4 New Scope Wizard, the Add Exclusions page (Figure 4.13) allows you to create exclusion ranges. Exclusions are TCP/IP numbers that are in the pool but do not get issued to clients. To exclude one address, put it in the Start IPv6 Address field. To exclude a range, also fill in the End IPv6 Address field.

Setting a Lease Duration

The Scope Lease Duration page (Figure 4.14) allows you to set how long a device gets to use an assigned IP address before it has to renew its lease. You can set two different lease durations. The section labeled Non Temporary Address (IANA) is the lease time for your more permanent hosts (such as printers and system towers). The one labeled Temporary Address (IATA) is for hosts that might disconnect at any time, such as laptops.

FIGURE 4.13   Add Exclusions page of the New Scope Wizard

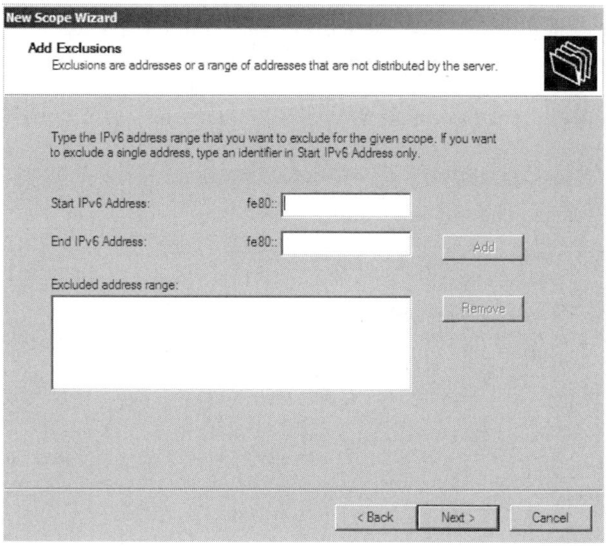

FIGURE 4.14   Scope Lease Duration page of the New Scope Wizard

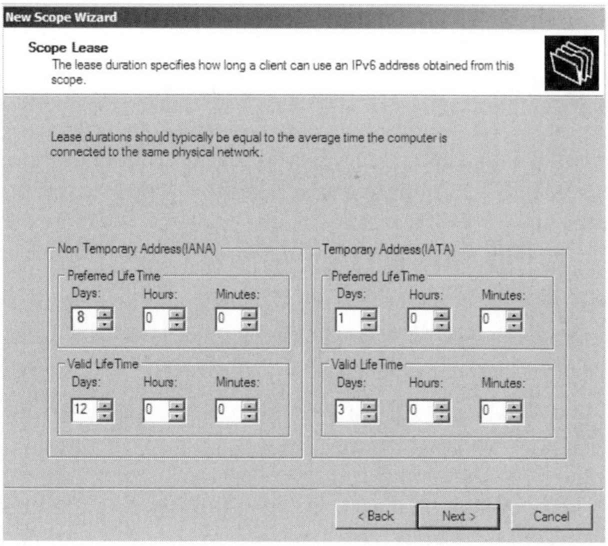

Activating the Scope

The Completing The New Scope Wizard page (Figure 4.15) gives you the option to activate the scope immediately after creating it. By default, the wizard will assume you want the scope activated. If you want to wait on activating the scope, choose No in the Activate Scope Now box.

FIGURE 4.15   Completing The New Scope Wizard page of the New Scope Wizard

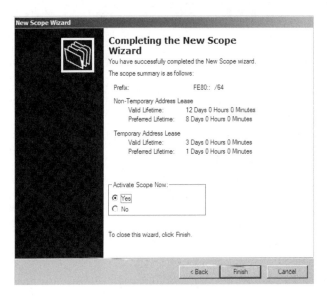

Changing Scope Properties (IPv4 and IPv6)

Each scope has a set of properties associated with it. Except for the set of options assigned by the scope (more about this in the next section), you can find these properties on the General tab of the scope's Properties dialog box (Figure 4.16). Some of these properties, such as the scope name and description, are self-explanatory. Others require a little more explanation:

- The Start IP Address and End IP Address fields allow you to set the range of the scope.
- For IPv4 scopes, the settings in the section Lease Duration For DHCP Clients control how long leases in this scope are valid.

    The IPv6 scope dialog box includes a Lease tab where you set the lease properties.

When you make changes to these properties, they have no effect on existing leases. For example, say you create a scope from 172.30.1.1 to 172.30.1.199. You use that scope for a while and then edit its properties to reduce the range from 172.30.1.1 to 172.30.1.150. If a client has been assigned the address 172.30.1.180—which was part of the scope before you changed it—the client will retain that address until the lease expires but will not be able to renew it.

FIGURE 4.16   General tab of the scope's Properties dialog box for an IPv4 scope

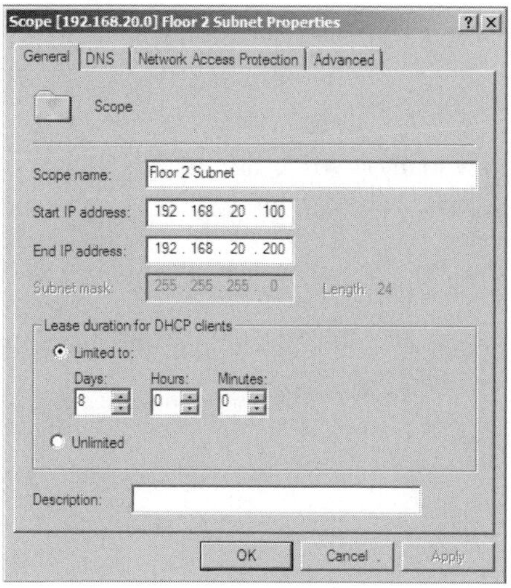

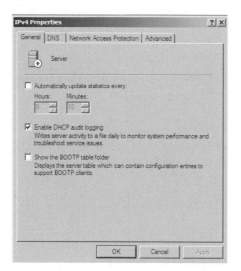

Changing Server Properties

Just as each scope has its own set of properties, so too does the server itself. You access the server properties right-clicking the IPv4 or IPv6 object within the DHCP management console and selecting Properties.

IPv4 Server Properties

Figure 4.17 shows the IPv4 Properties dialog box.

FIGURE 4.17   General tab of the IPv4 Properties dialog box for the server

The IPv4 Properties dialog box has four tabs: General, DNS, Network Access Protection, and Advanced.

The Advanced tab, shown in Figure 4.18, contains the following configuration parameters:

- Audit Log File Path is the location for log files.
- Conflict Detection Attempts specifies how many ICMP echo requests (pings) the server sends for an address it is about to offer. The default is 0.

FIGURE 4.18   The Advanced tab of the IPv4 Properties dialog box for the server

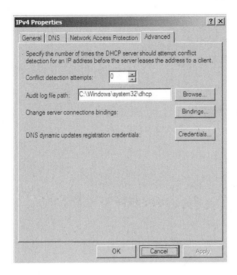

The Network Access Protection (Figure 4.19) tab allows you to set up Network Access Protection (NAP). With NAP, which is a new Windows Server 2008 service, an administrator can perform the following tasks:

- Carry out computer health policy validation.
- Ensure ongoing compliance with health policies.
- Optionally restrict the access of computers that do not meet with the computer health requirements.

IPv6 Server Properties

The IPv6 Properties dialog box for the server has two tabs: General and Advanced. On the General tab (see Figure 4.20), you can configure the following settings:

- Frequency with which statistics are updated
- DHCP auditing

FIGURE 4.19   The Network Access Protection tab of the IPv4 Properties dialog box for the server

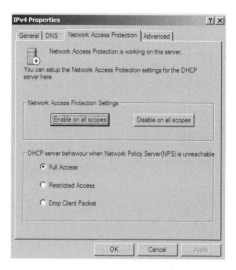

FIGURE 4.20   Server's IPv6 Properties, General tab

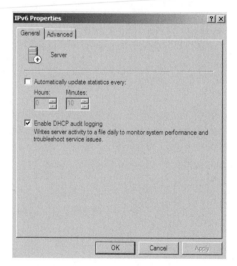

The Advanced tab (see Figure 4.21) allows you to configure the following settings:

- Database path for the audit file path

- Connection bindings

- Registration credentials for dynamic DNS. The registration credential is the user account that DHCP will use to register clients with Active Directory.

FIGURE 4.21   Server's IPv6 Properties, Advanced tab

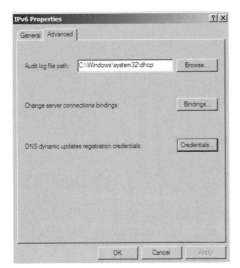

Managing Reservations and Exclusions

After defining the address pool for your scope, the next step is to create reservations and exclusions, which reduce the size of the pool. In the following sections, you will learn how to add and remove exclusions and reservations.

Adding and Removing Exclusions

When you want to exclude an entire range of IP addresses, you need to add that range as an *exclusion*. Ordinarily, you'll want to do this before you enable a scope, because that prevents any of the IP addresses you want excluded from being leased before you have a chance to exclude them. In fact, you can't create an exclusion that includes a leased address—you have to get rid of the lease first.

Adding an Exclusion Range

Here's how to add an exclusion range:

1. Open the DHCP snap-in and find the scope to which you want to add an exclusion (either IPv4 or IPv6).

2. Expand the scope so you can see its Address Pool item for IPv4 or the Exclusion section for IPv6.

3. Right-click Address Pool or Exclusion section, and choose the New Exclusion Range command.

4.   When the Add Exclusion dialog box appears (see Figure 4.22), enter the IP addresses you want to exclude. To exclude a single address, type it in the Start IP Address field. To exclude a range of addresses, also fill in the End IP Address field.

5.   Click the Add button to add the exclusion.

FIGURE 4.22   Add Exclusion dialog boxes for IPv4 and IPv6

IPv4 Add Exclusion dialog box   IPv6 Add Exclusion dialog box

When you add exclusions, they appear in the Address Pool node, which is under the scope for IPv4 and under the Exclusion section of IPv6.

Removing an Exclusion Range

To remove an exclusion, just right-click it, and choose the Delete command. After confirming your command, the snap-in removes the excluded range, and the addresses become immediately available for issuance.

Adding and Removing Reservations

Adding a reservation is simple as long as you have the MAC address of the device for which you want to create a reservation. Because reservations belong to a single scope, you create and remove them within the Reservations node beneath each scope.

Adding a Reservation

To add a reservation, perform the following tasks:

1.   Right-click the scope, and select New Reservation.

This displays the New Reservation dialog box, shown in Figure 4.23.

2.   Enter the IP address and MAC address or ID for the reservation.

To find the MAC address of the local computer, use the `ipconfig` command. To find the MAC address of a remote machine, use the `nbtstat -a` *computername* command.

FIGURE 4.23   New Reservation dialog boxes for IPv4 and IPv6

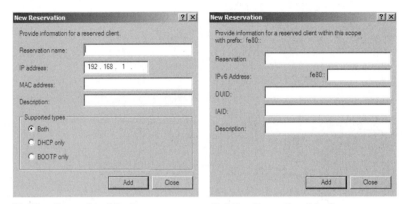

IPv4 New Reservation dialog box   IPv6 New Reservation dialog box

3.   If you want, you can also enter a name and description.

4.   For IPv4, in the Supported Types section, choose whether the reservation will be made by DHCP only, BOOTP only (useful for remote-access devices), or both.

Removing a Reservation

To remove a reservation, right-click it, and select Delete. This removes the reservation but does nothing to the client device.

There's no way to change a reservation once it has been created—if you want to change any of the associated settings, you'll have to delete and re-create the reservation.

Setting Scope Options for IPv4

Once you've installed a server, authorized it in Active Directory, and fixed up the address pool, the next step is to set scope options that you want sent out to clients, such as router (that is, default gateway) and DNS server addresses. You must configure the options you want sent out before you activate a scope. If you don't, clients may register in the scope without getting any options, rendering them virtually useless. Scope options, along with the IP address and subnet mask that you configured earlier in this chapter, complete the standard TCP/IP settings you saw in Chapter 2.

In the following sections, you will learn how to configure and assign scope options on the DHCP server.

Understanding Option Assignment

You can control which DHCP options are doled out to clients in five (slightly overlapping) ways.

Predefined Options

Predefined options are templates that are available in the Server, Scope, or Client Options dialog box.

Server Options

Server options are assigned to all scopes and clients of a particular server. That means if there's some setting you want all clients of a DHCP server to have, no matter what scope they're in, this is where you assign it. Specific options (those that are set at the class, scope, or client level) will override server-level options. That gives you an escape valve; it's a better idea, though, to be careful about which options you assign if your server manages multiple scopes.

Scope Options

If you want a particular option value assigned only to those clients in a certain subnet, you should assign it as a scope option. For example, it's common to specify different routers for different physical subnets; if you have two scopes corresponding to different subnets, each scope would probably have a separate value for the router option.

Class Options

You can assign different options to clients of different types. For example, Windows 2000, XP, Vista, Server 2003, and Server 2008 machines recognize a number of DHCP options that Windows 98, Windows NT, and Mac OS machines ignore, and vice versa. By defining a Windows 2000 or newer class (using the `ipconfig /setclassid` command you saw earlier), you could assign those options only to machines that report themselves as being in that class.

Client Options

If a client is using DHCP reservations, you can assign certain options to that specific client. You attach client options to a particular reservation. Client options override scope, server, and class options. The only way to override a client option is to manually configure the client. The DHCP server manages client options.

 Client options override class options, class options override scope options, and scope options override server options.

Assigning Options

You can use the DHCP snap-in to assign options at the scope, server, reserved address, or class level. The mechanism you use to assign these options is identical; the only difference is where you set the options.

When you create an option assignment, remember that it applies to all the clients in the server or the scope from that point forward. Option assignments aren't retroactive, and they don't migrate from one scope to another.

Creating and Assigning a New Option

To create a new option and have it assigned, follow these steps:

1. Select the scope or server where you want the option assigned.

2. Select the corresponding Options node, and choose Action ➤ Configure Options.

   To set options for a reserved client, right-click its entry in the Reservations node, and select Configure Options.

   You'll then see the Scope Options dialog box (Figure 4.24), which lists all the options you might want to configure.

3. To select an individual option, check the box next to it, and then use the controls in the Data Entry control group to enter the value you want associated with the option.

4. Continue to add options until you've specified all the ones you want attached to the server or scope. Then click OK.

Configuring the DHCP Server for Classes

You saw how to assign classes to individual machines earlier in the chapter. Now you will learn how to configure the DHCP server to recognize your customized classes and configure options for them. In Exercise 4.5, you will create a new user class and configure options for the new class. Before you begin, you should make sure that the computers you want to use in the class have been configured with the `ipconfig /setclassid` command as described in the section "*ipconfig* Lease Options" earlier in this chapter.

FIGURE 4.24   The Scope Options dialog box

EXERCISE 4.5

Configuring User Class Options

1. Open the DHCP snap-in by selecting Start ➢ Administrative Tools ➢ DHCP.

2. Right-click the IPv4 item, and select Define User Classes.

3. Click the Add button in the DHCP User Classes dialog box.

4. In the New Class dialog box, enter a descriptive name for the class in the Display Name field. Enter a class ID in the ID field. (Typically, you will enter the class ID in the ASCII portion of the ID field.) When you are done, click OK.

5. The new class appears in the DHCP User Classes dialog box. Click the Close button to return to the DHCP snap-in.

6. Right-click the Scope Options node, and select Configure Options.

7. Click the Advanced tab. Select the class you defined in step 4 from the User Class pop-up menu.

8. Configure the options you want to set for the class. Click OK when you are done. Notice that the options you configured (and the class they are associated with) appear in the right pane of the DHCP window.

About the Default Routing and Remote Access Predefined User Class

Windows Server 2008 includes a predefined user class called the Default Routing and Remote Access class. This class includes options important to clients connecting to Routing and Remote Access, notably the 051 Lease option.

 Be sure to know that the 051 Lease option is included within this class and that it can be used to assign a shorter lease duration for clients connecting to Routing and Remote Access.

Activating and Deactivating Scopes

When you've completed the steps in Exercise 4.5 and you're ready to unleash your new scope so that it can be used to make client assignments, the final required step is activating the scope. When you activate a scope, you're just telling the server that it's OK to start handing out addresses from that scope's address pool. As soon as you activate a scope, addresses from its pool may be assigned to clients. Of course, this is a necessary precondition to getting any use out of your scope.

If you later want to stop using a scope, you can, but beware because it's a permanent change. When you deactivate a scope, DHCP tells all clients registered with the scope that they need to immediately release their leases and renew them someplace else—the equivalent of a landlord who evicts his tenants when the building is condemned!

 Don't deactivate a scope unless you want clients to stop using it immediately.

Creating a Superscope for IPv4

A superscope allows the DHCP server to provide multiple logical subnet addresses to DHCP clients on a single physical network. You create superscopes with the New Superscope command, which triggers the New Superscope Wizard.

 You can have only one superscope per server.

Creating a Superscope

The following steps take you through the process of creating a superscope:

1. Open the DHCP snap-in by selecting Start ➢ Administrative Tools ➢ DHCP.

2. Follow the instructions in Exercise 4.4 to create two scopes: one for 192.168.0.2 through 192.168.0.127 and one for 192.168.1.12 through 192.168.1.127.

3. Right-click IPv4, and choose the New Superscope command. The New Superscope Wizard appears. Click the Next button.

4. On the Superscope Name page, name your superscope, and click the Next button.

5. The Select Scopes page appears, listing all scopes on the current server. Select the two scopes you created in step 2, and then click the Next button.

6. The wizard's summary page appears; click the Finish button to create your scope.

7. Verify that your new superscope appears in the DHCP snap-in.

Deleting a Superscope

You can delete a superscope by right-clicking it and choosing the Delete command. A superscope is just an administrative convenience, so you can safely delete one at any time—it doesn't affect the "real" scopes that make up the superscope.

Adding a Scope to a Superscope

To add a scope to an existing superscope, find the scope you want to add, right-click it, and choose Action ➢ Add To Superscope. A dialog box appears, listing all the superscopes known to this server. Pick the one you want the current scope appended to, and click the OK button.

Removing a Scope from a Superscope

To remove a scope from a superscope, open the superscope, and right-click the target scope. The pop-up menu provides a Remove From Superscope command that will do the deed.

Activating and Deactivating Superscopes

Just as with regular scopes, you can activate and deactivate superscopes. The same restrictions and guidelines apply. You must activate a superscope before it can be used, and you must not deactivate it until you want all your clients to lose their existing leases and be forced to request new ones.

To activate or deactivate a superscope, right-click the superscope name, and select Activate or Deactivate, respectively, from the pop-up menu.

Creating IPv4 Multicast Scopes

Multicasting occurs when one machine communicates to a network of subscribed computers rather than specifically addressing each computer on the destination network. It's much more efficient to *multicast* a video or audio stream to multiple destinations than it is to unicast it to the same number of clients, and the increased demand for multicast-friendly network hardware has resulted in some head scratching about how to automate the multicast configuration.

In the following sections, you will learn about MADCAP, the protocol that controls multicasting, and about how to build and configure a multicast scope.

Understanding the Multicast Address Dynamic Client Allocation Protocol

DHCP is usually used to assign IP configuration information for *unicast* (or one-to-one) network communications. With multicast, there's a separate type of address space assigned from 224.0.0.0 through 239.255.255.255. Addresses in this space are known as *Class D* addresses or simply *multicast* addresses. Clients can participate in a multicast just by knowing (and using) the multicast address for the content they want to receive. However, multicast clients also need to have an ordinary IP address.

How do clients know what address to use? Ordinary DHCP won't help because it's designed to assign IP addresses and option information to one client at a time. Realizing this, the Internet Engineering Task Force (IETF) defined a new protocol: Multicast Address Dynamic Client Allocation Protocol (MADCAP). MADCAP provides an analog to DHCP but for multicast use. A MADCAP server issues leases for multicast addresses only. MADCAP clients can request a multicast lease when they want to participate in a multicast.

DHCP and MADCAP have some important differences. First, you have to realize that the two are totally separate. A single server can be a DHCP server, a MADCAP server, or both; no implied or actual relation exists between the two. Likewise, clients can use DHCP and/or MADCAP at the same time—the only requirement is that every MADCAP client has to get a unicast IP address from somewhere.

Remember that DHCP can assign options as part of the lease process, but MADCAP cannot. The only thing MADCAP does is dynamically assign multicast addresses.

Building Multicast Scopes

Most of the steps you go through when creating a multicast scope are identical to those required for an ordinary unicast scope. Exercise 4.6 highlights the differences.

EXERCISE 4.6

Creating a New Multicast Scope

1. Open the DHCP snap-in by selecting Start ≻ Administrative Tools ≻ DHCP.

2. Right-click IPv4, and choose New Multicast Scope. The New Multicast Scope Wizard appears. Click the Next button on the welcome page.

3. In the Multicast Scope Name page, name your multicast scope (and add a description if you'd like). Click the Next button.

4. The IP Address Range page appears. Enter a start IP address of **224.0.0.0** and an end IP address of **224.255.0.0**. Adjust the TTL to 1 to make sure that no multicast packets escape your local network segment. Click the Next button when you're done.

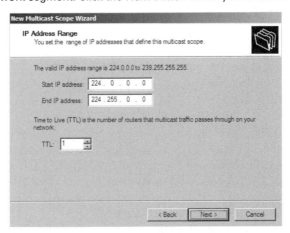

5. The Add Exclusions page appears; click its Next button.

6. The Lease Duration page appears. Since multicast addresses are used for video and audio, you'd ordinarily leave multicast scope assignments in place somewhat longer than you would with a regular unicast scope, so the default lease length is 30 days (instead of 8 days for a unicast scope). Click the Next button.

7. The wizard asks you whether you want to activate the scope now. Click the No radio button and then the Next button.

8. The wizard's summary page appears; click the Finish button to create your scope.

9. Verify that your new multicast scope appears in the DHCP snap-in.

Setting Multicast Scope Properties

Once you create a multicast scope, you can adjust its properties by right-clicking the scope name and selecting Properties.

The Multicast Scope Properties dialog box has two tabs. The General tab (Figure 4.25) allows you to change the scope's name, its start and end address, its Time to Live (TTL) value, its lease duration, and its description—in essence, all the settings you provided when you created it in the first place.

FIGURE 4.25   General tab of the Multicast Scope Properties dialog box

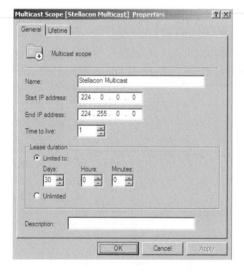

The Lifetime tab (see Figure 4.26) allows you to limit how long your multicast scope will be active. By default, a newly created multicast scope will live forever, but if you're creating a scope to provide MADCAP assignments for a single event (or a set of events of limited duration), you can specify an expiration time for the scope. When that time is reached, the scope disappears from the server, but not before making all its clients give up their multicast address leases. This is a nice way to make sure the lease cleans up after itself when you're done with it.

FIGURE 4.26   Lifetime tab of the Multicast Scope Properties dialog box

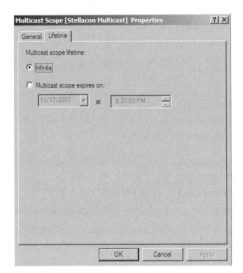

Integrating Dynamic DNS and IPv4 DHCP

DHCP integration with Dynamic DNS is a simple concept but powerful in action. By setting up this integration, you can pass addresses to DHCP clients while still maintaining the integrity of your DNS services.

The DNS server can be updated in two ways. One way is for the DHCP client to tell the DNS server what its address is. Another is for the DHCP server to tell the DNS server when it registers a new client.

However, neither of these updates will take place unless you configure the DNS server to use Dynamic DNS. You can make this change in two ways:

- If you change it at the scope level, it will apply only to the scope.

- If you change it at the server level, it will apply to all scopes and superscopes served by the server.

Which of these options you choose depends on how widely you want to support Dynamic DNS; most of the sites we visit have enabled DNS updates at the server level.

 You also have to instruct the DNS server to accept Dynamic DNS updates. For more on how to do so, see Chapter 3.

To update the settings at either the server or scope level, you need to open the scope or server properties by right-clicking the appropriate object and choosing Properties. The DNS tab of the Properties dialog box (Figure 4.27) includes the following options:

Enable DNS Dynamic Updates According To The Settings Below   This check box controls whether this DHCP server will attempt to register lease information with a DNS server. It must be checked to enable Dynamic DNS.

> **Dynamically Update DNS A And PTR Records Only If Requested By The DHCP Clients**
> This radio button (which is on by default) tells the DHCP server to register the update only if the DHCP client asks for DNS registration. When this button is active, DHCP clients that aren't hip to DDNS won't have their DNS records updated. However, Windows 2000, XP, Vista, Server 2003, and Server 2008 DHCP clients are smart enough to ask for the updates.

> **Always Dynamically Update DNS A And PTR Records**   This radio button forces the DHCP server to register any client to which it issues a lease. This setting may add DNS registrations for DHCP-enabled devices that don't really need them, such as print servers; however, it allows other clients (such as Mac OS, Windows NT, and Linux machines) to have their DNS information automatically updated.

Discard A And PTR Records When Lease Is Deleted   This check box has a long name but a simple function. When a DHCP lease expires, what should happen to the DNS registration? Obviously, it would be nice if the DNS record associated with a lease vanished when the lease expired; when this check box is checked (as it is by default), that's exactly what happens. If you uncheck this box, your DNS will contain entries for expired leases that are no longer valid; when a particular IP address is reissued on a new lease, the DNS will be updated, but in between leases you'll have incorrect data in your DNS—something that's always best to avoid.

FIGURE 4.27   DNS tab of the scope's IPv4 Properties dialog box

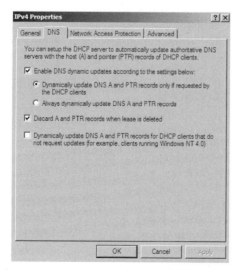

Dynamically Update DNS A And PTR Records For DHCP Clients That Do Not Request Updates   This check box lets you handle these older clients graciously by making the updates using a separate mechanism.

In Exercise 4.7, you will enable a scope to participate in Dynamic DNS updates.

EXERCISE 4.7   o

Enabling DHCP-DNS Integration

1. Open the DHCP snap-in by selecting Start ≻ Administrative Tools ≻ DHCP.

2. Right-click the IPv4 item, and select Properties.

3. The Server Properties dialog box appears. Click the DNS tab.

4. Verify that the check box labeled Enable DNS Dynamic Updates According To The Settings Below is checked, and verify that the radio button labeled Dynamically Update DNS A And PTR Records Only If Requested By The DHCP Clients is selected.

5. Verify that the check box labeled Discard A And PTR Records When Lease Is Deleted is checked. If not, then check it.

6. Click the OK button to apply your changes and close the Server Properties dialog box.

Using Multiple DHCP Servers

DHCP can become a single point of failure within a network if there is only one DHCP server. If that server becomes unavailable, clients will not be able to obtain new leases or renew existing leases. For this reason, it is recommended that you have more than one DHCP server in the network. However, more than one DHCP server can create problems if they both are configured to use the same scope or set of addresses. Microsoft recommends the 80/20 rule for redundancy of DHCP services in a network.

Implementing the 80/20 rule calls for one DHCP server to make approximately 80 percent of the addresses for a given subnet available through DHCP while another server makes the remaining 20 percent of the addresses available. For example, with a /24 network of 254 addresses, say 192.168.1.1 to 192.168.1.254, you might have Server 1 offer 192.168.1.10 to 192.168.1.210 while Server 2 offers 192.168.1.211 to 192.168.254.

Windows Server 2008 Hyper-V

As we discussed in Chapter 3, Windows Server 2008 has a role-based utility called Hyper-V. Hyper-V is a hypervisor-based virtualization feature. (A *hypervisor* is a virtual machine monitor.) It includes all the necessary features to support machine virtualization. Using machine virtualization allows a company to reduce costs, improve server utilization, and create a more dynamic IT infrastructure.

Server Core Installation

In Chapter 3 we discussed how DNS is a feature of *Server Core*, a low-maintenance, limited-functionality Windows Server 2008 environment. Another function that Server Core can provide is DHCP.

Because Server Core has limited functionality, it actually provides some strong benefits, including reduced servicing requirements, reduced management requirements, reduced attack surface, and reduced disk space usage.

Besides DHCP, Server Core functionality includes the following:

- Active Directory (AD)
- Active Directory Lightweight Directory Services (AD LDS)
- DNS server
- File server
- Media services
- Print server

Monitoring and Troubleshooting DHCP

DHCP doesn't require a lot of ongoing care. However, it's useful to know how to monitor and troubleshoot it for those rare occasions when something does go wrong. In the following sections, you will see how to monitor DHCP leases, log DHCP activity, work with the DHCP server log files and database files, reconcile DHCP scopes, and figure out how to manage multiple DHCP servers and scopes.

Monitoring DHCP Leases

You monitor which DHCP leases have been assigned using the Address Leases view associated with a particular scope. When you open the scope and click the Address Leases item under the scope name, you'll see an easy-to-read list of all the leases currently in force for that scope. The list includes the following information:

- Client IP address
- Client DNS name
- Lease duration
- Client's unique DHCP ID (if there is one)

If you want to remove a client lease, you can do so by right-clicking it in the Address Leases view and selecting Delete. This cancels and removes the lease. Usually, it's better to let leases expire rather than manually canceling them, but sometimes circumstances dictate otherwise.

In Exercise 4.8, you will create a tab-delimited text file containing information about all leases in a scope—the same data that you see in the Address Leases view. You can use this file for analysis or record keeping long after leases have expired or been renewed. Before performing this exercise, make sure you have at least one or two leases in use.

EXERCISE 4.8

Inspecting Leases

1. Open the DHCP snap-in by selecting Start ➢ Administrative Tools ➢ DHCP.

2. Expand IPv4, and click the target scope in the MMC.

3. Right-click the target scope, and click Export List on the pop-up menu.

4. When the Save As dialog box appears, select a location for the list file. Type a meaningful name in the Filename field, and click the Save button.

5. In WordPad, Word, Excel, or any other tool that honors Tab settings, open the file you just created. Notice that the contents of the file mirror what you saw in the DHCP snap-in. If the lease list is empty, you will see only a header row in the text file.

Logging DHCP Activity

In the Windows Server 2008 family, DHCP server log files use audit logging. Log files don't require added monitoring or administering to manage their growth or to conserve disk resources.

By default, the DHCP service automatically logs all DHCP activity to a daily log file in the *systemroot*/System32/DHCP folder. The log file's name is DhcpSrvLog-*Day* where *Day* is the three-letter abbreviation for the day of the week.

The following sections outline the format of these log files and describe how you can use them to gather more information about DHCP server service operations on the network.

DHCP Server Log File Format

DHCP server logs are comma-delimited text files. Each log entry represents a single line of text. The following fields appear in a log file entry:

ID, Date, Time, Description, IP Address, Host Name, MAC Address

Table 4.1 describes these fields in detail.

TABLE 4.1   DHCP Log File Fields

Field	Description
ID	A DHCP server event ID code
Date	The date on which this entry was logged on the DHCP server
Time	The time at which this entry was logged on the DHCP server
Description	The type of DHCP server event that occurred
IP Address	The IP address of the DHCP client
Host Name	The hostname of the DHCP client
MAC Address	The media access control address used by the network adapter hardware of the client

Common DHCP Server Log Event Codes

DHCP server audit log files use reserved event ID codes to provide information about the type of server event or activity logged. Table 4.2 describes these event ID codes.

TABLE 4.2   Common DHCP Log File Event IDs

Event ID	Description
00	The log was started.
01	The log was stopped.
02	The log was temporarily paused because of low disk space.
10	A new IP address was leased to a client.
11	A lease was renewed by a client.
12	A lease was released by a client.
13	An IP address was found in use on the network.
14	A lease request could not be satisfied because the address pool of the scope was exhausted.
15	A lease was denied.
16	A lease was deleted.
17	A lease was expired.
20	A BOOTP address was leased to a client.
50 and greater	Codes greater than 50 are used in relation to detecting rogue DHCP servers.

When the DHCP server is configured to perform DNS dynamic updates on behalf of DHCP clients, you can use the DHCP audit logs to monitor update requests by the DHCP server to the DNS server, DNS record update successes, and DNS record update failures. Table 4.3 lists the event IDs that are used for DNS dynamic update events.

TABLE 4.3   DNS Dynamic Update Events

ID number	DHCP Event
30	DNS dynamic update request
31	DNS dynamic update failed
32	DNS dynamic update successful

The IP address of the DHCP client computer is included in the DHCP audit log, providing the ability to track the source in the event of a denial-of-service attack.

The following is a sample output of a DHCP log file:

```
ID,Date,Time,Description,IP Address,Host Name,MAC Address
00,04/10/03,12:36:22,Started,,,,
64,04/10/03,12:36:22,No static IP address bound to DHCP server,,,,
56,04/10/03,12:38:59,Authorization failure, stopped servicing,,sybex.com,,
24,04/10/03,13:36:25,Database Cleanup Begin,,,,
25,04/10/03,13:36:25,0 leases expired and 0 leases deleted,,,,
25,04/10/03,13:36:25,0 leases expired and 0 leases deleted,,,,
24,04/10/03,14:36:28,Database Cleanup Begin,,,,
25,04/10/03,14:36:28,0 leases expired and 0 leases deleted,,,,
25,04/10/03,14:36:28,0 leases expired and 0 leases deleted,,,,
55,04/10/03,14:44:49,Authorized(servicing),,sybex.com,,
```

The messages show that the DHCP service failed to start at first because the server didn't have a static IP address. This made it impossible to authorize the services, as shown in the next line. After a few database cleanup logs, DHCP was authorized, probably because an administrator assigned a correct static IP address to the server and manually authorized DHCP.

Examining DHCP Activity in the Event Viewer

DHCP activity is also recorded in the system log, which you can see using the Event Viewer utility, located in the Administrative Tools folder. The Event Viewer logs most of the same events as the DHCP log.

To quickly look up DHCP events, click the System section, and sort the entries by the Source field. Scroll down until you see DHCP entries.

Working with the DHCP Database Files

DHCP uses a set of database files to maintain its knowledge of scopes, superscopes, and client leases. These files, which live in the *systemroot*\System32\DHCP folder, are always open when the DHCP service is running.

 You shouldn't modify or alter the DHCP database files when the service is running.

The primary database file is dhcp.mdb—it has all the scope data in it. The following files are also part of the DHCP database:

-   Dhcp.tmp is a backup copy of the database file created during reindexing of the database. You normally won't see this file, but if the service fails during reindexing, it may not remove the file when it should.

- J50.log (plus a number of files named J50xxxxx.log, where *xxxxx* stands for 00001, 00002, 00003, and so on) is a log file that stores changes before they're written to the database. The DHCP database engine can recover some changes from these files when it restarts.
- J50.chk is a checkpoint file that tells the DHCP engine which log files it still needs to recover.

In the following sections, you will see how to manipulate the DHCP database files.

Removing the Database Files

If you're convinced that your database is corrupt because the lease information you see doesn't match what's on the network, the easiest repair mechanism is to remove the database files and start over with an empty database.

   If you think the database is corrupt because the DHCP service fails at start-up, you should check the event log.

To start over, follow these steps:

1. Stop the DHCP service by typing **net stop dhcpserver** at the command prompt
2. Remove all the files from the *systemroot*\system32\DHCP folder.
3. Restart the service.
4. Reconcile the scope (as described in the section "Reconciling IPv4 DHCP Scopes" later in this chapter) to rebuild the database contents.

Changing the Database Backup Interval

By default, the DHCP service backs up its databases every 60 minutes. You can adjust this setting by editing the Backup Interval value under HKEY_LOCAL_MACHINE\SYSTEM\ CurrentControlSet\Services\DHCPServer\Parameters. This allows you to make backups either more frequently (if your database changes a lot or if you seem to have ongoing corruption problems) or less often (if everything seems to be on an even keel).

Moving the DHCP Database Files

You may find that you need to dismantle or change the role of your DHCP server and offload the DHCP functions to another computer. Rather than spend the time re-creating the DHCP database on the new machine by hand, you can copy the database files and use them directly. This is especially helpful if you have a complicated DHCP database with lots of reservations and option assignments.

By copying the files, you also minimize the amount of human error that could be introduced by reentering the information by hand.

Incorrectly editing the registry can render Windows completely unusable. Always have a backup available and use caution when working with the registry.

Exercise 4.9 shows how to move the DHCP database from one Windows 2000, Windows 2003, or Server 2008 machine to another.

EXERCISE 4.9

Moving the DHCP Database Between Servers

1. Stop the DHCP service on the source computer by typing **net stop dhcpserver** at the command prompt.

2. Copy the *systemroot*\System32\DHCP folder on the source server to a temporary folder that is accessible from the target server.

3. Run regedit.exe, and view the HKEY_LOCAL_MACHINE\SOFTWARE\Microsoft\DhcpServer\ Configuration Registry key. Highlight the Configuration key, and select Registry ≻ Save Key. Save the key and note the filename that you used.

4. Install DHCP on the target server, and then stop the service by typing **net stop dhcpserver** at the command prompt.

5. Rename the System.mdb file in the temporary folder to System.src.

6. Delete all the file and subfolders in the *systemroot*\System32\DHCP folder on the target computer. Copy the temporary folder on the source computer to the new *systemroot*\ System32\DHCP folder on the target computer.

7. Use regedit to find the HKEY_LOCAL_MACHINE\SOFTWARE\Microsoft\DhcpServer\ Configuration key on the target computer. Highlight the key, and select Registry ≻ Restore. Select the file that you saved in step 3, and click Yes to overwrite the current settings.

8. Start the DHCP service on the target computer by typing **net start dhcpserver** at the command prompt, and choose Reconcile All Scopes in the DHCP administrative tool (more on this in the next section).

9. If the target computer is part of a Windows 2000, Windows Server 2003, or Windows Server 2008 domain, then it must be authorized. (See "Authorizing DHCP for Active Directory" earlier in this chapter.)

If you need to transfer the DHCP database from a Windows NT 4 server, you should copy the Edb500.dl_file from the Windows 2000, Server 2003, or Server 2008 CD and expand it to the System32 folder before proceeding. Also note that you will receive an error message after you start the target DHCP server service. This is normal.

Reconciling IPv4 DHCP Scopes

As time passes, you may experience what we call *DHCP drift*, which means the contents of your DHCP database no longer reflect accurately what's on your network. To fix this problem, you can reconcile the database. You can also reconcile scopes to recover from a corrupt DHCP database.

Although Microsoft doesn't make any prominent mention of this fact in the DHCP documentation, the DHCP server actually records lease information in two places: the DHCP database and the server's registry. When you reconcile a scope, the DHCP server will cross-check the database contents with the contents of the registry, reporting (and fixing) any inconsistencies it finds.

Reconciling a Single Scope

To reconcile, you first remove the database files and then reconcile the server's scopes.

To reconcile a single scope, follow these steps:

1. Open the DHCP snap-in by selecting Start ➤ Administrative Tools ➤ DHCP.

2. Expand IPv4 in the MMC until you see the target scope.

3. Right-click the target scope, and choose Reconcile.

4. The Reconcile dialog box appears, but it's empty, as shown in Figure 4.28. To start the reconciliation, click the Verify button.

5. If the database is consistent, you'll see a dialog box telling you so. If there are any inconsistencies, the dialog box will list them and allow you to repair them.

FIGURE 4.28 The Reconcile dialog box

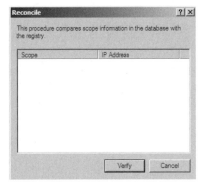

Reconciling All Scopes

You can use a similar procedure to reconcile all scopes on a server:

1. Open the DHCP snap-in by selecting Start ➢ Administrative Tools ➢ DHCP.

2. Right-click IPv4 in the MMC, and choose Reconcile All Scopes.

3. Click the Verify button.

Recovering a Broken DHCP Server

The preferred way to recover a broken DHCP server is as follows:

1. Remove the database files. (See "Removing the Database Files" earlier in this chapter.)

2. Reconcile all scopes on the server to rebuild the database. (See the previous section, "Reconciling All Scopes.")

Correcting Client Problems

Problems with DHCP configurations can show up on the client side. These problems might include the following:

- The client fails to obtain an IP address.

- There are address conflicts.

- The client obtains an address from the wrong scope.

When problems are encountered with the client's IP network settings, you can use the Repair button to perform a variety of actions in an attempt to reconfigure the network settings to a valid state.

To use the Repair button, right-click a connection, and choose Status. A Connection Status dialog box appears, and the Repair button is on the Support tab, as shown in Figure 4.29.

When clicked, the Repair button performs a series of specific actions:

- If the network connection is configured as a DHCP client, the current settings are released, and a DHCPREQUEST message is broadcast in an attempt to obtain new IP settings. This is the functional equivalent to performing an `ipconfig /release` and `ipconfig /renew`, though there is technically not an exact equivalent to what the repair process does.

- The ARP cache is flushed, as with the `arp -d *` command.

- The NetBIOS cache is flushed, as if the `nbtstat -R` command was run.

- The DNS cache is flushed, as if `ipconfig /flushdns` was entered from the command line.

- The client's NetBIOS name and IP address are reregistered with the WINS server, as if `nbtstat -RR` was entered.

- The client is reregistered with DNS as if `ipconfig /registerdns` was entered from the command line.

FIGURE 4.29 Use the Repair button to try to correct network settings.

Summary

This chapter covered the DHCP lease process as it relates to TCP/IP configuration information for clients. The following stages were covered: IP discovery, IP lease offer, IP lease selection, and IP lease acknowledgment. We covered how to install and configure the DHCP server on Windows Server 2008 as well as how to create and manage DHCP scopes and scope options. We also discussed the authorization of DHCP servers within Active Directory and scopes for IPv4 and IPv6 and showed how to create them. We cover superscopes as well as managing client leases with the options therein. Finally, we showed how to monitor and troubleshoot DHCP.

Exam Essentials

Understand the four stages of the DHCP process. The first phase of the DHCP process is the discovery stage. In the second phase, any DHCP server that received the discover message broadcast and that has valid address information to offer responds with an offer message. Once the client has received at least one offer, the client machine selects an offer from those it received. Once the chosen DHCP server receives the acceptance message from the client, it marks the selected IP address as leased and then sends an acknowledgment message back to the client.

Know how to install and authorize a DHCP server.   You install the DHCP service using the Add/Remove Windows Components Wizard. You authorize the DHCP server using the DHCP snap-in. When you authorize a server, you're actually adding its IP address to the Active Directory object that contains a list of the IP addresses of all authorized DHCP servers.

Know how to create a DHCP scope.   You use the New Scope Wizard to create a new scope for both IPv4 and IPv6. Before you start, you'll need to know what the IP address range is for the scope you want to create; which IP addresses, if any, you want to exclude from the address pool; which IP addresses, if any, you want to reserve; and the values for the DHCP options you want to set, if any.

Understand how relay agents help with multiple physical network segments.   A question about relay agents on the exam may appear to be a DHCP-related question. Relay agents assist DHCP message propagation across network or router boundaries where such messages ordinarily wouldn't pass.

Understand the difference between exclusions and reservations.   When you want to exclude an entire range of IP addresses, you need to add that range as an exclusion. Any IP addresses within the range for which you want a permanent DHCP lease are known as reservations. Remember that exclusions are TCP/IP numbers in a pool that do not get issued and reservations are numbers in a TCP/IP pool that get issued only to the same client each time.

Understand what a IPv4 superscope is used for.   A superscope allows the DHCP server to provide multiple logical subnet addresses to DHCP clients on a single physical network.

Understand how to integrate IPv4 Dynamic DNS with DHCP.   By setting up Dynamic DNS and DHCP integration, you can pass out addresses to DHCP clients and still maintain the integrity (and utility) of your DNS services. You can apply integration at either the scope level or the server level.

Understand how to troubleshoot DHCP problems.   If one or more client machines that obtain their addresses dynamically revert to APIPA, that's usually the first sign you have a problem. You should make sure the DHCP server is activated and authorized in Active Directory. You can check the DHCP log files and examine all past DHCP activity. You can solve lease-related problems by examining lease information in the Address Leases item under the scope name. When lease information on the network doesn't match lease information on the DHCP server, it's a sure sign that the database is corrupt and needs to be reset. When you reconcile a scope, the DHCP server will cross-check the database contents with the contents of the registry, reporting (and fixing) any inconsistencies it finds. You can also reconcile scopes to recover from a corrupt DHCP database.

Review Questions

1. You are in the process of upgrading your network to Windows XP and Server 2008, and during the process, you are including DHCP to help manage the IP addressing. You have created the scope with your 10.0.0.0/16 private address range. You now have 50 Windows Professional workstations completed. You still have 100 Windows 95 workstations to migrate to XP. Everything went smoothly during the migration of the Windows XP Professional workstations and has worked properly for a month. When you arrived at the office this morning, however, there was havoc everywhere. You were told that the Windows 95 workstations can no longer connect to the Windows Server 2008 computers; in addition, the XP workstations cannot access the servers, but they can communicate peer to peer. When you look at one of the Windows XP workstations, you notice that the address is 169.254.0.27. What is the next step you should take to resolve this problem?

   A. Install the DHCP relay agent on a Windows 2008 Server.

   B. Attempt to ping the DHCP server from a client with a valid IP address.

   C. Enable the conflict-resolution protocol on the DHCP server.

   D. Enable the APIPA protocol on the Windows 95 clients.

   E. Enable the APIPA protocol on the Windows 2008 and XP clients.

2. You are the administrator of a network in a single location. The network has grown dramatically. You have a router that you want to use to break the network into three subnets in order to control the overall bandwidth utilization. You also want to avoid the amount of work entailed in changing the static IP configurations if you make changes again in the future. For that reason, you are going to implement DHCP to manage the IP addresses centrally. What should you ensure before you start implementing your plan? (Choose all that apply.)

   A. Make sure you have identified a Windows 2008 Server computer on each subnet you will install the DHCP services on.

   B. Make sure your router supports BOOTP.

   C. If your router supports BOOTP, make sure you install a DHCP server on each subnet.

   D. If your router supports BOOTP, make sure you install a DHCP relay agent on each subnet.

   E. If your router does not support BOOTP, make sure you install a DHCP relay agent on each subnet.

3. You administer a network that assigns IP addresses via DHCP. You want to make sure that one of the clients always receives the same IP address from the DHCP server. You create an exclusion for that address, but you find that the computer isn't being properly configured at bootup. What's the problem?

   A. You excluded the wrong IP address.

   B. You need to make a reservation for the client that ties the IP address to the computer's MAC address. Delete the exclusion.

   C. You need to create a superscope for the address.

   D. You must configure the client manually. You cannot assign the address via the DHCP server.

4. Your DHCP server crashed in the middle of the day. You rebooted the server and got it running within five minutes, and nobody but you seemed to notice that it had gone down at all. What additional steps must you take?

    A. None. If there were no lease renewal requests during the five-minute period in which the DHCP server was down, none of the clients will ever know that it went down.

    B. You need to renew all the leases manually.

    C. None. The DHCP server automatically assigned new addresses to all the clients on the network transparently.

    D. You must reboot all the client machines.

5. Your employer, the Huggy Buggy Bear Company, has used networking for years, starting with LAN Manager in the early 1990s. You migrated to Windows NT as an early adopter, and recently you also migrated to Windows Vista and 2008 Server. You are using DHCP on your newly upgraded network, and you still have 100 Windows NT workstations to migrate before you're finished. You have added a new DNS server to the network and modified the scope on the DHCP server to reflect the new addition. You know the command for the Windows NT machines, but what command would you use to verify the IP configuration on the Windows Vista machines?

    A. `w2kipcfg /all`

    B. `ipconfig /all`

    C. `dhcpcfg /all`

    D. `tcpcfg /all`

    E. `winipcfg /all`

6. You have just finished migrating your workstations to Windows XP Professional. Along with this migration, you changed all your static IP addresses to DHCP. Four subnets are connected by a single router, which supports BOOTP. The DHCP server has been installed on subnet 1, and it's functioning properly in delivering addresses. When you bring up the clients on subnet 3, the clients boot properly and can communicate with each other, but they cannot communicate with devices on the other subnets. When you run `ipconfig /all`, you discover that the computers on subnets 2, 3, and 4 are in the 169.254.*x*.*y* address block, which is not the correct network address for any of the subnets. What is the likely cause of this outcome?

    A. The DHCP server evaluated the scope for subnet 3, found it invalid, and substituted the default subnet information for the machines in that subnet.

    B. The DHCP discover request isn't reaching the DHCP server on subnet 1, and the clients are configuring themselves with APIPA addresses.

    C. DHCP servers can support only three subnets, and an additional DHCP server needs to be added to the network.

    D. One of the users has brought another DHCP server online, and it's conflicting with the administrator's DHCP server.

7. You are going to modify the IP configuration on your network to take advantage of DHCP. This will be new to your staff, and you need to explain how DHCP works so that they'll be able to troubleshoot problems if they arise. You particularly want your staff to understand how a client obtains an address from the DHCP server. What steps that occur in the initial DHCP lease process do you need to explain to your staff? (Choose all that apply.)

   A. DHCP lease search

   B. DHCP lease offer

   C. DHCP lease acknowledgment

   D. DHCP lease announce

   E. DHCP lease request

   F. DHCP discovery

   G. DHCP lease selection

   H. DHCP selection

8. You assign two DNS server addresses as part of the options for a scope. Later you find a client workstation that isn't using those addresses. What's the most likely cause?

   A. The client didn't get the option information as part of its lease.

   B. The client has been manually configured with a different set of DNS servers.

   C. The client has a reserved IP address in the address pool.

   D. There's a bug in the DHCP server service.

9. Your Spring Flowers Florist Company in Las Vegas has been migrated to Windows XP and Server 2008 using Active Directory to manage the users and desktops with group policies. The company is in one location, and all the machines are on the same subnet. More recently, you decided to use DHCP to manage the address space more efficiently, so you installed the DHCP server on one of the Windows Server 2008 computers. The scope was created and activated for use. You also configured all the Windows XP Professional workstations to use DHCP. However, when you reboot the Windows XP Professional workstations, they cannot obtain an IP address from the DHCP server. What is the most likely reason for the problem on this network?

   A. The DHCP relay agent has not been enabled for this subnet.

   B. The DHCP server has not been authorized to provide addresses in Active Directory.

   C. The DHCP relay agent needs to be installed on the DHCP server to pass the requests to the DHCP service.

   D. The Windows Server 2008 computer that hosts the DHCP server needs to be rebooted before the DHCP service will start.

10. You are working on a client machine that gets its IP configuration via DHCP. You notice that the client received different configuration information the last few times its lease was renewed. Which of the following would cause this to occur?

   A. The DHCP server is not working properly.

   B. Another computer on the network has taken over your machine's configuration information since the last renewal.

   C. The client is receiving only the information that has changed since the last renewal. An administrator is changing the configuration information between lease renewals.

   D. When clients renew their leases, they receive all their configuration information. An administrator is changing the configuration information between lease renewals.

11. Because of a recent acquisition, your company has two locations, East and West, running Windows Server 2003. The acquired company had been using DHCP on its East network. Soon after the acquisition, you decided to give DHCP a try, and you used BOOTP through your router to configure your West network to utilize the DHCP server that was running on the East network. Everything worked fine. You then migrated both of your Windows Server 2003 networks to Windows Server 2008, and the DHCP service still works fine. However, all the support staff members who ran the East network on the other subnet have left the company, and you now want to have the DHCP East server physically reside on your side of the network so that you can manage the machine more efficiently. What are some of the steps you must take to move the DHCP service on the East server to your subnet on the West server and still use the old DHCP database? (Choose all that apply.)

   A. Pause the DHCP service on East.

   B. Stop the DHCP service on West.

   C. Save the DHCP server registry subkey of East to a text file.

   D. Copy the *systemroot*\System32\DHCP folder from East to West.

   E. Scavenge all the scopes in West.

   F. Reconcile all the scopes in West.

   G. Enter the IP addresses of West and East into the DHCP configuration tools, and select Move Service.

12. You have a Windows Server 2008 network that supports a midsize business that refurbishes bowling balls for the Rock & Bowl Lanes in Cleveland, Ohio. You decide to use DHCP to help manage the IP addresses. You configure the DHCP server, two DNS servers, nine file and print servers, and the IIS server with static IP addresses from your private address range of 192.168.1.1 through 192.168.1.254. When you bring up the workstations over the weekend to test your new DHCP network, everything appears to be working fine. But on Monday, you receive calls from some of the users complaining that they cannot access their servers. What is the most likely cause of this sporadic networking problem?

    A. You didn't create client reservations for the static IP addresses in the scope.

    B. You didn't create a separate scope for the servers that have been configured with the static IP addresses.

    C. You didn't exclude the IP addresses of the servers that have been configured with the static IP addresses.

    D. You didn't configure the servers that have been configured with static IP addresses for interoperability with a DHCP server.

13. You administer a network that consists of 300 Windows XP and Server 2008 machines, all on a single subnet. You are deploying DHCP using two Windows Server 2008 DHCP servers named Dynamo1 and Dynamo2. Dynamo1 will assign IP addresses in the range 208.45.231.1 through 208.45.231.254. Dynamo2 will assign IP addresses in the range 208.45.232.1 through 208.45.232.254. What should you do to ensure that the DHCP configuration works efficiently?

    A. Configure each DHCP server with one superscope and two member scopes. Configure the first member scope on each server with the range 208.45.231.1 through 208.45.231.254 and the second member scope on each server with the range 208.45.232.1 through 208.45.232.254. On Dynamo1, exclude the range 208.45.232.1 through 208.45.232.254. On Dynamo2, exclude the range 208.45.231.1 through 208.45.231.254.

    B. Configure a scope on Dynamo1 with the range 208.45.231.1 through 208.45.231.254. Configure a scope on Dynamo2 with the range 208.45.232.1 through 208.45.232.254.

    C. Configure a scope on both servers with the range 208.45.231.1 through 208.45.232.254. Exclude the range 208.45.232.1 through 208.45.232.254 on Dynamo1, and exclude the range 208.45.231.1 through 208.45.231.254 on Dynamo2.

    D. Configure one superscope and two member scopes on each DHCP server. Configure the first member scope on each server with the range 208.45.231.1 through 208.45.231.254 and the second member scope on each server with the range 208.45.232.1 through 208.45.232.254.

14. Your network consists of three logical subnets named Subnet A, Subnet B, and Subnet C. They are all on the same physical network. Subnet A contains addresses in the range 208.44.0.1 through 208.44.0.50, Subnet B contains addresses in the range 208.44.0.60 through 208.44.0.100, and Subnet C contains addresses in the range 208.44.0.110 through 208.44.0.120. You are setting up a single DHCP server that will provide DHCP services for Subnet A and Subnet B only. The address of the server must be set to 208.44.0.10.

In the following diagram, each address listed in the Choices column on the left will fit into only one of the empty boxes in the other two columns. Select each address and place it in its appropriate position within the network.

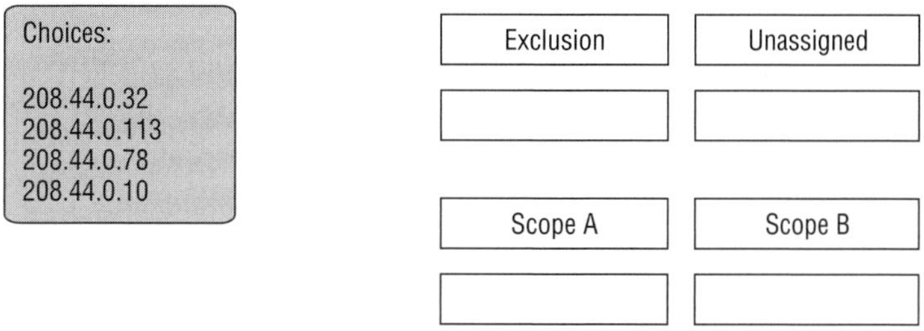

Choices:

208.44.0.32
208.44.0.113
208.44.0.78
208.44.0.10

Exclusion		Unassigned	

Scope A		Scope B	

15. Your network consists of 100 Windows XP Professional machines, 2 Windows Server 2008 machines, and 3 NetWare clients. All the machines need to access resources on the Windows Server 2008. You want to use the TCP/IP protocol with all the Windows computers and IPX/SPX on all the NetWare computers. You also want to minimize setup time as much as possible.

In the following diagram, the items in the Choices box represent various configuration options for the three different machine types. Select the configuration options, and place them in their appropriate places within the network.

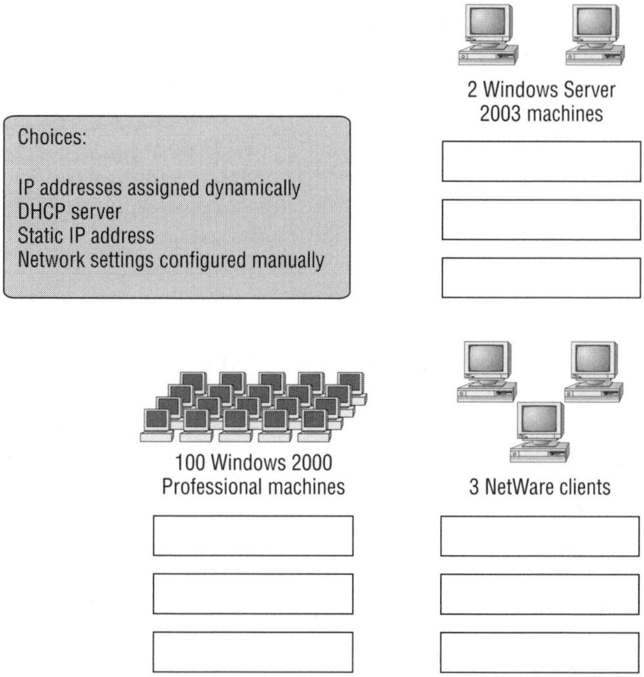

2 Windows Server
2003 machines

Choices:

IP addresses assigned dynamically
DHCP server
Static IP address
Network settings configured manually

100 Windows 2000
Professional machines

3 NetWare clients

16. When creating a new scope, what is the default lease time for that scope, and approximately how long would it be until a client begins attempting to renew the address?

    A. Three days is the lease time, and the client will attempt to renew at the end of the three days.

    B. Three days is the lease time, and the client will attempt to renew after approximately one and a half days.

    C. Five days is the lease time and, the client will attempt to renew after approximately three days.

    D. Eight days is the lease time, and the client will attempt to renew after approximately four days.

17. You are the administrator for a network using DHCP. The configuration calls for the first 31 addresses to be reserved for servers within the 192.168.1.0/24 network. You've created exclusions for the servers that will be statically configured within this range and also the servers that have reservations. You attempt to add a new server with a reservation, but it is not obtaining any DHCP information. After assigning the server an IP address manually, you ensure connectivity by using ping. The server can indeed ping the DHCP server. What else might you look for in order to get this server to use DHCP?

    A. On the server trying to use DHCP, make sure that DNS is enabled in order to obtain an address.

    B. On the DHCP server, make sure that the reservation isn't one of the addresses configured to be excluded.

    C. On the DHCP server, type ipconfig /renewall in order to force all clients to renew their addresses.

    D. See whether you can browse the Web to check higher-level protocols.

18. Windows Server 2008's DHCP service can be configured on certain types of servers or servers with certain roles. From the list, choose the roles that can act as a DHCP server, assuming they are authorized in Active Directory. (Choose all that apply.)

    A. Relay agent

    B. Router

    C. Domain controller

    D. Master server

    E. Member server

    F. Stand-alone server

19. When troubleshooting a DHCP problem, you notice an event ID in the 50s within the DHCP log. What does an event ID greater than 50 indicate?

    A. A problem related to leases, such as the 051 Lease option

    B. An issue with a client not receiving an address in time

    C. A problem with the client being unable to renew its address

    D. A problem with a rogue server

20. DHCP's four-step process sees messages of specific types exchanged between the client and network and the client and server. What is the name of the message that a DHCP client sends to initially obtain configuration parameters?

A. DHCPOFFER

B. DHCPREQUEST

C. DHCPDISCOVER

D. DHCPACK

Answers to Review Questions

1. B. When a DHCP-enabled XP workstation cannot locate a DHCP server, it uses APIPA to automatically configure itself with an address in the 169.254.0.0/16 address range. If you cannot ping the DHCP server from a correctly configured machine, it's likely that the DHCP server is down—which is why the XP machines have autoconfigured themselves. In this particular situation, the Windows Server 2008 computers have configured themselves using APIPA, which is why the other workstations can still see the servers. Because the Windows 95 machines didn't participate in the APIPA configuration, they were left without IP addresses. Conflict-resolution protocol on a DHCP server is used to determine duplicate addresses, not bad ones, so option C is incorrect. APIPA is already enabled on the XP machines, which is why the network is behaving in the manner described, so options D and E are incorrect. The DHCP relay agent is used to pass requests through routers that don't support the BOOTP protocol for DHCP broadcasts, so option A is incorrect.

2. B, E. DHCP depends on the client machines delivering a specific type of broadcast that includes their IP configuration information. By design, broadcasts are not propagated through routers. However, BOOTP is a specialized and standard broadcast recognized by many routers and is passed through from one subnet to another, allowing DHCP to function properly. If the routers don't support BOOTP, you can use a DHCP relay agent, which recognizes the DHCP requests from the clients and passes those requests to DHCP servers through their known IP addresses.

3. B. An exclusion just marks addresses as excluded; the DHCP server doesn't maintain any information about them. A reservation marks an address as reserved for a particular client.

4. A. When the DHCP server crashed, the scope was effectively deactivated. Deactivating a scope has no effect on the client until it needs to renew the lease.

5. B. ipconfig /all is still the command to display the IP configuration on Windows 2000, XP, Vista, Server 2003, and Server 2008 machines. The /all switch is needed to show the details that include the DNS server address. The winipcfg command is used for Windows 9x workstations. The other commands are not valid.

6. B. TCP/IP is the standard protocol of choice, but it also increases the complexity of configuring Windows XP operating systems. Because of this complexity, Microsoft has implemented Automatic Private IP Addressing (APIPA). When an APIPA IP stack is configured for DHCP and a server isn't located, the stack is automatically configured with an address in the 169.254.0.0/16 range. This allows an IP network to be set up fairly easily. The other options are incorrect for the following reasons: DHCP servers can support any number of subnets or scopes, within reason. A DHCP server doesn't validate the scope information while clients are communicating with it. Finally, a user cannot bring a DHCP server online because the user needs administrative capability to add the service.

7. B, C, E, F. The key word to remember is DORA. IP lease discovery is used when a DHCP-enabled IP stack is initialized to locate a DHCP server with this specialized broadcast. When a DHCP server receives the discover packet, it sends out an IP lease offer containing an available address. The client responds to the DHCP offer with an IP lease acceptance message, showing that this address is acceptable. Finally, when the DHCP request is received, the server sends out an IP lease acknowledgment, which contains configuration options for the IP stack and adds the information to the DHCP database.

8. B. Manual settings override DHCP options.

9. B. When you install a DHCP server using Windows Server 2008 and Active Directory, the server won't be permitted to provide DHCP services until it has been authorized. When you authorize a server, you are actually adding its IP address to the Active Directory object that contains a list of DHCP servers. If the address of the server isn't on the list, the DHCP service will fail. The other options are incorrect for the following reasons: DHCP relay agents are used to send DHCP requests across routers that don't support BOOTP. Windows Server 2008 computers don't need to be rebooted after DHCP has been installed in order to start the service.

10. D. During lease renewal, the client gets all configuration information offered by the server, not a subset of that information.

11. B, C, D, F. Options B, C, D, and F are not all the steps necessary to complete this procedure, but all four are necessary. To move the DHCP database from one server to another, you must first stop the DHCP service. Then, copy the *systemroot*\system32\DHCP folder on the East server to a temporary folder that is accessible from the West server. Next, copy the DHCP server registry key to a text file using REGEDT32. Next, install DHCP on the West server, stop the service, and then rename the System.mdb file in the temporary *systemroot*\System32\DHCP folder to System.src. Then copy the temporary *systemroot*\ System32\DHCP folder to the new *systemroot*\System32\DHCP folder. Then, use REGEDT32 to restore the DHCP server registry key to West from the text file saved from the East server. Finally, start the DHCP service on West, and choose Reconcile All Scopes.

12. C. If you configure static IP addresses and then don't exclude those addresses from the scope in the DHCP server, the same addresses will be available to be delivered to clients. If clients lease those addresses, they won't be available to the servers to which you assigned them. The best practice is to exclude a block of addresses large enough to cover all the devices on your network that should be static. Having just one block also makes it easier for you to recognize the excluded addresses when you're looking at network traffic. The other options are incorrect because client reservations are used to deliver the same address to the same machine each time and are not used to recognize statically configured clients. In addition, a scope identifies a subnet, and the servers and the workstations exist on the same subnet. Finally, there is no configuration for a static IP address to interoperate with a DHCP server.

13. A. A superscope allows the DHCP server to provide multiple logical subnet addresses to DHCP clients on a single physical network. In each superscope, you should exclude the range of addresses that you want the other server to assign. If you just created a single scope on each DHCP server, you would probably end up with a lot of unused leases.

14. The address 208.44.0.10 needs to be excluded so that the DHCP server can use it. 208.44.0.113 is part of Subnet C and is not assigned by the DHCP server. 208.44.0.32 is part of Scope A, and 208.44.0.78 is part of Scope B.

Exclusion	Unassigned
208.44.0.10	208.44.0.113

Scope A	Scope B
208.44.0.32	208.44.0.78

15. Because you have a large number of Windows clients that need to use TCP/IP, you should assign IP addresses to them dynamically. To do this, you need to configure the Windows Server 2008 computer as a DHCP server and assign its IP address manually. The NetWare clients will not use TCP/IP, so their network settings cannot be assigned via DHCP.

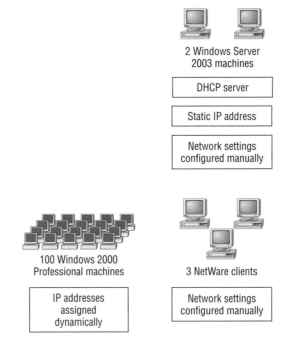

16. D. The default lease time is eight days for a scope, which means that its T1 time is approximately four days. At four days, the client will begin trying to renew the address with the server that gave it the lease. The T2 time is approximately 87.5 percent of the lease duration, at which point a client will attempt to renew with any DHCP server.

17. B. On the DHCP server, make sure the reservation isn't one of the addresses configured to be excluded. Option A is incorrect because DNS is meaningless in this context. Without an IP address, the machine can't use DNS. Option C is incorrect because there is no /renewall option for `ipconfig`. Option D is used by some people to troubleshoot, but `ping` is a better method.

18. C, E, F. The three roles that can act as authorized DHCP servers are domain controllers, member servers, and stand-alone servers. A relay agent is used to forward requests from one subnet to a server on another subnet.

19. D. Event IDs greater than 50 are used for rogue server detection to indicate a server that hasn't been authorized to serve DHCP. The 051 Lease option is a DHCP option sent to clients, not an event ID.

20. C. DHCPDISCOVER is used to initially request configuration parameters. When a server receives it, the server will send a DHCPOFFER. The client receives this offer and, if it accepts it, sends a DHCPREQUEST broadcast. The server, if it accepts the DHCPREQUEST, sends a DHCPACK.

Chapter 5

Managing Routing and Remote Access

MICROSOFT EXAM OBJECTIVES COVERED IN THIS CHAPTER:

✓ **Configuring Routing**

- May include but is not limited to: static routes, persistent routing, Routing Internet Protocol (RIP), Open Shortest Path First (OSPF)

✓ **Configuring remote access**

- May include but is not limited to: Virtual Private Networks (VPN), Network Address Translation (NAT), Routing and Remote Access Server (RRAS), inbound/outbound filters

As the use of TCP/IP internetworking has grown, so has the demand for easy-to-install and easy-to-configure routers. Not every small business that wants to connect to the Internet or connect two remote offices can afford an expensive router and a certified professional to administer it. Microsoft's first attempt to solve this problem was the version of the Routing and Remote Access Services (RRAS) included in the Windows NT 4.0 Option Pack, which is the direct ancestor of the RRAS components included in Windows Server 2008.

The Windows Server 2008 version of RRAS is a fully functional multiprotocol router. Third parties can also extend it to add network protocols or routing methods. The idea behind using RRAS for routing is that you can just enable RRAS on a Windows Server 2008 machine and use it as a router in addition to whatever else you have it doing. For example, you could use a Windows Server 2008 computer with RRAS for routing, Internet Information Services (IIS) for Simple Mail Transfer Protocol (SMTP) mail and web service, and two network interface cards (NICs) to serve as a combination firewall/router/Internet server.

We will begin the chapter by discussing how routing works and covering the ways that routing is integrated into Windows Server 2008.

Understanding Routing

Routing is the process of delivering traffic to the correct destination. IP routing is simple to understand at the most basic level. Packets have addresses, and the process of routing involves getting a packet from its source to its destination. The mechanics of how that happens are a little more complicated, though. In the following sections, you will see exactly what routing does, how routing works, and how Windows Server 2008 handles routing.

What Routing Does

An *internetwork* is just a network of networks. A sample internetwork might contain five distinct networks, which might be named after the cities they are based in, for example—Atlanta, Boston, Orlando, Portland, and San Diego. The internetwork is the collection of all these networks, any of which could ordinarily stand alone.

An internetwork is not the same as the Internet. Actually, it's the other way around. The Internet we all use is just a really large, really complex internetwork.

Complex internetworks like the Internet require routing. Consider what happens when you try to send a file over the Internet. Suppose you're on the East Coast and the destination is in California. If you look at a map of the physical topology of the Internet, you'll see that there are a large number of potential routes to get from here to there. Some may be better than others; for instance, one route would carry packets east, across the Atlantic, through Europe, and across Russia and the Pacific Ocean to the West Coast of the United States. That's a legal route, but it would be inefficient.

Routing associates the routes a message might take with costs. Routing systems allow administrators to attach a metric, or *cost*, to each leg of a route. In a bit, you'll see how routing systems use this metric information to calculate the most efficient route for packets to take.

The actual way in which the metric information is used in calculations varies depending which routing protocol is being used. The routing protocols are Routing Information Protocol (RIP) version 1, RIP version 2, and Open Shortest Path First (OSPF—which is no longer supported in Windows Server 2008 Routing and Remote Access). The important point to remember is that all three routing protocols (discussed in more detail throughout this chapter) use metrics to figure out the "best" route in any situation.

How Routing Works

The basic underlying idea in the routing process is that each packet on a network has a source address and a destination address, which means any device that receives the packet can inspect its headers to determine where it came from and where it's going. If such a device also has some information about the network's design and implementation—such as how long it takes packets to travel over a particular link—it can intelligently change the routing to minimize the total cost.

Figure 5.1 shows an imaginary network consisting of six interconnected local networks. These networks, named A through F, are connected by links of varying speeds and costs. This accurately mirrors what happens in the real world, where it's common for internal networks (or Internet service providers) to have multiple ways to establish a link between two points.

Imagine that a client machine on network B wants to send traffic to a machine on network E. The most obvious route would probably be B to F to E, but you could also use B to C to D to E. Notice the costs: B-F-E has a total cost of 12, while the seemingly longer B-C-D-E actually has a lower cost of 8. That doesn't appear to make sense because the latter route has a longer path. When you consider what cost really means, though, you'll understand why this makes sense.

Assigning link costs is entirely up to you. Usually, you assign costs that reflect your preference for how you want traffic to flow. An expensive or slow link would probably deserve a higher cost than a cheaper or faster link; if you assign a high cost to your most financially expensive links (for example, metered ISDN connections), they would not be used if there were more cost-efficient links available.

Now, revisit Figure 5.1 with the assumption that each circle is really a router. You can hide all the complexity of the network behind a router, because only the router is in charge of moving packets. Call your client machine X and your server Y. When X wants to send traffic to

Y, it already knows the destination IP address of its target. X will build a packet, including its IP address as the source and Y's address as the destination. X will then use its default gateway setting to send that packet to router B.

FIGURE 5.1 An example network

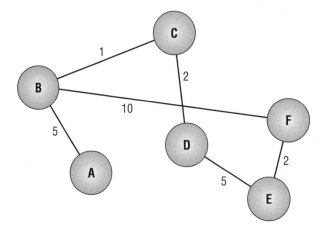

According to the Open Systems Interconnection (OSI) model, a gateway and a router are two different things. However, Microsoft uses the terms interchangeably, and so will we. We discussed OSI models in Chapter 1, "Understanding Windows Server 2008 Networking."

Router B receives the packet and has both source and destination address information. By examining the IP addresses, it can determine that it doesn't "know" a direct route to the network where Y is located. However, two intermediate nodes claim to know how to reach Y: C and F. Because C has the lowest link cost, the router at B will send the packet to C in a simple routing algorithm. When C receives it, it will go through the same process, forwarding the packet on to D, and so on. Eventually the packet arrives at its destination.

Let's take a look at some of the specific ways in which RRAS actually performs the steps in the preceding example.

Routing Tables

A routing table is a database that stores route information. Think of it as a road map for the internetwork—the routing table lists which routes exist between networks, so the router or host can look up the necessary information when it encounters a packet bound for a foreign network. Each entry in the routing table contains the following five pieces of information:

- The network address of the remote host or network
- The netmask associated with the entry
- The forwarding address to which traffic for the remote network should be sent

- The network interface that should be used to send the packet to the forwarding address
- A cost, or metric, that indicates what relative priority should be assigned to this route

For example, you could write the San Diego–Atlanta route as 10.1.1.0:255.255.255.128: 10.10.1.254:ATL:1, assuming that the interface name is ATL and you want to use a metric of 1. The actual format in which these entries are stored isn't important (in fact, it's not visible in RRAS); what's important for you to know is that every routing table entry contains that information.

Routing tables actually can contain these three different kinds of routes:

- Network routes provide a route to an entire network. For example, the route from San Diego to Atlanta is a network route because it can be used to route traffic from any host in San Diego to any host in Atlanta.

- Host routes provide a route to a single system or to a broadcast address. Think of them as shortcuts—they provide a slightly more efficient way for a router to "know" how to get traffic to a remote machine, so they're usually used when you want to direct traffic to remote networks through a particular machine.

- Default routes are where packets go when there's no explicit route for them. They are similar to the default gateway you're used to configuring for IP clients. Anytime a router encounters a packet bound for some remote network, it will first search the routing table; if it can't find a network or host route, it will use the default route instead. This saves you from having to configure a network or host route for every network to which you might ever want to talk.

Static Routing

Static routing provides predefined routes in a table called, predictably, a *static routing table*. Static routing systems don't make any attempt to discover other routers or systems on their networks. Instead, you manually tell the routing engine how to get data to other networks; specifically, you tell it what other networks are reachable from your network by specifying the network addresses, subnet masks, and a metric for each network. This information goes into the system's routing table. When an outgoing packet arrives at the routing engine, the engine can examine the routing table to select the lowest-cost route to the destination. If there's no explicit entry in the routing table for that network, the packet goes to the default gateway, which is then entrusted with getting the packet to where it needs to go.

Static routing is faster and more efficient than dynamic routing. Static routing works well with a small network that doesn't change much. You can identify the remote networks to which you want to route and then add static routes to them to reflect the costs and topology of your network. In Windows Server 2008, you maintain static routes with the route command, which allows you to either see the contents of the routing table or modify it by adding and removing static routes to individual networks.

Dynamic Routing

Unlike static routing, *dynamic routing* doesn't depend on your adding fixed, unchangeable routes to remote networks. Instead, a dynamic routing engine can discover its surroundings by finding and communicating with other nearby routers in an internetwork.

This process, usually called *router discovery*, enables a newly added (or rebooted) router to configure itself. This is roughly equivalent to the process that happens when you move into a new neighborhood. Within a short time of your arrival, you'll probably meet most of the people who live nearby, either because they come to you or because you go to them. At that point, you have useful information about the surrounding environment that could come only from people who were already there.

The dynamic routing protocol in Windows Server 2008 is the Routing Information Protocol (RIP). In previous versions, the Open Shortest Path First (OSPF) protocol was also used, but in Windows Server 2008, OSPF has been discontinued. RIP has its advantages and disadvantages. Each router (whether a hardware device, a Windows Server 2008 machine, or otherwise) is connected to at least two separate physical networks. When the router starts, the only information it has comes from its internal routing table. Usually, that means it knows about all the attached networks plus whatever static routes have been previously defined. The router then receives configuration information that tells it about the state and topology of the network.

As time goes on, the network's physical topology can change. For example, take a look at the network in Figure 5.2. If network G suddenly lost its connection, the routers in sites A, D, and E would need to readjust their routing tables because they could no longer route traffic directly to G. The process by which this adjustment happens is what makes the routing dynamic, and it's also the largest area of difference between the two dynamic routing protocols for IP.

FIGURE 5.2   A more complex, dynamically routed network

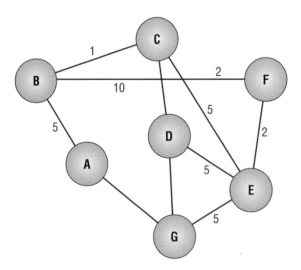

In the following sections, we will look at both RIP and OSPF more closely.

Even though OSPF is not used in Windows Server 2008, we will cover it because many third-party routers use it and you may see it on the Microsoft exam.

The Routing Information Protocol

RIP is a distance-vector routing protocol that is generally simple and easy to configure, but it has performance limitations that restrict its usefulness on medium and large networks. RIP routers begin with a basically empty routing table, but they immediately begin sending out announcements that they know will reach the networks to which they're connected.

RIP uses UDP as a transport protocol and port 520 by default.

RIP announcements may be broadcast or multicast. Routers on other networks that hear these announcements can add the advertised routes to their own routing tables. The process works both ways, of course; your router will hear announcements from other routers and add the advertised routes to its list of places it knows how to reach. Unfortunately, RIP supports a maximum of 15 hop counts only (the number of routers that a packet can pass through).

Microsoft's RIP implementation in Server 2008 supports RIPv2. You should be aware of these important differences between RIPv1 and RIPv2:

- The primary, or most important, difference between versions 1 and 2 of RIP is that RIPv2 supports variable-length subnet masking (VLSM). VLSM helps preserve IP address space by enabling networks to be subdivided into smaller blocks based on need.

- RIPv2 supports simple (that is, plain text) username/password authentication, which is handy to prevent unwanted changes from cluttering your routing tables.

- RIPv2 routers add the ability to receive triggered updates. When you know that your network topology is changing (perhaps because you've added connectivity to another network), you can send out a trigger that contains information about the changes. This trigger forces all the RIP routers you own to assimilate the changes immediately. Triggered updates are also useful because routers that detect a link or router failure can update their routing tables and announce the change, making their neighbors aware of it sooner rather than later.

You can use the Routing And Remote Access snap-in to set up two kinds of filters that screen out some types of RIP updates:

- Route filters allow you to pick and choose the networks that you want to admit knowing about and for which you want to accept announcements.

- Peer filters give you control over the neighboring routers to which your router will listen.

RIP also incorporates features that attempt to prevent route loops. In Figure 5.2 (shown earlier in the chapter), the network topology has the potential to cause a route loop. For instance, say that someone in E wants to send a packet to a machine in A, but the G-A and D-C links are down. E sends the packet to G, which recognizes that it can't reach A. Also, G knows that the route D-C-B-A will work, so it sends the packet to D. When the packet reaches D, D knows it can't talk to C, so it sends the packet to E because E-G-A is usually a valid route. You can see that the packet will never reach its destination and will loop continually. This might seem like a contrived example, but in real life, where internetwork links are often concentrated among a small number of physical links, it's a real problem. RIP offers several methods for resolving and preventing loops, including the split-horizon and poison-reverse algorithms. (Despite their cool names, it's not important to understand how these algorithms work to pass the exam—it's enough to know what they're for and that RIP implements them to protect against routing loops.)

RIP has two operation modes:

- In *periodic update* mode, a RIP router sends out its list of known routes at periodic intervals (which you define). The router marks any routes it learns from other routers as RIP routes, which means they remain active only while the router is running. If the router is stopped, the routes vanish. This mode is the default for RIP on LAN interfaces, but it's not suitable for demand-dial connections because you don't want your router bringing up a connection just to announce its presence.

- In *autostatic update* mode, the RRAS router broadcasts the contents of its routing table only when a remote router asks for it. Better still, the routes that the RRAS router learns from its RIP neighbors are marked as static routes in the routing table, and they persist until you manually delete them—even if the router is stopped and restarted or if RIP is disabled for that interface. Autostatic mode is the default for demand-dial interfaces.

One drawback to RIP in either version is that it causes the router to send its entire routing table with every update. This can generate a large amount of traffic and makes RIP inappropriate for many of today's networks. Another routing protocol, Open Shortest Path First, solves this problem by sending updates for only routes that have changed.

The Open Shortest Path First Protocol

RIP is designed for fairly small networks; it can handle only 15 router-to-router hops. If you have a network that spans more than 16 routers at any point, RIP won't be able to cache routes for it, and some parts of the network will appear to be (or in fact will be) unreachable. The OSPF routing protocol is a link-state protocol designed for use on medium, large, or very large networks. It's much more efficient than RIP, but it also requires more knowledge and experience to set up and administer. Also, as stated earlier in the chapter, OSPF is no longer supported by Windows Server 2008 RRAS.

RIP routers continually exchange routing data with one another, which allows incorrect route entries to propagate. Instead of exchanging routing data, each OSPF router maintains a map of the state of the internetwork. This map, called a *link-state map*, provides a continually updated reference to the state of each internetwork link. Neighboring routers group into an *adjacency* (similar to a neighborhood). Within an adjacency, routers synchronize any changes to the link-state map. When the network topology changes, whichever router notices it first floods the internetwork with change notifications. Each router that receives the notification updates its copy of the link map and then recalculates its internal routing table.

The "shortest path first" in OSPF refers to the algorithm that OSPF systems use to calculate routes. Routes are calculated so that the shortest path (the one with the lowest cost) is used first. SPF-calculated routes are always free of loops, which is another nice advantage over RIP.

OSPF networks are broken down into subparts called *areas*; an area is a collection of interconnected networks. Think of an area as a subsection of an internetwork. Areas are interconnected by backbones. Each OSPF router keeps a link-state database only for the areas to which it's connected. Special OSPF routers called *area border routers* interlink areas. Figure 5.3 shows how this looks.

FIGURE 5.3   A simple OSPF network

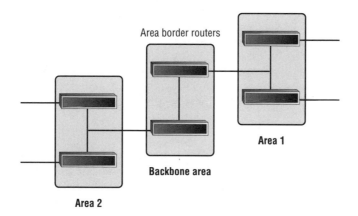

Area border routers

Area 1

Backbone area

Area 2

Border Routing

Internal routing refers to routing that occurs within your internetwork. By contrast, *border routing* is what happens when packets leave your internetwork and go to another router someplace else. Consider what happens when you use your home computer to browse a website. TCP/IP packets from your machine go to your ISP (probably via PPP, over an analog, cable, DSL, or ISDN connection). The ISP examines the destination address of the packets and determines that they should go to some other network, usually a network for which the ISP doesn't maintain a direct connection.

For example, when you want to fetch a web page from Microsoft's website, you essentially lease an Internet connection from a local ISP, which likely leases lines from another, larger provider, which maintains peering connections at national access points (NAPs). These peering connections maintain routing tables for various networks on the Internet. They forward your packet to the next nearest hop, and then on to the next nearest hop, until the packet reaches its destination.

Figure 5.4 shows an example of the Internet service provider where one of this book's authors used to work: Core Digital Communication Services (later ExecPC/Voyager). The local router represents a home user or business connected to the ISP. From there, the Stevens Point router forwarded packets over a DS3 to Appleton; from there they traveled to Milwaukee and on to the NAP in Chicago. The thick black lines between borders indicate backbone links that join border areas together. Even though this network was all owned by ExecPC/Voyager, it utilized different OSPF areas up to the NAP where Border Gateway Protocol (BGP) was used. The true border of this network was at the NAP.

FIGURE 5.4   Networks are divided into areas linked by backbones.

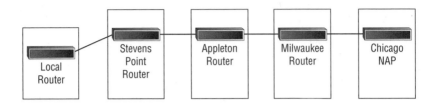

In a border routing network, some routers are responsible for handling packets inside the area, while others manage network communication with other areas. These border routers are responsible for storing routes to other borders that they can reach over the backbone.

Multicast Routing

IP multicasting works by sending to a single IP address a packet that is read by many hosts. The hosts all have individual IP addresses, but they belong to a multicast group that shares a single, separate IP address. As you saw in Chapter 4, "Managing Dynamic Host Configuration Protocol (DHCP)," multicast group membership is dynamic, and groups can contain unlimited hosts on separate IP networks, provided that routers between the networks support multicast traffic. In fact, even computers that aren't part of a multicast group can send multicast packets.

Multicasting uses a special range of IP addresses, called the *Class D address space*, that is reserved exclusively for multicasting. The multicast address range contains the IP addresses 224.0.0.0 through 239.255.255.255. Each multicast group uses a single address in the Class D address space. In addition, just as with regular IP addresses, the multicast address range reserves a few special addresses used for specific purposes. Table 5.1 contains a partial list of these special multicast addresses.

TABLE 5.1   Special Multicast Addresses

Address	Description
224.0.0.0	Base address (reserved)
224.0.0.1	All Hosts, all systems on the same network segment
224.0.0.2	All Routers, all routers on the same network segment
224.0.0.5	All OSPF Routers, used to send routing information to all OSPF routers on the network

TABLE 5.1   Special Multicast Addresses *(continued)*

Address	Description
224.0.0.6	All Designated OSPF Routers, used to send routing information to all designated OSPF routers
224.0.0.9	All RIP 2 Routers, used to send routing information to all RIPv2 routers on the network
224.0.1.24	Used to support replication for WINS servers

 Real World Scenario

Is a Multihomed Computer a Router?

For several years, your company has been growing steadily, from a small network of 50 Windows NT workstations and 5 Windows NT servers to a medium-sized network of more than 200 Vista and XP Professional workstations and more than 10 Windows Server 2008 servers. Everything functions properly, but performance is beginning to suffer. After analyzing the network traffic, you realize that you need to segment the network into subnets to control the traffic and improve the performance. You are considering using multihomed computers to save money when purchasing dedicated routers.

Windows Server 2008 has expanded support with the RIP routing protocol. But before you leap at the cost savings of using a multihomed Windows Server 2008 computer, you want to take a closer look.

Despite some added cost, there is a lot to be said for using specialized routing computers for the connection points in networks. When there is a significant utilization of bandwidth across your network, it's questionable whether the multihomed host will be able to provide the level of service you need. General-purpose operating systems such as Windows Server 2008 will always pale in comparison to a computer that's designed to perform singular tasks. In addition, with the basic routing protocols, you can use many tools and services to guarantee levels of service and to set up filters and access control lists.

Windows Server 2008 doesn't really make sense as a router for small offices either, with the cost of basic routers being so low. Make sure you are applying these Windows Server 2008 routing services in the areas that are appropriate for the particular load and scale of your situation.

Internet Group Management Protocol (IGMP) is used to exchange multicast group membership information between multicast-capable routers. You can configure RRAS in two modes:

- *IGMP router mode* listens for IGMP membership report packets and tracks group membership. IGMP router mode must be attached to any interfaces that connect to multicast-configured hosts.

- *IGMP proxy mode* essentially acts like a multicast host, except that it forwards IGMP membership report packets to an IGMP router. This provides a list of multicast-enabled hosts to an upstream router that normally wouldn't be aware of the hosts. Typically, IGMP proxy is used on single-router networks connected to the Internet. The IGMP proxy sends the list of multicast hosts to the multicast-capable portion of the Internet known as the *Internet multicast backbone*, or MBone, so that the hosts can receive multicast packets.

You may need to send multicast traffic across non-multicast-compatible routers. This is made possible through the use of *IP-in-IP interfaces* (or *IP-in-IP tunnels*). An IP-in-IP interface actually encapsulates packets with an additional IP header. The encapsulated packets can be sent across any router because they appear to be ordinary IP packets. You create and manage IP-in-IP interfaces in RRAS the same way you configure other interfaces.

Routing in Windows Server 2008

RRAS provides a multiprotocol router. In other words, the RRAS routing engine can handle multiple network protocols and multiple routing methods on multiple NICs. RRAS provides some specific features of interest when the conversation turns to network routing:

- Demand-dial routing can open connections to specific networks when the router receives packets addressed to those networks. This feature allows you to use on-demand links instead of permanent connections. It's especially nice for Integrated Services Digital Network (ISDN), which combines per-minute fees in most places with really fast call setup times. Point-to-Point Tunneling Protocol (PPTP) connections can be demand-dialed, too, or you can use demand-dial interfaces to make long-distance connections only when they're needed.

- You can establish static routes that specify where packets bound for certain networks should go. The most common use of this feature is to link a remote network with your LAN. The remote network gets one static route that basically says, "Any traffic leaving my subnet should be sent to the router." RRAS handles it from there.

- Dynamic routing using RIPv1 and RIPv2 protocols provides ways for your router to share routing information with other routers "near" it in network space.

- Packet filtering screens out undesirable packets in both directions. For example, you can create a packet filter to keep out FTP traffic, or you can add a filter to a demand-dial interface so that it will be opened only for web or mail traffic. Other traffic types will pass if the link is up, but they won't cause RRAS to open the link if it's not already open. (See the section "Configuring TCP/IP Packet Filters" later in the chapter for more details.)

- In unicast routing, one machine sends directly to one destination address. In multicast routing, one machine sends to an entire network. RRAS supports both methods.

- Network Address Translation (NAT) is a service that allows multiple LAN clients to share a single public IP address and Internet connection.

 Real World Scenario

About NAT

NAT provides an advantage with routing. NAT (also referred to as *network masquerading*) allows a router to translate one IP address to another.

For example, let's say you have two networks (10.10.0.0 and 192.168.1.0) and they are configured with two separate sets of TCP/IP addresses. The router can use NAT so that a user from the 10.10.0.0 network goes to the 192.168.1.0 network and gets a valid IP address for that network. Basically, the NAT swaps its 10.10.0.0 address for a 192.168.1.0 address.

NAT is also commonly used for Internet connections. For example, let's say you have an Internet service provider (ISP) that issues you only six valid Internet TCP/IP addresses for you to use on your network. You can set up NAT and program it to use those six valid addresses. Then, when a user from the network wants to access the Internet, NAT swaps the user's internal IP address for one of the valid IP addresses.

Installing RRAS

To use RRAS, you need to install the RRAS components on computers running Windows Server 2008, because they're not installed by default. You can do this through the Server Manager MMC's Add Roles Wizard. Exercise 5.1 leads you through the process of installing RRAS as a router.

EXERCISE 5.1

Installing RRAS for IP Routing

1. Open Server Manager by clicking Start ➢ Administrative Tools ➢ Server Manager.

2. In the left pane, click Roles. In the right pane, click Add Roles.

3. On the Select Server Roles page, check the Network Policy And Access Service box, and click Next.

EXERCISE 5.1 *(continued)*

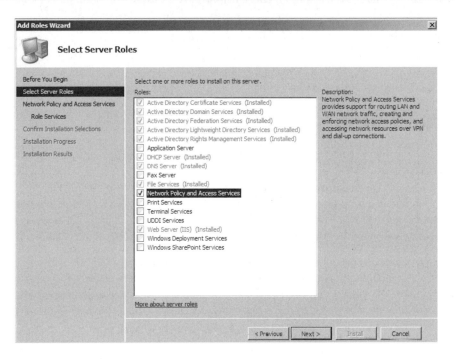

4. On the Introduction page, click Next.

5. On the Select Role Services page, check the Routing And Remote Access Services box, and click Next.

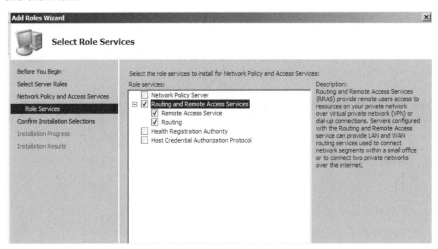

EXERCISE 5.1 *(continued)*

6. On the Confirm Installation Selections page, click Install.

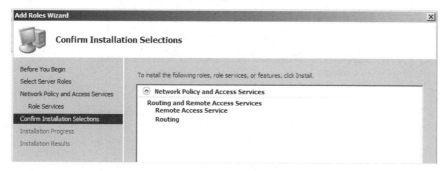

7. On the Installation Results page, verify that the installation was successful, and click Close.

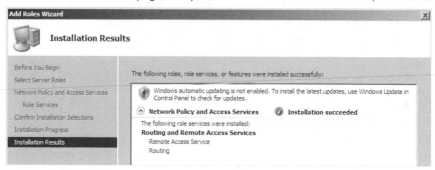

8. Close the Server Manager MMC.

9. Open the Routing And Remote Access snap-in by selecting Start ➢ Administrative Tools ➢ Routing And Remote Access.

10. Select the server you want to configure in the left pane of the MMC. Right-click the server, and choose Configure And Enable Routing And Remote Access.

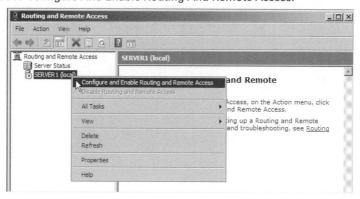

EXERCISE 5.1 *(continued)*

The Routing And Remote Access Server Setup Wizard appears. Click the Next button.

11. On the Configuration page, ensure that the Secure Connection Between Two Private Networks radio button is selected. Then click the Next button.

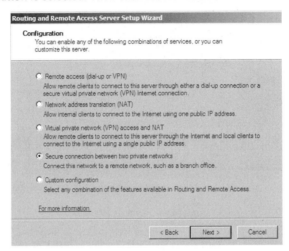

12. The Demand-Dial Connections page appears. It's there only to ask whether you want to use demand-dialed connections; you still have to set the connections up (either manually or using the Demand-Dial Wizard) after you complete the Routing And Remote Access Server Setup Wizard. Select Yes to use demand-dial connections. Click Next to continue.

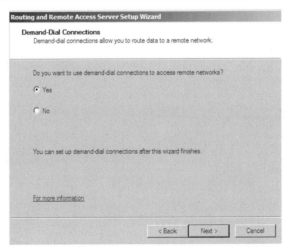

13. On the IP Address Assignment page, you can choose how RRAS assigns IP addresses to incoming demand-dial calls. If you want to use DHCP (either a DHCP server on your network or the built-in address allocator), leave the Automatically radio button selected. If you want to pick out an address range, select the From A Specified Range Of Addresses button. Click the Next button.

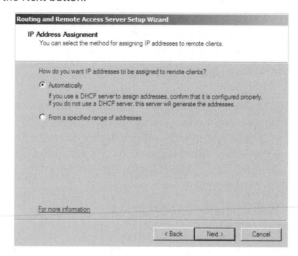

14. Click the Finish button on the summary page to close the wizard. If you chose to create a demand-dial interface, the Demand-Dial Interface Wizard appears automatically. Leave the computer in its current state because Exercise 5.2 will walk you through the Demand-Dial Interface Wizard.

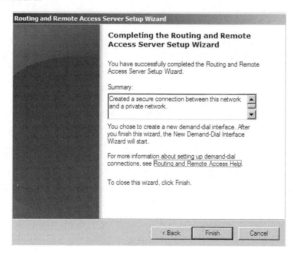

Configuring IP Routing

Continuing from the previous exercise, when the summary page of the Routing And Remote Access Server Setup Wizard appears, it's going to remind you to do the following things, depending on whether you chose to use demand-dial connections:

- Add demand-dial interfaces if you want to support demand dialing.

- Give each routable interface a network address for each protocol it carries. For example, if you're using IP and IPX on a computer with three NICs, each NIC that participates in routing needs to have distinct IP and IPX addresses.

- Install and configure the routing protocols (for example, RIP for IP in this case) on the interfaces that should support them.

These three actions form the core of what you must do to make your RRAS server into an IP router. In the following sections, we'll cover how RRAS treats LAN, demand-dial, and RIP interfaces. Next, we'll show how to configure properties that affect RRAS in general, such as error logging and route preferences. You'll also learn how to install and configure RIP. Finally, you'll see how to manage static routes with the `route` command.

Creating and Managing Interfaces

The Network Interfaces node in the Routing And Remote Access snap-in (shown in Figure 5.5) summarizes the routable interfaces available on your machine for *all* protocols. It lists all the LAN and demand-dial interfaces, plus two special interfaces maintained by RRAS: loopback and internal. Each of the interfaces displayed has a type, a status (either Enabled or Disabled), and a connection status associated with it. For example, a Windows Server 2008 machine in the default configuration with a single NIC displays the Local Area Connection interface. Each of those interfaces represents a potential destination for routed packets.

What "Unreachable" Really Means

A demand-dial interface can be in any of several different states:

- First, the Enabled and Disabled states that appear in the Status column indicate whether the link is administratively available—that is, whether you're allowing people to use it.

- The Connection State column shows you whether the connection is working. The default state for a demand-dial connection is Disconnected, which is perfectly reasonable. When RRAS tries to establish a connection, the state changes to Connected—also eminently logical. In both the connected and disconnected states, any static routes tied to the demand-dial interface are available.

- When RRAS tries to dial a number and fails to connect, it will continue to try until it reaches the redial limit set on the Dialing tab of the interface's Properties dialog box (the default redial limit is 10 minutes). If the redial limit is reached, the interface will be marked as Unreachable for a time-out period.

As long as the interface is unreachable, any static routes pointing to it will be unavailable— they'll actually disappear from the routing table. After the time-out period, RRAS will try again to dial; if it fails again, it tacks another 10 minutes onto the time-out and tries again. If the time-out period reaches the maximum (six hours by default), the counter will stop incrementing so RRAS will try again to connect every six hours until a successful connection is made or until you restart the RRAS service.

You can adjust both the minimum and maximum values for this time-out from their defaults (10 minutes and 6 hours, respectively). You make this change in the Registry, by adding two REG_DWORD values to HKLM\System\CurrentControlSet\Services\Router\Interfaces\Interface-Name (where InterfaceName matches the name of the interface you want to change). The MinUnreachabilityInterval value controls both the minimum retry interval and how much the retry interval is incremented after each failure; the MaxUnreachabilityInterval sets the upper limit. Both of these values must be expressed in seconds.

You can right-click each interface to get a pop-up menu with some useful commands, including Disable, Enable, and Unreachability Reason (which tells you why an interface is marked as Unreachable). The menu also contains some commands specific to demand-dial interfaces, which will be covered in the following sections.

FIGURE 5.5   The Network Interfaces node

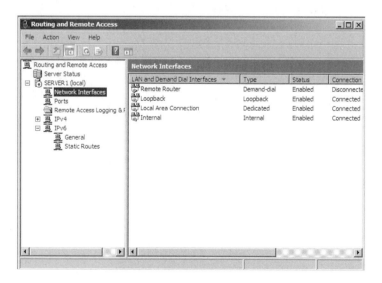

Managing LAN Interfaces

LAN interface options appear when you select the General node under the IPv4 node in the Routing And Remote Access snap-in. These options correspond to the LAN interfaces you've defined in RRAS. You can set general properties for the LAN interfaces. After you add specific routing protocols to the interfaces, you can configure those protocols individually (as you'll see later in this chapter).

To see the properties for an interface, select the General node in the console, click the interface in the pane on the right, and select Action ➢ Properties, which opens the Local Area Connection Properties dialog box (Figure 5.6).

FIGURE 5.6 The General tab of the Local Area Connection Properties dialog box

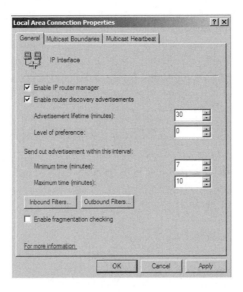

The General tab allows you to set some useful parameters for the entire interface, including whether this interface will send out router discovery advertisements so that other routers on your network can find it.

The controls on the General tab do the following:

- The Enable IP Router Manager check box controls whether this interface allows IP routing at all. When it's checked, the administrative status of this interface will appear as Up, indicating that it's available for routing traffic. When it's unchecked, the interface will be marked as Down; it won't route any packets, and other routers won't be able to communicate with it.

- The Enable Router Discovery Advertisements check box controls whether this router will broadcast router discovery messages. These messages allow clients to find a "nearby" (in network terms) router without any manual configuration on your part. When this check box is enabled, the controls below it become active so you can set the following properties:

  - The Advertisement Lifetime (Minutes) field determines how long advertisements are valid. Clients will ignore any advertisement they receive after its lifetime has expired.

  - The Level Of Preference field determines how clients use this router in comparison with other routers on your network. Clients use routers with higher preferences first; if there are routers with equal preference levels, the client can randomly select one.

  - RRAS will send out advertisements at a randomly chosen interval that falls between the minimum and maximum time intervals for sending advertisements. The default settings mean RRAS will send an advertisement every 7 to 10 minutes.

- The Inbound Filters and Outbound Filters buttons allow you to selectively accept or reject packets on the specified interface. You can accept all packets that don't trigger a filter or accept only those packets that match filter criteria. Each type of filter can use the source or destination IP address and netmask as filter criteria. For example, you can construct a filter that rejects all packets from 206.151.234.0 with a netmask of 255.255.255.0; that effectively screens out any traffic from that subnet.

- The Enable Fragmentation Checking check box tells your router to reject any fragmented IP packets instead of accepting them for processing. Because flooding a router with fragmented IP packets is a popular denial-of-service attack, you may want to check this box.

Setting Up Demand-Dial Interfaces

When you install RRAS, it will automatically create an interface for each LAN connection it can find. If you want to create new demand-dial interfaces, you'll have to do it yourself. Fortunately, there's an easy way to do this with the Demand-Dial Interface Wizard. To activate the wizard, right-click the Network Interfaces node in the Routing And Remote Access snap-in, and choose the New Demand-Dial Interface command.

In the following sections, we cover the steps involved in setting up demand-dial interfaces.

Naming the Interface

The first page of the wizard is the Interface Name page, where you specify the name you want the new interface to have. This is the name you'll see in the Routing And Remote Access snap-in, so you should choose a name that identifies the source and destination of the connection (for example, HSV-ATL for a connection between Huntsville and Atlanta). This is particularly useful when you want to use one RRAS console somewhere on a network to manage many RRAS servers, because having an easy way to see which link you're working with can be very valuable.

Choosing a Connection Type

The Connection Type page of the wizard allows you to specify which type of demand-dial interface you will create. Demand-dial interfaces can use a physical device (such as a modem or an ISDN adapter) or a virtual private network (VPN) connection. For example, you can have a demand-dial connection that opens a VPN tunnel to a remote network when it sees traffic destined for that network. Depending on which option you choose here, the remaining wizard pages will differ.

Assuming you choose to use a physical device as the basis for your network, the Select A Device page of the wizard prompts you to choose a device (such as a modem or ISDN terminal adapter) to use for this demand-dial interface. If the device you want to use isn't already set up, you'll need to add it; for that reason, you're probably better off adding and configuring modems before setting up RRAS.

If you specify that you want to use a VPN connection, you'll see the VPN Type page, where you can specify what type of VPN connection to use. You have the following three choices:

- The Automatic radio button tells RRAS to figure out the connection type when negotiating with the remote server. This is the most flexible choice, so it's selected by default.

- The Point-To-Point Tunneling Protocol (PPTP) radio button tells RRAS that this connection will always use PPTP.

- Likewise, the Layer 2 Tunneling Protocol (L2TP) radio button indicates that you want this connection to always use L2TP.

Determining Who to Call

The next step is the same for both VPN and physical connections, even though the wizard page is labeled differently. For VPNs, you'll see the Network Address page. For ordinary dial-up connections, the page is labeled Phone Number. In either case, you should enter the phone number or IP address (whichever is appropriate) of the remote router.

Setting Routing and Security Options

The next page is the Protocols And Security page, which contains four configuration check boxes:

- The Route IP Packets On This Interface Or Route IPX Packets On This Interface box controls whether this interface will handle the specified packet types. By default, IP routing is enabled, but IPX routing isn't.

- If you want to add a user account so that a remote router (running RRAS or not) can dial in, check the Add A User Account So A Remote Router Can Dial In box.

- Some routers can handle Password Authentication Protocol (PAP), Challenge Handshake Authentication Protocol (CHAP), or Microsoft Challenge Handshake Authentication Protocol (MS-CHAP) authentication, but others can handle only PAP. If your remote partner works only with PAP, make sure the Send A Plain-Text Password If That Is The Only Way To Connect box is checked.

- If your RRAS server is calling a system that isn't running RRAS, the system may expect you to manually interact with it, perhaps through a terminal window. This is what the last check box, Use Scripting To Complete The Connection With The Remote Router, is for—check it, and you'll get a terminal window after the modem connects so you can provide whatever commands or authenticators you need.

Setting Dial-in Credentials

If you choose to allow remote routers to dial in to the RRAS machine you're setting up, you'll have to create a user account with appropriate permissions. The Demand-Dial Interface Wizard handles the account creation process for you, assuming you fill out the fields on the Dial-In Credentials page.

Setting Dial-out Credentials

If you want your router to initiate calls to another router, you'll need to tell your local RRAS installation what credentials to use when it makes an outgoing call. Although RRAS uses the information you enter in the Dial-In Credentials page, it makes no attempt to do anything with the credentials you provide on the Dial-Out Credentials page. The credentials you provide here must match the credentials the remote router expects to see. If they don't match, your router won't be able to authenticate itself to the remote end.

In Exercise 5.2 you will continue from Exercise 5.1 with configuring the Demand-Dial Interface Wizard. In this exercise, you'll create a simple demand-dial interface. This requires you to have the phone number, username, and password for the remote end as well as a demand-dial-capable device installed in the machine.

 The Demand-Dial Interface Wizard automatically appears after you complete Exercise 5.1.

EXERCISE 5.2

Creating a Demand-Dial Interface

1. The Demand-Dial Interface Wizard should be open if you just finished Exercise 5.1. Click Next.

2. On the Interface Name page, you can specify a name for the interface. Accept the default of Remote Router. Click Next.

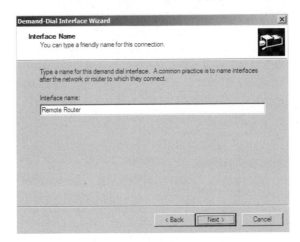

3. The Connection Type page appears. You can connect to the remote router via a VPN interface or through a Point to Point over Ethernet (PPPoE) connection. Make sure the Connect Using Virtual Private Networking (VPN) option is selected, and click Next.

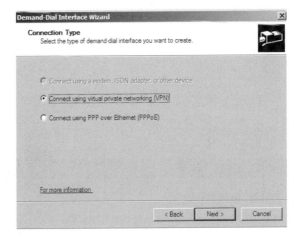

4. On the VPN Type page, choose Automatic Selection. This page allows you to choose which VPN connection you want to use.

5. The Destination Address page appears next. Here is where you enter the IP address of the other router to which you are connecting. Type the IP address of one of your routers (if you are at home and have a small home router, type that IP address). For this example, we entered **192.168.1.1**. Click Next after you've entered the IP address.

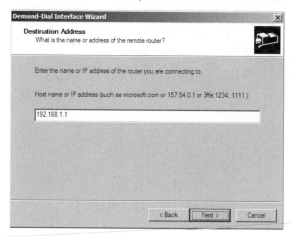

6. On the Protocols And Security page, make sure the Route IP Packets On This Interface box is the only one checked.

7. If you have not defined any static routes yet, you will be asked to do so before you can activate the demand-dial connection. On the Static Routes For Remote Networks page, click the Add button, and enter the IP address, subnet mask, and metric of the remote router. Click OK when you're done. You will notice the new static route in the list. Click Next.

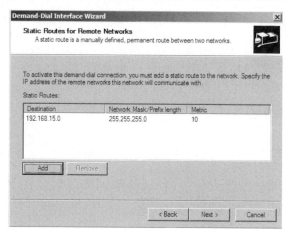

8. In the Dial-Out Credentials page, fill in the username, domain (if any), and password needed to connect to the remote network. Click Next.

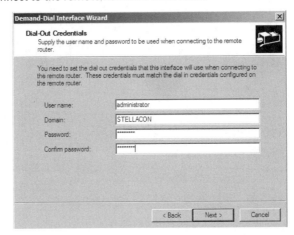

9. When the wizard's summary page appears, click the Finish button to create the interface.

Creating and Removing RIP Interfaces

After you create the physical interfaces (using either demand-dial or LAN interfaces), the next step you have to take is create an interface for the routing protocol you want to use. After you install the routing protocols (the section "Managing Routing Protocols" later in this chapter), RIP nodes appear in the Routing And Remote Access snap-in. To create an interface, right-click the RIP node, and choose New Interface. That displays the New Interface dialog box, which lists all the physical interfaces that are available for the selected protocol.

Once you select the interface you want to use, if RRAS can create the interface, the interface is added to the appropriate item in the console, and the corresponding Properties dialog box opens.

You can remove a RIP interface by selecting it in the appropriate folder and pressing the Delete key, by selecting Action ➤ Delete, or by choosing Delete from the pop-up menu.

Setting RIP Interface Properties

RIP interfaces have their own properties, all of which are specific to RIP. You adjust these settings by selecting the RIP node, clicking the appropriate RIP interface in the right pane, and selecting Properties from the pop-up or Action menu.

In the following sections, we'll cover the various options available in a RIP interface's Properties dialog box.

The General Tab

The General tab of the RIP interface's Properties dialog box (Figure 5.7) lets you control the router's operational mode, which protocols it uses to send and accept packets, and a couple of other useful things.

FIGURE 5.7   The General tab of the RIP interface's Properties dialog box

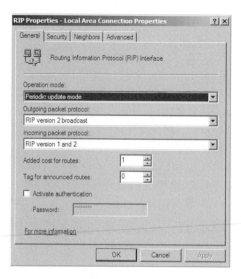

Here's what you can do with the General tab:

- The Operation Mode drop-down list controls the router's mode. By default, demand-dial interfaces will be set to Auto-Static Update Mode, while LAN interfaces will be set to Periodic Update Mode.

- The Outgoing Packet Protocol drop-down list controls what kind of RIP packets this router sends:

  - If your network has all RIPv2 routers, choose RIP Version 2 Multicast to make RRAS send efficient RIP multicasts

  - If you have a version 1 or a mix of version 1 and version 2, there are selections for those, too.

  - The fourth choice, Silent RIP, is useful when you want your RRAS router to listen to other routers' routes but not advertise any of its own. Typically, you'll use Silent RIP when you're using RRAS to connect a small network (such as a branch office) that doesn't have any other routers to a larger network—the small network doesn't have any routes to advertise because it's connected to only one remote network.

- Use the Incoming Packet Protocol drop-down list to specify what kinds of RIP packets this interface will accept. You can choose to accept any of the following:

  - Only RIPv1 packets

  - Only RIPv2 packets

  - Both version 1 and version 2 packets

  - No packets at all

  The default setting is to accept both version 1 and version 2 packets.

- The Added Cost For Routes field lets you control how much this router will increase the route cost. Usually, it's best to leave this set to 1 because setting it too high may increase the interface's cost so much that no one uses it.

- The Tag For Announced Routes field gives you a way to supply a tag included in all RIP packets sent by this router. RRAS doesn't use RIP tags, but other routers can use them.

- The Activate Authentication check box and Password field give you an identification tool for use with your routers. If you turn on authentication, all incoming and outgoing RIP packets must contain the specified password. Therefore, all of this router's neighbors need to use the same password. The password is transmitted as clear text, so this option doesn't provide you with any security.

 Real World Scenario

Assessing Risk

In the list of options for the General tab of the RIP interface's Properties dialog box, we've chosen to leave the last bullet point as is from the first edition of this book to highlight a problem found all too often in the real world. The last sentence of the final bullet point refers to the transmission of passwords in clear text between routers and ends with "so this option doesn't provide you with any security." That sentence indicates a problem with risk assessment and is unfortunately found all over the field of information technology. The statement that a clear-text password doesn't provide "any security" is very misleading. A password, even one transmitted in clear text, can provide a significant amount of security depending on the application and the environment.

In this case, the environment is one in which routers are passing routing information to one another using a routing protocol. Risks include the following:

- An attacker could inject malicious routes and black-hole traffic or cause the traffic to be lost.

- An attacker might cause traffic to be routed through a machine under their control and thus be able to intercept the traffic.

If you use a password, even one transmitted in clear text, the attacker must first guess the password in order to be able to inject malicious routes.

How might an attacker learn the password? Aside from brute-force guessing, the attacker could find the password by sniffing or listening to the network traffic between routers. But to do that, they would need to be able to place a sniffing tool within the network. Is it possible? Certainly. But how likely is it that an attacker could place a sniffer in a strategic location such as between routers? It's not that likely. If an attacker does indeed manage to get the sniffer into that strategic location, it's even less likely that they would care about listening for routing protocol information. It's more likely that they would be interested in all the other traffic passing between those routers than sniffing the routing protocol password and injecting their own routes. Yes, this is possible, but it's not something that we, or any of our colleagues in network departments, lose any sleep over. If an attacker is able to place a sniffer that deep into a network, it's already "game over."

As you can see, it's important to be able to assess risk vs. cost and determine just how much benefit you can obtain by a given mitigating factor. In this case, the risk is that an attacker can inject routes into a router maliciously. A mitigating factor for this risk is the use of a password transmitted along with the routes. This mitigating factor provides a great deal of safety but is not a perfect solution. This is not a perfect solution because the password is transmitted in the first place. It's slightly worse because the password is transmitted in clear text, but the solution isn't perfect simply because the password is transmitted, clear text or not.

Even if the password were encrypted prior to being transmitted, it would still be susceptible to any number of attacks. A replay attack can be made against even an encrypted password—the attacker sniffs the encrypted password and then simply transmits the encrypted password along with the malicious route injection. To do this, the attacker would again need to have a sniffer on the network. So as you can see, clear text or encrypted, a password being transmitted with the routing information provides the same amount of security. But to say that it doesn't provide "any security" is false.

The Security Tab

The Security tab (see Figure 5.8) helps you regulate which routes your RIP interface will accept from and broadcast to its peers. There are good reasons to be careful about which routes you accept into your routing table because a malicious attacker could simply flood your router with bogus routes and watch, laughing, as your routers send traffic off on a wild goose chase. Likewise, you may not want to advertise every route in your routing table, particularly if the same routers handle both Internet and intranet traffic. You can use the controls on this tab to discard routes that fall within a particular range of addresses, or you can accept only those routes that fall within a particular range.

FIGURE 5.8   The Security tab of the RIP interface's Properties dialog box

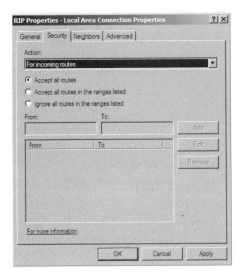

The default setting is to accept all routes, but you can change it using these controls:

- The Action drop-down list lets you choose whether you want to impose settings on incoming routes that your router hears from its peers or on outgoing routes that it announces. Depending on which of these options you choose, the wording of the three radio buttons below the drop-down will change.

- The restriction radio buttons in the center of the dialog box control the action applied to incoming or outgoing routes:

  - The default setting, Announce All Routes (for outgoing routes) or Accept All Routes (for incoming routes), does just that—all routes are accepted or announced, no matter the source.

  - Announce All Routes In The Ranges Listed (outgoing) or Accept All Routes In The Range Listed (incoming) causes RRAS to silently ignore any routes that fall outside the specified ranges. You'd usually use this option when you wanted to limit the scope of routes over which your router can exchange traffic.

  - Do Not Announce All Routes In The Range Listed (outgoing) or Ignore All Routes In The Ranges Listed (incoming) tells RRAS to silently ignore any routes that fall within the specified ranges. This is useful for filtering out routes that you don't want to make available or those you don't want to use to reach remote systems.

- The From and To fields; the Add, Edit, and Remove buttons; and the address range list are all used to specify which set of addresses you want to use with the restriction radio buttons.

The Neighbors Tab

The Neighbors tab (Figure 5.9) gives you a finer degree of control over how this particular interface interacts with its peer RIP routers. By specifying a list of trusted neighbor routers, you can choose to use neighboring routers' routes in addition to, or instead of, broadcast and multicast RIP announcements.

FIGURE 5.9   The Neighbors tab of the RIP interface's Properties dialog box

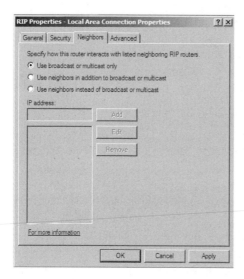

You will see the following radio buttons on the Neighbors tab:

- The Use Broadcast Or Multicast Only radio button tells RRAS to ignore any RIP neighbors. This is the default setting. It means that any router that can successfully broadcast or multicast routes to you can load its routes into your routing table.

- The Use Neighbors In Addition To Broadcast Or Multicast radio button tells RRAS to accept routes from RIP peers as well as from the neighbors you've specified.

- The Use Neighbors Instead Of Broadcast Or Multicast radio button indicates that you don't trust RIP announcements that your router picks up from the network; instead, you're telling RRAS to trust only those neighbors that are defined in the neighbor list.

You manage the list of trusted neighbor routers using the IP Address field; the Add, Edit, and Remove buttons; and the list itself. These controls are enabled when you specify that you want to use neighbor-supplied routing information; once the controls are activated, you can add router IP addresses to the neighbor list.

The Advanced Tab

The Advanced tab (Figure 5.10) contains 12 controls that govern some fairly esoteric RIP behavior.

FIGURE 5.10 The Advanced tab of the RIP interface's Properties dialog box

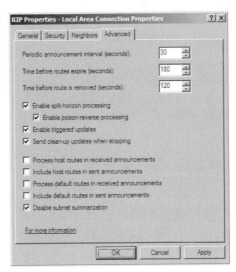

The first three controls are active only when you turn on Periodic Update Mode on the General tab:

- The Periodic Announcement Interval (Seconds) field controls the interval at which periodic router announcements are made.

- The Time Before Routes Expire (Seconds) field controls how long the route may stay in the routing table before it's considered to be expired. The arrival of a new RIP announcement for the route resets the timer—it will be marked as invalid only if it reaches the expiration timer without being renewed through a new announcement.

- The Time Before Route Is Removed (Seconds) field controls the interval that may pass between the time a route expires and the time it's removed.

The next group of check boxes update processing and loop detection:

- The Enable Split-Horizon Processing check box turns on split-horizon processing, in which a route learned by a RIP router on a network is not rebroadcast to that network. Split-horizon processing helps prevent routing loops, so it's on by default.

  - The Enable Poison-Reverse Processing check box is active only when the Enable Split-Horizon Processing check box is on. This option modifies the way split-horizon processing works. When poison-reverse processing is turned on, routes learned from a network are rebroadcast to the network with a metric of 16, a special value that tells other routers that the route is unreachable. This option prevents routing loops while still keeping the routing tables up-to-date.

- The Enable Triggered Updates check box indicates whether you want routing table changes to be immediately sent out when they're noticed (the default). Triggered updates help keep the routing table up-to-date with minimum latency.

- The Send Clean-Up Updates When Stopping check box controls whether RRAS will send announcements that mark the routes it was handling as unavailable. This immediately lets its RIP peers know that the routes it was servicing are no longer usable.

The last set of controls governs what happens with host and default routes:

- By default, RRAS ignores any host routes it sees in RIP announcements. Check the Process Host Routes In Received Announcements box if you want it to honor those routes instead of ignoring them.

- The Include Host Routes In Sent Announcements check box directs RRAS to send host route information as part of its RIP announcements; normally it won't do this.

- The Process Default Routes In Received Announcements and Include Default Routes In Sent Announcements check boxes have the same function as their host route check boxes described earlier.

- The Disable Subnet Summarization check box is active only if you have RIPv2 specified as the outbound packet type for the router. When subnet summarization is turned off, RIP won't advertise subnets to routers that are on other subnets.

Setting IP Routing Properties

The IPv4 and IPv6 nodes in the Routing And Remote Access snap-in have several subnodes, including the General node. When you click the General node and select Properties from the Action menu, you'll find settings that apply to all installed IP routing protocols on the server. These settings give you some additional control over how routing works.

In the following sections, we'll look at the options in the General Properties dialog box. These options are available for configuring settings that apply to IP routing in general.

 The Multicast Scopes tab of the General Properties dialog box is for setting and managing multicast scopes.

The Logging Tab

The Logging tab (shown in Figure 5.11) contains four radio buttons that you use to control what information the IP routing components of RRAS log:

- The Log Errors Only radio button instructs the server to log IP routing–related errors and nothing else. This gives you adequate indication of problems after they happen, but it doesn't point out potential problems noted by warning messages.

- The Log Errors And Warnings radio button is the default choice; it instructs RRAS to log error and warning messages to the event log without adding any informational messages. If you get in the habit of carefully reviewing your event logs, these warning messages may give you welcome forewarning of incipient problems.

- The Log The Maximum Amount Of Information radio button causes the IP routing stack to log messages about almost everything it does. This gives you a lot of useful fodder when you're troubleshooting, but it can flood your logs with minutiae if you're not careful—don't turn it on unless you're trying to isolate and fix a problem.

- The Disable Event Logging radio button turns off all IP routing event logging.

 Don't use the Disable Event Logging option because it will keep you from being able to review the service's logs in case of a problem.

FIGURE 5.11   The Logging tab of the General Properties dialog box

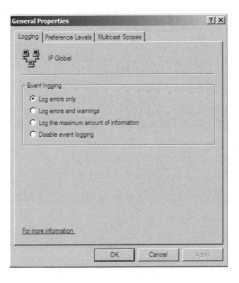

The Preference Levels Tab

The Preference Levels tab (Figure 5.12) gives you a way to change the router's behavior by telling it what class of routes to prefer. In the earlier discussion of routing, you read that the router selects routes based on cost metric information. The other factor that comes into play is the preference level of the routing source. The default configuration for RRAS causes it to prefer local and static routes over dynamically discovered routes.

For example, say there are two routing table entries indicating routes to 216.80.*—one that you've entered as a static route and one that your router has discovered via a RIP peer.

In the example shown in Figure 5.12, the router will always try to use the static route first; if it can't, it will try to use the RIP-generated route. You can change the router's class preference by selecting the class you want to change and using the Move Up and Move Down buttons.

FIGURE 5.12   The Preference Levels tab

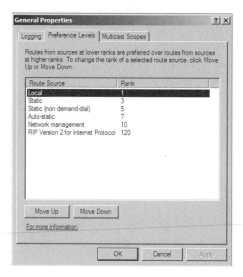

Managing Routing Protocols

Routing protocols typically don't take a lot of management; once you install RIP, the protocol engine takes care of exchanging routes with remote routers. You can't directly edit the contents of the routing table generated by dynamic routing protocols (this feature is available only with dedicated routers using a router operating system such as Cisco's IOS). That means your management of these protocols is pretty much limited to installing them, configuring them to meet your needs, and watching them as they run.

In the following sections, you will learn how to install routing protocols and set routing protocol properties.

Installing RIP

You add routing protocols from the General subnode of the IPv4 node in the Routing And Remote Access snap-in. This is different from the way you manage network protocols in Windows NT, but it makes sense—there's no reason to install RIP unless you're using RRAS, so it's logical that you would install it from there.

Exercise 5.3 explains how to install RIP; you'll need the protocol installed to complete the exercises later in the chapter.

EXERCISE 5.3

Installing the RIP Protocols

1. Open the Routing And Remote Access snap-in by selecting Start ≻ Administrative Tools ≻ Routing And Remote Access.

2. Select the server you want to configure in the left pane of the MMC. Expand it until you see the General node beneath IPv4.

3. Right-click the General node, and select New Routing Protocol.

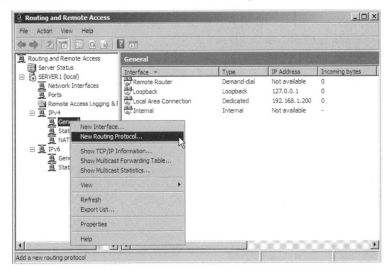

The New Routing Protocol dialog box appears.

4. Select the routing protocol you want to install. In this case, choose RIP Version 2 For Internet Protocol, and click the OK button.

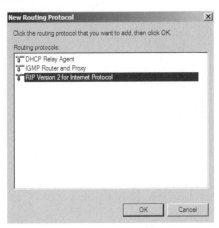

5.   The RRAS console refreshes its display, revealing a new node labeled RIP under the IP
     Routing node.

Setting RIP Properties

RIP is pretty much self-tuning. Once you configure an RRAS router to use RIP, the router will
look for peer routers and exchange routing information without a whole lot of effort on your
part. You can make a few settings through the RIP Properties dialog box. To open RIP Properties, select the RIP node under IP Routing in the Routing And Remote Access snap-in, and
then choose Action ➢ Properties.

   We will cover the various tabs of the RIP Properties dialog box in the following sections.

The General Tab

The General tab (Figure 5.13) has the same logging controls as the General tab of the IPv4
General Properties dialog box. The Maximum Delay control governs how long the router will
wait to send an update notification to its peers.

FIGURE 5.13   The General tab of the RIP Properties dialog box

The Security Tab

The Security tab (Figure 5.14) lets you control what router announcements your router will
accept. By default, the RRAS RIP implementation will ingest routes supplied by any other
router; you can restrict this behavior by supplying either a list of routers to trust or a list of
routers whose routes you want to ignore.

FIGURE 5.14 The Security tab of the RIP Properties dialog box

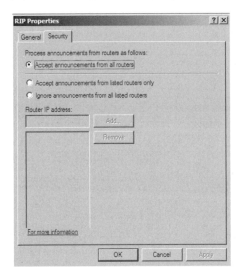

Managing Static Routes

Static routes are simple to manage and configure because they don't participate in any kind of automatic discovery process. Static routes are conceptually very simple—they combine a destination network address with a subnet mask to provide a list of potential destinations. The destination addresses are reached through a particular interface on your router, and they're sent to a specified gateway (normally another router). Finally, there's a metric associated with the static route.

You create new static routes in two ways: by using the route add command from the command line or by right-clicking the Static Routes node in the Routing And Remote Access snap-in and selecting New Static Route.

In the following sections, we'll show how those methods work.

Using *route add* to Create a Static Route

With the route add command, you can add new static routes and choose whether these routes remain in the routing table after the system reboots. Routes that stick around in this manner are called *persistent routes*. To make a route persistent, you need to add the -p switch to the route add command. The command syntax itself is simple:

```
route add –p destinationMask netMask gateWay metric interfaceID
```

You specify the destination, netmask, gateway, metric, and interface ID on the command line. These parameters are all required. The route add command does some basic checking to make sure that the netmask and destination match and that you haven't omitted anything.

You have to specify the interface as a number, not as a name. However, the `route print` command (which will be covered a little later in this chapter) lists its interfaces and the associated numbers.

Using RRAS to Create a Static Route

To create a new static route using the RRAS console, right-click the Static Routes node in the Routing And Remote Access snap-in, and select New Static Route. This opens the IPv4 Static Routes dialog box (Figure 5.15).

FIGURE 5.15 Use the IPv4 Static Routes dialog box to create new static routes.

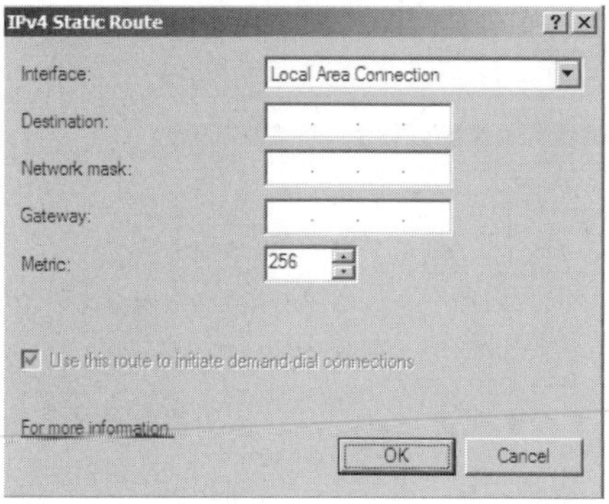

You have to provide the same parameters as with the `route add` command—the interface you want to use to connect, the destination and network mask, the gateway for the outbound packets, and a metric.

If you're creating a route that's not bound to a LAN interface, you can use the Use This Route To Initiate Demand-Dial Connections check box to specify that the route should open a new demand-dial connection on the specified interface.

Exercise 5.4 shows you how to add and remove static routes. To complete Exercise 5.4, you must have completed Exercise 5.1.

EXERCISE 5.4

Adding and Removing Static Routes

1. Open the Routing And Remote Access snap-in by selecting Start ➢ Administrative Tools ➢ Routing And Remote Access.

2. Select the server you want to configure in the left pane of the MMC. Expand IPv4 until you see the Static Routes node beneath.

3. Right-click the Static Routes node, and select New Static Route. The Static Route dialog box appears.

EXERCISE 5.4 *(continued)*

4. Select the interface you want to use from the Interface drop-down list. The choices are Local Area Connection and Remote Router. Choose Local Area Connection for this exercise.

5. Enter the destination address (try **10.10.10.0**), and enter a netmask of **255.255.255.0**.

6. For the gateway address, enter the IP address of your RRAS server.

7. Click the OK button. The Routing And Remote Access snap-in reappears.

8. Right-click the Static Routes item, and choose Show IP Routing Table. The IP Routing Table window appears. Verify that your newly added static route is present in the table.

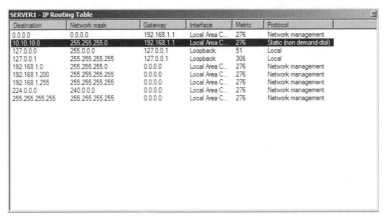

SERVER1 - IP Routing Table					
Destination	Network mask	Gateway	Interface	Metric	Protocol
0.0.0.0	0.0.0.0	192.168.1.1	Local Area C...	276	Network management
10.10.10.0	255.255.255.0	192.168.1.1	Local Area C...	276	Static (non demand-dial)
127.0.0.0	255.0.0.0	127.0.0.1	Loopback	51	Local
127.0.0.1	255.255.255.255	127.0.0.1	Loopback	306	Local
192.168.1.0	255.255.255.0	0.0.0.0	Local Area C...	276	Network management
192.168.1.200	255.255.255.255	0.0.0.0	Local Area C...	276	Network management
192.168.1.255	255.255.255.255	0.0.0.0	Local Area C...	276	Network management
224.0.0.0	240.0.0.0	0.0.0.0	Local Area C...	276	Network management
255.255.255.255	255.255.255.255	0.0.0.0	Local Area C...	276	Network management

9. Close the IP Routing Table window.

10. Right-click the static route you added, and use the Delete command to remove it.

Configuring TCP/IP Packet Filters

One of the most useful features in RRAS is its ability to selectively filter TCP/IP packets in both directions.

Filters are usually used to block out undesirable traffic. In general, the idea is to keep out packets that your machines doesn't need to see. You can construct filters that allow traffic into or deny traffic out of your network based on rules that specify source and destination addresses and ports.

The basic idea behind packet filtering is simple:

1. You specify filter rules.

2. Incoming packets are measured against those rules.

There are two types of filter rule:

- Accept all packets except those prohibited by a rule.

- Drop all packets except those permitted by a rule.

Filters are associated with a particular interface; the filters assigned to one interface are totally independent of those on all other interfaces. Inbound and outbound filters are likewise separate. The following are some examples of filters:

- Block all packets to a web server except those on TCP ports 80 and 443.

- Block all outgoing packets on the ports used by the MSN and AOL instant messaging tools.

- Filters on a PPTP or L2TP server can screen out everything except VPN traffic. This allows you to expose a Windows Server 2008 VPN server without fear of compromise.

You create and remove filters by using the Input Packet Filters and Output Packet Filters buttons on the General tab of the Local Area Network Properties dialog box. The mechanics of working with incoming and outbound filters are identical; just remember the following guidelines:

- You create inbound filters to screen traffic coming to the interface.

- You create outbound filters to screen traffic going back out through that interface.

To create a filter, find the interface on which you want the filter and then open its Properties dialog box. Click the appropriate packet filter button, and you'll see the Inbound Filters dialog box (Figure 5.16).

FIGURE 5.16   The Inbound Filters dialog box

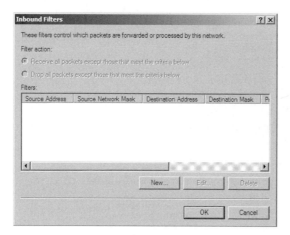

This dialog box has the following six parts:

- Receive All Packets Except Those That Meet The Criteria Below excludes the packets you specify and accepts everything else.

  This option is inactive until you create a filter rule.

- Drop All Packets Except Those That Meet The Criteria Below accepts only those packets you specify and excludes everything else.

  This option is inactive until you create a filter rule.

- The Filters list, which is initially empty, shows you which filters are defined on this interface. Each entry in the list shows the following:

  - Source address and mask

  - Destination address and mask

  - Protocol, port, and traffic type specified in the rule

- The New, Edit, and Delete buttons allow you to add, edit, and remove filters.

To create a filter, click the New button, and you'll see the Add IP Filter dialog box (Figure 5.17). The conditions you specify here must all be true to trigger the rule. For example, if you specify both the source and destination addresses, only traffic from the defined source to the defined destination will be filtered.

FIGURE 5.17   The Add IP Filter dialog box

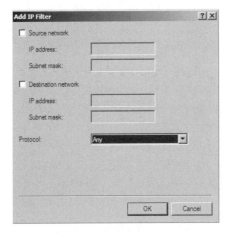

Use these tips to fill out the Add IP Filter dialog box:

- To create a filter that blocks packets by their origin or source address, check the Source Network box, and supply the IP address and subnet mask for the source you want to block.

- To create a filter that blocks packets according to their destination address, check the Destination Network box, and fill in the appropriate address and subnet mask.

- To filter by protocol, choose the protocol you want to block:

  - Any, which blocks everything

  - TCP

  - TCP (Established)

This means that the TCP/IP has an established connection already.

- IP
- UDP
- ICMP
- Other, with a fill-in field for a protocol number

For each of these protocols, you'll have to enter some additional information; for example, if you select TCP, you have to specify the source or destination port numbers (or both).

Once you've specified the filter you want, click the OK button, and you'll see it in the filter list. Filters go into effect as soon as you close the interface's Properties dialog box; you can go back and add, edit, or remove filters at any time.

Configuring VPN Packet Filters

Packet filters provide a useful security mechanism for blocking unwanted traffic on particular machines. It's a good idea to use packet filters to keep non-VPN traffic out of your VPN servers. The rules for doing this are fairly straightforward, as you will see in the following sections.

PPTP Packet Filters

You need at least two filters to adequately screen out non-PPTP traffic:

- The first filter allows traffic with a protocol ID of 47—the Generic Routing Encapsulation (GRE) protocol—to pass to the destination address of the PPTP interface.
- The second filter allows inbound traffic bound for TCP port 1723 (the PPTP port) to come to the PPTP interface.

You can add a third filter if the PPTP server also works as a PPTP client; in that case, the third filter needs the interface's destination address, a protocol type of TCP (established), and a source port of 1723.

Once you've created these filters, you open the Inbound Filters dialog box and select the radio button labeled Drop All Packets Except Those That Meet The Criteria Below.

Then you repeat the process on the Outbound side, creating two or three corresponding output filters that screen out any traffic not originating from the VPN interface and using the correct protocols.

In Exercise 5.5, you'll set up RRAS IP packet filters that block everything except PPTP traffic on the specified interface.

 Don't attempt this exercise on your production VPN server until you've been successful in trying it on another, less-critical machine.

EXERCISE 5.5

Configuring PPTP Packet Filters

1. Open the Routing And Remote Access snap-in by selecting Start ➤ Administrative Tools ➤ Routing And Remote Access. Expand the server and IPv4 nodes to expose the General node of the server on which you're working. Select the General node.

2. Right-click the Local Area Connection interface, and choose Properties.

3. In the General tab of the interface's Properties dialog box, click the Inbound Filters button. The Inbound Filters dialog box appears.

4. Click the New button, and the Add IP Filter dialog box appears.

5. Fill out the Add IP Filter dialog box as follows:

   Check the Destination Network check box.

   Fill in the destination IP address field with the IP address of the remote VPN interface. (For this exercise, we entered **192.168.1.254**. You can use the same.)

   Enter a destination subnet mask of **255.255.255.255**.

   Select a protocol type of TCP, and then specify a source port of 0 and a destination port of 1723.

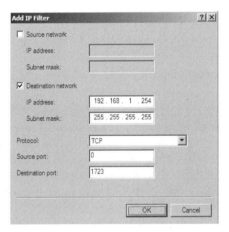

   Click the OK button.

6. The Inbound Filters dialog box reappears, listing the new filter you created in step 5. Add another new filter using the same IP address and subnet mask, but this time specify Other in the Protocol field and fill in a protocol number of 47.

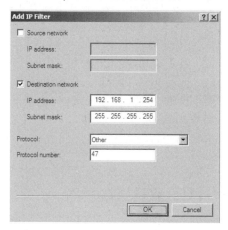

When you're done, click the OK button to return to the Inbound Filters dialog box.

7. In the Inbound Filters dialog box, click the Drop All Packets Except Those That Meet The Criteria Below radio button, and click the OK button.

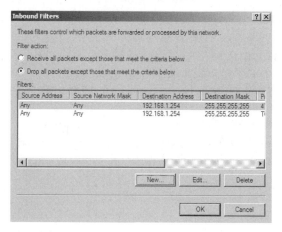

8. Close the interface's Properties dialog box.

L2TP Packet Filters

To use L2TP packet filters, you have to go through the same basic process as you do with PPTP packet filters (see the previous section), but the filters you need are slightly different. Four filters are required—two input filters and two output filters:

- Two input filters with a destination of the VPN interface address and a netmask of 255.255.255.255, filtering UDP:
  - One with a source and destination port of 500
  - The second with a source and destination port of 1701
- Two output filters with a source of the VPN interface address and a netmask of 255.255.255.255, filtering UDP:
  - One with a source and destination port of 500
  - The second with a source and destination port of 1701

Managing IP Routing

Managing IP routing is fairly simple. If you understand how the options described earlier in this chapter work, you know most of what you need to know to keep IP routing working smoothly. All the remaining skills you'll need center around monitoring your routers to make sure traffic is flowing smoothly and troubleshooting the occasional problem.

A number of status displays are built into the Routing And Remote Access snap-in. Knowing that they exist, and what they display, makes it much easier to see all the various health and status data that RRAS maintains. Each of these commands shows you something different:

The General ➤ Show TCP/IP Information command   As you would expect, this display shows a broad general selection of IP routing data, including the number of routes in the route table, the number of IP and UDP datagrams received and forwarded, and the number of connection attempts. To customize the view, you can right-click in the TCP/IP Information window and choose the Select Columns command.

The Static Routes ➤ Show IP Routing Table command   This command shows you the entire contents of the routing table, including the destination, netmask, and gateway for each route. This version of the routing table doesn't show you where the route came from (for example, whether it was learned by RIP).

The RIP ➤ Show Neighbors command   This command shows you which RIP neighbors exist; for each router, you can see how many bad packets and bad routes that neighbor has tried to foist off on your router.

Exercise 5.6 shows you how to monitor IP routing.

EXERCISE 5.6

Monitoring Routing Status

1. Open the Routing And Remote Access snap-in by selecting Start ➤ Administrative Tools ➤ Routing And Remote Access.

2. Select the server whose status you want to monitor in the left pane of the MMC.

3. Select the Network Interfaces node. Notice that the right pane of the MMC now lists all known interfaces along with their status and connection state.

4. Select the General node beneath IPv4. Notice that the right pane of the MMC updates to show the IP interfaces, their IP addresses, their administrative and operational states, and whether IP filtering is enabled on each interface.

5. Right-click the General node, and choose the Show TCP/IP Information command. Check the number of IP routes shown.

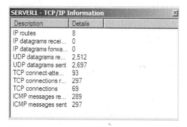

SERVER1 - TCP/IP Information	
Description	Details
IP routes	8
IP datagrams recei...	0
IP datagrams forwa...	0
UDP datagrams re...	2.512
UDP datagrams sent	2.697
TCP connect-atte...	93
TCP connections r...	297
TCP connections	69
ICMP messages re...	289
ICMP messages sent	297

6. Right-click the Static Routes node, and choose the Show IP Routing Table command. Note that the number of routes listed corresponds to the route count in the TCP/IP Information window and that some of the routes listed are automatically generated.

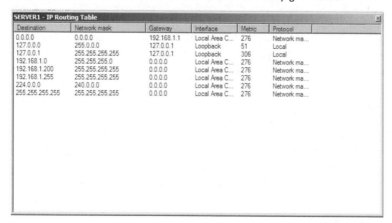

SERVER1 - IP Routing Table					
Destination	Network mask	Gateway	Interface	Metric	Protocol
0.0.0.0	0.0.0.0	192.168.1.1	Local Area C...	276	Network ma...
127.0.0.0	255.0.0.0	127.0.0.1	Loopback	51	Local
127.0.0.1	255.255.255.255	127.0.0.1	Loopback	306	Local
192.168.1.0	255.255.255.0	0.0.0.0	Local Area C...	276	Network ma...
192.168.1.200	255.255.255.255	0.0.0.0	Local Area C...	276	Network ma...
192.168.1.255	255.255.255.255	0.0.0.0	Local Area C...	276	Network ma...
224.0.0.0	240.0.0.0	0.0.0.0	Local Area C...	276	Network ma...
255.255.255.255	255.255.255.255	0.0.0.0	Local Area C...	276	Network ma...

Now let's revisit the route command you saw earlier but in the context of route monitoring.

Using the *route print* Command

You already learned how to use the route add command to add a new static route from the command line. The route print command can show you all or part of the routing table from the command line. Just entering **route print** into a command window gives you a complete dump of the entire routing table. Adding a wildcard IP address displays only routes that match the address you specify. For example, route print 206.151.* displays only routes that match 206.151.

 Real World Scenario

Bringing in Experts to Help the Experts

Your company has finally realized that using its multihomed computers as routers isn't the most effective means for supporting your network. You decide to explore using dedicated routers and switches to segment and control network traffic. You also want to make sure that you have evaluated the differences between the two approaches thoroughly and professionally. How exactly should you proceed?

Part of the MCSE certification covered in this chapter is TCP/IP routing and the RIP routing protocol. Those concepts are important because you are most likely placing the Windows Server 2008 information system in a routed environment. Just as it is important to understand that expertise regarding Windows Server 2008 is essential, it's also important to understand the need for experts in the world of RIP and other routing protocols.

Although these concepts are covered in this book and although the certification exam tests your understanding of the concepts, the book and certification don't fully prepare you to design a network with all the nuances that the operating systems from vendors such as Cisco, Nortel, and Lucent provide. This is a deep field, just as Windows Server 2008 is a deep field. As an analogy, both a vascular surgeon and an orthopedic surgeon are technically proficient, and there is a great deal of crossover knowledge between the two—but when your bones are sticking out and the blood is flowing, you want the two doctors to cover their own fields. The same is true in networking. If you are not as experienced and knowledgeable in internetworking as you are in networking, you would be well served to run your routing or IP designs by an internetworking specialist. The specialist may have some insight that has been honed over time, which will reap benefits to your information system. No single person knows everything, and one of the hallmarks of a professional is to know when to call in another professional. Both professionals need to work together to build an infrastructure that will support the requirements of the new services available in Windows Server 2008.

Troubleshooting IP Routing

A comprehensive overview of IP routing troubleshooting is beyond the scope of this book. Microsoft's online help is pretty good at suggesting probable causes and solutions for most routing problems. If you understand the topics presented in this chapter, then you shouldn't have many troubleshooting problems in RRAS as long as you verify the following points:

- The RRAS service is running and configured to act as an IP router.
- The router's TCP/IP configuration is correct (including a static IP address).
- You have IP routing protocols attached to each interface on which you need them.

    Next, you need to verify the following routing-specific settings and behaviors:

- Check to be sure that your router is receiving routes from its peers. Do this by opening the routing table and looking at the Protocol column. Seeing entries marked as RIP tells you that at least some peers are getting routing information through. If you don't see any RIP routes, that's a bad sign.
- You need to have a static default route enabled if your router hasn't received any default routes. To do this, add a new static route with a destination of 0.0.0.0, a netmask of 0.0.0.0, and either a demand-dial or a LAN interface appropriate for your network setup.

Troubleshooting Example

In Exercise 5.7, you will perform some troubleshooting, and the exercise assumes the following:

- Your Windows Server 2008 server doesn't have any packet filters or firewall running.
- Your server uses the IP address of 192.168.1.64 as its main interface address.

    The goal is to allow only necessary traffic to this server using an IP packet filter. It was your understanding that another network administrator was going to enable a firewall outside the Windows Server 2008 server. However, after performing a scan of the server using nmap from a nearby Linux server, you find these ports open:

```
PORT      STATE  SERVICE
53/tcp    open   domain
135/tcp   open   msrpc
139/tcp   open   netbios-ssn
445/tcp   open   microsoft-ds
1025/tcp  open   NFS-or-IIS
1723/tcp  open   pptp
```

    Obviously the other firewall is not in place yet. The server acts as a PPTP VPN server for a Windows network and therefore needs only port 1723/TCP open for inbound connections.

Your job is to enable some type of filtering as soon as possible in order to protect this Windows Server 2008 server.

EXERCISE 5.7

Troubleshooting Your Server

1. Open the Routing and Remote Access snap-in by clicking Start ➢ Administrative Tools ➢ Routing And Remote Access.

2. Expand IPv4 or IPv6, and click the General node.

   If you don't have an IPv4 or IPv6 node, open the server's Properties dialog box, and make sure the Router box is checked. If it's not, select it.

3. In the General window of the IPv4 node in the Routing and Remote Access snap-in, right-click the main network interface for the server, which is Local Area Connection by default, and then select Properties.

4. Click the Inbound Filters button. This opens the Inbound Filters dialog box.

5. In the Inbound Filters dialog box, click New. This opens the Add IP Filter dialog box.

6. The first order of business is to allow established TCP connections into the server. These are necessary for any connection that originates from the computer. Within the Add IP Filter dialog box, use the Protocol drop-down, and select TCP [Established]. Leave the Source Port and Destination Port text boxes empty. Click OK to return to the Inbound Filters dialog box.

7. In the Inbound Filters dialog box, which now has one filter in it, change the filter action to Drop All Packets Except Those That Meet The Criteria Below. This is an important step because it changes the policy from "accept everything by default" to "deny everything by default," which is a better filtering policy.

8. Add another filter by clicking New in the Inbound Filters dialog box. For this filter, change the protocol to UDP, and set the source port at 53. This allows the server to receive responses from DNS queries that it sends. Click OK to return to the Inbound Filters dialog box.

9. Back at the Inbound Filters dialog box, click New once again. This time add a filter for PPTP traffic, which runs on 1723/TCP. To do this, select TCP from the Protocol drop-down box, and type **1723** in the Destination Port text box. Then click OK.

10. Check the final group of filters in the Inbound Filters dialog box. Click OK at the Inbound Filters dialog box and OK again at the Local Area Connection Properties dialog box.

Scanning the server again reveals that the only port open from a remote location is 1723/TCP:

```
PORT      STATE SERVICE
1723/tcp open   pptp
```

You've now effectively blocked access to this server except for traffic on the PPTP port of TCP/1723. Outbound traffic has not been filtered.

As extra credit, you could enable ICMP echo requests and replies by adding inbound filters. You could also add outbound filters to ensure that only authorized traffic is being sent from the server. For example, only PPTP traffic and HTTPS traffic to Windows Update might be allowed from this server.

In this exercise, you worked with RRAS to create packet filters for inbound traffic. These were created through the IP Routing section of the Routing And Remote Access snap-in. You added filters were added for established TCP connections, for responses to outgoing DNS requests, and finally for the PPTP traffic itself. The policy for the filter was set to a "deny by default" policy.

Summary

In this chapter, you learned how IP routing connects networks by intelligently delivering network traffic to the correct destination in the internetwork, how to create and manage demand-dial and the RIP interface for IP routing, how to install RIP and set routing parameters, how to manage static routes with the `route add` command and the Routing And Remote Access snap-in, how to configure TCP/IP packet filters for blocking undesirable traffic, and finally how to manage demand-dial routing. We also discussed the OSPF routing protocol and how OSPF is no longer supported by Windows Server 2008 RRAS.

We then discussed VPN connections and protocols. We talked about the inbound and outbound filters that you can set up on your VPN connection. We also discussed NAT and how it can help minimize TCP/IP numbers needed for Internet and remote network connections.

Exam Essentials

Know the difference between static routing and dynamic routing.   Static routing systems don't make any attempt to discover other routers or systems on their networks. Instead, you tell the routing engine how to get data to other networks. Dynamic routing doesn't depend on your adding fixed, unchangeable routes to remote networks. Instead, a dynamic routing engine can discover its surroundings by finding and communicating with other nearby routers in an internetwork.

Understand RRAS.   RRAS provides Windows Server 2008 computers with routing capabilities. You can establish static routes that specify where packets bound for certain networks should go. RRAS provides dynamic routing using versions 1 and 2 of the Routing Information Protocol (RIP). It also provides packet filtering to screen out undesirable packets in both directions.

Understand the difference between RIP and OSPF.   A RIP-capable router periodically sends out announcements while simultaneously receiving announcements from its peers. This exchange of routing information enables each router to learn what routers exist on the network and which destination networks each router knows how to reach. OSPF networks are broken down into areas; an area is a collection of interconnected networks. Think of an area as a subsection of an internetwork. Areas are interconnected by backbones. Each OSPF router keeps a link-state database only for the areas to which it's connected.

Know how to install RRAS and configure IP routing.   The RRAS components are not installed by default on computers running Windows Server 2008. To enable your server to route IP packets, you have to install, activate, and configure RRAS using the Routing And Remote Access Server Setup Wizard in the Routing And Remote Access snap-in. You then need to add demand-dial interfaces if you want to support demand-dialing, give each routable interface a network address for each protocol it carries, and install and configure the routing protocols on the interfaces that should support them.

Know how to configure TCP/IP packet filters.   You can construct filters that allow or deny traffic into or out of your network based on rules that specify source and destination addresses and ports. To create a filter, find the interface on which you want the filter, open its Properties dialog box, and click the appropriate packet filter button.

Review Questions

1. You work on a network with four subnets whose addresses are 208.45.231.0, 208.45.232.0, 208.45.233.0, and 208.45.234.0. Your routers are configured with these IP addresses:

   Router 1: 208.45.231.1 and 208.45.232.1

   Router 2: 208.45.231.2 and 208.45.233.1

   Router 3: 208.45.232.2 and 208.45.234.1

   Router 4: 208.45.233.2 and 208.45.234.2

   Router 2 is connected to the Internet. The connection between Router 2 and Router 4 is a very slow 56K dial-up line. Your computer's IP address is 208.45.231.25. Your default gateway is 208.45.231.2, because that's the address of the router that's connected to the Internet. You want to make sure your computer always routes information to 208.45.234.0 through Router 1 (unless Router 1 becomes unavailable) because the 56K line is so slow. Which command should you use to accomplish this?

   A. `route add 208.45.231.1 mask 255.255.255.0 208.45.234.0 metric 1`
      `route add 208.45.231.2 mask 255.255.255.0 208.45.234.0 metric 2`

   B. `route add 208.45.234.0 mask 255.255.255.0 208.45.231.1 metric 2`
      `route add 208.45.234.0 mask 255.255.255.0 208.45.231.2 metric 1`

   C. `route add 208.45.234.0 mask 255.255.255.0 208.45.231.1 metric 1`
      `route add 208.45.234.0 mask 255.255.255.0 208.45.231.2 metric 2`

   D. `route add 208.45.234.0 mask 255.255.255.0 208.45.232.1 metric 1`
      `route add 208.45.234.0 mask 255.255.255.0 208.45.233.1 metric 2`

2. You administer a network that consists of four subnets. Your manager wants to reduce costs as much as possible. You decide to configure at least one Windows Server 2008 computer on each subnet with RRAS and a nonpersistent demand-dial connection. You want to have the routers dynamically update themselves. Which of the following should you use to accomplish these goals?

   A. RIPv2

   B. OSPF

   C. EIGRP

   D. Area border routers

3. Leigh is setting up an RRAS router at a remote site so that it can connect to the corporate LAN. Which of the following interfaces will Leigh need?

   A. A demand-dial interface for connecting the remote and LAN routers

   B. RIP for routing discovery

   C. A demand-dial interface as well as RIP or OSPF

   D. None of the above

4. You upgraded all your locations to Windows Server 2008 and implemented the routing capability built into the servers. You chose to implement RIP. After implementing the routers, you discover that routes that you don't want your network to consider are updating your RIP routing tables. What can you do to control which networks the RIP routing protocol will communicate with on your network?

A. Configure TCP/IP filtering.

B. Configure RIP route filtering.

C. Configure IP packet filtering.

D. Configure RIP peer filtering.

E. There is no way to control this behavior.

5. You are the network administrator for your organization. You need to see the routing table from the command line. What command-line utility can you use?

A. `route add`

B. `route view`

C. `route print`

D. `route monitor`

6. Joe set up a new RRAS router that seems to be functioning properly, but it isn't routing traffic. He has already verified that RRAS is running and properly configured. Which of the following are possible causes of the problem? (Choose all that apply.)

A. No routes are being learned from peer routers.

B. There is no static default route.

C. No RIP neighbors are defined.

D. The router's authentication credentials are wrong.

7. Your company has six locations that have been connected in a hub-and-spoke design with your location as the center. The network is designed that way because it grew over time and you simply added another connection to your Windows NT server each time one was needed. You are concerned that if your connection goes down, the entire network will go down and all your users across the country will lose connectivity. You have now migrated all your servers to Windows Server 2008, and you are well on your way to migrating the Windows NT workstations to Vista and XP Professional. You decide that each RRAS server will have at least three separate connections to other RRAS servers in the network so that you will always have a way to find a path through the network. You want to accomplish this with the least amount of administrative effort. How should you configure the RRAS computers to ensure these objectives?

A. Configure RIPv2 on all routing interfaces.

B. Configure OSPF on all routing interfaces.

C. Configure RIPv1 and OSPF on all routing interfaces.

D. Configure static routes.

E. Configure RIP version 2 and OSPF on all routing interfaces.

8. You work for a very large accounting company that has more than 1,000 workstations in three locations over a routed network. You have upgraded all the servers to Windows Server 2008 and are well underway in bringing all the workstations to Windows 2000 and XP Professional. Two of the locations are connected to the central office, which has a T1 connection to the Internet. All the users on all three networks are funneled through this RRAS server for Internet access. Your company has a policy that personal Internet browsing from company equipment is not acceptable. The main purposes of Internet access within the company are email connectivity and VPN traffic to your business partners. Also, some staff members occasionally download new regulations and forms from a few government websites. How can you implement this policy using the tools and services on your Windows Server 2008 network?

    A. Configure TCP/IP filters to control access to the Internet.

    B. Configure IP packet filters to control access to the Internet.

    C. Configure the Internet browsers through global policies to control which websites users can and cannot visit.

    D. Create static routing tables to control which websites, based on address, the users can reach.

9. You notice that packets sent to your RRAS router aren't being routed. You determine that the packets are indeed reaching the router. What should you check in order to troubleshoot the problem?

    A. The RRAS service status

    B. The RRAS routing configuration

    C. The RRAS server's TCP/IP configuration

    D. All of the above

10. You are the administrator of a network consisting of six subnets that are routed together through an ISP that doesn't support multicasting. You are connected to the ISP at all locations with Windows Server 2008 RRAS servers. The marketing department is interested in providing audio and video presentations between the corporate office and one of the other locations; these presentations will be a test of how audio and video presentations could be used throughout the entire company. Your company is growing rapidly, and you plan to build a private network to support more flexibility in your routing capability—but that isn't going to happen in time for the test. What can you do on your side of the network to allow the multicasting traffic to reach the intended destinations?

    A. Configure multicast boundaries on each of the appropriate RRAS routers.

    B. Install RIPv2 to carry the multicast traffic.

    C. Configure an IP-in-IP tunnel interface on the appropriate RRAS routers.

    D. Configure the multicast heartbeat on the appropriate RRAS routers.

11. You are the network administrator for your company. You're planning to upgrade the network to Windows 2008 to take advantage of the various new services available and the general overall stability that it promises to provide. Your network is located in one large building and is not connected to remote locations; the entire network is on one subnet and has poor performance because of the amount of network traffic it is supporting. You want to break the network into smaller pieces, but your company doesn't want to spend money on a third-party dedicated router. After you get your servers up and running Windows 2008, you plan to build one Windows 2008 server with multiple NICs so that you can break the network into four subnets. When you're ready to set up this solution for this network, what would be the best way to configure the multihomed Windows 2008 router?

    A. Install and configure the OSPF routing protocol, and let it figure out the routing tables automatically.

    B. Install and configure RIPv1 so that the broadcasts will fill in the tables and keep them up-to-date automatically.

    C. Install and configure RIPv2 so that the broadcasts will fill in the tables and keep them up-to-date automatically.

    D. Configure the multihomed host with a static routing table.

    E. Install and configure RIPv1 and RIPv2 so that the broadcasts will fill in the tables and keep them up-to-date automatically.

12. You are part of a small support staff of a medium-sized company that is growing. No one on your staff is experienced with routers, and because your company has a hiring freeze that extends to your support staff, you cannot bring routing expertise on board in the foreseeable future. However, you are charged with connecting eight offices together. You are almost finished upgrading your servers to Windows 2008 Server, and you've read that you can use them as routers. When it comes time to connect the servers between the various offices using the routing functionality offered in Windows 2008, what routing protocol would make the most sense for your particular situation?

    A. OSPF

    B. RIP

    C. BGP

    D. Dynamic routing file

    E. Static routing tables

13. Your network has three subnets; each subnet has at least two connections to the other subnets. This design was created because you wanted to make sure that every subnet was accessible from every other network if any connection went down. You want to implement this design as effectively as possible, and you want the network to recover as quickly as possible if a link should go down. You are going to implement this design in the near future and use Windows 2008 Server servers as the routers as you bring each subnet online. Which routing protocol supported by Windows 2008 Server would be most appropriate for this design?

    A. RIPv1

    B. RIPv2

    C. OSPF

    D. Static routing tables as a backup to RIP

    E. Static routing tables as a backup to OSPF

14. You are building four networks—each in a different city—to support the regional activities of the Sunrise Flower Shop. Each region needs to communicate with each of the others so that it can take orders for the other regions and then transmit the delivery instructions, including JPEG images, to the appropriate location. To save costs, you decide to set up demand-dial connections with a bandwidth that's sufficient to support the images. However, you don't want routing updates to be broadcast throughout the network—although you do want any changes to the network to be sent to the other routers so that communications can be reliable. Which routing protocol should you use when you configure the Windows 2008 Server servers that you are using for the connection points?

A. OSPF

B. RIPv2

C. Static routing tables

D. RIPv1

E. CHAP

15. You need to create a new demand-dial interface. What would you do in the following exhibit in order to begin the Demand-Dial Interface Wizard?

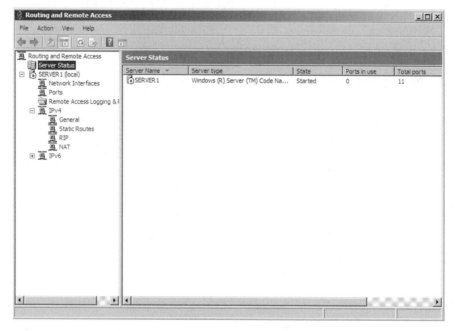

A. Right-click SERVER1, select New, and select Interface.

B. Right-click Network Interfaces, and select New Demand-Dial Interface.

C. Right-click SERVER1, and select Properties.

D. Right-click Routing Interfaces, and select Properties.

16. Which network protocol can Windows Server 2008 route?

    A. TCP

    B. NetBEUI

    C. SNA

    D. IP

17. Which routing protocols available in Windows Server 2008 are described as link-state protocols that transmit the entire routing table? (Choose all that apply.)

    A. RIPv1

    B. RIPv2

    C. OSPF

    D. EIGRP

18. You will be configuring Windows Server 2008 as a demand-dial router, but you need to enable the feature first. From where do you enable Windows Server 2008 to be a demand-dial router?

    A. From the General tab of the Properties dialog box of the local area connection

    B. From the General tab of the server Properties dialog box within the Routing and Remote Access snap-in

    C. From the IP tab of the server Properties dialog box within the Routing and Remote Access snap-in

    D. From the routing interface's Properties dialog box for the routing protocol, either RIP or OSPF

19. You are the network administrator for organization. Your organization has three subnets controlled by two multihomed Windows Server 2008 servers. You have discovered that subnetA is sending ICMP traffic to subnetC. You want to stop the ICMP traffic from being sent to the other subnet. What do you need to set up?

    A. Traffic filters

    B. Traffic rules

    C. Traffic denials

    D. Traffic relays

20. Which routing protocols are not available in Windows Server 2008? (Choose all that apply.)

    A. RIPv1

    B. RIPv2

    C. OSPF

    D. EIGRP

Answers to Review Questions

1. C. The correct syntax for the `route add` command is as follows: `route add` *destination_mask subnet_mask gateway_metric cost_metric*. In option A, the destination and gateway addresses are reversed. Option B uses incorrect metrics. Option D uses gateways that are not on the host's subnet.

2. A. The only way to accomplish all the goals is to use RIPv2. OSPF and EIGRP cannot be used in Windows Server 2008 RRAS. Area border routers are simply special versions of OSPF routers.

3. A. RIP is optional; you can use static routes on a remote dial-up router to avoid dealing with dynamic routing protocols.

4. B. RIP route filters allow you to configure your routers to either ignore or accept updates from specific network addresses or a range of addresses. TCP/IP filtering is configured at each individual host to control the traffic at a granular level, such as a specific address, UDP port, or TCP port. IP packet filtering is used on the router interface to control IP traffic based on subnet masks, IP address, or port. RIP peer filtering is used to control communication between individual routers rather than control the entire network address.

5. C. The `route print` command can show you all or part of the routing table from the command line. Just typing **route print** into a command window will give you a complete dump of the entire routing table.

6. A, B, D. RIP neighbors are optional. If no routes are arriving or if there is no static default route, the router may not be able to route traffic.

7. A. RIP is a distance-vector protocol that periodically broadcasts routes to the other servers. It's useful for a very simple routed network. Your environment is much too complex to configure static routes. Every time something changed, you would have to modify all the routing tables manually. OSPF cannot be used in Windows Server 2008.

8. B. IP packet filters are applied at the RRAS server and can control access based on rules that act on source and destination addresses and ports. For example, you could build a rule that specifies the IP address of all acceptable web destinations while dropping all other requests, or you could create a rule that would use IP addresses to prevent requests from reaching specific sites.

    TCP/IP filters are configured at each workstation; although they can control specific communication, the administrative overhead is unacceptable for a broad-based policy. Configuring each browser through global policies is not a valid option. Using static routing tables applies only to communication between routers; it wouldn't involve the ultimate destinations of the packets.

9. D. Any of these factors could prevent traffic from flowing, and therefore all should be checked.

10. C. An IP-in-IP tunnel encapsulates IP datagrams inside other IP headers. This allows you to send packets that are not supported—such as multicasts—to other locations that are supported. Multicast boundaries use the multicast scope, rate of traffic, or IP header to control the forwarding of the traffic, but this does not allow that traffic to flow across a section of the network that does not support it. This is also the case for multicast heartbeat, which is used to look for multicast support connectivity on the network. RIP is a routing protocol that manages the tables that locate routes through the network. It is not involved in the support or lack of support of multicast traffic.

11. D. Configuring the multihomed router with a static routing table is the simplest approach for this environment. Although you could spend the time configuring the server with the more sophisticated routing protocols, there is no compelling advantage in this situation because every subnet will always be one hop away from the others. The more sophisticated protocols become useful when there are multiple routes available or when there are subnets across multiple routers. Finally, remember that OSPF support has been discontinued in Windows Server 2008.

12. B. RIP is the easiest dynamic routing protocol among the choices you have with Windows 2008. RIP will automatically discover the other RIP routers and build the tables necessary for the routing to take place. Although there is broadcast traffic associated with RIP on a small network, it won't have an impact. Even as you add new paths to this network, RIP will update its tables appropriately. Static routing tables are a bit too cumbersome and error prone for a network with multiple routes. There is no such thing as a dynamic routing file. Border Gateway Protocol (BGP) is used to connect large, independently managed networks and isn't an option with the Windows 2008 product.

13. B. RIPv2 is the best protocol that is supported by Windows Server 2008. Building static routes to back up dynamic routing protocols is self-defeating, and OSPF cannot be used.

14. B. RIPv2 uses a multicast method for communicating changes to the other routers when routing changes are detected on the network. This minimizes any traffic on the network, but this protocol is still easy to configure and is reliable. RIPv1 broadcasts every 30 seconds to communicate with the other routers. OSPF cannot be used with Server 2008. Static routing tables must be edited manually and won't update other routers. CHAP is an authentication protocol, not a routing protocol.

15. B. To create a new demand-dial interface, you need to right-click the Network Interfaces node that is under the server on which you want to create the interface. Then select New Demand-Dial Interface from the pop-up menu.

16. D. Windows Server 2008 can route IP. Don't be confused by TCP being one of the options. Internet Protocol (IP) is the routable protocol. TCP knows nothing about routes. Contrary to the belief of some IT individuals in the industry, NetBEUI isn't a routable protocol.

17. A, B. Both RIPv1 and RIPv2 are link-state protocols that transmit the entire routing table. Open Shortest Path First (OSPF) is a link-state protocol but is not available in Windows Server 2008. EIGRP is a proprietary protocol used by Cisco and thus not available in Windows Server 2008.

18. B. The server's Properties dialog box's General tab contains the button to enable demand-dial routing in Windows Server 2008.

19. A. ICMP traffic can be filtered so that it does not pass through the router. One of the most useful features in RRAS is its ability to selectively filter TCP/IP packets in both directions. You can construct filters that allow or deny traffic into or out of your network based on rules that specify source and destination addresses and ports.

20. C, D. Open Shortest Path First (OSPF) is a link-state protocol but is not available in Windows Server 2008. EIGRP is a proprietary protocol used by Cisco and thus not available in Windows Server 2008.

Chapter 6

Managing Remote Access Services

MICROSOFT EXAM OBJECTIVES COVERED IN THIS CHAPTER:

✓ **Configure Remote Access**

- ▪ May include but not limited to: Dial-up, Internet Connection Sharing (ICS), VPN, Routing and Remote Access Services (RRAS), Inbound/outbound filters, Configure Remote Authentication Dial-In User Service (RADIUS) server, Configure RADIUS proxy, Remote access protocols

✓ **Configure Network Authentication**

- ▪ May include but not limited to: RAS authentication using MS-CHAP, MS-CHAP v2 and EAP

✓ **Configure Wireless Access**

- ▪ May include but not limited to: Set Service Identifier (SSID), Wired Equivalent Privacy (WEP), WI-FI Protection Access (WPA), WI-FI Protection Access 2 (WPA2), Ad hoc versus infrastructure mode, Group policy for wireless

Now that you understand how routing works, it's time to discuss how clients connect using remote access. Dial-up networking (on the client side) and remote access services (on the server side) provide another way, in addition to LANs, to carry the network protocols you're already using.

Routing and Remote Access Services (RRAS) includes some security features necessary to effectively provide remote access. For example, you'll probably want to have the ability to restrict user dial-up access by group membership, time of day, or other factors. You'll also need a way to specify the various callback, authentication, and encryption options that the protocols support. In this chapter, you'll learn about both dial-up and remote access.

You will also learn about virtual private networks (VPNs), which provide remote access to private networks across public connections. That is, using the Internet, clients can dial in to an Internet service provider (ISP) and connect to your private network. The main benefit of VPNs is reduced cost, because it means long-distance calls are unnecessary. VPNs are becoming more popular because of the increased popularity of high-speed Internet connections such as cable and digital subscriber line (DSL).

We understand that in this day and age, few of us use dial-up. Most hotels give you high-speed Internet, and most homes also use high-speed connections. But dial-up is still an option, so we must discuss it.

Many of the features included in Windows Server 2008 are simply carried over from Windows 2003, with a few minor additions. Thus is the case with the Routing and Remote Access console. RRAS itself actually dates back to the Windows NT 4 Option Pack, and Windows 2000 sported a completely revised version. Windows Server 2008 adds a few new features to RRAS, but it remains mostly intact from the previous generation of Windows.

Before we can get into the details of what these features do and how to configure them to provide remote access for your network, you need to understand some of the terms and concepts specific to RRAS. That's where we'll begin in this chapter, and then we'll move on to reviewing the features and configuration settings that you need to understand to meet the exam objectives.

Overview of Dial-Up Networking (DUN)

LANs provide relatively high-speed connectivity to attached machines, but where does that leave those of us who work from home, who travel, or who need to access data on a remote computer? Until wireless access is available worldwide, we have the option of using dial-up networking, in which the client computer uses a modem to dial in and connect to a remote server. Once the connection is established, a variety of protocols and services make it possible for us to view web pages, transfer files and email, and do pretty much anything we could do with a hardwired LAN connection, albeit at a reduced speed.

In the following sections, you will learn more about what dial-up networking does and how it works by examining the specific technologies and protocols associated with remote access.

What DUN Does

From Chapter 1, "Understanding Windows Server 2008 Networking," you already understand that Windows Server 2008 network protocols are actually implemented as drivers. These drivers normally work with hardware network interfaces to get data from point A to point B. How do dial-up connections fit in?

Think back to the OSI model. Each layer has a function, and each layer serves as an intermediary between the layer above it and the one below. By substituting one driver for another at some level in the stack, you can dramatically change how things work. That's exactly what Windows Server 2008's Dial-Up Networking (DUN) subsystem does. It makes the dial-up connection appear to be just another network adapter. The DUN driver takes care of the work of making a slow asynchronous modem appear to work just like a fast LAN interface. Applications and services that use TCP/IP on your DUN connection never know the difference. In fact, you can configure Windows Server 2008 to use your primary connection first and then pass traffic over a secondary connection (such as a dial-up link) if the primary connection is down—this does not affect the applications you're working with (except that they might run more slowly).

On the server side, DUN allows you to host one or more network users who dial into your Windows Server 2008 machine. Windows Vista and XP Professional allow up to 10 concurrent dial-up connections, and Windows Server 2008 allows up to 255. (But by the time you allow 255 concurrent connections, you'll probably be overloading your server.)

 Real World Scenario

Dial-Up Using ISPs

When you dial into an ISP, chances are you're not dialing into a server running RRAS on Windows. You're probably dialing into a bank of modems, but these modems don't resemble the modems you see on the store shelf at all. The modems used by ISPs—called *network access servers* (NASs)—are made by a few companies, including 3Com, U.S. Robotics, Cisco, and Ascend. These NASs hook directly into T1 interfaces or primary-rate interfaces (PRIs). Each such interface is equivalent to either 24 or 23 phone lines, respectively. The NASs, along with one or more RADIUS servers (which you'll learn about later), are responsible for handling the connection and negotiation of PPP. The NAS can handle hundreds of calls without problems and provides the best solution for dial-in access.

Depending on how you configure the DUN server, users who dial in can see the whole network or only specific resources on the server. You also get to control who can log on, when they can log on, and what they can do once they've logged on. As far as Windows Server 2008 is concerned, a user connected via DUN is no different from one using resources over your LAN, so all the access controls and permissions you apply remain in force for DUN users.

How DUN Works

A lot of pieces are required to successfully complete a dial-up call from your computer to a server at another physical location. Understanding what these pieces are, how they work, and what they do for you is important. In the following sections, we will cover the DUN infrastructure, how the Point-to-Point Protocol (PPP) helps in this connection, the relationship between PPP and the network protocols, and how multilink can be used to increase the speed and efficiency of your remote connections.

The DUN Infrastructure

We'll start with a look at the physical layer that underlies voice and data calls. Most of the following material will be familiar to anyone who has ever used a modem, but you should still understand the details that you might not have thought of before.

Plain Old Telephone Service

Plain Old Telephone Service (POTS) connections offer a theoretical maximum speed of 56Kbps; in practice, many users routinely get connections at 51 or 52Kbps.

The word *modem* is actually short for "modulator-demodulator." The original Bell System modems took digital data and modulated it into screechy analog audio tones suitable for use on regular phone lines. Because phone lines are purposely designed to pass only the low end of the audible frequency range that most can hear, the amount of data was limited. However, in the early 1990s, an engineer discovered that you could communicate much faster when the path between the sender and receiver was all digital. An all-digital path doesn't have any analog components that induce signal loss, so it preserves the original signal quality faithfully, which in turn makes it possible to put more information into the original signal. As it happens, phone companies nationwide were in the process of making major upgrades to replace their analog equipment with newer, better, digital equivalents. These upgrades made it possible for people in most areas to get almost-56Kbps speeds without changing any of the wiring in their homes or offices. The connection between the house and the phone office was still analog, but the connections between phone offices were digital, ensuring high-quality connections.

Integrated Services Digital Network

In the mid-1970s, Integrated Services Digital Network (ISDN) was designed. At the time, no one had any idea that you'd be able to get 56Kbps speeds out of an ordinary phone line. ISDN's speeds of up to 128Kbps over a single pair of copper wires seemed pretty revolutionary. In addition, ISDN had features such as call forwarding, caller ID, and multiple directory numbers (so you could have more than one number, perhaps with different ringing patterns, associated with a single line).

Unfortunately, ISDN requires an all-digital signal path. It also requires special equipment on both ends of the connection. The phone companies were slow to promote ISDN as a faster alternative to regular dial-up service, so customers avoided it.

ISDN still has some advantages, though. Because it's all digital, call setup times are much shorter than they are for analog modems—it takes only about half a second to establish a new ISDN call. Modern ISDN adapters and ISDN-capable routers can seamlessly stitch together multiple ISDN channels to deliver bandwidth in 64Kbps increments. Because you can use ISDN lines for regular analog voice, data, and fax traffic, you can make a single ISDN act like two voice lines, a single 128Kbps data line, or a 64Kbps data line plus a voice line.

ISDN is quickly being replaced by faster broadband services such as DSL and cable modems. In fact, you should resort to ISDN only if these other solutions are not available in your area. Note that DSL (a misnomer because they are all digital) and cable modems do not use PPP—discussed later—so they are technically not considered dial-up connections.

Other Connection Methods

Any other on-demand connection that's established using the Point-to-Point Protocol (PPP) can be thought of as a dial-up connection, and Windows Server 2008 doesn't make any distinction between POTS, ISDN, and other dial-ups—they're all treated identically.

Connecting with PPP

The Point-to-Point Protocol enables any two devices to establish a TCP/IP connection over a serial link. That usually means a dial-up modem connection, but it could just as easily be a direct serial cable connection, an infrared connection, or any other type of serial connection. When one machine dials another, the machine that initiates the connection is referred to as a *client*, and the machine that receives the call is a *server*—even though PPP itself makes no such distinction.

PPP negotiation involves three phases that are required to establish a remote access connection. The three phases invoke one or more protocols, as you can see in Figure 6.1.

Actually, at least six distinct protocols run on top of PPP. Understanding what they do helps make the actual PPP negotiation process clearer. These protocols include the following:

The Link Control Protocol (LCP)   The Link Control Protocol (LCP) handles the details of establishing and configuring the lowest-level PPP link; in that regard, you can think of it almost as if it were part of the Physical layer. When one PPP device calls another, the devices use LCP to agree that they want to establish a PPP connection.

The Challenge Handshake Authentication Protocol (CHAP)   The Challenge Handshake Authentication Protocol (CHAP)—as well as MS-CHAPv2 and PAP, which will be covered in Chapter 7, "Managing Security for Remote Access Services"—allows the client to authenticate itself to the server. This authentication functions much like a regular network logon; once the client presents its logon credentials, the server can figure out what access to grant.

FIGURE 6.1 The PPP negotiation process

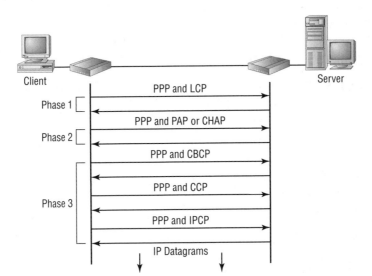

The Callback Control Protocol (CBCP) The Callback Control Protocol (CBCP) is used to negotiate whether a callback is required, whether it's permitted, and when it happens. Once the client has authenticated itself, the server can decide whether it should hang up and call the client back. The client can also request a callback at a number it provides; although this isn't as secure as having the server place a call to a predetermined number, it provides some additional flexibility. If a callback occurs, the connection is reestablished and reauthenticated, but the CBCP stage is skipped.

The Compression Control Protocol (CCP) The Compression Control Protocol (CCP) allows the two sides of the connection to determine what kind of compression, if any, they want to use on the network data. Because PPP traffic actually consists of wrapped-up IP datagrams and because IP datagram headers tend to be fairly compressible, negotiating effective compression can significantly improve overall PPP throughput.

The IP Control Protocol (IPCP) At this point in the call, the two sides have agreed to authentication, compression, and a callback. They haven't yet agreed on what IP parameters to use for the connection. These parameters, which include the maximum packet size to be sent over the link (the maximum transmission unit, or MTU), have a great impact on the overall link performance, so the client and server use the IP Control Protocol to negotiate them based on the traffic they expect to be passed.

The Internet Protocol (IP) Once the IPCP negotiation has been completed, each end has complete knowledge of how to communicate with its peer. That knowledge allows the two sides to begin exchanging IP datagrams over the link just as they would over a standard LAN connection.

Figure 6.1 (earlier in the chapter) shows how these protocols work together to lead up to establishing the link. Remember this diagram because you'll see it again when you start reading about PPTP. Now you can see what happens after the link is established and traffic begins flowing.

The Relationship Between PPP and Network Protocols

Usually when you hear about network communication, you hear about using TCP/IP on a hardwired LAN. How does this protocol fit in with PPP? In the case of TCP/IP, that's an easy question to answer: the client routes all (or some) of its outgoing TCP/IP traffic to its PPP peer, which can then inspect the IP datagrams it gets back from the PPP stack to analyze and route them properly.

Windows Server 2008 supports only TCP/IP, so consider what has to happen when a client using AppleTalk needs to connect via dial-up. Because the server will not use those other protocols, it will drop the call or cause the client to warn its user (that's what Windows Server 2008 does). After the other PPP setup steps are finished, the client and server can wrap other types of network traffic inside an IP datagram. This process, called *encapsulation*, allows the client to take a packet with some kind of private content, wrap it inside an IP datagram, and send it to the server. The server, in turn, processes the IP datagram, routing real datagrams normally and handling any encapsulated packets with the appropriate protocol. At that point, the client can communicate with the server without knowing that its non-TCP/IP packets are being encapsulated in any way—that detail is hidden deep in the layers of the OSI model.

Understanding the Benefits of Multilink

Many parts of the world don't have high-speed broadband access yet. In fact, many places don't have ISDN or even phone lines that support 56Kbps modems. The *multilink* extensions to the Point-to-Point Protocol provide a way to take several independent PPP connections and make them look like one line so that they act as a single connection.

For example, if you use two phone lines and modems to place a two-line multilink call to your ISP, instead of getting the usual 48Kbps connection, you would end up with an apparent bandwidth of 96Kbps. The multilink PPP software on your Windows Server 2008 machine and on the ISP's router takes care of stringing all the packets together to make this process seamless. Windows Server 2008's RRAS supports multilink PPP for inbound and outbound calls.

 The primary drawback to multilink calls is that they take up more than one phone line apiece.

Overview of Virtual Private Networks

Private networks offer superior security. You own the wires, so you have control over what they're used for, who can use them, and what kind of data passes over them. However, they're not very flexible, because they require you to configure and manage costly leased lines between remote locations. To make things worse, most private networks face a dilemma: implementing enough capacity to handle peak loads almost guarantees that much of that capacity will sit idly much of the time, even though it still has to be paid for.

One way to work around this problem is to maintain private dial-up services. Such services allow, for example, a field rep in Chicago to dial the home office in Boston. But dial-ups are expensive, and they have the same excess capacity problem that truly private networks do. As an added detriment, someone has to pay long-distance or toll-free number charges.

Virtual private networks (VPNs) offer a solution. You get the security of a true private network with the flexibility, ubiquity, and low cost of the Internet. In the following sections, we will cover VPNs, including what they are used for and how they work (in general and with Windows Server 2008).

What VPNs Do

At any time, two parties can create a connection over the Internet. The idea behind a VPN is that you can use these connections to let two parties establish an encrypted *tunnel* between them using the Internet as a transportation medium. The VPN software on each end takes care of encrypting the VPN packets as they go; when the packets leave one end of the tunnel, their payloads are encrypted and encapsulated inside regular IP packets that cause them to be delivered to the remote machine. Figure 6.2 shows one way to conceptualize this process.

FIGURE 6.2   Drilling a tunnel through the Internet

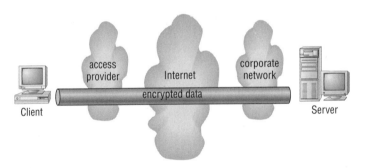

As an example, let's say you're in the field at a client site. As long as you're somewhere that your ISP serves, you can dial into the client's local point of presence and get connected to the Internet. At that point, you can open a VPN connection back to the servers at your office and do whatever you could do when sitting in front of a regular desktop machine.

VPNs and Windows Server 2008

Windows Server 2008 includes support for Microsoft's proprietary Point-to-Point Tunneling Protocol and Layer 2 Tunneling Protocol. Layer 2 Tunneling Protocol (L2TP) provides a more generic tunneling mechanism than PPTP; when combined with IPSec, L2TP also allows you to establish VPNs using a wide range of Microsoft or non-Microsoft hardware and software products, including routers and access devices from companies such as Cisco, Red Creek, and Nortel.

Worthwhile features in Windows Server 2008's VPN support include the following:

- You can set up account lockout policies for dial-up and VPN users; this capacity has existed for network and console users for some time.

- The Extensible Authentication Protocol (EAP) allows Microsoft or third parties to write modules that implement new authentication methods and retrofit them to servers. One example is the EAP-TLS module, which implements access control based on smart cards and certificates for VPN and dial-up users.

- If you're using Active Directory in the domain native mode, you can use remote access policies to apply and enforce consistent policies to all users in a site, domain, or organizational unit. These policies can include which encryption and authentication protocols users may, or must, use when talking to your servers.

How you enable VPN support on your Windows Server 2008 machine depends on whether you're using a server or a client (Vista, XP, and so on).

Client configuration is easy, as you'll see later in this chapter. Just install the Dial-Up Networking service and then use the Make New Connection Wizard to create a new VPN connection. On the server side, you'll need to install and configure RRAS and then enable it to accept incoming VPN connections.

How VPNs Work

The VPN client assumes that the VPN server is already connected to the Internet in some way. Here's how the VPN connection process works:

1. The client establishes a connection to the Internet. Dial-up networking or any other connection method can be used for this connection. The client must be able to send packets to the Internet.

2. The client sends a VPN connection request to the server. The exact format of the request varies, depending on whether the VPN is using PPTP or L2TP.

3. The client authenticates itself to the server. Again, the exact process varies according to the VPN protocol in use. If the client can't provide valid credentials, the connection is terminated.

4. The client and server negotiate parameters for the VPN session. This negotiation allows the two ends to agree on an encryption algorithm and strength.

5. The client and server go through the PPP negotiation process (see "Connecting with PPP" earlier in this chapter) because both L2TP and PPTP depend on the lower-level PPP protocols (you will see why later in the section "Configuring a VPN").

Because the contents of data passed around in steps 2 and 3 vary according to the tunneling protocol in use, we'll explain the differences. First, though, you should understand encapsulation and how VPNs use it to wrap one kind of data inside another.

An Encapsulation Primer

Most of yesterday's networks could carry only one kind of data. Each network vendor had its own protocol, and most of the time there was no way to intermingle data using different protocols on the same line. Over time, vendors began to find ways to allow a single network to carry many different types of traffic, resulting in the current assortment of traffic types found on most large networks. However, the Internet works only with IP, which is why it's called Internet Protocol. If you need to send other types of traffic—such as AppleTalk—across the Internet, you can encapsulate it within IP.

How does encapsulation work? Software at each level of the OSI model has to see header information to figure out where a packet is coming from and where it's going. But the payload contents aren't important to most of those components, and the payload is what's encapsulated. By fabricating the right kind of header and prepending it to whatever you want in the payload, you can route foreign traffic types through IP networks with no trouble.

VPNs depend on encapsulation because their security method depends on being able to keep the payload information encrypted. The following steps demonstrate what happens to a typical packet as it goes from being a regular IP datagram to a PPTP packet (see Figure 6.3):

1. An application creates a block of data bound for a remote host. In this case, it's a web browser.

2. The client-side IP stack takes the application's data and turns it into an IP packet, first by adding a TCP header and then by adding an IP header. This can be called the *IP datagram* because it contains all the necessary addressing information to be delivered by IP.

3. The client is connected via PPP, so it adds a PPP header to the IP datagram. This PPP+IP combination is called a *PPP frame*.

4. If you are using PPP instead of a VPN protocol, the packet goes across the PPP link without further modification. When you are using a VPN (as in this example), the next step is for the VPN to encrypt the PPP frame, turning it into unreadable information to be transported over the Internet.

5. A Generic Routing Encapsulation (GRE) header is combined with the encrypted payload. GRE really is generic; in this case, the protocol ID field in the GRE header says that this is an encapsulated PPTP packet.

6. Now that there is a tag to tell you what's in the payload, the PPTP stack can add an IP header (specifying the destination address of the VPN server) and a PPP header.

7. Now the packet can be sent out over your PPP connection. The IP header specifies that it should be routed to the VPN server.

8. When the packet arrives at the VPN server, the server reverses steps 1–6 to extract the payload.

Encapsulation allows the use of VPN data inside ordinary-looking IP datagrams, which is part of what makes VPNs so powerful—you don't have to change any of your applications, routers, or network components (unless they have to be configured to recognize and pass GRE packets).

FIGURE 6.3   The encapsulation process

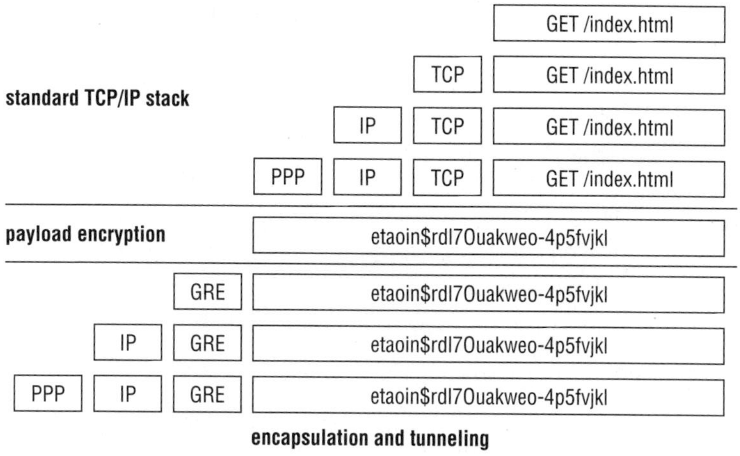

PPTP Tunneling

PPTP is a pretty straightforward protocol. It works by encapsulating packets using the mechanism described in the previous section, "An Encapsulation Primer," and performs encryption (step 4) using the Microsoft Point-to-Point Encryption (MPPE) algorithm. The encryption keys used to encrypt the packets are generated dynamically for each connection; in fact, the keys can be changed periodically during the connection.

When the client and server have successfully established a PPTP tunnel, the authorization process begins. This process is an exchange of credentials that allows the server to decide whether the client is permitted to connect:

1. The server sends a challenge message to the client.

2. The client answers with an encrypted response.

3. The server checks the response to see whether the answer is right. The challenge-response process allows the server to determine which account is trying to make a connection.

4. The server determines whether the user account is authorized to make a connection.

5. If the account is authorized, the server accepts the inbound connection; any access controls or remote access restrictions still apply.

L2TP/IPSec Tunneling

L2TP is much more flexible than PPTP, but it's also more complicated. It was designed to be a general-purpose tunneling protocol not limited to VPN use.

L2TP itself doesn't offer any kind of security. When you use L2TP, you're setting up an unencrypted, unauthenticated tunnel. Using L2TP by itself over the Internet, therefore, would be dangerous, because anyone who wanted to could read your traffic.

To address this issue, you can use L2TP in conjunction with IPSec (see Chapter 2, "TCP/IP").

The overall flow of an L2TP/IPSec tunnel session looks a little different from that of a PPTP session because IPSec security is different. Here's how the L2TP/IPSec combination works:

1. The client and server establish an IPSec security association using the ISAKMP and Oakley protocols discussed in Chapter 2. At this point, the two machines have an encrypted channel between them.

2. The client builds a new L2TP tunnel to the server. Because this happens after the channel has been encrypted, there's no security risk.

3. The server sends an authentication challenge to the client.

4. The client encrypts its answer to the challenge and returns it to the server.

5. The server checks the challenge response to see whether it's valid; if so, the server can determine which account is connecting. Subject to whatever access policies you've put in place, at this point the server can accept the inbound connection.

Note that steps 3–5 mirror the steps described for PPTP tunneling. This is because the authorization process is a function of the remote access server, not the VPN stack. All VPN does is provide a secure communications channel, and something else has to decide who gets to use it.

Configuring Your Remote Access Server

Most of the configuration necessary for a remote access server happens at the server level. You use the server's Properties dialog box to control whether the server allows remote connections, what protocols and options it supports, and so forth. Because all the protocols are carried via PPP, you can set some generic PPP options as well. We will cover these options in the following sections. You also have to configure settings for your users, which you'll read about in the next section.

 Chapter 5, "Managing Routing and Remote Access," covers how to configure the RRAS general properties.

Configuring PPP Options

You can use the PPP tab of the RRAS server's Properties dialog box (see Figure 6.4) to control the PPP-layer options available to clients that call in. The settings you specify here control whether the related PPP options are available to clients; you can use remote access policies to control whether individual connections can use them.

FIGURE 6.4   The PPP tab of the RRAS server's Properties dialog box

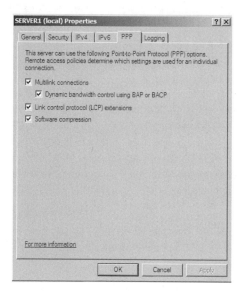

This tab has four check boxes:

- The Multilink Connections check box, which is selected by default, controls whether the server will allow clients to establish multilink connections when they call in.

- The Dynamic Bandwidth Control Using BAP Or BACP check box determines whether clients and servers are allowed to dynamically add or remove links during a multilink session. If you enable this feature, you can throttle the amount of available bandwidth up or down on demand. It's available only when the Multilink Connections check box is selected.

  BAP stands for Bandwidth Allocation Protocol, and BACP stands for Bandwidth Allocation Control Protocol.

- The Link Control Protocol (LCP) is used to establish a PPP link and negotiate its settings. A variety of LCP extensions are defined in various RFCs; these extensions allow a client and server to dynamically agree on which protocols are being passed back and forth, among other things. The Link Control Protocol (LCP) Extensions check box controls whether these extensions are available. Windows 9*x*, NT, 2000, Vista, and XP clients depend on the LCP extensions, so you should leave this check box selected.

- The Software Compression check box controls whether RRAS will allow a remote client to use the Compression Control Protocol (CCP) to compress PPP traffic. In some cases, hardware compression at the modem level is more efficient, but not everyone has a compression-capable modem. You should leave this check box selected as well.

It doesn't make sense to enable multilink connections if you have only one phone line; in addition, you may want to turn them off to keep a small number of users from using all your lines. Exercise 6.1 will take you through the process of controlling multilink for incoming calls.

EXERCISE 6.1

Controlling Multilink for Incoming Calls

1.   Open the RRAS MMC console by selecting Start ➢ Administrative Tools ➢ Routing And Remote Access.

2.   Right-click the server you want to configure in the left pane of the MMC, and choose Properties. The server's Properties dialog box appears.

3.   Click the PPP tab.

4.   To turn the multilink capability off, make sure the Multilink Connections check box is not selected. To turn it on, simply select the check box.

5.   If you decide to turn the multilink capability on, you should also enable BAP/BACP to make it easier for your server to adjust to the load placed on it. To do so, make sure the Dynamic Bandwidth Control Using BAP Or BACP check box is selected.

6.   Click the OK button.

Configuring IP-Based Connections

TCP/IP is far and away the most commonly used remote access protocol; coincidentally, it's also the most configurable of the protocols that Windows Server 2008 supports. Both of these facts are reflected in the IPv4 and IPv6 tabs of the server's Properties dialog box. Figure 6.5 shows the IPv4 tab.

FIGURE 6.5   The IPv4 tab of the RRAS server's Properties dialog box

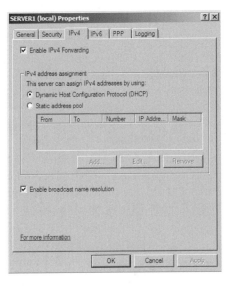

The controls on the IPv4 tab do the following:

- The Enable IPv4 Forwarding check box controls whether RRAS will route IPv4 packets between the remote client and other interfaces on your RRAS server. When this box is checked, as it is by default, remote clients' packets can go to the RRAS server or to any other host to which the RRAS server has a route. To allow clients to access resources on the RRAS server only, uncheck this box.

- The IP Address Assignment control group lets you specify how you want remote clients to get their IP addresses. The default settings here depend on what you told the RRAS Setup Wizard during setup:

  - If you want to use a DHCP server on your network as the source of IP addresses for remote clients, select the Dynamic Host Configuration Protocol (DHCP) radio button and make sure you have the DHCP relay agent installed and running.

  - If you'd rather use static address allocation, select the Static Address Pool radio button. Then in the list below, specify which IP address ranges you want issued to clients.

> If you choose to use static addressing, be sure you don't use any address ranges that are part of a DHCP server's address pool. Better still, you can add the ranges you want reserved for remote access as excluded ranges in the DHCP snap-in. (See Chapter 4.)

- The Enable Broadcast Name Resolution option allows remote clients to resolve TCP/IP names without the use of a WINS or DNS server. This feature is enabled by default and is new for Windows Server 2008.

Figure 6.6 shows the IPv6 tab of the RRAS server's Properties dialog box.

FIGURE 6.6   The IPv6 tab of the RRAS server's Properties dialog box

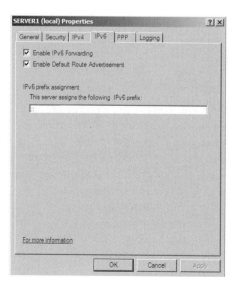

The controls on the IPv6 tab do the following:

- The Enable IPv6 Forwarding check box controls whether RRAS will route IPv6 packets between the remote client and other interfaces on your RRAS server. When this box is checked, as it is by default, remote clients' packets can go to the RRAS server or to any other host to which the RRAS server has a route. To allow clients to accessing resources on the RRAS server only, uncheck this box.

- The Enable Default Route Advertisement check box (enabled by default) makes the Border Gateway Protocol (BGP) routing protocol available. BGP can exchange routing information between Windows Server 2008 routers. When this box is checked, your Windows Server 2008 router can announce its route to other routers.

- On the IPv6 tab, you can also set up your IPv6 prefix assignment (assigning IPv6 prefixes was discussed in Chapter 2).

In Exercise 6.2, you'll configure your RRAS server so it accepts only those inbound calls that use the IP protocol.

EXERCISE 6.2

Configuring Incoming Connections

1. Open the RRAS MMC console by selecting Start ≻ Administrative Tools ≻ Routing And Remote Access.

2. Right-click the server you want to configure in the left pane of the MMC, and choose the Properties command. The server's Properties dialog box appears.

3. Click the IPv4 tab. Verify that the Enable IPv4 Forwarding check box is selected.

4. Make sure the Dynamic Host Configuration Protocol (DHCP) radio button is selected.

5. Click the OK button.

Installing a VPN

Conventional dial-up access works well, but as you saw earlier, it can be expensive to implement, painful to manage, and extremely slow by today's standards. VPNs offer a way around these problems by providing low initial and ongoing costs, easy management, and excellent speeds (depending on your connection). Windows Server 2008's RRAS component includes two complete VPN implementations: one using Microsoft's PPTP and one using a combination of the Internet-standard IPSec protocol and L2TP.

The basic process of setting up a VPN is simple, but you need to think some things through before plunging ahead. Getting the VPN installation right may require small hardware or networking changes plus proper configuration of the VPN service. We will look at this process in the following sections.

PPTP VPNs

PPTP has a reputation for being a less-secure method for VPN connections, and frankly, it is. PPTP is generally easier to configure than an L2TP/IPSec VPN, though, and therefore it's a common choice among Windows administrators.

Security requires constant assessment of the risks and costs associated with mitigating or eliminating those risks. The risk in choosing a less-secure protocol for VPN connections is that an attacker will be able to compromise the data channel. The cost associated with VPNs is largely (though not completely) that of configuring the VPN connections both on the server and on the client. The assessment of cost vs. risk can be done only by the information owner, considering the value of the data and the amount of time it takes to configure a PPTP vs. an L2TP-type VPN.

How VPN Works

A VPN sits between your internal network and the Internet, accepting connections from clients in the outside world. In Figure 6.7, clients 1 and 2 are using different ISPs (probably because they're at different physical locations). For example, a packet from client 1 goes from its computer to its ISP and then through some route, unknown to you, that eventually delivers it to the VPN server, which transforms it into a packet suitable for use on the internal network.

FIGURE 6.7   VPNs provide private connections between clients and servers across the Internet.

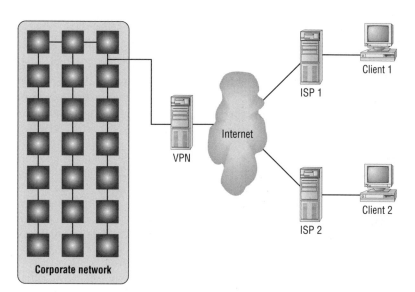

Imagine a line around the internal network, and think of it as a security boundary. In general, you'll want your VPN server to be outside any firewalls or network security measures you have in place. The most common configuration is to use two NICs: one connects to the Internet, and the other connects either to the private network or to an intermediate network that itself connects to the private network. Of course, you can use any type of Internet connection you want for the VPN server: cable modems, DSL, T1, satellite, or whatever.

The point behind giving the VPN its own network adapter is that your VPN clients need a public IP address to connect to, and you probably don't want them calling directly into your internal network. That also means that things will be easiest for your VPN users if the IP address for your VPN server's external interface is statically assigned so it won't be changing on them when they least expect it.

Avoiding Some Subtle L2TP Pitfalls

As you learned in Chapter 2, IPSec uses a fairly complex process to negotiate security agreements (SAs) between two endpoints of a secure connection. Part of this process involves using what Microsoft calls *machine certificates*. These are nothing more than digital certificates issued to machines instead of users. These certificates allow both ends of the connection to authenticate the computers involved, not just the people. In fact, machine-level authentication is a prerequisite step—on an L2TP VPN, the machine endpoints are authenticated before the VPN client ever sends an authentication request.

In most cases, these certificates will be issued automatically, assuming, of course, that you've configured your certificate authority (CA) to issue certificates automatically to machines when they join a Windows Server 2008 domain. If you haven't already set up your certificate authority in this manner, you can manually enroll machines by using the certificate authority tools to request a computer certificate for each machine that needs one; you can also force the CA to issue a certificate to the VPN server by restarting the VPN server or refreshing the local security policy.

In addition, your remote machines must be able to join the domain in the first place. Let's say you want to allow employees to use VPN from home but you don't want those machines joining your domain. In that case, you might be able to issue certificates manually to those users who are running Windows 2000 or newer operating systems, but your best bet will probably be to turn on PPTP instead until the L2TP infrastructure catches up.

With Windows Server 2008, you can also configure a VPN server to use preshared keys instead of certificates. Preshared keys are much easier to configure and manage than certificates because you do not need to set up a certificate server (or use a third-party certificate service). But they are slightly less secure because you need to give the same key to every remote access user. Also, if the preshared key is changed, your users will need to manually change their key configurations, which might not seem like a problem for you, but many users balk at the thought of computer configuration.

Enabling RRAS as a VPN

If you're already using RRAS for IP routing or remote access, you can enable it as a VPN server without reinstalling.

Recall that the General tab of the server's Properties dialog box allows you to specify whether your RRAS server is a router, a remote access server, or both. The first step in converting your existing RRAS server to handle VPN traffic is to make sure the IPv4 Remote Access Server or IPv6 Remote Access Server check box is selected on this tab (see Figure 6.8).

FIGURE 6.8   Enabling your RRAS server as a remote access server

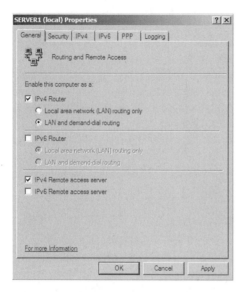

Making this change requires you to stop and restart the RRAS service, but that's OK because the snap-in will do it for you. Then you must configure VPN ports, as shown in the following sections.

Configuring a VPN

VPN configuration is extremely simple, at least for PPTP. Either a server can accept VPN calls or it can't. If it can, it will have a certain number of VPN ports, all of which are configured identically. You don't have to change or tweak much to get a VPN server set up, but you can adjust a few things as you like.

Configuring VPN Ports

The biggest opportunity to configure your VPN server is to adjust the number and kind of VPN ports available for clients to use. You can enable or disable either PPTP or L2TP, depending on what you want your remote users to be able to access. You accomplish this through the Ports Properties dialog box (see Figure 6.9).

FIGURE 6.9   The Ports Properties dialog box

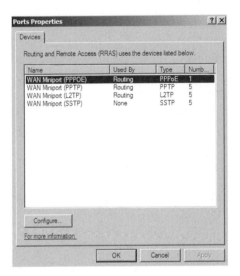

For conventional remote access servers, this dialog box shows you a list of hardware ports, but for servers that support VPN connections, there two WAN Miniport device selections, one for PPTP and one for L2TP. (These aren't really devices; they're actually virtual ports maintained by RRAS for accepting VPN connections.) You configure these ports by selecting one and clicking the Configure button, which displays the Configure Device – WAN Miniport (PPTP) dialog box (see Figure 6.10).

FIGURE 6.10   The Configure Device – WAN Miniport (PPTP) dialog box

Three controls are pertinent to a VPN configuration:

- The Remote Access Connections (Inbound Only) check box must be activated in order to accept VPN connections with this port type. To disable a VPN type (for instance, if you want to turn off L2TP), uncheck this box.

- The Demand-Dial Routing Connections (Inbound And Outbound) check box controls whether this VPN type can be used for demand-dial connections. By default, this box is checked; you'll need to uncheck it if you don't want to use VPN connections to link your network with other networks.

- The Maximum Ports control lets you set the number of inbound connections that this port type will support. By default, you get 5 PPTP and 5 L2TP ports when you install RRAS; you can use from 0 to 250 ports of each type by adjusting the number here.

You can also use the Phone Number For This Device field to enter the IP address of the public interface to which VPN clients connect. You might want to do this if your remote access policies accept or reject connections based on the number called by the client. Because you can assign multiple IP addresses to a single adapter, you can control VPN traffic by throttling which clients can connect to which addresses through a policy.

Chapter 7 discusses remote access policies in more detail.

Troubleshooting VPNs

The two primary problems you might encounter with VPN are as follows:

- Inability to establish a connection at all
- Inability to reach some needed resource once connected

There's a lot of common ground between the process of troubleshooting a VPN connection and the process of troubleshooting an ordinary remote access connection.

The following are some extremely simple—but sometimes overlooked—things to check when your VPN clients can't connect. First, make sure your clients can make the underlying connection to its ISP, and then check the following:

- Is RRAS installed and configured on the server?

    - Is the server configured to allow remote access? Check the General tab of the server's Properties dialog box.

    - Is the server configured to allow VPN traffic? Check the Ports Properties dialog box to make sure that the appropriate VPN protocol is enabled and that the number of ports for that protocol is greater than 0.

    - Are there any available VPN ports? If you have 10 L2TP ports allocated, the 11th caller will not be able to connect.

- Do the client and server match?

  - Is the VPN protocol used by the client enabled on the server? Windows 2000 and newer clients will try L2TP first and switch to PPTP as a second choice. However, clients on other OSs (including Windows NT) can normally expect either L2TP or PPTP.

- Are the client and server authenticated correctly?

  - Are the username and password correct?

  - Does the user account in question have remote access permissions, either directly on the account or through a policy?

  - Do the authentication settings in the server's policies (if any) match the supported set of authentication protocols?

If you check all the simple stuff and find nothing wrong, it's time to move on to checking more complex issues. These tend to affect more than one user, as opposed to the simple (and generally user-specific) issues just outlined. The problems include the following:

Policy problems   If you're using a native-mode Windows Server 2008 domain and you're using policies, those policies may cause some subtle problems that show up under some circumstances:

  - Are there any policies whose Allow or Deny settings conflict with each other? Remember that all conditions of all policies must match to gain user access; if any condition of any policy fails or if there are any policies that deny access, the connection will be denied.

  - Does the user match all the necessary conditions that are in place, such as time and date?

Network problems   If you're using dynamic IP addressing, are there any addresses left in the pool? If the VPN server can't assign an address, it won't accept the connection.

Domain problems   Windows Server 2008 RRAS servers can coexist with Windows NT RRAS servers, and both of them can interoperate with RADIUS servers from Microsoft and other vendors. Sometimes, though, this interoperation doesn't work exactly as you'd expect. Some questions to ask include the following:

  - Is the RRAS server's domain membership correct? Your RRAS servers don't have to be domain members unless you want to use native-mode features such as remote access policies.

  - If you're in a domain, are the server's group memberships correct? The server account must be a member of the RAS group and Internet Authentication Servers security group.

Managing Your Remote Access Server

RRAS server management is generally pretty easy because, in most cases, there's not much to manage. You set up the server, and it answers calls. You'll probably find it necessary to monitor the server's ongoing activity, however, and you may find it necessary to log activity for accounting or security purposes.

You can monitor your server's activity in a number of ways, including having the server keep local copies of its logs or having it send logging data to a remote RADIUS server. In addition, you can monitor the current status of any of the ports on your system.

Microsoft's documentation distinguishes between event logging, which records significant things that happen such as the RRAS service starting up and shutting down, and authentication and accounting logging, which tracks things such as when a user logged on and logged off. The settings for both types of logging are intermingled in the RRAS snap-in.

Managing Remote Users with a RADIUS Server

Remote Authentication Dial-In User Service (RADIUS) allows for maintaining and managing your remote users. A RADIUS server allows Remote Access Service (RAS) clients and dial-up routers to be authenticated.

Network Policy Server (NPS) is Microsoft's implementation of a RADIUS server in Windows Server 2008. NPS is replacing Windows Server 2003 Internet Authentication Service (IAS). NPS, working as a RADIUS server, allows for authentication, authorization, and accounting for wireless and VPN networks.

NPS allows a server to perform the duties of a RADIUS proxy. A RADIUS proxy allows the routing of RADIUS messages between RADIUS clients (RAS) and RADIUS servers. NPS also gives you the ability to record information about forwarded messages in an accounting log.

Monitoring Overall Activity

The Server Status node in the RRAS snap-in shows you a summary of all the RRAS servers known to the system. Depending on whether you use the features discussed in Chapter 5 to manage multiple RRAS servers from one console, you may see only the local server's information here. When you select the Server Status item, the right pane of the MMC will list each known RRAS server. Each entry in the list tells you whether the server is up, what kind of server it is, how many ports it has, how many ports are currently in use, and how long the server has been up. You can right-click any Windows Server 2008 RRAS server in this view to start, stop, restart, pause, or resume its RRAS service (see Figure 6.11); disable RRAS on the server; or remove the server's advertisement from Active Directory (provided, of course, that you're using Active Directory).

Controlling Remote Access Logging

A standard RRAS installation will always log some data locally, but that's pretty useless unless you know what gets logged and where it goes. Each RRAS server on your network has its own set of logs, which you manage through the Remote Access Logging folder. Within that folder, you'll usually see a single item labeled Local File, which is the log file stored on that particular server.

 If you don't have Windows accounting or Windows authentication turned on, you won't have a local log file. Depending on whether you're using RADIUS accounting and logging, you may see additional entries.

FIGURE 6.11 The All Tasks menu item for the RRAS server

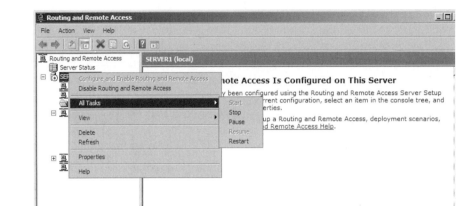

Setting Server Logging Properties

You can control server logging at the server level. You use the Logging tab (see Figure 6.12) to control what level of detail you want in the server's event log.

 These controls regulate all logging by RRAS, not just remote access log entries.

You have four choices for the level of logged detail:

- The Log Errors Only radio button instructs the server to log errors and nothing else. This gives you an adequate indication of problems after they happen, but it doesn't point out potential problems noted by warning messages.

- The Log Errors And Warnings radio button is the default choice. This forces the server to log error and warning messages to the event log, giving you a nice balance between information content and log volume.

- The Log All Events radio button causes the RRAS service to log mass quantities of messages, covering literally everything the server does. Although this voluminous output is useful for troubleshooting (or even for getting a better understanding of how remote access works), it's overkill for everyday use.

- The Do Not Log Any Events radio button turns off all event logging for RRAS.

FIGURE 6.12   The Logging tab of the server's Properties dialog box

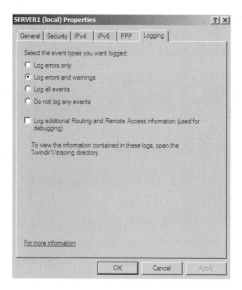

 WARNING   Don't use the Do Not Log Any Events option. The service's logs are important in case of a problem.

The Log Additional Routing And Remote Access Information check box allows you to turn on the logging of all PPP negotiations and connections. This can provide valuable information when you're trying to figure out what's wrong, but it adds a lot of unnecessary bulk to your log files. Don't turn it on unless you're trying to pin down a problem.

Setting Log File Properties

By selecting an individual log file in the snap-in, you can change what events will be logged in that file. This dialog box has two tabs:

- The Settings tab (see Figure 6.13) controls what gets logged in the file:

  - Accounting Requests governs whether events related to the service will be logged (as well as accounting data). You should always leave this checked.

  - Authentication Requests adjusts whether successful and failed logon requests are logged. You should always leave this checked.

  - Periodic Status controls whether interim accounting packets are permanently stored on disk. You should usually leave this checked.

  - Periodic Authentication Requests adjusts whether successful and failed logon requests are periodically logged. You should always leave this checked.

FIGURE 6.13 The Settings tab of the Local File Logging dialog box

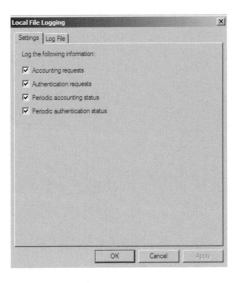

- The Log File tab (see Figure 6.14) controls the format of the file, specifically, how the log file is written to disk. You use this tab to designate three things:

  - The Directory field shows where the log file is stored. By default, each server logs its data in *systemroot*\system32\LogFiles. You can change this location to wherever you want.

  - The Format controls determine the format of the log file. By default, Windows Server 2000, 2003, and 2008 use the database-compatible file format. This format makes it easy for you to take log data and store it in a database, enabling more sophisticated postprocessing for things such as billing and chargebacks.

  - The Create A New Log File controls determine how often new log files are created. For example, some administrators prefer to start a new log file each week or each month, whereas others are content to let the log file grow without end. You can choose to have RRAS start new log files every day, week, month, never, or when the log file reaches a certain size.

Having correct accounting and authorization data is critical to maintaining a good level of security. Exercise 6.3 walks you through configuring remote access logging.

FIGURE 6.14   The Log File tab of the Local File Logging dialog box

Changing Remote Access Logging Settings

1. Open the RRAS MMC snap-in by selecting Start ➢ Administrative Tools ➢ Routing And Remote Access.

2. Navigate to the Remote Access Logging and Policies folder. Right-click the folder, and select Launch NPS.

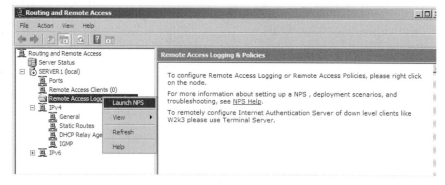

3. On the left pane, click Accounting. On the right side, click Configure Local File Logging.

EXERCISE 6.3 *(continued)*

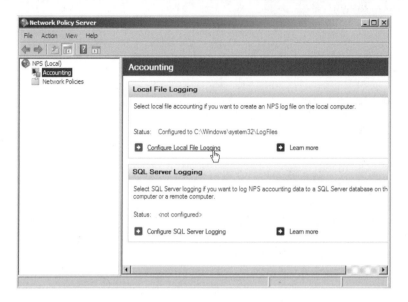

4. The Local File Logging dialog box appears. On the Settings tab, make sure all check boxes are marked.

5. Switch to the Log File tab in the Create A New Log File control group, select the When Log File Reaches This Size option, and enter **50** to set the maximum size of the log file to 50 MB.

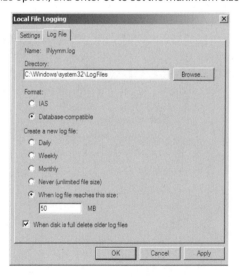

6. Click the OK button. Close the Network Policy Server window.

Reviewing the Remote Access Event Log

You use the Log File tab to specify the format, size, and location of the log file. But once you have a log file, what do you do with the log information? Windows Server 2008 online help has an exhaustive list of all the fields logged for each connection attempt and accounting record. Because of the availability of online help, you don't need to have all those fields memorized, and you don't have to remember exactly how to make sense of the log entries.

Why bother reviewing the logs? One nice feature is that each entry in the authentication log indicates which remote access policy was applied (either to accept or to reject the connection). This is a good way to identify problems with policies, because sometimes multiple policies can combine to have an effect you didn't expect.

Furthermore, if it's desirable in your environment, you can use the logged data to generate accounting reports to tell you things such as the average utilization of your dial-in ports, the top-ten users of dial-in connect time, or how much online time accounts or certain Windows groups use.

Monitoring Ports and Port Activity

You can monitor port status and activity from the RRAS snap-in. The Ports folder under the server contains one entry for each defined port. When you select the Ports folder, you'll see a list of the ports and their current status. The list indicates whether each port is a dial-in or VPN port and whether it's active, so you can get a quick summary of your server's workload at any time.

Double-clicking an individual port displays the Port Status dialog box (see Figure 6.15). This dialog box shows information such as a port's line speed (Line BPS), the amount of transmitted and received data (Bytes In and Bytes Out), and the network address for each protocol being carried on the port. This is a useful tool for verifying whether a port is in active use, and it gives you a count of the number of transmission and reception errors on the port.

FIGURE 6.15   The Port Status dialog box

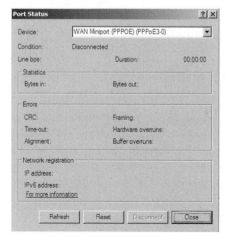

Integrating RRAS with DHCP

As you briefly learned in Chapter 4, "Managing Dynamic Host Configuration Protocol (DHCP)," each network that has a DHCP client on it must have either a DHCP server or a DHCP relay agent. Otherwise, the client has no way to reach a DHCP server and get a lease.

What does this mean for your remote access deployment? It depends on your network configuration, as described by the following:

- On a small or simple network, you may choose to use static IP addressing and assign each dial-in client a fixed IP address. In this case, you don't have to fool with DHCP at all.

- If your RRAS server is also a DHCP server, you're OK because dial-in clients will get an IP address from that server's address pool.

- If your RRAS server is on a different IP network from your DHCP servers or if you want to assign client addresses using of an address range that's not part of any DHCP scope, you need a relay agent.

The RRAS snap-in includes a DHCP relay agent that you install as an additional routing protocol. Once you install and configure it, it can tie your remote access clients to whatever DHCP infrastructure you want to use.

Installing the DHCP Relay Agent

You should know the following before installing a DHCP relay agent:

- You can't install the relay agent on a computer that's already acting as a DHCP server.

- You can't install it on a system running Network Address Translation (NAT) with the addressing component installed.

As long as your setup meets these requirements, the Server 2008 implementation of RRAS will install the DHCP relay agent automatically when you first enable remote access. You can also install the DHCP relay agent manually if necessary (for example, if you recently disabled the DHCP server component on your RRAS server). You will see how to install the relay agent in Exercise 6.4.

Configuring the DHCP Relay Agent

As is typical of other RRAS components, you configure the DHCP relay agent in two places: in the DHCP Relay Agent Properties dialog box and again on each individual interface. The configuration settings available in each place are different. In the following sections, you will see how to set a DHCP relay agent's properties, how to assign the relay agent to specific interfaces, and how to set an interface's properties.

Setting DHCP Relay Agent Properties

When you select the DHCP Relay Agent item under the IP Routing node in the RRAS snap-in and open its Properties dialog box, you'll see the controls shown in Figure 6.16. The only thing you can do here is specify which DHCP servers will receive forwarded requests from this particular DHCP relay agent. The only restriction is that the RRAS server that's running the DHCP relay agent must be able to route IP packets to the destination network. The servers you specify here apply to all network interfaces to which you attach the relay agent; there's no way to configure independent forwarding addresses for individual network interfaces.

FIGURE 6.16   DHCP Relay Agent Properties dialog box

In Exercise 6.4, you will learn how to install the DHCP relay agent on an RRAS server as well as configure it. You can complete this exercise if the DHCP relay agent was not previously installed and the local computer isn't running DHCP or NAT.

EXERCISE 6.4

Installing and Configuring the DHCP Relay Agent on an RRAS Server

1. Open the Routing and Remote Access snap-in by selecting Start ➤ Administrative Tools ➤ Routing And Remote Access.

2. Locate the server on which you want to install the DHCP relay agent.

EXERCISE 6.4 *(continued)*

3.   Expand the server until you see IPv4 and DHCP Relay Agent.

4.   Right-click DHCP Relay Agent, and choose Properties.

5.   In the DHCP Relay Agent Properties dialog box, add the IP addresses of the DHCP servers to which you want DHCP requests forwarded. Then click the OK button.

Assigning the Relay Agent to Specific Interfaces

Once you've configured the list of servers to which you want DHCP requests forwarded, you still have to attach the relay agent to particular network interfaces. To create a relay agent interface, right-click the DHCP Relay Agent item, and select New Interface. When the New Interface For DHCP Relay Agent dialog box appears, select the network interface to which you want the relay agent bound. Once you do, the interface-specific Properties dialog box (discussed in the following section) appears.

Setting Interface Properties

Each relay agent–enabled interface has its own set of properties, which are exposed through the interface-specific Properties dialog box (see Figure 6.17). The topmost control, the Relay DHCP Packets check box, lets you control whether DHCP relaying is active on this interface—you can turn it on or off without restarting the RRAS service.

FIGURE 6.17   The interface-specific Properties dialog box

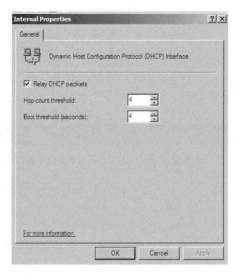

The other two controls affect how long relayed DHCP requests will bounce around your network:

- The Hop-Count Threshold field sets a limit on the number of intervening routers between the client and the DHCP server that the DHCP traffic can traverse.

- The Boot Threshold (Seconds) field controls how long the relay agent waits before forwarding any DHCP messages it hears. If you want to give a local DHCP server first crack at incoming requests, adjust the boot threshold up so that the local server has a chance to respond before the message is forwarded.

In Exercise 6.5, you'll add a new DHCP relay agent interface for your LAN connection and then specify configuration parameters for it. In practice, you'd need to add the DHCP relay agent to whichever interface remote clients use, but because we can't assume anything about the configuration of your lab machine, we've simplified this exercise.

EXERCISE 6.5

Configuring the DHCP Relay Agent on a Network Interface

1. Verify that the DHCP relay agent is installed. If not, refer to Exercise 6.4.

2. Right-click the DHCP Relay Agent item, and choose New Interface.

3. The New Interface For DHCP Relay Agent dialog box appears, listing each of the interfaces to which you could attach the relay agent. Select Local Area Connection, and click the OK button.

4. The interface-specific Properties dialog box appears. If you have a DHCP server on your local network, increase the boot threshold to 5 seconds; if you don't, decrease it to 0.

5. Click the OK button. Note that the list of DHCP relay agent interfaces has been updated to reflect the new interface.

Configuring a RAS or VPN Client

Dial-up RAS clients and VPN clients are similar. Almost all the options that are available when you set up a RAS client are also available when you set up a VPN client. The main differences are as follows:

- VPN clients specify the server's IP address, whereas RAS clients specify the server's phone number.

- VPN clients require an underlying connection to the Internet.

Client configuration is not a focus of the exam, so in this chapter you will learn how to configure a VPN client, but not a RAS client. Just remember that the RAS client configuration is extremely similar.

VPN connections are almost always created on client workstations, so this section describes the settings in Windows XP Professional.

When you establish a virtual private network connection, you're actually building an encrypted tunnel between you and some other machine. The tunneled data is carried over an insecure network, such as the Internet.

Once you've created a connection, you can change its properties at any time by opening its Properties dialog box. The Dial-Up Connection Properties dialog box has a total of five tabs you can use to adjust all the pertinent settings for each connection.

Don't confuse these settings with the ones in the Local Area Connection Properties dialog box; they serve entirely different purposes.

The General Tab

The General tab of the Connection Properties dialog box (the box is called Dial-Up Connections or VPN Connections, depending on whether you're configuring dial-up RAS or VPN) is where you specify either the IP address of the VPN server or the modem and phone number to use with this particular connection. Some fields have already been filled in from when you used the Network Connection Wizard. Figure 6.18 shows the VPN settings.

The General tab has a field where you enter the VPN server address or host name. The First Connect group lets you specify which dial-up connection, if any, you want brought up before the VPN connection is established.

With the General tab, you can also do the following:

- Change whether the connection shows a status/progress icon in the system tray whenever the connection is active. By default, dial-up connections show an icon when connected.
- Set VPN options:
  - Enter the VPN server address or host name.
  - Specify whether to automatically dial another connection first, and then specify the connection to dial.
- Set RAS options:
  - Change the modem this connection uses, or settings for the modem you already have, with the Configure button.

FIGURE 6.18   General tab of the VPN Connection Properties dialog box

 When configuring dial-up, you can also use the Phone And Modem Options control panel to adjust a broader range of modem settings.

- Enter the phone number to dial.

- Change whether dialing rules (for example, "I am now in area code 770") are used when DUN decides how to dial the number for this connection. When the Use Dialing Rules check box is selected, the Rules button becomes active, allowing you to define new locations and edit the dialing rules attached to each.

The Options Tab

The Options tab (see Figure 6.19) holds settings that control how DUN dials and redials the connection. The controls in this dialog box are segregated into two groups. The Dialing Options group holds controls that govern DUN's interface behavior while dialing, and the Redialing Options group controls whether and how DUN will redial if it doesn't immediately connect.

FIGURE 6.19   Options tab of the VPN Connection Properties dialog box

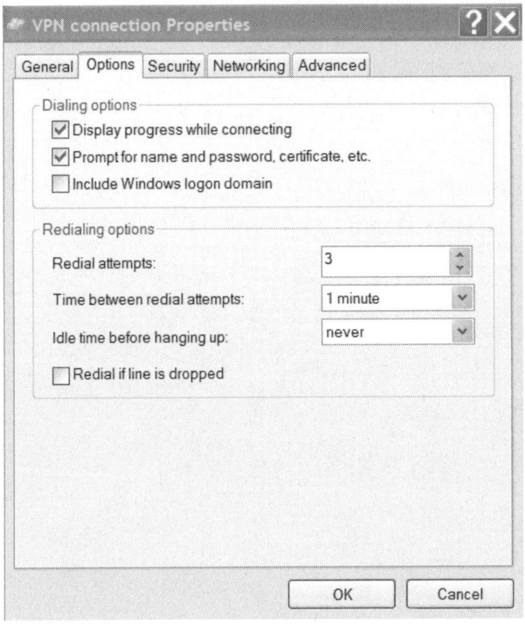

Dialing Options

Four dialing options are available in the Dialing Options group:

- The Display Progress While Connecting check box (selected by default) instructs DUN to keep you updated on its progress as it attempts to raise the connection.

- The Prompt For Name And Password, Certificate, Etc. check box is also selected by default. When it's on, Windows will prompt you for any credentials it needs to authenticate your connection to the remote server. This may be a username, a password, a public-key certificate, or some combination of the three, depending on what the remote end requires.

- The Include Windows Logon Domain check box is unchecked by default. It forces DUN to include the domain name of the domain you're logged on to as part of the authentication credential. Leave this unchecked unless you're dialing into a Windows NT/2000 network that has a trust relationship with your logon domain.

- For RAS connections, a Prompt For Phone Number check box (not shown in Figure 6.19) tells DUN to display the phone number in the connection dialog box. This box is checked by default. This gives you a chance to edit the phone number before dialing; you may want to uncheck it if you (or your users) are prone to making accidental changes.

Redialing Options

The settings in the Redialing Options group control how DUN will attempt to redial the specified number if the remote end is busy or doesn't answer with a recognizable carrier tone. These settings include the following:

- The Redial Attempts field controls how many attempts DUN will make to raise the other end before giving up. The default value is 3, but you can set any value from 0 (meaning that DUN won't attempt to redial) to 999,999,999.

- The Time Between Redial Attempts drop-down menu controls how long DUN will wait after each failed call before it tries again. Values in the drop-down menu range from 1 second all the way to 10 minutes, with various increments in between.

- The Idle Time Before Hanging Up drop-down menu lets you specify an inactivity timer. If your connection is idle for longer than the specified period, your client will terminate the call. Note that the remote end may drop the call sooner than your client, depending on how it's configured. By default, this drop-down menu is set to Never, meaning that your client will never drop a call. If you want an inactivity timer, you can pick values ranging from 1 minute to 24 hours.

- The Redial If Line Is Dropped check box automatically redials the number if you are disconnected.

The Security Tab

How useful you find the Security tab (see Figure 6.20) will depend on whom you're calling. The default settings it provides will work fine with most Internet service providers and corporate dial-up facilities, but Windows XP has a broad range of security settings you can change if you require. The Security Options group contains controls that directly affect the security of your connection. The Advanced (Custom Settings) radio button controls settings such as encryption and authentication protocols.

Security Options

The controls in the Security Options group are pretty straightforward. The security settings in effect for this connection are governed by your choice between the Typical (Recommended Settings) and Advanced (Custom Settings) radio buttons.

Typical (Recommended Settings)

Usually, it's best to stick with the Typical (Recommended Settings) option and use its subordinate controls to pick a canned setting that matches your needs. These subordinate controls include the following:

- The Validate My Identity As Follows drop-down menu lets you choose among the following authentication methods:
  - Unsecured passwords (the default, and the only type of authentication that most networks support)

- Secured passwords
- Smart card authentication (useful only when calling another Windows 2000, 2003, or 2008 network)

- If you choose to require a secured password, the Automatically Use My Windows Logon Name And Password (And Domain If Any) check box instructs DUN to offer to the remote end the logon credentials you used to log on to the computer or domain. This is useful only if you're dialing into a network that has access to your domain authentication information.

- If you require a secured password or smart card authentication, the Require Data Encryption (Disconnect If None) check box allows you to have either an encrypted connection or none at all. If you check this box, your client and the remote server will attempt to negotiate a common encryption method. If they can't (perhaps because the remote end doesn't offer encryption), your client will hang up.

FIGURE 6.20   Security tab of the VPN Connection Properties dialog box

Advanced (Custom Settings)

If you select the Advanced (Custom Settings) radio button and then click the Settings button, you'll see the Advanced Security Settings dialog box. Its controls are more complex than the ones on the Security tab.

The first field is the Data Encryption drop-down menu. Windows XP offers you the opportunity to encrypt both sides of network connections using IPSec. This capability extends to dial-up connections, too. The drop-down menu gives you the following four choices:

- No Encryption Allowed means that the server will drop your call if it requires encryption because you can't provide it.

- Optional Encryption tells the client to request encryption but to continue the call if it's not available.

- Require Encryption tells the client to request encryption and to refuse to communicate with servers that don't support it.

- Maximum Strength Encryption tells the client to communicate only with servers that offer the same strength encryption it does. For example, with this setting in force, a North American Windows Server 2008 machine running 3DES won't communicate with a French Windows XP machine because the French machine uses the weaker exportable encryption routines.

The Logon Security group controls which authentication protocols this client can use. The default setting, Use Extensible Authentication Protocol (EAP), is for standard Windows authentication (using the MD5-Challenge method) or certificate-based authentication (using the Smart Card Or Other Certificate choice in the drop-down menu).

The Allow These Protocols radio button is followed by a long list of authentication protocols. Although the specifics of how they work are different, the basic idea behind all these protocols is the same. Each provides a secure way for a client to prove its identity to a server. By selecting the appropriate check boxes, you can make your client use the same protocols as the remote end. For more details, see "Introduction to Authentication Protocols" later in this chapter as well as Chapter 7.

The Networking Tab

You use the Networking tab (see Figure 6.21) to control which protocols your client will attempt to use when communicating with other servers. When setting up RAS, you have to tell DUN what kind of server it's calling in the first place by using the Type Of Dial-Up Server I Am Calling field. Your choices are PPP or the Serial Line Internet Protocol (SLIP, now relegated to older Unix machines and dial-up hardware). By default, PPP will be selected, and it's unlikely that you'll need to change it.

When setting up VPN, the top drop-down menu is labeled Type Of VPN, and you use it to indicate what kind of VPN call you're making. Automatic is the default setting, but you can select a PPTP or L2TP connection if you prefer.

The list box in the middle of the tab shows the network protocols installed on the client. Protocols marked with a check are available for use with this connection. Usually, when configuring RAS, you'll see TCP/IP and Client For Microsoft Networks marked, which indicates that those two protocols can be used over the connection.

FIGURE 6.21   Networking tab of the VPN Connection Properties dialog box

The Install, Uninstall, and Properties buttons work just as they do in the Local Area Connection Properties dialog box—by using them you can control which protocols are on your machine and what their settings are.

It's worth mentioning that selecting Internet Protocol (TCP/IP) in the protocols list and opening its Properties dialog box gives you access to a set of properties that are completely distinct from any TCP/IP settings that may apply to your LAN interfaces. Usually, the dial-up TCP/IP settings are configured to obtain an IP address and DNS information from the remote server, although if you need to, you can override these settings.

The Advanced Tab

The Advanced tab (Figure 6.22) contains a few important settings:

- The Settings button under Windows Firewall allows you to configure the same firewall settings as the control panel.

- Internet Connection Sharing allows other users to connect to the Internet through this machine. The machine you enable this on works like a gateway to the Internet.

Creating a VPN Connection on a Windows XP Client

In Exercise 6.6, you will learn how to create a VPN connection on a Windows XP client.

FIGURE 6.22   The Advanced tab of the VPN Connection Properties dialog box

EXERCISE 6.6

Configuring Windows XP Professional as a VPN Client

1. Choose Start, right-click My Network Places, and select Properties.

2. Click the Create A New Connection icon. The New Connection Wizard appears. Click the Next button.

3. Choose the Connect To The Network At My Workplace button, and click Next.

4. Choose the VPN Connection radio button, and click Next.

5. Enter a descriptive name for the connection, and click Next.

6. Choose the Do Not Dial The Initial Connection radio button, and click Next.

7. Enter the IP address of the VPN server. Click Next when you're done.

8. The wizard's Summary page appears. Click Finish.

9. The Connect dialog box appears. Make sure you are connected to the Internet, enter a username and password, and click the Dial button to connect.

 **Real World Scenario**

Servers as Remote Access Clients

We mentioned earlier that remote access clients are usually workstations dialing in to the network from home or on the road. This represents the majority of remote access activity in the world, but you might not realize that servers often communicate with each other across remote access connections as well. Most small businesses (and some medium-sized businesses) with multiple locations cannot afford dedicated leased lines between sites, so they rely on daily, hourly, or even persistent dial-up or VPN connections to replicate their Active Directory databases or to share data between locations. In situations such as this, the server at one location represents the remote access client, and the server at the other end represents the remote access server, even though technically they might be peers in Active Directory.

Server-to-server VPN connections are more and more common as high-speed Internet access becomes ubiquitous. Because most high-speed Internet connections are always on, you don't even need to establish the initial connection to the Internet before "dialing in" to the VPN server. In fact, traditional WAN solutions are rapidly being replaced by persistent VPN connections that are always on and always connected. In this situation, the VPN connection is a two-way initiated connection. The connection is initiated from either one of the servers. Two-way initiated connections require the creation of demand-dial interfaces, remote access policies, IP address pools, and packet filters on the routers on both sides of the connection. In cases such as this, the distinction between the *client* and the *server* is not so clear, so always remember to use those terms with caution.

Introduction to Authentication Protocols

The authentication protocols available when setting up VPN or dial-up connections include the following:

- PAP
- SPAP
- CHAP
- MS-CHAP version 1 (MS-CHAPv1)
- MS-CHAP version 2 (MS-CHAPv2)

SPAP and MS-CHAPv1 are no longer supported by Windows Server 2008 for authentication protocols for PPP-based connections. We will continue to discuss these protocols so that you have an understanding of them for older operating systems and clients.

The sheer number of authentication protocol choices means that it's quite easy to miss the subtleties inherent within each choice and version. It is important that you understand the differences between these protocols—not only for your career as an administrator but also for the exam! Both this chapter and Chapter 7 will cover these authentication protocols in some detail since you'll likely encounter questions about them on the exam.

Challenge Handshake Authentication Protocol (CHAP)   CHAP is an authentication protocol that calls for the authenticating server to send a challenge to the NAS, which then combines that challenge with a preshared secret and performs the authentication. Passwords for use with CHAP are stored with a reversible encryption, which makes CHAP a poor choice for most scenarios.

Extensible Authentication Protocol-Transport Level Security (EAP-TLS)   EAP-TLS is a certificate-based authentication framework that's usually used with smart cards. EAP-TLS can be used only on servers that are members of a domain and is found only in Windows Server 2003 and Server 2008.

Extensible Authentication Protocol-Message Digest 5 Challenge Handshake Authentication Protocol (EAP-MD5 CHAP)   EAP-MD5 CHAP is a version of EAP that uses CHAP. This algorithm hashes encryption information using MD5. This algorithm can be used for compatibility with other, non-Microsoft systems. Windows Server 2008 no longer supports this protocol for authentication protocols for PPP-based connections.

MS-CHAPv1   MS-CHAPv1 is Microsoft's implementation of a one-way authentication and encryption algorithm. MS-CHAPv1 is supported on older versions of Windows, including Windows 95 and Windows 98. Windows Server 2008 no longer supports this protocol for authentication protocols for PPP-based connections.

MS-CHAPv2   MS-CHAPv2 is an implementation by Microsoft of a two-way authentication system. It is available in Windows 2000, Server 2003, Vista, XP, and Server 2008. MS-CHAPv2 solves many of the problems with MS-CHAPv1 but still leaves much to be desired.

Password Authentication Protocol (PAP)   PAP is an authentication mechanism found at many Internet providers. PAP sends user credentials in plain text between the NAS and the authentication server and therefore is susceptible to man-in-the-middle attacks.

Shiva Password Authentication Protocol (SPAP)   SPAP encrypts authentication information between the NAS and the authentication server and is mainly used with Shiva remote access servers. Windows Server 2008 no longer supports this protocol for PPP-based connections.

Unauthenticated access   This method enables connections to be established without providing credentials. You shouldn't use this method in a live network, but it can be helpful for testing and troubleshooting.

 For the exam, you should know which authentication protocols support which features and which ones are available on various versions of operating systems.

Table 6.1 lists some features and the protocols that support them.

TABLE 6.1   Features of Authentication Protocols

Feature	Authentication Protocol
Encryption of both authentication and connection data with Windows operating systems	MS-CHAPv1*, MS-CHAPv2, EAP-TLS
Encryption of authentication information for non-Microsoft operating systems	CHAP, EAP-MD5 CHAP*
Mutual authentication of both client and server	MS-CHAPv2, EAP-TLS
No encryption of authentication information or connection data	PAP
No authentication of credentials	Unauthenticated access
Encryption for Shiva-related servers and clients	SPAP*

*This protocol is not supported in Windows Server 2008.

The nuances of support for authentication protocols between Microsoft operating systems can be difficult to remember. Table 6.2 describes which protocols are supported by which operating systems.

TABLE 6.2   Authentication Protocols and the Operating Systems That Support Them

Authentication Protocol	Operating Systems Supporting	Recommendations
MS-CHAPv1	Windows 95, Windows 98, Windows Me, Windows NT 4	Recommended.
MS-CHAPv2	Windows 95, Windows 98, Windows Me, and Windows NT 4 if they have the latest upgrades; Windows 2000, Windows XP, Vista, Windows Server 2003, and Windows Server 2008 natively	Recommended. The default for Windows 2000, XP, Vista, Windows Server 2003, and Windows Server 2008.
EAP-TLS	Windows Server 2003 and 2008	Can be used only on servers that are members of a domain.

TABLE 6.2 Authentication Protocols and the Operating Systems That Support Them *(continued)*

Authentication Protocol	Operating Systems Supporting	Recommendations
EAP-MD5 CHAP	All but Windows Server 2008	If running an OS other than Windows Server 2008, use for compatibility with non-Microsoft systems.
CHAP	All	Recommended.
PAP	All	Avoid unless you must talk to an older device that doesn't use CHAP or MS-CHAPv2.
Unauthenticated access	All	Avoid except for testing and troubleshooting.
SPAP	All but Windows Server 2008	Avoid unless you must talk to an older device that doesn't use CHAP or MS-CHAPv2.

Overview of Wireless Access

In today's computer world, it seems like everyone has a laptop. We do a lot of traveling, and when you go to any airport in America, it seems like everyone is working on a laptop while they wait for their plane.

Because laptops have grown in popularity, we IT professionals must account for them on our networks. Laptops offer IT administrators a unique set of challenges that we must deal with on a day-to-day basis.

One major concern for IT administrators is security. Years ago we never had to worry about users copying documents to a desktop computer and then walking out with the computer. But today, users can copy company documents to laptop computers and then walk out the door with the computer and the documents. In this section, we will discuss wireless networks, protocols, and security.

Windows Vista and Windows Server 2008 have enhanced the IEEE 802.11 wireless support to include some of the following changes:

- Single sign-on
- 802.11 wireless diagnostics
- WPA2 support
- Native WiFi architecture

- Wireless Group Policy enhancements
- Changes in Wireless Auto Configuration
- Integration with Network Access Protection when using 802.1X authentication
- EAPHost infrastructure
- Command-line support for configuring wireless settings
- Network Location Awareness and network profiles
- Next-generation TCP/IP stack enhancements for wireless environments

Configuring Wireless Access

Windows Vista, Windows XP, Windows Server 2003, and Windows Server 2008 provide built-in support for 802.11 wireless LAN networking. Inside the Network Connections folder, an installed 802.11 wireless LAN network adapter appears as a wireless network connection. The following are some of the items you can configure:

Operating modes   There are two types of operating modes:

- *Infrastructure mode*: This uses at least one wireless access point (AP) and/or a device that bridges the wireless computers to each other
- *Ad hoc mode*: Wireless network computers connect directly to each other without the use of an AP or bridge.

Wired Equivalent Privacy (WEP)   All of us (on a laptop) have tried to find a wireless network at one time or another. Wired Equivalent Privacy (WEP) is a wireless encryption that was originally defined in 802.11. WEP helps prevent unauthorized wireless users from accessing your wireless network by the use of a shared secret key:

- If your wireless network is using the infrastructure mode, the WEP key must be configured on the wireless AP and all the wireless clients.
- If your wireless network is using the ad hoc mode, the WEP key must be configured on all the wireless clients.

The WEP key can be either 40-bit or 104-bit depending on what your hardware can accommodate.

Wi-Fi Protected Access (WPA)   An organization of wireless equipment vendors called the Wi-Fi Alliance created an interim standard called Wi-Fi Protected Access (WPA) while the IEEE 802.11i wireless LAN security standard was still being completed. WPA uses a strong encryption method called the Temporal Key Integrity Protocol (TKIP) to replace the weaker WEP standard. You have the ability to use the Advanced Encryption Standard (AES) for encryption that is provided by WPA.

WPA can be used in two different mode types:

- WPA-Personal is used for a home office or small company.
- WPA-Enterprise was designed for a midsize to large organization.

Wi-Fi Protected Access 2 (WPA2)   Wi-Fi Protected Access 2 (WPA2) was designed to officially replace the WEP standard. WPA2 certifies that equipment used in a wireless network is compatible with the IEEE 802.11i standard. This certification is used to help standardize the use of the additional security features of the IEEE 802.11i standard that are not already included in WPA.

WPA2 can be used in two different mode types:

- WPA2-Personal is used for a home office or small company.
- WPA2-Enterprise was designed for a midsize to large organization.

Service set identifier (SSID)   To specify a wireless network by name, you specify the service set identifier (SSID), also known as the *wireless network name*:

- In infrastructure mode, the SSID is configured on the wireless access point.
- In ad hoc mode, the SSID is configured on the initial wireless client.

To help wireless clients discover and join the wireless network, the wireless AP or the initial wireless client periodically advertise the SSID (this can be disabled for security).

Group policies for wireless   You have the ability to use Group Policy settings for Vista and Windows Server 2008 for WPA2. If you have systems running Windows XP, you must first install the XP Service Pack 2 in order to configure the WPA2 authentication options. Group Policy settings allow you to configure WPA2 options at the server for all wireless clients.

Internet Connection Sharing

Internet Connection Sharing (ICS) gives networked computers the ability to access a single connection to the Internet. Think of ICS as a form of gateway to the Internet. You can have multiple users connected to the Internet through one connected computer.

This can work well with wireless access. You can use ad hoc mode (users connecting directly to each other) and allow all of your users to connect to the Internet using one computer. You also have the ability to do this in infrastructure mode, but it isn't advised. If all your users are going to connect to a device or AP, you can set up the Internet through the device.

Summary

In this chapter, you learned how to install and configure the Routing and Remote Access Services to handle dial-in connections, how to configure appropriate encryption and security settings so that communication between the client and server is encrypted and authenticated, how to install RRAS to provide VPN service using the PPTP and L2TP protocols, how to configure VPN services on the server and client, and finally how to troubleshoot common problems with VPNs.

We also discussed using wireless networking and what types of security encryption you can use to help support your wireless network. We talked about the different components of wireless access and using group policies to configure wireless clients. Finally, we discussed Internet Connection Sharing and the benefits of using it.

Exam Essentials

Understand how multilink works.   The multilink extensions to the Point-to-Point Protocol (PPP) provide a way to combine several independent PPP connections so that they act as a single connection. Windows Server 2008's RRAS supports multilink PPP for inbound and outbound calls.

Know how to install and configure RAS at the server level.   The RAS installation process is driven by the Routing And Remote Access Server Setup Wizard, which you use to set up a dial-up server. You can specify whether the server acts as a remote access server, specify what authentication providers and settings you want the server to use, control the settings applied to each protocol you have installed, specify which PPP protocols (including multilink) the clients on this server are allowed to use, and control what level of log detail is kept for incoming connections.

Know the different components you can use to manage the remote access server.   The Server Status node in the RRAS snap-in shows you a summary of all the RRAS servers known to the system. Each RRAS server on your network has its own set of logs, which you manage through the Remote Access Logging folder. You can monitor port status and activity from the RRAS snap-in, too. The Ports folder under the server contains one entry for each defined port; when you select the Ports folder, you'll see a list of the ports and their current status.

Know how to integrate RRAS with DHCP using the DHCP relay agent.   If no DHCP server is available on the network where the client is located, you can use a DHCP relay agent to forward DHCP messages from the client to the DHCP server's network. The relay agent acts like a radio repeater, listening for DHCP client requests and retransmitting them on the server's network.

Know how to install and configure a VPN server.   If you don't have RRAS installed, you'll need to install it, activate it, and configure it as a VPN server. If you're already using RRAS for IP routing or remote access, you can enable it as a VPN server without reinstalling. VPN configuration is extremely simple, at least for PPTP. Either a server can accept VPN calls or it can't. If it can, it will have a certain number of VPN ports, all of which are configured identically.

Understanding Internet Connection Sharing.   Internet Connection Sharing allows you to share one connected Internet computer with multiple users. The users can all access the Internet through the one connected computer.

Know how to troubleshoot a VPN.   Verify that the RRAS server is installed and configured on the server, that the client and server protocols match, and that authentication is working properly. Then check for policy problems, network problems, and domain problems.

Know how to configure an RRAS client.   Most client connections are made on Vista or XP Professional workstations. Dial-in and VPN connections are configured very similarly, but when creating a VPN connection, you must substitute an IP address for a phone number.

Understand wireless access.   Understand what wireless access does and the different types of security encryption to help support your wireless network. Understand the difference between infrastructure mode and ad hoc mode.

Review Questions

1. You have a local DHCP server for your dial-in clients, but you also want to use the DHCP relay agent to forward requests to a remote DHCP server if the local server doesn't answer a request. To do this, you must do which of the following?

   A. Add a static route to the remote server.

   B. Adjust the boot threshold on the DHCP relay agent interface for the remote network so that the local server has enough time to respond.

   C. Adjust the DHCP Forwarding Time parameter in the registry.

   D. Adjust the forwarding time in the DHCP Relay Agent Global Properties dialog box.

2. Your sales force consists of 1,000 people who use laptops that are standardized on Windows 98 and Windows NT Workstation. In a migration that's well underway, you have already upgraded all your servers and services to Windows Server 2008 and a half of your internal Windows NT and Windows 98 machines to Windows 2000 and XP Professional. As soon as you finish the internal migration, you'll begin to bring all the remote users up to Windows 2000 and XP Professional. Recently, you were told that your CEO is concerned about network security, and you were ordered to make sure that all your external network connections are secure and that any data paths outside your network are encrypted. Which of the following steps can you take to meet these new requirements? (Choose all that apply.)

   A. Configure IPSec for all your network communications.

   B. Upgrade all your remote users immediately to Windows 2000 and XP Professional.

   C. Configure your RRAS servers to use MS-CHAP.

   D. Configure your RRAS servers to accept only PPTP and MPPE connections.

   E. Disable remote connections until you complete the Windows Server 2008 migration.

3. Your company has offices in five locations around the country. Most of the users' activity is local to their own network. Occasionally, some of the users in one location need to send confidential information to one of the other four locations or to retrieve information from one of them. The communication between the remote locations is sporadic and relatively infrequent, so you have configured RRAS to use demand-dial lines to set up the connections. Management's only requirement is that any communication between the office locations be appropriately secured. Which of the following steps should you take to ensure compliance with this requirement? (Choose all that apply.)

   A. Configure CHAP on all the RRAS servers.

   B. Configure PAP on all the RRAS servers.

   C. Configure MPPE on all the RRAS servers.

   D. Configure L2TP on all the RRAS servers.

   E. Configure MS-CHAPv2 on all the RRAS servers.

4. Your small financial consulting company has a stand-alone Windows 2008 server that provides a central location for your home-based consultants to upload and download spreadsheet files using Vista. A few of the consultants use Windows XP Professional workstations. You want to set up VPN connections between the consultants and the RRAS server. The RRAS server is connected to a small peer-to-peer network of five Windows XP Professional workstations that use the network for storing files, including the files that the consultants are uploading and downloading. What authentication protocol should you use for the VPN?

   A. CHAP

   B. MS-CHAPv2

   C. EAP-TLS

   D. PAP

5. You recently migrated your company's Windows NT network to Windows Server 2008. This migration includes 300 Windows XP Professional workstations and 8 Windows Server 2008 servers. Your company has just acquired another company with offices down the street. It has a Windows NT network that needs to be migrated to Windows Server 2008 as well, and you have already begun to move the servers to the new operating system and associated services. Because you have a tight cap on expenses for network additions, you presently can't afford leased lines between the buildings. Until you can get support for them, you are going to create a VPN that is both encrypted and authenticated between the two facilities over the Internet connections that already exist. What do you need to implement in order to achieve this goal? (Choose all that apply.)

   A. L2TP

   B. PPTP

   C. IPSec

   D. RADIUS

   E. MS-CHAPv2

6. You have implemented VPNs to connect the various locations of your organization. These locations include offices in New York, Sacramento, Memphis, and Omaha, with a significant LAN in each one. The RRAS server is set up such that the users aren't aware of the intricacies of the connections. You are beginning to have problems with the connections between the offices, and as a result, the number of support calls is growing dramatically. What configurations could you use to troubleshoot the communication problems?

   A. L2TP using MPPE

   B. L2TP unencrypted

   C. L2TP using IPSec in transport mode

   D. L2TP using IPSec in tunnel mode

7. Your company's 450 sales reps are finally going to receive laptops so that they can communicate with the corporate office whenever they need information stored on the corporate network. The corporate network is fully upgraded to Windows Server 2008, including the default configuration of the RRAS server for the remote connectivity over VPNs. You have installed Windows XP Professional with the default configuration on all the laptops and have added the sales reps to a special group in Active Directory. After testing the laptops, everything appears to work fine. You ship them out, and as they reach the sales reps, you monitor their initial connections. During the next few days, you begin receiving support calls from people complaining they cannot connect to the network. What is the most likely cause of the problem?

    A. The Windows XP clients are not configured to support a VPN.

    B. The default RRAS configuration does not support VPNs.

    C. The default RRAS configuration does not support enough VPN connections.

    D. The default RRAS configuration does not support L2TP.

    E. The Windows XP client default configuration does not support L2TP.

8. You are the network administrator for a company with two offices: one located on the East Coast and the other on the West Coast. Sales information needs to be sent from the East Coast office to the West Coast office on the regular basis, and some accounting reports and payroll information needs to be sent back to the East Coast. The owner of your company has been reading stories in the press about security problems on the Internet and refuses to allow any company information to travel through the Internet, regardless of how much you talk about securing those transmissions. The communications between the sites occur approximately once a week. What steps would you take to ensure secure authentication and secure transmission while not spending too much money? (Choose all that apply.)

    A. Configure PAP as the authentication method between the servers.

    B. Install RRAS on a server at each location, and keep the line open with an ISDN connection that will always be available for the communication.

    C. Install RRAS on a server at each location, and configure demand-dial to open the connection each time the transmission occurs.

    D. Configure CHAP as the authentication method between the servers.

    E. Configure MS-CHAPv2 as the authentication method between the servers.

    F. Configure IPSec as the encryption method between the servers.

    G. Configure MPPE as the encryption method between the servers.

    H. Configure L2TP as the encryption method between the servers.

9. You are using an RRAS server to manage remote access to your small Windows Server 2008 network that serves a single location. RRAS provides access to several remote users and to the people who have machines on the local network but occasionally want to access the network from home or from hotels when on the road. Regardless of the category of user, everyone is authenticated through Active Directory. You haven't spent much time reviewing the use of this remote connectivity since you configured the system, but now there is a concern about unauthorized users as well as intermittent problems that remote users are experiencing when connecting to the network. You've been asked to prepare a report for management describing the extent of these problems in the company. You recall that when you set up the system, you configured the logging to track all connection attempts using local Windows accounting. Where will you find the logging information that you need for preparing your report?

   A. The Performance Monitor log

   B. Active Directory

   C. The *systemroot*\System32\LogFiles folder

   D. The system event log

   E. The RRAS authentication log

10. Your area of responsibility at the All Terrain Vehicle Rentals Company is to build, deploy, and maintain the remote access system for the Windows Server 2008 network. The system consists of four RRAS servers, which serve 200 users across the country. The users often travel from location to location, and they access different servers depending upon where they call in. You put together a management station to monitor all the RRAS servers so you can keep an eye on this critical aspect of your network. What tool do you use to accomplish this?

   A. The Server Monitor of the RRAS snap-in

   B. The Server Status node of the RRAS snap-in

   C. The System Monitor snap-in

   D. The MMC

11. You have an RRAS server for your dial-in clients, but you want to use the DHCP relay agent to forward requests to a remote DHCP server. You don't want the requests to travel through more than three routers to get to the DHCP server. How can you make this happen?

   A. Add a static route to the DHCP server.

   B. Adjust the boot threshold on the DHCP relay agent interface for the network so that the local server has enough time to respond.

   C. Adjust the hop-count threshold on the DHCP relay agent interface for the network.

   D. Adjust the forwarding time in the DHCP Relay Agent Properties dialog box.

12. After your company acquired another company, you were given the responsibility for connecting the two together. One company is in Los Angeles, and the other is in Sacramento. Both systems ran Windows NT, and you migrated them to Windows Vista, XP, and Server 2008 using Active Directory to manage the users and desktops with group policies. You connected the two locations using one of the Windows Server 2008 computers in Los Angeles. You then decided to use DHCP to manage the address space more efficiently. You installed DHCP service on one of the Windows Server 2008 computers in Los Angeles and installed DHCP relay agent on the multihomed Windows Server 2008 computer that is connecting the two locations. Everything looks great in Los Angeles, but when the clients in Sacramento try to obtain a DHCP lease, there is no reply. What is the most likely problem with this configuration?

A. The DHCP relay agent is configured on the wrong NIC and with the wrong address on the multihomed router.

B. The DHCP relay agent needs to be installed on the DHCP router to forward the requests.

C. None of the addresses has been reserved for the Windows NT machine in Sacramento.

D. The clients in Sacramento need to register with the DHCP server for security purposes.

13. You administer a network consisting of 100 client computers and 2 Windows Server 2008 computers. You must configure a VPN solution for your company using L2TP/IPSec. Unfortunately, you don't have a certificate server in-house, and the management would prefer to not pay for a third-party service. What should you do to ensure that VPN communication is secure? Choose the best answers. (Choose all that apply.)

A. Implement a solution with preshared keys.

B. Use CHAP.

C. Use PPTP.

D. Install a certificate server on the other Windows Server 2008 computer.

14. You recently took over the network administration job at a small company. The network consists of 20 client computers and 2 Windows Server 2008 computers. The network does not contain a DNS or WINS server. Clients on the LAN are able to resolve names to IP addresses without any problem using broadcasts, but you find that remote users cannot do the same. What is the best solution to solve the remote users' problem?

A. Install and enable DNS on one of the Windows Server 2008 computers.

B. Install and enable WINS on one of the Windows Server 2008 computers.

C. Configure the Enable Broadcast Name Resolution option on the RRAS server.

D. Instruct the remote users to access internal computers by IP address.

15. Your RRAS server's NIC is configured with multiple IP addresses. You want to restrict VPN access to only one of the IP addresses. Look at the following graphic to determine the steps you should take to enable this configuration.

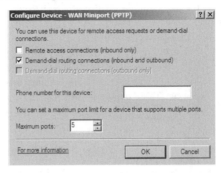

   A. Select the Remote Access Connections (Inbound Only) check box.

   B. Select the Demand-Dial Routing Connections (Inbound And Outbound) check box.

   C. Enter the appropriate IP address in the Phone Number For This Device field.

   D. Increase the number of available ports to match the number of IP addresses assigned to the NIC in the computer.

16. You will be performing authentication through your remote access server using smart cards. Which authentication protocol should you use in order to achieve this?

   A. EAP-TLS

   B. MS-CHAPv2

   C. MS-CARD

   D. EAP-MD5 CHAP

17. You are the administrator of a network running a Windows Server 2008 server called VPN-SERVER, which is a member of the domain `example.com`. This server is in charge of authentication for remote users of a VPN. The VPN runs PPTP. A user who is using Windows XP on a computer called `client1.example.com` is unable to make a VPN connection. You've performed some troubleshooting, including pinging `client1.example.com` successfully from the server. From these choices, what might be a possible cause?

   A. There is a problem with DNS that is preventing `client1.example.com` from being resolved correctly by the default gateway.

   B. The VPN client is unable to ping `vpnserver.example.com` and therefore has network connectivity problems.

   C. The client's VPN configuration is using an invalid key length.

   D. There are not enough VPN ports configured, or the ports were never configured for PPTP connections.

18. Thinking of the protocols involved in creating a PPP connection, this protocol is responsible for establishing and configuring the PPP connection.

   A. Challenge Handshake Authentication Protocol (CHAP)

   B. Link Control Protocol (LCP)

   C. Internet Protocol Control Protocol (IPCP)

   D. Link Establishment Protocol (LEP)

19. You have been given directions to create a secure method for communication between two offices, the main office in Chicago and a remote office in Los Angeles. The Los Angeles office runs all Linux and Macintosh computers. Because of the prohibitive costs, management has ruled out a private line connection between the two locations. You've decided instead to implement a secure protocol over the Internet in order to meet this goal. Which of the following combinations is valid for this task? (Choose all that apply.)

   A. L2TP with IPSec

   B. PPTP with L2TP

   C. Installing a Windows Server 2008 server running Routing and Remote Access

   D. MPPE with L2TP

20. You are considering multilink PPP in order to increase bandwidth available for a dial-up client. Which of the following is not a benefit of multilink?

   A. Multilink can make the client experience faster by combining multiple phone lines and creating one logical PPP connection.

   B. Multilink enables the encryption of data between the client and the server.

   C. Multilink can be relatively low in cost and can utilize already existing infrastructure.

   D. Multilink is easy to use and included in Windows Server 2008 for both inbound and outbound calls.

Answers to Review Questions

1. B. The boot threshold for an interface controls how long the relay agent will wait before forwarding DHCP requests it hears on that interface.

2. C, D. Because your entire set of client machines are Windows clients, you can use MS-CHAP to provide password encryption when establishing a connection to the network. PPTP and MPPE provide encryption of data between the client machine and the RRAS server. IPSec provides encryption from the client all the way to the resource it's connecting to, which is more than required by the directives. Upgrading the remote clients will not, by itself, provide the encryption required, and the Windows NT clients already support MS-CHAP. Disabling all remote connections until you finish the migration isn't necessary because the pieces are already in place to satisfy the requirements.

3. C, E. MS-CHAPv2 provides encrypted and mutual authentication between the respective RRAS locations. MPPE works with MS-CHAPv2 and provides encryption for all the data between the locations. CHAP provides encrypted authentication, but MS-CHAPv2 is needed for MPPE to work. PAP is the lowest level of authentication providing passwords, but it sends passwords in clear text, which is not the most secure solution. L2TP needs to team up with IPSec to provide the data encryption for the secure transfer of information between the locations.

4. B. MS-CHAPv2 authentication allows you to create VPN connections with a stand-alone server using PPTP and MPPE. MPPE employs keys that are created via MS-CHAPv2 or EAP-TLS authentication. EAP-TLS is not the correct answer because only domain controllers or member servers support EAP-TLS. Stand-alone servers support only MPPE. Neither PAP nor CHAP is supported with MPPE.

5. A, C. L2TP connections can be used to authenticate both sides of the VPN. L2TP needs IPSec to provide the encryption for the connection. These two together will provide the secure and authenticated transmission of data across the Internet between the two sites. PPTP connections provide encryption only using MPPE but don't provide authentication between the machines. RADIUS is a service that provides dial-in connectivity. MS-CHAPv2 is an authentication protocol for clients accessing the network.

6. B. L2TP and IPSec each has its own negotiation procedure for making a connection. If you remove the IPSec portion of the connection and the problem is alleviated, it is likely that IPSec is the problem, and you can then focus on IPSec. If the problem remains, you can work on the L2TP portion of the connection. IPSec has two modes: tunnel mode and transport mode. But because L2TP is a tunneling protocol, there is no sense in using IPSec tunneling. IPSec transport mode is used with L2TP and should be set aside for troubleshooting, as discussed. The L2TP implementation in Windows Server 2008 doesn't support MPPE.

7. C. The default configuration for RRAS supports five PPTP ports and five L2TP ports. There are up to 150 sales reps trying to connect to the server, but only the first 10 will be able to connect. You can increase the number of ports available, up to 1,000, by using the Ports Properties dialog box. The Windows XP Professional clients are by default ready to support VPNs; they will first try L2TP and then switch over to PPTP if ports are unavailable.

8. C, E, G. Because the communication is not a continuous or frequent occurrence, it doesn't make sense to have the line always available, so RRAS with demand-dial will be less expensive than ISDN, which is always up. MS-CHAPv2 provides encryption and a mutual authentication process. The MPPE provides the encryption of the actual data that travels across the connection. PAP is a clear-text authentication method, and CHAP provides only one-way authentication. L2TP doesn't provide any encryption by itself.

9. C. When you use Windows accounting, the local Windows account logs are found in the `systemroot\System32\LogFiles` folder. These logs can be stored in one of two formats for later analysis—Open Database Connectivity (ODBC) or Internet Authentication Service. The Performance Monitor Log tool that came with Windows NT has been replaced with the system event log. This keeps track of global service errors such as initialization failures and service starts and stops. There is no RRAS authentication log. You do have RADIUS logging available; when it's used, the log files are stored on the RADIUS servers. This is useful when you have multiple RRAS servers because you can centralize RRAS authentication requests. Active Directory is not used to log events from the various services in Windows Server 2008.

10. B. The Server Status node in the RRAS snap-in shows you a summary of all the RRAS servers known to the system. Each server entry displays whether the server is up, what kind of server it is, how many ports it has, how many ports are currently in use, and how long the server has been up.

11. C. The hop count threshold controls the number of intervening routers that the DHCP traffic can traverse between the client and the DHCP server.

12. A. If the relay agent isn't installed on the subnet that needs the service, the requests cannot be forwarded and the Sacramento subnet won't have DHCP services. You can't install the relay agent on the DHCP server because they share the same UDP ports and will conflict. Client reservations are used to make sure that a machine always receives the same address from the scope; they don't apply in this situation. For security purposes, clients don't register with DHCP servers.

13. A, D. Windows Server 2008 introduces the ability to use preshared keys with L2TP/IPSec. This can be useful when you don't have access to a certificate server, but you should use certificates if possible because they are more secure.

14. C. A new feature of Windows Server 2008 allows remote clients to resolve names to IP addresses using broadcasts. Previously, you would have needed a DNS or WINS server in order for remote clients to do this, but this is no longer necessary.

15. A, C. Although it may sound strange, you should enter the IP address that you want to apply the VPN to in the Phone Number For This Device field. Then you can click the Remote Access Connections (Inbound Only) check box to accept inbound connections only on the appropriate IP address.

16. A. EAP-TLS is used for smart card authentication.

17. D. The most likely cause listed here is that there aren't enough ports configured or that the ports were never configured in the first place for VPN access. (There are many other possible causes.) Options A and B are incorrect because you were able to ping the remote computer by its name. Option C is not a real issue.

18. B. Link Control Protocol (LCP) is responsible for establishing and configuring a PPP connection. CHAP and IPCP are also involved. No protocol called Link Establishment Protocol (LEP) exists.

19. A, C. You can accomplish the goal by implementing L2TP with IPSec or by installing a Windows Server 2008 server running RRAS (although it could be argued that this isn't necessarily required). Options A and C are correct for this question, though it could be argued that option C isn't necessarily required. PPTP with L2TP and MPPE with L2TP are invalid combinations.

20. B. Multilink PPP has nothing to do with encryption of data. Multilink is easy to set up, is relatively low in cost, and makes the connection faster.

Chapter

7

Managing Security for Remote Access Services

MICROSOFT EXAM OBJECTIVES COVERED IN THIS CHAPTER:

✓ **Configuring network authentication.**

- May include but is not limited to: LAN authentication by using NTLMv2 and Kerberos., WLAN authentication by using 802.1x, RAS authentication by using MS-CHAP, MS-CHAPv2 and EAP, Remote Access Policy, Network Address Translation (NAT), Connection Manager.

✓ **Configuring Network Access Protection (NAP).**

- May include but is not limited to: Network layer protection, DHCP enforcement, Default user profiles, VPN enforcement, Configure NAP health policies, IPsec enforcement, 802.1x enforcement, Flexible host isolation.

✓ **Configuring firewall settings.**

- May include but is not limited to: Incoming and outgoing traffic filtering, Active Directory account integration, Identify ports and protocols, Windows Firewall vs. Windows Firewall with advanced security, Configure firewall by using group policy, Isolation policy.

One of the more important goals for a network administrator is keeping the network secure, including when your users remotely access the network. The Windows Server 2008 Group Policy Object (GPO) provides a way to apply dial-up permission and capability settings to groups of users.

This chapter explains how network access policies and profiles are used to grant or deny user access to resources on the network across remote connections. We'll begin by looking in more detail at the authentication protocols included with Windows Server 2008 (introduced in Chapter 6, "Configuring RADIUS and Wireless Access"). You'll also see how the operating system handles remote access security. Then we'll dive into the details of configuring user access with profiles and policies. You'll also learn how to configure your server to use Windows authentication or RADIUS authentication.

Remote Access Security

In the past, remote access was seldom part of most companies' networks. It was too hard to implement, too hard to manage, and too hard to secure. It's reasonably easy to secure your networks from unauthorized physical access, but it was perceived to be much harder to do so for remote access. Recently, a number of security policies, protocols, and technologies have been developed to ease this problem. First we'll discuss the user authentication protocols.

User Authentication

One of the first steps in establishing a secure remote access connection involves allowing the user to present some credentials to the server. You can use any or all of the following authentication protocols that Windows Server 2008 supports:

Password Authentication Protocol The Password Authentication Protocol (PAP) is the simplest authentication protocol. It transmits all authentication information in clear text with no encryption, which makes it vulnerable to snooping if attackers can put themselves between the modem bank and the remote access server. However, this type of attack is unlikely in most networks. The security risk with PAP is largely overemphasized considering the difficulty of setting up a sniffer in between the modems and the remote access server. If an attacker has the ability to install a sniffer this deep in the network, you have larger problems to address.

PAP is the most widely supported authentication protocol, and you therefore may find that you need to leave it enabled.

Microsoft CHAPv2   Microsoft CHAPv2 (MS-CHAPv2) was created by Microsoft as an extension of the CHAP protocol to allow the use of Windows authentication information. Version 2 is more secure than version 1, which is not supported by Windows 2008. Some other operating systems support MS-CHAP version 1.

Extensible Authentication Protocol   The Extensible Authentication Protocol (EAP) doesn't provide any authentication itself. Instead, it relies on external third-party authentication methods that you can retrofit to your existing servers. Instead of hardwiring any one authentication protocol, a client/server pair that understands EAP can negotiate an authentication method. The computer that asks for authentication—the *authenticator*—is free to ask for several pieces of information, making a separate query for each one. This allows the use of almost any authentication method, including smart cards, secure access tokens such as SecurID, one-time password systems such as S/Key, or ordinary username/password systems.

Each authentication scheme supported in EAP is called an *EAP type*. Each EAP type is implemented as a plug-in module. Windows Server 2008 can support any number of EAP types at once; the Routing and Remote Access Services (RRAS) server can use any EAP type to authenticate if you've allowed that module to be used and the client has the module in question.

Windows Server 2008 comes with EAP-Transport Level Security (TLS). This EAP type allows you to use public-key certificates as an authenticator. TLS (discussed in Chapter 6, "Configuring RADIUS and Wireless Access") is similar to the familiar Secure Sockets Layer (SSL) protocol used for web browsers. When EAP-TLS is turned on, the client and server send TLS-encrypted messages back and forth. EAP-TLS is the strongest authentication method you can use; as a bonus, it supports smart cards. However, EAP-TLS requires your RRAS server to be part of a Windows 2000, Windows Server 2003, or Windows Server 2008 domain.

EAP-RADIUS is another authentication method included with Windows Server 2008. EAP-RADIUS is a fake EAP type that passes any incoming message to a Remote Authentication Dial-In User Service (RADIUS) server for authentication.

NTLMv2   NTLMv2 helps the authentication process for Windows NT 4 systems or earlier and allows for transactions between any two computers running these older systems. Networks that use NTLMv2 are referred to as *mixed mode*, which is the default setting in the Windows Server 2008 domain.

Kerberos   Active Directory domain authentication is done by using the Kerberos authentication protocol. By default, all computers joined to a Windows Server 2008 domain use the Kerberos authentication protocol. Kerberos allows for single sign-on to network resources on a domain or on a trusted domain. Administrators have the ability to control certain parameters through the Kerberos security settings of the account policies.

802.1X   The IEEE has a standard for wireless authentication called 802.1X. 802.1X allows wireless networks to authenticate onto a wired Ethernet networks or wireless 802.11 networks. The IEEE 802.1X standard uses EAP for exchanging messages during the authentication process.

Connection Security

You can use some additional features to provide connection-level security for your remote access clients:

- The Callback Control Protocol (CBCP) allows your RRAS servers or clients to negotiate a callback with the other end. When CBCP is enabled, either the client or the server can ask the server at the other end to call the client back at a number supplied by the client or a prearranged number stored on the server.

- You can program the RRAS server to accept or reject calls based on the caller ID or automatic number identification (ANI) information transmitted by the phone company. For example, you can instruct your primary RRAS server to accept calls from only your home analog line. That means you can't call the server when you're on the road—and it also keeps the server from talking to strangers.

- You can specify various types and levels of encryption to protect your connection from interception or tampering.

 Real World Scenario

The Limits of Caller ID

It's risky to rely on ANI information for any type of authentication or caller verification. First, caller ID information can be forged. Therefore, if an attacker knows the telephone numbers from which your network accepted calls, they could make their ANI report as one of those numbers and be authenticated into the network.

Another problem with relying on ANI for authentication is that not all telephone companies pass ANI information with the call. Therefore, if your users are in remote locations (which is why they'd be dialing in anyway), they might not be able to authenticate. Even when ANI information is sent, some telephone companies pass different pieces of the information, which can also result in authentication failures.

Finally, not all incoming line types support ANI. If your site uses a network access server or modem bank that doesn't receive this information based on the type of T1 connection used for incoming calls, the ANI information might not be there at all.

Access Control

Apart from the connection-level measures you can use to prohibit outside callers from talking to your servers, you can restrict which users can make remote connections in a number of ways:

- You can allow or disallow remote access from individual user accounts. This is the same limited control you have in Windows NT, but it's just the start for Windows Server 2008.

- You can use network access policies to control whether users can get access.

  Like group policies, network access policies give you an easy way to apply a consistent set of policies to groups of users. However, the policy mechanism is a little different: you create rules that include or exclude the users you want in the policy.

  Unlike group policies, network access policies are available only in Windows 2000 native, Windows Server 2003, and Windows Server 2008 domain functional level (that is, in domains in which there are no Windows NT domain controllers present). That means you may not have the option to use network access policies until your Windows 2000, Windows Server 2003, and Windows Server 2008 deployment is further along.

  In the next section, you will learn how to configure user access control.

Configuring User Access

In the previous chapter, you set up the server to accept incoming calls. Now it's time to determine who can actually use the remote access services. You do this in two ways:

- By setting up remote access profiles on individual accounts
- By creating and managing network access policies that apply to groups of users

  This distinction is subtle but important because you manage and apply profiles and policies in different places.

Setting Up User Profiles

Windows Server 2008 stores a lot of information for each user account. Collectively, this information is known as the account's *profile*, and it's normally stored in Active Directory. Some settings in the user's profile are available through one of the two user-management snap-ins:

- If your RRAS server is part of an Active Directory domain, the user profile settings are in the Active Directory Users and Computers snap-in.
- If your RRAS server is *not* part of an Active Directory domain, the user profile settings are in the Local Users and Groups snap-in.

  In either case, the interesting part of the profile is the Dial-In tab of the user's Properties dialog box (see Figure 7.1). This tab has a number of controls that regulate how the user account can be used for dial-in access.

Most aspects of Active Directory are beyond the scope of this book and the related exam. For more information, see *MCTS: Windows Server 2008 Active Directory, Configuring Study Guide (70-640)* by William Panek with James Chellis (Sybex, 2008).

FIGURE 7.1   The Dial-In tab of the user's Properties dialog box

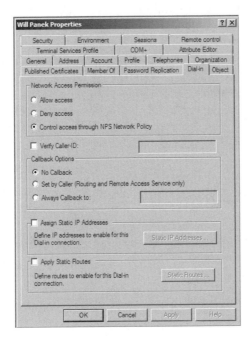

These controls include the following:

Network Access Permission control group   The first, and probably most familiar, controls on this tab are in the Network Access Permission control group. These options control whether the user has dial-in permission. They're similar to the controls you may remember from the Windows NT User Manager; however, Windows Server 2008 has a new feature: in addition to explicitly allowing or denying access, you can control access through Network Access Policy (see Chapter 6).

Verify Caller-ID controls   RRAS can verify a user's caller ID information and use the results to allow or deny access. When you check the Verify Caller-ID check box and enter a phone number in the field, you're telling RRAS to reject a call from anyone who provides that username and password but whose caller ID information doesn't match what you enter. This means the user can call in only from a single phone number.

Callback Options control group   The Callback Options control group gives you three choices for regulating callback:

- No Callback (the default setting) means the server will never honor callback requests from this account.

- Set By Caller allows the calling system to specify a number at which it wants to be called back. The RRAS server will call the client back at that number.

- Always Callback To allows you to enter a number that the server will call back no matter from where the client is actually calling. This option is less flexible but more secure than the Set By Caller option.

Assign A Static IP Address controls   If you want this user to always get the same static IP address, you can arrange it by selecting the Assign A Static IP Address check box and then entering the desired IP address. This allows you to set up nondynamic DNS records for individual users, guaranteeing that their machines will always have a valid DNS entry. On the other hand, this can be more prone to typographical errors on setup than the dynamic DNS-DHCP combination you could be using instead.

Apply Static Routes check box   In an ordinary LAN, you don't have to do anything special to clients to enable them to route packets—just configure them with a default gateway, and the gateway handles the rest. For dial-up connections, though, you may want to define a list of static routes that will enable the remote client to reach hosts on your network, or elsewhere, without requiring that packets be sent to a gateway in between. Depending on the remote access server, though, the client may be able to use Address Resolution Protocol (ARP) for local devices too. If you want to define a set of static routes on the client, you'll have to do it manually. If you want to assign static routes on the server, select the Apply Static Routes check box, and then use the Static Routes button to add and remove routes as necessary.

Remember that these settings apply to individual users, so you can assign different routes, caller ID, or callback settings to each user.

Using Network Access Policies

Windows Server 2008 includes support for two additional configuration systems:

- Network access policies (which used to be called *remote access policy*)
- Remote access profiles (covered later in this chapter)

Policies determine who can and cannot connect; you define rules with conditions that the system evaluates to see whether a particular user can connect.

You can have any number of policies in a native Windows Server 2008 domain; each policy must have exactly one profile associated with it.

Settings in an individual user's profile override settings in a network access policy.

You manage network access policies through the Remote Access Logging and Policies folder in the RRAS snap-in. Policies contain conditions that you pick from a list. When a caller connects, the policy's conditions are evaluated, one by one, to see whether the caller gets in. All the conditions in the policy must match for the user to gain access. If there are multiple policies, they're evaluated according to an order you specify.

In the following sections, you will see how to create and configure network access policies.

Network Policy Attributes

To create a policy, right-click the Remote Access Logging and Policies folder, and select Launch NPS (see Figure 7.2). Then right-click Network Policies, and choose New. This command starts the New Network Policy Wizard, which uses a series of steps to help you define the policy.

FIGURE 7.2   The Launch NPS option in RRAS

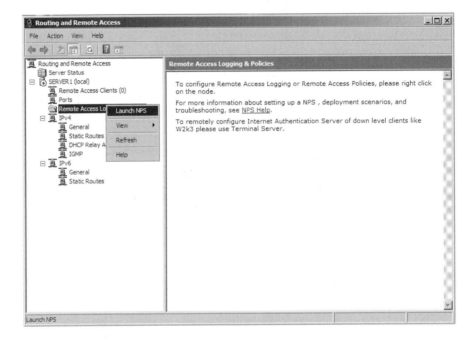

The Select Condition dialog box (see Figure 7.3) is part of the New Network Policy Wizard. It lists the attributes that you can evaluate in a policy. Table 7.1 lists the attributes that you can set. These attributes are drawn from the RADIUS standards, so you can (and in some cases, should) intermix your Windows Server 2008 RRAS servers with RADIUS servers.

When setting up any policies, you must base your policy on company rules and standards. Remember, policies can allow or restrict users from remotely accessing your network. The needs of the organization determine the policy and when to use it.

Once you choose an attribute and click the Add button, its corresponding editor appears. You use the editor to set the value of the attribute. For example, if you select the Day-And-Time-Restrictions attribute, you'll see the Time Of Day Constraints dialog box, a calendar grid that lets you select which days and times are available for logging on.

FIGURE 7.3   Select Condition dialog box of New Network Policy Wizard

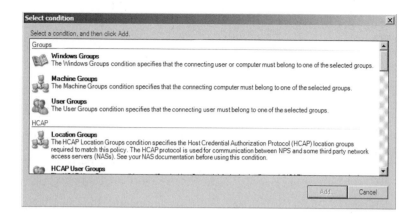

TABLE 7.1   Network Access Policy Attributes

Attribute Name	What It Specifies
Authentication Type	Specifies the authentication methods required to match this policy.
Allowed EAP Types	Specifies the EAP types required for client computer authentication method configuration to match this policy.
Called-Station-Id	Specifies the phone number of the remote access port called by the caller.
Calling-Station-Id	Specifies the caller's phone number.
Client-Friendly-Name	Specifies the name of the RADIUS server that's attempting to validate the connection.
Client-IP-Address (IPv4 and IPv6)	Specifies the IP address of the RADIUS server that's attempting to validate the connection.
Client-Vendor	Specifies the vendor of remote access server that originally accepted the connection. This is used to set different policies for different hardware.
Day-And-Time Restrictions	Specifies the weekdays and times when connection attempts are accepted or rejected.

TABLE 7.1 Network Access Policy Attributes *(continued)*

Attribute Name	What It Specifies
Framed-Protocol	Specifies the protocol to be used for framing incoming packets (for example, PPP, SLIP, and so on).
HCAP (Host Credential Authorization Protocol) User Groups	Used for communications between NPS and some third-party network access servers (NAS).
Location Groups	Specifies the HCAP location groups required to match this policy. This is used for communications between HCAP and some third-party network access servers (NAS).
MS-RAS Vendor	Specifies the vendor identification number of the network access server (NAS) that is requesting authentication.
NAS-Identifier	Specifies the friendly name of the remote access server that originally accepted the connection.
NAS-IP-Address (IPv4 and IPv6)	Specifies the IP address of the remote access server that originally accepted the connection.
NAS-Port-Type	Specifies the physical connection (for example, ISDN, POTS) used by the caller.
Service-Type	Specifies Framed or Async (for PPP) or login (Telnet).
Tunnel-Type	Specifies which tunneling protocol should be used (L2TP or PPTP).
Windows-Groups	Specifies which Windows groups are allowed access.

After you select an attribute and give it a value, you can add more attributes or move to the next page by clicking the Next button on the Select Conditions page.

Once you're finished setting attributes, you arrive at the Specify Access Permission page of the wizard. This page has only two radio buttons—Grant Remote Access Permissions and Deny Remote Access Permissions—which specify whether the policy you create *allows* users to connect or *prevents* users from connecting. The page also includes an Access Is Determined By User Dial-In Properties check box. If this box is checked and there is a conflict between the network policy and user dial-in properties, the user dial-in properties take precedence.

⊕ **Real World Scenario**

Using Attributes with Authentication

Be careful when using attributes for network access policies. You can effectively prevent any-one from authenticating if you specify an attribute incorrectly or if the value for an attribute changes unexpectedly.

For example, if you use the NAS-Port-Type attribute to specify the type of line from which a user may authenticate and that NAS-Port-Type changes, the user will be unable to authenticate.

Different network access server vendors define the NAS-Port-Type differently. What might be called Framed on a one vendor's device is called Async on another vendor's equipment, even though both describe a typical dial-up line connected to a modem. Additionally, the values for certain attributes might change between versions of the vendor's software. Imagine updating the firmware on thousands of modems only to find that an attribute's name has changed and now no one can dial in!

Creating a Network Access Policy

In Exercise 7.1, you'll create an adjunct policy that adds time and day restrictions to the default policy. (An adjunct policy is used in conjunction with another policy.) This exercise requires you to be in Windows 2000 native, Windows Server 2003, or Windows Server 2008 domain functional level, and you must have completed the exercises in Chapter 6.

EXERCISE 7.1

Creating a Network Access Policy

1. Open the RRAS MMC snap-in by selecting Start ➢ Administrative Tools ➢ Routing And Remote Access.

2. Expand the server you want to configure in the left pane of the MMC.

3. Right-click the Remote Access Logging And Policies folder.

4. Right-click, and then select Launch NPS.

5. Once the Network Policy Server page appears, right-click Network Policies and then choose New.

6. The New Network Policy Wizard starts. In the Policy Name box, enter **Test Policy** and then click Next (leave the other settings as they are).

EXERCISE 7.1 *(continued)*

7. On the Specify Conditions page, click the Add button.

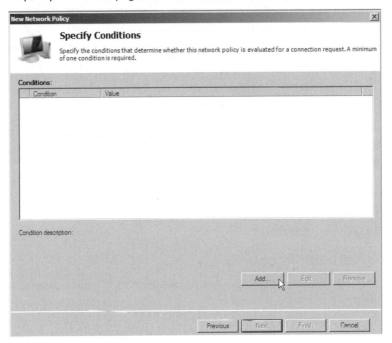

8. In the Select Condition dialog box, scroll down, and click Day and Time Restrictions. Next click Add.

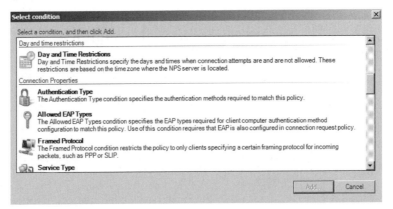

EXERCISE 7.1 *(continued)*

9. The Time Of Day Constraints dialog box appears. Use the calendar controls to allow remote access Monday through Saturday from 7 a.m. to 7 p.m. and then click the OK button.

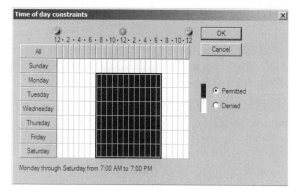

10. The Select Conditions dialog box reappears, this time with the new condition listed. Click the Next button.

11. The Specify Access Permission page appears. Select the Access Granted radio button, and click Next to continue.

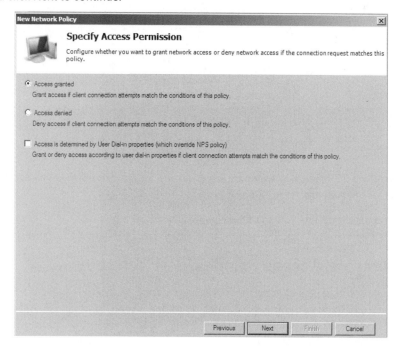

12. Next the Configure Authentication Methods page appears. This page is where you choose which authentication methods will be used for this connection. Make sure that MS-CHAP and MS-CHAPv2 are both checked along with the check boxes associated with them. Click Next.

13. The Configure Constraints page appears. Under Constraints, click Session Timeout. On the right side, click the Disconnect After The Following Maximum Session Time box, and type **60** in the field (the value represents minutes). Click Next.

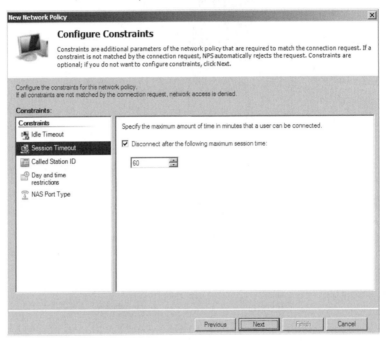

14. The Configure Settings page appears. This page allows you to configure any additional settings for this network policy. Click Next.

15. On the Completing New Network Policy page, click Finish.

Using Remote Access Profiles

Remote access profiles are an integral part of network access policies. Profiles determine what happens during call setup and completion. Each policy has a profile associated with it; the profile determines what settings will be applied to connections that meet the conditions stated in the policy.

For security reasons, it's usually a good idea to limit access to the administrative accounts on your network. In particular, as consultants, we usually tell clients to restrict remote access for the Administrator account; that way, the potential exposure from a dial-up compromise is reduced. In Exercise 7.2, you will learn how to configure the Administrator account's user profile to restrict dial-up access.

EXERCISE 7.2

Restricting a User Profile for Dial-In Access

1. Log on to your computer using an account that has administrative privileges.

2. If you're using an RRAS server that's part of an Active Directory domain, open the Active Directory Users And Computers snap-in by selecting Start ➤ Administrative Tools ➤ Active Directory Users And Computers. If not, open the Local Users And Groups snap-in by selecting Start ➤ Administrative Tools ➤ Computer Management ➤ Local Users And Groups.

3. Expand the tree to the Users folder. Right-click the Administrator account in the right pane, and choose Properties. The Administrator Properties dialog box appears.

4. Switch to the Dial-In tab. On machines that participate in Active Directory, make sure the Control Access Through NPS Network Policy option (in the Permissions group) is selected.

5. Click the Deny Access radio button to prevent the use of this account over a dial-in connection.

6. Click the OK button.

You can create one profile for each policy. The profile contains settings that fit into specific areas; each area has its own link in the profile's Properties dialog box.

The Constraints Tab

The Constraints tab has most of the settings that you think of when you consider dial-in access controls. The controls here allow you to adjust how long the connection can be idle before it gets dropped, how long it can be up, the dates and times for establishing the connection, and what dial-in port and medium can be used to connect.

Authentication Link

In the Authentication Methods pane (see Figure 7.4), you can specify which authentication methods are allowed on this specific policy. Note that these settings, like the other policy settings, will be useful only if the server's settings match. For example, if you turn EAP authentication off in the server's Properties dialog box, turning it on in the Authentication Methods pane of the profile's Properties dialog box will have no effect.

FIGURE 7.4 Authentication Methods settings

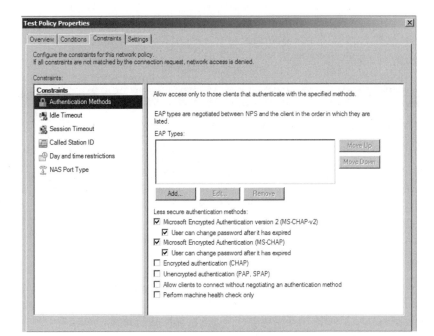

You'll notice that each authentication method has a check box. Check the appropriate boxes to control the protocols that you want this profile to use. If you enable EAP, you can also choose which specific EAP type you want the profile to support. You can also choose to allow totally unauthenticated access (which is unchecked by default).

Settings Tab

The Settings tab of the policy's Properties dialog box has several useful sections, described in the following list:

IP Settings pane   The IP Settings pane (see Figure 7.5) gives you control over the IP-related settings associated with an incoming call. If you think back to the server-specific settings covered in Chapter 6, you'll remember that the server preferences include settings for protocols other than IP; this is not so in the network access profile. In this pane, you can specify where the client gets its IP address.

Multilink And Bandwidth Allocation Protocol (BAP) pane   The profile mechanism gives you a degree of control over how the server handles multilink calls; you exert this control through the Multilink And Bandwidth Allocation Protocol (BAP) pane of the profile Properties dialog box (see Figure 7.6). Your first choice is to decide whether to allow multilink calls at all and, if so, how many ports you want to let a single client use at once. Normally, this setting is configured so that the server-specific settings take precedence, but you can override them.

FIGURE 7.5   IP Settings pane of the Settings tab

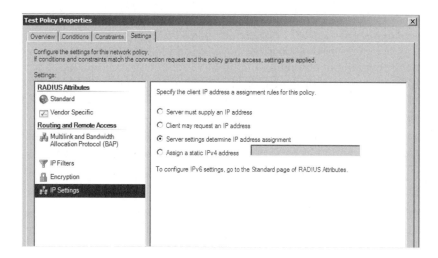

FIGURE 7.6   The Multilink And Bandwidth Allocation Protocol (BAP) pane of the Settings tab

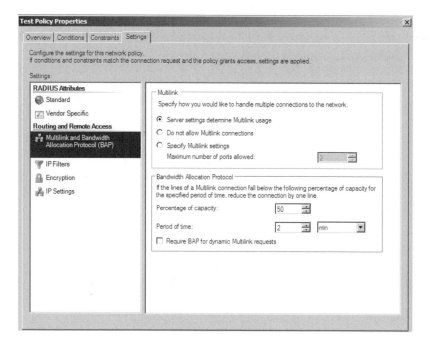

Bandwidth Allocation Protocol (BAP) Settings group   The Bandwidth Allocation Protocol (BAP) Settings control group gives you a way to control what happens during a multilink call when the bandwidth usage drops below a certain threshold. For example, why tie up three analog lines to provide 168Kbps of bandwidth when the connection is using only 56Kbps? You can tweak the capacity and time thresholds; by default, a multilink call will drop one line every time the bandwidth usage falls to less than 50 percent of the available bandwidth and stays there for two minutes. The Require BAP For Dynamic Multilink Requests check box allows you to refuse calls from clients that don't support BAP; this is an easy way to make sure that no client can hog your multilink bandwidth.

Encryption tab   The Encryption tab (see Figure 7.7) controls which type of encryption you want your remote users to be able to access. The following radio buttons are on the Encryption tab:

- Basic Encryption (MPPE 40-Bit) means single Data Encryption Standard (DES) for IPSec or 40-bit Microsoft Point-to-Point Encryption (MPPE) for Point-to-Point Tunneling Protocol (PPTP).

- Strong Encryption (MPPE 56 Bit) means 56-bit encryption (single DES for IPSec; 56-bit MPPE for PPTP).

- Strongest Encryption (MPPE 128 Bit) means triple DES for IPSec or 128-bit MPPE for PPTP connections.

- No Encryption allows users to connect using no encryption at all. Unless this button is selected, a remote connection must be encrypted, or it'll be rejected.

FIGURE 7.7   Encryption pane of the Settings tab of the policy's Properties dialog box

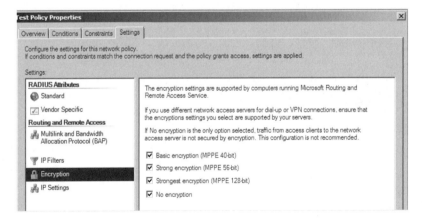

In Exercise 7.3, you'll force all connections to your server to use encryption. Any client that can't use encryption will be dropped. You must complete Exercise 7.1 before you do this exercise.

    Don't do this exercise on your production RRAS server unless you're sure that all your clients are encryption capable.

EXERCISE 7.3

Configuring Encryption

1. Open the RRAS MMC snap-in by selecting Start ➢ Administrative Tools ➢ Routing And Remote Access.

2. Expand the server you want to configure in the left pane of the MMC.

3. Right-click the Remote Access Logging And Policies folder.

4. Select Launch NPS.

5. Once the Network Policy Server page appears, click the hours policy you created in Exercise 7.1 (we named ours Test Policy).

6. Select Action ➢ Properties. The policy's Properties dialog box appears.

7. Click the Settings tab. Select Encryption in the left pane.

8. In the right pane, uncheck the No Encryption check box. Make sure that the Basic, Strong, and Strongest check boxes are all selected.

9. Click the OK button. When the policy Properties dialog box reappears, click the OK button.

Setting Up a VPN Network Access Policy

Earlier in this chapter, you learned how to use the network access policy mechanism on a Windows Server 2008 domain. Now it's time to apply what you've learned to a virtual private network (VPN). Recall that you have two ways to control which specific users can access a remote access server:

- You can grant and deny dial-up permission to individual users in each user's Properties dialog box.

- You can create a network access policy that embodies whatever restrictions you want to impose.

It turns out that you can do the same thing for VPN connections, but there are a few additional things to consider.

Granting and Denying Per-User Access

To grant or deny VPN access to individual users, all you have to do is make the appropriate change on the Dial-In tab of each user's Properties dialog box. Although this is the easiest method to understand, it gets tedious quickly if you need to change VPN permissions for more than a few users. Furthermore, this method offers you no way to distinguish between dial-in and VPN permissions.

> ### 🌐 Real World Scenario
>
> #### Remote Access Is More Than Technology
>
> You are the network administrator of a Windows Server 2008 network that supports the sales organization of a national training company. In an effort to cut costs, your management wants the sales representatives to work out of their homes and on the road. You jump to the task with the immediate intention of implementing RRAS, which you know has the necessary components to provide secure remote access.
>
> However, one thing you want to keep in mind is that the simplicity of RRAS creates a tendency for administrators to rely too much on the technology and to take their eyes off the ball of proper processes and procedures. If your users can get into your network, then unauthorized intruders will surely try. The first step in dealing with the malicious users is to prepare a properly detailed written network access policy. This should include a description of how you want to enable remote access, what resources should be available, and what consistent type of technical mechanism you will deploy to facilitate remote access. There is no one right or wrong answer for every organization, but there needs to be a well-thought-out rationale for how you deploy remote services. As you can see, this is not simply a technical problem to solve.
>
> The approach to this network access policy should be based on an analysis of risk and liability. The analysis should cover what the implications would be if various levels of information were breached. Then you can objectively determine the cost necessary to protect the resource. This determination will affect all decisions regarding the variety of technologies that are included with RRAS, such as types of authentication, control of who can access the network remotely, encryption levels, and callback. A failure to complete a process of this nature will most likely result in a situation in which unauthorized access results in damage to your network—and by extension, damage to your career.

Creating a Network Access Policy for VPNs

You may find it helpful to create network access policies that enforce the permissions you want end users to have. You can accomplish this result in a number of ways; which one you use will depend on your overall use of network access policies.

The simplest way is to create a policy that allows all your users to use a VPN. Earlier in this chapter, you learned how to create network access policies and specify settings for them; one thing you may have noticed was that there's a NAS-Port-Type attribute that you can use in the policy's conditions. That attribute is the cornerstone of building a policy that allows or denies remote access via VPN, because you use it to accept or reject connections arriving over a particular type of VPN connection. For best results, you'll use Tunnel-Type attribute in conjunction with the NAS-Port-Type attribute, as described in Exercise 7.4.

EXERCISE 7.4

Creating a VPN Network Access Policy

1. Open the RRAS MMC snap-in by selecting Start ➢ Administrative Tools ➢ Routing And Remote Access.

2. Expand the server you want to configure in the left pane of the MMC.

3. Right-click the Remote Access Logging And Policies folder.

4. Select Launch NPS.

5. Once the Network Policy Server page appears, right-click Network Policies, and choose New.

6. The New Network Policy Wizard starts. In the Policy Name box, enter **VPN Network Policy**, and click Next (leave the other settings as they are).

7. On the Specify Conditions page, click the Add button.

8. On the Select Condition page, scroll down, click NAS-Port-Type Attribute, and click Add. When the NAS Port Type page appears, click Virtual VPN in the Common Dial-Up And VPN Tunnel Types box. Click OK, and then click the Next button.

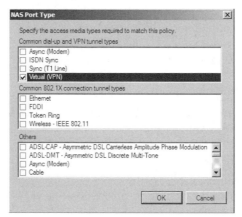

9. The Specify Conditions page reappears, this time with the new condition listed. Click the Next button.

10. The Specify Access Permission page appears. Select the Access Granted radio button, and click Next to continue.

11. Next the Configure Authentication Methods page will appear. This page is where you choose which authentication methods will be used for this connection. Make sure that MS-CHAP and MS-CHAPv2 are both checked along with their associated check boxes. Click Next.

12. The Configure Constraints page appears. Under Constraints, click Session Timeout. On the right side, click the Disconnect After The Following Maximum Session Time box, and type **60** in the box (the value specifies minutes). Click Next.

13. The Configure Settings page appears. This page allows you to configure any additional settings for this network policy. Click Next.

14. At the Completing New Network Policy page, click Finish.

If you don't want to grant VPN access to everyone, you can make some changes to the process in Exercise 7.4 to fine-tune it. First, you'll probably want to move the VPN policy to the top of the list. (When you first add the policy described in the exercise, it is placed at the end of the policy list. Unless you move it, the default policies will take effect before the VPN-specific policy does.)

Second, you can create an Active Directory group and put your VPN users in it. You can then create a policy using the two conditions outlined in Exercise 7.4 plus a condition that uses the Windows-Groups attribute to specify the new group. You can also use this process to allow everyone dial-up access and reserve VPN capability for a smaller group.

Connection Manager

To help administrators create and manage remote access connections, Microsoft includes within Windows Server 2008 a suite of components called Connection Manager. Connection Manager is not installed by default. You can install the Connection Manager by using Server Manager, Add Roles, and then Network Access Services.

Connection Manager allows an administrator to create remote access connections called *service profiles*. These profiles then appear on client machines as network connections. You can use these network connections to connect client machines to VPNs or remote networks.

Configuring Security

When configuring remote access security, you must consider several aspects, the most fundamental of which involves configuring the types of authentication and encryption the server will use when accepting client requests. We will look at each of these in the following sections.

Planning VPN Security

The CEO of your company has just returned from a seminar that promised lower communication costs through the use of VPNs tunneled through the Internet. She can't wait to start ripping out the fixed leased lines so that she can see the saved dollars move down to the bottom line. As the network administrator, you are now charged with implementing VPNs to provide secure communications across the network.

You know that along with the increase in mobile computing, there has been a correlating increase in the use of VPNs. This trend has been, and will continue to be, a boon to productivity. This growth is akin to the benefit that the public highway system has provided to private organizations for their economic activities. For this reason, VPNs will continue to grow in importance in the explosion of remote communication that's taking place today.

However, you know that a VPN is only part of an overall security implementation for a network; you can't assume that a company's communications are secure simply because it's using a VPN. A written network access policy needs to include a written security policy that is based on an analysis of risk and liability. You can make the effort to create a VPN solution for the users on your network, but they may have NetBIOS with file and printer sharing enabled on their network connections. With this type of configuration, communications with your network are secure, but any confidential company information that the users have downloaded to their computers is exposed to the Internet. Windows Firewall, included with Windows Server 2008, Windows Vista, and Windows XP SP2, has luckily alleviated some of this concern.

Here are some other security risks to consider:

- Clients may download Java applets and ActiveX controls that have the capability to run their own remote control activities, hidden from view.

- Hackers may use your system to gain access to your network so that they can use it as a platform for a future denial-of-service (DoS) attack on another network.

You need to ensure that you have considered as many aspects as possible when you are planning your remote systems. As you deploy VPNs to secure your company's communications, make sure you aren't plugging one narrow crack in your system while leaving another gaping hole that's too big to see.

Controlling Server Security

The Security tab of the server's Properties dialog box (see Figure 7.8) allows you to specify which authentication and accounting methods RRAS uses. You can choose one of two authentication providers by using the Authentication Provider drop-down list.

FIGURE 7.8 The Security tab of the RRAS server's Properties dialog box

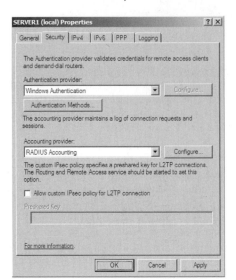

Your choices include the following:

- Windows Authentication, a built-in authentication suite included with Windows Server 2008
- RADIUS Authentication, which allows you to send all authentication requests heard by your server to a RADIUS server for approval or denial

You can also use the Accounting Provider drop-down list on the Security tab to choose between the following:

- Microsoft-Developed Accounting, in which connection requests are maintained in the event log
- RADIUS Accounting, in which all accounting events such as call start and call stop are sent to a RADIUS server for action

---

 Real World Scenario

RADIUS Accounting

RADIUS accounting is used to determine when a given session started and stopped for a user. It is a distinctly separate function from RADIUS authentication; it even operates on a different UDP port (1646 or 1813, depending on the version). Where authentication is the process of verifying a user's credentials, accounting is used for back-end purposes. Internet accounts are billed on a per-minute or per-hour basis using the RADIUS accounting data. Clients first authenticate, and then after authentication is successful, the NAS sends an Accounting-Request.

Here's a real-life Accounting-Request from a 3Com NAS (some of the values have been changed for privacy):

```
Code: Accounting-Request
Identifier: 214
Authentic: 000000
Attributes:
     Acct-Session-Id = "00001ebd"
     User-Name = "afunuser"
     NAS-IP-Address = 192.168.1.8
     NAS-Port = 24
     Acct-Status-Type = Start
     Acct-Authentic = RADIUS
     Called-Station-Id = "5559332"
     Calling-Station-Id = "7155550101"
     USR-Connect-Speed = 26400_BPS
     USR-Modulation-Type = v32Terbo
     USR-Simplified-MNP-Levels = v42Etc2
     USR-Simplified-V42bis-Usage = NONE
     USR-Chassis-Call-Slot = 0
     USR-Chassis-Call-Span = 0
     USR-Chassis-Call-Channel = 2
     USR-Unauthenticated-Time = 30
     NAS-Identifier = "nas001"
     NAS-Port-Type = Async
     Service-Type = Framed-User
     Framed-Protocol = PPP
     Framed-IP-Address = 192.168.1.23
     Acct-Delay-Time = 0
```

With this information, the RADIUS server can place an entry into its database indicating that *afunuser* has started a connection as indicated by the Acct-Status-Type attribute being set to Start. The user was assigned the IP address of 192.168.1.23 (the Framed-IP-Address attribute). When the user terminates the call, the NAS will send an Accounting-Request with the Acct-Status-Type of Stop. Later, if an abuse report is received, the Internet service provider will be able to go back through the RADIUS Accounting database and see that *afunuser* was connected during the time that the abuse occurred.

RADIUS Authentication Settings

When you select the RADIUS Authentication option from the Authentication Provider drop-down menu, you are enabling a RADIUS client that passes authentication duties to a RADIUS server. This communication is sent via UDP on port 1645 or 1812, depending on the version of RADIUS being used.

Click the Configure button to open the RADIUS Authentication dialog box. From here, you can set the following options:

- Click the Add button to add the name or address of a RADIUS server to which the RAS server will pass authentication duties.

- You must also enter the correct secret, which is initially set by the RADIUS server.

- The Time-Out option determines how long the RRAS server will attempt to authenticate the remote user before giving up.

- The Initial Score option is similar to the cost value used by routers. The RAS server will attempt to authenticate users on the RADIUS server with the highest score first. If that attempt fails, the RAS server will use the RADIUS server with the next highest score, and so on.

- Although the Port option can be changed, the default setting is part of RFC 2866, "RADIUS Accounting," and should not be altered unless extraordinary circumstances call for it.

The Internet Assigned Numbers Authority (IANA) is the official source for port number assignment. You can view current port number assignments and other valuable information at www.iana.org/assignments/port-numbers.

Windows Authentication Settings

Select the Windows Authentication option from the Authentication Provider drop-down menu if you want the local machine to authenticate your remote access users. To configure the server by telling it which authentication methods you want it to use, click the Authentication Methods button, which displays the Authentication Methods dialog box (see Figure 7.9). If you look at the list of authentication protocols earlier in the chapter, you'll find that each one has a corresponding check box here: EAP, MS-CHAPv2, CHAP, and PAP. You can also turn on unauthenticated access by checking the Allow Remote Systems To Connect Without Authentication box, but that is not recommended because it allows anyone to connect to, and use, your server (and thus by extension your network).

There's actually a special set of requirements for using CHAP because it requires access to each user's encrypted password. Windows Server 2008 normally doesn't store user passwords in a format that CHAP can use, so you have to take some additional steps if you want to use CHAP:

1. Enable CHAP at the server and policy levels.

2. Edit the default domain GPO's Password Policy object to turn on the Store Password Using Reversible Encryption policy setting (see Figure 7.10).

FIGURE 7.9   Authentication Methods dialog box

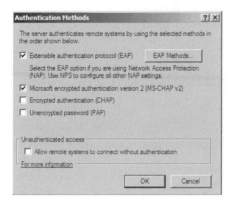

FIGURE 7.10   The default domain GPO's Password Policy

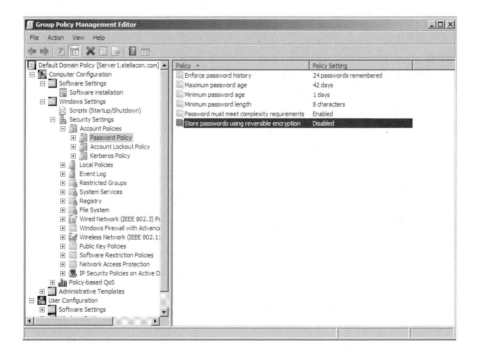

3. Change or reset each user's password, which forces Windows Server 2008 to store the password using reversible encryption.

After these steps are completed for an account, that account can be used with CHAP.

These steps aren't required for MS-CHAPv2; for that protocol, you just enable MS-CHAPv2 at the server and policy levels.

Configuring Network Access Protection

Another way you can have security is to allow users to access resources based on the identity of the client computer. This new security solution is called Network Access Protection (NAP). Determined by the client needs, network administrators now have the ability to determine granular levels of network access using NAP. NAP also allows administrators to determine client access based on compliancy with corporate governance policies. The following are some of the NAP features:

Network layer protection   Network layer protection is the ability to secure communications at the Network layer of the OSI model.

As explained in Chapter 1, "Understanding Windows Server 2008 Networking," all communications travel through the seven layers of the OSI model. Starting at the top (layer 7), the seven layers are the Application, Presentation, Session, Transport, Network, Data-Link, and Physical layers.

DHCP enforcement   If a computer wants to receive unlimited IPv4 network access, the computer must be compliant with corporate governance policies. DHCP enforcement verifies that a computer is compliant before granting unlimited access. If a computer is noncompliant, the computer receives an IPv4 address that has limited network access and a default user profile.

When a client computer attempts to receive an IP address from DHCP, the DHCP enforcement checks the health policy requirements of the system to make sure they meet the compliancy.

VPN enforcement   VPN enforcement works a lot like DHCP enforcement except that VPN enforcement verifies the compliancy of the system before the VPN connection is given full access to the network.

IPSec enforcement   IPSec enforcement will allow a computer to communicate with other computers as long as the computers are IPSec compliant. You have the ability to configure the requirements for secure communications between the two compliant computer systems. You can configure the IPSec communications based on IP address or TCP/UDP port numbers.

802.1X enforcement   For a computer system to have 802.1X unlimited access to network connections (Ethernet 802.11 or wireless access point), the computer system must be 802.1X compliant. 802.1X enforcement verifies that the connecting system is 802.1X connection compliant. Noncompliant computers will obtain only limited access to network connections.

Flexible host isolation   Flexible host isolation allows a server and domain to isolate computers to help make it possible to design a layer of security between computers or networks. Even if a hacker gains access to your network using an authorized username and password, the server and domain isolation can stop the attack because the computer is not an authorized domain computer.

Configuring Firewall Options

Before we can start talking about firewall options, you must first understand what a firewall does. A *firewall* is a software or hardware device that checks the information that is received from an outside (Internet) or external network and determines from that information whether the packet is accepted or declined.

Depending on the firewall, you have the ability to check all potential remote users against Active Directory to verify that the remote user has an authorized domain account. This process is called Active Directory *account integration*.

Microsoft Windows Server 2008 has a built-in firewall. The following are some of the configuration options included in the Windows Firewall Settings dialog box:

Windows Firewall Settings—General tab   On the Windows Firewall Settings dialog box's General tab, you have the ability to turn the firewall on and off. When turning the firewall on, you also have the ability to block all incoming traffic (see Figure 7.11). This stops all traffic from accessing your server.

FIGURE 7.11   General tab of Windows Firewall Settings

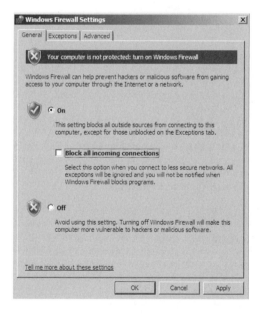

Windows Firewall Settings—Exceptions tab   The Exceptions tab gives you the ability to exclude applications from the firewall settings (see Figure 7.12).

If you enable the firewall, this tab gives you the following options:

- You can allow certain applications to continue to access the firewall.
- You also have the ability to add programs to the exceptions.

- You also have the ability to do traffic filtering by ports and protocols (explained in the next section).

- Finally, you have the ability to see the properties of any of the applications you exclude.

Traffic filtering   When setting up Microsoft Windows Server 2008 firewall, the administrator has the ability to filter traffic by ports and by protocols (see Figure 7.13).

FIGURE 7.12   Exceptions tab of Windows Firewall Settings

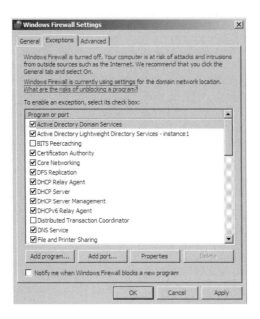

FIGURE 7.13   Add A Port dialog box of Windows Firewall

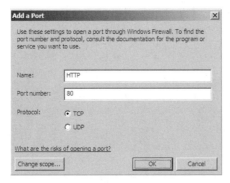

FIGURE 7.14   Advanced tab of Windows Firewall Settings

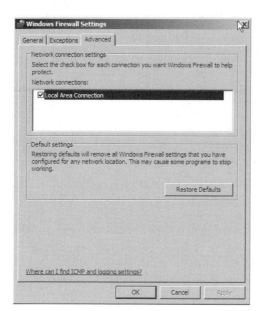

Windows Firewall Settings—Advanced tab   The Windows Firewall Settings dialog box's Advanced tab allows you to choose the network connection you want to enable for the firewall (see Figure 7.14). For example, if you have multiple network cards, you can choose to which connections the firewall settings will apply.

Firewall With Advanced Security   Windows Server 2008 takes firewalls a step further than just the normal firewall settings in the control panel. An MMC snap-in called Windows Firewall With Advanced Security (see Figure 7.15) can block all incoming and outgoing connections based on its configuration.

One of the major advantages to using the Firewall With Advanced Security snap-in is the ability to set firewall configurations on remote computers using group policies.

Group policies are beyond the scope of this book and the related exam. For more information, see *MCTS: Windows Server 2008 Active Directory Configuration Study Guide (70-640)* by William Panek with James Chellis (Sybex, 2008).

Another advantage to using this MMC is the ability to set up firewalls using IPSec security. The Firewall With Advanced Security snap-in allows an administrator to set more in-depth rules for Microsoft Active Directory users and groups, source and destination Internet Protocol (IP) addresses, IP port number, ICMP settings, IPSec settings, specific types of interfaces, and services.

FIGURE 7.15   Firewall With Advanced Security snap-in

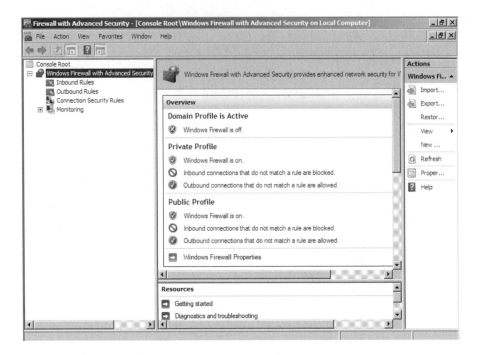

Troubleshooting Techniques

When you're troubleshooting authentication, use the same logical approach you would use when troubleshooting any computer or network problem:

- Is the problem being reported by one user, a group of similar users, or all users?
- Can you independently verify the problem by dialing in or attempting what the users are attempting?
- If you can verify the problem, what events are you seeing in the Event Viewer?
- If Event Viewer doesn't show any problems, what does Network Monitor or tracing show?

These are just some of the things you can do when troubleshooting remote access. Let's look at an example.

This example describes some troubleshooting tips for a RADIUS server running NPS on Windows Server 2008. It will use a RADIUS test client that is part of the FreeRADIUS package that runs on Linux. Similar software is available for Windows, and FreeRADIUS may run on Windows too.

In this example, attempting to authenticate with a RADIUS Access-Request for an account that exists on the local server was resulting in a failure. Specifically, the following Access-Reject message was generated:

```
rad_recv: Access-Reject packet from host 192.168.1.64:1812, id=225, length=20
```

Tracking down this issue led first to the Event Viewer, where a number of warning messages were available related to NPS. These messages are not particularly helpful, so we elected to enable logging for NPS. Within the NPS management console, the NPS Accounting folder offers two options—Local File Logging and SQL Server Logging—as shown in Figure 7.16.

With logging enabled, you can generate additional authentication requests. The resulting log file was placed in the location specified with the Local File Properties, which by default is `C:\Windows\System32\LogFiles\`.

You can further troubleshoot a problem like this by using a sniffer program such as Network Monitor or a program such as TCPDump or WinDump in order to analyze the network traffic as it is sent and received.

FIGURE 7.16   NPS Accounting folder in the Network Policy Server console

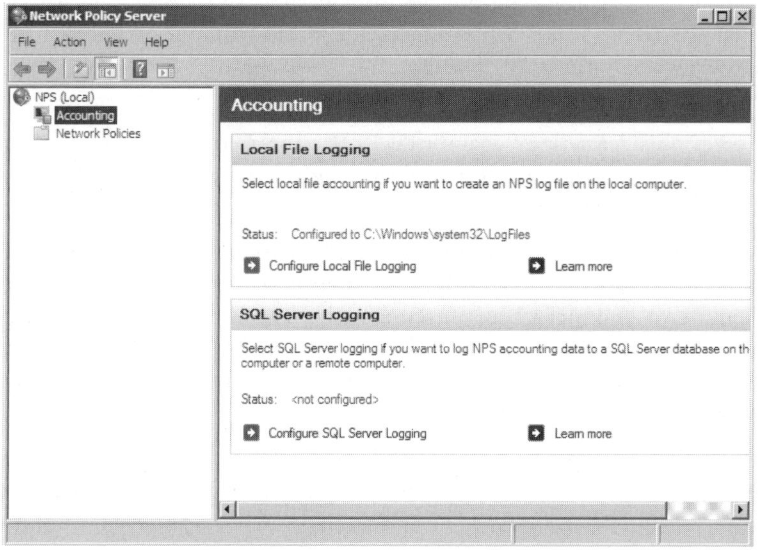

Summary

In this chapter, you learned about remote access and authentication. You learned that the user authentication protocols included with Windows Server 2008 are PAP, CHAP, MS-CHAPv2, Kerberos, NTLMv2, 802.1X, and EAP. You also learned that the Dial-In tab of a user's Properties dialog box has a number of interesting controls that regulate how the user account may be used for dial-in access. We covered how to use network access policies to determine who may and may not connect, as well as the process for defining rules with conditions that the system evaluates to see whether a particular user can connect. You also learned about the Windows Firewall options and the Windows Firewall With Advanced Security MMC. We discussed the Network Access Protection (NAP) options and features. In addition, you learned how to use network access profiles that contain settings that determine what happens during call setup and completion. Finally, you learned how to configure which accounting and authentication methods RRAS uses.

Exam Essentials

Know how to use network access policies. Policies determine who can and cannot connect; you define rules with conditions that the system evaluates to see whether a particular user can connect. You manage network access policies through the NPS snap-in. Policies contain conditions that you pick from a list. When a caller connects, the policy's conditions are evaluated, one by one, to see whether the caller gets in.

Know how to use remote access profiles. Each network access policy has a profile associated with it; the profile determines what settings will be applied to connections that meet the conditions stated in the policy. The settings fit into distinct areas, and each area has its own tab or link in the profile's Properties dialog box.

Know how to configure remote access security. Several different aspects are involved with remote access security configuration, the most fundamental of which involves configuring the types of authentication and encryption the server will use when accepting client requests. You can choose one of two authentication providers by using the Authentication Provider drop-down list: Windows Authentication and RADIUS Authentication. You can apply authentication restrictions at the policy level too.

Know how to configure Network Access Protection (NAP). Network Access Protection (NAP) allows you to set security for accessing resources, based on the identity of the client computer. Determined by the client needs, network administrators have the ability to determine granular levels of network access using NAP.

Know how to create a network access policy for VPNs. The simplest way is to create a policy that allows all your users to use a VPN. To allow VPN access to a smaller group, create an Active Directory group, and put your VPN users in it. You can then create a policy by setting the NAS-Port-Type attribute to Virtual (VPN).

Know how to troubleshoot user access.   The main things to look for are missing or misconfigured policies. Without a default network access policy, no user will be allowed access through the RRAS server. All connection requests are evaluated against the criteria contained in the network access policy. If there is no network access policy, there are no conditions to compare, and any request is thereby denied.

Understand Windows Firewall.   A firewall helps protect your network from unauthorized access. Windows Server 2008 has two different ways to configure a firewall: the Windows Firewall Settings control panel and the Firewall With Advanced Security MMC.

Review Questions

1. You are the network administrator for Worldwide Sales Organization, Inc., and you have hundreds of salespeople who need to connect to the network from all over the world. The sales representatives' computers all have smart cards that they use with a Cisco RADIUS server for authentication into the network. The network consists of a Windows NT LAN as well as several Unix servers and a mainframe. You are in the process of migrating the Windows NT portion of the network to Windows Server 2008. You have included Windows Server 2008 RRAS, and you want to incorporate the RADIUS authentication for use with the RRAS server. Which authentication protocol should you select for the RRAS server to use the RADIUS server?

   A. MS-CHAP

   B. Kerberos

   C. EAP

   D. PAP

2. You receive a phone call from Carlos, the new network administrator for the Enterprise Shoe Sales To Your Door Company. The majority of the users of this company's network are the hundreds of remote salespeople who connect throughout the day to the network to update and track sales orders. For quite a while, they have been experiencing intermittent problems, which have increased in frequency since the last administrator left the company. Carlos attempted to modify the default network access policy with little success, so he decided to begin from scratch. To make sure no one is negatively affected by the modifications, he deleted the now-confusing default network access policy that he was trying to modify. During his telephone call, Carlos asks for your help in building the new network access policy. What will happen to the remote users until the new network policy is created?

   A. Only users who have standard remote access permission set to Allow Access will connect to the server.

   B. All connection attempts will be rejected.

   C. Anyone who dials the server will be connected.

   D. Only users in Active Directory will be connected.

   E. All users will be connected except those who are configured to be allowed access through the network access policy.

3. You are building an ISP around the technology available with Windows Server 2008. You are marketing personalized services that will ultimately allow you to provide voice, data, and video services to your customers by integrating Active Directory with the infrastructure of the network. For example, you plan to sell bandwidth on demand based on the customer's account in Active Directory. Your long-range plans notwithstanding, you start providing basic services to your customers by offering both dynamic and static IP addressing. Some ISPs offer static IP addresses based on a particular machine, but you want to provide a particular address based on the individual user. How can you provide this level of service for the users?

A. Create an IP address reservation for the users in the Windows Server 2008 DHCP server.

B. Assign a unique IP address to the users' accounts in Active Directory.

C. Create a network access policy that provides an assigned static IP address to the appropriate users.

D. You can't provide a static IP address per user using Windows Server 2008 services.

4. You are the network administrator for the Beach Party Bingo Apparel Company. You serve offices in three cities, with support people for the network in each location. The support people need to access the network from home occasionally when they get paged for network problems during weekends and evenings. You also have more than 100 salespeople who travel incessantly as they try to get your company's product in boutiques across the country. They need to access the network on a regular basis. You want all remote communication to be logged for security purposes so you can track the locations where connections originate. How can you configure the RRAS server to accommodate these requirements?

A. Configure Set By Caller for the sales staff and No Callback for the support staff.

B. Configure Set By Caller for the sales staff and for the support staff.

C. Configure Set By Caller for the sales staff and Always Callback for the support staff.

D. Configure No Callback for the sales staff and Set By Caller for the support staff.

E. Configure Set By Caller for the sales staff.

5. You are configuring RAS on your network, and you have installed RRAS on a Windows Server 2008 server. Users can dial in to one of two phone numbers, 420-4200 and 420-4201, in order to establish RAS connectivity. The Remote Access Permission for each user is set to Control Access Through Network Access Policy.

You are required to apply the following rules: Administrators and power users can connect at any time, but power users must dial in to 420-4200. If a user is a member of both the Administrators group and the Power Users group, that user must be treated as an administrator. Members of the Domain Users group can connect only between the hours of 5 p.m. and 11 p.m. but can connect to either phone number.

Using the following diagram, design the simplest network access policies possible by selecting the items in the Choices column and placing them in the appropriate empty boxes. Policy A is always processed first, and Policy C is always processed last. The default network access policy has been deleted. Use the Default item if the default setting is required for an element. If no setting is required, then leave its box blank. Note that some items might be used more than once and some items might not be used at all.

Choices:

420-4200
420-4201
5 P.M.–11 P.M.
11 P.M.–5 P.M.
Administrators
Allow
Default
Deny
Domain Users
Power Users

	Conditions	Permission	Profile
Policy A			
Policy B			
Policy C			

6. The AVO import/export company has offices in Canada and throughout South America. The buyers for the company have laptop computers that dial into the network, usually from hotels and from company facilities of AVO's clients. Because financial and proprietary client information will be included in these communications, you want to make sure they are secure. You plan to encrypt the authentication and data transfers during the VPN communication sessions. Many of the remote sites don't support 128-bit encryption, but you do want to make sure that all sessions are using 56-bit keys. How do you configure the network access policy for the RRAS server to support these requirements?

A. Basic Encryption

B. Enhanced Encryption

C. Strong Encryption

D. Strongest Encryption

7. Mildred's Natural Pharmaceuticals is in the process of gobbling up other health food and homeopathic companies and integrating them into a national organization. Because the acquisition process for many of the companies that are coming on board hasn't been completed, you don't want them to have complete access to your network. Your company is halfway through a migration from Windows NT and 2000 to Windows Server 2008 at the corporate level. You are still running the Windows 2000 network using Active Directory in mixed mode. Most of the new locations are small, mom-and-pop health food stores, and many of them aren't computerized at all. You are in the process of sending out stand-alone Windows Server 2008 servers so that each of those locations can connect to the corporate RRAS server. The other locations represent a mix of Windows 95, Windows 98, and Windows NT workstations. You want to use VPNs to enable each location to connect to the corporate network through the location's local Internet connection. What is the best way for you to grant and control VPN access to the RRAS server for all the locations for which the acquisition process has been completed?

A. Use the default network access policy for VPN.

B. Grant access per user.

C. Create a network access policy with a NAS port type that uses tunnel type.

D. Create an Active Directory group containing your VPN users, add a condition that uses the Windows-Groups attribute, and put this policy ahead of the default network access policy in order to ensure execution.

8. You are the network administrator of the New Products Development Company, which has offices in Southern California. The employees at the corporate office are a combination of administrative support staff and technical engineers in the lab. The engineers also frequently work from home at all hours of the night, and they are supported via RRAS. You were involved with the migration of the network from a hodgepodge of different network operating systems, but predominantly Windows clients and a smattering of Macintosh client computers. The CIO decided that the network operating system would be based upon Windows Server 2008 and that the Novell and Banyan hardware would be removed. Coupled with this was the decision to disallow passing through the network any credentials that were not encrypted. This was completed last year, and everything appears to be fine. Recently, and increasingly, you have been getting calls from development engineers who are working with the Linux operating system complaining that they cannot connect to the RAS server. You are now told that even though the fundamental network for the company will continue to be based on Windows Server 2008, it is still important to support the work of the development engineers. What steps do you need to take in order for the Linux clients to be able to connect to the RRAS servers so that they can securely access resources at the office from home? (Choose all that apply.)

A. Select Store Password Using Reversible Encryption For All Users in the GPO for the engineers.

B. Select The User Must Change Password At Next Logon for the engineers.

C. Reset the passwords for the engineers.

D. Enable PAP on RRAS and in the engineers' network access policy.

E. Enable MS-CHAPv2 on RRAS and in the engineers' network access policy.

F. Enable CHAP on RRAS and in the engineers' network access policy.

9. The Risk Assessment Insurance Company has five main offices across the United States. The cities are Los Angeles, Dallas, Atlanta, Chicago, and New York. Each city acts as the hub for the many individual sales offices each agent represents in their respective region. You have been involved in the migration from Windows NT to Windows Server 2008 over the last year. The main reason for the migration as directed by the CIO was to reduce administrative costs, a benefit promised by the new operating system platform. The migration has been completed, and the domain has finally been switched over from mixed mode to native mode. Although the software has been upgraded across all the workstations and servers, you still have not taken full advantage of the administrative opportunities available with the system. You still spend a great deal of time managing all the remote connections used by the agents from their home offices. You are instructed to reduce the amount of time you spend supporting these tasks. What should you do to accomplish this?

   A. Create and implement consistent remote access rules for the agents in a Group Policy object, and place it in the root domain of the forest with the No Override option set.

   B. Create and implement consistent remote access rules for the agents in a Group Policy object, and place it in each domain of the forest with the No Override option set.

   C. Create a master network access policy, and implement it systematically on each RRAS server.

   D. Implement Network Policy Server (NPS).

10. Rick needs to set up RRAS callbacks for a single group of users who work from home. He could accomplish this by enabling callbacks for each individual user in each user's Properties dialog box, but there is a more efficient method. Which of the following accomplishes the task more efficiently?

   A. Creating a Windows Server 2008 security group and then configuring a network access policy for the group

   B. Creating a remote access profile for the group

   C. Moving the users to a server that has callbacks enabled

   D. Enabling callbacks on the server

11. Hannah's manager has asked her to configure a remote access server so that it restricts what times of day users can dial in. She creates a network access policy that contains time-of-day restrictions, but it doesn't work. What is the most likely cause?

   A. The Day-And-Time-Restrictions policy hasn't been replicated throughout the domain.

   B. The Day-And-Time-Restrictions policy doesn't have a high enough priority.

   C. The Day-And-Time-Restrictions policy has a priority that's too high.

   D. The Day-And-Time-Restrictions policy is not linked to an active remote access profile.

12. You have already upgraded all your network servers and the services that run on them, including RRAS, to Windows Server 2008. You are responsible for building the remote access system for all your remote users. The requirements are that you must support Windows 98, Windows NT, Windows 2000/XP Professional, and also the growing number of Linux machines that the users are authorized to use from home or on the road. Because most of the users have machines on the local network as well as the need to connect from home, another requirement is that all forms of authentication use encrypted passwords to protect the passwords across the Internet and the ISP networks through which users connect to the RRAS servers. What authentication protocol should you use to satisfy these requirements?

    A. MS-CHAPv1

    B. MS-CHAPv2

    C. CHAP

    D. PAP

    E. EAP

13. The Windows Server 2008 network that you administer has about 250 people with accounts that give them access to resources. Of these 250 people, only 35 are supposed to have unlimited remote access while they are on the road. Another 10 managers are allowed remote access at certain specified times. In addition, five administrators are authorized to have remote access from home so they can support the network. You have implemented network access polices to make sure that only the people you have approved have access to the Windows Server 2008 network. Some of the people are in more than one group. These people are having problems accessing the network remotely, so you take a look at the various policies to find the cause. How are network access policies evaluated?

    A. The most restrictive policy first

    B. By name

    C. By date of creation

    D. By priority

14. ABC's Sailing Company provides weeklong trips up and down the Atlantic and Pacific coasts of the United States. The company's administrative offices are in North Carolina, providing support to the crews on the six ships in the fleet. You have built a policy-based remote access system that includes several conditions. When a crew member covered by the policy tries to access the network to download the guest lists and their meal requests, he is denied access. As the network administrator, you are trying to troubleshoot the problem. Which of the following is true regarding network access policies?

    A. The crew member does not need to meet any of the policy conditions as long as he has dial-in permission.

    B. The crew member must meet at least one condition in order to be granted access.

    C. The crew member must meet all conditions in order to be granted access.

    D. The crew member does not need to meet any of the conditions as long as the correct credentials are supplied.

15. The Happy Trails Riding Club has a small network of about 25 Windows XP Professional workstations and 1 Windows Server 2008 computer. The company provides its clients with weeklong vacations in the mountains featuring a rugged outdoor experience. The owner of the company and two sales representatives need remote access to the network. As the network administrator, you must make sure that the remote access network is always available to these three users but that it is restricted to normal business hours for all other users. What steps should you take to accomplish this task? (Choose all that apply.)

A. Create a new group, and add only the three users.

B. Create a policy that includes the Day-And-Time Restrictions and the Windows-Groups policies for the three-user group.

C. Create a new group, and add every employee except for the three users.

D. Create a policy that includes the Windows-Groups policy for the three-user group.

E. Create a policy that includes the Day-And-Time Restrictions and the Windows-Groups policies for the larger group.

16. You want to restrict the IP addresses that users can use when connecting to your site. They are dialing in with regular modems and using a mix of Windows XP SP2 and Windows 2000 Professional operating systems. What method should you use to specify how IP address assignment is done (users are not allowed to request specific IP addresses) while not adding undue administration overhead?

A. Use the NPS/RADIUS attribute Client-IP-Address to specify the IP address.

B. Use a network access policy to change the dial-in profile to the Server Must Supply An IP Address option.

C. Use a network access policy to set a static IP address for each client.

D. Use the NPS/RADIUS attribute IP-Address to specify the address upon connection.

17. The CIO of the company has mandated that the dial-in communication should be encrypted as strongly as possible. You've decided to implement a remote access profile that requires the strongest encryption available. Within which tab of the Dial-In Profile Properties would you set this option, and what are the parameters for the strongest encryption available?

A. The settings are found on the Security tab, and the strongest available is 3DES for IPSec or 128-bit MPPE for PPTP connections.

B. The settings are found on the Encryption tab, and the strongest available is 3DES for IPSec or 128-bit MPPE for PPTP connections.

C. The settings are found on the Encryption tab, and the strongest available is EAP-MD5 for IPSec or 56-bit MPPE for PPTP connections.

D. The settings are found on the Security tab, and the strongest available is EAP-MD5 for IPSec or 56-bit MPPE for PPTP connections.

18. Your network uses a RADIUS passthrough that calls for a Linux server in between the modems and the Windows Server 2008 remote access server running NPS. You have about 4,200 users who use a mix of operating systems, including Windows in all forms, Linux, and various Apple operating systems. Clients also use POTS modems from different vendors and connect from a wide array of locations. Because of these factors, you've had to enhance the security of the dial-in access. You have a number of attributes employed for authentication including Called-Station-ID and NAS-Port-Type. Your NASs are all 3Com/USR with incoming T1s, but recently you began purchasing Cisco AS5300s and using incoming PRI. You find that users are unable to authenticate when they hit the Cisco gear. You've verified with the Cisco Technical Assistance Center (TAC) that the configuration on the AS5300s is correct. What might be the cause of this issue?

   A. The Called-Station-ID is not sent by some remote locations or telephone companies.

   B. The client modems are incompatible with the Cisco AS5300s.

   C. The NAS-Port-Type is different for the Cisco gear than it is for the 3Com gear.

   D. There is not enough information to determine the cause or troubleshoot further.

19. When using RADIUS authentication, what ports and protocols must be allowed through the firewall?

   A. Either port 1645 or 1812 using UDP transport

   B. Either port 1445 or 1433 using TCP transport

   C. Port 1645 using EAP-TLS transport

   D. Port 1813 using UDP transport

20. Which of the following authentication protocols offers encryption of authentication data and communication alike?

   A. PAP

   B. SPAP

   C. TLS-MD5-SHA-1

   D. MS-CHAPv2

Answers to Review Questions

1. C. RRAS supports multiple authentication methods that can be used for different purposes. The Extensible Authentication Protocol (EAP) allows requests to the RRAS server to be properly formatted and forwarded to the RADIUS server. MS-CHAP is an incorrect answer because the Microsoft Challenge Handshake Authentication Protocol is used in a pure-Microsoft environment. Kerberos is an incorrect answer because it is a standard that's used to authenticate a user to Active Directory, not to a RADIUS server. The Password Authentication Protocol (PAP) is incorrect because it is a simple protocol that provides little security and does not forward requests to third-party authentication authorities.

2. B. Without a default network access policy, no user will be allowed access through the RRAS server. All connection requests are evaluated against the criteria contained in the network access policy. If there is no network access policy, there are no conditions to compare, and any request is thereby denied. Removing the network access policy does not leave the remote connection to your network open. Therefore, partial connectivity to your network is not possible if there is no network access policy. The options are either granularity of access through a policy or no access at all with no policy.

3. B. In Active Directory, dial-in users can be assigned a static IP address as part of the user account settings. You need to make sure you have removed these IP addresses from any scope being delivered through DHCP so that you won't create conflicts. DHCP delivers addresses based on the machine, and reservations are assigned based on a particular MAC address. Remote policies don't allow you to deliver a unique IP address.

4. C. The Always Callback option for the support staff will ensure that their remote connections are always made from their homes. The Set By Caller option for the sales staff will allow them to travel around the country and enter the number where they are at any given time for the callback, thereby allowing you to keep records of all connections. Using No Callback would allow anyone configured with this option to call from anywhere and connect to the system without any callback requirements.

5. Administrators need to be able to connect to either line at any time of the day, so this policy should be listed first. The policy allowing members of the Power Users group to connect should come second; this will make it possible for members of both the Administrators and the Power Users groups to take advantage of the unlimited access enjoyed by administrators. The policy that applies to Domain Users needs to come last; otherwise, users who are members of both Power Users and Domain Users would be allowed to dial in to 420-4201.

	Conditions	Permission	Profile
Policy A	Administrators	Allow	Default
Policy B	Power Users	Allow	420-4200
Policy C	Domain Users	Allow	Default
	5 P.M.–11 P.M.		

6. C. Strong Encryption in the network access policy will configure the RRAS server to use 56-bit DES encryption for L2TP/IPSec VPN connections as well as 56-bit MPPE dial-up connections. Basic Encryption will support L2TP/IPSec 56-bit encryption but only 40-bit encryption for MPPE dial-up connections. Strongest Encryption uses 128-bit encryption for MPPE dial-up connections and supports triple DES encryption for L2TP/IPSec connections. Enhanced Encryption is not a valid option in RRAS.

7. B. In this situation, you are forced to grant access per user because you can implement network access policies only if you are running your Windows Server 2008 Active Directory network in Windows 2000 native mode or Windows Server 2003 or 2008 domain functional level. Ideally, you would use Active Directory and create groups so that you could manage access to the network via network access policies, but this solution doesn't apply in this situation.

8. A, C, F. PAP uses clear-text passwords and therefore cannot be used according to your security policy. MS-CHAP supports only Microsoft clients. CHAP supports encryption across the wire but not in storage, so the encryption must be reversible. Selecting this option does not affect existing passwords, so after you select this option, you need to reset the engineers' passwords. However, if you select the option that forces a password change at the next login, then the engineers will be unable to access the system in the first place from their Linux machines because CHAP does not support this feature.

9. D. The Windows Server 2008 RRAS server can be configured to behave as a RADIUS server. This allows configuration information to be shared by multiple machines through NPS. In this configuration, when the RRAS server receives a request, it forwards that request to the NPS server for processing and authorizes or denies access based upon a centralized policy. Network access polices cannot be set in GPOs. The problem of creating a master policy and trying to keep all the RRAS servers in sync will expand geometrically as the number of servers you are trying to manage increases.

10. A. Network access policies allow you to create policies that target specific groups (provided you're in Windows 2000, 2003, or 2008 native domain functional level).

11. B. Policies are evaluated in order, so if the time-of-day restrictions have too low a priority, another policy may allow the connection to proceed.

12. C. The Challenge Handshake Authentication Protocol (CHAP) is a standard remote access authentication that is available on Microsoft and non-Microsoft clients. It provides the use of encrypted passwords. The MS-CHAP protocol is based on CHAP but is not available for non-Microsoft clients. If MS-CHAP is the only authentication protocol available on the RRAS server, the Linux clients won't be able to connect to the server. PAP is available on Linux clients, but it doesn't provide the encryption you need. EAP is an authentication protocol that allows RRAS to interact with other authentication enforcement entities such as RADIUS servers.

13. D. Policies are evaluated in the order of their priority. If a policy set to restrict remote access has a lower priority and another policy set to allow the connection to proceed has a higher priority, the latter will prevail.

14. C. To gain access to the system, users must meet all the conditions in at least one network policy as well as have dial-in permission and supply the correct credentials.

15. A, C, D, E. In this case, you should create two groups, one for the three unique users and one for the other users in the company. Then apply a policy that allows access unconditionally to the smaller group and a policy that includes Day-And-Time Restrictions and Windows-Groups policies for the larger group.

16. B. You would use a network access policy and set the Server Must Supply An IP Address option to meet the requirements in this scenario. You could also theoretically assign a static IP address for each user, but that would not meet the requirements for the scenario since it adds much administration overhead. The Client-IP-Address attribute is a valid RADIUS attribute, but it specifies the NAS that sent the request.

17. B. The Encryption tab contains four options—Basic, Strong, Strongest, and No Encryption—offering varying levels of encryption. There is no Security tab in the Dial-In Profile Properties.

18. C. This question gave you a lot of information, some of which is not relevant to the answer. Both on the exam and in real life, you often have to weed out superfluous information in order to identify the real issues. In this case, you can rule out the Called-Station-ID attribute since it is actually sent by the NAS and not by the remote telco. Granted, it could be a problem if the Cisco NAS isn't sending the attribute correctly, but the option specifically stated that it was sent by the remote telephone company and therefore had to be false. It is also very unlikely that the client modems are incompatible with the Cisco gear since the question stated that a variety of vendor modems were being used by the clients. Out of these options, the most likely cause is that the NAS-Port-Type attribute is being sent differently.

19. A. RADIUS authentication uses port 1645 or 1812, depending on the version of RADIUS. RADIUS uses UDP as the transport mechanism. Port 1813 is used by RADIUS accounting, not authentication.

20. D. MS-CHAPv2 offers encryption of both authentication data and communication. PAP doesn't encrypt anything but is widely used at ISPs because of its compatibility with a wide array of client computers. Shiva Password Authentication Protocol (SPAP) is used for Shiva dial-up gear. Option C is not a valid protocol.

Chapter

8

Managing File and Print Services

MICROSOFT EXAM OBJECTIVES COVERED IN THIS CHAPTER:

✓ **Configure a file server.**

▪ May include but is not limited to: file share publishing, Offline Files, share permissions, NTFS permissions, encrypting file system (EFS)

✓ **Configure Distributed File System (DFS).**

▪ May include but is not limited to: DFS namespace, DFS configuration and application, creating and configuring targets, DFS replication

✓ **Manage disk quotas.**

▪ May include but is not limited to: quota by volume or quota by user, quota entries, quota templates

✓ **Configure and monitor print services.**

▪ May include but is not limited to: printer share, publish printers to Active Directory, printer permissions, deploy printer connections, install printer drivers, export and import print queues and printer settings, print pooling, print priority

Now that we have covered remote access, we'll explain how to set up your servers so that your network users have something to access. Before you can set up a server, you have to decide what the server is going to be used for. Is it going to be a print server, a file storage server, a remote access server, or a domain controller?

After you have decided how the machine is going to help your network, you must implement your decision. In this chapter, we'll show you how to set up a print server and a file server. In addition, we will discuss how to set up permissions and security for these servers. Finally, we will also discuss how you can limit the amount of space your users can have on a server.

> All the server types covered in this chapter use Microsoft Windows Server 2008. Although other operating systems can do these tasks, this chapter refers only to Windows Server 2008.

Understanding File Servers

Before you configure a file server, you must understand what a file server does. *File servers* are machines on your network that store data files to share among network clients. The same machine can be a file server and another type of server. For example, a machine can both be hosting network files and be running Exchange Server 2007. Such a machine would have both file server and application server functions. (*Application servers* are machines that host applications used by network clients.)

 Real World Scenario

Multiple Server Types on One Machine

In today's computer world, most IT departments must worry about budgets. The problem with the IT department is that most of the time it gets the smallest budget in the company. You are usually stuck between a rock and a hard place, because if your network is running well, people (including executives) forget about you. This makes it hard when you ask for your budget.

Because of the lack of money, many times you must use one machine to do many server tasks. We have been IT managers in many companies where the IT department had to have the same machine running both as an application server and as a file server.

You must consider many factors before allowing a machine to run multiple server types. How many processors do you have? What are the processor speeds? How much RAM does the machine have? What is the hard drive speed? What type of applications will be hosted on the machine?

After you have gathered all your information about the machine, then you can decide whether the machine can host multiple server types. However, keep this one fact in mind: because of the requirements and demands on the computer system, it's always a good idea to host SQL Server on a dedicated machine.

We have been doing consulting for many years, and one thing we stress to all clients is to perform regular backups. After all, most organizations would not be able to recover from losing all of their data. Usually, companies back up only their servers, and this is why home folders are so important. *Home folders* are one of the most common file types on a file server; they are folders set up on the server for users to store information. Users have a location on the server to store their important data, and therefore that data will be backed up when the company does its regular backups.

Home folders are just one example of how to use a file server. We will be discussing other examples throughout this chapter.

Backing up will be discussed in Chapter 9, "Monitoring and Managing a Network Infrastructure."

Configuring File Servers

Now that you have an understanding of what a file server does, it's time to discuss how to configure these servers. Setting up a file server properly encompasses many steps. One major concern, as always, is security. In the following sections, first we will describe how to share and publish online and offline files and folders. Then we will discuss the two types of security—shared permissions and NTFS security—that an administrator can set when sharing files or folders.

Sharing Folders

A file server is for sharing and storing data. To use one, you need to know how to set up a share, or a shared folder, on your server. A *shared folder* is exactly what it says; it's a folder that is shared on your network so users can access the data within that folder. You, as an administrator, have the ability to determine which users can access which files within that shared folder.

One of the main goals of Active Directory is to make resources easy to find. Active Directory also makes it easy to determine which files are available to users. With that said, we will explain how Active Directory manages to publish shared folders.

 The next section discusses publishing objects in Active Directory. To learn more about Active Directory, read *MCTS: Windows Server 2008 Active Directory Configuration Study Guide* by William Panek and James Chellis (Sybex, 2008).

Making Active Directory Objects Available to Users

With Active Directory, a system administrator can control which objects users can see. The act of making an Active Directory object available is known as *publishing*. The two main publishable objects are Printer objects and Shared Folder objects.

The general process for creating server shares and shared printers has remained unchanged from previous versions of Windows: you create the various objects (printers or file system folders) and then enable them for sharing.

To make these resources available via Active Directory, however, there's an additional step: you must publish the resources. Once an object has been published in Active Directory, clients will be able to use it.

You can also publish Windows NT 4 resources through Active Directory by making Active Directory objects out of them. Without Active Directory, Windows NT 4 shares and printers are accessible only by using NetBIOS-based shares. If you're planning to disable the NetBIOS protocol in your environment, you must be sure that these resources have been published, or they will not be accessible.

When you publish objects in Active Directory, you should know the server name and share name of the resource. However, this information doesn't matter to your users. A system administrator can change the resource to which the object points without having to reconfigure or even notify clients. For example, if you move a share from one server to another, all you need to do is update the Shared Folder object's properties to point to the new location. Active Directory clients still refer to the resource with the same path and name as they used before.

In Exercise 8.1, we will walk you through the steps of sharing and publishing a folder for use on your network.

EXERCISE 8.1

Creating and Publishing a Shared Network Folder

1. Create a new folder in the root directory of your C: partition, and name it **Test Share**.

2. Right-click the Test Share folder, and choose Share.

3. In the File Sharing dialog box, enter the names of users you want to share this folder with. In the upper box, enter **Everyone,** and then click Add. Note that Everyone appears in the lower box. Click in the Permission Level column next to Everyone, and choose Contributor from the drop-down menu. Then click Share.

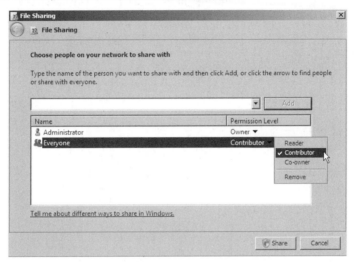

4. You see a message that your folder has been shared. Click Done.

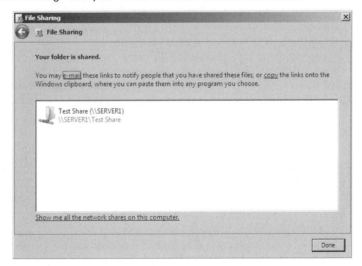

EXERCISE 8.1 *(continued)*

5. Open the Active Directory Users And Computers tool. Expand the current domain, and right-click RD OU. Select New ➢ Shared Folder.

6. In the New Object – Shared Folder dialog box, type **Shared Folder Test** for the name of the folder. Then type the UNC path to the share (for example, **\\server1\Test Share**). Click OK to create the share.

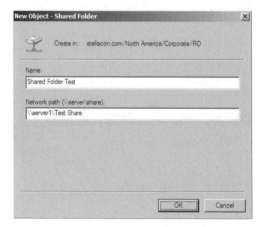

 One of the main benefits of having all your resource information in Active Directory is that you can easily find what you're looking for using the Find dialog box. When setting up objects in Active Directory, we recommend you always enter as much information as possible for the objects you're creating. The extra effort will begin to pay off when your users start doing searches for these objects. The more information you enter, the more users can search to find the appropriate resource they need.

Configuring Offline Folders

If you have been in this industry long enough, you have seen a major change in the computers that end users now use. Years ago, only a few select users had laptops. They were big and bulky, and they weighed almost as much as today's desktop.

The pendulum has swung in the opposite direction. It probably seems like every one of your end users now has a laptop. This gives you as an IT administrator a whole new set of challenges and problems to address.

One challenge you have to address is how users can work on files while outside the office. If you have a user who wants to work at home, how do you give them the files they need to get their work done?

The answer is *offline folders*. These folders contain data that can be worked on by users while outside the office. An IT administrator can set up offline folders through the use of Group Policy Objects (GPOs).

When you decide to make folders available for offline use, these folders need to synchronize with the laptops so that all the data matches between both systems. One decision that you should make as an administrator is when the offline folders will be synchronized. You have three synchronization options you can set in the GPO (see Figure 8.1).

FIGURE 8.1   Synchronization options in a GPO

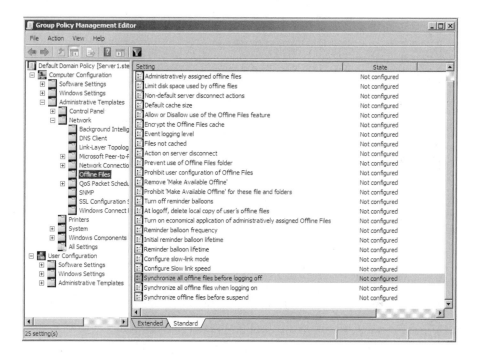

You can set up any combination of these options:

- When you select Synchronize All Offline Files Before Logging Off, offline folders are synchronized when the user logs off the network.

- When you select Synchronize All Offline Files When Logging On, offline folders are synchronized when the user logs on to the network.

- When you select Synchronize Offline Files Before Suspend, offline folders are synchronized before the user does a system suspend.

In Exercise 8.2, we will show you the steps necessary to configure offline folder options by using a GPO. This exercise uses the Group Policy Management console (GPMC). If your GPMC is not installed, use the Server Manager MMC (under Features) to install it.

EXERCISE 8.2

Configuring Offline Folder Options

1.   Open the Group Policy Management console by clicking Start ≻ Administrative tools ≻ Group Policy Management.

2.   In the left pane, expand your forest and then your domain. Under your domain name there should be a default domain policy.

3.   Right-click the default domain policy, and choose Edit.

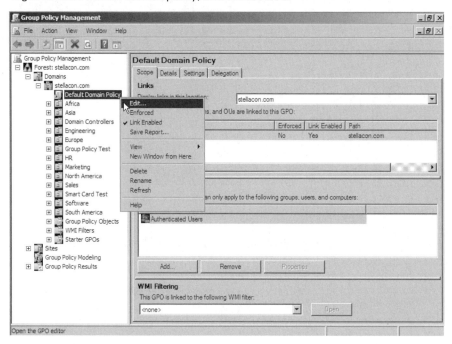

4.   In the User Configuration section, expand Administrative Templates ≻ Network, and then click Offline Files.

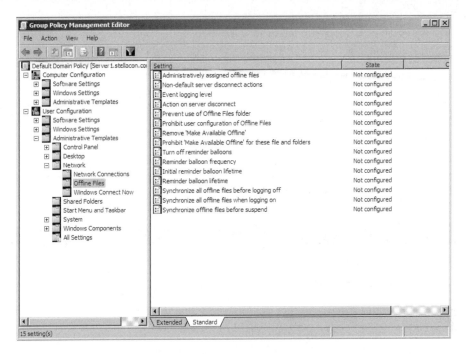

5. Right-click Synchronize All Offline Files Before Logging Off, and choose Properties. The Properties dialog box appears. Choose the Enabled option, and click OK.

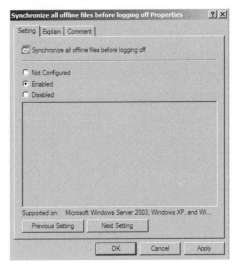

EXERCISE 8.2 *(continued)*

6. Right-click Synchronize All Offline Files When Logging On, and choose Properties. The Properties dialog box appears. Choose the Enabled option, and click OK.

7. Right-click Synchronize Offline Files Before Suspend, and choose Properties. The Properties dialog box appears. Choose the Enabled option. In the Action drop-down box, make sure Quick is selected. Click OK.

8. Close the GPMC.

Now that you have set up a GPO for synchronization, it's time to share a folder for offline usage. In Exercise 8.3, we will show how to set up a folder for offline access. You must complete Exercise 8.1 before doing this exercise.

EXERCISE 8.3

Configuring a Shared Network Folder for Offline Access

1. Right-click the Test Share folder you created in Exercise 8.1, and choose Properties.

2. Click the Sharing tab, and then click the Advanced Sharing button.

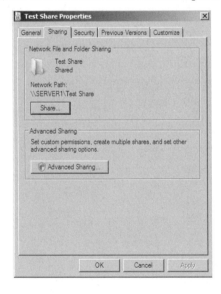

3. When the Advanced Sharing dialog box appears, click the Caching button.

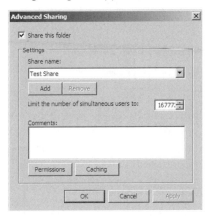

4. When the Offline Settings dialog box appears, choose the All Files And Programs That Users Open From The Shares Will Be Automatically Available Offline option. Click OK.

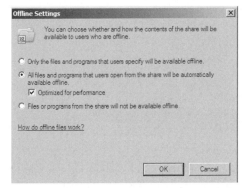

5. Click OK twice more to close the Properties dialog box.

Understanding Permissions

You have gone through the steps to set up a shared folder, publish it to Active Directory, and set it up for offline access. Now we will discuss how you can protect these files and folders by using permissions.

You can secure folders using permissions in two ways, and you can secure files in one way. You can set up permissions and security through NTFS or through sharing.

Understanding NTFS

NTFS is an option that you have when you are formatting a hard drive. You can format a hard drive for a Microsoft operating system in three ways:

- File Allocation Table (FAT) is supported on older operating systems only (Server 2003, Server 2000, XP, and so on).

- FAT32 is supported on Windows Server 2008.

- NTFS is supported on Windows Server 2008.

NTFS has many advantages over FAT and FAT32. They include the following:

Compression   Compression helps compact files or folders to allow for more efficient use of hard drive space. For example, a file that usually takes up 20 MB of space might use only 13 MB after compression. To enable compression, just open the Advanced Attributes dialog box for a folder and check the Compress Contents To Save Disk Space box (see Figure 8.2).

FIGURE 8.2   Setting up compression on a folder

Quotas   Quotas allow you to limit how much hard drive space users can have on a server. Quotas are discussed in greater detail later in the section "Configuring Disk Quotas."

Encryption   Encrypting File System (EFS) allows a user or administrator to secure files or folders by using encryption. Encryption employs the user's security identification (SID) number to secure the file or folder. To implement encryption, open the Advanced Attributes dialog box for a folder, and check the Encrypt Contents To Secure Data box (see Figure 8.3).

If you use EFS, it's best not to delete users immediately when they leave a company. Administrators have the ability to recover encrypted files, but it is much easier to gain access to the user's encrypted files by logging in as the user who left the company and unchecking the encryption box.

FIGURE 8.3   Setting up encryption on a folder

Security   One of the biggest advantages of NTFS is security. As we stated in previous chapters, security is one of the most important aspects of an IT administrator's job. An advantage of NTFS security is that the security can be placed on individual files and folders. It does not matter whether you are local to the share (in front of the machine where the data is) or remote to the share (coming across the network to access the data), the security is always in place with NTFS.

The default security permission is Users = Read on new folders or shares.

NTFS security is *additive*. In other words, if you are a member of three groups (Marketing, Sales, and R&D) and these three groups have different security settings, you get the highest level of permissions. For example, let's say you have a user by the name of *wpanek* who belongs to all three groups (Marketing, Sales, and R&D). Figure 8.4 shows this user's permissions. The Marketing group has Read and Execute permissions to the Stellacon Documents folder. The Sales group has Read and Write, and the R&D group has Full Control. Since wpanek is a member of all three groups, wpanek would get Full Control (the highest level).

The only time that this does not apply is with the Deny permission. Deny overrides any other group setting. So in the same example, if Sales had the Deny permission to the Stellacon Documents folder, the user wpanek would be denied access to the folder. The only way around this Deny is if you added wpanek directly to the folder and gave him individual permissions (see Figure 8.5). Individual permissions override a group Deny. In this example, the individual right of wpanek would override the Sales group's Deny. The user's security permission for the Stellacon Documents folder would be Full Control.

Give users only the permissions necessary to do their jobs. Do not give them higher levels than necessary.

FIGURE 8.4   Security settings on the Stellacon Documents folder

Stellacon Documents

Marketing	Sales	R&D
RX	RW	FC

FIGURE 8.5   Security settings with individual settings

Stellacon Documents

Marketing	Sales	R&D	wpanek
RX	Deny	FC	FC

Understanding Shared Permissions

When you set up a folder to be shared, you have the ability to assign that folder permissions. *Shared permissions* can be placed only on the folder and not on individual files. Files inherit their permissions from the parent folder.

Shared folder permissions are in effect only when users are remote to the shared data. In other words, if computer A shares a folder called Downloads and assigns that folder shared permissions, those permissions would apply only if you connected to that share from a machine other than computer A. If you were sitting in front of computer A, the shared permissions would not apply.

Like NTFS permissions (discussed in the previous section), shared permissions are additive, so users receive the highest level of permissions granted by the groups they are members of.

Also like NTFS permissions, the Deny permission (see Figure 8.6) overrides any group permission, and an individual permission overrides a group Deny.

The default shared permission is Administrators = Full Control. The shared permissions going from lowest to highest are: Read, Change, Full Control, and Deny. Table 8.1 compares the two different types of permissions and security.

How NTFS Security and Shared Permissions Work Together

When you set up a shared folder, you need to set up shared permissions on that folder. If you're using NTFS, you will also need to set up NTFS security on the folder. Since both shared permissions and NTFS security are in effect when the user is remote, what happens when the two conflict?

FIGURE 8.6   Setting up permissions on a shared folder

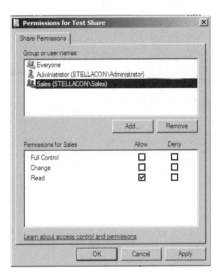

TABLE 8.1   NTFS Security vs. Shared Permissions

Description	NTFS	Shared
Folder-level security	Yes	Yes
File-level security	Yes	No
In effect when local to the data	Yes	No
In effect when remote to the data	Yes	Yes
Permissions are additive	Yes	Yes
Group Deny overrides all other group settings	Yes	Yes
Individual settings override group settings	Yes	Yes

There are two basic rules of thumb:

- The local permission is the NTFS permission.
- The remote permission is the more restrictive set of permissions between NTFS and shared.

This is easy to do as long as you do it in steps. Let's look at Figure 8.7 and walk through the process of figuring out what wpanek has for rights.

As you can see, wpanek belongs to three groups (Marketing, Sales, and R&D), and all three groups have settings for the Stellacon Documents folder. In the figure, you will notice that there are two questions: Remote = ? and Local = ? That's what you need to figure out—what are wpanek's effective permissions when he is sitting at the computer that shares the folder, and what are his effective permissions when he connects to the folder from another computer (remotely)? To figure this out, follow these steps:

1. Add up the permissions on each side separately.

   Remember, permissions and security are additive. You get the highest permission. So if you look at each side, the highest shared permission is the Read permission. The NTFS security side should add up to equal Full Control. So, now you have Read permission on shared and Full Control on NTFS.

2. Determine the local permissions.

   Shared permissions do not apply when you are local to the data. Only NTFS would apply. So, the local permission would be Full Control.

3. Determine the remote permissions.

   Remember, the remote permission is the most restrictive set of permissions between NTFS and shared. Since Read is more restrictive than Full Control, the remote permission would be Read.

Let's try another. Look at Figure 8.8 and see whether you can come up with wpanek's local and remote permissions.

Your answer should match the following:

```
Local = Read
Remote = Read
```

FIGURE 8.7 NTFS security and shared permissions example

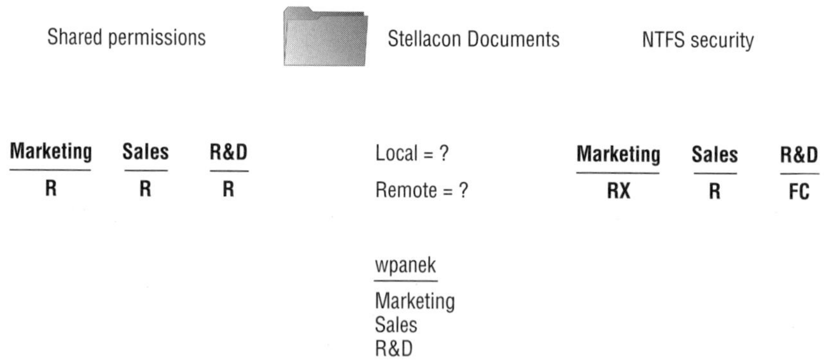

| Shared permissions | | | Stellacon Documents | NTFS security | | |

Marketing	Sales	R&D	Local = ?	Marketing	Sales	R&D
R	R	R	Remote = ?	RX	R	FC

wpanek
Marketing
Sales
R&D

FIGURE 8.8   NTFS security and shared permissions

Shared permissions   Stellacon Documents   NTFS security

Marketing	Sales	R&D
R	R	FC

Local = ?
Remote = ?

Marketing	Sales	R&D
R	R	R

wpanek
Marketing
Sales
R&D

Remember, first you add up each side to get the highest level of rights. NTFS would be Read, and shared would be Full Control. The local permission is always just NTFS (shared does not apply to local permissions), and remote permission is whichever permission (NTFS or Shared) is the most restrictive (which would be Read, on the NTFS side).

Exercise 8.4 walks you through the process of setting both NTFS and shared permissions. You must complete Exercise 8.1 before doing this exercise.

EXERCISE 8.4

Configuring Shared and NTFS Settings

1. Right-click the Test Share folder you created in Exercise 8.1, and choose Properties.

2. Click the Sharing tab, and then click the Advanced Sharing button. (You will set the shared permissions first.)

3. Click the Permissions button. Click the Add button. When the Select User page appears, choose a group from Active Directory (we used our Sales group). Once you find your group, click OK.

4. The Permissions dialog box appears. With your group highlighted, click the Allow check box next to Full Control, and click OK. (All the other Allow check boxes will automatically become checked.)

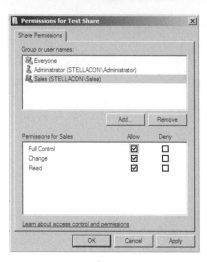

5. On the Advanced Sharing page, click OK. Now click the Security tab. (This allows you to set the NTFS security settings.)

6. Click the Edit button. That takes you to the Permissions page. Now click the Add button. When the Select User page appears, choose a group from Active Directory (we used our Sales group). Once you find your group, choose OK.

7. The Permissions dialog box appears. With your group highlighted, click the Allow check box next to Modify, and click OK. (All of the check boxes below Modify will automatically become checked.)

8. Click Close.

Configuring Disk Quotas

In this chapter so far, you have seen how to set up a share and publish it to Active Directory. You've also learned how to set up permissions and security and how NTFS and shared permissions work with each other. It's time to learn how to limit users' hard drive space on the servers.

Disk quotas give administrators the ability to limit how much storage space a user can have on a hard drive. As mentioned earlier in this chapter, disk quotas are an advantage of using NTFS over FAT32. If you decide to use FAT32 on a volume or partition, quotas will not be available.

You have a few options available to you when you set up disk quotas. You can set up disk quotas based on volume or on users.

A good rule of thumb is to set up an umbrella quota policy that covers the entire volume and then let individual users exceed the umbrella as needed.

 Real World Scenario

Disk Quotas

You are the administrator for a research company. The company policy states that all users should get only 1,000 MB of disk space on the server. The problem is that the scientists need unlimited server space to log their reports and findings. You have been told by your boss to give the scientist unlimited space on the server.

First you need to set up the umbrella policy for all users on the server. You enable disk quotas and set all users to 1000 MB. Then you have to allow scientists to exceed the limit.

This is a common problem within the industry. Many times as an administrator you are asked to set up a disk quota and then have executives and managers exceed this umbrella quota.

Setting quotas by volume   One way to set up disk quotas is by setting the quota by volume, on a per-volume basis. This means that if you have a hard drive with C:, D:, and E: volumes, you would have to set up three individual quotas (one for each volume). This is your umbrella. This is where you set up an entire disk quota based on the volume for all users.

Setting quotas by user   You have the ability to set up quotas on volumes by user. Here is where you would individually let users have independent quotas that exceed your umbrella quota.

Specifying quota entries   You use quota entries to configure the volume and user quotas. You do this on the Quotas tab of the volume's Properties dialog box. (See Exercise 8.5.)

Creating quota templates Quota templates are predefined ways to set up quotas. Templates allow you to set up disk quotas without needing to create a disk quota from scratch. One advantage to using a template is that when you want to set up disk quotas on multiple volumes (C:, D:, and E:) on the same hard drive, you do not need to re-create the quota on each volume.

Exercise 8.5 will show you how to set up an umbrella quota for all users and then have an individual account in your Active Directory exceed this quota.

EXERCISE 8.5

Configuring Disk Quotas

1. Open Windows Explorer by right-clicking the Start menu and choosing Explore.

2. Right-click the Local Disk (C:), and choose Properties.

3. Click the Quotas tab.

4. Check the Enable Quota Management check box. Also check the Deny Disk Space To Users Exceeding Quota Limit box.

5. Click the Limit Disk Space To option, and enter **1000 MB** in the boxes.

6. Enter **750 MB** in the Set Warning Level To boxes.

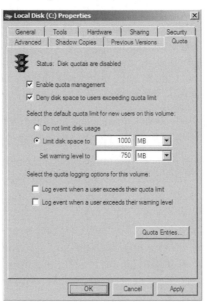

7. Click the Apply button. If a warning box appears, just click OK. This warning is just informing you that the disk may need to be rescanned for the quota.

8. Now that you have set up an umbrella quota to cover everyone, you'll set up a quota that exceeds the umbrella. Click the Quota Entries button.

9. The Quotas Entries for (C:) window appears. You will see some users already listed. These are users who are already using space on the volume. Click the Quota menu at the top, and choose New Quota Entry.

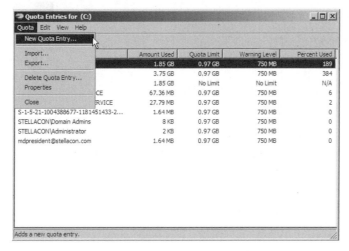

Notice the N/A entry in the Percent Used column. This belongs to the Administrator account, which by default has no limit.

10. On the Select User page, choose a user that you want to allow to exceed the quota (for this example, we used the wpanek account). Click OK.

11. This opens the Add New Quota Entry dialog box. Click the Do Not Limit Disk Usage option, and click OK.

12. You will notice that the new user has no limit. Close the disk quota tool.

Configuring Distributed File System (DFS)

One problem that we have had as network administrators is deciding how to share folders and communicating to the end users how to find our shares. For example, if you share a folder called Stellacon Documents on server A, how do you make sure that your users will find the folder and files within it? The users have to know the server name and the share name. This can be a huge problem if you have hundreds of shares on multiple servers. If you want to have multiple copies of the folder called Stellacon Documents for fault tolerance and load balancing, the problem becomes even more complicated.

Distributed File System (DFS) in Windows Server 2008 offers a simplified way for users to access geographically dispersed files. DFS allows you to set up a tree structure of virtual directories that allow users to connect to shared folders throughout the entire network.

Administrators have the ability to take shared folders that are located on different servers and transparently connect them to one or more DFS namespaces—virtual trees of shared folders throughout an organization.

Administrators can use the DFS tools to choose which shared folders will appear in the namespace and also decide how the names of these shared folders will show up in the virtual tree listing.

Advantages of DFS

One of the advantages of DFS is that when a user views this virtual tree, the shared folders appear to be located on a single machine. Other advantages to DFS include the following:

Simplified data migration   DFS gives you the ability to move data from one location to another without the user needing to know the physical location of the data. Because the users do not need to know the physical location of the shared data, administrators can simply move data from one location to another.

Increased availability of file server data   Other advantages of DFS are availability and reliability. If a client tries to connect to a shared folder in DFS and that folder becomes unavailable, the DFS system will automatically route the user to another replica of the share.

Load sharing   DFS replication allows you to have multiple copies of a shared folder on multiple file servers. The DFS server will balance the load between these multiple folder replicas.

Security integration   Administrators do not need to configure additional security for the DFS shared folders. The shared folders use the NTFS and shared folder permissions that an administrator has already assigned when the share was set up.

Types of DFS

The following are types of DFS:

DFS Replication   Administrators have the ability to manage replication scheduling and bandwidth throttling using the DFS management console. Replication is the process of sharing data between multiple machines. As explained earlier in the section, replicated shared folders allow you balance the load and have fault tolerance.

DFS Namespaces   The DFS Namespace service is the virtual tree listing in the DFS server. An administrator can set up multiple namespaces on the DFS allowing for multiple virtual trees within DFS. DFS Namespaces was previously known just as Distributed File System in Windows 2000 Server and Windows Server 2003.

In Exercise 8.6 we will show how to install the DFS Namespace service on the file server. You need to start the installation using the Server Manager MMC.

EXERCISE 8.6

Installing the DFS Namespace Service

1. Open Server Manager by clicking Start ➢ Administrative Tools ➢ Server Manager.

2. Expand the Roles link in the left window under Server Manager.

3. Click File Services (if File Services has not been installed, install it under New Roles). In the window on the right, scroll down until you see Role Services. Click Add Role Services.

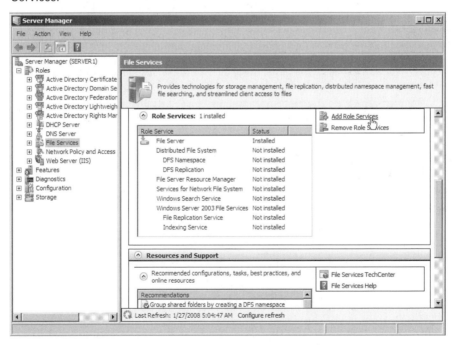

4. On the Select Role Services page, select the Distributed File System box, and click Next.

EXERCISE 8.6 *(continued)*

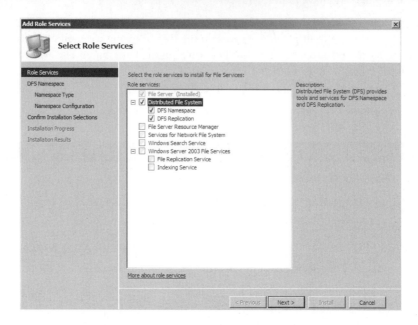

5. On the Create a DFS Namespace page, leave the default of Namespace1, and click Next.

6. On the Select Namespace Type page, make sure Domain-Based Namespace is selected, and click Next.

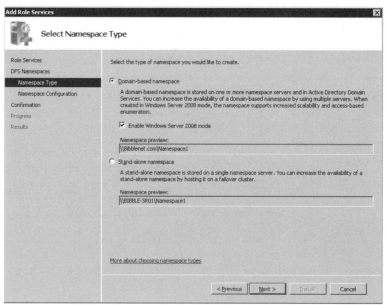

7.   On the Configure Namespace page, click the Add button. This is where you add the shared folders that are going to be part of the DFS tree. The Add Folder window will appear. Click the Browse button, and choose your server name. After you put in your server name, all your shared folders will appear. Choose the Test Share folder you created in Exercise 8.1. Click OK.

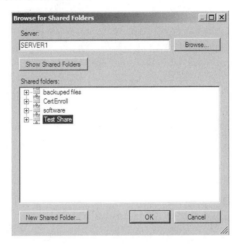

8.   The Add Folder To Namespace page reappears. Test Share should be listed under Folder Name. Click OK.

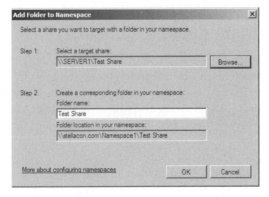

9.   On the Configure Namespace page, click the Next button.

EXERCISE 8.6 *(continued)*

10. On the Confirm Installation Selections page, choose Install.

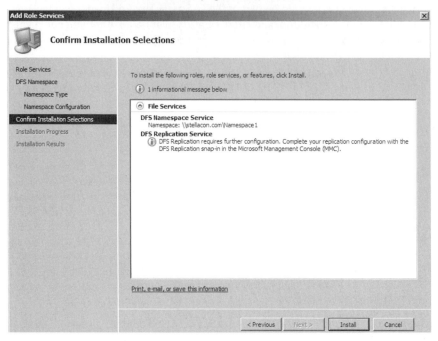

Using the DFS Management Console

Once you have installed DFS, it's time to learn how to manage DFS with the DFS Management MMC. The DFS Management console (see Figure 8.9) gives you one place to do all your DFS configurations. The DFS Management console allows you to set up DFS Replication and DFS Namespace. Another task you can do in the DFS Management console is add a folder target—a folder that you add to the DFS Namespace (the virtual tree) for all your users to share.

In Exercise 8.7, you will create and share a folder and then add that folder target to the DFS namespace you created in Exercise 8.6 (which you must complete before doing Exercise 8.7).

FIGURE 8.9   DFS Management console

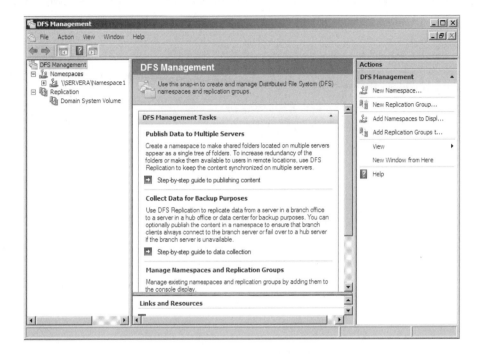

Configuring DFS

1. Create a new folder in the root directory of your C: partition, and name it **DFS Test Folder**.

2. Right-click the DFS Test Folder, and choose Share.

3. In the File Sharing dialog box, enter the names of users you want to share this folder with. In the upper box, enter **Everyone** and then click Add. Note that Everyone appears in the lower box. Click in the Permission Level column next to Everyone, and choose Contributor from the drop-down menu. Then click Share.

4. You see a message that your folder has been shared. Click Done.

5. Open the DFS Management console by clicking Start ➢ Administrative Tools ➢ DFS Management.

EXERCISE 8.7 *(continued)*

6. Under DFS Management, expand Namespaces, right-click your server name, and choose New Folder.

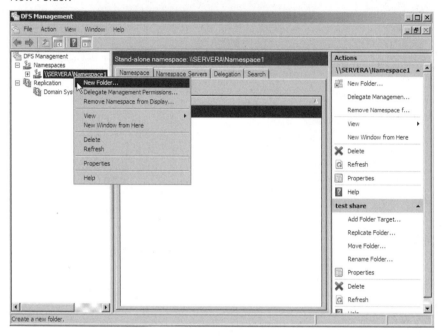

7. On the New Folder page, click the Add button. On the Add Folder Target page, click the Browse button. When the Browse For Shared Folders page appears, choose the new DFS Test Folder you created in step 1. Click OK.

8. The Add Folder Target page reappears. Click OK.

9. The New Folder page reappears. In the Name box, type a display name that will show on the DFS Namespace. We used DFS Test Folder for our example. Click OK.

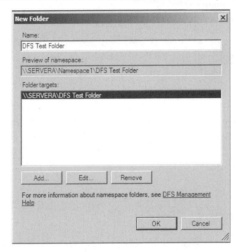

10. You will notice that the new folder has been added to the Namespace listing. Close the DFS Management console.

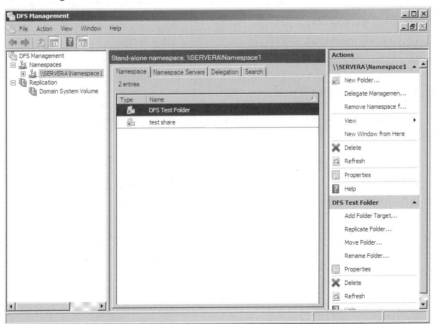

Understanding Printing

One of the most important components on a network is the printer. Printers today are almost as important as the computers themselves. Think about your network. What would your network be like without a printer? Even small networks or home networks have a printer today.

How many printers do you want on your network? It is not feasible to put a printer on every user's desk. What if some users need black and white and some need color? Do you give each user two printers? What if they need laser printing for reports but ink jets will work fine for every other type of print job? These are all questions you must answer before buying any printers for your networks.

This is also where network printers and print servers come into play. *Network printers* are printers that can be directly connected to the network, through some form of network interface card. These printers usually have settings that can be configured for your network needs. For example, if your network uses DHCP, you can set the printer to be a DHCP client.

 Real World Scenario

DHCP and Printing

If you decide to use DHCP, it is a good idea to set up a DHCP reservation. (See Chapter 4.) A DHCP reservation issues the same TCP/IP number to the printer based on the printer's MAC address. This guarantees that your printer will get the same TCP/IP address every time from DHCP.

This helps you when you set the printer up on your client machines. One way to install a printer to a client machine is by the printer's TCP/IP address. If the printer is using DHCP and there is no reservation, the TCP/IP number could change. This would make it almost impossible for you to set the printer up on the client machines by using the printer's TCP/IP address.

By using DHCP reservations, you can hook clients up to the printer by the printer's TCP/IP number, thus giving you another option for your setup strategy.

Print servers are servers that have a connected printer, where the server handles all printing issues. This is an excellent solution for printers that cannot directly connect to the network. Once the printer is connected to the network (through the use of a NIC or a server), the end user just connects to the printer and prints. To the end user, there is no real difference between the two options.

Before an end user can print to a network printer, an administrator must connect, set up, share, and publish the printer for use. An administrator must also set the permissions on the printer to allow users to print to that printer. The following sections will discuss these items in detail.

Creating and Publishing Printers

Once your printer is installed, you must share the printer and then publish the printer to Active Directory before users can print to it. Printers can be published easily within Active Directory. This makes them available to users in your domain.

Exercise 8.8 walks you through the steps you need to take to share and publish a Printer object by having you create and share a printer. To complete the printer installation, you need access to the Windows Server 2008 installation media (via the hard disk, a network share, or the CD drive). If you do not have a printer for this exercise, just choose one from the list and continue the exercise.

EXERCISE 8.8

Creating and Publishing a Printer

1. Click Start ➤ Control Panel ➤ Printers ➤ Add Printer. This starts the Add Printer Wizard.

2. On the Choose A Local Or Network Printer page, select Add A Local Printer. This should automatically take you to the next page. If it does not, click Next.

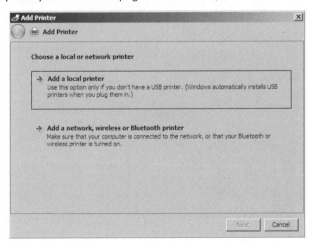

3. On the Choose A Printer Port page, select Use An Existing Port. From the drop-down list beside that option, make sure LPT1: (Printer Port) is selected. Click Next.

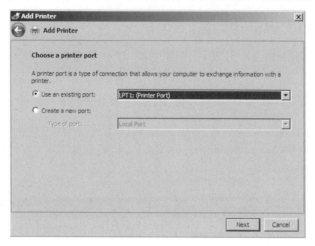

4. On the Install The Printer Driver page, select Generic for the manufacturer, and for the printer, highlight Generic / Text Only. Click Next.

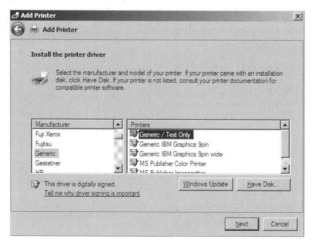

5. On the Type A Printer Name page, type **Text Printer**. Uncheck the Set As The Default Printer box and then click Next.

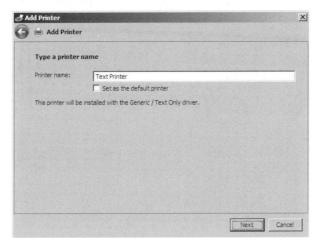

6. The Installing Printer page appears. After the system is finished, the Printer Sharing page appears. Make sure the Share This Printer So That Others On Your Network Can Find And Use It box is selected, and accept the default share name of Text Printer.

7. In the Location section, type **Building 203,** and in the Comment section, add the following comment: **This is a text-only Printer**. Click Next.

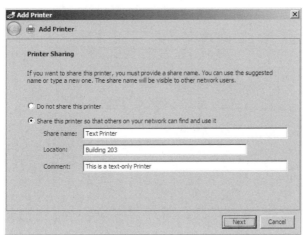

EXERCISE 8.8 *(continued)*

8. On the You've Successfully Added Text Printer page, click Finish.

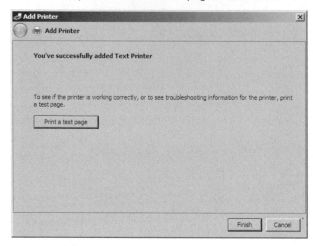

9. Next, you need to verify that the printer will be listed in Active Directory. Click Start ➤ Control Panel ➤ Printers, right-click the Text Printer icon, and select Properties.

10. Next, select the Sharing tab, and ensure that the List In The Directory box is checked. Note that you can also add printer drivers for other operating systems using this tab. Click OK to accept the settings.

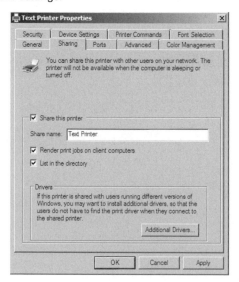

Note that when you create and share a printer this way, an Active Directory Printer object is not displayed within the Active Directory Users And Computers tool. The printer is actually associated with the Computer object to which it is connected. Printer objects in Active Directory are manually created for sharing printers from Windows NT 4 and earlier shared printer resources.

Configuring Printers

The printer has now been installed and published to Active Directory. It's time to set all the different configuration options. To get to the options, right-click the Printer object, and choose Properties. The following are just some of the tabs you can configure:

The General tab   The General tab (see Figure 8.10) allows you to set some basic printer attributes:

- The field at the top of the dialog box contains the display name of the Printer object.
- The Location field should contain text helping users physically locate the printer.
- The Comments field allows an administrator to put in any additional information, such as the printer type.
- The Printing Preferences button takes you to controls allowing you to change the layout and paper type of the printer.

FIGURE 8.10   The General tab of the printer's Properties dialog box

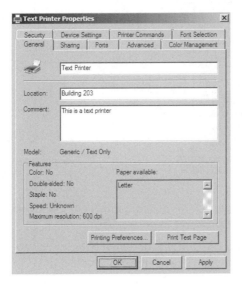

The Sharing tab   The Sharing tab (see Figure 8.11) allows you to configure your printer for sharing on your network. This is what allows users to use a network printer (if they have the proper permissions on the printer).

- The Share This Printer check box allows you to share the printer on the network.

- Share Name is the name your users will see on the network.

- When Render Print Jobs On Client Computers is checked, the client computer caches the print job until the printer is ready to print. If unchecked, the print server will cache the entire job before it prints to the printer.

- When List In The Directory is checked, users can search the directory for the printer.

- The Additional Drivers button allows you to load additional drivers for your clients. It is especially useful for giving access to drivers for older client systems. One advantage of a print server is that the server will automatically download drivers to client computers.

FIGURE 8.11   The Sharing tab of the printer's Properties dialog box

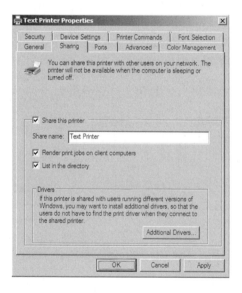

The Ports tab   The Ports tab (see Figure 8.12) allows you to configure the port to which your printer is connected. You can add ports or configure existing ports.

- The port check boxes allow you to choose to which port your printer is connected. Options are the printer port, serial port, local port, and print to file port.

- The Add Port button allows you to add a custom port (for example, a TCP/IP port).

- The Delete Port button allows you to remove a port from the port list.

- The Configure Port button gives you settings to configure an existing port. For example, if you use TCP/IP, this button allows you to change the TCP/IP options.

- Enable Bidirectional Support allows your printer and computer to communicate back and forth. If this check box is disabled, your printer cannot support two-way communications.

- A *printer pool* allows two or more identical printers to share the print load. When a document is sent to the printer pool, the first available printer receives the print job and prints it. Enable Printer Pooling allows a large department or organization to get print jobs done faster. Users do not have to wait for one printer to get their print job. You should follow a couple of rules when setting up a printer pool:

  - All printers in the pool need to be the same model and type.

  - All printers in the pool should be in the same physical location. Print jobs will be printed to the first available printer. If these printers are located all over the company, it may take a user too long to find their print job.

FIGURE 8.12   The Ports tab of the printer's Properties dialog box

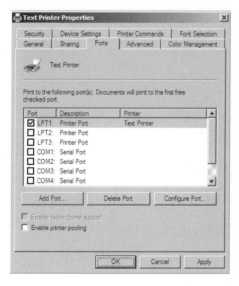

The Advanced tab   The Advanced tab (see Figure 8.13) is where you can set availability, priority, and many other options:

- The availability controls let you set the hours when this printer can be used. You can set it to be always available or available only between the hours you set.

- If multiple print shares are set up to go to the same printer, you can specify a priority with the Priority field for each share. The higher the number, the faster a print job sent to that share will access the printer. The highest priority is 99, and the default (lowest) is 1. If two users send jobs to the same printer at the same time, one with a 99 priority and the other with a 1 priority, the 99 priority would print first.

- Driver is the default driver that the printer is using.

- The print spooling controls let you decide how the print job will spool. You can choose to have the entire job spool first before printing (this ensures that the entire job is received by the print queue before printing), to start printing immediately while the job is still spooling, or to print directly to the printer without spooling (the last option requires a printer with a large amount of RAM on the motherboard).

- Hold Mismatched Documents allows the spooler to hold any print jobs that don't match the setup for the print device.

- Print Spooled Documents First allows a completely spooled printer job to be printed first even if it has a lower-priority number than a job that is still spooling.

- Usually after a print job has been printed, the print queue deletes the print job. If you check the Keep Printed Documents box, the print queue will not delete the print job after it is printed.

- Enable Advanced Printing Features allows you to set some advanced features such as the Page Order and Pages Per Sheet settings.

Color Management tab   This tab allows you to adjust the color of your printing jobs.

FIGURE 8.13   Advanced tab of the printer's Properties dialog box

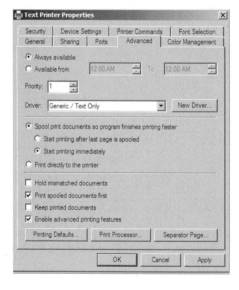

Security tab   The Security tab (see Figure 8.14) is where you can set the permissions for your printer. This allows users to print, manage printers, manage documents, and take advantage of special permissions:

- The Add button allows you to add users and groups to the printer.

- The Remove button allows you to remove users and groups from the printer.

- The following controls, available in the Permissions For Everyone box, apply to everyone on your network:

    - Print gives everyone the right to print to this printer.

    - Manage Printers gives everyone the right to manage this printer, including deleting print jobs, setting priorities, setting availability, and so on.

    - Manage Documents gives everyone the right to manage print jobs.

    - Special Permissions allows you to set unique permissions such as Print, Manage Printers, Read permissions, Change permissions, and Take Ownership.

Migrating Print Servers

In a network environment, an administrator may find it necessary to replace older print servers or to consolidate multiple print servers into one.

FIGURE 8.14   Security tab of the printer's Properties dialog box

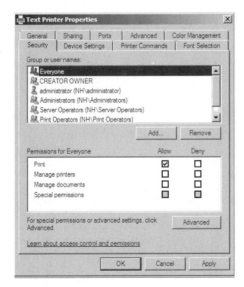

To do this print server migration or replacement, you can use the Printer Migration Wizard or the `Printbrm.exe` command-line tool. These two utilities allow you to export print queues, printer settings, printer ports, and language monitors. These utilities then allow you to import these settings on another print server running Windows Server 2008.

Summary

In this chapter, we discussed file servers and how they can be effective on your network. We discussed sharing folders for users to access, and then we discussed how to publish those share folders to Active Directory.

We discussed NTFS security vs. shared folder permissions. We also discussed how to limit users' hard drive space by setting up disk quotas. We also talked about the Encrypting File System (EFS) and how users can encrypt and compress files.

Next, we discussed Distributed File System (DFS). DFS allows you to set up a tree structure of virtual directories that allow users to connect to shared folders throughout the entire network.

Finally, we discussed print servers and configuring printers. We talked about how to share and publish printers within Active Directory. We discussed print permissions and printer priorities along with print pooling.

Exam Essentials

Learn how resources can be published.   A design goal for Active Directory was to make network resources easier for users to find. With that in mind, you should understand how using published printers and shared folders can simplify network resource management.

Know how to configure offline folders.   Offline folders give you the opportunity to set up folders so that users can work on the data while outside the office and later synchronize it with a master copy. You can set up GPOs to help with offline folder synchronization.

Know how to configure NTFS security.   One of the major advantages of using NTFS over FAT32 is access to additional security features. NTFS allows you to put security at the file and folder layers. NTFS security is in effect whether the user is remote or local to the computer with the data.

Know how to configure shared permissions.   Shared permissions allow you to determine the access a user will receive when connecting to a shared folder. Shared permissions are allowed only at the folder layer and are in effect only when the user is remote to the computer with the shared data.

Understand how NTFS and shared permissions work together.   NTFS and shared permissions are individually additive—you get the highest level of security and permissions within each type. NTFS is always in effect and is the only security available locally. Shared permissions are in effect only when connecting remotely to access the shared data. When the two types of permissions meet, the most restrictive set of permissions applies.

Know how to configure disk quotas.   Disk quotas allow an organization to determine the amount of disk space users can have on a volume of a server. An administrator can set up disk quotas based on volumes or by users. Each volume must have its own separate set of disk quotas.

Know how to configure DFS.   Distributed File System (DFS) in Windows Server 2008 offers a simplified way for users to access geographically dispersed files. The DFS Namespace service allows you to set up a tree structure of virtual directories that allow users to connect to shared folders throughout the entire network.

Know how to configure printing.   We discussed network printers vs. print servers. Understand that when you create a printer, you want to publish the printer within Active Directory so your users can find it throughout the domain. Understand the different printer permissions and how to install print drivers.

Review Questions

1. The company you work for has a multilevel administrative team that is segmented by departments and locations. There are four major locations, and you are in the Northeast group. You have been assigned to the administrative group that is responsible for creating and maintaining network shares for files and printers in your region. The last place you worked was a large Windows NT 4 network, where you had a much wider range of responsibilities. You are excited about the chance to learn more about Windows Server 2008.

    For your first task, you have been given a list of file and printer shares that need to be created for the users in your region. You ask how to create them in Windows Server 2008, and you are told that the process of creating a share is the same as with Windows NT. You create the shares and use NET USE to test them. Everything appears to work fine, so you send out a message that the shares are available. The next day, you start receiving calls from users who say they cannot see any of resources you created. What is the most likely reason for the calls from the users?

    A. You forgot to enable NetBIOS for the shares.

    B. You need to force replication for the shares to appear in the directory.

    C. You need to publish the shares in the directory.

    D. The shares will appear within the normal replication period.

2. You want to publish a printer to Active Directory. In the following dialog box, where would you click in order to accomplish this task?

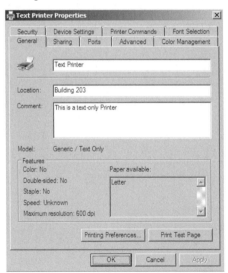

    A. The Sharing tab

    B. The Advanced tab

    C. The Device Settings tab

    D. The Printing Preferences button

3. A systems administrator creates a local Printer object, but it doesn't show up in Active Directory when a user executes a search for all printers. Which of the following are possible reasons for this? (Choose all that apply.)

    A. The printer was not shared.

    B. The printer is offline.

    C. The client does not have permission to view the printer.

    D. The printer is malfunctioning.

4. You are the network administrator for a midsize coffee bean distributor. Your company's network has four Windows 2008 servers, and all clients are running either XP or Vista. Most of your end users use laptops to do their work, and many of them work away from the office. What should you configure to help them work on documents when away from the office?

    A. Online file access

    B. Offline file access

    C. Share permissions

    D. NTFS permissions

5. Your company has decided to implement a Windows 2008 server. The company IT manager before you always used FAT32 as the system partition. Your company wants to know whether it should move to NTFS. Which of the following are some advantages of NTFS? (Choose all that apply.)

    A. Security

    B. Quotas

    C. Compression

    D. Encryption

6. Will, the IT manager for your company, has been asked to give Tylor the rights to read and change documents in the Stellacon Documents folder. The following table shows the current permissions on the shared folder:

Group/User	NTFS	Shared
Sales	Read	Change
Marketing	Modify	Change
R&D	Deny	Full Control
Finance	Read	Read
Tylor	Read	Change

Tylor is a member of the Sales and Finance groups. When Tylor accesses the Stellacon Documents folder, he can read all the files, but the system won't let him change or delete files. What do you need to do to give Tylor the minimum amount of rights to do his job?

A. Give Sales Full Control to shared permissions.

B. Give Tylor Full Control to NTFS security.

C. Give Finance Change to shared permissions.

D. Give Finance Modify to NTFS security.

E. Give Tylor Modify to NTFS security.

7. You are the administrator of your network, which consists of two Windows Server 2008 systems. One of the servers is a domain controller, and the other server is a file server for data storage. The hard drive of the file server is starting to fill up. You do not have the ability to install another hard drive, so you decide to limit the amount of space everyone gets on the hard drive. What do you need to implement to solve your problem?

A. Disk spacing

B. Disk quotas

C. Disk hardening

D. Disk limitations

8. You are the IT manager for your company. You have been asked to give the Admin group the rights to read, change, and assign permissions to documents in the Stellacon Documents folder. The following table shows the current permissions on the Stellacon Documents shared folder:

Group/User	NTFS	Shared
Sales	Read	Change
Marketing	Modify	Change
R&D	Deny	Full Control
Finance	Read	Read
Admin	Change	Change

What do you need to do to give the Admin group the rights to do their job? (Choose all that apply.)

A. Give Sales Full Control to shared permissions.

B. Give Tylor Full Control to NTFS security.

C. Give Admin Full Control to shared permissions.

D. Give Finance Modify to NTFS security.

E. Give Admin Full Control to NTFS security.

9. You are the administrator for a large organization. You have multiple Windows Server 2008 systems that all contain files that need to be shared for all users. The files and folders constantly move among servers, and users are having a hard time finding files they need. What can you implement to help your users out?

A. Encrypting File System (EFS)

B. Distributed File System (DFS)

C. Shared File System (SFS)

D. Published File System (PFS)

10. You have been hired by a small company to implement new Windows Server 2008 systems. The company wants you to set up a server for users' home folder locations. What type of server would you be setting up?

A. PDC server

B. Web server

C. Exchange server

D. File server

11. You are the IT manager for your company. You have been asked to give Jason the rights to read, delete, and change documents in the Stellacon Documents folder. The following table shows the current permissions on the Stellacon Documents shared folder:

Group/User	NTFS	Shared
Sales	Full Control	Change
Marketing	Modify	Change
R&D	Deny	Full Control
Finance	Read	Read
Admin	Change	Change

Jason is a member of the Sales and R&D groups. What do you need to do to give Jason the ability to do his job?

A. Add Jason directly to the folder permissions, and give him the Full Control permission to the NTFS security.

B. Add Jason directly to the folder permissions, and give him the Full Control permission to the Shared permissions.

C. Add Jason directly to the folder permissions, and give him the Modify permission to the NTFS security.

D. Add Jason directly to the folder permissions, and give him the Modify permission to the Shared permission.

12. You are the IT manager for your company. You have been asked to give the Admin group the rights to delete print jobs for any user and also to give users the rights to use the printer. The following table shows the current permissions on the company printer:

Group/User	Printer Permission
Sales	Print
Marketing	Manage Documents
R&D	Manage Documents
Finance	Print
Admin	Print

What do you need to do to give the Admin group the rights to do their job?

A. Give the Admin group Manage Documents rights.

B. Give the Admin group Manage Printer rights.

C. Give the Admin group Manage Users rights.

D. Give the Admin group Manage Print Jobs rights.

13. You have been asked by your company to set up disk quotas. You need to set 250 MB as the maximum amount anyone can use. You want to set a 200 MB warning on all users. You want to make sure that if any user hits the 250 MB limit, they cannot store additional data on the hard drive. Open the following exhibit. Which of the following would you need to do to set up disk quotas? (Choose all that apply.)

    A. Check the Enable Quota Management checkbox

    B. Check the Deny Disk Space To Users Exceeding Quota Limit checkbox

    C. Enable Do Not Limit Disk Usage radio button

    D. Set Limit Disk Space To 250MB and Set Warning Level To 200MB

14. Your company has purchased six new HP laser printers that are all the same model. They want you to set it up so that when a user prints to one of the HP laser printers, any one of the six HP lasers that are available can print the job. How do you set this up?

    A. Printer group

    B. Printer spooling

    C. Printer pool

    D. Printer sharing group

15. You are the administrator for your organization. You have two groups, Sales and Marketing, which use a laser printer. The Sales group prints a lot of invoices and quotes for companies. The Marketing group usually prints large presentations that take a long time to print. You want the Sales group's documents to print before the Marketing group. How do you set this up?

   A. Assign the Marketing group a priority of 100 and the Sales group a priority of 1.

   B. Assign the Marketing group a priority of 99 and the Sales group a priority of 1.

   C. Assign the Marketing group a priority of 1 and the Sales group a priority of 100.

   D. Assign the Marketing group a priority of 1 and the Sales group a priority of 99.

16. Alexandria is a member of the Sales and Marketing departments. There is a shared folder that everyone uses called Stellacon Documents. The following table shows the current permissions on the Stellacon Documents shared folder:

Group/User	NTFS	Shared
Sales	Full Control	Read
Marketing	Modify	Read
R&D	Deny	Full Control
Finance	Read	Read
Admin	Change	Full Control

When Alexandria logs onto the Stellacon Documents folder, what will her local and remote permissions be?

   A. Local would be Full Control, and Remote would be Full Control.

   B. Local would be Read, and Remote would be Read.

   C. Local would be Read, and Remote would be Full Control.

   D. Local would be Full Control, and Remote would be Read.

17. Paige is a member of the R&D and Marketing departments. There is a shared folder that everyone uses called Stellacon Documents. The following table shows the current permissions on the Stellacon Documents shared folder:

Group/User	NTFS	Shared
Sales	Full Control	Read
Marketing	Full Control	Read
R&D	Deny	Full Control
Finance	Read	Read
Admin	Change	Full Control

When Paige logs onto the Stellacon Documents folder, what will her local and remote permissions be?

A. Local would be Full Control, and Remote would be Full Control.

B. Local would be Deny, and Remote would be Deny.

C. Local would be Deny, and Remote would be Full Control.

D. Local would be Full Control, and Remote would be Read.

18. You are the administrator for your organization. You have two groups, Sales and Marketing, that use a laser printer. The sales group prints a lot of invoices and quotes for companies. The Marketing group usually prints large presentations that take a long time to print. You want the Marketing group to print jobs only between 6 p.m. and 6 a.m. How do you set this up?

A. Create two shares to the laser printer. Share 1 would be able to print any time, and Share 2 can print only after 6 p.m. until 6 a.m. Assign the Marketing group to Share 1 and the Sales group to Share 2.

B. Create two shares to the laser printer. Share 1 would be able to print anytime, and Share 2 can print only after 6 a.m. until 6 p.m. Assign the Sales group to Share 1 and the Marketing group to Share 2.

C. Create two shares to the laser printer. Share 1 would be able to print anytime, and Share 2 can print only after 6 a.m. until 6 p.m. Assign the Marketing group to Share 1 and the Sales group to Share 2.

D. Create two shares to the laser printer. Share 1 would be able to print anytime, and Share 2 can print only after 6 p.m. until 6 a.m. Assign the Sales group to Share 1 and the Marketing group to Share 2.

19. Adriana is a member of the Admin, Sales, and Marketing departments. There is a shared folder that everyone uses called Stellacon Documents. The following table shows the current permissions on the Stellacon Documents shared folder:

Group/User	NTFS	Shared
Sales	Full Control	Deny
Marketing	Full Control	Read
R&D	Deny	Full Control
Finance	Read	Read
Admin	Change	Full Control

When Adriana logs onto the Stellacon Documents folder, what will her local and remote permissions be?

A. Local would be Full Control, and Remote would be Deny.

B. Local would be Deny, and Remote would be Deny.

C. Local would be Full Control, and Remote would be Full Control.

D. Local would be Change, and Remote would be Read.

20. Rick is the IT administrator for your company. Rick needs to set up offline file access. Rick wants all users to synchronize with the server when they either log on or log off the network. What is the easiest way to set up synchronization options for all users?

   A. Manually configure synchronization with all users.

   B. Configure a GPO to set synchronization with all users.

   C. Configure the server with the synchronization options.

   D. Configure a GPO to set synchronization with all servers.

Answers to Review Questions

1. C. You need to publish shares in the directory before they are available to the users of the directory. If NetBIOS is still enabled on the network, the shares will be visible to the NetBIOS tools and clients, but you do not have to enable NetBIOS on shares. Although replication must occur before the shares are available in the directory, it is unlikely that the replication will not have occurred by the next day. If this is the case, then you have other problems with the directory as well.

2. A. The Sharing tab contains a check box that you can use to list the printer in Active Directory.

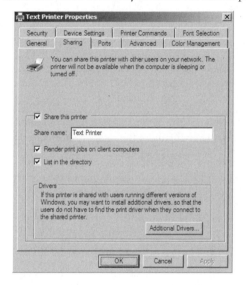

3. A, C. A printer may not show up within Active Directory if the printer has not been shared or if the client does not have permission to view the printer. The printer will appear as an object in Active Directory even if it is offline or malfunctioning.

4. B. Offline files give you the opportunity to set up files and folders so that users can work on the data while outside the office.

5. A, B, C, D. Improved security, quotas, compression, and encryption are all advantages of using NTFS over FAT32. These features are not available in FAT32. The only security you have in FAT32 is shared folder permissions.

6. E. By giving Tylor Modify on the NTFS security setting, you're giving him just enough to do his job. You could also give Sales or Finance the Modify permission, but then everyone in those groups would be able to delete, change, and do more than they all need. Also, Tylor does not need Full Control to change or delete files.

7. B. Disk quotas allow you to limit the amount of space on a volume or partition. You can set an umbrella quota for all users and then implement individual users quotas to bypass the umbrella quota.

8. C, E. The Admin group needs Full Control on the NTFS security and shared permission settings in order to do their job. To be able to give other users permissions, you must have the Full Control permission.

9. B. The Distributed File System (DFS) Namespace service in Windows Server 2008 offers a simplified way for users to access geographically dispersed files. DFS allows you to set up a tree structure of virtual directories to allow users to connect to shared folders throughout the entire network.

10. D. File servers are used for storage of data, especially for users' home folders. Home folders are folder locations for your users to store data that is important and that needs to be backed up.

11. C. By giving Jason Modify on the NTFS security setting, you're giving him just enough to do his job. You could also give R&D Modify, but then everyone in that group would be able to delete, change, and do more than they all need.

12. B. By giving Admin the Manage Printer setting, you're giving the Admin group the right to manage the printer, including giving users the rights to use the printer.

13. A, B, and D. To set up disk quotas, you need to make sure the Enable Quota Management and Deny Disc Space To Users Exceeding Quota limit checkboxes are checked, and set the disk space limit to 250MBs, and set the warning to 200MBs.

14. C. A printer pool allows two or more identical printers to balance the print load among multiple printers. When a document is sent to the printer pool, the first available printer receives the print job and prints it.

15. D. The higher the priority number, the faster the print job gets printed. The lowest-priority number is 1, and the highest-priority number is 99.

16. D. Permissions are additive among themselves. This means you get the highest level of permissions. But when the two permission sets meet, the most restrictive set of permission applies. Local is always the same as NTFS, because shared permissions do not apply locally. So, the Local (NTFS only) would be Full Control. When accessing the folder remotely, the two permission sets meet, and the most restrictive permission, Read, applies.

17. B. Permissions are additive among themselves. This means you get the highest level of permissions. When the two permission sets meet, the most restrictive set of permission applies. Local is always the same as NTFS, because shared permissions do not apply locally. So the Local (NTFS) permissions would be Deny. When accessing the folder remotely, the two permission sets meet, and the most restrictive permission, Deny, applies again.

18. D. Marketing should be able to print only from 6 p.m. until 6 a.m. You need to create two shares and set one share up to print anytime and the other share to be available only during the 6 p.m. until 6 a.m. time frame.

19. A. Permissions are additive among themselves. This means you get the highest level of permissions. When the two permission sets meet, the most restrictive set of permissions applies. Local is always the same as NTFS, because shared permissions do not apply locally. So, the Local (NTFS) permissions would be Full Control. When accessing the folder remotely, the two permission sets meet, and the most restrictive permission, Deny, applies.

20. B. The easiest way to configure synchronization is by using a GPO that applies to all users. In the GPO, you can configure three options for synchronization: Synchronize All Offline Files Before Logging Off, Synchronize All Offline Files When Logging On, and Synchronize Offline Files Before Suspend.

Chapter 9

Monitoring and Managing a Network Infrastructure

MICROSOFT EXAM OBJECTIVES COVERED IN THIS CHAPTER:

✓ **Configure Windows Server Update Services (WSUS) server settings**

- May include but is not limited to: Update type selection, Client settings, Group Policy Object (GPO), Client targeting, Software updates, Test and approval, Disconnected networks

✓ **Gather network data**

- May include but is not limited to: Simple Network Management Protocol (SNMP), Baseline Security Analyzer, Network Monitor

✓ **Monitor event logs**

- May include but is not limited to: Custom views, Application and services logs, Subscriptions, DNS log

✓ **Capture performance data**

- May include but is not limited to: Data Collector Sets, Performance Monitor, Reliability Monitor, Monitoring System Stability Index

✓ **Configure and monitor print services**

- May include but is not limited to: Add counters to Reliability and Performance Monitor to monitor print servers

✓ **Configure shadow copy services**

- May include but is not limited to: Recover previous versions, Set schedule, Set storage locations

✓ **Configure backup and restore**

- May include but is not limited to: Windows Server 2008 Backup Utility, Backup types, Backup schedules, Managing remotely, Restoring data

In this book, we have discussed how to set up clients on a network, and we have discussed how to keep their systems running on the network. In this chapter, we will discuss how to keep their systems updated using Windows Server Update Services (WSUS).

Another important task of an IT team is to keep the network up and running quickly and efficiently. Keeping your network running at its peak performance is one way to make sure your end users continue to use the network and its resources without problems or interruptions. Remember, everyone has clients—salespeople have theirs, and so do we as system administrators. Our clients are the end users. And it's our job to make sure our clients can do their jobs.

When you are working with servers, it is important that you make sure your system's information is safely backed up. Backups become useful when you lose data because of system failures, file corruptions, or accidental modifications of information. As consultants, we can tell you from experience that backups are among the most important tasks that an IT person performs daily. In this chapter, we'll cover the many different types of backup strategies.

Sometimes, performance optimization can feel like a luxury, especially if you can't get your domain controllers to the point where they are actually performing the services you intended for them, such as servicing printers or allowing users to share and work on files. The Windows Server 2008 operating system has been specifically designed to provide high-availability services intended solely to keep your mission-critical applications and data accessible even in times of disaster. Occasionally, however, you might experience intermittent server crashes on one or more of the domain controllers or other computers in your environment.

The most common cause of such problems is a hardware configuration issue. Poorly written device drivers and unsupported hardware can cause problems with system stability. So can failed hardware components (such as system memory). Memory chips can be faulty, electrostatic discharge can ruin them, and other hardware issues can occur. No matter what, a problem with your memory chip spells disaster for your server.

Usually, third-party hardware vendors provide utility disks with their computers that can be used for performing hardware diagnostics on machines to help you find problems. These utilities are a good first step to resolving intermittent server crashes. When these utility disks are used in combination with the troubleshooting tips provided in this and other chapters of this book, you should be able to pinpoint most network-related problems that might occur.

In this chapter, we'll cover the tools and methods for measuring performance and troubleshooting failures in Windows Server 2008. Before you dive into the technical details, however, you should thoroughly understand what you're trying to accomplish and how you'll meet this goal.

Knowing How to Locate and Isolate Problems

It would be almost impossible to cover everything that could go wrong with your Windows Server 2008 system. This book covers many of the most likely and common issues you might come across, but almost anything is possible. Make sure you focus on the methodology used and the steps to locate and isolate a problem even if you are not 100 percent sure what the problem may be. Use online resources to help you locate and troubleshoot the problem. And don't believe everything you read (some things that are posted online can be wrong or misleading); test your changes in a lab environment and try to read multiple sources. Always use Microsoft Support (http://support.microsoft.com/) as one of your sources, because this site is most likely the right source of information (since it's the product vendor). You won't be able to find and fix everything, but knowing where to find critical information that will aid you definitely won't hurt you either. One of the tools that many of us in the industry use is Microsoft TechNet. The full version of TechNet (paid subscription) is a resource that will help you find and fix many real-world issues.

Configuring Windows Server Update Services

To keep your Windows operating systems up-to-date and secure, you can use Windows Update, Automatic Updates, WSUS, and the Microsoft Baseline Security Analyzer:

- Windows Update attaches to the Microsoft website through a user-initiated process and allows Windows users to update their operating systems by downloading updated files (critical and noncritical software updates).

- Automatic Updates extends the functionality of Windows Update by automating the process of updating critical files. With Automatic Updates, you can specify whether you want updates to be automatically downloaded and installed or whether you just want to be notified when updates are available.

- Windows Server Update Services is used to deploy a limited version of Windows Update to a corporate server, which in turn provides the Windows updates to client computers within the corporate network. This allows clients that are limited to what they can access through a firewall to be able to keep their Windows operating systems up-to-date.

- Microsoft Baseline Security Analyzer (MBSA) is a utility you can download from the Microsoft website to ensure that you have the most current security updates.

In the following sections, you will learn how to use these tools.

Windows Update

Windows Update is available through the Microsoft website and is used to provide the most current files for Windows operating systems. Examples of updates include security fixes, critical updates, updated help files, and updated drivers.

You can download Windows Update through the Help And Support page on the Microsoft website. Once it's installed, to search for new updates, click the Scan For Updates link on the Welcome To Windows Update screen.

The results of the Windows Update search will be displayed on the left side of the Windows Update screen. You will see the following options:

- Pick Updates To Install, which lists what updates are available for your computer and includes the following categories:

  - Critical Updates And Service Packs

  - Windows Server 2008 Family

  - Driver Updates

- Review And Install Updates, which allows you to view all updates you have selected to install and installs the updates

- View Installation History, which allows you to track all the updates you have applied to your server

- Personalize Windows Update, which customizes what you see when you use Windows Update

- Get Help And Support, which displays help and support information about Windows Update

Sometimes the updates that are installed require that the computer be restarted before they can take effect. In this event, Windows Update uses a technology called *chained installation*. With chained installation, all updates that require a computer restart are applied before the computer is restarted. This eliminates the need to restart the computer more than once.

The information that is collected by Windows Update includes the operating system and version number, the Internet Explorer version, the software version information for any software that can be updated through Windows Update, the Plug and Play ID numbers for installed hardware, and the region and language settings. Windows Update will also collect the product ID and product key to confirm you are running a licensed copy of Windows, but this information is retained only during the Windows Update session and is not stored. No information that can be used to personally identify users of the Windows Update service is collected.

Windows Automatic Updates

The Automatic Updates application extends the functionality of Windows Update by automating the update process. With Automatic Updates, Windows Server 2008 recognizes when you have an Internet connection and will automatically search for any updates for your computer from the Windows Update website.

If any updates are identified, they will be downloaded using Background Intelligent Transfer Services (BITS). BITS is a bandwidth-throttling technology that allows downloads to occur using idle bandwidth only. This means that downloading automatic updates will not interfere with any other Internet traffic.

If Automatic Updates detects any updates for your computer, you will see an update icon in the notification area of the taskbar.

> To configure Automatic Updates, you must have local administrative rights to the computer on which Automatic Updates is being configured. Requiring administrative rights prevents users from specifying that critical security updates not be installed. In addition, Microsoft must digitally sign any updates that are downloaded.

You configure Automatic Updates by selecting Start ➢ Control Panel ➢ Windows Update. You will see the Check For Updates button shown in Figure 9.1.

FIGURE 9.1   Windows Update control panel

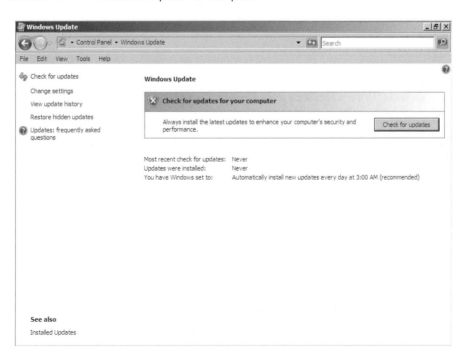

You enable Automatic Updates by clicking the Change Settings link. With this setting enabled, Windows Update software may be automatically updated prior to applying any other updates (see Figure 9.2).

FIGURE 9.2 Change Settings window of the Windows Update control panel

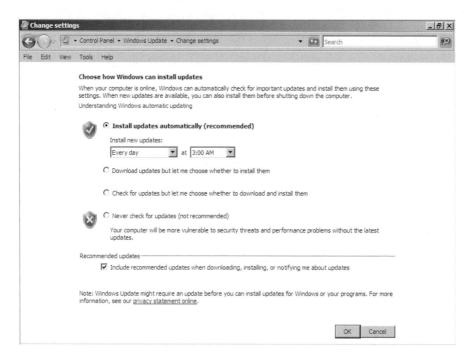

Using Windows Server Update Services

WSUS, formerly known as Software Update Services (SUS), is used to leverage the features of Windows Update within a corporate environment. WSUS downloads Windows updates to a corporate server, which in turn provides the updates to the internal corporate clients. This allows administrators to test and have full control over what updates are deployed within the corporate environment.

WSUS is designed to work in medium-sized corporate networks that are not using System Center Essentials 2007.

We'll cover these topics in the following sections:

- Advantages of using WSUS
- WSUS server requirements
- Configuring the WSUS servers
- WSUS client requirements
- Configuring the WSUS clients

Advantages of Using WSUS

Using WSUS has many advantages:

- WSUS allows an internal server within a private intranet to act as a virtual Windows Update server.

- Administrators have selective control over what updates are posted and deployed from the public Windows Update site. No updates are deployed to client computers unless an administrator first approves them.

- Administrators can control the synchronization of updates from the public Windows Update site to the WSUS server either manually or automatically.

- Administrators can configure Automatic Updates on client computers to access the local WSUS server as opposed to the public Windows Update site.

- WSUS checks each update to verify that Microsoft has digitally signed it. Any updates that are not digitally signed are discarded.

- Administrators can selectively specify whether clients can access updated files from the intranet or from Microsoft's public Windows Update site, which is used to support remote clients.

- Administrators can deploy updates to clients in multiple languages.

- Administrators can configure a WSUS statistics server to log update access, which allows them to track which clients have installed updates. The WSUS server and the WSUS statistics server can coexist on the same computer.

- Administrators can manage WSUS servers remotely using HTTP or HTTPS if their web browser is Internet Explorer 5.5 or newer.

WSUS Server Requirements

To act as a WSUS server, the server must meet the following requirements:

- Must be running Windows 2000 Server with Service Pack 4 or newer, Windows Server 2003, or Windows Server 2008

- Must be using Internet Explorer 6.0 with Service Pack 1 or newer

- Must have all the most current security patches applied

- Must be running Internet Information Services (IIS)

- Must be connected to the network

- Must have an NTFS partition with 100 MB free disk space to install the WSUS server software and 6 GB of free space to store all the update files

- Must use BITS version 2.0

If your WSUS server meets the following system requirements, it can support up to 15,000 WSUS clients:

- Pentium III 700 MHz processor

- 512 MB of RAM

Installing the WSUS Server

WSUS should run on a dedicated server, meaning the server will not run any other applications except IIS, which is required. Microsoft recommends you install a clean or new version of Windows Server 2003 or Windows Server 2008, and apply any service packs or security-related patches.

 WARNING   You should not have any virus-scanning software installed on the server. Virus scanners can mistake WSUS activity for a virus.

Exercise 9.1 walks you through the installation process for WSUS. This exercise requires Internet access to download the free version of WSUS.

EXERCISE 9.1

Installing a WSUS Server

1.   Download the WSUS software from the Microsoft website. The URL for accessing the WSUS home page is http://go.microsoft.com/fwlink/?LinkId=47374.

2.   Double-click WSUSSetup.exe to install the WSUS server.

3.   The welcome screen appears. Click the Next button.

4.   The Installation Mode Selection page appears. Choose Full Server Installation Including Administration Console. Click Next.

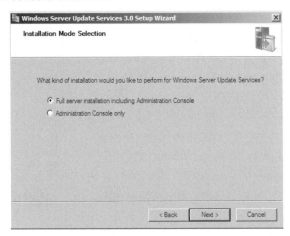

5.   The End-User License Agreement page appears. Carefully read the agreement, and select the I Accept The Terms In The License Agreement option. Click the Next button.

6. On the Required Components Warning page, click Next.

7. The Select Update Source page appears. On this page, you can select the location where update files will be stored. Make sure the Store Updates Locally box is checked. Type the path **C:\WSUS**, and then click Next.

8. The Database Options page appears next. Use Existing Windows Internal Database On This Computer (C:\WSUS) is the default. Leave this default, and click Next.

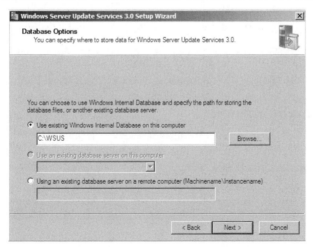

9. The Connecting To SQL Server Instance page appears. Click Next.

10. The Web Site Selection page comes next, where you can choose to serve updates from the default IIS installation or create a specific WSUS website listening on a different TCP port. Since the WSUS server should be dedicated solely to WSUS, you can go with the default here. Click Next.

If you're already running the IIS server to serve web pages and don't want to change that, then you'll need to choose the option to create a WSUS website.

11. The Ready To Install page appears. The client self-update download URL is `http://yourservername/selfupdate` by default. Click Next to begin the installation.

12. The Completing The Windows Server Update Services Setup Wizard page appears. Click the Finish button.

Configuring a WSUS Server

In Exercise 9.2 you will learn how to set the WSUS server options. The sections that follow describe how to set synchronization, approve updates, view the synchronization log, view the approval log, and monitor the WSUS server.

Setting WSUS Server Options

1. If the WSUS administration website is not open, you can open it from Internet Explorer through the URL `http://yourservername/WSUSadmin`.

2. The Windows Server Update Services page appears. Click Options.

3. On the Options page, you can do the following:

Select a proxy server configuration.

Specify the name your clients will use to locate this update server.

Select which server to synchronize content from (Microsoft Windows Update servers or a local Software Update server).

Select how you want to handle new versions of previously approved updates, that is, whether you want them automatically approved.

Select where you want to store updates (maintain the updates on a Windows Server Update Services server or save the updates to a local update folder).

Select which specific products and classifications of updates to synchronize.

Synchronize installation packages for certain locales (specify locales/languages for which you are storing update packages).

Click the Save Settings button when you are done with your configuration settings.

Setting WSUS Server Synchronization

By default, WSUS server synchronization is not defined. You can manually synchronize your server with the Windows Update server, or you can set a synchronization schedule to automate the process.

Test and Approving Updates

Before updates can be deployed to WSUS clients, the administrator should test and approve the updates. The testing should be done on a test machine that is not used for daily tasks.

To approve updates, from the welcome screen, click Updates on the site's toolbar. Make your settings on the Updates page that appears.

Viewing the Synchronization Log

To view the synchronization log, from the welcome screen, click the Reports button on the site's toolbar. The Reports page will appear. Click Synchronization Results to view the results.

Configuring a Disconnected Network

You have the ability to use WSUS on a disconnected network. To do this, you download the updates to the Internet-connected WSUS server. After the download is complete, you can export the updates and then import the updates to the disconnected network.

WSUS Client Requirements

WSUS clients run a special version of Automatic Updates that is designed to support WSUS. The following enhancements to Automatic Updates are included:

- Clients can receive updates from a WSUS server as opposed to the public Microsoft Windows Update site.
- The administrator can schedule when the downloading of updated files will occur.
- Clients can be configured via Group Policy or through editing the registry.
- Updates can occur when an administrative account or nonadministrative account is logged on.

The following client platforms are the only ones that WSUS currently supports:

- Windows 2000 Professional (with Service Pack 3 or newer)
- Windows 2000 Server (with Service Pack 3 or newer)
- Windows 2000 Advanced Server (with Service Pack 2 or newer)
- Windows XP Home Edition (with Service Pack 1 or newer)
- Windows XP Professional (with Service Pack 1 or newer)
- Windows Server 2003 (all platforms)
- Windows Vista (all platforms)
- Windows Server 2008 (all platforms)

Configuring the WSUS Clients

You can configure WSUS clients in two ways. The method you use depends on whether you use Active Directory in your network.

In a nonenterprise network (not running Active Directory), you would configure Automatic Updates through the control panel using the same process that was defined in the section "Windows Automatic Updates" earlier in this chapter. Each client's registry would then be edited to reflect the location of the server providing the automatic updates.

Within an enterprise network, using Active Directory, you would typically see Automatic Updates configured through Group Policy. Group policies are used to manage configuration and security setting via Active Directory. Group Policy is also used to specify what server a client will use for Automatic Updates. If Automatic Updates are configured through Group Policy, the user will not be able to change Automatic Updates settings by choosing Control Panel ➤ System (for XP and prior) or Windows Update (for Vista and Server 2008).

Configuring a Client in a Non–Active Directory Network

The easiest way to configure the client to use Automatic Updates is by using the control panel. However, you can also configure Automatic Updates through the registry. The registry is a database of all your server settings; you can access it by choosing Start ➤ Run and typing **regedit** in the Run dialog box. Automatic Updates settings are defined through HKEY_LOCAL_MACHINE\ Software\Policies\Microsoft\Windows\WindowsUpdate\AU.

Table 9.1 lists some of the registry options that you can configure for Automatic Updates.

TABLE 9.1   Selected Registry Keys and Values for Automatic Updates

Registry Key	Options for Values
NoAutoUpdate	0: Automatic Updates are enabled (default).
	1: Automatic Updates are disabled.
	2: Notify of download and installation.
	3: Autodownload and notify of installation.
	4: Autodownload and schedule installation.
	5: Automatic Updates is required but end users can configure.
ScheduledInstallDay	1: Sunday.
	2: Monday.
	3: Tuesday.
	4: Wednesday.
	5: Thursday.
	6: Friday.
	7: Saturday.
UseWUServer	0: Use public Microsoft Windows Update site.
	1: Use server specified in WUServer entry.

To specify what server will be used as the Windows Update server, you edit two registry keys, which are found at HKEY_LOCAL_MACHINE\Software\Policies\Microsoft\Windows\ WindowsUpdate:

- The WUServer key sets the Windows Update server using the server's HTTP name, for example, http://intranetSUS.

- The WUStatusServer key sets the Windows Update intranet WSUS statistics server by using the server's HTTP name, for example, http://intranetSUS.

Configuring a Client in an Active Directory Network

If the WSUS client is part of an enterprise network using Active Directory, you would configure the client via Group Policy. In Exercise 9.3, we will walk through the steps needed to configure the GPO for WSUS clients. The Group Policy Management Console (GPMC) needs to be installed to complete this exercise. If you don't have the GPMC installed, you can install it using the Server Manager utility.

EXERCISE 9.3

Configuring a GPO for WSUS

1. Open the GPMC by clicking Start ➢ Administrative Tools ➢ Group Policy Management.

2. Expand the forest, domains, and your domain name. Under your domain name, click Default Domain Policy. Right-click, and choose Edit.

3. Under the Computer Configuration section, expand Administrative Templates ➢ Windows Components ➢ Windows Update.

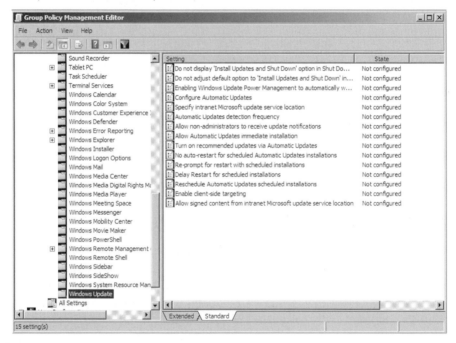

4.   In the right pane, double-click the Configure Automatic Updates option. The Configure Automatic Updates Properties dialog box appears. Click the Enabled button. Then in the drop-down list, choose Auto Download And Notify For Install. Click OK.

The Configure Automatic Updating drop-down list has four options:

Notify For Download And Notify For Install

Auto Download And Notify For Install

Auto Download And Schedule The Install

Allow Local Admin To Choose Settings

The schedule settings apply only if you choose Auto Download And Schedule The Install. The settings you can choose are the install day and the install time.

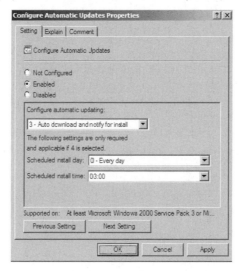

5.   Double-click Specify Intranet Microsoft Update Service Location Properties. This setting allows you to specify the server from which the clients will get the updates. Click Enabled. In the two server name boxes, enter *//**servername** (the name of the server you installed WSUS on in Exercise 9.1). Click OK.

EXERCISE 9.3 *(continued)*

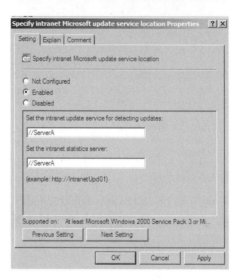

6. To configure the rescheduling of automatic updates, double-click Reschedule Automatic Updates Scheduled Installations. You can enable and schedule the amount of time that Automatic Updates waits after system start-up before it attempts to proceed with a scheduled installation that was previously missed. Click Enabled. Enter **10** in the Startup (Minutes) box. Click OK.

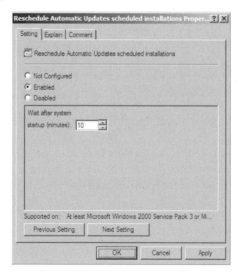

7. To configure autorestart for scheduled Automatic Updates installations, double-click No Auto-Restart For Scheduled Automatic Updates Installations. By enabling this option, the computer is not required to restart after an update. Enable this option, and click OK.

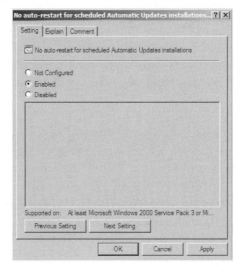

8. Close the GPMC.

Overview of Windows Server 2008 Performance Monitoring

The first step in any performance optimization strategy is to accurately and consistently measure performance. The insight that you'll gain from monitoring factors such as network and system utilization will be extremely useful when you measure the effects of any changes.

The overall process of performance monitoring usually involves the following steps:

1. Establish a baseline of current performance.

2. Identify the bottleneck(s).

3. Plan for and implement changes.

4. Measure the effects of the changes.

5. Repeat the process, based on business needs.

Note that the performance optimization process is never really finished because you can always try to gain more performance from your system by modifying settings and applying other well-known tweaks. Before you get discouraged, realize that you'll reach some level of performance that you and your network and system users consider acceptable enough that it's not worth the additional effort it'll take to optimize performance further. Also note that as your network and system load increases (more users or users doing more), so will the need to reiterate this process. By continuing to monitor, measure, and optimize, you will keep ahead of the pack and keep your end users happy.

Now that you have an idea of the overall process, let's focus on how changes should be made. Some important ideas to keep in mind when monitoring performance include the following:

Plan changes carefully   Here's a rule of thumb we always try to follow: an hour of planning can save you a week of work. When you are working in an easy-to-use GUI-based operating system like Windows Server 2008, it's tempting to randomly remove a check mark here or there and then retest the performance. You should resist the urge to do this because some changes can cause large decreases in performance or can impact functionality. Before you make haphazard changes (especially on production servers), take the time to learn about, plan for, and test your changes. Plan for outages and testing accordingly.

Utilize a test environment   Test in a test lab that simulates a production environment. Do not make changes on production environments without first giving warning. Ideally, change production environments in off-hours when fewer network and system users will be affected. Making haphazard changes in a production environment can cause serious problems. These problems will likely outweigh any benefits you could receive from making performance tweaks.

Make only one change at a time   The golden rule of scientific experiments is that you should always keep track of as many variables as possible. When the topic is server optimization, this roughly translates into making only one change at a time.

One of the problems with making multiple system changes is that, although you may have improved performance overall, it's hard to determine exactly *which* change created the positive effects. It's also possible, for example, that changing one parameter increased performance greatly, while changing another decreased it slightly. Although the overall result was an increase in performance, you should identify the second, performance-reducing option so the same mistake is not made again. To reduce the chance of obtaining misleading results, always try to make only one change at a time.

But the main reason to make one change at a time is that if you do make a mistake or create an unexpected issue, you can easily "back out" of the change. If you make two or three changes at the same time and are not sure which one created the problem, you will have to undo all the changes and then make one alteration at a time to find the problem. If you make only one change at a time and follow that methodology every time, you won't find yourself in this situation.

WARNING   It's important to remember that many changes (such as registry changes) take place immediately; they do not need to be explicitly applied. Once the change is made, it's live. Be careful to plan your changes wisely.

Ensure consistency in measurements   When you are monitoring performance, consistency is extremely important. You should strive to have repeatable and accurate measurements. Controlling variables, such as system load at various times during the day, can help.

Assume, for instance, that you want to measure the number of transactions that you can simulate on the accounting database server within an hour. The results would be widely different if you ran the test during the month-end accounting close than if you ran the test on a Sunday morning. By running the same tests when the server is under a relatively static amount of load, you will be able to get more accurate measurements.

Maintain a performance history   In the introduction to this chapter, we mentioned that the performance optimization cycle is a continuous improvement process. Because many changes may be made over time, it is important to keep track of the changes that have been made and the results you experienced. Documenting this knowledge will help solve similar problems if they arise. We understand that many IT professionals do not like to document, but documentation can make life much easier in the long run.

As you can see, you need to keep a lot of factors in mind when optimizing performance. Although this might seem like a lot to digest and remember, do not fear; as a systems administrator, you will learn some of the rules you need to know to keep your system running optimally. Fortunately, the tools included with Windows Server 2008 can help you organize the process and take measurements. Now that you have a good overview of the process, let's move on to look at the tools that can be used to set it in motion.

Using Windows Server 2008 Performance Tools

Because performance monitoring and optimization are vital functions in network environments of any size, Windows Server 2008 includes several performance-related tools.

Introducing the Reliability and Performance Monitor

The first and most useful tool is the Windows Server 2008 Reliability and Performance Monitor, which was designed to allow users and systems administrators to monitor performance statistics for various operating system parameters. Specifically, you can collect, store, and analyze information about CPU, memory, disk, and network resources using this tool, and these are only a handful of the things you can monitor. By collecting and analyzing performance values, system administrators can identify many potential problems. As you'll see later in this chapter, you can also use the Reliability and Performance Monitor to monitor the performance of your network and its various components.

You can use the Reliability and Performance Monitor in the following ways:

Reliability and Performance Monitor ActiveX control   The Windows Server 2008 Reliability and Performance Monitor is an ActiveX control that you can place within other applications.

Examples of applications that can host the Reliability and Performance Monitor control include web browsers and client programs such as Microsoft Office's Word XP or Excel XP. This functionality can make it easy for applications developers and systems administrators to incorporate the Reliability and Performance Monitor into their own tools and applications.

Reliability and Performance Monitor MMC   For more common performance monitoring functions, you'll want to use the built-in Microsoft Management Console (MMC) version of the Reliability and Performance Monitor called the Performance Monitor.

System Stability Index   The System Stability Index is a numerical value from 1 (least stable) to 10 (most stable) that represents the stability of your network. The Reliability and Performance Monitor calculates and creates the System Stability Index. You can view a graph of this index value. The graph can help a network administrator identify when the network started encountering problems. The System Stability Index also offers side-by-side comparisons. An administrator can view when system changes occurred (installing applications, devices, or drivers) and when system problems started to occur. This way you can determine whether any system changes caused the problems that you are encountering.

Data Collector Sets   Windows Server 2008 Reliability and Performance Monitor includes the new Data Collector Set. This tool works with performance logs, telling Performance Monitor where the logs are stored and when the log needs to run. The Data Collector Sets also define the credentials used to run the set.

To access the Reliability and Performance Monitor MMC, you open Computer Management in the Administrative Tools program group within your Start menu. This launches the Reliability and Performance MMC and loads and initializes Reliability and Performance Monitor with a handful of default counters.

You can choose from many different methods of monitoring performance when you are using Performance Monitor. A couple of examples are listed here:

- You can look at a snapshot of current activity for a few of the most important counters; this allows you to find areas of potential bottlenecks and monitor the load on your servers at a certain point in time.

- You can save information to a log file for historical reporting and later analysis. This type of information is useful, for example, if you want to compare the load on your servers from three months ago to the current load.

You'll get to take a closer look at this method and many others as you examine Performance Monitor in more detail.

In the following sections, you'll learn about the basics of working with the Windows Server 2008 Performance Monitor and other performance tools. Then, you'll apply these tools and techniques when you monitor the performance of your network.

Your Performance Monitor grows as your system grows, and whenever you add services to Windows Server 2008 (such as installing Exchange Server 2007 SP1), you also add to what you can monitor. You should make sure that, as you install services, you take a look at what it is you can monitor.

Deciding What to Monitor

The first step in monitoring performance is to decide *what* you want to monitor. In Windows Server 2008, the operating system and related services include hundreds of performance statistics that you can track easily. All these performance statistics fall into three main categories that you can choose to measure:

Performance objects   A performance object within Performance Monitor is a collection of various performance statistics that you can monitor. Performance objects are based on various areas of system resources. For example, there are performance objects for the processor and memory, as well as for specific services such as web services.

Counters   Counters are the actual parameters measured by Performance Monitor. They are specific items that are grouped within performance objects. For example, within the Processor performance object, there is a counter for % Processor Time. This counter displays one type of detailed information about the Processor performance object (specifically, the amount of total CPU time all the processes on the system are using). Another set of counters you can use will allow you to monitor print servers.

Instances   Some counters will have *instances*. An instance further identifies which performance parameter the counter is measuring. A simple example is a server with two CPUs. If you decide you want to monitor processor usage (using the Processor performance object)—specifically, utilization (the % Total Utilization counter)—you must still specify *which* CPU(s) you want to measure. In this example, you would have the choice of monitoring either of the two CPUs or a total value for both (using the Total instance).

To specify which performance objects, counters, and instances you want to monitor, you add them to Performance Monitor using the Add Counters dialog box. Figure 9.3 shows the various options that are available when you add new counters to monitor using Performance Monitor.

The items that you will be able to monitor will be based on your hardware and software configuration. For example, if you have not installed and configured the IIS, the options available within the Web Server performance object will not be available. Or, if you have multiple network adapters or CPUs in the server, you will have the option of viewing each instance separately or as part of the total value. You'll see which counters are generally most useful later in this chapter.

Viewing Performance Information

The Windows Server 2008 Performance Monitor was designed to show information in a clear and easy-to-understand format. Performance objects, counters, and instances may be displayed in each of three views. This flexibility allows systems administrators to quickly and easily define the information they want to see once and then choose how it will be displayed based on specific needs. Most likely you will use only one view, but it's helpful to know what other views are available depending on what it is you are trying to assess.

FIGURE 9.3 Adding a new Performance Monitor counter

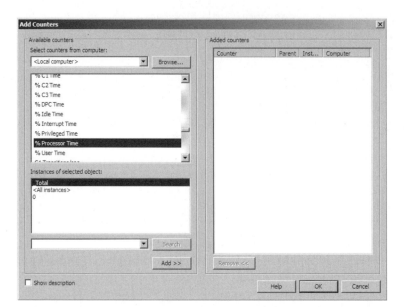

You can use the following main views to review statistics and information on performance:

Graph view The Graph view is the default display that is presented when you first access the Windows Server 2008 Performance Monitor. The chart displays values using the vertical axis and time using the horizontal axis. This view is useful if you want to display values over a period of time or see the changes in these values over that time period. Each point that is plotted on the graph is based on an average value calculated during the sample interval for the measurement being made. For example, you may notice overall CPU utilization starting at a low value at the beginning of the chart and then becoming much higher during later measurements. This indicates that the server has become busier (specifically, with CPU-intensive processes). Figure 9.4 provides an example of the Graph view.

A quick way to get to the Performance Console and view Performance Monitor is to select Start ➤ Run and enter **perfmon** in the Open box. The Performance Console opens directly to Performance Monitor.

Histogram view The Histogram view shows performance statistics and information using a set of relative bar charts. This view is useful if you want to see a snapshot of the latest value for a given counter. For example, if you were interested in viewing a snapshot of current system performance statistics during each refresh interval, the length of each of the bars in the display would give you a visual representation of each value. It would also allow you to visually compare measurements relative to each other. You can set the histogram to display an average measurement as well as minimum and maximum thresholds. Figure 9.5 shows a typical Histogram view.

FIGURE 9.4   Viewing information in Performance Monitor Graph view

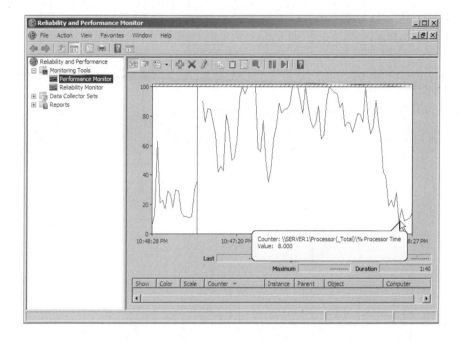

FIGURE 9.5   Viewing information in Performance Monitor Histogram view

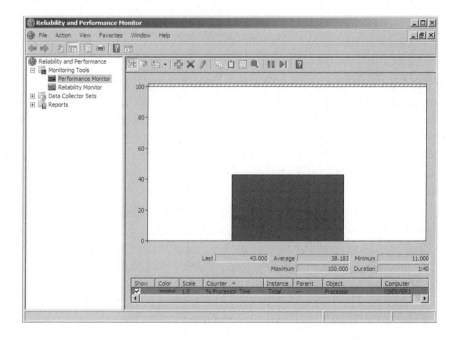

Report view   Like the Histogram view, the Report view shows performance statistics based on the latest measurement. You can see an average measurement as well as minimum and maximum thresholds. This view is most useful for determining exact values because it provides information in numeric terms, whereas the Chart and Histogram views provide information graphically. Figure 9.6 provides an example of the type of information you'll see in the Report view.

FIGURE 9.6   Viewing information in Performance Monitor Report view

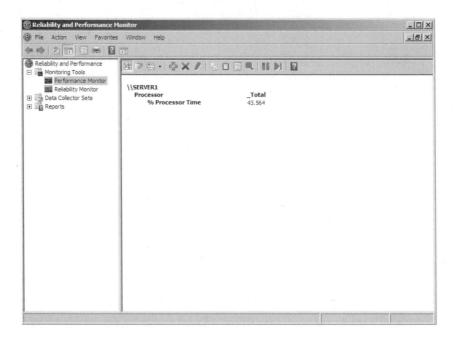

Managing Performance Monitor Properties

You can specify additional settings for viewing performance information within the properties of Performance Monitor. You can access these options by clicking the Properties button in the taskbar or by right-clicking Performance Monitor display and selecting Properties. You can change these additional settings by using the following tabs:

General tab   On the General tab (shown in Figure 9.7), you can specify several options that relate to Performance Monitor views:

- You can enable or disable legends (which display information about the various counters), the value bar, and the toolbar.

- For the Report and Histogram views, you can choose which type of information is displayed. The options are Default, Current, Minimum, Maximum, and Average. What you see with each of these options depends on the type of data being collected. These options are not available for the Graph view, because the Graph view displays an average value over a period of time (the sample interval).

- You can also choose the graph elements. By default, the display will be set to update every second. If you want to update less often, you should increase the number of seconds between updates.

Source tab   On the Source tab (shown in Figure 9.8), you can specify the source for the performance information you want to view. Options include current activity (the default setting) or data from a log file. If you choose to analyze information from a log file, you can also specify the time range for which you want to view statistics. We'll cover these selections in the next section.

FIGURE 9.7   General tab of Performance Monitor Properties dialog box

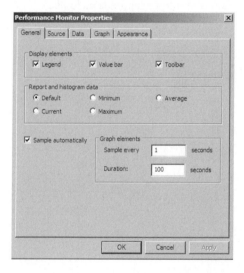

FIGURE 9.8   Source tab of Performance Monitor Properties dialog box

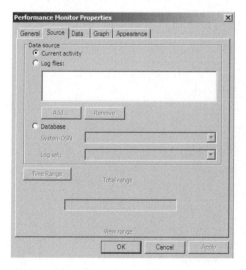

Data tab   The Data tab (shown in Figure 9.9) lists the counters that have been added to the Performance Monitor display. These counters apply to the Chart, Histogram, and Report views. Using this interface, you can also add or remove any of the counters and change the properties, such as the width, style, and color of the line and the scale used for display.

Graph tab   On the Graph tab (shown in Figure 9.10), you can specify certain options that will allow you to customize the display of Performance Monitor views. First you can specify what type of view you want to see (Line, Histogram, or Report). Then you can add a title for the graph, specify a label for the vertical axis, choose to display grids, and specify the vertical scale range.

FIGURE 9.9   The Data tab of Performance Monitor Properties dialog box

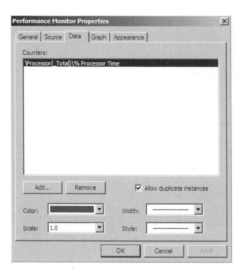

FIGURE 9.10   The Graph tab of Performance Monitor Properties dialog box

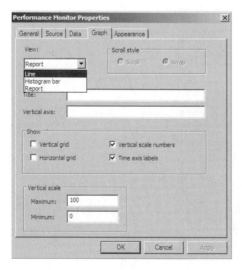

Appearance tab   Using the Appearance tab (see Figure 9.11), you can specify the colors for the areas of the display, such as the background and foreground. You can also specify the fonts that are used to display counter values in Performance Monitor views. You can change settings to find a suitable balance between readability and the amount of information shown on one screen. Finally, you can set up the properties for a border.

FIGURE 9.11   The Appearance tab of Performance Monitor Properties dialog box

Now that you have an idea of the types of information Performance Monitor tracks and how this data is displayed, take a look at another feature—saving and analyzing performance data.

Saving and Analyzing Data with Performance Logs and Alerts

One of the most important aspects of monitoring performance is that it should be done over a given period of time (referred to as a *baseline*). So far, we have discussed how you can use Performance Monitor to view statistics in real time. We have, however, also alluded to using Performance Monitor to save data for later analysis. Now let's take a look at how you can do this.

When viewing information in Performance Monitor, you have two main options with respect to the data on display:

View Current Activity   When you first open the Performance icon from the Administrative Tools folder, the default option is to view data obtained from current system information. This method of viewing measures and displays various real-time statistics on the system's performance.

View Log File Data   This option allows you to view information that was previously saved to a log file. Although the performance objects, counters, and instances may appear to be the same as those viewed using the View Current Activity option, the information itself was actually captured at a previous point in time and stored into a log file.

Log files for the View Log File Data option are created in the Performance Logs and Alerts section of the Windows Server 2008 Performance tool.

Three items allow you to customize how the data is collected in the log files:

Counter logs   *Counter logs* record performance statistics based on the various performance objects, counters, and instances available in Performance Monitor. The values are updated based on a time interval setting and are saved to a file for later analysis.

Circular logging   In *circular logging*, the data that is stored within a file is overwritten as new data is entered into the log. This is a useful method of logging if you want to record information only for a certain time frame (for example, the past four hours). Circular logging also conserves disk space by ensuring that the performance log file will not continue to grow over certain limits.

Linear logging   In linear logging, data is never deleted from the log files, and new information is added to the end of the log file. The result is a log file that continually grows. The benefit is that all historical information is retained.

Now that you have an idea of the types of functions that are supported by the Windows Server 2008 Performance tools, you can learn how you can apply this information to the task at hand—monitoring and troubleshooting your Windows network.

 Real World Scenario

Real-World Performance Monitoring

In our daily jobs as systems engineers and administrators, we come across systems that are in need of our help...and may even ask for it. You, of course, check your Event Viewer and Performance Monitor and perform other tasks that help you troubleshoot. But what is really the most common problem that occurs? From our experience, we'd say that many times you suffer performance problems if you have your Windows Server 2008 operating system installed on a subpar system. Either the server hardware isn't enterprise class or the minimum hardware requirements weren't addressed. Most production servers suffer from slow response times, lagging, and so on, because money wasn't spent where it should have been—on the server's hardware requirements.

Take a look at www.microsoft.com/windowsserver2008/evaluation/overview.mspx to see the minimum Windows Server 2008 requirements. You have to make sure you follow these minimum requirements. That's not all, though; as you will see in this chapter, most times the minimum requirements are just that—the bare minimum and not necessarily good enough, especially if you are running many services on your server or you have many network clients who will access the server.

Would you drive a truck over a glass bridge? No. Then why would you run an enterprise-class server operating system hosting a mission-critical application such as Active Directory, email, and messaging on an antiquated desktop system? This seems illogical when you read it, but in practice, it's common to find budgets squeezed to the point where your secondary domain controller is running on a high-end desktop. Just make sure you consider this when you deploy a new system. Once you deploy it, open Performance Monitor, and see whether you are having issues just opening and running programs on the server itself.

It's also common to blame the network first, but that is usually not the problem at all. Be careful of false positives, and keep your mind focused on finding the root of the problem. If you come across other problems, document them, but continue to focus on finding (and fixing) the real issue.

If your enterprise-level servers aren't running with Redundant Array of Independent Disks (RAID), then you will most likely need an upgrade on your system hardware. Most enterprise-level server systems come with RAID as the minimum fault tolerance you should have on any server of any size. RAID can help you in a pinch; when you lose a disk—and you will, based on the Mean Time Between Failure (MTBF)—you can quickly recover with minimal downtime and no loss of data.

Using Other Performance Monitoring Tools

Performance Monitor allows you to monitor different parameters of the Windows Server 2008 operating system and associated services and applications. However, you can also use three other tools to monitor performance in Windows Server 2008. They are the Network Monitor, Task Manager, and Event Viewer. All three of these tools are useful for monitoring different areas of overall system performance and for examining details related to specific system events. In the following sections, you'll take a quick look at these tools and how you can best use them.

The Network Monitor

Although Performance Monitor is a great tool for viewing overall network performance statistics, it isn't equipped for packet-level analysis and doesn't give you much insight into what types of network traffic are traveling on the wire. That's where the Network Monitor tool comes in. The Network Monitor has two main components: the Network Monitor Agent and the Network Monitor tool.

The Network Monitor Agent is available for use with Windows 2000, XP, Server 2003, and Server 2008. The agent allows you to track network packets. When you install the Network Monitor Agent, you will also be able to access the Network Segment System Monitor counter.

On Windows Server 2008 computers, you'll see the Network Monitor icon appear in the Administrative Tools program group. You can use the Network Monitor tool to capture data as it travels on your network.

A version of Network Monitor is available for free with Windows Server 2008. The full version of Network Monitor is available at Microsoft's download server. For more information, see www.microsoft.com/downloads/.

Once you have captured the data of interest, you can save it to a capture file or further analyze it using the Network Monitor. Experienced network and systems administrators can use this information to determine how applications are communicating and the types of data that are being passed via the network.

 For the exam, you don't need to understand the detailed information that Network Monitor displays, but you should be aware of the types of information that you can view and when you should use Network Monitor.

The Task Manager

Performance Monitor is designed to allow you to keep track of specific aspects of system performance over time. But what do you do if you want to get a quick snapshot of what the local system is doing? Creating a System Monitor chart, adding counters, and choosing a view is overkill. Fortunately, the Windows Server 2008 Task Manager has been designed to provide a quick overview of important system performance statistics without requiring any configuration. Better yet, it's always readily available.

You can easily access the Task Manager in several ways:

- Right-click the Windows taskbar, and then click Task Manager.

- Press Ctrl+Alt+Del, and then select Task Manager.

- Press Ctrl+Shift+Esc.

Each of these methods allows you to quickly access a snapshot of the current system performance.

Once you access the Task Manager, you will see the following five tabs:

Applications tab   The Applications tab (see Figure 9.12) lists the applications currently running on the local computer. This is a good place to determine which programs are running on the system. You can also use this tab to shut down any applications whose status is listed as Not Responding (meaning either that the application has crashed or that it is performing operations and not responding to Windows Server 2008).

Processes tab   The Processes tab shows you all the processes that are currently running on the local computer. By default, you'll be able to view how much CPU time and memory a particular process is using. By clicking any of the columns, you can quickly sort by the data values in that particular column. This is useful, for example, if you want to find out which processes are using the most memory on your server.

By accessing the performance objects in the View menu, you can add columns to the Processes tab. Figure 9.13 shows a list of the current processes running on a Windows Server 2008 computer.

FIGURE 9.12   The Applications tab of the Task Manager

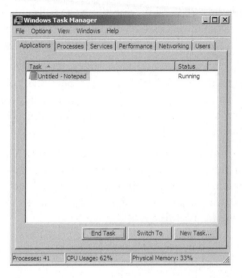

FIGURE 9.13   Viewing process statistics and information using the Task Manager

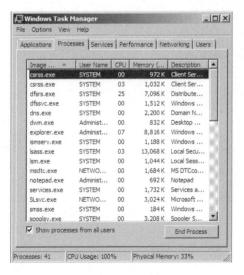

Services tab   The Services tab (see Figure 9.14) shows you what services are currently running on the system. From this location you can stop a service from running by right-clicking the service and choosing Stop. The Services button launches the Services MMC.

Performance tab   One of the problems with using Performance Monitor to get a quick snapshot of system performance is that you have to add counters to a chart. Most systems administrators are too busy to take the time to do this when all they need is basic CPU and memory information. That's where the Performance tab of the Task Manager comes in. Using the Performance tab, you can view details about how memory is allocated on the computer and how much of the CPU is utilized (see Figure 9.15).

Networking tab   Like the Performance tab, the Networking tab (see Figure 9.16) displays a graph of the current network utilization. The active connections are displayed at the bottom of the tab along with their connection speed, percentage of utilization, and status. The graph in the top part of the tab displays the percentage of utilization in real time.

Users tab   The Users tab (see Figure 9.17) lists the currently active user accounts. This is particularly helpful if you want to see who is online and quickly log off or disconnect users. You can also send a console message to any remote user in the list by clicking the Send Message button. (The button is grayed out in Figure 10.15 because you cannot send a message to yourself. If you select a different user, the button will be available.)

FIGURE 9.14   Viewing services information using the Task Manager

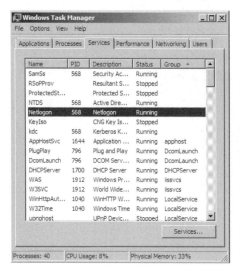

FIGURE 9.15   Viewing CPU and memory performance information using the Task Manager

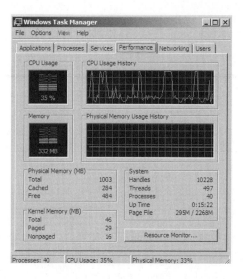

FIGURE 9.16   Viewing network information using the Task Manager

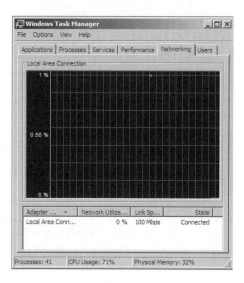

FIGURE 9.17 Viewing user information using the Task Manager

As you can see, the Task Manager is useful for quickly providing important information about the system. Once you get used to using the Task Manager, you won't be able to get by without it!

 Make sure you use Task Manager and familiarize yourself with all that it can do; you can end processes that have become intermittent, kill applications that may hang the system, view NIC performance, and so on. In addition, you can access this tool quickly to get an idea of what could be causing you problems. Event Viewer, Network Monitor, and Performance Monitor are all great tools for getting granular information on potential problems.

The Event Viewer

The Event Viewer is also useful for monitoring network information. Specifically, you can use the logs to view any information, warnings, or alerts related to the proper functioning of the network. You can access the Event Viewer by selecting Start ➤ Programs ➤ Administrative Tools ➤ Event Viewer. Clicking any of the items in the left pane displays the various events that have been logged for each item. Figure 9.18 shows the contents of Directory Service log.

Each event is preceded by a blue "i" icon. That icon designates that these events are informational and do not indicate problems with the network. Rather, they record benign events such as Active Directory start-up or a domain controller finding a Global Catalog server.

FIGURE 9.18   The Directory Service log in Event Viewer

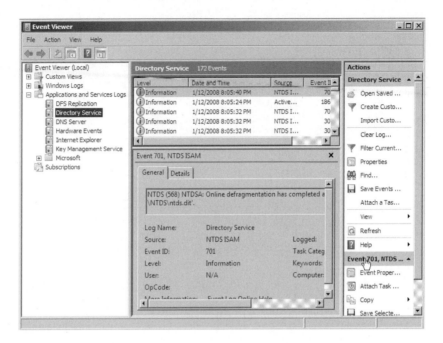

Problematic or potentially problematic events are indicated by a yellow warning icon or a red error icon, both of which are shown in Figure 9.19. Warnings usually indicate a problem that wouldn't prevent a service from running but might cause undesired effects with the service in question. For example, we were configuring a site with some fictional domain controllers and IP addresses. Our local domain controller's IP address wasn't associated with any of the sites, and the Event Viewer generated a warning. In this case, the local domain controller could still function as a domain controller, but the site configuration could produce undesirable results.

Error events almost always indicate a failed service, application, or function. For instance, if the dynamic registration of a DNS client fails, the Event Viewer will generate an error. As you can see, errors are more severe than warnings, because in this case, the DNS client cannot participate in DNS at all.

Double-clicking any event opens the event's Properties dialog box, as shown in Figure 9.20. The Event Properties dialog box displays a detailed description of the event.

The Event Viewer can display thousands of different events, so it would be impossible to list them all here. The important points to be aware of are the following:

- Information events are always benign.

- Warnings indicate noncritical problems.

- Errors indicate showstopping events.

FIGURE 9.19 Information, errors, and warnings in Event Viewer

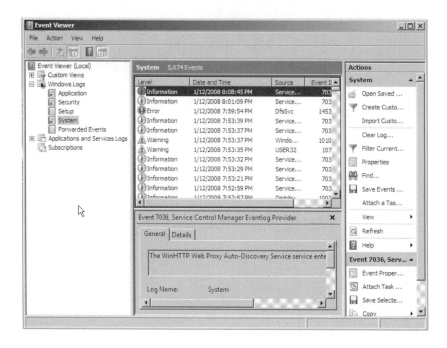

FIGURE 9.20 An Event Properties dialog box

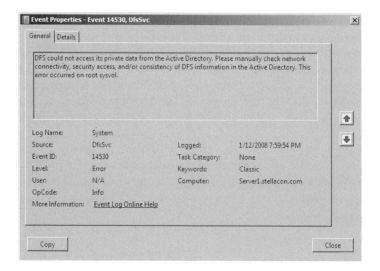

Let's discuss some of the logs and ways you can view data:

Application and services   The application and services logs are part of Event Viewer where applications (for example, Exchange) and services (DNS) log their events. In Chapter 8, we showed how to install and work with DFS. DFS events would be logged in this part of Event Viewer. An important log in this section is the DNS log (see Figure 9.21). This is where all your DNS events get stored.

FIGURE 9.21   The application and services DNS Server log

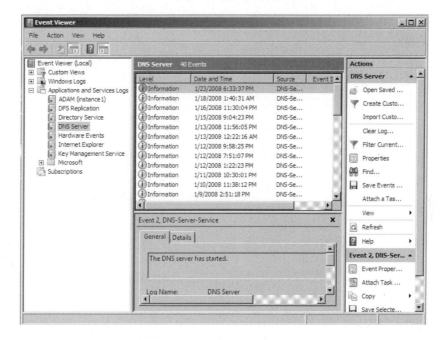

Custom views   Custom views allow you to filter events (see Figure 9.22) to create your own customized look. You can filter events by event level (critical, error, warning, and so on), by logs, and by source. You also have the ability to view events occurring within a specific time frame. This allows you to look only at the events that are important to you.

Subscriptions   Subscriptions allow a user to receive alerts about events that you predefine. In the Subscriptions Properties dialog box (see Figure 9.23), you can define what type of events you want notifications of and the notification method. The Subscriptions section is an advanced alerting service to help you watch for events.

FIGURE 9.22 Create Custom View dialog box

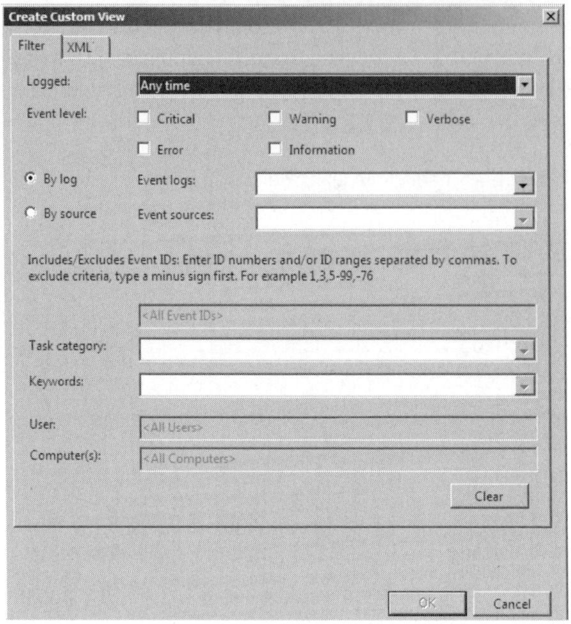

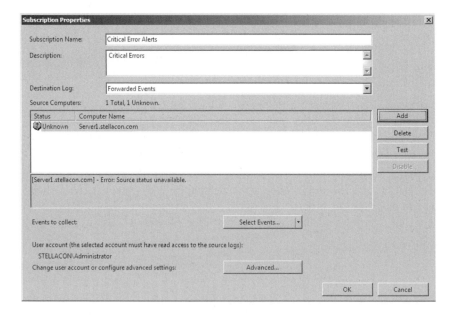

FIGURE 9.23 Subscriptions Properties dialog box

Microsoft Baseline Security Analyzer

The MBSA is a security assessment utility that you can download from the Microsoft web-site. The filename of the download is `mbsasetup.msi`. It verifies whether your computer has the latest security updates and whether there are any common security violation configura-tions that have been applied to your computer. MBSA can scan the following programs and operating systems:

- Windows NT 4
- Windows 2000
- Windows XP
- Windows Vista
- Windows Server 2003
- Windows Server 2008
- IIS 4 or newer
- Internet Explorer, versions 5.01 and newer
- SQL Server 7 or newer
- Microsoft Office 2000 or newer
- Windows Media Player, versions 6.4 and newer

To use MBSA, the computer must meet the following requirements:

- Must be running Windows NT 4, 2000, Windows XP, Vista, Windows Server 2003, or Windows Server 2008 (MBSA is not supported by Windows 95, Windows 98, or Windows Me)
- Must be running Internet Explorer 5.01 or newer
- Must have an XML parser installed for full functionality
- Must have the Workstation and the Server service enabled
- Must have Client for Microsoft Networks installed

 MBSA replaces the Microsoft Personal Security Advisor (MPSA), which was an application previously used to scan for possible security threats to your computer.

Using the GUI Version of MBSA

Once you have installed MBSA, you can access it by selecting Start ➤ All Programs ➤ Microsoft Baseline Security Analyzer or by opening the command prompt and executing `mbsa.exe`. This opens the Baseline Security Analyzer utility, shown in Figure 9.24. You can select from Scan A Computer, Scan More Than One Computer, and View Existing Security Reports.

FIGURE 9.24   Baseline Security Analyzer

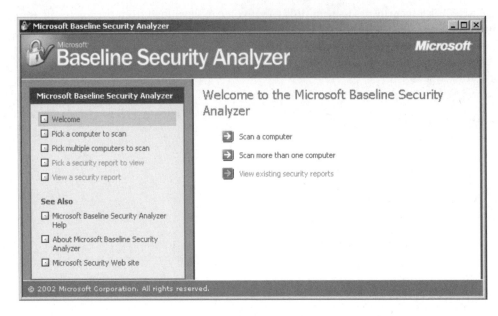

When you click Scan A Computer, the Pick A Computer To Scan dialog box appears (Figure 9.25). You can specify that you want to scan a computer based on a computer name or IP address. You can also specify the name of the security report that will be generated.

The following are options for the security scan:

- Check For Windows Vulnerabilities

- Check For Weak Passwords

- Check For IIS Vulnerabilities

- Check For SQL Vulnerabilities

- Check For Security Updates (if you use this option and are using WSUS, you can specify the name of the WSUS server that should be checked for the security updates)

Once you have made your selections, click Start Scan. When the scan is complete, the security report will be automatically displayed. If you have scanned multiple computers, you can sort the security reports based on issue name or score (worst first or best first).

Using the MBSA Command-Line Utility *mbsacli.exe*

The MBSA command-line utility is located in *Drive:*\Program Files\Microsoft Baseline Security Analyzer. You can specify several options. Enter **mbsacli.exe /hf**, and then customize the command execution with any of the options defined in Table 9.2.

FIGURE 9.25 The Pick A Computer To Scan dialog box

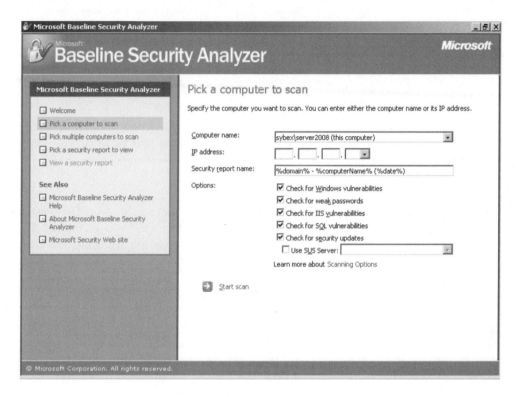

TABLE 9.2 mbsacli.exe /hf Command-Line Options

Option	Description
-h *host name[, host name,...]*	Scans the specified host. You can specify that you want to scan multiple host computers by separating the host names with commas.
-fh *filename*	Scans the NetBIOS names of each computer that is to be scanned and saves the information as text within a file specified by *filename*.
-i *xxxx.xxxx.xxxx.xxxx [, xxxx.xxxx.xxxx.xxxx,...]*	Scans a computer based on the specified IP address. You can scan multiple computers by IP address by separating the IP addresses with commas.

TABLE 9.2   mbsacli.exe /hf Command-Line Options *(continued)*

Option	Description
-fip *filename*	Looks in the text file specified by *filename* for IP addresses and scans the computers with those IP addresses. The file can have up to a maximum of 256 IP addresses.
-d *domainname*	Scans the specified domain.
-n	Scans all of the computers on the local network.

Simple Network Management Protocol

The Simple Network Management Protocol (SNMP) is a TCP/IP protocol monitor. The SNMP service creates trap messages that are then sent to a trap destination. One way you might use SNMP is to trap messages that don't contain an appropriate host name for a particular service.

When you set up SNMP, you set up communities. *Communities* are groupings of computers that help monitor each other.

Windows Server 2008 includes SNMP with the operating system. To install the service, you must use Server Manager. In Exercise 9.4, we will walk you through the process of installing the SNMP service.

EXERCISE 9.4

Installing SNMP

1. Open Server Manager by clicking Start ➢ Administrative Tools ➢ Server Manager.

2. In the left pane, click Features.

3. In the right pane, click Add Features.

4. When the Select Features window appears, click the SNMP Services check box. Click Next.

5. The Confirm Installation page appears. Click Install.

6. Click Close. Exit the Server Manager application.

Now that you have installed the SNMP service, you have to set up your community so that you can start trapping messages. As stated earlier, communities are a grouping of computers to help monitor each other. After you have created the initial community, you can add other computer systems to the community.

In Exercise 9.5, we will walk you through the steps to set up the SNMP service and also set up your first community name. To complete this exercise, you must have completed Exercise 9.4.

EXERCISE 9.5

Configuring SNMP

1. Open Computer Management by clicking Start ➤ Administrative Tools ➤ Computer Management.

2. Expand Services and Applications. Click Services. In the right pane, double-click SNMP Service.

3. The SNMP Service properties window will open. Click the Traps tab. In the Community Name box, enter **Community1**. Click the Add To List button.

4. Click the General tab. Click the Start button to start the service. Click OK.

5. Close Computer Management.

Backup and Recovery

If you have deployed file and application servers in your network environment, your users now depend on it to function properly in order to do their jobs, from network authentications to file access to print and web services. Therefore, the importance of backing up the network servers should be evident. It is important to have multiple servers available to provide backup in case of a problem. The same goes for Active Directory itself—it too should be backed up by being saved. This way, if there is a massive disaster in which you need to restore your directory services, you will have that option available to you.

Backups are just good common sense, but there are several specific reasons to back up data, including the following:

Protect against hardware failures   Computer hardware devices have finite lifetimes, and all hardware eventually fails. We discussed this when we mentioned MTBF earlier. MTBF is the average time a device will function before it actually fails. There is also a rating derived from benchmark testing of hard disk devices that tells you when you may be at risk for an unavoidable disaster. Some types of failures, such as corrupted hard disk drives, can result in significant data loss.

Protect against accidental deletion or modification of data   Although the threat of hardware failures is very real, in most environments mistakes in modifying or deleting data are much more common. For example, suppose a systems administrator accidentally deletes all the files within a specific folder. Clearly, it's important to be able to retrieve this information from a backup.

Keep historical information   Users and systems administrators sometimes modify files and then later find that they require access to an older version of the file. Or a file is accidentally deleted, and a user does not discover that fact until much later. By keeping multiple backups over time, you can recover information from prior backups when necessary.

Protect against malicious deletion or modification of data   Even in the most secure environments, it is conceivable that unauthorized users (or authorized ones with malicious intent!) could delete or modify information. In such cases, the loss of data might require valid backups from which to restore critical information.

Windows Server 2008 includes a Backup utility that is designed to back up operating system files and the Active Directory data store. It allows for basic backup functionality, such as scheduling backup jobs and selecting which files to back up. Figure 9.26 shows the main screen for the Windows Server 2008 Backup utility.

FIGURE 9.26   The main screen of the Windows Server 2008 Backup utility

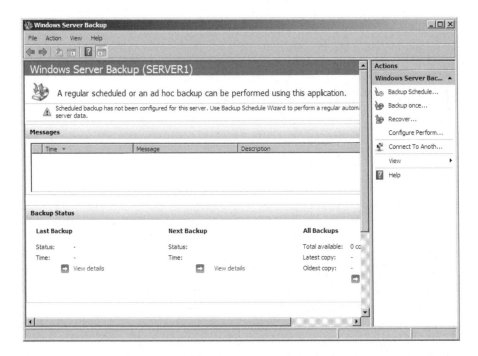

In the following sections, we'll look at the details of using the Windows Server 2008 Backup utility and how you can restore the network when problems do occur.

Overview of the Windows Server 2008 Backup Utility

Although the general purpose behind performing backup operations—protecting information—is straightforward, system administrators must consider many options when determining the optimal backup and recovery scenario for their environment. Factors include what to back up, how often to back up, and when the backups should be performed.

In the following sections, you'll see how the Windows Server 2008 Backup utility makes it easy to implement a backup plan for many network environments.

Although the Windows Server 2008 Backup utility provides the basic functionality required to back up your files, you may want to investigate third-party
products that provide additional functionality. These applications can provide
options for specific types of backups (such as those for Exchange Server and
SQL Server), as well as disaster recovery options, networking functionality,
centralized management, and support for more advanced hardware.

Backup Types

One of the most important issues when dealing with backups is keeping track of which files
have been backed up and which files need to be backed up. Whenever a backup of a file is
made, the Archive bit for the file is set. You can view the attributes of system files by right-
clicking them and selecting Properties. By clicking the Advanced button in the Properties dialog box, you will see the option File Is Ready For Archiving in the Advanced Attributes dialog
box. Figure 9.27 shows an example of the attributes for a file.

FIGURE 9.27   Viewing the Archive attributes for a file

Although it is possible to back up all the files in the file system during each backup operation, it's sometimes more convenient to back up only selected files (such as those that have
changed since the last backup operation).

The Windows Server 2008 Backup utility supports normal (full) and incremental
backups. We also explain other backup methods in the event that you use a
third-party backup utility.

Several types of backups can be performed:

Normal   *Normal backups* (also referred to as *full backups*) back up all the selected files and
then mark them as backed up. This option is usually used when a full system backup is made.

Copy *Copy backups* back up all the selected files but do not mark them as backed up. This is useful when you want to make additional backups of files for moving files offsite or make multiple copies of the same data or for archival purposes.

Incremental *Incremental backups* copy any selected files that are marked as ready for backup (typically because they have not been backed up or have been changed since the last backup) and then mark the files as backed up. When the next incremental backup is run, only the files that are not marked as having been backed up are stored. Incremental backups are used in conjunction with normal (full) backups. The most common backup process is to make a full backup and then to make subsequent incremental backups. The benefit to this method is that only files that have changed since the last full or incremental backup will be stored. This can reduce backup times and disk or tape storage space requirements.

When recovering information from this type of backup method, a systems administrator must first restore the full backup and then restore each of the incremental backups.

Differential *Differential backups* are similar in purpose to incremental backups with one important exception: differential backups copy all files that are marked for backup but do not mark the files as backed up. When restoring files in a situation that uses normal and differential backups, you need to restore only the normal backup and the latest differential backup.

Daily *Daily backups* back up all files that have changed during a single day. This operation uses the file time/date stamps to determine which files should be backed up and does not mark the files as having been backed up.

Figure 9.28 shows the Windows Server 2008 Backup utility's Optimize Backup Performance dialog box and the three choices for backup types.

FIGURE 9.28 Options for optimizing backup performance

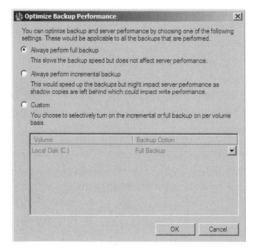

Note that system administrators might choose to combine normal, daily, incremental, and differential backup types as part of the same backup plan. In general, however, it is sufficient to use only one or two of these methods (for example, normal backups with incremental backups). If you require a combination of multiple backup types, be sure you fully understand which types of files are being backed up.

Scheduling Backups

In addition to specifying which files to back up, you can schedule backup jobs to occur at specific times. Planning *when* to perform backups is just as important as deciding what to back up. Performing backup operations can reduce overall system performance; therefore, you should plan to back up information during times of minimal activity on your servers. Figure 9.29 shows the Backup Schedule Wizard of the Window Server 2008 Backup utility.

FIGURE 9.29   Scheduling jobs using the Windows Server 2008 Backup utility

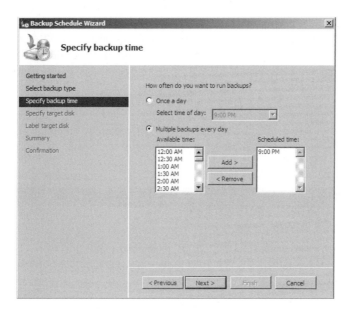

To add a backup operation to the schedule, you can simply click the Add button on the Specify backup time windows.

Restoring Data

In some cases, the servers or user data may become corrupt or unavailable. This could be because of many different reasons. A hard disk failure might, for example, result in the loss of data. Or the accidental deletion of a folder and all of its files might require a restore operation to be performed.

In a worst-case scenario, all the information on a server has been lost, or a hardware failure is preventing the machine from properly booting. If this is the case, you must take several steps in order to recover user or server data:

1. Fix any hardware problem that might prevent the computer from booting (for example, replace any failed hard disks).

2. Reinstall the Windows Server 2008 operating system. This should be performed like a regular installation on a new system.

3. Reinstall any device drivers that may be required by your backup device. If you backed up information to the file system, this will not apply.

4. Restore the system state data using the Windows Server 2008 Backup utility.

Backing Up Active Directory

The Windows Server 2008 Backup utility makes it easy to back up the system data (including Active Directory) as part of a normal backup operation. We've already covered the ideas behind the different backup types and why and when they are used. Exercise 9.6 walks you through the process of backing up the domain controller. To complete this exercise, the local machine must be a domain controller, and you must have sufficient free space to back up the system state (usually at least 500MB).

Windows Server 2008 Backup utility is not installed by default. If you have already installed Windows Server 2008 Backup utility, skip to step 5.

EXERCISE 9.6

Backing Up Active Directory

1. To install the Windows Server 2008 Backup utility, click Start ➢ Administrative Tools ➢ Server Manager. In the left pane, click Features. In the right pane, click Add Features.

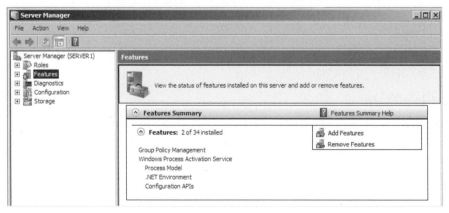

2. In the Select Features page, scroll down and check the Windows Server Backup box. Click Next.

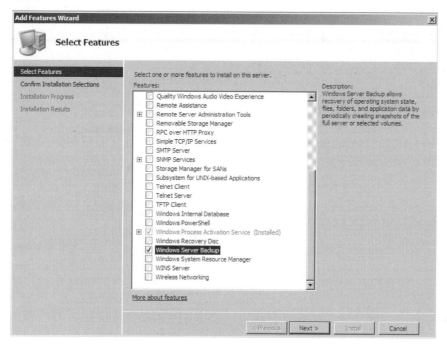

3. On the Confirm Installation Selections page, click the Install button.

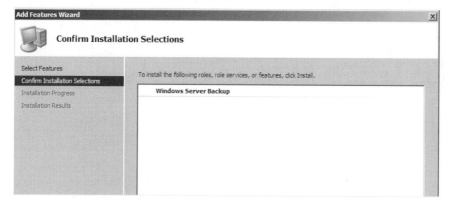

4. After the installation is complete, close Server Manager.

5. Open the Backup utility by clicking Start ➢ Administrative Tools ➢ Backup.

EXERCISE 9.6 *(continued)*

6. In the Windows Server Backup utility, click Action ➢ Backup Once. This is how you sched-
    ule a one-time backup. The Action menu also contains the Backup Schedule (set a daily
    backup time), Recover, and Configure Performance Settings commands.

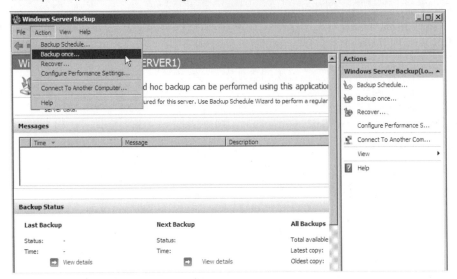

7. The Backup Once Wizard appears. Make sure the Different Options option is checked, and
    click Next.

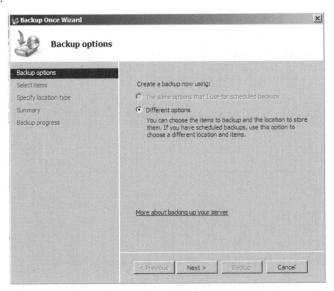

8. On the Select Items page, click the Custom button. Click Next.

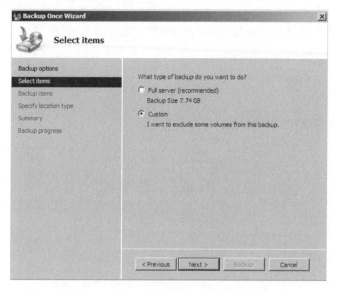

The Full Server (Recommended) option does a complete backup of the system.

9. On the Backup Items page, make sure that the I Want To Be Able To Perform A System Recovery Using This Backup box is checked. Once this box is checked, the local disk box will also be checked. Click Next.

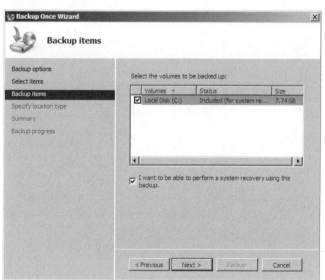

EXERCISE 9.6 *(continued)*

10. On the Specify Location Type page, choose Local Drives. These options help you determine where your backup file is going to be stored. Click Next.

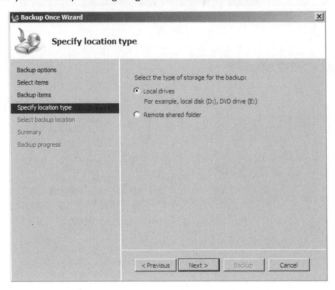

11. On the Select Backup Location page, choose a local drive that has enough space for the
backup. Click Next.

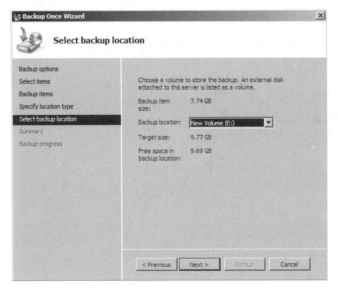

12. Verify all your choices in the Summary screen, and click the Backup button.

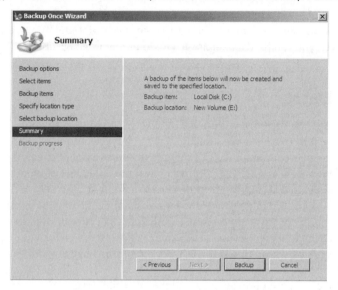

13. The Backup Progress page shows you the status of your backup. Once the backup is complete, close the Windows Server 2008 Backup utility.

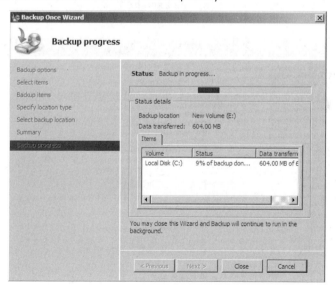

Remote Backup Administration

A new feature of the Windows Server 2008 Backup utility is the ability to do remote administration. The Backup utility is a MMC snap-in that allows you to remotely administer backups on other machines: just choose Action ➢ Connect To Another Computer. After you connect to the other computer, you can repeat Exercise 9.6 to do the remote backup.

Restoring Data

Your network should be designed with fault tolerance in mind. For example, it is highly recommended that each Active Directory domain have at least two domain controllers. Each of these domain controllers contains a copy of the Active Directory data store. Should one of the domain controllers fail, the available one can take over the failed server's functionality. When the failed server is repaired, it can then be promoted to a domain controller in the existing environment. This process effectively restores the failed domain controller without incurring any downtime for end users because all the Active Directory data is replicated to the repaired server in the next scheduled replication. The same needs to be done for your file servers.

In many cases, you may need to restore network data from a backup. For example, suppose a system administrator accidentally deletes several hundred files from the server and does not realize it until the change has been propagated to all the other file servers. Manually re-creating the folders and files is not an option. Clearly, a method for restoring from backup is the best solution.

In Exercise 9.7, you will walk through the process of restoring data to a system. You need to have completed Exercise 9.6 before starting Exercise 9.7.

EXERCISE 9.7

Restoring from Backup

1. Open the Backup utility by clicking Start ➢ Administrative Tools ➢ Backup.

2. The Backup utility starts. Open the Action menu, and choose Recover.

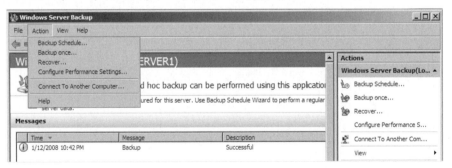

EXERCISE 9.7 *(continued)*

3. The Recovery Wizard appears. Make sure the This Server option is selected, and click Next.

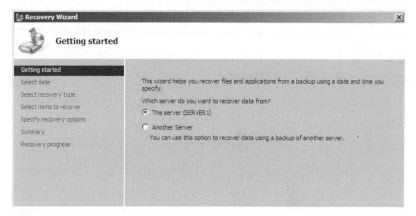

4. On the Select Date page, click the date of the backup that you created in Exercise 9.6. Click Next to continue.

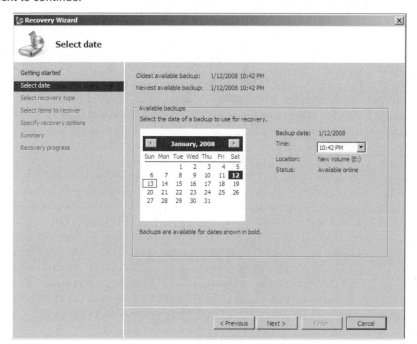

5. On the Select Recovery Type page, click the Files And Folders option. Click Next to continue.

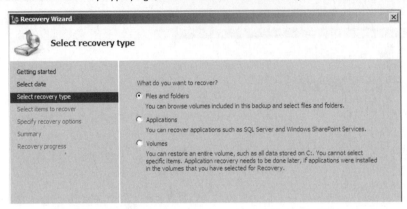

6. On the Select Items To Recover page, you will see the server you backed up Exercise 9.6. Click Local Disk (C:), and then click Next.

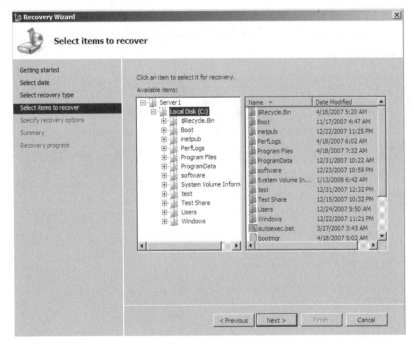

7. If a warning box appears, just click OK.

8. On the Specify Recovery Options page, choose Another Location, and click the Browse button. Choose a location on your hard disk to restore the files. Do not overwrite your hard disk! Click Next.

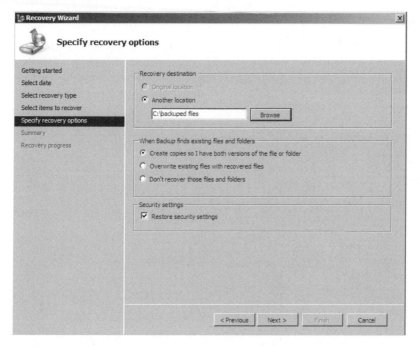

9. On the Summary page, click Finished.

10. You will be asked whether you want to restart the computer. Select No.

11. Close the Backup Utility.

Understanding Shadow Copies

An excellent way to protect your shared folders is by using *shadow copies*. Shadow copies allow an administrator to back up shared folders to a remote location. Shadow copies are designed to help recover files that were accidentally deleted, were overwritten, or have become corrupt. One major advantage to shadow copies is that open files can be backed up. This means that even if users are currently working on files in a shared folder that has shadow copies enabled, the shadow copies will continue to function.

Once administrators have configured and enabled shadow copies (using the Computer Management snap-in), network users can restore earlier versions of files. After the initial shadow copy of the shared folder is created, only changes are copied and not the entire file.

You can enable shadow copies of entire volumes.

The following are some of the settings you can configure when setting up shadow copies:

Schedule You have the ability to set the schedule (see Figure 9.30) of the shadow copies. You can set this schedule to run daily, weekly, monthly, once, at system start-up, at logon, or when the system is idle. You can also set the time at which the shadow copy will run.

FIGURE 9.30 Scheduling shadow copies

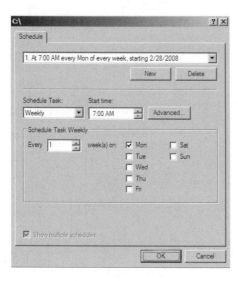

Storage locations An administrator needs to set the location (see Figure 9.31) of the shadow copy backup. If you are on a network, it is a good idea to place the shadow copy on a network drive.

Maximum size You can set a maximum size on your shadow copies, or you can specify that they have no size limit. One of the predetermined settings is 64 shadow copies per volume.

In Exercise 9.8, you'll set up a volume to make shadow copies every Monday at 7 a.m. To set up the shadow copies, you will use the Computer Management MMC snap-in.

FIGURE 9.31   Setting the storage location for shadow copies

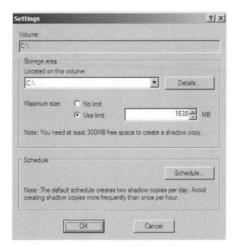

EXERCISE 9.8

Configuring a Shadow Copy on a Volume

1. Open Computer Management by clicking Start ➢ Administrative Tools ➢ Computer Management.

2. Expand Storage, and then right-click Disk Management. Choose All Tasks ➢ Configure Shadow Copies.

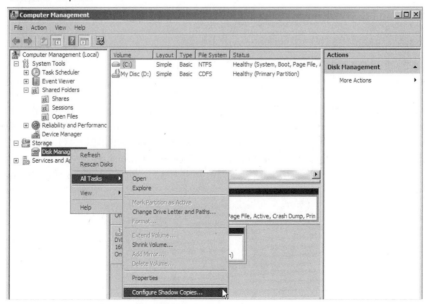

3. When the Shadow Copies dialog box appears, click the Settings button.

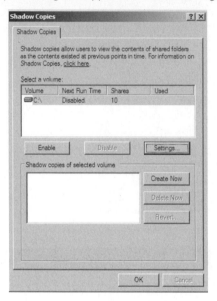

4. When the Settings windows appears, click the Schedule button.

5. In the Schedule window, set the schedule task to weekly and the start time for 7 a.m. Uncheck all the days of the week boxes except Mon. Click OK.

6. When the Settings windows reappears, click OK.

7. If the Enable button is enabled, click it. Then click OK.

8. Exit the Computer Management MMC.

To recover a previous version of a file from a shadow copy, you use the *servername*\ *sharename* path. The operating system determines how you will gain access to the shared folders and shadow copies. Shadow copies are built into Windows XP (SP1), Windows Vista, Windows Server 2003, and Windows Server 2008. If you are using a different Microsoft operating system, you need to download the Shadow Copy Client pack from the Microsoft download center.

Summary

We started this chapter with a discussion on WSUS and what Windows Updates can do for your network. We discussed why you would want to use a WSUS server instead of having clients manually connect to the Internet to receive their updates.

In this chapter, we also covered file server and print server optimization and reliability, including many tools that can help you monitor and manage your systems, and the basics of troubleshooting the network in times of disaster.

Monitoring performance on servers is imperative to rooting out any issues that may affect your network. If your systems are not running at their best, your end users may experience issues such as latency—or, worse, you may experience corruption in your network data. Either way, it's important to know how to monitor the performance of your servers. In this chapter, you also looked at ways system administrators can optimize the operations of servers to ensure that end users receive adequate performance.

You also looked at how to use the various performance-related tools that are included with Windows Server 2008. Tools such as the Performance Monitor, Task Manager, Network Monitor, and Event Viewer can help you diagnose and troubleshoot system performance issues. These tools will help you find typical problems related to memory, disk space, and any other hardware-related issues you may experience. Knowing how to use tools to troubleshoot and test your systems is not only imperative to passing the exam but also to performing your duties at work. To have a smoothly running network environment, it is vital that you understand the issues related to the reliability and performance of your network servers and domain controllers.

We also covered the details of performing backups, the most commonly used form of reliability you can implement. You learned how to back up and restore data using the Windows Server 2008 Backup utility. Through the use of wizards and prompts, this backup tool can simplify an otherwise tedious process. Knowing how to restore data can really put you a cut above the rest, especially in times of disaster. Finally, we discussed shadow copies and how you can set up shadow copies to run at specific intervals.

Exam Essentials

Understand WSUS.   Windows Server Update Services is one way to have your end users receive important updates from Microsoft. WSUS gives administrators the ability to download, test, and approve updates before they get released onto the network.

Understand the methodology behind troubleshooting performance.   By following a set of steps that involves making measurements and finding bottlenecks, you can systematically troubleshoot performance problems.

Be familiar with the features and capabilities of the Windows Server 2008 Performance Monitor tool for troubleshooting performance problems.   The Performance Monitor administrative tool is a very powerful method for collecting data about all areas of system performance. Through the use of performance objects, counters, and instances, you can choose to collect and record only the data of interest and use this information for pinpointing performance problems.

Know the importance of common performance counters.   Several important performance-related counters deal with general system performance. Know the importance of monitoring memory, print server, CPU, and network usage on a busy server.

Understand the role of other troubleshooting tools.   The Windows Task Manager, Network Monitor, SNMP, Baseline Security Analyzer, and Event Viewer can all be used to diagnose and troubleshoot configuration- and performance-related issues.

Understand how to troubleshoot common sources of server reliability problems.   Windows Server 2008 has been designed to be a stable, robust, and reliable operating system. Should you experience intermittent failures, you should know how to troubleshoot device drivers and buggy system-level software.

Understand the various backup types available with the Windows Server 2008 Backup utility.   The Windows Server 2008 Backup utility can perform full and incremental backup operations. Some third-party backup utilities also support differential and daily backups. You can use each of these operations as part of an efficient backup strategy.

Know how to back up network data.   All data on a server can be backed up using Windows Server 2008 and the Backup utility. Understand how to perform a backup and the reasons why you need to back up network servers.

Know how to restore network data.   Recovering data on a server is one of the most important tasks you can know as an IT administrator. Know how to recover data using the Windows Server 2008 Backup utility. Understand how to perform a restore and the reasons why you would recover your network servers.

Understand shadow copies.   Shadow copies are an excellent way to protect shared folder data. By using shadow copies, you have the ability to recover files that were accidentally deleted, were overwritten, or have become corrupted.

Review Questions

1. Paige is a systems administrator who is responsible for performing backups on several servers. Recently, she has been asked to take over operations of several new servers. Unfortunately, no information about the standard upkeep and maintenance of those servers is available. Paige wants to begin by making configuration changes to these servers, but she wants to first ensure that she has a full backup of all the data on each of these servers.

   Paige decides to use the Windows Server 2008 Backup utility to perform the backups. She wants to choose a backup type that will back up all files on each of these servers, regardless of when they were last changed or if they have been previously backed up. Which of the following types of backup operations store all the selected files, without regard to the Archive bit setting? (Choose all that apply.)

   A. Normal

   B. Incremental

   C. Copy

   D. Differential

2. You are the network administrator for a Fortune 500 company. You are responsible for all client computers at the central campus. You want to make sure that all the client computers are secure. You decide to use MBSA to scan your client computers for possible security violations. You want to use the command-line version of MBSA to scan your computers based on IP address. Which of the following commands should you use?

   A. `mdsacli.exe /hf -i xxxx.xxxx.xxxx.xxxx`

   B. `mdsacli.exe /ip xxxx.xxxx.xxxx.xxxx`

   C. `mbsa.exe /hf -ip xxxx.xxxx.xxxx.xxxx`

   D. `mbsa.exe /ip xxxx.xxxx.xxxx.xxxx`

3. You are the network administrator for a Fortune 500 company. You are responsible for all client computers at the central campus. You want to make sure all the client computers have the most current software installed for their operating systems, including software in the categories Critical Updates and Service Packs, Windows Server 2008 Family, and Driver Updates. You want to automate the process as much as possible, and you want the client computers to download the updates from a central server you are managing. You decide to use Windows Server Update Services. The WSUS server software has been installed on a server called WSUSServer. You want to test the WSUS server before you set up group policies within the domain. You install Windows XP Professional with the latest service pack on a test client. Which of the following registry entries needs to be made for the client to specify that the client should use WSUSServer for Windows Update? (Choose all that apply.)

    A. Use HKEY_LOCAL_MACHINE\Software\Policies\Microsoft\Windows\ WindowsUpdate\AU\UseWUServer, and specify 0 data.

    B. Use HKEY_LOCAL_MACHINE\Software\Policies\Microsoft\Windows\ WindowsUpdate\AU\UseWUServer, and specify 1 for data.

    C. Use HKEY_LOCAL_MACHINE\Software\Policies\Microsoft\Windows\ WindowsUpdate\AU\WUServer, and specify http://WSUSServer.

    D. Use HKEY_LOCAL_MACHINE\Software\Policies\Microsoft\Windows\ WindowsUpdate\AU\WUServer, and specify WSUSServer.

    E. Use HKEY_LOCAL_MACHINE\Software\Policies\Microsoft\Windows\ WindowsUpdate\WUServer, and specify http://WSUSServer.

    F. Use HKEY_LOCAL_MACHINE\Software\Policies\Microsoft\Windows\ WindowsUpdate\WUServer, and specify WSUSServer.

4. Which of the following types of backup operations should be used to back up all the files that have changed since the last full backup or incremental backup and mark these files as having been backed up?

    A. Differential

    B. Copy

    C. Incremental

    D. Normal

5. You are a network administrator for your company. The network consists of a single Active Directory domain. All servers run Windows Server 2008. Windows Server Update Services (WSUS) is installed on two servers, SERVERA and SERVERB. SERVERA receives software updates from Microsoft Windows Update servers. You manually synchronized SERVERB with the Windows Update servers and now need to complete the WSUS configuration on SERVERB. Which of the following is *not* a step you might take to complete the configuration of WSUS on SERVERB?

    A. Approve the current updates.

    B. Set SERVERB to receive updates from SERVERA and automatically synchronize with approved updates on SERVERA.

    C. Set SERVERB to automatically draw updates from whichever sources SERVERA is set to draw from.

    D. Set SERVERB to automatically receive daily updates at a given time.

6. You are the network administrator for your company. The network consists of a single Active Directory domain. All servers run Windows Server 2008. All client computers run Windows XP Professional. The company has 16 mobile sales representatives that are all members of the Power Users local group on their computers. From 6 p.m. until 7 a.m., the sales representatives' portable computers are usually turned off and disconnected from the corporate network. The mobile sales representatives' computers must receive software updates every day with minimal user interaction. While verifying the recent updates on one of the portable computers, you notice that the updates from the Windows Update servers were not applied. On the Automatic Updates tab of the System Properties dialog box of the mobile computer, what should you do to make sure that software updates are applied to the computer? (Choose three.)

    A. Set the scheduled time to every day at 12 a.m.

    B. Select the option Automatically Download The Updates, And Install Them On The Schedule That I Specify.

    C. Select the option Notify Me Before Downloading Any Updates And Notify Me Again Before Installing Them On My Computer.

    D. Select the Keep My Computer Up To Date check box.

    E. Select the option Download The Updates Automatically And Notify Me When They Are Ready To Be Installed.

    F. Set the scheduled time to every day at 12 p.m.

7. You are responsible for managing several Windows Server 2008 domain controller computers in your environment. Recently, a single hard disk on one of these machines failed, and the Active Directory database was lost. You want to perform the following tasks:

    - Determine which partitions on the server are still accessible.

    - Restore as much of the system configuration (including the Active Directory database) as possible.

Which of the following could be used to help meet these requirements?

A. Event Viewer

B. Performance Monitor

C. A hard disk from another server that is not configured as a domain controller

D. A valid system state backup from the server

8. You have been hired as a consultant to research a network-related problem at a small organization. The environment supports many custom-developed applications that are not well documented. A manager suspects that some computers on the network are generating excessive traffic and bogging down the network. You want to do the following:

- Determine which computers are causing the problems.

- Record and examine network packets that are coming to/from specific machines.

- View data related only to specific types of network packet.

What tool should you use to accomplish all of the requirements?

A. Task Manager

B. Performance Monitor

C. Event Viewer

D. Network Monitor

9. You are the network administrator for your company. The network consists of a single Active Directory domain. All servers run Windows Server 2008. All client computers run either Windows 2000 Professional or Windows XP Professional. You install Windows Server Update Services (WSUS) on a computer named SUSSERVER. You create a Group Policy Object (GPO) that configures all client computers to receive their software updates from SUSSERVER. Later, you run Microsoft Baseline Security Analyzer (MBSA) on all client computers to find out whether all updates are being applied. You discover that all the Windows 2000 Professional client computers receive updates, but the Windows XP Professional client computers do not receive updates. You confirm that the GPO setting was applied on all Windows XP Professional computers. How can you be sure that the Windows XP Professional client computers receive their updates from SUSSERVER.

A. Make all users of the Windows XP Professional client computers members of the Administrators local group.

B. On all Windows XP Professional client computers, install Service Pack 1.

C. On all Windows XP Professional client computers, restart Automatic Updates.

D. On all Windows XP Professional client computers, delete the NoAutoUpdate value under HKEY_LOCAL_MACHINE\SOFTWARE\Policies\Microsoft\Windows\ WindowsUpdate\AU.

10. You are the administrator for a small company. You have noticed lately that users are accidentally deleting files from shared folders. You want to implement a way to have your users recover the deleted files. What can you implement?

A. Backups

B. Shadow copies

C. Recovery console

D. File restoration utility

11. You want to set up Simple Network Management Protocol (SNMP) on your network. What is the name of the grouping of computers that will monitor each other?

A. Groupings

B. Trap groups

C. Communities

D. Agents

12. Robert is a systems administrator who is responsible for performing backups on several servers. Recently, he has been asked to take over operations of several new servers, including backup operations. He has the following requirements:

- The backup must finish as quickly as possible.

- The backup must use the absolute minimum amount of storage space.

- He must perform backup operations at least daily with a full backup at least weekly.

Robert decides to use the Windows Server 2008 Backup utility to perform the backups. He wants to choose a set of backup types that will meet all these requirements. He decides to back up all files on each of these servers every week. Then, he decides to store only the files that have changed since the last backup operation (regardless of type) during the weekdays. Which of the following types of backup operations should he use to implement this solution? (Choose two.)

A. Normal

B. Daily

C. Copy

D. Differential

E. Incremental

13. A systems administrator suspects that a domain controller is not operating properly. Another systems administrator has been monitoring the performance of the server and has found that this is not a likely cause of the problems. Where can the first systems administrator look for more information regarding details about any specific problems or errors that may be occurring?

A. Task Manager

B. Network Monitor

C. Performance Monitor

D. Event Viewer

14. Which of the following System Monitor views displays performance information over a period of time?

   A. Graph

   B. Histogram

   C. Report

   D. Current Activity

15. You are using the Backup Wizard to back up Active Directory. You want to ensure that the entire Active Directory is backed up while maintaining a minimum backup file size. In the following screen, where would you click in order to accomplish this task?

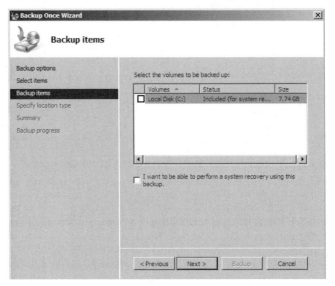

   A. I Want To Be Able To Perform A System Recovery Using This Backup

   B. Local Disk (C:)

   C. Nowhere—this screen does not back up the system state data

   D. The Next button

16. In your current capacity as network administrator, you are looking to diagnose a problem with your current network infrastructure. You have 20 Windows Server 2008 servers and 1,000 Windows XP Professional workstations spread out across 6 subnets. You need to test the connections between each pair of servers and determine how each server connects to the network switches that are used to build the core of the network. All servers run fine except for one. Of the options listed, what tools would you use to troubleshoot this server?

   A. Event Viewer, Performance Monitor, and Network Monitor

   B. Task Manager, Network Monitor, and Server Monitor

   C. Performance Monitor, System logs, and Task Manager

   D. Event Viewer, Network Sniffer, and NTBACKUP

17. You are the systems engineer responsible for 123 Ltd.'s new division. You need to deploy five new Windows Server 2008 systems. What do you need to do in order to make sure you understand the normal load put on the systems under normal operations?

    A. Set up Task Manager.

    B. Establish a baseline of current performance.

    C. Deploy the alerts in the Performance Console.

    D. Use Network Monitor to see current and future load.

18. As the IT manager for your company's technology division, you are asked to deploy a method of finding problems on your connection to the network. You have three Windows Server 2008 systems, and each is set up as a domain controller. What tools are incorporated with each server that will help you find problems on the network and, more specifically, on the network medium?

    A. Task Monitor

    B. Performance Monitor

    C. Network Monitor

    D. Event Monitor

19. You have decided as the network administrator to implement shadow copies for your shared folders. In which application do you set up shadow copies?

    A. Server Manager

    B. Computer Management

    C. Reliability Manager

    D. Backup Utility

20. You have been asked to deploy counters to monitor your CPU on a server that is performing poorly. What is the process of adding the % Processor Time counter and the _Total instance counter on a Windows Server 2008 system?

    A. In the Add Counters dialog box, select Use Local Computer Counters. Choose the CPU performance object from the Performance Object list, and then click Select Counters From List. Select the % Processor Time counter and the _Total instance counter.

    B. In the Add Counters dialog box, select Use Local Computer Counters. Choose the PROC performance object from the Performance Object list, and then click Select Counters From List. Select the % Processor Time counter and the _Total instance counter.

    C. In the Add Counters dialog box, select Use Local Computer Counters. Choose the DISK performance object from the Performance Object list, and then click Select Counters From List. Select the % Processor Time counter and the _Total instance counter.

    D. In the Add Counters dialog box, select Use Local Computer Counters. Choose the Processor performance object from the Performance Object list, and then click Select Counters From List. Select the % Processor Time counter and the _Total instance counter.

Answers to Review Questions

1. A. Normal and copy backup operations do not use the Archive bit to determine which files to back up, and they will include all files that are selected for backup on the server. The other backup types will store only a subset of files based on their dates or whether they have been previously backed up. The Windows Server 2008 Backup utility supports normal backups but does not support copy backups. For this reason, Paige should choose a normal backup to ensure that she performs a valid backup of all files on the servers before she makes any configuration changes.

2. A. If you use MBSA from the command-line utility `mdsacli.exe`, you can specify several options. You type **`mdsacli.exe /hf`** (from the folder that contains `Mdsacli.exe`) and then customize the command execution with an option such as `/i xxxx.xxxx.xxxx.xxxx`, which specifies that the computer with the specified IP address should be scanned.

3. B, E. You can set the registry key `HKEY_LOCAL_MACHINE\Software\Policies\Microsoft\Windows\WindowsUpdate\AU\UseWUServer` set to 0 to use the public Windows Update server, or you can set it to 1, which means you will specify the server for Windows Update in the `HKEY_LOCAL_MACHINE\Software\Policies\Microsoft\Windows\WindowsUpdate` key. The `WUServer` key sets the Windows Update server using the server's HTTP name, for example, `http://intranetSUS`.

4. C. Incremental backup operations copy files and mark them as having been backed up. Therefore, they are used when a systems administrator wants to back up only the files that have changed since the last full or incremental backup. Differential backups, although they will also back up only those files that were created or changed since the last full or incremental backup, will not mark the files as having been backed up.

5. C. All options are valid steps to complete the configuration, except option C, because SERVERB cannot automatically draw updates from whichever sources on SERVERA.

6. B, D, F. Option A schedules the updates to occur at a time when the computers are generally not connected to the corporate network. Options C and E require more user interaction than would be considered minimal. By setting updates to occur with no user interaction at noon, you satisfy the requirements.

7. D. You can recover system state data from a backup, which always includes the Active Directory database. In this case, the Event Viewer and System Monitor wouldn't help you recover the database, but they might help you determine why the hard drive crashed in the first place.

8. D. By using the Network Monitor, you can view all the network packets that are being sent to or from the local server. Based on this information, you can determine the source of certain types of traffic, such as pings. The other types of monitoring can provide useful information, but they do not allow you to drill down into the specific details of a network packet, and they don't allow you to filter the data that has been collected based on details about the packet.

9. B. Specifying a schedule for updates, as well as the server from which to draw the updates, is supported on the minimum platform of Windows Server 2003, Windows XP with SP1, and Windows 2000 with SP3.

10. B. Shadow copies are an excellent way to protect shared folder data. By using shadow copies, users have the ability to recover files that were accidentally deleted, were overwritten, or have become corrupted.

11. C. Communities are groupings of computers within SNMP. The computers work together and trap predefined messages.

12. A, E. To meet the requirements, Robert should use the normal backup type to create a full backup every week and the incremental backup type to back up only the data that has been modified since the last full or incremental backup operation.

13. D. The Event Viewer is the best tool for viewing information, warnings, and alerts related to Windows Server 2008 functions.

14. A. Using the Graph view, you can view performance information over a period of time (as defined by the sample interval). The Histogram and Report views are designed to show the latest performance statistics and average values.

15. A. I Want To Be Able To Perform A System Recovery Using This Backup is what you want to click. Once this check box is selected, the Local Disk (C:) box will automatically become selected.

16. A. Event Viewer shows you informational- and warning-based events tracked by the system. The logs are useful for finding problems in your system. Performance Monitor is used to monitor performance objects, set counters, and establish a baseline of your system. Network Monitor is used to look at the traffic (to the packet level) on your network. All these tools can help find problems in your system.

17. B. By establishing a baseline of the current performance of your systems, you get an idea of how they perform normally, and then you will know when they aren't performing as expected because the charts will be off. Make sure you document this procedure, and consider setting up a linear rather than a circular log.

18. C. Network Monitor is used to find network problems at the packet level. Make sure you are familiar with this tool for both the exam and in production environments where you can use it.

19. B. To set up shadow copies, you use the Computer Management MMC. If you want to set up shadow copies on shared folders, you right-click the Shared Folders section and choose Configure Shadow Copies. If you want to set up shadow copies on the entire volume, right-click the volume, and choose Configure Shadow Copies.

20. D. In the Add Counters dialog box, you first need to select Use Local Computer Counters. Then you need to choose the Processor performance object from the Performance Object list, and then click Select Counters From List. Finally, select the % Processor Time counter and the _Total instance.

Appendix

About the Companion CD

IN THIS APPENDIX:

- ✓ What you'll find on the CD
- ✓ System requirements
- ✓ Using the CD
- ✓ Troubleshooting

What You'll Find on the CD

The following sections are arranged by category and provide a summary of the software and other goodies you'll find on the CD. If you need help with installing the items provided on the CD, refer to the installation instructions in the "Using the CD" section of this appendix.

Some programs on the CD might fall into one of these categories:

Shareware programs are fully functional, free, trial versions of copyrighted programs. If you like particular programs, register with their authors for a nominal fee and receive licenses, enhanced versions, and technical support.

Freeware programs are free, copyrighted games, applications, and utilities. You can copy them to as many computers as you like—for free—but they offer no technical support.

GNU software is governed by its own license, which is included inside the folder of the GNU software. There are no restrictions on distribution of GNU software. See the GNU license at the root of the CD for more details.

Trial, *demo*, or *evaluation* versions of software are usually limited either by time or functionality (such as not letting you save a project after you create it).

Sybex Test Engine

For Windows

The CD contains the Sybex Test Engine, which includes all of the Assessment Test and Chapter Review questions in electronic format, as well as two bonus exams located only on the CD.

PDF of the Book

For Windows

We have included an electronic version of the text in `.pdf` format. You can view the electronic version of the book with Adobe Reader.

Adobe Reader

For Windows

We've also included a copy of Adobe Reader so you can view PDF files that accompany the book's content. For more information on Adobe Reader or to check for a newer version, visit Adobe's website at `http://www.adobe.com/products/reader/`.

Electronic Flashcards

For PC, Pocket PC, and Palm

These handy electronic flashcards are just what they sound like. One side contains a question or fill-in-the-blank, and the other side shows the answer.

System Requirements

Make sure that your computer meets the minimum system requirements shown in the following list. If your computer doesn't meet most of these requirements, you may have problems using the software and files on the companion CD. For the latest and greatest information, please refer to the ReadMe file located at the root of the CD-ROM.

- A PC running Microsoft Windows 98, Windows 2000, Windows NT4 (with SP4 or later), Windows Me, Windows XP, or Windows Vista
- An Internet connection
- A CD-ROM drive

Using the CD

To install the items from the CD to your hard drive, follow these steps:

1. Insert the CD into your computer's CD-ROM drive. The license agreement appears.

Windows users: The interface won't launch if you have Autorun disabled. In that case, click Start ➢ Run (for Windows Vista, Start ➢ All Programs ➢ Accessories ➢ Run). In the dialog box that appears, type *D*:\Start.exe. (Replace *D* with the proper letter if your CD drive uses a different letter. If you don't know the letter, see how your CD drive is listed under My Computer.) Click OK.

2. Read through the license agreement, and then click the Accept button if you want to use the CD.

The CD interface appears. The interface allows you to access the content with just one or two clicks.

Troubleshooting

Wiley has attempted to provide programs that work on most computers with the minimum system requirements. Alas, your computer may differ, and some programs may not work properly for some reason.

The two likeliest problems are that you don't have enough memory (RAM) for the programs you want to use, or you have other programs running that are affecting installation or running of a program. If you get an error message such as "Not enough memory" or "Setup cannot continue," try one or more of the following suggestions and then try using the software again:

Turn off any antivirus software running on your computer. Installation programs sometimes mimic virus activity and may make your computer incorrectly believe that it's being infected by a virus.

Close all running programs. The more programs you have running, the less memory is available to other programs. Installation programs typically update files and programs; so if you keep other programs running, installation may not work properly.

Have your local computer store add more RAM to your computer. This is, admittedly, a drastic and somewhat expensive step. However, adding more memory can really help the speed of your computer and allow more programs to run at the same time.

Customer Care

If you have trouble with the book's companion CD-ROM, please call the Wiley Product Technical Support phone number at (800) 762-2974. Outside the United States, call +1 (317) 572-3994. You can also contact Wiley Product Technical Support at http://sybex.custhelp.com. John Wiley & Sons will provide technical support only for installation and other general quality-control items. For technical support on the applications themselves, consult the program's vendor or author.

To place additional orders or to request information about other Wiley products, please call (877) 762-2974.

Glossary

6to4 An integration/migration tool in IPv6 allowing native IPv6 client machines to communicate through IPv4 clouds. This method is used for nondual stack machines running IPv6 only. The edge or border devices (connecting IPv6 and IPv4 networks) need to be configured to forward IPv6 traffic to IPv6 networks "tunneling" the IPv6 addresses through the IPv4 space. The IPv6 prefix for 6to4 functionality is 2002:: /16.

A

Active Directory Microsoft's implementation of the LDAP directory service networking database. Active Directory stores information about objects in a central database and makes it available to users.

Active Directory account integration Feature of some firewalls that allows the network administrator to check all potential remote users against Active Directory to verify that they have authorized domain accounts.

Active Directory–integrated DNS zone Primary zone with Active Directory integration. The zone database is stored in Active Directory.

ad hoc mode A form of wireless communication in which computers connect directly to each other without using an access point or bridge.

additive security Security in which the user's permissions are those of the group with the greatest access. If a user is in two groups, one of which has Read permissions to an item and another of which has Full Control permissions, that user has Full Control. NTFS security is additive.

address pool The range of IP addresses that the DHCP server can assign to clients.

adjacency A term used to describe neighboring routers that are grouped (think neighborhood). Within an adjacency, routers synchronize any changes to the link-state map. When the network topology changes, whichever router notices it first floods the internetwork with change notifications.

AnonymousAddress Used in Windows Server 2008 to set IPv6 to use a random value in an EUI-64 instead of using the device's MAC address. The MAC address provides uniqueness, but some consider it less than secure and consider a random or anonymous address to be better.

Anycast IPv6 (also defined for IPv4 but not generally used) packet type that defines a unique address for an interface that can be applied to multiple devices as well. Communication occurs between only two devices, typically the closest devices on the network. Anycast is described as one-to-"one of many."

application server Windows Server machines that host applications that all users access.

area border router Special OSPF router that connects adjacent areas.

authentication header   IPSec header used to authenticate data or a data stream included in the IPv6 protocol as an extension header.

authorization   In the context of DHCP, a registration process used with Active Directory to ensure that only DHCP servers that have been approved or authorized are allowed to allocate DHCP addresses. Authorization prevents nonauthorized DHCP servers from issuing TCP/IP numbers on your network.

Automatic Updates   Feature that extends the functionality of Windows Update by automating the update process.

autostatic update mode   RIP update mode in which the RIP router broadcasts the contents of its routing table only when a peer router asks for it. See also *periodic update mode*.

B

backbone   A technology associated with interconnecting networks through a central network.

Background Intelligent Transfer Services (BITS)   Bandwidth-throttling technology, used by the Automatic Updates application, that downloads updates during times when bandwidth is idle. This means that downloading the updates doesn't interfere with other Internet traffic.

background zone loading   An Active Directory feature that allows an Active Directory–integrated DNS zone to load in the background. This means that a DNS server can service client requests while the zone is still loading into memory.

binding   The process of linking together software components. For example, binding links the protocol stack to the network device driver for the network interface adapter.

Border Gateway Protocol (BGP)   Routing protocol allowing a Windows Server 2008 router to announce its route to other routers.

border routing   The passing of packets from one autonomous internetwork to another.

C

Callback Control Protocol (CBCP)   Allows RRAS servers or clients to negotiate a callback with another server.

chained installation   Technology that applies all updates requiring a computer restart before the computer is restarted, eliminating the need to restart the computer more than once.

Challenge Handshake Authentication Protocol (CHAP)   Remote access authentication protocol that uses encrypted challenge and response messages instead of sending passwords and usernames in plain text. It has cryptographic weaknesses and is not supported by all platforms.

circular logging   Logging in which old data is overwritten as new data is entered into the log. Conserves disk space by limiting the size of the log file.

Connection Manager   Suite of components provided by Microsoft to help administrators create and manage remote access connections. See also *service profile*.

copy backup   A backup type that backs up selected folders and files but does not set the archive bit.

counter logs   Files that contain information collected by the Windows Performance tool. Counter logs can be used to track and analyze performance-related statistics over time.

cyclic redundancy check (CRC)   A mathematical calculation that is computed on a data stream input (a packet at the source and destination). The output value is used to determine whether a packet has been damaged or altered in transmission.

D

daily backup   A backup type that backs up all the files that have been modified on the day that the daily backup is performed. The Archive attribute is not set on the files that have been backed up. The Windows Server 2008 Backup utility does not support daily backups.

default route   The route packets take when there is no explicit route. If a router encounters a packet bound for some remote network whose route cannot be resolved in the routing table, the packet takes the default route.

default subnet mask   Network IDs and host IDs within an IPv4 address are distinguished by using a subnet mask. The default subnet mask is assigned based on the class of the address in question, such as a Class A, B, or C address. These addresses are characterized by 8, 16, or 24 bits to specify the network portion of the address—one octet for a Class A network (255.0.0.0), two octets for a Class B network (255.255.0.0), and three octets for a Class C network (255.255.255.0). It's not the subnet mask that determines the class of an address; it is the first octet numerical value.

delegation   The process by which a higher security authority assigns administrative permissions to a lesser authority, such as another administrator or user.

demand-dial routing   Type of routing that allows the use of an impermanent connection, such as an analog modem or ISDN, to imitate a dedicated Internet connection.

DHCP discover message   Message broadcast by a DHCP client that's looking for a nearby DHCP server. Contains the hardware MAC address, among other information.

DHCP relay agent   Service that allows DHCP requests to be processed on a multisegment network. The DHCP relay agent or proxy is used to forward requests through a router to a DHCP server. (Without a relay agent, non-BootP routers prevent all broadcasts, including DHCP broadcasts, from passing through.)

DHCP request message   Message a client sends to the DHCP server to request or renew the lease of its IP address.

DHCPACK   Acknowledgment message sent by the DHCP server to the client after the server marks the selected IP address as leased.

DHCPNACK   Negative acknowledgment sent by the DHCP server to the client. This generally occurs when the client is attempting to renew a lease for its old IP address after the address has been reassigned elsewhere.

differential backup   A backup type that copies only the files that have been changed since the last normal backup (full backup) or incremental backup. A differential backup backs up only those files that have changed since the last full backup, but it does not reset the archive bit. The Windows Server 2008 Backup utility does not support differential backups.

disk quota   A way in Windows Server 2008 NTFS to limit the amount of hard drive space on which users can store data. You can set up quotas on a volume and on individual users.

Distributed File System (DFS)   Allows Windows Server 2008 servers to offer a simplified way for users to access geographically dispersed files. DFS Namespace allows you to set up a tree structure of virtual directories that allow users to connect to shared folders throughout the entire network. DFS Replication allows you to replicate the target folders to other DFS servers.

DNS aging   Windows Server 2008 feature that, with DNS scavenging, cleans up and removes stale resource records.

DNS client   Any machine issuing queries to a DNS server. The client host name may or may not be registered in a Domain Name System (DNS) database.

DNS forwarding   The ability of a DNS server to send a request to another DNS server. There are several types of forwarding, including external forwarding (forwarding to a server outside your organization) and conditional forwarding (forwarding based on rules set up by an administrator).

DNS name server   Any computer providing domain name resolution services.

DNS Notify   A mechanism that allows the process of initiating notifications to secondary servers when zone changes occur (RFC 1996).

DNS scavenging   Windows Server 2008 feature that, with DNS aging, cleans up and removes stale resource records. You can specify the scavenging interval.

DNS Server list   Configured on a DNS client, a set of DNS servers the client can contact to resolve names.

DNS Suffix search order   Configured on a DNS client, a list of suffix names associated with the client.

domain   In Microsoft networks, a logical arrangement within an organization of client and server computers referenced by a specific name and sharing a single security permissions database.

Domain Name System (DNS)　A set of network protocols. DNS resolves domain names/host names to a TCP/IP address.

dual stack　Device (end node or network device) that has both IPv4 and IPv6 installed and enabled. The implementation can be dual IP layer (as in Windows Server 2008) or a complete TCP/IP stack (software) for both IPv4 and IPv6.

dynamic　In computer terms, a system or application that builds its own records.

Dynamic DNS (DDNS)　A standard that allows clients or DHCP to register with DNS automatically. This means DNS can build its zone database on the fly.

Dynamic Host Configuration Protocol (DHCP)　A protocol that automatically assigns TCP/IP addresses to DHCP clients.

dynamic routing　Type of routing in which a router can discover its surroundings by finding and communicating with other nearby routers.

E

EAP-RADIUS　A "fake" EAP type that passes any incoming message to a RADIUS server for authentication. See also *EAP type*, *Extensible Authentication Protocol (EAP)*, and *Remote Authentication Dial-In User Service (RADIUS)*.

EAP type　Authentication scheme supported in Extensible Authentication Protocol (EAP). See also *Extensible Authentication Protocol (EAP)*.

Encapsulating Security Payload　IPSec header (and specification) used to provide security by encrypting data or a stream of data. Included in IPv6 as an extension header.

encapsulation　A process in which a client sending data wraps the data or encapsulates it within an IP datagram before it is sent through the network. Each OSI layer adds its own header and sometimes trailer information onto the data.

Event Viewer　A Windows Server 2008 utility that tracks information about the computer's hardware and software, as well as security events. This information is stored in three log files: the Application log, the Security log, and the System log.

exclusion　A range of IP addresses that DHCP does not automatically assign to clients.

Extended User Interface 64-bit (EUI-64) format　Extended unique identifier using 64 bits. The EUI-64 address uses the 48-bit MAC address (6 bytes) and adds 2 bytes between the Organizationally Unique Identifier (the first 3 bytes of the MAC address) and the last 3 bytes. The added 2 bytes are FF:FE. Also, the first byte of the MAC has its sixth bit flipped so the value is 02.

Extensible Authentication Protocol (EAP)　A protocol that allows third parties to write modules that implement new authentication methods and retrofit them to fielded servers.

Extensible Authentication Protocol-Transport Level Security (EAP-TLS)   EAP-TLS is a certificate-based authentication framework that's usually used with smart cards. EAP-TLS can be used only on servers that are members of a domain and is found only in Windows Server 2003 and Server 2008. See also *EAP type* and *Extensible Authentication Protocol (EAP)*.

extension headers   A component of IPv6 that allows additional or new information to be included as part of the layer 3 data, but as an extension or addition to the base frame. IPv4 had similar functionality, but it was part of the base header making the header variable length and harder to work with as far as software/device evaluation. By using extension headers, IPv6 becomes more efficient and extensible.

F

file server   Windows Server machines on your network that store data files for users to access.

firewall   Software or hardware device that checks the information received from the Internet or another external network and determines from that information whether the packet should be accepted or declined.

G

Generic Routing Encapsulation (GRE) header   A header that is combined with an encrypted payload to transmit information over IP.

global unicast address   In the IPv6 address space, addresses assigned to devices that will be accessible to the global IPv6 Internet space. This is similar to the public IP addresses of IPv4, but there are a lot more of them. The current allocation of the global unicast address space is 2000:: /3 (this leaves only 125 bits for uniqueness).

H

hexadecimal   Notation used to represent 8 bits (a byte) using two characters (each representing 4 bits or a nibble). The valid 4 byte values are 0–9 and A–F. Any of these two characters together represent a byte. (*C0* in hex, for example, is a C and a 0. A C is 1100 in binary, a zero is 0000 in binary; the 8 bits are then 1100 0000, or 192, in decimal.)

hierarchical address   In IP addressing, one part (the leftmost) is designated as the network address, and the other part is designated as a node address. The highest-order bits are shared by devices on a network. This allows you to summarize routes in routing tables so routers have the fewest route entries upon which to make layer 3 decisions.

host record   A record that is used to statically associate a host's name to its IP addresses. This is also called an *A record* for TCP/IP version 4 and an *AAAA record* for TCP/IP version 6.

host route   Route to a single system; normally used when you want to direct traffic to remote networks through a particular machine.

Hyper-V   Windows Server 2008 role-based utility that offers hypervisor-based virtualization, including all the features necessary to support machine virtualization.

I

incremental backup   A backup type that backs up only the files that have changed since the last normal or incremental backup. It sets the archive attribute on the files that are backed up.

infrastructure mode   A form of wireless communication that uses one or more wireless access points (APs) and/or a bridging device.

internal routing   The process of moving packets around on your own internetwork.

Internet Connection Sharing (ICS)   Gives networked computers the ability to access a single connection to the Internet. This is helpful when clients are using wireless access.

Internet Protocol (IP)   The Network layer protocol upon which the Internet is based. IP provides a simple connectionless packet exchange. Other protocols such as TCP use IP to perform their connection-oriented (or guaranteed delivery) services.

Internet Protocol next generation (IPng)   Also known as IPv6. Early in the development of the new IP protocol, it was not known which concepts and ideas (and even version) of IP would be the replacement for IPv4. Many folks took to calling the next generation of IP *IPng*. You will still see this term in documentation today.

Internet Protocol Security (IPSec)   IPSec is a set of protocols and functionality providing an authenticated and/or secure channel (tunnel) between end nodes and/or network devices. IPSec uses several protocols to protect against certain security concerns (providing authentication, data integrity, and encryption, for example). In IPv4 you had to add components to allow IPSec to function. In IPv6 headers carry the IPSec information as part of the protocol. These are called IPv6 *extension headers*. The authentication header (AH) and encapsulating security payload (ESP) header are the components of IPSec included within IPv6.

Internet Protocol version 6 (IPv6)   The next generation of IP, also called *IPng*, is being implemented and standardized today. IPv6 is simply a replacement of the layer 3 components of the TCP/IP protocol suite. The layer 4 components (TCP and UDP) are not modified. IPv6 uses a 128-bit address space, much larger than IPv4's 32-bit address space.

Intra-Site Automatic Tunnel Addressing Protocol (ISATAP)   An IPv4 to IPv6 integration/migration utility that allows dual-stack nodes to discover ISATAP routers and communicate with other IPv6 networks on the other side of an IPv4 cloud.

IP datagram   The structure that enables a client and server to transfer other types of data by wrapping the data within an IP packet.

IPv6 mobility   Built-in IPv6 functionality that allows a client node to move between IP networks without disrupting TCP connectivity. The client establishes a TCP connection with a home address. When changing networks, the client continues to communicate with the original endpoint from a care-of address that sends all traffic back through the home address. This functionality is extremely useful when considering wireless networks and even wireless VoIP in the near future.

L

Layer 2 Tunneling Protocol (L2TP)   A generic tunneling protocol that allows encapsulation of one network protocol's data within another protocol. It is used in conjunction with IPSec to enable virtual private network (VPN) access to Windows 2008 networks. It is more secure than PPTP VPNs and also has greater interoperability with devices and software from other vendors.

linear logging   Logging in which data is never deleted from the log file. New information is added to the end of the log file. The log file continually grows, but all historical information is retained.

link-local address   Address used on a local link (a link in IPv6 terms is a network segment) that allows devices on the same link to communicate (for example, to share files) without needing to be configured. Link-local addresses use the prefix FE80:: /10. Link-local addresses are not globally routable.

Link-Local Multicast Name Resolution (LLMNR)   Peer-to-peer name resolution protocol for use in small, temporary networks that don't use DNS.

link-state map   Used with OSPF, a routing table that contains the current links or paths that are available for routers to use and determines what router should service a route request.

LMHOSTS file   ASCII flat file associated with WINS, similar to a HOSTS file. See also *Windows Internet Name Service (WINS)*.

load balancing   A method of distributing network load among multiple network hosts.

Logical Link Control (LLC) sublayer   A sublayer in the Data-Link layer of the Open Systems Interconnection (OSI) model. The LLC sublayer defines flow control; that is, it establishes and maintains the logical communication links between the communicating devices.

M

machine certificate   Digital certificate issued to a machine instead of to a user.

masked   When you apply the subnet mask to an IP address to see the network value (subnet value), the IP addresses is said to be masked.

Media Access Control (MAC) sublayer A sublayer in the Data-Link layer of the Open Systems Interconnection (OSI) model. The MAC sublayer is used for physical addressing; that is, it provides hardware addressing that allows for multiple devices or network nodes to communicate within the network.

metric Cost information used to calculate the most efficient route for packets to take.

Microsoft Baseline Security Analyzer (MBSA) A utility you can download from the Microsoft website to ensure that you have the most current security updates. There is a GUI version and a command-line utility, `mbsacli.exe`.

Microsoft CHAP (MS-CHAP) A remote access authentication protocol and Microsoft's extension to CHAP. It is designed to work with computers and networks that are using Windows 98, Windows Me, Windows NT 4 (all versions), Windows 2000 (all versions), Windows XP (all versions), Windows Vista, Windows Server 2003, and Windows Server 2008. There are two versions of this protocol, MS-CHAPv1 and MS-CHAPv2. Windows Server 2008 does not support MS-CHAPv1.

Microsoft Point-to-Point Encryption (MPPE) algorithm Method of encrypting packets for sending via PPTP tunneling.

MS-CHAPv1 See *Microsoft CHAP (MS-CHAP)*.

MS-CHAPv2 See *Microsoft CHAP (MS-CHAP)*.

Multicast IPv4 and IPv6 packet type defining a single address that can be received by multiple devices at the same time, but not by everyone. Multicast allows a server to send a stream of data to multiple clients. Client computers subscribe to a group and communicate by sending packets to the multicast address. In unicast communication, by contrast, the server needs to send the same packets to each computer individually. IPv6 uses multicast functionality to let a device query multiple network devices for their MAC addresses. This facilitates network communication (IPv4 broadcast ARP functionality).

multicast routing A special type of routing where a packet is sent to multiple host computers based on a special Class D IP address.

multilink Extensions to the Point-to-Point Protocol (PPP) that provide a way to take several independent PPP connections and make them look like one line and act as a single connection.

N

name server A server that can give an authoritative answer to name resolution queries about that domain.

name server (NS) record This record lists the name servers for a domain and allows other name servers to look up names in your domain.

neighbor discovery   Protocol used in IPv6 that allows devices to discover other devices on the same link. Neighbor discovery uses multicast packets and can retrieve router information. Neighbor discovery is the IPv6 functionality that replaces the IPv4 ARP. Neighbor discovery also participates in the IPv6 stateless autoconfiguration feature.

network access policies   Like group policies, network access policies (which used to be called *remote access policy*) allow the administrator to control whether users can get access. Unlike group policies, network access policies are available only in native Windows 2003 or 2008 domains.

network address   A value that uniquely identifies a network. Every machine on the network shares that network address as part of its IP address. In IPv4, the classful address (As in class A, class B, or class C). In classless addressing, this is the number of network bits defined by the subnet mask. In IPv6, this is the hexadecimal value specified by the number of bits in the prefix (or by the slash notation value). In the IPv4 address 130.57.30.56, for example, 130.57 is the network address.

Network Address Translation (NAT)   Service that allows multiple LAN clients to share a single public IP address and Internet connection by translating and modifying packets to reflect the correct addressing information. Also called *network masquerading.*

Network Driver Interface Specification (NDIS)   An application programming interface (API) that allows multiple protocols to be bound to the same network interface cards (NICs) or the same protocol to multiple cards. NDIS was developed by Microsoft and 3Com Corporation for Microsoft Networks.

Network Monitor   A Windows Server 2008 utility that can be used for monitoring and decoding packets that are transferred to and from the local server.

Network Policy Server (NPS)   Microsoft's implementation of a RADIUS server in Windows Server 2008. It replaces Windows Server 2003 Internet Authentication Service (IAS).

network printer   Printer connected directly to the network by its own network interface card (NIC) or that is available on the network through the use of a print server. Network printers in Active Directory must be shared and published before use.

network route   IP network segments are interconnected by routers, which pass IP datagrams from one network segment to another. Network routes are the paths that are in the configurations of the routers.

node address   A value that uniquely identifies a device in a network. In IPv4, the node has a single node address, but in IPv6, a node will typically have more than one IPv6 address—one for the physical interface and addresses for the virtual or pseudointerfaces as well.

Nondynamic DNS (NDDNS)   A DNS database that needs to be built manually. Clients cannot automatically update the DNS server.

normal backup   A backup type that backs up all selected folders and files and then marks each file that has been backed up as archived.

`nslookup`   Command-line utility for testing a DNS server.

NTFS   Formatting option for a hard drive for a Microsoft operating system. NTFS has many advantages over the FAT and FAT32 formatting, including support for compression, disk quotas, encryption, and permissions on files and folders.

O

offline folder   Network folder containing data that can be changed by users outside the office or on laptops. The data in offline folders needs to be synchronized with the network data. Synchronizing can occur when users log off, log on, or suspend their systems.

Open Data-link Interface (ODI)   Driver interfaces that allow multiple network interface cards (NICs) to be bound to multiple protocols. ODI was developed by Apple and Novell for NetWare and Macintosh environments.

Open Shortest Path First (OSPF)   A link-state routing protocol that transmits only the changes to the routing table involving neighbors. OSPF is not supported in Windows Server 2008.

OSI model   A reference model for network component interoperability developed by the International Standards Organization (ISO) to promote cross-vendor compatibility of hardware and software network systems. The OSI model splits the process of networking into seven distinct services, or *layers*. Each layer uses the services of the layer below it to provide its service to the layer above. The ISO began developing the OSI model in 1977. It has since become the most widely accepted model for understanding network communication.

P

packet   Small chunks of data that are constructed, modified, and disassembled by network protocols at various levels of the OSI model during the process of transmitting data across the network. Each packet, also called an *envelope*, consists of three parts: a header, data, and a trailer.

packet filtering   Technology that applies rules to determine what type of traffic is allowed into and out of the router.

packet payload   The data within a network packet that is to be transmitted to the remote computer.

packet sniffer   A utility that allows an individual to watch or retrieve packets from a network cable.

Password Authentication Protocol (PAP)   PAP is an authentication mechanism used by many Internet providers. PAP sends user credentials in plain text between the NAS and the authentication server and therefore is susceptible to a man-in-the-middle attack.

peer filter   Technology used by routers that specifies the neighboring routers to which a local router will listen.

periodic update mode   RIP update mode in which routing table updates are automatically sent to all other RIP routers on the internetwork. See also *autostatic update mode*.

persistent route   Static route that remains in the routing table after the system reboots.

Point-to-Point Protocol (PPP)   A protocol for transmitting information over point-to-point links. Widely used as the protocol for dial-in Internet access using modems.

Point-to-Point Tunneling Protocol (PPTP)   A Microsoft-specific VPN protocol that encapsulates IP, IPX, or NetBEUI information inside IP packets.

pointer (PTR) record   Used to associate an IP address to its host's name. This record is necessary because IP addresses begin with the least-specific portion first (the network) and end with the most-specific portion (the host), whereas host names begin with the most specific portion at the beginning and the least specific at the end.

PPP frame   PPP header added to an IP datagram.

prefix notation   IPv4 and IPv6 notation for showing the network portion of an IP address by specifying the number of network bits after a forward slash. For example, /16 (pronounced "slash 16") indicates 16 network bits (out of 32 for IPv4 and out of 128 for IPv6).

primary zone   This zone is responsible for maintaining all the records for the DNS zone. It contains the primary copy of the DNS database, and all record updates occur here. You create a new primary zone whenever you create a new DNS domain.

print server   Server with a connected printer attached. The print server can handle all the printing options for the connected printer.

printer pool   Allows two or more identical printers to balance the print load among multiple printers. When a document is sent to the printer pool, the first available printer receives the print job and prints it.

protocol stack   A group of protocols, arranged in layers, that implements an entire communication process. TCP/IP is an example of a protocol stack. TCP is one protocol and IP is another. They are stacked together to allow communications.

pseudo-interface   Virtual or logical interface of an IPv6 device. A Teredo interface or an ISATAP interface is an example of a pseudo-interface. The pseudo-interfaces of a network device will have their own IPv6 addresses.

publishing   The act of making an Active Directory object available for network users to locate and use.

R

Reliability and Performance Monitor   A Windows Server 2008 utility used to log and view performance-related data. The Reliability and Performance Monitor includes chart, histogram, and report views.

reliable   Something that can be counted on. Dependable. TCP/IP is an example of a reliable protocol.

remote access profiles   A profile that is associated with a user and allows an administrator to determine who can actually use dial-up capabilities. Remote access profiles work on individual accounts, whereas remote access policies work on groups of users.

Remote Authentication Dial-In User Service (RADIUS)   A common protocol used for authentication, authorization, and accounting services, allowing you to maintain and manage remote users. A RADIUS server allows Remote Access Service (RAS) clients and dial-up routers to be authenticated.

reservation   IP-to-MAC mapping that allows a DHCP server to always give the same IP address to a DHCP client. Reserved IP numbers are part of a DHCP pool that are set aside for machines with specific ID numbers or MAC addresses.

resolver   Any machine issuing queries to a DNS server is a resolver, although technically a resolver is a software process that finds answers to queries for DNS data. Clients issue DNS requests through processes called resolvers.

resource record (RR)   An entry in a DNS database that specifies the availability of specific DNS services. For example, an MX record specifies the IP address of a mail server, and (A) host records specify the IP addresses of workstations on the network.

route filter   Sets of rules used by routers. You use route filters to configure from which networks you want to accept network traffic.

router discovery message   Message that allows clients to find a "nearby" (in network terms) router without any manual configuration on your part.

Routing Information Protocol (RIP)   IP routing protocol that allows routers to exchange information about the presence and routes of other routers on the network. There are two versions—RIPv1 and RIPv2. Windows Server 2008 supports RIPv2, which accommodates variable-length subnet masking (VLSM), among other features.

S

scope   Contiguous range of addresses for DHCP. There's usually one scope per physical subnet. A scope can cover a Class A, Class B, or Class C network address or a IPv6 address.

secondary DNS zone   Noneditable copy of the DNS database that is used for load balancing (also referred to as *load sharing*). A secondary zone gets its database from the primary zone and provides for fault tolerance and increased network performance, especially in organizations with WAN connections.

Server Core   Limited version of Windows Server 2008 intended to provide a low-maintenance, reduced disk-space server environment.

service access point (SAP)   A technology provided by the LLC sublayer so that other computers can transfer information through this sublayer to the upper OSI layers. When a computer receives an incoming frame, the SAP identifies which protocol handler should process the frame.

service profile   Remote access connection, created through Connection Manager, that appears on a client machine as a network connection. See also *Connection Manager*.

service set identifier (SSID)   Method for specifying a wireless network by name. To help wireless clients discover and join the wireless network, the wireless AP or the initial wireless client periodically advertises the SSID (this can be disabled for security).

service (SRV) record   Ties the location of a service (such as a domain controller) to information about how to contact the service.

shadow copy   Shared folder backed up to a remote location. Open files can be backed up. After the initial shadow copy is created, only changes, and not the entire file, are copied.

shared folder   Folder the contents of which are accessible over the network. In Active Directory, sharing a folder is known as *publishing*. The administrator can determine what access users have to the folder's contents.

shared permissions   Permissions on a shared folder. (Files inherit permissions from the parent folder.) Shared permissions are in effect only when users are accessing the shared data remotely. Shared permissions are additive.

Simple Network Management Protocol (SNMP)   TCP/IP protocol monitor that creates trap messages. The messages are sent to a destination you specify to help you monitor your network. When you set up SNMP, you also set up a community—a group of computers that monitor each other.

stateless autoconfiguration   In IPv6, a network node can automatically find the network it is on and the address of the network's router. The node can then assign itself an IPv6 address and default gateway. This functionality is similar to the APIPA feature of IPv4, but unlike APIPA, it provides access not only to the local network but to the bigger routed network as well.

static routing   A specification that determines where packets bound for certain networks should go, based on static route tables.

subnet   A logical division of IP addresses. In IPv4 and IPv6, subnets allow you to divide your network into smaller segments or links. This permits your routers to make more efficient decisions, and it prevents routers outside the subnet from knowing what you're doing internally.

subnet address   The portion of an IP address that your routers are using to make routing decisions on your network infrastructure. Routers find this value by looking at the bits of the IP address as defined by the 1s of the subnet mask for that network and making all the other bits (the host bits) 0 and converting the address back to decimal (or hex in the IPv6 world). What's nice about IPv6 is you can just put a :: in at the end of the Network/Subnet portion.

subnet mask   In IP addressing, masking is the function of letting the device evaluate the network portion of the IP address to make routing decisions. The device uses the mask (or subnet mask) to find the network portion by logically ANDing the IP address and the subnet mask (which essentially makes all the non-network bits (host bits) zero). The dotted decimal or slash (/) value indicates the network portion of an IP address. The subnet mask is the stream of 1s in the dotted decimal mask for IPv4 or the number of bits defined by the slash for IPv4 in CIDR or slash notation as well as the number of bits defined by the slash in IPv6.

superscope   Enables the DHCP server to provide addresses from more than one scope to clients on the same physical subnet.

T

Task Manager   A Windows Server 2008 utility that can be used to quickly and easily obtain a snapshot of current system performance.

TCP/IP   Transmission Control Protocol/ Internet Protocol. TCP/IP is a protocol suite and is the primary communication protocol on a Windows Server 2008 network. Transmission Control Protocol (TCP) is a reliable connection-oriented protocol on the Transport layer of the OSI Model, part of the TCP/IP protocol suite.

Temporal Key Integrity Protocol (TKIP)   Strong encryption method used by the WPA wireless encryption standard. See also *Wi-Fi Protected Access (WPA)*.

Teredo   Protocol used for unicast IPv6 communication with an IPv4 NAT implementation across an IPv4 infrastructure. Allows IPv6 addresses to be available to hosts through one or more layers of NAT. Teredo works by tunneling packets through the IPv4 space using UDP. The Teredo service encapsulates the IPv6 data within a UDP segment (packet) and uses an IPv4 address to get through the IPv4 cloud. Other IPv6 integration/migration methods do not work behind a NAT.

Tunnel   A technology usually associated with VPNs that establishes a secure channel of communications over a network such as the Internet.

U

Unicast   A type of network communication in which a packet is sent from a source host to a single destination host. The unicast packet type defines a unique address for each node (IPv4) or interface (IPv6).

unicast routing   Routing in which one machine sends data directly to one destination address.

unmasked   When you apply the subnet mask to an IP address and can see the network value (subnet value), the host portion of the address is said to be unmasked.

unreliable   Something that cannot be counted on. Undependable. UDP is an example of an unreliable protocol.

User Datagram Protocol (UDP)   A connectionless protocol on the Transport layer of the OSI Model and part of the IP protocol suite.

V

virtual private network (VPN)   Private network that uses links across private or public networks (such as the Internet). When data is sent over the remote link, it is encapsulated and encrypted and requires authentication services.

W

Wi-Fi Protected Access (WPA)   A wireless encryption standard that uses the Temporal Key Integrity Protocol (TKIP). It is stronger encryption than WEP. See also *Wired Equivalent Privacy (WEP)*.

Windows Internet Name Service (WINS)   A service that resolves a NetBIOS name to a TCP/IP address. WINS is used primarily in older operating systems (Windows 95, 98, and NT).

Windows Server Update Services (WSUS)   Deploys a limited version of Windows Update to a corporate server, which in turn provides the updates to client computers on the corporate network. This allows clients behind a firewall to keep their operating systems up-to-date. The replacement for Software Update Services, WSUS enables greater management and control capabilities as well as enhanced reporting.

Windows Update   A utility that connects the computer to Microsoft's website and checks software to look for newer versions with bug and security fixes.

Wired Equivalent Privacy (WEP)   Wireless encryption standard originally defined in 802.11. Security is achieved through the use of a shared 40-bit or 104-bit secret key.

Index

Note to the reader: Throughout this index **boldfaced** page numbers indicate primary discussions of a topic. *Italicized* page numbers indicate illustrations.

Numbers

Wiley Publishing, Inc.
End-User License Agreement

THE ABSOLUTE BEST MCTS: WINDOWS SERVER 2008 NETWORK INFRASTRUCTURE, CONFIGURING BOOK/CD PACKAGE ON THE MARKET!

Get ready for your MCTS: Windows Server 2008 Network Infrastructure, Configuring or MCITP: Enterprise or Server Administrator certifications with the most comprehensive and challenging sample tests anywhere!

The Sybex Test Engine features:

- All the review questions, as covered in each chapter of the book

- Challenging questions representative of those you'll find on the real exam

- Two full-length bonus exams available only on the CD

- Assessment Test to narrow your focus to certain objective groups

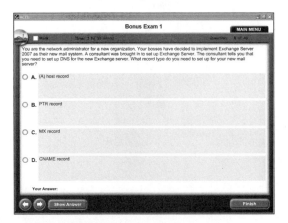

Search through the complete book in PDF!

- Access the entire *MCTS: Microsoft Windows Server 2008 Network Infrastructure Configuration Study Guide* complete with figures and tables, in electronic format.

- Search the *MCTS: Microsoft Windows Server 2008 Network Infrastructure Configuration Study Guide* chapters to find information on any topic in seconds.

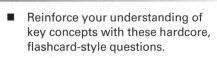

Use the Electronic Flashcards for PCs or Palm devices to jog your memory and prep last minute for the exam!

- Reinforce your understanding of key concepts with these hardcore, flashcard-style questions.

- Download the Flashcards to your Palm device and go on the road. Now you can study for the MCTS: Windows Server 2008 Network Infrastructure, Configuring (70-642) exam any time, anywhere.

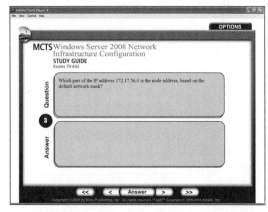

- CD also includes PrepLogic's robust Audio+ exam preparation product for Exam 70-642, exclusive for Sybex Study Guides.